John Calvin's Ideas

John Calvin's Ideas

✳

PAUL HELM

OXFORD
UNIVERSITY PRESS

OXFORD
UNIVERSITY PRESS

Great Clarendon Street, Oxford OX2 6DP

Oxford University Press is a department of the University of Oxford.
It furthers the University's objective of excellence in research, scholarship,
and education by publishing worldwide in

Oxford New York

Auckland Cape Town Dar es Salaam Hong Kong Karachi
Kuala Lumpur Madrid Melbourne Mexico City Nairobi
New Delhi Shanghai Taipei Toronto

With offices in

Argentina Austria Brazil Chile Czech Republic France Greece
Gautemala Hungary Italy Japan Poland Portugal Singapore
South Korea Switzerland Thailand Turkey Ukraine Vietnam

Oxford is a registered trade mark of Oxford University Press
in the UK and in certain other countries
Published in the United States
by Oxford University Press
in the UK and in certain other countries

Published in the United States
by Oxford University Press Inc., New York

© Paul Helm, 2004

First published in paperback 2006

British Library Cataloguing in Publication Data

Data available

Library of Congress Cataloging in Publication Data
Data available

Typeset by Footnote Graphics Limited, Warminster, Wilts
Printed in Great Britain
on acid-free paper by
Biddles Ltd., King's Lynn

ISBN 0-19-925569-5 978-0-19-925569-6
ISBN 0-19-920599-X (Pbk.) 978-0-19-920599-8 (Pbk.)

To Mark and Cindy Talbot

Preface

Most of this book has not been published before. But antecedents of parts of some of the chapters may be found in the following published material:

'John Calvin on "Before All Ages"', *Tyndale Bulletin*, 52/2 (2002), 143–8. (Chapter 2)

'Calvin (and Zwingli) on the Providence of God', *Calvin Theological Journal*, 29/2 (Nov. 1994), 388–405. (Chapter 4)

'Calvin and Bernard on Freedom and Necessity: A Reply to Brümmer', *Religious Studies*, 30 (1994), 457–65. (Chapter 5)

'John Calvin on Divine Accommodation', *Baptist Review of Theology*, 4/2 (Fall 1994), 41–53. (Chapter 7)

'Moses Maimonides and John Calvin on Accommodation', in Paul Helm (ed.), *Referring to God* (Richmond: Curzon Press, 2000). (Chapter 7)

'God in Dialogue', in A. N. S. Lane (ed.), *Interpreting the Bible* (Leicester: Apollos, 1997). (Chapter 7)

'John Calvin, the *sensus divinitatis* and the Noetic Effects of Sin', *International Journal for the Philosophy of Religion* (1998). (Chapter 8)

'Calvin and Natural Law', *Scottish Bulletin of Evangelical Theology*, 2 (1984), 5–22. Reprinted in Richard C. Gamble (ed.), *Articles on Calvin and Calvinism*, vii; *The Organizational Structure of Calvin's Theology* (Hamden, Conn.: Garland Publishing Inc., 1993), 177–94. (Chapter 12)

'Faith and Self-Reflection', chapter 9 of Paul Helm, *Faith With Reason* (Oxford: Clarendon Press, 2000). (Chapter 13)

Quotations from the 1559 *Institutes* are from the Ford Lewis Battles translation. I have mostly used the Calvin Translation Society's edition of his commentaries, and the English translations of various treatises and letters. Though the language is in many cases dated much of this material has been recently reprinted and so is more or less accessible to all. In my view the ideas of John Calvin are the common property of anyone who may be interested in them, and not the special preserve of scholars and others involved in something called 'Calvin Studies'. Nothing much in what I have written turns on nuances in the original, and where I think it may, I have provided the original, or other translations.

The book is longer than I would have wished. This is because I have tried where possible to let Calvin speak for himself. Also I have found it surprising how little detailed work there is on his ideas and arguments. He is often pigeonholed, and left to gather dust. Where there has been such work I have tried to interact with it with some care. This also has added to the book's length.

A good bit of the work published here for the first time was tried out under the auspices of the Rutherford House Calvin Group and of the Systematic Theology Research Seminar at King's College London. I have also benefited from the comments of audiences at Keele and Oxford. I should like to thank all who helped me for their expertise and good judgement which provided me with useful stimulus. I especially thank my friend Mark Talbot, who in the midst of a busy schedule made time meticulously to read through the first half of the book, saving me from many blunders and making numerous helpful suggestions, most of which I have adopted. Hilary O'Shea, Lucy Qureshi, and Enid Barker of the Press have provided excellent support during the various stages of the publishing process. I am particularly grateful to my friend and former student Oliver Crisp for the use of his portrait of Calvin which adorns the dustjacket. Lastly but most of all I thank Angela and Alice, who patiently made space and time for me to work, more space and more time as the book grew in size and scope.

P.H.

Vancouver,
British Columbia.

The preparation of a reprint (2006) makes it possible to correct small errors of fact and some typographical mistakes in the first edition. It also provides the opportunity to amend the statement made on p. 197 that Calvin does not use the idea of accommodation in connection with the Incarnation. This is contradicted by his endorsement of the view of Irenaeus (*Institutes* II. 6. 4) and also by what he writes in his *Commentary* on 1 Peter 1: 21.

Fifield,
Oxon.

Contents

Shall we say that the philosophers were blind in their fine observation and artful description of nature? Shall we say that those men were devoid of understanding who conceived the art of disputation and taught us to speak reasonably?

Human reason, therefore, neither approaches, nor strives toward, nor even takes a straight aim at, this truth: to understand who the true God is or what sort of God he wishes to be toward us.

John Calvin, Institutes of the Christian Religion

Introduction

JOHN CALVIN was a theological genius, but that genius did not express itself in a vacuum. This book does not study Calvin's theology as such, but some of the context in which he worked, and some of the ideas he inherited. It is concerned with Calvin as a receiver, user, and transmitter of theological ideas, and particularly of those theological ideas that have philosophical aspects and histories to them. Calvin was neither a philosopher nor a philosophical theologian but his first-rate intellect had a systematizing bent that is congenial to a philosopher and that was receptive to philosophical ideas. It is interesting and important to see where Calvin used philosophical ideas and arguments, and also to study those places in which he refuses to follow an argument wherever it may lead, and the reasons he has for this.

Calvin is frequently taken to stand apart from the late medieval theological tradition. He is portrayed as a biblicist, a humanist-influenced lawyer by training, who lacked an education in scholastic theology (although not in scholastic philosophy). His theological interest is taken to be practical rather than theoretical. This kept him from speculating about God's character or purposes or from seeing or seeking a three- or fourfold sense in Scripture while leading him to stick to commenting on the grammatical text tersely and sparingly. He invariably writes theology for the Church, writing in the first or second person of the knowledge of God and ourselves and, because he is convinced that Scripture is theologically sufficient for present purposes, he delights in the concrete rather than in the abstract. On this view, if theology is a science, then Calvin is an applied rather than a pure scientist who sees theology's worth more in encouraging appropriate religious responses than in increasing metaphysical comprehension.

In these respects his work is said to stand in sharp relief both to the Catholic medieval tradition, which he is invariably portrayed as condemning for being sophistical and speculative, as well as to the tradition of later Reformed Scholasticism.[1] The latter, legend has it, is an un-Calvinian

---

[1] For such judgements, see, for example, Brian G. Armstrong, *Calvin and the Amyraut Heresy: Protestant Scholasticism and Humanism in Seventeenth Century France* (Madison: University of Wisconsin Press, 1969), 31–2. On Reformed Scholasticism and its significance, see for example Richard Muller, 'Calvin and the Calvinists: Assessing Continuities and Discontinuities Between the Reformation and

aberration that followed from the reintroduction of the scholastic method into Reformed churches and that used the doctrine of the double predestination as its methodological axiom. Theodore Beza, appointed as Calvin's deputy sheriff, became the guy in the black Stetson who succeeded in running all the good guys out of town. True Calvinists, so the legend goes, have never forgiven him.

This view of Calvin's relation to his forebears and successors is currently in the process of being severely reshaped, if not totally dismantled, by the influence of four or so separate lines of scholarly inquiry.

The first is research into the medieval tradition, particularly into the world of late medieval Augustinianism, that shows it to be much more multiform than previously thought and to contain strands congenial to the incipient Reform movement, strands that fed directly into the education and experience of Martin Luther and Peter Martyr Vermigli, for example, as well as into Calvin.[2] Important elements of this tradition were in the air that each of them breathed, although it may be that Calvin's more detailed acquaintance with scholastic theology came later in his career; suggestions that he learned theology from John Major seem unfounded.[3] He seems to have picked up scholastic theology on the hoof.

So considerable attention is being paid to Calvin's situation as an heir to the later Middle Ages, an inheritor of a mind-set strongly imbued with scholasticism. Though Calvin repeatedly inveighs against speculation, whether

Orthodoxy, Part I', *Calvin Theological Journal* (1995), Part II, *Calvin Theological Journal* (1996); Muller, *Christ and the Decree: Christology and Predestination in Reformed Theology from Calvin to Perkins* (Durham, N C: Labyrinth Press, 1986), and Carl R. Trueman and R. S. Clark (eds.), *Protestant Scholasticism: Essays in Reassessment* (Carlisle: Paternoster Press, 1999). A selection of translated texts may be found in *Reformed Dogmatics*, ed. and trans. by John W. Beardslee III (New York: Oxford University Press, 1965).

[2] See, for example, Richard A. Muller, *The Unaccommodated Calvin* (New York: Oxford University Press, 2000). H. A. Oberman, *The Dawn of the Reformation: Essays in Late Medieval and Early Reformation Thought* (Edinburgh: T. & T. Clark, 1986); Oberman, *The Harvest of Medieval Theology: Gabriel Biel and Late Medieval Nominalism* (3rd edn., Grand Rapids, Mich.: Baker, 2000); David C. Steinmetz, *Calvin in Context* (New York: Oxford University Press, 1997), and *Luther in Context* (Grand Rapids, Mich.: Baker, 1995); Denis R. Janz, *Luther and Late Medieval Thomism: A Study in Theological Anthropology* (Waterloo: Wilfrid Laurier University Press, 1983); *The Peter Martyr Library*, vol. 4: *The Philosophical Works*, trans. Joseph C. McClelland (Kirkville, Mo.: Sixteenth Century Essays and Studies, 1996); Frank James III, *Peter Martyr Vermigli and Predestination* (Oxford: Clarendon Press, 1998). On Theodore Beza, see Jeffrey Mallinson, *Faith, Reason, and Revelation in Theodore Beza (1519–1605)* (Oxford: Oxford University Press, 2003); Mallinson draws attention to the strong theological parallels between Calvin and Beza.

[3] For arguments against the claim that Calvin learned scholastic theology from Major, see Alexandre Ganoczy, *The Young Calvin*, trans. David Foxgrover and Wade Provo (Philadelphia: Westminster Press, 1987), ch. 16. See also A. N. S. Lane, *John Calvin: Student of the Church Fathers* (Edinburgh: T. & T. Clark, 1999), and Muller, *The Unaccommodated Calvin*, 45–6.

scholastic or not, this should not blind us to his indebtedness to such modes of thought, nor to his own occasional speculative flights, any more than should his own style of doing theology. The judgement that Calvin was virulently anti-scholastic cannot be sustained, not at least from references to the scholastics that one finds in the *Institutes*. For instance, when Calvin dissents from some scholastic he often does so simply over the substance of the view, what that scholastic believed, and not to the scholastic method as such. He appropriates without embarrassment the distinctions of the schools when he judges that it is necessary or useful to do so. In fact, when we separate Calvin's criticism of the scholastics for 'speculation' or 'excessive speculation' from the other things that Calvin has to say about them, we find him making a range of judgements.

Take, for example, part of his discussion of free will in *Institutes* II. 2. Calvin shows that, though Lombard and the scholastics are basically August- inian in their approach, they make certain distinctions of their own, for example, *arbitrium* referring to reason and *liberum* to the will, and he recog- nizes that the schools distinguish freedom from necessity as well as from sin and from misery, declaring 'I willingly accept this distinction, except in so far as necessity is falsely confused with compulsion'.[4] By contrast, a few pages later he makes it clear that he believes that the schoolmen pervert the meaning of Romans 7.[5] Elsewhere he makes distinctions between sounder and less sound schoolmen,[6] reserving particular venom for theologians at the Sorbonne, 'mothers of all errors'.[7] The 'Sorbonnists' in question were his contemporaries at the Sorbonne, whom he saw as obstructing reform. It is interesting that Calvin's French versions of the Latin *Institutes* often use 'Sorbonnist' in place of 'scholastic'.[8]

Even to say that Calvin's own theological style was non-scholastic or anti- scholastic needs to be qualified; for while Calvin's *Institutes* is not patterned on the model of, say, Aquinas's *Summae* and no doubt owes a great deal to Renaissance rhetorical style, there are nevertheless many discussions in it that have the pattern of thesis/objections/responses that was characteristic of the schools. Richard Muller observes that the

pattern of argument in many of the chapters of the *Institutes* ... reflects a fairly strict observation of the form of scholastic disputation, moving from the initial statement of a point to various objections and replies to objections. ... It is also clear from Calvin's usage that technical *distinctiones* occupied virtually the same place in his theological method as they did in the development of Lombard's *Sententiae*: the

---

[4] *Inst.* II. 2. 5. All quotations from the *Institutes* are from *Institutes of the Christian Religion*, trans. F. L. Battles (London: SCM Press, 1961).

[5] *Inst.* II. 2. 27.   [6] *Inst.* II. 2. 6.   [7] *Inst.* III. 15. 7.

[8] Muller, *The Unaccommodated Calvin*, 50–2. See also Oberman, *The Dawn of The Reformation*, 248.

distinctio offered a means of dealing with difficulties and even potential contradictions in the text of Scripture or between a biblical statement and a truth known from some other perspective.[9]

This is equally true of Calvin's polemical works devoted to single issues. He valued the patterns of logic and rhetoric that he had inherited, not only from the Renaissance but also from ancient and medieval worlds: 'Shall we say that the philosophers were blind in their fine observation and artful description of nature? Shall we say that those men were devoid of understanding who conceived the art of disputation and taught us to speak reasonably?'[10]

Occasionally we find Calvin writing in a fairly self-conscious way about the Renaissance and its beneficial effects and of God in his own day having 'revived the human sciences, which are both proper and profitable for the guidance of our lives and which, while being used for our benefit, can also serve his glory'.[11] And occasionally the influence of the new learning is seen in Calvin's willingness to offer purely rational and empirical arguments against some particular view. Thus in the work against astrology just quoted he argues that if the principles of astrology are sound, then it should be the moment of conception that is relevant to a person's fate and not the date of his birth.

The discriminating judgements that Calvin makes of the scholastics—he usually reserves the term 'sophist' for those speculative thinkers whose trains of thought he rejects as a matter of principle—are paralleled in his judgements of 'the philosophers'. For example, he rejects Aristotle's views on immortality[12] and on praise and blame,[13] but commends him for his shrewdness in his account of incontinence.[14] In *Institutes* II. 2. 3 he approves of what Cicero writes about the effect of wicked opinions but several lines later he rejects Cicero's view that it is in our own power whether or not we live virtuously.

Consequently, the days are past when Calvin could be seen as a purely 'biblical' Reformer, a theologian of 'the Word'. As if he wrote his *Institutes* and his voluminous commentaries, preached and carried on controversy, in a way that was uncontaminated either by Renaissance or scholastic influences, and instead delighted in paradox and mystery in a way that made him a forerunner of many a 'dialectical' theologian. If a dialectical theologian is someone who strives to balance one theological element against another, say a high view of created human nature balanced by a radical view of fallen-

[9] Muller, *The Unaccommodated Calvin*, 45–6. [10] *Inst.* II. 2. 15.

[11] *Advertissement contre l'astrologie qu'on appelle iudiciaire, et autre curiosité qui regnent aujourd'huy au monde* (1549), trans. Mary Potter as *A Warning Against Judiciary Astrology and Other Prevalent Curiosities, Calvin Theological Journal* (1983), 163.

[12] *Inst.* I. 5. 5. [13] *Inst.* II. 5. 2. [14] *Inst.* II. 2. 23.

ness, then certainly Calvin was a dialectical theologian. But if a dialectical theologian is someone who opposes one theological element to another in order to effect some novel synthesis, then Calvin was not among their number. John Calvin was a Reformer and a reformer is a re-former. He re-formed his Christian inheritance, with its intricate interplay of theological and philosophical themes, along distinctly evangelical lines, but he did not abandon it.

A second line of scholarly inquiry that is reshaping our understanding of Calvin's relation to his forebears and successors is research into the onset and character of Protestant scholasticism. We now can see that Protestant scholasticism was not the exclusive preserve of the so-called High Calvinists but a pervasive phenomenon embracing the style of early Calvinists such as Peter Martyr Vermigli and Hieronymus Zanchi as well as non-Calvinists such as Jacobus Arminius. Thus, sole responsibility for Calvinistic doctrinal development (or, if you prefer, doctrinal deterior-ation) on faith and assurance, say, or on limited atonement, cannot be laid at the door of scholasticism as such, for scholasticism is merely a method of intellectual inquiry.[15] Establishing links between Calvin's ideas and those of the medieval world makes it more plausible to ascribe doctrinal continuity between Calvin and later Reformed scholasticism, because some of the sources of such scholasticism are to be found in Calvin's own method. But to examine the strands of such continuity largely falls outside the scope of this book.

A third line of inquiry is the attention that is being paid to Calvin's own words, both in his writings and more surprisingly, perhaps, in his sermons. Looking at this material while being alert to the possibility of the influence of earlier theological styles on Calvin, we shall see that Calvin conveys to his readers and hearers an intimate knowledge of scholastic distinctions and their associated doctrines. He had mastered them in the sense that he was prepared to endorse or reject them whenever it suited him to do so. As Aquinas ran with Aristotle when he judged it appropriate but parted company from him when he thought that revealed truth was at stake (on the eternity of matter, say, or the nature of angelic intelligence), so Calvin the preacher, while mostly eschewing a scholastic method of organizing his material, effortlessly appropriated not only their distinctions but a doctrinal outlook similar to that of many scholastics.

All three strands of inquiry into Calvin's ideas and their legacy are found in this book. I do not argue over, propose, or speculate about precisely who were Calvin's mentors, those singular figures through whom the tradition

---

[15] See Muller, *The Unaccommodated Calvin*, ch. 3.

was transmitted to him, and transmuted in the process.[16] How dominant was
the dominance of Augustine? How significant, if at all, was the influence of
the later medieval philosopher John Major? What was the precise significance of his legal education? In what sense was Calvin's first work, his
commentary on Seneca's *De Clementia*, a Renaissance work? In what sense
is the *Institutes* itself a Renaissance work? There is scholarly consensus on
the answers to at least some of these questions as well as some excellent work
on Calvin's overall relation to philosophy, for example, Charles Partee's
Calvin and Classical Philosophy.[17] No attempt is made to address any of these
questions nor to consider the equally interesting but murkier issues about
Calvin's temperament and its effect on his theology.

Did Calvin's theology change over the years? Unlike his hero Augustine,
Calvin published no retractions. I shall simply assume, unless there is explicit
evidence to the contrary (as occasionally there is), that, prompted by controversy and by what he judged to be the needs of the church, Calvin articulated
and developed but did not substantially modify his early ideas. I shall
endeavour to take what we might call the literary deposit of Calvin's work,
particularly in his *Institutes* and his controversial works, and study it as
someone might study any philosophical or theological text from 500 years
ago—Descartes's *Meditations*, say, or Hobbes's *Leviathan*. This is to study
Calvin's writings for the ideas and arguments that they contain. We are interested in the provenance of those concepts and arguments only where that
can throw light on his concepts and arguments and thus help us to avoid
howlers and promote interpretations that are appropriately nuanced.

A further major contemporary influence on the study of Calvin is the
sudden growth in contemporary analytical philosophy of what has come to
be called 'Reformed' epistemology. 'Reformed' epistemology criticizes the
classical foundationalism of the Enlightenment and defends the reasonableness of religious belief in a way that finds inspiration in Calvin's remarks on
the universal *sensus divinitatis* and (more recently) in what Calvin called
the internal testimony of the Holy Spirit.[18] Alvin Plantinga, the *fons* if not
the *origo* of 'Reformed' epistemology, also makes the bold claim that Calvin,
and with him any true Calvinist, has philosophical objections to natural
theology.[19] So in this quite unexpected way the ideas of a non-philosopher,

[16] The extent to which it is safe to draw conclusions about the way in which Calvin was directly influenced by the Church Fathers and others, through their writings, has been meticulously researched by
A. N. S. Lane. See his *John Calvin: Student of the Church Fathers*.

[17] (Leiden: E. J. Brill, 1977).

[18] Alvin Plantinga, *Warranted Christian Belief* (New York: Oxford University Press, 2000), part III.

[19] Alvin Plantinga, 'The Reformed Objection to Natural Theology', *Proceedings of the American
Catholic Philosophical Association*, (1980).

John Calvin, have taken on contemporary philosophical significance. We shall look at this appeal to Calvin, and the interpretation of him by the proponents of 'Reformed' epistemology.

I hope that my evaluation of that appeal, together with my broader assessment of Calvin's philosophical inheritance and his use of philosophical materials, will put 'Reformed' epistemology in true perspective. It will be argued that the proponents of 'Reformed' epistemology have misinterpreted Calvin's appeal to the *sensus divinitatis*, and I shall also try to show, particularly by looking at what Calvin has to say about the *sensus divinitatis*, equity, and natural law, as well as in other ways, that Calvin cannot easily be pressed into a communitarian rather than into a natural theological mould.[20] Calvin is, I believe, an evidentialist rather than fideist or a 'Reformed' epistemologist, with real but modest expectations as far as the natural knowledge of God is concerned. On the other hand, I shall argue that 'Reformed' epistemology's appeal to the internal testimony of the Holy Spirit is more faithful to Calvin.

Because this book looks at philosophical issues and theological ideas rather than being a treatise on Calvin's theology, we shall consider topics and themes that sometimes cut across the main loci of his theology. So while we shall be considering what, for example, Calvin has to say about the soul and its powers, and while in his view this forms part of the *imago dei*, we shall not consider how Calvin understood the *imago dei*. Whether he understood it in ontological, or ethical, or relational terms, or in some of each, are properly the concern of the theologian.

This material is organized in a way that will be more immediately familiar to philosophers than to theologians. We shall examine certain aspects of Calvin's metaphysics, his doctrine of God, including its Trinitarian and Christological aspects, and divine providence; his doctrine of the human self, including human freedom; certain aspects of his epistemology, notably his pervasive appeal to accommodation and his use of the *sensus divinitatis*; his

---

[20] Plantinga has frequently argued that the first responsibility of the Christian philosopher is not to present arguments for the reasonableness of his religious beliefs that will convince any rational man, but arguments that will establish for the Christian believer the reasonableness of taking the existence of God and many other theological claims as 'properly basic', claims he is entitled to believe without argument. 'The Christian will of course suppose that belief in God is entirely proper and rational; if he does not accept this belief on the basis of other propositions, he will conclude that it is basic for him and quite properly so. Followers of Bertrand Russell and Madelyn Murray O'Hare may disagree; but how is that relevant? Must my criteria, or those of the Christian community, conform to their examples? Surely not. The Christian community is responsible to *its* sets of example, not to theirs.' 'Reason and Belief in God', in Alvin Plantinga and Nicholas Wolterstorff (eds.), *Faith and Rationality* (Notre Dame: University of Notre Dame Press, 1983), 77. See also Alvin Plantinga, 'Advice to Christian Philosophers', *Faith and Philosophy*, (1984).

treatment of divine power and goodness, and the way in which his under-standing of angels throws light on this; and his ethics, particularly his appeal to natural law and the use to which he puts it in his ethics, and his underlying appeal to equity. Only the chapter on the atonement will at first seem to be more exclusively theological, but even there I shall be more concerned with Calvin's understanding of divine freedom and his handling of the issues of causation, time, and change than with the substantive theological issues themselves. Attention will also be paid to the logical consistency of Calvin's thought, both in the sense in which its disparate strands may be shown to cohere as well as with the question of the extent to which Calvin himself thinks that logical consistency is an important theological virtue.

Even when looking at his ideas philosophically we shall find that Calvin takes for granted matters that a contemporary philosophical theologian might find important, such as an account of divine omnipotence or of divine omniscience. For example, in his treatment of predestination he notes that to God's knowledge there is nothing future or past, but all things are present.[21] In eternity there is no before or after.[22] In his treatment of the Trinity, he upholds a notion of divine simplicity,[23] believing (with the mainstream Christian tradition) that God is both without parts but yet tri-personal. In his discussion of necessity, he emphasizes that the necessity of God's good-ness does not detract from its praiseworthiness,[24] the precise issue that has been the subject of numerous discussions in contemporary philosophical theology.[25]

There are principally two reasons for Calvin's relative disinterest in several of what are currently regarded as central ideas in philosophical theology. First, he did not question the theological tradition unless he had what he regarded as very good reason. For instance, if we compare his attitude to the idea of divine omnipotence, say, to that of human merit, we find that he inherits theories of each, accepts the former without demur, but subjects the latter to withering analysis and refutation. Secondly, Calvin never forgot that the *Institutes* was not a textbook or a *summa* but a manual of instruction in the Christian faith for believers, which set him against anything that would distract him from this task. So the *Institutes* is not a full system of theology, a textbook in which every locus is given equal weight, but an 'occasional' writing. We shall attempt to respect these contours of Calvin's thought, attempting to look at his own concerns in his own terms, rather than trying to press his ideas into an alien theological mould.

---

[21] *Inst.* III. 21. 5.   [22] *Inst.* I. 13. 8.   [23] *Inst.* I. 13. 2, 16–19.   [24] *Inst.* II. 3. 5.

[25] e.g. Thomas V. Morris, 'Duty and Divine Goodness', in Thomas V. Morris (ed.), *The Concept of God* (Oxford: Oxford University Press, 1987).

In the popular mind and to some extent even in the scholarly mind Calvin had only one theological idea, the idea of predestination. Obsessed with this, the central dogma of his system, he made it function as an axiom from which all of his other ideas are derived. I intend the plural 'ideas' used in the book's title to repudiate this way of thinking about Calvin. Calvin had numerous theological ideas, each of which he believed to be derived from or endorsed by Scripture, and each one of which he believed to be consistent with each of the others. In order to underline this point further, no discussion of predestination is included in the book.

We ought not to infer from Calvin's neglect of a topic such as God's nature or natural theology that it was not important to him.[26] We need to contrast what Calvin gives prominence to because it is controversial and needs settling in order to carry forward the project of the Reformation, and what is intellectually central to his system of thought, even though he may be relatively silent on it. For example, he says little or nothing about the idea of creation, but it is nevertheless clear that he regards *creatio ex nihilo* as absolutely crucial, along with the corollary that all truths about the creation, whatever their proximate source, have their ultimate source in God.[27] If anything were a candidate for the axiom of Calvin's theology, then the following statement would be a strong contender:

Not only does he [God] sustain this universe (as he once founded it) by his boundless might, regulate it by his wisdom, preserve it by his goodness, and especially rule mankind by his righteousness and judgment, bear with it in his mercy, watch over it by his protection; but also that no drop will be found either of wisdom and light, or of righteousness or power or rectitude, or of genuine truth, which does not flow from him, and of which he is not the cause.[28]

But in fact nothing is axiomatic for Calvin in this sense. Reasoning *more geometrico* was not his style.

In most of my chapters Calvin's relation to his medieval antecedents is explored and even stressed. Yet this is not to be understood as implying any diminution of Calvin's distinctiveness as a theologian of the Reformation. In order to underline this point, and to end the book on this note, the final chapter is concerned with Calvin's understanding of the central Reformation idea of *sola fide*. I try to show how Calvin uses distinctions about causation that come to him from Aristotle via the medievals to elucidate his distinctive

---

[26] Muller, *The Unaccommodated Calvin*, 115. In order to form an overall estimate of Calvin's treatment of natural theology, in addition to the much-discussed passages in book 1 of the *Institutes*, Calvin's treatment of biblical texts such as Acts 17 should also be consulted. See ch. 8 of the present work for an assessment of this material.

[27] *Inst.* II. 2. 15. See also Calvin's brief treatment of the eternity of matter in his commentary on Acts 17.

[28] *Inst.* I. 2. 1.

Reformation claims about the role of faith in salvation; and I compare his views to the revisionary position of Karl Barth. So in endeavouring to set out Calvin's ideas it is my aim to work with them, not only by placing them within a spectrum of other ideas, but also by making them interact with past and contemporary discussions on similar themes.

1

God *in Se* and *Quoad Nos*

CALVIN draws a fundamental distinction between God as he is in himself and God as he is revealed to us. This distinction applies to all of his discussions of God. So in his deliberations about the Trinity that we shall consider more fully in the next chapter, God is in himself (*in se*) Trinitarian, as he is Trinitarian toward us (*quoad nos*). It is not as if God is Trinitarian simply in his relations with us; he is Trinitarian in his relations with himself. This distinction is of considerable importance for Calvin. It plays a prominent part in the *Institutes* and it recurs frequently in his commentaries and sermons. In fact, it is a controlling theme in Calvin's idea of God and in his entire attitude to theology.

In this chapter I shall first examine this distinction in Calvin and then try to show that it corresponds to one familiar in the Middle Ages—in Aquinas, for example. Here and elsewhere the argument is that Aquinas offers illuminating precedents for Calvin's distinctions, even if he is not the direct intellectual source of them.[1] If these precedents can be established, then even if Aquinas was not the source of Calvin's views, it is likely that there were others who thought similarly to him who were. Some have claimed that the thought of Duns Scotus was more 'in the air' in later medievalism than Aquinas's thought, and therefore that Scotus is more likely to have influenced Calvin. Even so, to show that the thoughts of Aquinas and Calvin follow similar patterns at various points provides evidence of a more general or pervasive medieval influence on Calvin.[2] I shall consider the relation between Calvin and Scotus in Chapter 11.

Having looked at Aquinas and Calvin on the distinction between God in himself and God as he is toward us, it will be argued that understanding

---

[1] A similar theme—that God is hidden outside his revelation of himself to us—is found in Martin Luther. The dazzlingly transcendent God hides himself in his revelation, which substitutes at the epistemological level for God as he is in himself. Because of the centrality and sufficiency of that revelation, speculation about God as he is in himself is pointless. See David C. Steinmetz, 'Luther and the Hidden God', *Luther in Context* (Grand Rapids, Mich.: Baker, 1995).

[2] Moreover, there is good precedent for a comparison between the views of Calvin and Aquinas. See Arvin Vos, *Aquinas, Calvin, and Contemporary Protestant Thought* (Grand Rapids, Mich.: Eerdmans, 1985). The infrequency with which Calvin refers to Aquinas explicitly is highlighted by Anthony N. S. Lane, *John Calvin: Student of the Church Fathers*, 44–5.

this distinction enables us to focus more clearly on exactly where Calvin's dislike of speculation about God is to be located. Aquinas will also help us to guard Calvin's views against possible misunderstanding. Does deploying this distinction indicate a disparaging of the metaphysics of theism on Calvin's part? I shall argue that this was no more so for Calvin than it was for Thomas.

The Distinction in Calvin

What is God? Men who pose this question are merely toying with idle speculations. It is far better for us to inquire 'What is his nature?' and to know what is consistent with his nature.[3]

Indeed, his essence is incomprehensible; hence, his divineness far escapes all human perception. But upon his individual works he has engraved unmistakable marks of his glory.[4]

Here is a somewhat nuanced distinction between God's *nature* and his *essence*. Calvin believes that we cannot perceive God's essence but that we can know his nature. God's nature and essence are distinct but connected. When Calvin says that 'God cannot be unlike himself' or that God 'cannot divest himself of his mercy, for he remains ever the same'[5] these expressions refer, I hazard, to God's activities as they characterize his nature and partly express to us his immutable and incomprehensible essence. God's activities, according to Calvin, partly reveal his nature and are, so to speak, endorsed or guaranteed by his immutable essence.

He [the Psalmist] does not speak of the hidden and mysterious essence of God which fills heaven and earth, but of the manifestations of his power, wisdom, goodness, and righteousness, which are clearly exhibited, although they are too vast for our limited understandings to comprehend.[6]

---

[3] *Inst.* I. 2. 2.

[4] *Inst.* I. 5. 1. Cf. I. 11. 3. Such quotations could be multiplied almost indefinitely. See, for instance, the additional quotations found in n. 6.   [5] *Comm.* Jonah 4: 2.

[6] *Comm.* Ps. 77: 14. Here are more statements of a similar kind: 'Consequently, we know the most perfect way of seeking God, and the most suitable order, is not for us to attempt with bold curiosity to penetrate to the investigation of his essence, which we ought more to adore than meticulously to search out, but for us to contemplate him in his works whereby he renders himself near and familiar to us, and in some manner communicates himself' (*Inst.* I. 5. 9). 'In understanding faith it is not merely a question of knowing that God exists, but also—and this especially—of knowing what is his will toward us. For it is not so much our concern to know who he is in himself, as what he wills to be toward us' (*Inst.* III. 2. 6). 'God is in himself invisible; but as his majesty shines forth in his works and in his creatures everywhere, men ought in these to acknowledge him, for they clearly set forth their Maker' (*Comm.* Rom. 1: 20). 'God has given us, throughout the whole framework of this world, clear evidence of his eternal wisdom, goodness, and power; and though he is in himself invisible, he in a manner becomes visible to us in his works' (*Comm.* Heb. 11: 3).

Although we cannot know God's essence, we can know that, because God is simple, his essence is immutable. God's essence is what he is; his accidents are what he has freely chosen to do.[7] And because the nature and the essence of God are connected insofar as the first is a partial revelation of the second we know that faithfulness is part of God's essence (part of what God is). Even though we cannot perceive or fully comprehend that essence, we can say that it is impossible for God to fail to be faithful (to fail to be what he is). Given that God has said this or done that, we can know that his incomprehensible essence underwrites, guarantees, or endorses the immutability—that is to say, the utter trustworthiness—of what he has said and done. God freely decrees this or that, but his freedom is always a freedom exercisable only in accordance with his immutable essence.

Why, then, in addition to God's essence, does Calvin speak of God's nature? Perhaps because Calvin needs a substantive expression that will serve as the logical subject for and an abbreviation of the predicates that express God *quoad nos*. Like the essence of God itself, God's nature is immutable because it is backed by his essence. We can know some things about the divine essence, such as that it is immutable. So God's essence, what God is, is not a *substratum* or *noumenon*, 'something I know not what'.[8] We can come to know, by inference from what God has disclosed of himself, some of the positive and negative characteristics of his essence even though we cannot perceive that essence or know it comprehensively.[9] Through God's gracious disclosure of himself we can know his nature—what God is toward us, and, because we know that what God says and does accords with his immutable essence, we can know that what he says and does is utterly reliable. More on this later.

[7] Calvin does not, as far as I am aware, entertain the question of what sort of change is involved in God's having extrinsic relations. But given Calvin's commitment to divine simplicity God's coming to be related to something other than himself cannot result in a real change in God, only the mere change that results in his relation to that thing. On this distinction, see Peter Geach, 'What Actually Exists' and 'Praying for Things to Happen', in *God and the Soul* (London: Routledge, 1969). We shall discuss this matter further in the final chapter.

[8] In Kant's philosophy a *noumenon*, such as the idea of the self or of material substance, cannot be an object of knowledge. Such concepts perform a regulative function only, postulated to account for the unity of our experience of sets of phenomena.

[9] Calvin here and elsewhere endorses (though not in so many words) the distinction between archetypal and ectypal theology, a distinction common in the medieval period and in later Reformed scholasticism. That is, the distinction between the knowledge of God known by God alone, and the knowledge of himself that he has communicated to his creatures. (For discussion of the distinction in Reformed scholasticism and its roots in Calvin, see Richard Muller, *Post-Reformation Reformed Dogmatics* (Grand Rapids, Mich.: Baker, 2003), 244, and Willem J. van Asselt, 'The Fundamental Meaning of Theology: Archetypal and Ectypal Theology in Seventeenth-Century Reformed Thought', *Westminster Theological Journal*, (2002), 324.)

God's nature, then, is expressed and summed up in what he is towards us. What God does, including what God reveals of himself, is what God has chosen to do. So we know God's nature through those activities that God has chosen to undertake. These activities express God's nature directly—for example, in the wisdom and righteousness that they display—but they express his essence only obliquely. Nevertheless, because what God has said and done are free, voluntary acts of condescension on his part, we must be guarded in drawing conclusions about his essence from what we know of his nature as expressed in his works lest we give ourselves the impression, an expression of *hubris*, that we thereby have a window into what is necessarily incomprehensible to us (God's very essence) or contingently unknowable by us (because it is God's secret will, or because it represents what God might have done but hasn't done and which he hasn't told us about).

I shall try to make good on all of these claims in what follows. But let us first look more closely at Calvin's attitude to God's essence and then at the connection between his essence and his immutability.

For Calvin, God's essence, God himself, is simple and incomprehensible, 'simple and undivided'.[10] We can make distinctions about God—between his attributes or among the persons of the Trinity, say—but these distinctions do not correspond to divisions in God. Presumably Calvin's reasoning here goes like this: only what has parts is divided (or divisible); God is without parts; therefore, God is undivided. But *distinctions* in God are not *divisions* of him. Even if we can distinguish between God's wisdom and his power, these are characteristics of one and the same God, just as distinguishing between Father, Son, and Spirit does not imply that there are three gods, or three parts to God.[11]

Such remarks about the divine essence's simplicity and incomprehensibility seem most at home with a rather negative approach to that essence, although this is not to say that Calvin was a 'negative theologian' in the style of Moses Maimonides.[12] We speak most sense about God's essence when we say what it is not (e.g. it is not changeable) and when we exercise reserve and restraint. In other words, we cannot know God—we cannot perceive

---

[10] *Inst.* I. 13. 2.

[11] Calvin explicitly draws the contrast between distinction and division in connection with the Trinity in *Inst.* I. 13. 17. Of course there is a potential difficulty here. Although the persons of the Trinity are distinct from each other, and yet God is not divided, nevertheless the persons are not merely modes of God, nor merely ways of thinking about God imposed by human finitude, in the way in which the distinctions between the divine attributes are.

[12] The Jewish thinker (1135–1204) who held that because of God's utter transcendence our language about God must be wholly negative, confined to stating what God is not, rather than attempting to say what God is.

God or completely comprehend him—as he is in himself. And we may also say that for Calvin, as for the entire tradition that accepts the idea of divine simplicity, God is incomprehensible to us partly at least *because* he is simple. Yet as we have seen, to say that God's essence is incomprehensible to us is not to say that we cannot know anything about it. We can know what has been revealed to us, thus giving us an insight into the character of God's nature, from which we can draw some conclusions about his essence. Yet that essence itself has not been revealed to us and could not presently be. Perhaps it can never be.

The fact that we know God only as he is to us does not mean, however, that our knowledge of him is only relational. So B. B. Warfield may be mistaken when he says: 'This much we know, [Calvin] says, that God is what His works and acts reveal Him to be; though it must be admitted that His works and acts reveal not His metaphysical Being but His personal relations—not what he is *apud se* [in himself], but what he is *quoad nos*.'[13] This confuses what God is to us with what God is in personal relation to us. It also assumes that what God is to us does not have a metaphysical character. There are ways in which what God is like to us is expressed in non-relational language but which, according to Calvin, do not reveal God as he is in himself.[14] For example, God is said to be wise, and good. In addition, we may say that God reveals himself, his being, through the relations he enters into. Warfield, however, may be correct to this extent, that Calvin believes that every way in which God accommodates himself to us is for soteric ends.

Thus what Calvin refers to separately as the 'nature' and the 'essence' of God are linked; and what links them is the immutability of God's essence. His nature cannot but give evidence of his essence. Randall Zachman correctly notes this; but the inseparability of God's goodness from his essence simply acknowledges that, in view of this linkage, God's works of goodness take on the quality of constancy or immutability.[15] 'The goodness of God is so inseparably connected with his essence as to render it impossible for him not to be merciful'[16]—impossible in the sense that having promised his mercy God cannot, in view of what he essentially is, renege on what he has promised.[17]

---

[13] 'Calvin's Doctrine of God', in *Calvin and Calvinism* (New York: Oxford University Press, 1931), 154.

[14] The index of the Battles edition of the *Institutes* lists both the essence and attributes of God under God 'in himself' whereas it is more faithful to Calvin, I am arguing, that the only entries under God in himself should be references to his essence.

[15] 'Calvin as Analogical Theologian', *Scottish Journal of Theology* (1998), 169.

[16] *Comm.* Ps. 77: 9.

[17] See also *Comm.* Lam. 3: 8: 'We may be content with this one thing, that when God claims to himself this prerogative, that he answers prayers, he intimates that it is what cannot be separated from his eternal essence and godhead; that is, that he is ready to hear prayer.'

God's essence, then, is incomprehensible. Yet we can nevertheless say that his actions are grounded in his essence; and from this we may infer that his actions, and especially his promises, are immutable.

THE DISTINCTION IN THOMAS AQUINAS

Aquinas also distinguishes between God *in se* and God *quoad nos*; and this distinction is of considerable theological importance for him. For instance, he marks the transition from *Summa Theologiae*, 1a, 12. 11 to 1a, 12. 12 by contrasting what he calls 'what God is in himself' to 'how in fact he is known by his creatures?'[18] Through 1a, 12. 11, Aquinas has been considering what God is in himself. Then he turns to 'what our minds can make of him; how in fact is he known by his creatures'. How God is known by his creatures is precisely *not* by knowing what God is in himself; by our reason, we may know that God exists, and then 'by grace we have a more perfect knowledge of God than we have by natural reason. . . . [H]uman knowledge is helped by the revelation of grace . . . although in this life revelation does not tell us what God is'.[19] That is, it does not reveal what God is *in se*.

What is the significance of this? Earlier, after expounding his Five Ways, Aquinas says that:

> Having recognized that a certain thing exists, we have still to investigate the way in which it exists, that we may come to understand what it is that exists. Now we cannot know how God is, but only how he is not; we must therefore consider the ways in which God does not exist, rather than the ways in which he does . . . The ways in which God does not exist will become apparent if we rule out from him everything inappropriate, such as compositeness, change, and the like.[20]

Under the heading 'what God is in himself' Aquinas considers God's simplicity (Q3), his perfection (Q4), his goodness (Q6), his limitlessness (Q7), his unchangeableness (Q9), and his eternity (Q10). These are all ways of knowing what God is not. Many if not all of these aspects of the godhead are implied by the reasoning and the conclusions of the Five Ways. Thus by the First Way, God is changeless; by the Second Way, he is first cause (and consequently eternal); and by the Fourth Way, he is the cause of goodness. (By the Third Way, he is necessary—'something which must be'; and by the Fifth Way, he is the ultimate director of the universe.)

A governing principle of the Five Ways is that God's existence is made evident by God's effects but that these effects 'cannot help us to know him

---

[18] *Summa Theologiae*, 1a, 2. 12, trans. Thomas Gilbey. All translations of the *Summa Theologiae* are from that published by Blackfriars, London: in connection with Eyre & Spottiswoode, 1963–80.

[19] *Summa Theologiae*, 1a, 12. 13.   [20] *Summa Theologiae*, 1a, 2. 2.

comprehensively for what he is'.[21] Nevertheless, they do enable us to come to certain conclusions about the God whose existence we can be sure of, albeit conclusions expressed in rather negative language.

So the contrast that we find in Calvin is already present in Thomas, both in his treatment of God's being (where he draws the contrast) and in the kind and source of the knowledge of God possessed by his creatures (where we know God primarily as he is revealed to us). Calvin stresses the negative character of our knowledge of God as he is in himself less than Thomas does. He also does not explicitly link our knowledge (*scientia*) of God to the possibility of establishing God's existence by proof. One way that Thomas characteristically puts these points is to say that we can know (by reason—*scientia*—via the Five Ways) *that* God is, but not (either by reason or by revelation) *what* God is, only how he has made himself known to us.[22] The Five Ways do not show us the way in which God exists; and, for Thomas, it is by knowing the way in which a thing exists that we know what that thing is.

Concerning our knowledge of anything, Thomas says:

One cannot have a complete [*perfecta*] cognition of any thing at all unless one has cognition of its activity [*operatio*], for the measure and the quality of a thing's power are evaluated by the mode and type of its activity; but a thing's power reveals its nature.[23]

But then, when we think this through with reference to God's essence:

The knowledge that is natural to us has its source in the senses and extends just so far as it can be led by sensible things; from these, however, our understanding cannot reach to the divine essence. Sensible creatures are effects of God which are less than typical of the power of their cause, so knowing them does not lead us to understand the whole power of God and thus we do not see his essence. They are nevertheless effects depending from[24] a cause, and so we can at least be led from them to know of God that he exists and that he has whatever must belong to a first cause of all things which is beyond all that is caused.

Thus we know about his relation to creatures—that he is the cause of them all; about the difference between him and them—that nothing created is in him; and that his lack of such things is not a deficiency in him but due to his transcendence. [25]

---

[21] *Summa Theologiae*, 1a, 2. 2.

[22] *Summa Theologiae*, 1a, 12. 1: 'As hitherto we have considered God as he is in himself, we now go on to consider in what manner he is in the knowledge of creatures.'

[23] Quoted in Norman Kretzmann, *The Metaphysics of Creation* (Oxford: Clarendon Press, 1999), 14 (*SCG* 1. 852). Kretzmann claims that in book 1 of the *Summa Contra Gentiles* Aquinas considers 'matters associated with God considered in himself' (*The Metaphysics of Theism* (Oxford: Clarendon Press, 1997), 2n). We have no cognition of what God is in himself (118, in reference to *Summa Contra Gentiles*, I. 14).

[24] That is, the effects arise from their cause in such a way that from them we are able to learn things about the cause.

[25] *Summa Theologiae*, 1a, 12. 12, trans. Herbert McCabe.

Can we on this basis understand, say, God's simplicity? No. When he treats divine simplicity, Aquinas says, 'So that when we talk of godhead or life or something of that sort residing in God, the diversity this implies is not to be attributed to God himself, but to the way in which we conceive him'.[26] That is, in attributing to God a diversity of properties our language does not correspond to the way in which God exists—for in himself he is simple—but merely to how we conceive of him. And even when we affirm God's simplicity, we still do not comprehend it as it actually is, because:

in talking about simple things we have to use as models the composite things from which our knowledge derives . . . God's effects resemble God as far as they can, but not perfectly. One of the defects in resemblance is that they can reproduce only manifoldly what in itself is one and simple. As a result they are composite, and so cannot be identified with their natures.[27]

Thus Calvin's contrast between division and distinction in God echoes Aquinas's practice.

The same point holds when we come to where natural reason cannot reach and where, consequently, we are dependent upon divine revelation: 'in this life revelation does not tell us what God is' but 'joins us to him as to an unknown'.[28] Even revealed knowledge of how God is *quoad nos* is oblique because it must use language that refers directly only to creation and its creatures and that, consequently, can only be applied analogically to God. To recognize this is not to denigrate revelation, which can still help us 'to know him better in that we are shown more and greater works of his and are taught things about him that we could never have known through natural reason, as for instance that he is both three and one'.[29] Yet even when revelation helps us to know God better by pointing out some of his greater works, those works still cannot fully reveal, for instance, the infinity of God's power, because creation and its creatures are only finite in power. It is similar with the revelation of each of God's other attributes.

In Exodus 34: 6 God reveals himself as Jehovah. Calvin's comments in the *Institutes* on this passage constitute a fundamental locus of his exposition of the divine nature as it is revealed in God's word:

Here let us observe that [God's] eternity and his self-existence are announced by that wonderful name twice repeated. Thereupon his powers are mentioned, by which he is shown to us not as he is in himself, but as he is toward us: so that this recognition of him consists more in living experience than in vain and high-flown speculation. Now we hear the same powers enumerated there that we have noted as shining in heaven and earth: kindness, goodness, mercy, justice, judgment and truth.[30]

---

[26] *Summa Theologiae*, 1a, 3. 3, trans. Timothy McDermott.   [27] *Summa Theologiae*, 1a, 3. 3.

[28] *Summa Theologiae*, 1a, 12. 13.   [29] *Summa Theologiae*, 1a, 12. 13.   [30] *Inst.* 1. 10. 2.

Each of the latter, more evangelical attributes of God is rooted in the former, more metaphysical attributes that are (to us) aspects of God's simple essence. In Thomas, the reasoning and conclusions about God found in the Five Ways governs all else. In Calvin there is something similar—namely, an account of theism in which some sort of priority is given to God's immutable power, truth, holiness, and goodness, even though Calvin does not ground these in the conclusions of arguments of natural theology. We must keep these divine attributes in mind if we are to understand properly everything else that God reveals to us about himself.

So like Aquinas, Calvin knows *that* God is eternal, self-existent, and all-good, but he does not know *what* God is. Thus Calvin affirms that he does not comprehend the divine essence of which eternity, self-existence, and complete goodness are aspects. Only God knows what God is. Yet the fact that we know that God is eternal, self-existing and all-good and that these are features of his essence does a great deal of theological and religious work for Calvin. Reference to God's essence or nature—even though that essence is incomprehensible to us—controls, in a kind of operational way, our understanding of and our attitude to God as he is to us:

The more violently [the Psalmist] was assailed, the more firmly did he lean upon the truth, That the goodness of God is so inseparably connected with his essence as to render it impossible for him not to be merciful. Whenever, therefore, doubts enter into our minds upon our being harassed with cares, and oppressed with sorrows, let us learn always to endeavour to arrive at a satisfactory answer to this question, Has God changed his nature so as to be no longer merciful?[31]

Likewise, God's revealed majesty and glory is inseparable from his essence.

The majesty, or the authority, or the glory of God does not consist in some imaginary brightness, but in those works which so necessarily belong to him, that they cannot be separated from his very essence. It is what peculiarly belongs to God, to govern the world, and to exercise care over mankind, and also to make a difference between good and evil, to help the miserable, to punish all wickedness, to check injustice and violence. When any one takes away these things from God, he leaves him an idol only.[32]

But this is not exhaustive of God's essence. God, as he reveals himself to us, must be a God whose actions *ad extra* are consistent with and reflect his incomprehensible essence—even though, because God is free, his essence does not necessitate these actions.

---

[31] *Comm.* Ps. 77: 9. '*To God belong lovingkindnesses*; therefore, as he can never deny himself, he will always be merciful. This attribute is inseparable from his eternal essence; and however we have rebelled against him, yet he will never either cast away nor disdain our prayers' (*Comm.* Daniel 9: 9).

[32] *Comm.* Zephaniah 1: 12.

Reference to God's incomprehensible essence also warns us against imagining what God is like, which would lead us inexorably down the road to idolatry. Recognizing God's infinite and spiritual essence keeps us from thinking that God can be represented in imagery. We should recognize pictorial and figurative language about God for what it is; a case of divine accommodation.

> For who even of slight intelligence does not understand that, as nurses commonly do with infants, God is wont in a measure to 'lisp' in speaking to us? Thus such forms of speaking do not so much express clearly what God is like as accommodate the knowledge of him to our slight capacity. To do this he must descend far beneath his loftiness.[33]

So the contrast between God as he is in himself and as he is towards us, in both Aquinas and Calvin, is warranted both by our position vis-à-vis God's incomprehensible essence and by the voluntariness of his creative and redemptive activities which, because they arise from God's free choice, do not and cannot reveal God as he is in himself, even if we were in a position to comprehend him in that way. This is not because God's activities are arbitrary but because they are contingent and so are not comprehensive accounts of the essence of God.

THE MEANING OF 'GOD AS HE IS IN HIMSELF'

Calvin contrasts God as he is in himself with God as he is toward us to highlight his refusal to speculate about God a priori and thus to respect the revealed knowledge of God. But what does he mean by the expression God 'as he is in himself'? What kind of knowledge of God are we not to seek? The clue to this lies in Calvin's idea of God's self-knowledge. In discussing the divine simplicity as part of his very restrained trinitarianism, Calvin says:

> Here, indeed, if anywhere in the secret mysteries of Scripture, we ought to play the philosopher soberly and with great moderation; let us use great caution that neither our thoughts nor our speech go beyond the limits to which the Word of God itself extends. For how can the human mind measure off the measureless essence of God according to its own little measure, a mind as yet unable to establish for certain the nature of the sun's body, though men's eyes daily gaze upon it? Indeed, how can the mind by its own leading come to search out God's essence when it cannot even get to its own? Let us then willingly leave to God the knowledge of himself. For, as Hilary

---

[33] *Inst.* I. 13. 1. Writing of the Second Commandment Calvin says it 'restrains our license from daring to subject God, who is incomprehensible, to our sense perceptions, or to represent him by any form' (*Inst.* II. 8. 17).

says, he is the one fit witness to himself, and is not known except through himself.[34] But we shall be 'leaving it to him' if we conceive him to be as he reveals himself to us.[35]

That is to say, only God can know God in a full and comprehensive fashion; and if we try to know God as he knows himself, then we are attempting to overturn the Creator/creature distinction. My claim that this is the kind of knowledge of God that we are not to seek gains support from considering what the medievals took as the sort of knowledge God has of himself.

The medieval tradition on God's knowability—on the precedent of which, I have been arguing, Calvin builds—stresses God's incomprehensibility to us. We can only apprehend God, not comprehend him. But it does not follow—indeed, it could not—that God is incomprehensible to himself. We may gain some insight into what this tradition thinks is necessarily denied to any finite knower if we consider its discussion of what God knows of himself and, in particular, of the nature of that knowledge.

It is obvious that, while you may know much about me, you do not know what it is to be me and to have my thoughts and desires. To have these thoughts and desires, you would have to be me. In this sense, I have a knowledge of myself that you do not and cannot possess. Bats navigate by a complicated sonar mechanism. We know that's how it is with bats. But what is it like to be a bat? To answer that question we would have to be bats, or sufficiently bat-like for appropriate analogies to work. Similarly, for Calvin, to know God as he is in himself we would ourselves have to be the infinite eternal spirit that God is, which we neither can be nor ought to aspire to be. This also means that there is a sense in which God does not know us, for he does not know me in the precise way that I know myself. But unlike in the case of our knowledge of God, his knowledge of us, even though he cannot have our own self-knowledge, is greatly assisted by the knowledge and power that he necessarily has as our Creator.

In the *Summa Theologiae*, Aquinas discusses at length God's knowledge of himself. Article 3 of 1a, 14 asks, 'Has God comprehensive knowledge of himself?' and answers like this:

---

[34] The passage from Hilary reads, 'Leave to God the privilege of knowing himself; for it is he only who is able to bear witness to himself who knows himself by himself alone. And we shall be leaving him what belongs to him if we understand him as he declares himself, and ask nothing at all concerning him except through his word.' (*On the Trinity* 1. xviii, quoted in F. Wendel, *Calvin: The Origins and Development of his Religious Thought* (London: Fontana Library, 1965), 152.)

[35] *Inst.* 1. 13. 21. H. A. Oberman observes that the formula *finitum non capax infiniti* does not occur in the works of Calvin (*The Dawn of the Reformation*, 253). Perhaps not. But this quotation shows that although the precise words may not be there, the idea certainly is.

God's power to know is equal to his actuality in existence: for his power to know comes from his actuality, his freedom from all matter and potentiality, as has been shown. Clearly, then, he knows himself to the extent to which he is knowable. Therefore he has completely comprehensive knowledge of himself.[36]

And thus it is clear from all that has gone before that in God intellect, and that which is known, and the knowledge-species, and the act of knowing, are entirely one and the same. Clearly, then, to say God is knowing is not to place any multiplicity in his substance.[37]

This has important consequences, Aquinas thinks, for our theological semantics. God's knowledge of himself is not discursive. He knows everything at once and not successively. More importantly, he does not know inferentially, passing from premises to conclusions as we do. By contrast, our thought and language about God are discursive, and our understanding is successive:

When we pass from principles to conclusions we are not considering both at the same time. . . . [Moreover,] this kind of discursiveness passes from known to unknown. So it is clear that when we know the first we are still ignorant of the second. Thus we do not know the second *in* the first, but *from* the first. And the process comes to an end when the second *is* seen in the first and the effects are found in their causes; at which point the discursive process ceases. Therefore, since God sees his effects in himself as in their cause, his knowledge is not discursive.[38]

So when Calvin contrasts God as he is in himself with God as he is toward us in order to highlight his decision to respect the revealed knowledge of God what he has in mind is the idea—found here in Aquinas, for example—that God alone can know God 'as he is in himself', an idea that has both scriptural warrant (in chapters 38–41 of the book of Job, say) and perhaps has some of its roots in Aristotle's claim in *Metaphysics* VI that in the case of divine thought the thought and the object of the thought are one and the same simple thing.

SPECULATION

God cannot reveal to us what he is in himself. But might we have access to this by some other route than by revelation? Calvin's resoundingly negative answer to this question can be discerned in a second, connected theme in his treatment of the doctrine of God. He refuses to speculate about God as he is in himself both because it is unwarranted, and therefore irreligious, but also because it is distracting, and therefore impious.

---

[36] *Summa Theologiae*, 1a, 14. 3, trans. Thomas Gornall.   [37] *Summa Theologiae*, 1a, 14. 4.
[38] *Summa Theologiae*, 1a, 14. 7. See also Article 14, Does God know propositions?

[T]he pious mind does not dream up for itself any god it pleases, but contemplates the one and only true God. And it does not attach to him whatever it pleases, but is content to hold him to be as he manifests himself.[39]

Thereupon his powers are mentioned, by which he is shown to us not as he is in himself, but as he is toward us: so that this recognition of him consists more in living experience than in vain and high-flown speculation.[40]

Calvin's anti-speculative emphasis is sometimes seen not only as characteristic of him but also as expressing a position that distinguished him from the stance of medieval theologians. Calvin's theology is portrayed as having a practical thrust that discouraged the kind of frigid speculation that was characteristic of scholastic theology. But we must go carefully here. For one thing, there is a clearly discernible anti-speculative strand in medievalism, such as in the tradition of monastic theology.[41] For another, there is a tradition in pre-Reformation theology that sees theology as more practical than theoretical, as leading to *sapientia* rather than *scientia*.

For a third, it may be best to see Calvin's anti-speculative thrust as recognizing a division of labour between theologians and philosophers. According to one medieval emphasis, theologians should restrict themselves to the study of revealed theology and not indulge in general metaphysics, not even in the branch of it that is concerned with natural theology. Metaphysics is not the business of the Faculty of Theology but of the Faculty of Arts. Calvin can fairly be placed within that tradition. Consider, for instance, his remarks on the soul, and in particular the contrast that he draws between his 'simple definition' of the soul and more subtle philosophical discussions of it.[42] This may be due to his insistence on the division between theology and philosophy. Another instance is where Calvin distinguishes between theology and medicine in discussing the views of the 'new Marcionites' who contend that women are 'without seed'. Calvin says that this is not a theological issue but belongs to philosophy and medicine; and, consequently, he says, he will not touch upon it (even though 'the reasons they bring forward . . . can be refuted without trouble') but content himself with answering those objections to the orthodox doctrine that are drawn from Scripture.[43]

Calvin's remarks on astronomy are perhaps his best-known recognition of such intellectual boundaries between disciplines. 'He who would learn

---

[39] *Inst.* I. 2. 2.   [40] *Inst.* I. 10. 2.

[41] See references to Gregory's letter against speculation, and to Albert the Great, in Lawrence Moonan, *Divine Power* (Oxford: Clarendon Press, 1994), 149. David Steinmetz also provides examples of anti-scholasticism in the medieval period (*Luther in Context*, ch. 5).

[42] 'I, indeed, agree that the things they [namely, the philosophers] teach are true, not only enjoyable, but also profitable to learn, and skillfully assembled by them. And I do not forbid those who are desirous of learning to study them' (*Inst.* I. 15. 6).   [43] *Inst.* II. 13. 3.

astronomy, and other recondite arts, let him go elsewhere'—elsewhere than to what Moses has to say about waters above the heaven.[44]

Astronomers investigate with great labour whatever the sagacity of the human mind can comprehend. Nevertheless, this study is not to be reprobated, nor this science to be condemned, because some frantic persons are wont boldly to reject whatever is unknown to them. For astronomy is not only pleasant, but also very useful to be known: it cannot be denied that this art unfolds the admirable wisdom of God.[45]

Calvin is a theologian, concerned with what God has in fact revealed; and, consequently, he is not given to speculation or to the discussion of philosophical, medical, or astronomical issues in their own right. But philosophy, as distinct from revealed theology, is legitimate, just as the study of medicine or astronomy is. Therefore, Calvin's warnings against speculation in theology ought not to be taken to express a root-and-branch opposition to all metaphysical investigation and speculation, any more than to the practice of medicine or astronomy.[46]

A further source of Calvin's anti-speculative stance involves his refusal to accept any conception of God in which God's power is abstracted from his justice or righteousness.

And we do not advocate the fiction of 'absolute might'; because this is profane, it ought rightly to be hateful to us. We fancy no lawless god who is a law unto himself. For, as Plato says, men who are troubled with lusts are in need of law; but the will of God is not only free of all fault but is the highest rule of perfection, and even the law of all laws.[47]

If we could break up the divine simplicity so as to be able to consider, say, divine power apart from divine justice, then it would be possible to speculate

---

[44] *Comm.* Gen. 1: 6.

[45] *Comm.* Gen. 1: 16. Calvin seems to have had a special appreciation of astronomy, just as he vehemently opposed astrology (though the term 'astrology' was used by him to cover both the legitimate and the bastard science). This comes out, for instance, in his 1549 *A Warning Against Judiciary Astrology and Other Prevalent Curiosities*, where, alongside excoriating the practice of divination, he comments positively on astronomy as the study of the planets and stars 'which involves estimating their office, property, and power and subjugating the entire science to God's end and God's use'. Praise and respect for the science comes out incidentally in a number of places, including his sermons on Job: The astronomers 'imagine things that are not in the skyes: but they imagin them not without reason: for they doo it to shewe by certayne degrees and measures, the things myght be to hygh and to deepe to comprehend. Well, and haue the Philosophers disputed much of this matter? Hathe God given them a greater grace than can bee beleeved, to note and marke out Gods secrets that are on hygh?' (*Sermons on Job*, trans. Arthur Golding (1574); repr. in facsimile (Edinburgh: Banner of Truth Trust, 1993), 158.)

[46] Alexander of Hales distinguishes between theology as the knowledge of God dependent upon divine grace and revelation and 'the theology of the philosophers', namely, natural theology. The theology of the theologians has an affective element as well as the purely cognitive element that it shares with the theology of the philosophers (Moonan, *Divine Power*, 131–2).   [47] *Inst.* III. 23. 2.

about what a God of pure power divorced from divine justice might command or perform. But Calvin will not countenance this. He abhors any thinking about God that separates his ruling power from his justice. We must hold together in fact what appears to be separable in thought. This is another way in which, according to Calvin, our knowledge that God has an immutable though incomprehensible essence must control all our thinking and speaking about God.

In his insistence on the unity of the divine essence we can also see that Calvin is echoing the recognition of many of his medieval predecessors that God can do what he does not do. For instance, for Aquinas God's decree is neither a matter of natural necessity nor the only decree that God could have made. In discussing this question in the *Summa Theologiae*, Thomas says:

There is no reason why something should not be within divine power which God does not will, and which is no part of the present order he has established. We conceive of understanding and wisdom as directing, will as commanding, and power as executing; as for what lies within power as such, God is able to do it by his absolute power . . . Accordingly we should state that by his absolute power God can do things other than those he foresaw that he would do and pre-ordained to do.[48]

That is, if we are speaking only of divine power, and abstracting it from other features of God's essence, then the range of things that God could have done that he has not done is governed solely by his 'absolute power'. Nevertheless, the exercise of such absolute power can never in fact be divorced from 'understanding and willing and wisdom and justice' because of the divine simplicity. We shall consider Calvin's attitude to divine power and justice more fully in Chapter 11.

A final source of Calvin's anti-speculative tendency is his principled refusal to inquire into what God might have done and hasn't done and which he hasn't told us about. This is characteristic of Calvin's theological thinking and especially of his reflections on God's will. Even though he recognizes the distinction between what God has done and what he might have done, he does not use that distinction to attempt to gain further insight into God's ways, because any such use of it would be speculative. 'Speculative' here contrasts with 'revealed'. Thus if some theological position might give rise to speculation—say, the idea that 'some distinction does exist in the one divinity of Father, Son, and Spirit' (something 'hard to grasp', as Calvin says)—then we do better to restrict ourselves to the terms in which Scripture speaks, 'even though they may fail to capture the height of the mystery', rather than indulge our curiosity about this and so enter a 'labyrinth'.[49]

---

[48] *Summa Theologiae*, 1a, 25. 5.   [49] *Inst.* I. 13. 21.

If God has revealed what he might have brought about but in fact hasn't brought about, then well and good. But it is impious and unprofitable to attempt to pry into what God has not revealed. In fact, Calvin sometimes seems reluctant to believe that God ever reveals what he did not do but might have done. One might reasonably take Christ's words, 'Woe unto thee, Chorazin!, woe unto thee, Bethsaida!, for if the mighty works, which were done in you, had been done in Tyre and Sidon, they would have repented long ago in sackcloth and ashes' (Matthew 11: 21), to refer to what might have taken place but hasn't. However, Calvin says:

Lest any should raise thorny questions about the secret decrees of God, we must remember, that this discourse of our Lord is accommodated to the ordinary capacity of the human mind. Comparing the citizens of *Bethsaida*, and their neighbours, with the inhabitants of *Tyre* and *Sidon*, he reasons, not of what God foresaw would be done either by the one or the other, but of what both parties would have done, so far as could be judged from the facts.[50]

Calvin pointedly fails to interpret this passage by invoking God's knowledge of conditionals, much less a 'middle knowledge', in spite of the fact that it gives him the opportunity to do so.[51] He prefers, instead, to understand the contrast Christ draws as based on empirical observation of the places in question.

And similarly with Calvin's treatment of what came to be the standard 'proof-text' of the Molinists, the incident of David's prayer to the Lord as to whether he should remain in the city of Keilah (I Sam. 23). In his lectures on the First Book of Samuel Calvin writes:

Now it ought not to be subtly disputed whether they would have handed David over or not, if he had awaited the arrival of Saul, with which idle questions, nevertheless, many are accustomed to show the sharpness of their genius by means of their sophistical imaginations . . . But it ought to be considered that the purpose of God is incomprehensible to us, concerning which things are able to happen. For whatever people call accidents or fortuitous events, they are nevertheless the most certain decrees of God, such that if we consider the plan of God there is nothing that may be determined to happen by chance or fortuitously. But when our senses, on account of

---

[50] *A Commentary on a Harmony of the Evangelists*, II. 27.

[51] Middle knowledge is the view that besides God's knowledge of every possibility, and his knowledge of what he has willed, there is knowledge of conditional propositions, in particular of what would be true if, in certain given circumstances, human beings were to act freely. It was brought into prominence by Luis de Molina (1535–1600) as a way of accounting for the harmony of God's foreknowledge and human freedom (Luis de Molina, *On Divine Foreknowledge, Part IV of the Concordia*, trans. with an Introduction and Notes by Alfred J. Freddoso (Ithaca and London: Cornell University Press, 1988)). Papers representative of the modern debate about middle knowledge can be found in William Hasker, David Basinger, and Eef Dekker (eds.), *Middle Knowledge: Theory and Applications* (Frankfurt: Peter Lang, 2000).

their weakness, are not able to search out the judgements of God, which are so lofty and profound, what they cannot grasp, they ought to adore within themselves. And yet, with certain phrases of Scripture God accommodates himself to our capacity, as when he says if you remain in the city, you shall die, but if you escape, you shall save your life. And there is no doubting that this is how it will be for God to be known as long as he may wish us to live on the earth and to conduct business with respect to which he protects our life; nevertheless God wills that we be kept within our small measure. For this reason, when the Lord says to David, if you should remain in the city you will be betrayed by the inhabitants, it ought not to be understood as if the Lord were incapable of arranging matters differently, or unable to bend the minds of the inhabitants of the city, but the Lord warned David concerning their treacherousness lest he rashly commit himself to their care.[52]

Nevertheless, it is not difficult to see that Calvin's views as expressed in this passage are in accord with the resolute anti-Molinism of later Reformed theologians.

We shall observe this anti-speculative tendency at work in connection with the atonement in Chapter 13. Whether Calvin always resolutely forbids all speculation, and eschews it, or whether he occasionally indulges in it himself, is something that we shall attend to later. It is obvious that Calvin must make a distinction between what God has in fact decreed and what he might have decreed as soon as we reflect with him on the fact that God's decrees are free rather than absolutely necessary. For example, atonement through the God-man is not absolutely necessary, but it has 'stemmed from a heavenly decree, on which men's salvation depended'.[53] So Calvin thinks that there is a viable distinction here, but he refuses point blank to raise questions about what God might have done unless we have information from God about the matter and (as we have just seen) perhaps not even then. And so Calvin rejects speculation about what God might have done not because there is nothing to speculate about, but because such speculation is pointless because it is in principle unsettlable; and it is unsettlable because it concerns matters that God knows about himself, matters about what he might have purposed but has not, but which he has chosen not to reveal to us, and which are, therefore, 'secret'.[54]

Perhaps we could express the point as follows. Take the case of an expression such as 'If Jones had been in situation X, then he would have ...'. If X is not too bizarre a situation, then we can reason intelligently about how we

---

[52] G. Baum, E. Cunitz, and E. Reuss (eds.), *Ioannis Calvinis Opera Quae Supersunt Omnia* (Brunschwig and Halle: Schwetschke, 1834–60), xxx. 527–8. I am grateful to Jon Balserak for supplying the translation.

[53] *Inst.* II. 12. 1. Calvin holds (or more strictly, came to hold) that though not absolutely necessary, there was no other way for God to procure human redemption. This matter is discussed more fully in ch. 11.

[54] 'Secret' is also used by Calvin in another, related sense, to refer to what God has in fact purposed but has not revealed to us, as in 'the secret providence of God'.

might complete the sentence because we know Jones and we know what other human beings like Jones have done in similar situations. So we might reasonably conclude, 'If Jones had been a millionaire, then he would have bought a yacht', based on what we know of Jones and what we know of how millionaires typically behave. But in the case of God almost all we know is what he has revealed about what he actually has done. He has revealed very little about what he might have done. So, since we lack experience of the activities of many gods, it would be unwise to draw conclusions about what God might have done.

Peter van Inwagen has plausibly argued for what he calls modal scepticism. Modal scepticism involves the claim that we know little (aside from what might be revealed to us) about what might and what might not be possible in areas that are remote from everyday life. We might apply this to Calvin's refusal to speculate. All we have to go on, Calvin says, in effect, is what God has actually done, including what he has revealed. To argue from what he has done to what he might have done when we don't have any guidance from revelation for so arguing is as vain as trying to argue about what might have been in areas that are remote from our everyday experience.[55]

Yet we must be careful to see what the phrase 'God as he is revealed to us' does and does not imply for Calvin. It implies the contrast between the unknowability of what God is in himself and the knowability of what he has revealed, but it does not imply that God as he has revealed himself to us presents no philosophical and theological problems. What God has revealed to us, and what God brings to pass in his providential government of the world, is on occasion incomprehensible to us, not because it is the will of absolute power divorced from every other essential feature of the divine character, nor because it is a revelation of how God is in himself, but because God has chosen not to disclose to us the reasons for doing what he has revealed to us that he will do.

We may briefly link these remarks about Calvin's attitude to the divine essence to the idea of divine accommodation. Divine accommodation is now recognized as a prominent and pervasive theme in Calvin—a theme that we shall consider in Chapter 7 and elsewhere. For Calvin, there is at least a twofold accommodation of God's nature to the capacities of his finite creatures. The first has to do with the human need to articulate and to infer in order to understand God. Theologians characteristically reason about God. They speak of him in subject–predicate language; they draw con-

---

[55] Peter van Inwagen, *God, Knowledge and Mystery: Essays in Philosophical Theology* (Ithaca: Cornell University Press, 1995), 11–14.

clusions about him from premisses about him; and so on. In these ways, God's simplicity is accommodated to us, for given our human condition his simple nature must inevitably be refracted into thought and language about numerous distinct attributes. His one decree may be spoken of as if it were many separate decrees. Further, God frequently presents himself to us in language that implies embodiment in human form, as well as his having passions and suffering change. In these ways, the first sort of accommodated language—language that sanctions talk of a plurality of divine attributes—is accommodated to a second degree, for in anthropomorphic and anthropopathic language God's immutable nature is further accommodated to us.

These are some of the central conditions under which God reveals himself to us. In a sense, we should be content with them, while not thinking that what God has revealed is all that could be revealed, or that it is exhaustive of God's very essence.

CALVIN'S METAPHYSICS OF THEISM

I come finally and briefly to emphasize a central consequence of Calvin's approach to the divine essence; namely, that Calvin's distinction between God as he is in himself and God as he is to us is consistent with and indeed requires a robust metaphysical theism.

In what is for the most part an admirable treatment of Calvin's doctrine of the knowledge of God, Edward A. Dowey has this to say about Calvin's idea of accommodation:

[Calvin] never ventured to attach anything but the name of incomprehensible mystery to what lay beyond that horizon, yet he maintained stoutly that it is God's mystery, not an abyss of nothingness. The mystery belongs to the unknowable side of the known God. Such a phenomenalism in the hands of a speculative thinker could lead as easily to skepticism as to faith.[56]

There is some good sense here, but also some exaggeration and a danger that we will be led astray in understanding Calvin's idea of God by certain patterns of thought and the use of a certain kind of philosophical terminology. In particular, the use of the term 'phenomenalism' conjures up an approach to the idea of God and our knowledge of him that is most certainly not Calvin's. It suggests that the contrast Calvin has in mind when applying the terms 'essence' and 'nature' to God is between an unknowable thing-in-itself—a Kantian *noumenon* or a Lockean *substratum*, 'something, I know

---

[56] Edward A. Dowey, *The Knowledge of God in Calvin's Theology* (expanded edn.; Grand Rapids, Mich.: Eerdmans, 1993), 17.

not what'—and sets of phenomena (as in Kant) or primary and secondary qualities (as in Locke).[57]

This would imply that Calvin's contrast between God as he is in himself and God as he is to us involves the contrast between a Kantian *noumenon* and phenomena. But then talk of God in himself could only perform a regulative function in our thought about God, for we would be forever and necessarily ignorant of any aspect of God's essence. Such an approach would make Calvin's views seem similar to those expressed by John Hick in his *An Interpretation of Religion*, where there is 'the Real' that is totally inscrutable to us and where the various 'great religions' represent equally valid attempts to access and to represent 'the Real'.

> It follows from this distinction between the Real as it is in itself and as it is thought and experienced through our religious concepts that we cannot apply to the Real *an sich* the characteristics encountered in its *personae* or *impersonae*. Thus it cannot be said to be one or many, person or thing, substance or process, good or evil, purposive or non-purposive. None of the concrete descriptions that apply within the realm of human experience can apply literally to the unexperiencable ground of that realm.[58]

Apart from being clearly anachronistic, this would be a highly misleading way of understanding what Calvin is saying, just as it would be if it were claimed that for Calvin God is 'wholly other'. For Calvin, the contrast between God as he is in himself and God as he is revealed to us is not between the knowable and the unknowable, nor is he saying that the idea of the essence of God is exhausted by some regulative role that the idea of such an unknowable essence plays in our thinking about God. He is drawing a contrast between two different kinds of knowledge; namely, the knowledge that we may have of God—which is partial, multiform, and accommodated to our capacity—and the knowledge that God, and only God, has of himself. In Jerome Gellman's terms, God has an 'inner life'.[59] My earlier contrast between human self-knowledge and the knowledge of others is but a shadowy analogy of the contrast between God's knowledge of his inner self and our knowledge of it.

At the same time, Aquinas and Calvin are to be distinguished from a number of modern philosophical theologians because their use of the distinction between God in himself and God as he is towards us signals the

[57] For an earlier discussion of Calvin's alleged 'Kantianism' see Auguste Lecerf, *An Introduction to Reformed Dogmatics* (London: Lutterworth Press, 1949), 168.

[58] John Hick, *An Interpretation of Religion* (London: Macmillan, 1989), 246. By 'personae' and 'impersonae' Hick refers to religions which do and those which do not worship a personal God.

[59] Jerome Gellman, 'Identifying God in Experience: On Strawson, Sounds and God's Space', in Paul Helm (ed.), *Referring to God* (Richmond, Surrey: Curzon Press, 1999), 74.

existence of a substantive 'epistemic gap' between God and ourselves. Those who acknowledge this distinction understand that it involves the recognition of cognitive limits on our part (whoever precisely 'we' are). Yet as important as this distinction was for the medieval philosophical theologians and for Calvin, it is not acknowledged in some modern philosophical theology.

There are perhaps two interconnected reasons for this. One is that modern philosophical discussion of the concept of God takes for granted that the language necessary to elucidate the concept of God is typically univocal. Modern philosophical theologians resist accounts of language about God that involve a theory of analogy or accommodation, for example. They prefer accounts that are univocal even while they stress human cognitive limitations.[60]

In both Aquinas and Calvin some of the human language about God is univocal, but it is couched mainly in negative terms. But apart from this (what we might call) 'negative core', all other language about God is analogical or accommodated language, with elements of univocity but also with elements of equivocity. Modern discussion recognizes that we readily employ metaphors, similes, and analogies when talking about God; nevertheless, it takes there to be a univocal core that is usually much more extensive than that envisaged by Aquinas or Calvin, for it embraces the entire concept of God. Consequently, when we say that God is wise, or all-good, it is presumed that what is predicated of God has the same meaning as what is predicated of individuals distinct from God. Only in this way, it is believed, can we have a rigorous or philosophically controlled account of our thought about God.

Behind this view of language lies a metaphysical thesis that involves a suspicion of, if not an outright rejection of, the idea of divine simplicity and with that a rejection of divine timeless eternity and of any strong sense of divine immutability and divine impassibility. Consequently, much modern philosophical theology takes God to be more human-like than the God of Calvin or of Aquinas: he exists in time, he has a memory, he hopes and (perhaps) fears, he acts and reacts to the actions of his creatures. Human language, developed by reference to empirically identifiable states of affairs and the changes that they undergo, is not then put under very much strain when it is applied to such a God.

[60] See, for example, William Alston, 'Can We Speak Literally of God?', in *Divine Nature and Human Language: Essays in Philosophical Theology* (Ithaca: Cornell University Press, 1989). In the entire discussion of Alvin Plantinga's *Does God Have A Nature?* (Milwaukee: Marquette University Press, 1980) there is no suggestion that human language needs qualifying when discussing the divine nature and actions. Likewise Richard Swinburne, *The Coherence of Theism* (Oxford: Clarendon Press, 1977), ch. 5, though his argument in ch. 14 should be noted.

Modern philosophical theologians may also be inclined to assert the transparency and literalness of our language about God because of the abiding influence of the argument from design, which assumes that God's character can be inferred from the perceived order of the world.[61] Of course, Aquinas and Calvin assert that God deliberately ordered the universe; but they also allege that this order is not easily or readily perceived by us. We cannot easily 'read off' truths about God from truths about nature. So an epistemological boundary between the infinite God and the finite universe that he has created must be maintained. Thus we should be cautious in drawing inferences from the character of the universe to the character of God.

God cannot will anything that is evil, according to Aquinas and Calvin, nor can his will (in the sense of what he decrees) be other than immutable. Yet we cannot say—either a priori or as a result of an empirical investigation—precisely what God will decree. The fact that there is change in the world is not per se a flouting of such immutability, since God can immutably will that there is change in the world. God can immutably will that the sun rises and that it sets. Part of what a negative, reserved theological approach to divine goodness and immutability implies is that we cannot draw valid conclusions about God's character either a priori or a posteriori. But if God has, by revelation, said that he wills to do such-and-such, then such-and-such either cannot be evil or it cannot be willed as evil by God; and if he has said in unconditional terms that he will do so-and-so, then he cannot not do so-and-so.

The second, connected point explaining the contrast between Aquinas's and Calvin's stance on our knowledge of God and the stance of much modern philosophical theology is the broad acceptance by contemporary thinkers of an epistemological thesis about God, a thesis which might be expressed as:

(R) It is unreasonable to believe that God has a justifying reason for doing A or for permitting someone else to do B that he may also have good reason not to disclose to us or that is such that were God to disclose it to us we would not understand it.

This thesis is linked with the previous point about language in the following way. On the univocal view of theistic language, God's wisdom or benevolence are readily recognizable from instances of human wisdom or benevolence (though of course divine wisdom and benevolence are on a far grander scale and are not infected with imperfection in the way that human benevolence or wisdom are). Consequently, it is also readily recognizable

---

[61] For this suggestion, see Moonan, *Divine Power*, 344–5, 352–4.

that some event is prima facie an instance of divine wisdom or benevolence, just as it is in human cases. Hence, the 'problem of evil' is a modern problem arising from the mismatch between the order that, given God's assumed character, it is assumed there should be and the actual world's perceived moral disorder. This is how 'the problem of evil'—a central topic in modern philosophical theology—is taken to arise; and these are the terms in which, by and large, it is discussed. In this context, it is not permissible to claim that one reasonable response to the problem of evil is simply to say that God's ways are inscrutable, that he must have reasons for permitting evil that he has chosen not to disclose to us or that are such that, were he to disclose them to us, we would not understand them—and, moreover, that there is good reason for this state of affairs. So 'the problem of evil', as usually discussed, is a modern problem and this problem is not the same one that Aquinas and Calvin discuss in their respective accounts of providence, as we shall see in Chapter 4.

There are exceptions to this general approach based on (R) or something like it. Alvin Plantinga has mounted an interesting defence of the claim that we do not know how God knows. 'So there are these analogies and similarities between God's knowledge and ours. But the main point is this: though there are these analogies, we don't really have any idea at all about how God knows.'[62] And in a number of papers Stephen J. Wykstra has defended the reasonableness of appealing to divine inscrutability when faced with cases of apparently pointless suffering, such as the case of a fawn dying agonizingly in a forest fire. Wykstra has argued that 'if there is a being who created and sustained this universe around us, the wisdom and vision of this being would be considerably greater than our own. Given what we independently know of our cognitive limits, I suggested that the vision of such a being might well be to ours, as a parent's is to that of a one-month-old human infant.'[63] Wykstra defends this view by an appeal to what he calls 'core theism', which includes the existence of God accompanied by other religious claims having to do with an afterlife, the end times, salvation, and the like. The crux of his appeal is to the respective scopes of our creaturely access to the future and God's. Given that we know that we cannot see, unassisted, what life will be like so many years from now, the goods that God purposes through permitting suffering may and perhaps must fall beyond our present cognitive horizon.[64]

[62] Alvin Plantinga, 'Divine Knowledge' in C. Stephen Evans and Merold Westphal (eds.), *Christian Perspectives on Religious Knowledge* (Grand Rapids, Mich.: Eerdmans, 1993).

[63] Stephen J. Wykstra, 'Rowe's Noseeum Arguments from Evil', in Daniel Howard-Snyder (ed.), *The Evidential Argument from Evil* (New York: Oxford University Press, 1996), 139. The book contains a number of essays on this theme. See also Alvin Plantinga, *Warranted Christian Belief* (New York: Oxford University Press, 2000), ch. 13. [64] 'Rowe's Noseeum Arguments from Evil', 143.

This, it seems to me, is a stance that Calvin would have wholeheartedly endorsed.

Calvin is not a modern Trinitarian theologian, one who sees in the Trinity the controlling idea of Christian theology. He makes what is for him an important distinction between *de Deo Uno*, which he considers in *Institutes* I. 12, and *de Deo Trino*, which he discusses in the next chapter. Nevertheless, he does not readily separate the doctrine of God from the doctrine of the Trinity. In the *Institutes* the first mark of God is his 'infinite and spiritual essence', which banishes popular delusions about God and also refutes the subtleties of secular philosophy.[65] The second is his Trinitarian character, by which he distinguishes himself from idols.[66] It follows that if the interpretation of Calvin's ideas presented in this chapter has been along the right lines then we shall find him also observing the distinction between *Trinitas in se* and *Trinitas quoad nos*. We now turn to explore this and other features of his doctrine of the Trinity, together with some of the misunderstandings of it that are to be found in recent interpretations of Calvin's ideas.

[65] *Inst.* I. 13. 1.   [66] *Inst.* I. 13. 2.

2

The Trinity

In the previous chapter we saw that Calvin makes a fundamental distinction between God as he is in himself and God as he is revealed to us. The distinction Calvin draws is not between a wholly mysterious and intractable inner divine essence or *substratum* and a revealed 'surface', but between God as he knows himself and God as he reveals himself to others. Only God can fully know God, but he reveals features of his nature, and, by implication, features of his essence (as in Exod. 34: 6), even though we do not know these features in the same comprehensive, intuitive way that God knows them.

This distinction, considered alone, may strongly suggest that Calvin has a very unitary conception of God. He is certainly an undeviating monotheist, committed to the idea of divine simplicity, although he is committed to a version of it that is consistent with distinctions in the godhead.

Indeed, the words 'Father,' 'Son,' and 'Spirit' imply a real distinction—let no one think that these titles, whereby God is variously designated from his works, are empty—but a distinction, not a division. The passages that we have already cited [e.g. Zech. 13: 7] show that the Son has a character distinct from the Father, because the Word would not have been with God unless he were another than the Father, nor would he have had his glory with the Father were he not distinct from the Father.[1]

The difference between a 'distinction' and a 'division' here is something like this: it is possible for A and B to be distinct while being features, and essential features, of the same subject. But if A and B are divided, then they become subjects in their own right. If an amoeba divides, it becomes two amoebas. Though necessarily related to the Father and the Spirit, the Son is distinct from the Father in that, say, the Son is incarnate, while the Father is not. But the Son and the Father are not divided, since each is wholly and necessarily God. Yet this difference cannot be pressed too far, for a division is a particular kind of distinction, and in any case whether A and B are distinct from each other is a matter of degree. Perhaps in recognition of this Calvin says that the Father is 'somehow' distinct from the Word,[2] otherwise a form of Trinitarian modalism is implied.

---

[1] *Inst.* I. 13. 17.

[2] *Inst.* I. 13. 17. For a sophisticated discussion of simplicity and trinitarianism in Aquinas, see Christopher Hughes, *On a Complex Theory of a Simple God* (Ithaca: Cornell University Press, 1989). Whether

For Calvin, God is essentially Trinitarian and this trinitarianism plays a fundamental role in his theology. He underlines this role by expounding it as an integral part of our knowledge of God the Creator. God is not only an immeasurable, spiritual being, but he is a trinity of distinct but indivisible persons.

But God also designates himself by another special mark to distinguish himself more precisely from idols. For he so proclaims himself the sole God as to offer himself to be contemplated clearly in three persons. Unless we grasp these, only the bare and empty name of God flits about in our brains, to the exclusion of the true God.[3]

[W]hen we profess to believe in one God, under the name of God is understood a single, simple essence, in which we comprehend three persons, or hypostases. Therefore, whenever the name of God is mentioned without particularization, there are designated no less the Son and the Spirit than the Father; but where the Son is joined to the Father, then the relation of the two enters in; and so we distinguish among the persons.[4]

This last sentence expresses one of several hermeneutical rules that Calvin propounds for interpreting scriptural references to the Trinity, as well as to Christ. This particular rule plays a pivotal role in Calvin's understanding of the *communicatio idiomatum*, as we shall see in the next chapter.

Calvin's approach to the doctrine of the Trinity is wholly a posteriori in intent. He believes in the Trinity because God has 'designated' himself in this fashion in Holy Scripture. He does not speculate on a proof of this doctrine nor is he in any way drawn to arguing for specific features of the Trinity a priori. For example, Calvin nowhere says that because God's nature is love his love must have a non-creaturely object—a divine person—and thus there must be more than one person in the godhead. Instead, believing (with Thomas Aquinas, say) that what we know of the Trinity we know only on account of God's revelation, he seeks to delineate the doctrine wholly from Scripture while at the same time paying respect—though, as we shall see, not wholly uncritical respect—to the church teaching that he inherited.

THE TRINITY AND HUMAN LANGUAGE

Calvin not only adheres to a version of the idea of divine simplicity, he is an eternalist; that is, he holds that God exists beyond or outside time. Perhaps the idea of divine simplicity entails eternalism, although Calvin does not say as much. Nonetheless, he clearly affirms both positions.

Calvin is open to Hughes's critique of Aquinas depends on his precise view of divine simplicity, about which he tells us very little.

[3] *Inst.* I. 13. 2.   [4] *Inst.* I. 13. 20.

When we attribute foreknowledge to God, we mean that all things always were, and perpetually remain, under his eyes, so that to his knowledge there is nothing future or past, but all things are present. And they are present in such a way that he not only conceives them through ideas, as we have before us those things which our minds remember, but he truly looks upon them and discerns them as things placed before him. And this foreknowledge is extended throughout the universe to every creature.[5]

The same view is expressed in connection with the Trinity. Writing of the 'order' of the persons in the Trinity, he says:

Indeed, although the eternity of the Father is also the eternity of the Son and the Spirit, since God could never exist apart from his wisdom and power, and we must not seek in eternity a *before* or an *after*, nevertheless the observance of an order is not meaningless or superfluous, when the Father is thought of as first, then from him the Son, and finally from both the Spirit.[6]

Although Calvin gives primary attention to Scripture's teaching on God's Trinitarian character, he is not biblicist. He thinks it is permissible, and even necessary, to use language and concepts drawn from extra-biblical sources to articulate—and in particular to defend—the biblical doctrine. There is tension here between, on the one hand, Calvin's commitment to the divine spirituality and immensity and to divine simplicity and atemporalism (which induce in him a reserve in his theological approach to God) and, on the other hand, the explicitly Trinitarian declarations of the New Testament. Within this tension, in discussing the mystery of the Trinity, Calvin warmly endorses Hilary's and Augustine's willingness to use terms such as *person* and *substance* in describing the Trinity, even though Scripture does not characterize the Trinity in these terms. Yet at the same time he also endorses their reticence to press the meaning of these terms. He cites this passage from Hilary:

The guilt of the heretics and blasphemers compels us to undertake what is unlawful, to scale arduous heights, to speak of the ineffable, and to trespass upon forbidden places. And since by faith alone we should fulfill what is commanded, namely, to adore the Father, to venerate the Son with Him, and to abound in the Holy Spirit, we are forced to raise our lowly words to subjects that cannot be described. By the guilt

---

[5] *Inst.* III. 21. 5.

[6] *Inst.* I. 13. 18. It has been suggested by Henri Blocher that Calvin disavows Augustine's view of time in his comments on 2 Tim. 1: 9 and Tit. 1: 2. ('Yesterday, Today, Forever: Time, Times, Eternity in Biblical Perspective', *Tyndale Bulletin*, 2001). But closer investigation suggests that Calvin is not objecting to Augustinian atemporalism so much as to Augustine's translation of *pro chronon aionion*. Calvin says that this phrase cannot refer to a state of affairs before time, because before time God would have had no one to promise to. Rather it refers to the time of the promise to Abraham (Gen. 22: 18). Thus according to Calvin, Tit. 1: 2 refers to God's promise, while 2 Tim. 1: 9 refers to God's pre-temporal decree. See Paul Helm, 'Calvin on "Before all Ages" ', *Tyndale Bulletin* (2002).

of another we are forced into guilt, so that what should have been restricted to the pious contemplation of our minds is now exposed to the dangers of human speech.[7]

In a passage that Calvin himself uses Augustine stated that 'on account of the poverty of human speech in so great a matter, the word "hypostasis" had been forced upon us by necessity, not to express what it is, but only not to be silent on how Father, Son, and Spirit are three'.[8] Augustine went on to say, in the passage to which Calvin refers,

For the sake, then, of speaking of things that cannot be uttered, that we may be able in some way to utter what we are able in no way to utter fully, our Greek friends have spoken of one essence, three substances; but the Latins of one essence or substance, three persons; because, as we have already said, essence usually means nothing else than substance in our language, that is, in Latin. And provided that what is said is understood only in a mystery, such a way of speaking was sufficient, in order that there might be something to say when it was asked what the three are, which the true faith pronounces to be three, when it both declares that the Father is not the Son, and that the Holy Spirit, which is the gift of God, is neither the Father nor the Son.[9]

Augustine's point, which Calvin appears unhesitatingly to endorse, seems to be something like this: the word 'person' when used of the Father, Son, and Spirit signals that certain kinds of thought and speech about God are warranted by the New Testament and certain other kinds are not warranted. In particular, when the New Testament speaks (say) about God the Son we are warranted in treating the Son as one who is a distinct subject of a certain range of properties, some of which he has in common with the Father, others he has distinct from the other two persons of the godhead. Calvin seems to have in mind here a rather mysterious relational property, differentiation by a 'peculiar quality' (*sed proprietate quadem esse distinctos*) as he calls it when referring to how the three persons are distinct.[10] Father, Son, and Spirit are three 'who's about whom we can and must say different things. That is, the use of the term 'person' allows us to say that there are properties possessed by the Son that are not possessed by the Father, properties possessed by the Father that are not possessed by the Son, and so on.[11] But if we think of the three persons of the Trinity as three individuals with a common nature, like Tom, Dick, and Harry are three persons with a human nature, then we err. For then we use language that implies division in the godhead. What would then stop us from thinking of the three divine persons as three gods? So the

---

[7] Saint Hilary of Poitiers, *The Trinity*, trans. Stephen McKenna (Washington, DC: Catholic University Press, 1954), II. 2.　　　　　　　　　　　　　　　　　　　　[8] *Inst.* I. 13. 5.

[9] *On the Trinity* VII. iv. 7, trans. A. W. Haddan (Edinburgh: T. & T. Clark, 1873).

[10] *Inst.* I. 13. 5.

[11] These are the 'incommunicable' qualities referred to by Calvin in *Inst.* I. 13. 6.

term 'person' is to be used with some reserve or restraint, but it is not to be abandoned.

A corollary of this is that as 'person' has a unique role in the doctrine of the Trinity, so does 'essence'. As we have just noted in the context of formulating a doctrine of the Trinity, 'essence' does not mean 'common nature'—as Tom, Dick, and Harry share the essence or common nature of being human beings. Applied to God, the term 'essence' is more like 'individual essence', in other words, that which is essential to God and to God alone and which constitutes God's very being. And so in an elucidation of the godhead the use of 'person' must be controlled by the use of 'essence', and vice versa.

So, in Calvin's view, the use of a certain kind of substantive expression for God's threeness and another kind of expression for God's oneness safeguards New Testament talk about the Father, the Son, and the Holy Spirit. It not only keeps us from manifest inconsistency; it also helps us to say the right kind of thing in turn about God the Father, about God the Son, and about God the Spirit that is not sayable of the others. Guided by the presence of the substantive 'person', we are prevented from entertaining and favouring certain thoughts about the threeness of the Trinity that would be at odds with the data of the New Testament. For example, we are prevented from thinking that the Father, Son, and Spirit are simply three different aspects in which the one God is revealed. For if they are merely three aspects of God, then the New Testament revelation about God the Father, say, is simply telling us about the fatherly aspect of God, a God who also has a filial and a spiritual aspect. The one God would then have fatherly, filial, and spiritual properties. The use of 'person' also prevents the opposite thought, that the Father, the Son and the Spirit are three gods; or the thought that the Spirit is an impersonal influence.

Yet while the terms 'person' and 'essence' have these positive functions, we ought not to suppose, in applying them to the Trinity, that we have more understanding of them than in fact we do. For example, we must not think that 'person', as applied to the Trinity, has the connotation of 'personality' as this normally applies to human beings. Rather, these terms have a strong negative role in our thinking, functioning *almost* as variables rather than as constants with a fixed sense. It is as if there is a rule to the effect that nothing that is an X can be a Y but three Xs may be one Y. God's nature is a case of this rule. Hence the values of X and Y must be distinct, not by being distinguished arbitrarily, but according to Scripture. Calvin, then, thought that we could know something about the Trinity as it is in itself, but he thought we must proceed with caution and reserve, in true Augustinian fashion.

For Calvin, there is also a sense in which human language about the Trinity functions primarily regulatively. It regulates what it is permissible for us to say and what we are forbidden from saying. But these regulations are not purely conventional. It is not as if we might have had different but equally usable rules had we chosen to construct them. Behind the rules that Scripture gives us to think and talk about the Trinity are realities that project these rules—realities that are, in themselves, incomprehensible to us. We cannot comprehend the inner life of the Trinity nor can we have any inkling what it is like to be Father or Son or Spirit.

Calvin's willingness to permit the use of the terms 'person', 'substance', and 'trinity' in Christian thinking about the godhead, given the place of this permission in his overall view of language about God, makes it clear that he in fact walks something of a tightrope. I am not aware of any place where he discusses his attitude to theological language in a way that attempts to provide us with an overall, consistent picture of it. On the one hand, he believes that some extra-biblical language is permissible—and even required—to identify and exclude heretical teaching. On the other hand, he hesitates to endorse models or analogies that attempt to explain the Trinitarian mystery. For instance, in an obvious allusion to Augustine's analogies in *On the Trinity*, Calvin says:

I really do not know whether it is expedient to borrow comparisons from human affairs to express the force of this distinction [between the persons of the Trinity]. Men of old were indeed accustomed sometimes to do so, but at the same time they confessed that the analogies they advanced were quite inadequate. Thus it is that I shrink from all rashness here: lest if anything should be inopportunely expressed, it may give occasion either of calumny to the malicious, or of delusion to the ignorant.[12]

Yet Calvin does not always shrink from such rashness. Overall, he is somewhat ambivalent about the use of models to aid theological understanding. He readily appeals to the relation between mind and body as an analogy of Christ's divine and human nature, as we shall see in the next chapter. But in Chapter 4 we shall also see that when Calvin debates the nature of divine providence he is opposed on principle to the taking of analogies of divine activity in providence from human affairs and not from Scripture. God's accommodation to us (see Chapter 7) is confined to the revelatory language of Holy Scripture. His general reluctance to use analogies drawn from

---

[12] *Inst.* 1. 13. 18. Compare Calvin's remarks in his *Commentary* on Gen. 1: 26. 'But Augustine, beyond all others, speculates with excessive refinement, for the purpose of fabricating a Trinity in man. For in laying hold of the three faculties of the soul enumerated by Aristotle, the intellect, the memory, and the will, he afterwards out of one Trinity derives many. If any reader, having leisure, wishes to enjoy such speculations, let him read the tenth and fourteenth books on the Trinity, also the eleventh book of the "City of God".'

outside Scripture, and to indulge in 'thought experiments', underlines his anti-speculative temper.

THE BEGOTTENNESS OF THE SON

Calvin's discussion of the nature of Christ's Sonship in the 1559 edition of the *Institutes* is clearly influenced by his controversy during 1556–7 over the anti-Trinitarian views of Giovanni Valentino Gentile, a member of the Italian refugee congregation in Geneva, a dispute that culminated in Gentile's trial in 1558. But Calvin's concern over what he regarded as perverse misinterpretations of the doctrine of the Trinity antedates this controversy. It is found, for example, in the 1536 edition of the *Institutes*.[13] Yet although Calvin always believed it was necessary to go beyond the very words of Scripture in order to elucidate the doctrine of the Trinity, were it not for controversy he would have been content to express the doctrine in a very simple form of words.

If, therefore, these terms [such as 'trinity', 'person'] were not rashly invented, we ought to beware lest by repudiating them we be accused of overweening rashness. Indeed, I could wish they were buried, if only among all men this faith were agreed on: that Father and Son and Spirit are one God, yet the Son is not the Father, nor the Spirit the Son, but that they are differentiated by a peculiar quality.[14]

Calvin here reveals an essentially conservative, catholic spirit. He was personally content with a minimalist expression of the Trinitarian formula, the essential deposit of Patristic reflection, in order to avoid speculation or extravagance that might ultimately prove to harbour heresy.[15] A doctrine of the Trinity, then, that mentions neither 'trinity', nor 'person' nor 'substance', nor the begetting of the Son nor the procession of the Spirit, is what Calvin in principle favours.

Calvin's growing appreciation of the subtleties of Arianism was nurtured by a series of controversies: with Pierre Caroli in 1537, Gentile, and Giorgio Blandrata from 1558 (all of whom were members of the Italian congregation in Geneva) and most notoriously in his correspondence with Michael Servetus in 1546.[16] According to Calvin, Gentile claimed that the Father 'in forming the Son and the Spirit, infused into them his own deity'. Calvin responded that deity 'is sometimes applied to the Father par excellence

---

[13] *Institution of the Christian Religion* (1536) trans. F. L. Battles (Atlanta: John Knox Press, 1975), ch. 2, ss. 7, 8, 9. [14] *Inst.* 1. 13. 5.

[15] Calvin's conservatism is nowhere better seen than in the *Institute*'s Prefatory Address to King Francis I, particularly in his appeal to the Church Fathers in refutation of the alleged 'novelty' of Reformation teaching.

[16] Calvin refers to Servetus and alludes to Gentile in *Inst.* 1. 13. 23, and he also alludes to Blandrata in *Inst.* 1. 13. 2.

because he is the fountainhead and beginning of deity—and this is done to denote the simple unity of essence'.[17] The Son of God is to be distinguished from the Father not by essence but by relation.

Certainly the Father would not differ from the Son unless he had in himself something unique, which was not shared with the Son. Now what can they find to distinguish him? If the distinction is in the essence, let them answer whether or not he has shared it with the Son. Indeed, this could not be done in part because it would be wicked to fashion a half-God. Besides, in this way they would basely tear apart the essence of God. It remains that the essence is wholly and perfectly common to Father and Son. If this is true, then there is indeed with respect to the essence no distinction of one from the other.[18]

Calvin's thought here seems to be that there is one whole, perfect, and simple divine essence; so the distinction between the persons of the Trinity cannot be sought in a 'partitioning' of that essence, a sharing out of it among them. The distinctions must lie elsewhere, in that while each is wholly and perfectly God, they have unique relations to each other.

For even though we admit that in respect to order and degree the beginning of divinity is in the Father, yet we say that it is a detestable invention that essence is proper to the Father alone, as if he were the deifier of the Son. For in this way either essence would be manifold or they call Christ 'God' in title and imagination only. If they grant that the Son is God, but second to the Father, then in him will be begotten and formed the essence that is in the Father unbegotten and unformed.[19]

In fact, when called upon by his controversialist Caroli to endorse the Nicene and Athanasian creeds Calvin refused to do so. 'We have professed faith in God alone, not in Athanasius, whose Creed has not been approved by any properly constituted Church.'[20] There appear to be two reasons for his refusal. One is, in B. B. Warfield's words, Calvin's 'constant and firm determination to preserve full liberty to deal with the doctrine [of the Sonship of God] free from all dictation from without or even prescription of traditional modes of statement'.[21] The second is his disinclination to speculate and to indulge in and endorse what one might call a theory or explanation of the Trinity; that is, a form of words that would take away or reduce its essential mystery as a reality beyond full human ken. (As we have already noted, there is nothing in Calvin to suggest sympathy with attempts

---

[17] *Inst.* I. 13. 23.   [18] *Inst.* I. 13. 23.   [19] *Inst.* I. 13. 24.

[20] Quoted by B. B. Warfield, 'Calvin's Doctrine of the Trinity', in *Calvin and Calvinism* (208–9) from Calvin's *Adversus Petri Caroli* (1545). Warfield's essay is a masterly treatment of Calvin's position. In his otherwise balanced treatment of Calvin's views Paul Owen fails to identify this strand in Calvin's anti-subordinationism ('Calvin and Catholic Trinitarianism', *Calvin Theological Journal*, 2000).

[21] Warfield, *Calvin and Calvinism*, 206.

to prove the Trinity a priori in the manner of Richard of St Victor or Jonathan Edwards or Richard Swinburne.)[22] Yet perhaps we can detect, following his controversies with Caroli and Gentile, a greater readiness on Calvin's part to be more specific in his account of the Trinity than he would otherwise have wished. In addition, the later episode with Gentile seems to have, if anything, sharpened Calvin's anti-subordinationism as expressed in his controversy with Caroli around twenty years earlier.

These controversies clarify that Calvin's objection to the traditional way of stating the Trinity—particularly the way the relation of the second person to the first person of the Trinity was expressed—is any language that suggests a subordination of the divinity of the Son to the divinity of the Father and so casts a shadow over the true, full deity of the second person and so compromises his aseity. Thus he objected to the battology of the Nicene Creed, 'God from God, Light from Light, true God from true God,' because, he said, it 'adds neither to the emphasis nor to the expressiveness of the document'.[23] Calvin thought the battology was more chant-like than creed-like. Yet he endorses the idea of the eternal begottenness of the Son at various places,[24] and so he does not so much offer a fundamental critique of the language of subordinationism as put his own gloss on it. His basic thought, however, is that each person of the Trinity is *autotheos*, God himself. This is how Calvin typically thinks about the Trinity, as expressed in I. 13 of the *Institutes*.

Scripture sets forth a distinction of the Father from the Word, and of the Word from the Spirit. Yet the greatness of the mystery warns us how much reverence and sobriety we ought to use in investigating this. And that passage in Gregory of Nazianzus vastly delights me:

'I cannot think on the one without quickly being encircled by the splendor of the three; nor can I discern the three without being straightway carried back to the one.' Let us not, then, be led to imagine a trinity of persons that keeps our thoughts distracted and does not at once lead them back to that unity.[25]

But because the peculiar qualities in the persons carry an order within them, e.g., in the Father is the beginning and the source, so often as mention is made of the Father and the Son together, or the Spirit, the name of *God* is peculiarly applied to the Father. In this way, unity of essence is retained, and a reasoned order is kept, which yet takes nothing away from the deity of the Son and the Spirit.[26]

---

[22] Richard of St Victor, *The Divine Trinity*, esp. bk. III; Jonathan Edwards, 'Essay on the Trinity', in *Treatise on Grace and other Posthumous Writings of Jonathan Edwards*, ed. Paul Helm (Cambridge: James Clarke, 1971); and Richard Swinburne, *The Christian God* (Oxford: Clarendon Press, 1994), ch. 8.

[23] Quoted Warfield, *Calvin and Calvinism*, 210.   [24] e.g. *Inst.* I. 13. 4, 7, 23, 24.

[25] *Inst.* I. 13. 17. The quotation is from Gregory Nazianzus, *Of Holy Baptism*, Oration XI. 41.

[26] *Inst.* I. 13. 20.

They object: if he is truly Son of God, it is absurd to think of him as the Son of a person. I reply that both are true: that is, he is the Son of God, because the Word was begotten by the Father before all ages . . . and yet for the sake of clarification we must have regard to the person, so as not to take the name of God here without qualification, but as used of the Father. For if we consider no one but the Father to be God, we definitely cast the Son down from this rank. Therefore whenever mention is made of deity, we ought by no means to admit any antithesis between Son and Father, as if the name of the true God applied to the latter alone. . . . For whoever says that the Son has been given his essence from the Father denies that he has being from himself.[27]

These assertions from the *Institutes* elaborate what Calvin said earlier in private correspondence about his controversy with Caroli.

Certainly if the distinction between the Father and the Word be attentively considered, we shall say that the one is from the other. If, however, the essential quality of the Word be considered, in so far as he is one God with the Father, whatever can be said concerning God may also be applied to him, the second person of the glorious Trinity.[28]

So Calvin, in effect, is proposing two rules that should govern our thinking when attending to the doctrine of the Trinity:

(1) Whenever we refer to God as such, that reference should be taken as denoting the entire Trinitarian character of God.

(2) Whenever we refer to the Son's begottenness, God the Father—rather than God as such—should be thought of as the begetter.

Thus Calvin distinguishes the language we use about God's Trinitarian nature according to how we are thinking and speaking. If we are thinking and speaking of God unqualifiedly, then the full, unqualified deity of the Son and of the Spirit is implied. But if we are speaking of the begetting of God the Son, then an orderly distinction between the persons is implied and the Father is to be understood as the begetter. In endeavouring to follow these rules, Calvin clarifies that for him the language of begottenness, when applied to the Son of God, refers not to the Son's *divinity* but to his *person*. Here again we find a regulative aspect in Calvin's remarks. Though he does not formulate these rules explicitly, as we have just done, nevertheless what he is in effect providing are rules for speaking about God. Talk of God *simpliciter* embraces the fully divine character of the Trinity of persons. Whatever is true of God in this unqualified way must therefore be true

[27] *Inst.* I. 13. 23.

[28] Letter to Simon Gryneus, May 1537, in *Selected Works of John Calvin, Tracts and Letters*, ed. Henry Beveridge and Jules Bonnet (Edinburgh, 1844, Philadelphia, 1858; repr. Grand Rapids, Mich.: Baker, 1983), iv. 55–6.

of each member of the Trinity. But if we are speaking of the Father alone, then we are using a relational term—the language of distinctness—and the begottenness of the person of the Son is implied. Matters are less clear, of course, in the case of the Holy Spirit, since 'spirit' is not a relational term in the straightforward way in which the terms 'father' and 'son' are. And Calvin has less to say about the procession of the Spirit. Nevertheless, one might expect him to adopt a set of rules consistent with those just given when treating of the relation of the Spirit to the Father and the Son, though appropriately modified to embrace the *filioque*.

There is an interesting parallel in the way in which Calvin treats the mysteries of the Incarnation and of the Trinity. With the Incarnation, as we shall see in Chapter 3, Calvin adopts a further set of rules for understanding New Testament assertions about the Son of God:

(3) Whenever Christ is the subject of a proposition, then both human and divine properties are ascribable to him.

(4) Whenever God (unqualified in any way) is the subject of a proposition, then human properties are ascribed to him only improperly, but with a reason, this being sanctioned by the *communicatio idiomatum*.

(5) Whenever the humanity of Christ (unqualified in any way) is the subject of a proposition, then divine properties are ascribed to him only improperly, but with a reason, this being sanctioned by the *communicatio idiomatum*.

Altogether these five rules (with a sixth to be added later) are intended by Calvin to govern thinking both about the Trinity and the Incarnation in ways that are faithful to the scriptural record yet which also avoid confusion and incoherence.

Thinking chiefly if not exclusively of Calvin, Gerald Bray claims that the Reformers believed that the persons of the Trinity are equal to one another in every respect.[29] But as we have now seen, this needs some qualification. Calvin believed that each person of the Trinity is fully God—and so as equally divine as any other person, since God is triune. In this foundational respect, all the persons are equal. No person has a derived or subordinate divine nature. Nevertheless, the persons of the Trinity are to be distinguished (there is a certain 'order' among the persons) and so they are not equal in every respect, since in virtue of this order each bears a unique relationship to the others. Whether for Calvin this order is ontological (an order in the very nature of God) or a merely functional order (an order of the role each of the persons of the godhead plays in creation and redemption) is an issue that will occupy us next.

---

[29] Gerald Bray, *The Doctrine of God* (Leicester: IVP, 1993), 200.

THE REVEALED TRINITY

Turning to a question already broached, how did Calvin see the relation between the Trinity as revealed in redemption (that is, the economic Trinity) and the immanent Trinity (that is, the Trinity in itself)? Clearly, they are closely related, but how closely?

In his otherwise excellent discussion of the place of the Trinity in Calvin's theology,[30] Philip Walker Butin causes himself unnecessary difficulties by unwarrantably stressing the identity of the immanent and economic trinities in Calvin's thought. He says that:

Calvin will tolerate no wedge between an 'immanent' and 'economic' Trinity, or between the divine essence and economic Trinitarian operations. The simple reason is that 'Word and Spirit are nothing less than the very essence of God' (*Inst.* I. 13. 16). Calvin spells out the implications of this identity by emphasizing the way the intra-trinitarian divine perichoresis of Son and Spirit is reflected in the parallel mutual, perichoretic interdetermination of the complementary movements of the divine self-revelation via Word and Spirit.[31]

What this reference to a 'wedge' implies is not very clear. Calvin's alleged intolerance of such a wedge seems to indicate that he holds that no distinction is to be made between the divine essence and the operations of the economic Trinity. A weaker relation between the essence and the operations appears to be implied by the metaphor of reflection, which Butin also uses. But all in all Butin seems to wish (somewhat anachronistically) to impute to Calvin the view of modern theologians such as Karl Barth, Karl Rahner, and T. F. Torrance[32] that the economic Trinity *is* the immanent Trinity. But if so, then his view of Calvin is wide of the mark.

Karl Rahner's so-called 'rule' states that 'The economic Trinity is the immanent Trinity and the immanent Trinity is the economic Trinity'.[33] There are at least three ways in which this assertion may be understood. First, as a reminder that in talk about the 'economic Trinity' and the 'immanent Trinity' there are not two trinities, only one. Such a reminder is unexceptionable; it is hard to imagine any Christian theologian dissenting from it.

---

[30] *Revelation, Redemption and Response* (New York: Oxford University Press, 1995).

[31] *Revelation, Redemption and Response*, 59. 'Perichoresis' is a term for the mutual indwelling of the three persons, implying indivisible will and understanding.

[32] Karl Barth, Karl Rahner, T. F. Torrance. Though note the following remark of Torrance, 'The economic Trinity cannot but point beyond itself to the theological or ontological Trinity, otherwise the economic Trinity would not be a faithful and true revelation of the transcendent Communion of Father, Son and Holy Spirit which the eternal being of God is in himself', *The Christian Doctrine of God* (Edinburgh: T. & T. Clark, 1996), 92.

[33] Karl Rahner, *The Trinity*, trans. J. Donceel (New York: Herder & Herder, 1970), 22, 34.

Secondly, as expressing in a rather exaggerated way the view that we only know of the immanent Trinity what is revealed to us about the economic Trinity. Thirdly, as indicating a metaphysical unity between the immanent and economic Trinities in the sense that the economic Trinity is the only way in which the immanent Trinity could reveal itself, and that the immanent Trinity must reveal itself thus. It is not clear that Calvin would subscribe to either the second or third senses of Rahner's rule, but Butin appears to think that he would or that he would be very sympathetic to doing so.

Having posited a very close relation or even an identity between of the economic and the immanent Trinity, Butin understandably discerns a tension between Calvin's Trinitarian theology and his view of the divine decrees, 'in which the divine will appears to be theologically prior to and more essential than God's triunity itself, not to mention the external operations'.[34] He says that Calvin's

emphasis on predestination is not easily reconciled with his overarching commitment to the economic-Trinitarian character of the divine–human relationship. The fact that he does not appear to have perceived any compelling theological contradiction between the two ways of understanding the divine–human relationship is both irritating and intriguing to many contemporary interpreters, for whom such a contradiction seems obvious.[35]

Butin's point here appears to be that Calvin's view of the sovereignty of the divine decrees—the fact that God could have decreed other than he did—is at odds with what Butin takes to be the 'economic-Trinitarian character of the divine–human relationship'.

Calvin failed to perceive a contradiction here because there isn't one; and there isn't one because Calvin does not affirm an identity between the immanent and economic trinities in the last two of the senses we distinguished earlier. He does not do so precisely because the work of Father, Son, and Holy Spirit in redemption is that of three fully divine persons who (in a way that is both hidden and inscrutable to us) decree to redeem[36]—a decree that, because it is freely taken, could have been other than it is. So both the decree to redeem at all and the decree to predestine only specific persons to salvation are, for Calvin, decrees that God freely took. Nothing in his writings suggests, however, that Calvin sees the decreeing divine will as 'prior' to God's triune character, or that his views entail such a priority. Such a view

---

[34] *Revelation, Redemption and Response*, 125. This is a remark about the Westminster Confession of Faith, but it is clearly intended as an accurate characterization of the predestinarian 'strand' in Calvin which Butin finds difficult to square with Calvin's trinitarianism.

[35] *Revelation, Redemption and Response*, 126.

[36] A decree intrinsic to what later covenant theologians called the Covenant of Redemption.

ignores the *in Christo* character of election and predestination according to Calvin.[37] In any case Butin's suggestion is impossible, if God is essentially triune and if the decree is the triune God's decree. For Calvin, election is 'God's eternal election'.[38] Observing his own first rule as stated above, if election is God's action then it is an act in which the three members of the Trinity unqualifiedly concur. Nevertheless, it decrees states of affairs that might not have been decreed. And if God could have decreed other than he has, as Calvin clearly holds, then his economic character could have been different from what in fact it is.[39] A 'wedge' is thus driven between the immanent and the economic Trinity. But this 'wedge' is necessary to preserve consistency in Calvin's account of the relation between God as he is in himself and God as he is to us.

This preserves the sovereignty of divine freedom. But how far is this disjunction between God *in se* and God *quoad nos* to go? The issue of determining the extent to which Calvin was willing to endorse the subordinationist language of Nicene Christology raises the question of how much the economic Trinity—the Trinity as it is revealed in connection with human redemption—mirrors the godhead as it is in itself? A more pointed and provocative way of posing this question is to ask: to what extent is the dogmatic construction of trinitarianism in the Patristic period, with its emphasis upon the subordination of the Son to the Father, based upon reading back into the godhead itself those roles that were only freely undertaken by the Trinity for human redemption? And if it is based upon such a reading back, to what extent is this theological procedure justified?

Given his view of God's simple essence and its essential moral perfection (which we noted in the previous chapter), Calvin would not subscribe to the idea that the relation between the economic and the immanent Trinity is arbitrary or potentially misleading. Calvin's reasoning, both with respect to the begottenness of the Son and to the procession of the Spirit, might be expressed by what we will call Principle A: *God necessarily reveals himself to us in a way that is consistent with his essential nature.*[40] So while there is no identity between the economic and the immanent Trinities, there is a consistent relation between them; the activities of the former express the nature or character of the latter. Thus there can be no disjunction between God as such and what is revealed about him regarding human redemption.

---

[37] *Inst.* III. 22. 1.   [38] *Inst.* III. 21. 1.

[39] Although not of course his Trinitarian character, since God is essentially Trinitarian.

[40] It is wrong in principle to attribute to Calvin the placing of a 'wedge' between the revelation of God's love and God himself. Such a misunderstanding is based partly on a misunderstanding of what Calvin meant by the unknowability of God. Appealing to the Trinity to eliminate the wedge is in any case no help unless it is accompanied by the dogma that if the hypostases are known then the substance is.

It would be very difficult, on Calvin's behalf, to deny Principle A, for it is implausible to suppose that God might reveal his role in the economy of redemption in a way that *contradicts* how he is in himself, or that in his revelation he is manifestly *misleading* as to his essence, or that he reveals himself in a way that is *irrelevant* to how he is in himself. This is because wisdom and love and grace and mercy are among God's essential attributes or perfections. For, as we saw in Chapter 1, Calvin maintains that, although we cannot know God as God, God reveals to us in Scripture something of his essential nature, quite apart from revealing to us his involvement in the economy of redemption, even though we cannot fully comprehend that nature or that involvement.[41] As we saw, God's essence is never represented to us by Calvin as a completely unknowable *noumenon*, as it is in Kantian and post-Kantian theologies. So in view of the fact that God reveals himself to us as one who is in himself a loving, just, and faithful God, we can be sure that God's revelation of himself and of the economy of redemption is not at variance with this but fully reflects his divine character.

Yet Principle A can be applied with such stringency as to reduce it to absurdity with regard to functional differences in the economy, differences such as submission, condescension, and obedience. In the economy of redemption the Son is revealed as utterly submissive to his Father's good pleasure. Does it follow from this submission in the economy that in his eternal relation to the Father the Son is utterly submissive to him? Is this a reasonable application of Principle A? May it not rather follow that there is something in the eternal relations of the Trinity that make the submission of the Son as incarnate an appropriate and a faithful expression of the divine nature?[42]

Principle A might be expressed with increasing degrees of stringency in the following way. Thinking of God's New Testament revelation of himself as a triune God—an electing Father, a redeeming Son, and a regenerating Spirit—this revelation is consistent with God as he is in himself being:

(a) An eternal Trinity of equal, undifferentiated, fully divine persons
(b) An eternal Trinity of coequal but ordered persons

---

[41] As Calvin says, God reveals his essence sparingly. See *Inst.* 1. 13. 1.

[42] '[T]he use of the temporal manifestations of God as models from which to draw analogies of the eternal nature of the trinitarian relationships, while it doubtless was a move in the right direction, had serious drawbacks of its own which Origen did not fully appreciate. In his earthly life and work, the Son had obviously been in submission to the Father. It followed, therefore, that submission was a basic ingredient of his divine personhood—hence the Son was eternally subordinate to the Father.' Gerald Bray, 'The Patristic Dogma', in Peter Toon and James Spiceland (eds), *One God in Trinity* (Westchester, Ill.: Cornerstone Books, 1980), 55. On the same point (though in the context of social trinitarianism), see the comment of David Brown, *The Divine Trinity* (London: Duckworth, 1985), 283.

    (*c*) An eternal Trinity of three ordered persons, ordered as the Father, the Son,
        and the Spirit
    (*d*) An eternal Trinity of a begetting Father, a begotten Son, and a processing
        Spirit.

Of course, there are more possibilities than these. Someone might think that
God's revelation of himself as a triune redeemer implies that God as he is in
himself is a *temporal* Trinity and this gives rise to another four possibilities.
There may be even more possibilities. For example, (*b*) could give rise to a
number of further options, depending on how the ordering is understood.
But this is sufficient to show that it is far from obvious what precisely a
revealed, economic Trinity must imply for God as he is in himself. Nor is it
clear how one might clearly and simply determine which possibility is most
likely or most reasonable.

    If we adopt Principle A, Calvin might say, we must conclude that the
temporal missions of the Father, Son, and Spirit will and must reflect their
eternal relations in the godhead. How could God not be faithful to himself? If
God reveals himself to us as the Father sending the Son, and as the Father and
the Son sending the Spirit, then this arrangement must correspond to eternal
relations of begottenness and procession in the godhead. So, given Principle
A, the Son must be eternally begotten, which corresponds to the begetting of
Jesus of Nazareth in the womb of Mary, and the Spirit must eternally process,
which corresponds to the Spirit being sent by the Father and the Son upon
Jesus' ascension. Similarly, if Trinitarian persons in their economic roles
undertake intelligent, willing, purposive action, then the persons of the
Trinity considered immanently cannot be less capable. And if the persons in
the economy manifest love and grace and mercy, then the persons of the
Trinity considered immanently cannot be other than loving, gracious, and
merciful. That is, in what he does, God is consistent with what he is.

    So while in the interests of preserving divine freedom for Calvin we
must not identify the immanent and economic Trinities, these Trinities are,
according to him, nevertheless closely allied, the one faithfully expressing the
character of the other.

CALVIN'S SOURCES

Calvin's stress on the equality of the persons, the fact that each is *autotheos*,
has been thought by some theologians—T. F. Torrance and Gerald Bray,
for example—to be evidence that Calvin drew on Eastern, Cappadocian
influences for his account of the Trinity. Bray says that:

Calvin held to a doctrine which said that the three persons were coequal in their
divinity and united with each other, not by sharing an impersonal essence, but

by their mutual fellowship and coinherence—the Cappadocian doctrine of peri-choresis in God, applies at the level of person, not essence.[43]

And T. F. Torrance:

Calvin directs the reader for further explanation to the fifth book of Augustine's work on the *Trinity*, but actually he takes his chief cue from Gregory Nazianzen, with whom he sides in his evident disagreement with his friends Basil and Gregory Nyssen. Thus in spite of his judicious deployment of citations from Augustine, the recognized *magister theologiae* of the West, Calvin's Trinitarian convictions were actually rather closer to those of the Greek Fathers Athanasius, Gregory Nazianzen, and Cyril of Alexandria.[44]

Torrance also claims that in developing his account of the Trinity, Calvin evidently has in mind certain statements of Gregory of Nazianzen[45] and of Basil and of Athanasius.[46] But as Tony Lane has recently shown the idea of such influences must remain speculative since there is no hard evidence that Calvin had access to their writings,[47] whereas he did have access to Augustine's writings, whose influence pervades other aspects of his theology. It is therefore not unreasonable to suppose that Calvin's views on the Trinity were strongly influenced by Augustine. Perhaps the views of Calvin and the Cappadocians coincide at certain points, and there may be even some general unspecifiable influence, but Warfield is surely on safer ground when he states:

If distinctions must be drawn, [Calvin] is unmistakably Western rather than Eastern in his conception of the doctrine, an Augustinian rather than an Athanasian. That is to say, the principle of his construction of the Trinitarian distinctions is equalisation rather than subordination.[48]

But whatever the intellectual and literary sources of Calvin's trinitarianism, there is in any case some tension between the subordinationism that prevailed in the East from Origen onwards because of the influence of Neo-platonism, and the idea of the Trinity as a perichoretic communion of equal persons, a view that is also said to be characteristic of the Cappadocians. Origen had used expressions such as 'there is one God, Father of the living

---

[43] *The Doctrine of God*, 202.

[44] 'Calvin's Doctrine of the Trinity', *Calvin Theological Journal* (1990), 179.

[45] Torrance, 'Calvin's Doctrine of the Trinity', 170.

[46] Torrance, 'Calvin's Doctrine of the Trinity', 177, 178.

[47] *John Calvin: Student of the Church Fathers*, ch. 3. However, he notes that Calvin's citation of Gregory of Nazianzen (in Greek with a Latin translation) in *Inst.* 1. 13. 17 (one of his very few direct references to the Greek Fathers) does not indicate pervasive influence, and concludes that, in general, the range of Calvin's reading in the Greek Fathers does not encourage the view that they were of great importance to him (85).

[48] Warfield, *Calvin and Calvinism*, 229–30.

Word . . . perfect begetter of the perfect begotten. . . . There is one Lord, unique out of unique, God out of God, impress and image of Godhead.'[49] For Origen, the Son had been begotten by the Father; thus he was not *autotheos*, for only the Father was that. In the words of J. N. D. Kelly, 'He ['the Son'] is not absolute goodness and truth, but His goodness and truth are a reflection and image of the Father's.'[50] According to Origen, 'we should not pray to any generate being, not even to Christ, but only to the God and Father of the universe, to Whom our Saviour Himself prayed'.[51]

This tension in the thought of the Cappadocians lies in the fact that, while they stressed that the one Godhead exists in three modes of being, they nevertheless wanted to do justice to their idea that the Father is the fountainhead of the Trinity: the Holy Spirit is 'out of the Father through the Son'.[52] So the parity and equal divinity of the perichoretically related persons is somewhat qualified by statements such as this by Gregory of Nazianzen: 'The Three have one nature, viz. God, the ground of unity being the Father, out of Whom and towards Whom the subsequent Persons are reckoned.'[53] This tension can be seen in the Athanasian Creed itself. On the one hand, the Creed strongly affirms the equality of the three persons.

the Godhead of the Father, of the Son, and of the Holy Spirit is all one, the glory equal, the majesty co-eternal. Such as the Father is, such is the Son, and such is the Holy Spirit. The Father uncreate, the Son uncreate, and the Holy Spirit uncreate. The Father incomprehensible, the Son incomprehensible, and the holy Spirit incomprehensible. . .

and yet

The Father is made of none, neither created, nor begotten. The Son is of the Father alone, not made, nor created, but begotten. The Holy Spirit is of the Father and of the Son, neither made, nor created nor begotten, but proceeding.

On the basis of what we have already learned about Calvin's trinitarianism, if Calvin were to be offered a choice between Origenesque subordinationism and Cappadocian *perichoresis*, then it seems that he would unhesitatingly have chosen *perichoresis*. But there are more choices than these; and while Calvin favours the coequality of the persons characteristic of Cappadocian *perichoresis*, he also favours an understanding of the Trinity as it is in itself that is not 'social',[54] for he stresses the oneness of the godhead in whom the Trinity are three equally divine persons.

[49] Quoted in J. N. D. Kelly, *Early Christian Doctrines* (5th edn.; London: A. & C. Black, 1977), 133.

[50] *Early Christian Doctrines*, 132. [51] *Early Christian Doctrines*, 132.

[52] *Early Christian Doctrines*, 263. [53] Quoted in *Early Christian Doctrines*, 265.

[54] Social trinitarianism is currently favoured among Christian analytic philosophers of religion as well as in others' discussions of the Trinity. See, for example, Richard Swinburne, *The Christian God*,

THE PERSON OF THE SON

Calvin stresses the co-equality of the persons of the Trinity—and especially the Son's full and unqualified divinity—and seeks to minimize speculation about God as he is in himself and to preserve the full deity of the Son by restricting the idea of begottenness to the *person* of the Son. So why, confronted with the mystery of the Trinity, and having delineated its bare features, doesn't Calvin appeal to the ineffability of the relation between the persons of the Trinity and leave matters there? It is because he thought that the data of the New Testament required him to have a positive view of those relations: the Father begets the *person* of the Son, and the *person* of the Spirit processes from both Father and Son. It is in this connection, rather than in discussing the economic Trinity, that Calvin writes about the 'reasoned order' that there is in the relation of the persons of the Trinity.[55]

So he carefully restricts the language of begottenness, where he uses it, to the begottenness of the *person* of the Son rather than to his essential deity: 'Therefore we say that deity in an absolute sense exists of itself; whence likewise we confess that the Son since he is God, exists of himself, but not in respect of his Person; indeed, since he is the Son, we say that he exists from the Father. Thus his essence is without beginning; while the beginning of his person is God himself.'[56] In reasoning like this, Calvin is seeking to establish certain non-negotiables. He emphasizes the full deity and equality of each of the persons, while at the same time assigning a primacy to the person of the Father from whom the Son derives his person. And so the language of subordinationism may be used, provided it relates to the personhood of the Son and not to his essential deity, while modes of thought about the inter-Trinitarian relations that encourage or are the result of speculation ought to be avoided.

For in each hypostasis the whole divine nature is understood, with this qualification—that to each belongs his own peculiar quality. The Father is wholly in the Son, the Son wholly in the Father . . . And ecclesiastical writers do not concede that the one is separated from the other by any difference of essence. By these appellations which set forth the distinction (says Augustine) is signified their mutual relationships and not the very substance by which they are one. In this sense the opinions of the ancients are to be harmonized, which otherwise would seem somewhat to clash. Sometimes, indeed, they teach that the Father is the beginning of the Son; sometimes they declare that the Son has both divinity and essence from

and Cornelius Plantinga, 'Social Trinity and Tritheism', and David Brown, 'Trinitarian Personhood and Individuality', both in Cornelius Plantinga and Ronald Feenstra (eds.), *Trinity, Incarnation and Atonement*, (Notre Dame: University of Notre Dame Press, 1989).

[55] *Inst.* I. 13. 20.　　　　　　　　　　　　　　　　　[56] *Inst.* I. 13. 25.

himself, and thus has one beginning with the Father. . . . Therefore, when we speak simply of the Son without regard to the Father, we well and properly declare him to be of himself; and for this reason we call him the sole beginning. But when we mark the relation that he has with the Father, we rightly make the Father the beginning of the Son. The whole fifth book of Augustine's *On the Trinity* is concerned with explaining this matter. Indeed, it is far safer to stop with that relation which Augustine sets forth than by too subtly penetrating into the sublime mystery to wander through many evanescent speculations.[57]

Brian Leftow, in his brilliant critique of social trinitarianism, unknowingly sums up Calvin's position exactly when he says: 'In LT [Latin trinitarianism], were there no processions, there would be no Persons, but simply God. The Persons are wholly equal: as ought to be so if they are equally divine. And yet . . . the Father does have a relevant priority. For given that there *are* persons, the others exist because the Father does.'[58] What Calvin says in effect adds a third rule about how to think about the Trinity to the other two we identified earlier, making six hermeneutical rules altogether:

(6) When the Son is referred without regard to his relation to the Father, he is to be thought of as unbegotten, as having his existence *a se*, as being fully divine.

Yet applying this rule presents some difficulty, for how could the Son be referred to without regard to the Father, since the very idea of sonship implies fatherhood? Calvin would answer that if we think of the Son in ways that do not explicitly involve his begottenness by the Father, then we are to think of the Son as self-begotten. Otherwise, we are to think of the Son as begotten as regards his person as Son.

As already noted, Calvin pays much less attention to the procession of the Spirit from the Father and the Son. But he does not deny it, upholding the *filioque* clause.

So then it is Christ who sends the Spirit, but it is from the heavenly glory, that we may know that it is not a gift of men, but a sure pledge of Divine grace. Hence it appears how idle was the subtilty of the Greeks, when they argued, on the ground of these words, that the Spirit does not *proceed* from the Son; for here Christ, according to his custom, mentions *the Father*, in order to raise our eyes to the contemplation of his Divinity.[59]

Note that Calvin here relies on a biblical text that involves the economic arrangements within the Trinity to warrant belief in the Spirit's immanent relation to Father and Son. In the *Institutes* he strongly affirms the Spirit's

[57] *Inst.* I. 13. 19.

[58] Brian Leftow, 'Anti Social Trinitarianism', in *The Trinity*, Stephen T. Davis, Daniel Kendall, Gerald O'Collins (eds.), (Oxford: Oxford University Press, 1999), 244.

[59] *Commentary on the Gospel According to John*, 15: 26.

divinity[60] and includes the Spirit in his discussion on sameness and difference among the persons of the Trinity. This discussion includes brief
remarks on the relation of the Spirit to the Father and the Son. But when it is
measured against the distinctive language of the Nicene formulation,
Calvin's language is muffled. Both the Son and the Spirit are said to 'come
forth', the former from the Father, the latter from the Father and the Son.
Calvin uses this relation to enforce the 'simple unity' of God by noting that
the Spirit is shared by the Father and the Son. Calvin eschews the subtleties
involved in making a clear distinction between 'eternal begottenness' and
'eternal procession'. From here on I will concentrate on his more extended
remarks about the relation of the person of the Son to the person of the
Father.

Isn't the idea of the begottenness of the *person* of the Son as obscure as the
idea of the begottenness of the *deity* of the Son, even if for Calvin the former
is acceptable speech while the latter is not? Why isn't the doctrine of the
begottenness of the person of the Son a doctrine that in turn invites the sort
of speculation that Calvin wishes to avoid?

Of course those who uphold the eternal begetting of the Son by the Father
do what they can to safeguard the idea. They are, almost without exception,
among those who hold that God is timelessly eternal. So the begetting of the
Son is an eternal begetting. In this vein, Calvin thinks of the Son's begottenness as a completed act, not an ongoing act (or activity). 'For what is the
point in disputing whether the Father always begets? Indeed, it is foolish to
imagine a continuous act of begetting, since it is clear that three persons have
subsisted in God from eternity.'[61] There was no time when the Son was not,
and no time when the Son was coming to be.

Despite this the Son, though equally God and eternally with the Father, is,
on Calvin's view, begotten as the Son from the unbegotten Father. What
could this possibly mean? Of course, all those who uphold the idea of
the eternal begetting of the Son distinguish between being begotten and
being created: the Son, though begotten, is not created; he is not a creature.
Nevertheless, being begotten is a causal concept, if it is anything at all: what is
begotten is caused to be by what begets. Yet in attempting to elucidate
the Son's begottenness, it is also customary to distinguish between being
begotten and having an origin. The Son is said to be eternally begotten but
not to have an origin, presumably because anything that has an origin has a
temporal point of origin, and the life of the eternal Son is not temporal. So
the usual meaning of 'begetting' is qualified in two or three important
respects. First, it is stripped of its causal connotations: the person of the Son

---

[60] *Inst.* I. 13. 14–15.   [61] *Inst.* I. 13. 29.

is not caused to be. And, secondly, it is stripped of the idea that begetting is an act of originating, that the one who is begotten does not exist until begotten by the begetter. Furthermore, in every case of begetting what is begotten has the same specific nature as the begetter but not the same numerical nature, except in the case of the alleged eternal begetting of the Son. For the Son, being essentially God, has the same numerical nature, in spite of being begotten (according to Calvin) as to his person by the person of the Father.

More than that, the Father's act of begetting the Son is necessary, not voluntary. It is an essential feature of the Father's person. And likewise the begottenness of the Son is essential to his person as Son. Father, Son, and Holy Spirit not only are essentially God, the relations to each other that they in fact have are equally essential. But if the Son of God essentially and necessarily has the person he has, then the begetting of the person of the Son by the Father cannot have any voluntariness about it. In a real sense, it was not up to the Father whether one of the divine persons should be the person of Son, since being the person of the Son is essential to the person who is the Son.

Here it is a little surprising that Gerald Bray holds that since according to Calvin each person of the Trinity is *autotheos*, this ensures that the relations between them must be voluntary, since no one person can claim the authority to impose his will on the others.[62] The point about authority is certainly fair, but it must be clear from the very idea of begetting as it is being used in this connection that it is not a voluntary act. It is a necessary expression of the Father's nature that he begets the person of the Son, and of the Son that he is begotten. Of course, this necessary relation of Father and Son is not *in*voluntary either, in the sense in which a knee-jerk or blinking may be involuntary acts. It can be represented as a relationship of love; but it is not a relationship that might not have been, and so it is not voluntary in the usual meaning of that word—it is not an act of the will distinct from the very nature of the Fatherly personality.

But if the usual meaning of 'beget' is so pared down, what is left of it? What truth is now being safeguarded by the assertion that the Son is begotten of the Father when this is understood in this pared-down sense? These are questions not only for Calvin but for the entire tradition that he represents.

Finally, it is not clear what other doctrinal truths Calvin is safeguarding by his careful modification of the Nicene expressions of eternal generation. Is he safeguarding the full divinity of the Son? No, for the full divinity of the Son is safeguarded by confessing him to be *autotheos*. Is he safeguarding the equality of the persons? No, again, for on this account they are not equal because, to use Calvin's and Tertullian's expression, there is a certain order

---

[62] *The Doctrine of God*, 203.

and economy among the persons that means not merely that each person has features not had by the other persons but that there is an asymmetrical relation of dependency of the Son upon the Father and of the Spirit upon the Father and the Son.

3

The *Extra*

OUR discussion in the last chapter, with its emphasis on Calvin's concern to understand the person of the Son in a way that safeguards his unqualified deity, prepares us for this chapter's topic, which is Calvin's assertion and defence of what has come to be known as the *extra Calvinisticum*. This is the view that in the Incarnation God the Son retained divine properties such as immensity and omnipresence and that therefore Christ was not physically confined within the limits of a human person. It is disputed whether this view is unique to Calvin. In an excellent study, *Calvin's Catholic Christology*,[1] E. David Willis shows that the *extra Calvinisticum* might equally well be called the *extra Catholicum*,[2] citing statements of it (or of its equivalent) from a host of Christian writers from Athanasius to Aquinas. So, at least on the strength of this evidence, the position that we shall discuss represents an important strand of Christian orthodoxy.

In the *Institutes* Calvin refers explicitly to the *extra* (as I shall call it) in two places. First, in his discussion of the Incarnation in book II:

They thrust upon us as something absurd the fact that if the Word of God became flesh, then he was confined within the narrow prison of an earthly body. This is mere impudence! For even if the Word in his immeasurable essence united with the nature of man into one person, we do not imagine that he was confined therein. Here is something marvelous: the Son of God descended from heaven in such a way that, without leaving heaven, he willed to be borne in the virgin's womb, to go about the earth, and to hang upon the cross; yet he continuously filled the world as he had done from the beginning![3]

And, second, in his discussion of the nature of the Lord's Supper in book IV:

But some are carried away with such contentiousness as to say that because of the natures joined in Christ, wherever Christ's divinity is, there also is his flesh, which

---

[1] (Leiden: Brill, 1966).　　　　　　　　　　　　　　[2] *Calvin's Catholic Christology*, 60.

[3] *Inst.* II. 13. 4. See also II. 14. 2, *Comm.* on Acts 20, *Comm.* on John 3: 13. Compare Augustine: 'Christian doctrine does not hold that God took on the flesh, in which He was born of the Virgin, in such wise as to abandon or lose His care of the government of the world, or to transfer this care, reduced and concentrated, so to speak, to that small body.' Saint Augustine, *Letters*, vol. iii, trans. Sister Wilfrid Parsons (Washington, DC: Catholic University of America Press, 1953), Letter 137, 20. I am grateful to Thomas Weinandy for drawing this passage to my attention.

cannot be separated from it. . . . But from Scripture we plainly infer that the one person of Christ so consists of two natures that each nevertheless retains unimpaired its own distinctive character. . . . Surely, when the Lord of glory is said to be crucified [1 Cor. 2: 8], Paul does not mean that he suffered anything in his divinity, but he says this because the same Christ, who was cast down and despised, and suffered in the flesh, was God and Lord of glory. In this way he was also Son of man in heaven [John 3: 13], for the very same Christ, who, according to the flesh, dwelt as Son of man on earth, was God in heaven. In this manner, he is said to have descended to that place according to his divinity, not because divinity left heaven to hide itself in the prison house of the body, but because even though it filled all things, still in Christ's very humanity it dwelt bodily [Col. 2: 9], that is, by nature, and in a certain ineffable way. There is a commonplace distinction of the schools to which I am not ashamed to refer: although the whole Christ is everywhere, still the whole of that which is in him is not everywhere. And would that the Schoolmen themselves had honestly weighed the force of this statement. For thus would the absurd fiction of Christ's carnal presence have been obviated.[4]

There is no need to become embroiled in the issue of classifying Calvin's Christology—whether or not Calvin displays Nestorian tendencies, for example—nor in the theology of the Lord's Supper, and particularly not in the controversy between Calvin and the Lutherans from which both passages were probably taken, except to say that it is inaccurate to say that Calvin's view of the *extra* was a product of that controversy. For though the two passages cited were added in the 1559 edition of the *Institutes*, and may be thought to express a later development in Calvin's ideas, the thoughts that they express are to be found in very similar terms in, for example, works of Augustine that Calvin had earlier access to. This section from Augustine's Letter to Volusian is very similar in style and emphasis to the first of our quotations.

And we think that something impossible to believe is told us about the omnipotence of God, when we are told that the Word of God, by whom all things were made, took flesh from a virgin and appeared to mortal senses without destroying His immortality or infringing His eternity, or diminishing His power, or neglecting the government of the world, or leaving the bosom of the Father, where He is intimately with Him and in Him![5]

Augustine's thought is similar to Calvin's: though incarnate, the Son of God retained the powers of deity undiminished.

Nor shall we be concerned about the implications of the *extra* for theories

---

[4] *Inst.* IV. 17. 30. In his Dedication to Frederick, Elector of Palatine, of his *Commentary on Jeremiah* (1563) Calvin also cites this 'commonplace distinction', from Lombard (*Sentences*, 3. 22).

[5] Augustine, Letter to Volusian (137), 22–3. Anthony N. S. Lane shows that Calvin had access to Augustine's *Epistolae* (*John Calvin: Student of the Church Fathers*, 154, 176).

of space and time. If Willis is correct, then it is hard to take seriously the contention of T. F. Torrance that the *extra* has essentially to do with such theories. Torrance claims that the Lutheran doctrine of the ubiquity of the human nature of Jesus Christ (against which the *extra* was asserted, and came to be known as such) could only have been affirmed on what he calls a 'receptacle' view of time and space, developed through the effect of Aristotelian influences upon Christian theology.[6] This influence is seen, according to Torrance, in connection with, for example, medieval views of sacramental grace. But denial of the 'receptacle' view is certainly not a necessary condition of maintaining the *extra*, even on Torrance's own understanding of what that view is. For Torrance claims that Thomas Aquinas held the receptacle view and upheld the *extra* (as Willis shows); while Augustine upheld the *extra* (as we have just seen) and yet denied the receptacle view, as Torrance admits. More plausibly, the *extra* had less to do with theories of time and space than with a concern to maintain the immensity and infinity of the divine nature.

Nor, finally, shall we be concerned about the significance of the *extra* for the nature of our knowledge of God, with whether, for example, there is a valid knowledge of God apart from reference to the Incarnation. Calvin clearly thought that there is. Rather we shall focus attention upon the central metaphysical aspects of what Calvin might be said to mean here. We shall, for instance, be concerned with what the implications of the *extra* are for the idea of the union of two natures, one divine and the other human. In what sense can God be wholly united with human nature if what Calvin says is true? Can A be *wholly* united with B without being *entirely* united with B? What does it mean to say that the Son of God became man, on this view? Finally, we shall examine Calvin's approach to the *communicatio idiomatum*.

The Chalcedonian Background to Calvin

According to the Chalcedonian view of the Incarnation (as theoretically unsatisfactory as that view may be), whatever is essential to the divine nature cannot be yielded up in the Incarnation. That is, if there are properties that are essential to God being God—for example, omnipotence or omniscience—then in becoming incarnate God cannot cease to be omnipotent or omniscient. Perhaps he could veil or hide the manifesting of his omnipotence, but he certainly cannot give up or empty himself of it, not even in his incarnate state, for in giving it up he would have ceased to be God. This is presumably part at least of what the Chalcedonian formula means by

---

[6] T. F. Torrance, *Space, Time and Incarnation* (New York: Oxford University Press, 1969), 25, 31.

claiming that the union of the Son of God and human nature is 'without change'. (And similarly, of course, with human nature; if there are properties that are essential to a person's being a human being, then these cannot be yielded up in the human nature to which the Son of God was united; this is also an implication of the 'without change' clause, but less relevant to us here.) As Calvin puts it, '[A]lthough Christ could justly have shown forth his divinity, he manifested himself as but a lowly and despised man'.[7]

It is important to understand that the Chalcedonian statement is not intended to be an *explanation* of the Incarnation, but a statement of what is essential to it and what is denied by it. This is seen by the fact that at the heart of the statement is a series of negations or denials respecting the two natures: 'without confusing . . . without transmuting . . . without dividing them, without contrasting them'. It is best to think of these denials as preventing the drawing of false inferences about the Incarnation. In essence they are negative theological claims.

As already noted, what came to be known as the *extra* was clearly present in the minds of the Fathers. For example, Athanasius of Alexandria says this of the Saviour:

For he was not, as might be imagined, circumscribed in the body, nor, while present in the body, was he absent elsewhere; nor, while he moved the body, was the universe left void of his working and providence; but, thing most marvelous, Word as he was, so far from being contained by anything, he rather contained all things himself; and just as while present in the whole of creation, he is at once distinct in being from the universe, and present in all things by his own power—giving order to all things, and over all and in all revealing his own providence, and giving life to each thing and all things, including the whole without being included, but being in his own Father alone wholly and in every respect—thus, even while present in a human body and himself quickening it, he was, without inconsistency, quickening the universe as well, and was in every process of nature, and was outside the whole, and while known from the body by his works, he was none the less manifest from the working of the universe as well.[8]

J. N. D. Kelly says that for Cyril of Alexandria the Logos 'remains what he was' in the Incarnation: 'What happened was that at the incarnation, while continuing to exist eternally in the form of God, He added to that by taking the form of a servant. Both before and after the incarnation He was the same Person, unchanged in his essential deity.'[9] As the consequence of this view it is said the Son suffered in the sense that those human properties or that

---

[7] *Inst.* II. 13. 2.

[8] Athanasius, *On the Incarnation of the Word*, trans. A Robertson, in Edwards R. Hardy (ed.), *Christology of the Later Fathers* (Philadelphia: Westminster Press, 1954), 70–1.

[9] J. N. D. Kelly, *Early Christian Doctrines*, 319.

human nature to which he was contingently united in the Incarnation suffered. He did not suffer in himself, in his divine nature.

Calvin supported this general outlook, as his comments on John 1: 14 show:

On this article of faith there are two things chiefly to be observed. The first is, that two natures were so united in one Person in Christ, that one and the same Christ is true God and true man. The second is, that the unity of person does not hinder the two natures from remaining distinct, so that his Divinity retains all that is peculiar to itself, and his humanity holds separately whatever belongs to it. . . . On the other hand, since he distinctly gives to the man Christ the name of *the Speech*, it follows that Christ, when he became man, did not cease to be what he formerly was, and that no change took place in that eternal essence of God which was clothed with *flesh*.[10]

By insisting on the *extra*, Calvin is arguing that the Son of God is God, and therefore has God's essence. In other words (although Calvin does not put it this way), the Son has all of God's essential properties, including—for Calvin—properties such as impassibility, immensity, and omnipresence. Therefore, if the Incarnation is truly the Incarnation of the Son of God, then it must preserve the divinity of the Son of God unaltered or unimpaired. For otherwise it would not be a true incarnation of the Son. So, even allowing for some poetic licence, Calvin would not have been best pleased with this couplet from Charles Wesley's Hymn 'Let Earth and Heaven Combine': 'Our God contracted to a span | Incomprehensibly made man.' In Calvin's view, God was not contracted to a span in the Incarnation but, rather, was in union with that which is only a 'span'—that is, with human nature. Calvin frequently invokes the principle of divine incomprehensibility elsewhere in his writings, but this is never to sanction what was in his eyes manifest metaphysical nonsense—as the essence of God being contracted to a span would be—but to safeguard the transcendence of the divine essence. So, incomprehensible or not, on Calvin's view God the Son was never contracted to a span, because he could not have been.

Here, by contrast, are some of the expressions that Calvin uses to convey the union of the divine and human in the Incarnation: the Son of God 'assumed' human nature, he was 'clothed with our flesh', divinity and human nature were mutually connected; 'he took our nature upon himself'; he 'came forth as true man and took the person and the name of Adam'; he 'coupled human nature with divine'.[11] But since the Son of God is essentially God and thus impassible, immense, and omnipresent, he must remain in his incarnation impassible, immense, and omnipresent. Consequently, whatever account may be given of the person of Jesus Christ, the relation of

---

[10] *Comm.* John 1: 14.   [11] These expressions are taken from *Inst.* II. 12 and 13.

the divine to the human is asymmetrical—in the Incarnation, the divine takes on human nature but human nature does not take on the divine: 'Christ emptied himself in a nature truly human. For what does "being found in fashion as a man" mean [Phil. 2: 8], save that for a time the divine glory did not shine, but only human likeness was manifest in a lowly and abased condition.'[12] Here Calvin does refer to the veiling of the glory of the Son of God in the Incarnation—'for a time the divine glory did not shine, but only human likeness was manifest in a lowly and abased condition'—but by this he does not mean that in the Incarnation the Son of God divested himself of the glory of deity. He means that, in virtue of his union with human nature, that glory was not manifest. It is essential to God that he is glorious, because this is a corollary of his perfection; but it is not essential to God that his glory shines, at least not if this means that everyone automatically recognizes its shining. For Calvin, kenotic christologies would have been unacceptable, not only because they are incoherent, but also because they require the Son of God to divest himself of properties that are essential to God and thus essential to the Son of God who is God.

According to Bruce McCormack, Karl Barth regarded Calvin's *extra* to be speculative and not consistently Christian because it requires Calvin to develop a contingent, adventitious connection between the *logos asarkos* and the incarnate Christ.[13] In McCormack's exposition of Barth's interpretation of Calvin, the Word must merely play the role of Christ, it is not essential to him to be the Christ.[14] This in turn, Barth claims, leads to Calvin postulating an unknown God. Why agnosticism about God follows on Calvin's alleged view is not made clear. In any case, Calvin could avoid these charges merely by asserting that becoming incarnate as the Christ is an apt and consistent expression of the character of the Word (a solution that McCormack mentions without discussing). When we consider passages from Calvin such as those just cited, it seems clear that this is what Calvin would have said.

Here the issue of God as he is in himself versus God as he is revealed to us revisits us. But previous discussion helps us to see how Calvin would

---

[12] *Inst.* II. 13. 2.

[13] Bruce McCormack, 'Grace and Being: The Role of God's Gracious Election in Karl Barth's Theological Ontology', in John Webster (ed.), *The Cambridge Companion to Karl Barth* (Cambridge: Cambridge University Press, 2000). The following is a typical statement of Barth's on Calvin's *extra*. The Reformed 'failed to show convincingly how far the *extra* does not involve the assumption of a two-fold Christ, of a *logos ensarkos* alongside a *logos asarkos*, and therefore a dissolution of the unity of the natures and hypostatic union, and therefore a destruction of the unequivocal Emmanuel and the certainty of faith and salvation based thereon' (*Church Dogmatics*, i/2, trans. G. T. Thomson and Harold Knight (Edinburgh: T. & T. Clark, 1956), 170). Why these conclusions follow is far from obvious and Barth offers no support. See also *CD* iv/1. 181.

[14] 'Grace and Being', 97, 98.

respond, namely, by saying that the Incarnation expresses the divine essence without exhaustively revealing it. As we saw when discussing the contrast between the immanent and the economic Trinity in the last chapter, there are various positive ways in which that relation may be understood. A corollary of that position is that there is a similar range of ways that the Word of God and Word of God incarnate might be related.

In any case it is not that God the Son in becoming man wills to lay aside features of his deity. For this language of 'laying aside' suggests that had he willed to do so the Son, instead of keeping his omnipresence could have divested himself of it, and this implies that omnipresence is a contingent feature of Godhood. Rather, given the divine will that the Word of God become incarnate, there was on this view a necessity to the limits of what subsequently happened, a necessity that is the product of the sort of thing a human being is and (if we can put it thus) the sort of thing that God is. Nothing could happen to make the humanity of Jesus Christ other than true humanity or his deity other than true deity. Given his commitment to the *extra* Calvin must reject a (so to speak) 'transfer' view of the Incarnation according to which in becoming man the Son of God became confined to a series of earthly locations. In this commitment, Calvin was echoing Chalcedonian orthodoxy as certainly as he was echoing Augustine.

Perhaps Calvin's view amounts to this: in the Incarnation there is uniquely powerful and loving and gracious focusing of the divine nature upon human nature, rather than a transfer of the Son of God to a spatio-temporal location. This focusing makes it possible for us to say that God the Son is so present with human nature that there is a union of natures in Jesus Christ. God in the person of the Son, through whom all things are created, focuses upon one unique aspect of his creation in uniting to human nature in the person of Jesus Christ. God the Son was not simply present by being active, he was present by being in union. The character of this divine presence sanctions the language of person with respect to the result.

The Logos, as Calvin liked to say, in true Chalcedonian fashion, 'remains what He was'; what happened was that at the Incarnation, while continuing to exist eternally in the form of God, the Logos, in Incarnation, took the form of a servant. Both before and after the Incarnation he was the same Person, unchanged (and unchangeable) in his essential deity. The only difference was that he who had existed 'with the Father' became 'embodied', that is, entered into a relationship with human nature of the closest possible kind.

Necessarily, you cannot get a quart of water into a pint pot. If you attempt to do so, and succeed in filling the pint pot, then necessarily some of the water will fail to get into the pot. This is nobody's fault, and certainly not the water's; it is a consequence of the respective volumes of pint and quart. A mono receiver receiving a stereo signal necessarily receives it in mono. If you look at a building, then necessarily the building will be seen from one particular vantage point.

These simple illustrations emphasize that in many circumstances what happens is circumscribed by the limited capacities or powers of the object or agent concerned. And so it is for Calvin in the case of the Incarnation. Suppose that God in the person of his Son eternally wills to become incarnate in Jesus Christ. *How* he can be incarnate depends on his own metaphysical powers and what it is possible and impossible to do given these powers. The divine nature is, so to speak, focused in and united with human nature in Jesus Christ as fully as this is metaphysically possible. To the extent that it is metaphysically impossible for the stereo life of the Son of God to become incarnate in the mono life of a human being, then not even God the Son can accomplish this.

The fundamental metaphysical thought behind Calvin's *extra* is that the union of human and divine that is implied in the Incarnation cannot be a case of strict or numerical identity. As Calvin puts it in the Dedication of his *Commentary on Jeremiah*:

There are two words commonly used, Union (*unio*) and Unity (*unitas*;) the first is applied to the two Natures, and the second to the Person alone. To assert the unity of the flesh and of Divinity, those would be ashamed to do, if I am not deceived, who yet inconsiderately adopt this absurdity; for, except the flesh differs and is distinct in its own peculiar properties from the Divine nature, they are by blending together become one.[15]

The Incarnation is a union of two natures each of which has its own distinct unity. For if God is essentially omnipresent (say) and forms a unity with human nature, then the divine and human would become one by blending together, each losing its own distinctive unity. Several undesirable consequences would flow from such a unity, including the consequence that whatever was true of God was true of human nature, and whatever was true of human nature was true of God, because God and man would when blended together to become one nature.

So for Calvin, Jesus of Nazareth, being God the Son incarnate, was God in the closest union with human nature that it is possible to be, but he was not identical with human nature, nor mixed with it. Unless the Incarnation was metaphysically necessary (which Calvin denies) such an identity would also flout the plausible metaphysical principle that if A is identical with B, A and B are necessarily identical. Calvin avoids scholastic expressions of the Incarnation such as that in it 'God is man' or 'Man is God', no doubt because

---

[15] Dedication to the *Commentary on Jeremiah*, xx.

such formulae are not found in Scripture and are also unduly abstract and paradoxical.[16] So for Calvin the sense of 'becoming' in which the Son of God became man, or the Son of God became flesh, cannot be such that in becoming flesh the Son of God ceased to be the Son of God in the way that, in becoming chocolate, the cocoa and milk cease to be cocoa and milk.

[W]e ought not to understand the statement that 'the Word was made flesh' [John 1: 14] in the sense that the Word was turned into flesh or confusedly mingled with flesh. Rather, it means that, because he chose for himself the virgin's womb as a temple in which to dwell, he who was the Son of God became the Son of man—not by confusion of substance, but by unity of person.[17]

We therefore hold that Christ, as he is God and man, consisting of two natures united but not mingled, is our Lord and the true Son of God even according to, but not by reason of, his humanity. Away with the error of Nestorius, who in wanting to pull apart rather than distinguish the nature of Christ devised a double Christ! Yet we see that Scripture cries out against this with a clear voice: there the name Son of God is applied to him who is born of the virgin [Luke 1: 32], and the virgin herself is called the 'mother of our Lord' [Luke 1: 43].[18]

For Calvin the unity of soul and body in a human person is an analogy of this 'very great mystery'[19]—not the great mystery of how the immensity of God could be united with human nature, for it is clearly not an analogy for that, but an analogy for the narrower point concerning the joining of two natures without each losing its distinctive character. Here again he follows the Patristic tradition, especially Augustine:

This Word took on human nature, and thereby became the one Jesus Christ, Mediator between God and men, equal to the Father in His divinity, less than the Father according to the flesh, that is, as man; unchangeably immortal according to His divinity which is equal to the Father, but likewise subject to change and death according to the weakness derived from us. . . . He condescended to become man and to be united to him. He did this in such manner that the whole of man was thus joined to Him, as the soul is to the body, but without changeableness of matter, into which God is not changed, but which we see present in the body and the soul.[20]

We shall shortly assess how important the body–soul analogy is to Calvin.

Given that he is committed to denying all of these possibilities, Calvin has therefore only one option. He must say that the union in question is a union of a new relationship, as when a man in becoming a husband has a new

---

[16] Thomas Aquinas discusses such sentences in *Summa Theologiae*, 3a, 116. 1, 2. For some discussion of these expressions, see Richard Cross, '*Alloiosis* in the Christology of Zwingli', (*Journal of Theological Studies*, NS 47 1996), 120, and *The Metaphysics of the Incarnation* (Oxford: Oxford University Press, 2002).

[17] *Inst.* II. 14. 1.   [18] *Inst.* II. 14. 4.   [19] *Inst.* II. 14. 1.

[20] Augustine, Letter 137, 27–8.

relationship but does not cease to be a man.[21] But if the Incarnation is such a relationship, in what sense can Christ be wholly divine? Perhaps the answer to this must take full account of the divine simplicity. Because God is simple the Son of God is simple, without parts, necessarily wholly divine. Being without parts, necessarily wholly divine, whatever he is in union with he is wholly in union with (without himself changing). He cannot change only partly, with a part of him not to be in union with human nature, since the Son of God does not have parts. If two circles touch at some point on their respective circumferences, then they may be said to be in union. Nevertheless, despite the union, parts of each circle's circumference are not in contact with parts of the other. They remain distinct circles. This analogy falls down in that it would not do to say that there was a part of God that was not united to human nature. Nevertheless, although the divine nature is not merely partly united to human nature, it is not confined within the bounds of human nature any more than either of the two circles that touch is confined within the bounds of the other. This may be what Calvin has in mind when (as we noted earlier) he endorses Peter Lombard's distinction that although the whole Christ is everywhere, still the whole of that which is in him is not everywhere.[22] This says, conversely, that the Son of God is omnipresent, but Christ's human nature, which is 'in' him by virtue of his union with it (although not of course physically or spatially in him) cannot be omnipresent (*contra* the Lutherans).

Calvin seems to suggest that we must also guard against falsely inferring from the fact that God is omnipresent that wherever God is present he is equally present. There may be degrees or intensities of that presence by which God is said to be omnipresent. Calvin guards against saying that if God is omnipresent then he is no more present to the human nature of Jesus than he is to the human nature of anyone else. He says that:

In this way he was also Son of man in heaven [John 3: 13], for the very same Christ, who, according to the flesh, dwelt as Son of man on earth, was God in heaven. In this manner he is said to have descended to that place according to his divinity, not because divinity left heaven to hide itself in the prison house of the body, but because even though it filled all things, still in Christ's very humanity it dwelt bodily [Col. 2: 9], that is, by nature, and in a certain ineffable way.[23]

---

[21] Compare Thomas Aquinas, 'The statement that "the Word was made flesh" does not indicate any change in the Word, but only in the nature newly assumed into the oneness of a divine person. "And the Word was made flesh" through a union to the flesh. Now a union is a relation. And relations newly said of God with respect to creatures do not imply a change on the side of God, but on the side of the creature relating in a new way to God,' Aquinas, *Commentary on the Gospel of St. John*, trans. James A. Weisheipl and Fabian Larcher (Albany, N Y: Magi, 1980), 86–7.

[22] *Inst.* IV. 17. 30. See also the Dedication to the *Commentary on Jeremiah.*   [23] *Inst.* IV. 17. 30.

In using the phrase 'by nature' Calvin apparently wants to affirm that while, in virtue of God's omnipresence, it makes sense to say of any place that 'God is here', God is present in Christ in a deeper sense. The contrast is between God as being omnipresent in the sense that he is everywhere active and God being present by identifying himself with human nature in the person of Jesus in a way that warrants statements such as 'The Word became flesh'. No doubt Calvin's phrase 'by nature' is a reference to the hypostatic union. It is scarcely surprising that he says that this union is 'ineffable'.

Of course, in recognizing the ineffability of this union Calvin is not going beyond what Christian theologians have always said, including the scholastics. Thus although Thomas Aquinas[24] engages in considerably more metaphysical analysis of the Incarnation than Calvin,[25] he is forced to acknowledge that how human nature is united to the person of the Word in order to form one thing is not accounted for by his metaphysics. He recognizes that the mode of union of the divine and human in the person of Christ is incomprehensible.[26]

When Calvin refers to the Incarnation as being 'incomprehensible' or 'ineffable' his precise point is that the truth of the Incarnation is above reason in the sense that it is not explicable in the way that other kinds of union or unity may be. He is thus tacitly endorsing the position of a predecessor such as Thomas Aquinas, as well as of a successor such as G. W. F. Leibniz.[27]

In view of Calvin's explicit contrast between 'union' and 'unity' and the importance that he attaches to it, it seems to me that the expression 'the unity of natures' is unhelpful when characterizing Calvin's position.[28] It suggests that the natures having unity cease to be two natures, which Calvin and the tradition declare to be impossible. So when Calvin writes of two natures being united,[29] 'two natures that each nevertheless retains unimpaired its own distinctive character',[30] it is preferable to think, instead, in terms of

---

[24] *Summa Theologiae*, 3. 2. 1, and 3. 4. 2; *Summa Contra Gentiles*, IV. 41.

[25] And some speculation about it that Calvin would not have endorsed. For example, he thinks it possible for a divine person other than the Son to have become incarnate and for the Son to have become incarnate more than once.

[26] On this see Eleonore Stump's treatment of Thomas's metaphysics of the Incarnation in *Aquinas*, (London: Routledge, 2003).

[27] See, for example, *Summa Contra Gentiles*, I. 6, 'That to Give Assent to the Truths of Faith is not Foolishness even though they are Above Reason'. For a discussion of Leibniz's treatment of truths above reason see Maria Rosa Antognazza, 'The Defence of the Mysteries of the Trinity and the Incarnation: An Example of Leibniz's "Other" Reason', *British Journal for the History of Philosophy* (2001).

[28] Cf. Robert A. Peterson, *Calvin and the Atonement* (2nd edn.; Fearn, Ross-shire: Mentor Books, 1999), 38.

[29] e.g. *Inst.* II. 14. 4.

[30] *Inst.* IV. 17. 30.

their union. It is a unity only by virtue of being a union of natures; hence its ineffability.

While it is possible, in abstraction, to consider Christ's divine and human natures, and to ascribe appropriate properties to each,[31] Calvin takes it to be impermissible to do this when considering Christ's characteristic actions as the Mediator, for then the union of the natures coming together to execute the mediatorial office must be stressed, since it is necessary to the Mediator's being such that he have divine and human natures. This seems to be the point of Calvin's remarks in his second letter to Stancaro when he says, 'What truly and suitably belongs to the totality ought not to be divided and assigned to the natures' and 'Expressions common to both natures are not to be separately ascribed to one'.[32] The privileges and powers of the mediatorial office cannot be ascribed either to human nature or to the divine person separately. What Christ did as Mediator he did in the unity of his office and so his official actions are not to be divided between the human and the divine. Christ's two natures can be separately identified and discussed, but they ought not to be held apart when his role as Mediator is specifically in view, and that role is ascribed indifferently to each.

Thus for Calvin reduplicative expressions—for example, 'as Mediator', 'as man', 'as God'—are confined to the Christ's role as Mediator. It is *as* Mediator that he is both divine and human, and therefore as Mediator he can both forgive sins, being divine, and sit on the side of the well, being human. For Calvin this is an official or functional reduplication rather than an ontological reduplication. We can say of some person that when considered as the Chancellor of the Exchequer, he has the power to set levels of taxation, while considered as a taxpayer he has not. Considered as the Mediator, Jesus Christ is both human and divine. He is not only divine, and not merely human. Considered solely as divine, the Son of God is not human. Considered solely in respect of his human nature, Christ is not divine. Calvin offers no speculation on the psychology of this union, unlike modern 'two minds' theories of the Incarnation.[33]

Calvin, then, provides his readers with rules about how to think of the unity of Christ's person as well as of the distinctness of his natures. What he proposes has a functional rather than an ontological thrust, but this does not imply that he held a 'functional' Christology. A small child may learn about

---

[31] As, according to Calvin, Paul does in passages such as Rom. 1: 1–4; 2 Cor. 13: 4; Rom. 9: 5—see his discussion *Inst.* II. 14. 6.

[32] 'The Controversy on Christ the Mediator: Calvin's Second Reply to Stancaro', trans. Joseph N. Tylenda, *Calvin Theological Journal* (1973), 149, 153.

[33] For example, Thomas V. Morris, *The Logic of God Incarnate* (Ithaca: Cornell University Press, 1986), and Richard Swinburne, *The Christian God*, ch. 9.

real objects and their shadows by learning what it makes sense to say about them. She may learn that it makes no sense to say that one can jump on one's own shadow, or that the shadow of a table may be present without the table. But this 'functional' approach to understanding objects and their shadows does not mean that there are no such things as tables and their shadows. So Calvin advises his readers to learn to talk about Christ in certain ways; it makes sense to say certain things about Christ, but other ways involve mistakes. Nevertheless, there are realities which warrant the talk. But because these realities are 'ineffable' it is wiser to stay at the functional level rather than to attempt to encompass them in a descriptive account, or—what for him would be worse—in a *theory* of the Incarnation.

One reason for holding together the union of the natures in the person and work of the Mediator is that Calvin held that the work of Mediator can only be performed by the God-man (although, as we shall briefly see in Chapter 11, there is reason to think that he did not always hold this view). A second reason is that in the case of Christ's mediatorship both the Son of God and that human nature to which he is united exemplify instances of the same moral and spiritual properties; the Son of God essentially and infinitely so, in virtue of his divinity, the human nature contingently and finitely so, in view of its creation in God's image. This is because by virtue of the union of the two natures the moral and spiritual properties that originate in God himself are communicated to the human nature of Christ. So this is a union of economy; it is in virtue of his role as Mediator of salvation that the Son of God, uniting with human nature, communicated to that nature (by the Spirit?) those graces by which Christ could effect salvation. '[T]hey could not have been given to a man who was nothing but a man.'[34]

Of course the human nature to which the Son of God is united is not an abstraction; it is a particular instance or expression of human nature, localized in Mary's womb, coming to exist not independently of the Son's incarnation, but precisely in incarnation. The nature of this particularity might be expressed like this: were it not to have been united to the Son of God this instance of human nature could have become a human being in its own right, though understandably enough Calvin does not express the point. Calvin would hold with Aquinas that 'Although a human nature is a kind of individual in the category of substance, in Christ it does not exist separately in itself but in another more perfect reality, namely in the person of the Word of God, and consequently does not have its own personality.'[35] Perhaps we ought to conclude from this that Calvin's is a 'parts' Christology. We shall consider this point more fully later. Yet Christ is surely a union of a divine

---

[34] *Inst.* II. 14. 3.   [35] *Summa Theologiae*, 3a, 2. 2, trans. T. R. J. Hennessey.

person, the Word or 'form' of God, and human nature, with that union making not a new person distinct from the person of the Word but that person in union with a particular expression of human nature.

An odd feature of Calvin's procedure is that in an effort to elucidate his Christology he is willing to use an analogy drawn from what he believes to be the nature of the human person. Why is this, given his reluctance to use a similar analogy to elucidate the Trinity and his more general unwillingness to countenance analogies not sanctioned by Scripture? As we shall see, when Calvin (following Augustine, though not in detail) offers an understanding of the person of Christ drawn from the constitution of the human person, this is because he thought of the person in pronouncedly dualistic fashion, and also no doubt because he thought that the human person is in the image of God.

THE *COMMUNICATIO IDIOMATUM*

In Calvin's Christological thinking an important role is played by the thought that there is a strong asymmetry between the person of the Son and the human nature that he 'assumed'. This asymmetry is underlined by Calvin's emphasis on the *extra*. The person of the Son has ontological priority. In an ontological if not in a temporal sense (for Calvin thinks that God exists atemporally), he exists before the existence of the human nature that he assumed. The asymmetry is strikingly seen in the fact that while the person of the Word can act independently of the human nature he assumed—this is the heart of the *extra*—his human nature has never acted and cannot act independently of the person of the Word. The hunger and tiredness referred to in the Gospels are not properly understood merely as facts about the human nature of Christ, but about Christ himself. The Word depends on nothing and on no one, retaining all the properties of Godhood, while his human nature utterly depends on him. Thus the Incarnation is an assuming of human nature by the eternal Word. The Word willed to become incarnate, but his human nature did not similarly will to be incarnated by the Son, for apart from that union it had no existence.

In elucidating the idea of Incarnation in a way that is consistent with the *extra*, Calvin appeals on more than one occasion to the idea of the *communicatio idiomatum* as a way of clarifying the distinctness of the natures that are in union in Christ. Thomas Weinandy claims that:

the whole of orthodox patristic christology, including the conciliar affirmations, can be seen as an attempt to defend the practice and to clarify the use of the communication of idioms. Why is this so? Simply, embedded within the communication of idioms are the . . . three truths essential for an authentic understanding of the

Incarnation, and it is only in the defense and clarification of the communication of idioms that these three truths became explicitly grasped and manifestly articulated. It is *truly* the Son of God who *truly* is man and so suffers *truly* as man. Historically, then, it was not an orthodox or a conciliar account of the Incarnation that gave rise to the communication of idioms, it was the communication of idioms that gave rise to the conciliar and orthodox account of the Incarnation.[36]

The *communicatio* held a less central position in Calvin's christology than this. He focuses not primarily on Patristic and later appeals to the *communicatio* as expressing a fundamental feature of the Incarnation but on the prima-facie Christological problem posed to him by a comparatively few scriptural statements. Yet it is no doubt true that his way of resolving this problem was undertaken with more than a sidelong glance at Lutheran views about the ubiquity of Christ's human nature. Consequently, while his view of the *communicatio* is not a central feature of his Christology, it nevertheless throws light on his view of the person of Christ. Here is one of his several references to the *communicatio*: 'It is equally senseless to despise the "communication of properties", a term long ago invented to some purpose by the holy fathers. Surely, when the Lord of glory is said to be crucified [1 Cor. 2: 8], Paul does not mean that he suffered anything in his divinity, but he says this because the same Christ, who was cast down and despised, and suffered in the flesh, was God and Lord of glory.'[37]

But what exactly is the *communicatio idiomatum*? Obviously, the expression refers to a transfer of attributes or properties. On the basis of the two-natures doctrine of Chalcedon, there are three logical possibilities for such a transfer: (1) The predicating of properties of the one or the other nature to the whole person of Christ. (2) The predicating of properties of the divine nature to the human nature of Christ. (3) The predicating of properties of the human nature to the divine nature of Christ. These possibilities are clearly not exclusive of each other.

Thus the term can be, and has been, variously used. The basic idea is that expressed in (1), that in view of the unity of Christ's person in the Incarnation both human and divine properties can be legitimately ascribed to him. This much seems hardly debatable by anyone in the Chalcedonian tradition and, in his discussion of the *communicatio*, Calvin does not dispute the unity of Christ's person, but emphasizes it. Nevertheless, he does not invoke the *communicatio* when discussing this. But several other questions arise, such as: In view of this union, can the divine nature of Christ be said to have human properties and vice versa? If so, is the possession of, say,

---

[36] Thomas Weinandy, *Does God Suffer?* (Edinburgh: T. & T. Clark, 1999), 175 (Weinandy's italics).

[37] *Inst.* IV. 17. 30. See also *Inst.* II. 14. 2.

divine properties by the human nature of Christ a real possession or is it only nominal or verbal? And in an expression such as 'God shed his blood' (legitimized from Acts 20: 28) how is the referring expression 'God' to be understood? These questions may also bring the *communicatio* into play and we shall touch on each of them later.

It is characteristic of Alexandrian and Cappadocian Christology, in view of its stress on the unity of Christ's person, to think of the *communicatio* not only as a way of sanctioning the application of divine and human predicates to Christ but also of thinking of the divine nature as having human properties and vice versa.[38] By contrast, it is characteristic of Antiochene Christology to restrict the *communicatio* to the concrete person of the Incarnate Son, the Mediator.[39] In discussing the *communicatio* in the thinking of Scotus and Aquinas, Richard Cross emphasizes that for the schoolmen the communication of properties ascribes divine and human properties to the divine person.[40]

In the *Summa Theologiae*, Aquinas discusses the *communicatio idiomatum* in the fourth and fifth articles of 3a, 16. He asks whether what belongs to the Son of Man may be predicated of the divine nature and whether what belongs to the Son of God of the human nature. What he has in mind is not 'human nature' or 'divine nature' as such, but the human and divine natures of Christ. He answers, in general, that 'whatever is predicated of Christ, in virtue either of his divine nature or of his human nature, may be predicated both of God and of the man'. So key to his answer to these questions is his conviction that since there is one hypostasis of both natures, the same hypostasis may be signified by the term for either nature. 'Whether, therefore, we speak of "the man" or of "God", the terms stand for the one subject subsisting in both divine and human nature. Consequently, we may predicate of the man what is attributed to the divine nature; and we may predicate of God what is attributed to the human nature.'

---

[38] 'Indeed, so close and real was the union [viz. the union of natures in the person of Christ] that Cyril [of Alexandria] conceived of each of the natures as participating in the properties of the other. . . Thus the humanity was infused with the life-giving energy of the Word, and itself became life-giving. Yet there were limits to this principle. As he explained, the Word did not actually suffer in His own nature; He suffered as incarnate . . .' (J. N. D. Kelly, *Early Christian Doctrines*, 322). It is this that J. F. Bethune-Baker refers to as a later usage of the *communicatio*, according to which the human and the divine natures were regarded as so interpenetrating each other that the properties of the one nature might be predicated of the other (*An Introduction to the Early History of Christian Doctrine* (3rd edn.), London: Methuen, 1923, 293–4).

[39] Thus the Antiochene Theodoret of Cyrus 'rejected the thoroughgoing use of the *communicatio idiomatum* advocated in the Alexandrian school; in his opinion it suggested a confusion or intermingling of the natures' (J. N. D. Kelly, *Early Christian Doctrines*, 326).

[40] *The Metaphysics of the Incarnation*, 183.

Aquinas implies, however, that we must not do this in an unthinking way.

While, accordingly, no distinction is to be made between the various Predicates attributed to Christ, it is necessary to distinguish the two aspects of the subject which justify the predication. For attributes of the divine nature are predicated of Christ in virtue of his divine nature, while attributes of the human nature are predicated of him in virtue of his human nature.[41]

So even granted the fact that the hypostasis of the human and divine natures in the person of the Mediator legitimizes such language, it does not do so by legitimizing a confusion or conflation of the natures nor, what would be worse, by a sort of transposition of them. It is the bare fact of the hypostatization that legitimizes the language, nothing else; and the character of that hypostatization must be respected. So the communication of the idioms does not flout the principle that contrary properties cannot be possessed by the same thing. For though Christ is 'one thing', he is a 'thing' with two natures. So both divine and human properties may be predicated of Christ (who was one hypostasis of the divine person of the Word and of human nature), but in the case of predicating what (for example) belongs to the human nature to the divine nature this is only possible in the concrete case of this particular hypostasis, and this concrete case licenses predicating indifferently what belongs to either nature. So for Aquinas the communication of properties is their being predicated, in their turn, of the one hypostasis of both natures as these are concretely instantiated or expressed in the person of the incarnate Son. The properties cannot be communicated to each other in the abstract, as if divine nature may have human properties, or human nature divine properties.

For Martin Luther also the language of the *communicatio* is mandated by the singularity of Christ's person. Nevertheless, Luther goes beyond the scholastics, invoking a minority tradition in the Patristic period (for example, that represented by John of Damascus)[42] in which the properties of divinity are ascribed not only to the divine person, but also to the human nature of Christ, and vice versa. 'Because the divinity and the humanity form in Christ one single person, the Scripture attributes to the divinity, on account of this personal unity, everything that concerns humanity, and conversely.'[43] At the time of the Reformation, in controversies over the

---

[41] *Summa Theologiae*, 3a, 16. 4, trans. Colman E. O'Neill.

[42] *The Metaphysics of the Incarnation*, 184.

[43] *Greater Confession of the Eucharist* (1528), quoted in Wendel, *Calvin: The Origins and Development of his Religious Thought*, 221. 'The catholic belief is this, that we confess the one Christ to be true God and man. From this truth of double substance and from the unity of the person follows what is called the communication of attributes, so that the things which belong to man may rightly be said concerning God

Supper, the later Lutherans (at least as judged by the Formula of Concord adopted in 1576) accepted (1), accepted (2) in the case of some divine properties, on the grounds that the divine nature is unchangeable (and thus in effect denied kenoticism), but denied (3).

> Therefore now not only as God, but also as man, he knows all things, can do all things, is present to all creatures, has under his feet and in his hand all things which are in heaven, in the earth, and under the earth ... This his power, being everywhere present, he can exercise, nor is anything to him either impossible or unknown.[44]

Because of the controversies over the Supper, and in particular the assertion by the Lutherans of the doctrine of consubstantiality, according to which the human nature of Christ takes on some of the properties of divinity, such as ubiquity, attention came to be focused on that sense or senses of the *communicatio* according to which the properties of the one nature of Christ were (or were not) predicable of the other. Calvin rejected this development; not a surprise, given his unwillingness to qualify the fully divine nature of Christ in any way.

> If anything like this very great mystery [of the Incarnation] can be found in human affairs, the most apposite parallel seems to be that of man, whom we see to consist of two substances. Yet neither is so mingled with the other as not to retain its own distinctive nature. For the soul is not the body, and the body is not the soul. Therefore, some things are said exclusively of the soul that can in no wise apply to the body; and of the body, again, that in no way fit the soul; of the whole man, that cannot refer—except inappropriately—to either soul or body separately. Finally the characteristics of the mind are [sometimes] transferred to the body, and those of the body to the soul. Yet he who consists of these parts is one man, not many.[45]

Here Calvin seems to be saying that there are properties of the whole man that are not properties of either the soul or the body alone. Of course, the Lutherans further argue that predicates of each part, since they can be ascribed to the whole, can also be ascribed to the other part.[46] Later in this chapter we shall return to the question of the place that the union of body and soul plays as a model for Calvin's Christology, and whether he is committed to a 'parts' Christology.

---

and on the other hand those which belong to God may be said of man. It is truly said, "This man created the world, and this God suffered" ' (*Disputation de divinitate and humanitate Christi*, in *Werke* (Weimar, 1932), 39: 199). If Luther really means that this man created the world, then this creates obvious difficulties. How could this man create the world if human nature is included in the creation?

[44] *Formula of Concord*, art. VIII. xi in Philip Schaff, *Creeds of Christendom* (6th edn.; 1919, repr. Grand Rapids, Mich.: Baker, 1977), iii. 152.   [45] *Inst.* II. 14. 1.

[46] *The Metaphysics of the Incarnation*, 196 n. 60.

With all of this as background, what is Calvin's view of the *communicatio*? In brief, he has no difficulty with the ascription of divine and human properties to the same person, the person of the Mediator; in this he follows the schoolmen. But he departs from them by not calling this an instance of the communication of properties. Rather, he seems to take up the Lutheran usage of the *communicatio*, especially senses (2) and (3) above, and particularly the ascription to divinity of human properties, *but he claims that such expressions are rhetorical and not literally the case.* Yet it is a usage that is warranted by the unity of the human and divine natures in the person of the Mediator. The metaphysics of the Incarnation is not a case of the *communicatio*, but warrants the language of *communicatio*, provided that this is understood not literally but rhetorically.

Perhaps it is best to think of Calvin's view as providing a hermeneutical rule that enables expositors or theologians to understand certain texts of Scripture in a way that displays their coherence with the rest. Thus by invoking the *communicatio idiomatum* we can permissibly speak of Mary as the mother of the Lord (Luke 1: 43) and of Christ's blood as the blood of God (Acts 20: 28) and of the Lord of glory as being crucified (1 Cor. 2: 8). God does not have a mother, nor does God have blood, nor can the Lord of glory be crucified; nevertheless, these are permissible modes of speech because they are warranted by the unity of the divine and human natures of the Mediator.[47]

Consequently Calvin took the first referring expression in 'God purchased the church by his own blood' to be 'God' in an unqualified way (and not as an elliptical expression for 'God in Christ', for example) thus following his own rule, identified in the previous chapter, that where the expression 'God' alone is found in Scripture, the entire Trinitarian godhead must be understood as its referent. He expressed this rule succinctly in a response to the questions put to him by the anti-Trinitarian Giorgio Blandrata in 1558.

When we profess a belief in one God, we understand by the word God the one simple essence in which we include the three persons or hypostases. Therefore, as often as the name God is used without qualification, we believe that it designates the Son and the Spirit no less than the Father. However, when the Son is added to the Father, then a relationship intervenes, and hence we distinguish the persons.[48]

---

[47] Joseph N. Tylenda, 'Calvin's Understanding of the Communication of Properties', *Westminster Theological Journal* (1975); 'Christ the Mediator: Calvin versus Stancaro', *Calvin Theological Journal* (1973); and 'The Controversy on Christ the Mediator: Calvin's Second Reply to Stancaro', *Calvin Theological Journal* (1973).

[48] *Responsum ad G. Blandrata Questiones*, trans. Jospeh N. Tylenda, 'The Warning That Went Unheeded. John Calvin on Giorgio Blandrata', *Calvin Theological Journal* (1977), 54.

It followed from this rule that the language of *communicatio*, though sanctioned by Scripture, is nevertheless figurative, metaphorical or 'improper', whenever it occurs. And in this respect at least Calvin's view coincides with that of Nestorius.[49] By contrast, later Reformed theologians such as Francis Turretin seem to have reverted to the scholastic position, insisting (against the Lutherans) that the communication of properties is to be restricted to the person of Christ. But this is because Turretin takes the referring expression in 'God shed his blood' not to be God unqualifiedly, as Calvin did, but to 'the man Christ and to the humanity of Christ as God'.[50]

The hermeneutical rule regarding the communication of properties is required, according to Calvin, because Scripture contains passages where human properties are ascribed to God and divine properties are ascribed to man. 'Let this, then, be our key to right understanding: those things which apply to the office of the Mediator are not spoken simply either of the divine nature or of the human.'[51] We break this hermeneutical rule, extending it beyond its proper bounds, if we say that God literally shed his blood, or that Mary was literally the mother of God. Calvin insists that these are properties of the one Mediator. The language of the *communicatio* is thus based upon or warranted by the nature of the Incarnation, even when there is no explicit, exclusive reference to the Mediator.

So the *communicatio* rule is to be invoked in the case of those relatively few passages that may seem to give rise to false inferences about the identity of God and man, passages such as Acts 20: 28, 1 Cor. 2: 8., 1 John 1: 1, 3: 16, and John 3: 13. For example, if 'The Lord of glory was crucified' is understood without this rule, then it warrants the inference that 'The Lord of glory died', since 'Necessarily, whoever is crucified dies'. But this inference must be ruled

---

[49] 'The corollary of this teaching was Nestorius's special treatment of the *communicatio idiomatum*. Strictly speaking, he contended, since the natures remained quite separate and neither was identical with the "*prosopon* of union", the human attributes, actions and experiences attributed to Jesus Christ should be predicated of the human nature, and *vice versa* the divine attributes, actions and experiences should be predicated of the divinity; but in virtue of the union both could be predicated indifferently of the "*prosopon* of the economy", i.e. the God-man Who united both natures in His single *prosopon*. It was even possible, he thought, in harmony with the usage of Scripture, to allow a certain interchange of predicates, describing "the man" as God, and God the Word as man, so long as it was clearly understood that this was done *omonumos*, i.e. as a mere matter of words' (J. N. D. Kelly, *Early Christian Doctrines*, 316).

[50] Francis Turretin, *The Institutes of Elenctic Theology*, trans. G. M. Giger, ed. J. T. Denison (Phillipsburg, NJ, 1992–7) XIII. VIII. In later Reformed theology (at least as exemplified by Turretin) the discussion was formalized as follows. Properties of either nature are predicable of the whole person of Christ in virtue of the union, no matter how that whole person is referred to, whether by an expression connoting his human nature, or his divine nature. But the communication of any human property to the divine nature, or vice versa, is invalid. Either under pressure of controversy over the Supper, or in the interests of doctrinal systematization, Calvin's references to certain expressions as permissible and yet 'improper' drops out.   [51] *Inst.* II. 14. 3.

out, because it is inconsistent with divinity. Otherwise, as Calvin says, we make 'man out of God and God out of man'.[52] So he invokes the *communicatio* only in the case of a restricted number of scriptural passages and in order to sanction language that is, strictly speaking, 'improper', a 'figure', a 'hard saying', even though its use is 'not without reason', the reason being the oneness of Christ's person, which lies in the background, together with the recognition of vividness and economy of expression in Scripture.[53]

Thus Calvin distinguishes two cases: first, the case of the mediatorship of Christ. It is permissible to ascribe both divine and human properties to the Mediator. Both divine and human properties are 'in harmony with the person of the Mediator'[54] because the Mediator is a union of the divine Word and human nature. So 'The Mediator was crucified' is to be understood straightforwardly. The Mediator was crucified because the Mediator has a human nature and his human nature underwent crucifixion. The second case is expressions that are justified only by appeal to the *communicatio idiomatum*. Here human properties are improperly and figuratively ascribed to God as such; and divine properties are ascribed to the human nature (although Calvin thinks this happens only rarely). Such expressions must be sanctioned by the *communicatio* rule. These expressions, although they are strictly speaking 'improper', that is, false, are rhetorical expressions whose economical form is warranted by the unity of Christ's person. Getting clear on this requires, consequently, distinguishing between language that accounts for the unity of Christ's person and other language that is warranted by that unity but is not strictly speaking true.

This is how Calvin puts the point in the Dedication of his *Commentary on Jeremiah*:

What they [the Lutherans] bring forward as to the communication of properties, it is unreasonable, and what I may say without offending them, they mistake in a matter that is very simple and plain; for to ascribe what is peculiar to Deity to the Son of man, and again to attribute to Deity what belongs only to humanity, is very improper and rash. To prevent the ignorant from stumbling by blending together different things, and to take away from the dishonest any occasion for contending, orthodox writers have called this figure, 'The communication of properties'.

What they have said of certain expressions, has been with little thought applied to the subject. While Christ was on earth he said that the Son of man was in heaven.

---

[52] *Inst.* IV. 17. 30.

[53] In the case of Luke 1: 43 Calvin says 'This denotes a unity of person in the two natures of Christ; as if she had said, that he who was begotten as a mortal man in the womb of Mary is, at the same time, the eternal God.' (*A Commentary on a Harmony of the Evangelists*, I. 50.) This is not a case of the *communicatio* because Elizabeth referred to 'the Lord', to Christ, and not to God in an unqualified sense.

[54] *Inst.* II. 14. 2.

That no-one, ill-informed, might think Christ's body to be infinite, it has been deemed necessary to meet this case by a plain admonition—that on account of the unity of the person what is suitable only to Divinity has been said of the Son of man. Paul says, as it is recorded by Luke, that God redeemed the Church by His own blood. (Acts 20: 28) Lest no one may hence conceive that God has blood, the same admonition ought to be sufficient to untie the knot; for as Christ was man and God, what is peculiar to His human nature is ascribed to His divinity. As it was the Father's design to employ this figure of speech for the purpose of teaching the simple and ignorant, it is absurd and even shameful to apply it for a different purpose, and to say that the communication of properties is the real blending of natures.[55]

Such expressions, then, do not express literal truths, there is no 'real blending'. It is not literally true that God purchased the church with his own blood. So the *communicatio* rule licenses ascribing divine properties to human nature, or human properties to divine nature, *but only as a figure of speech*. There can be no blending of natures.

In his treatment of Calvin's understanding of the communication of properties, Joseph Tylenda fails to appreciate why it is that in almost every place where Calvin discusses the *communicatio* positively he also says that expressions of the communication are 'improper' or 'figurative'. Tylenda claims that for Calvin the language of the *communicatio* is warranted only when one is referring to God and human nature in the concrete, as God and human nature are to be found in the Incarnation, and not in the abstract. But in fact Calvin does not invoke the *communicatio* for the concrete case. Given what the Incarnation implies, he thinks that this language needs no explanation. But an explanation is needed for those cases where the language of Scripture seems to entail that God has human properties (e.g. Acts 20: 28) or that human nature has divine properties (e.g. John 3: 13). Tylenda goes on to claim that it is Calvin's view that 'since Christ is a single subject having two real natures (he is true God and true man) we can truthfully say by the communication of idioms that "God purchased the church with his own blood"'.[56]

But as we have seen there is reason to doubt that Calvin thinks of the *communicatio* in this way. He thinks that it is only figuratively and not literally true that God purchased the church with his own blood, and so this is an 'improper' expression. Nevertheless it is a permissible way of talking— permissible on the grounds of vividness and economy[57]—that is sanctioned

---

[55] Dedication to the *Commentary on Jeremiah*, pp. xviii–xix. For Calvin the expression 'in heaven' does not indicate a bounded location, but the absence of one. It is an expression of divine ubiquity.

[56] Tylenda, 'Calvin's Understanding of the Communication of Properties', 60.

[57] In 'Calvin's Understanding of the Communication of Properties', (62 n. 18) Tylenda addresses Calvin's use of the word 'improper', blood improperly attributed to God, but properly applied to Christ.

by the union of the two natures in the Incarnation. In his Commentary on Acts 20: 28, Calvin says:

But because the speech which Paul useth seemeth to be somewhat hard, we must see in what sense he saith that God purchased the Church with his blood. For nothing is more absurd than to feign or imagine God to be mortal or to have a body. But in this speech he commendeth the unity of person in Christ; for because there be distinct natures in Christ, the Scripture does sometimes recite that apart by itself which is proper to either. But when it setteth God before us made manifest in the flesh, it doth not separate the human nature from the Godhead. Notwithstanding, because again two natures are so united in Christ, that they make one person, that is improperly translated sometimes unto the one, which doth truly and in deed belong to the other, as in this place Paul doth attribute blood to God; because the man Jesus Christ, who shed his blood for us, was also God. This manner of speaking is called, of the old writers, *communicatio idiomatum*, because the property of one nature is applied to the other.[58]

So although sanctioned by the unity of Christ's person, the expression is nevertheless 'somewhat hard' if taken literally, a case of improper imputation of a property of one nature to the other nature. But in virtue of the union of divine and human natures in Christ's person we can and must interpret such expressions figuratively.

Thus understood, Calvin's approach to the *communicatio idiomatum* also differs somewhat from the interpretation offered of it in a recent study by Thomas Weinandy. For Weinandy, the *communicatio idiomatum* is 'the predicating of divine and human attributes of one and the same person—the Son'. As already noted, he believes that, from the Patristic period onwards, the *communicatio idiomatum* plays a central role as a criterion for whether a Christology is orthodox or heretical because it was the communication of idioms that gave rise to a proper understanding of the Incarnation.[59] For Weinandy, 'the use and practice of the communication of idioms grew up and developed as a "shorthand" way of accenting the reality and intensifying the implications of the Incarnation. God as God could not be born, but if he became a man, he could truly be born. God as God could not suffer, but if he existed as man, he could actually suffer and die.'[60] As he understands the term, predicating divine and human properties of the same person, Jesus

---

But Calvin's own attitude is clear from his Dedication to his *Commentary on Jeremiah*. The language of Acts 20: 28, warranting expressions such as 'God purchased the church with his blood' is allowable because it is Scriptural. But it is 'improper', i.e. figurative language. Nevertheless its use is justified not because (as Tylenda claims) it is used of the unique case of Christ, who has both natures, because Calvin does not interpret the text in this fashion, but because of its pedagogic effectiveness.

[58] *Commentary on the Acts of the Apostles*, 20. 28.

[59] Thomas Weinandy, *Does God Suffer?* 174–5, 198.　　　　[60] *Does God Suffer?* 174.

Christ, is what the communication of idioms *is*. And this is justified because the Incarnation is an ontological union. Jesus Christ is not to be understood as a mere union of natures, but as the forming of one ontological entity from these natures, although not by a fusion of them, as fruit and cream may be mixed in an electric blender. He is one person, one entity, to be understood, following Cyril of Alexandria, as the union of the divine and human natures taking place within the person of the Son.[61]

The Incarnation does not involve the changing, mixing, or confusing of natures (as in the soul–body model), but rather the person of the Word taking on a new mode or manner of existence, that is, as man. There is a change or newness in the mode of the existence of the Son, though not a change or newness within the natures. The Son now newly exists as man. . . . [B]y correctly conceiving and articulating that it is the person of the Son who exists as man, Cyril, as we will fully examine momentarily, equally has validated the communication of idioms. Cyril's understanding of the Incarnation is what I have come to refer to as a personal/existential conception. Jesus is the *person* of the Son *existing* as a man. While the Incarnation remains a mystery, Cyril, in accordance with authentic doctrinal development, has clarified more exactly what the mystery is—it is truly the person of the divine Son who truly exists as a true man.[62]

So it is of the very same ontological subject that divine and human properties are ascribed, and the fact that such a Christological understanding entails the *communicatio* proves its orthodoxy. Hence the *communicatio* is a touchstone of orthodoxy or heterodoxy.

But as we have noted Calvin does not see things quite like this. Rather for him the union of the divine and the human in Christ's person is what justifies the *communicatio* without itself being a case of *communicatio*. This is obviously a much looser approach. As Calvin sees things, it is not so much the attribution of two sorts of properties to one person that is the communication of properties as it is the figurative, non-actual, transfer of properties, the predicating of human properties of God and divine properties of human nature. Weinandy says that 'Because Calvin interprets the incarnational act as the union of natures after the manner of the soul–body union, he has lost the authentic use of the communication of idioms, where all attributes, whether divine or human, are applied to one and the same person of the Son.'[63] But this is to mistake the word for the thing: Calvin upholds the unity of Christ's person, but does not think of that, in and of itself, as a case of the *communicatio*.

In his brief discussion of the *communicatio idiomatum* David Willis states that for Calvin the *communicatio* does not provide the ontological

---

[61] *Does God Suffer?* 197.

[62] *Does God Suffer?* 197. Emphasis in the original.

[63] *Does God Suffer?* 188.

foundation of the person of Christ, but it is nevertheless grounded in an ontological unity between both the natures. 'For Calvin, the *communicatio idiomatum* is primarily an hermeneutical tool to keep in balance the varied scriptural witness to the One Person; but it rests upon and presupposes the hypostatic union.'[64] This seems to me to get the matter exactly right.

In further elucidation of his understanding of the Incarnation, Weinandy has recourse to the reduplicative idiom. Mary is mother of God, but she is not the mother of God *as* God; when the Son of God suffered, he did not suffer *as* God, for God *as* God cannot suffer. He who is impassible *as* God is passible as man.[65] 'It is actually the Son of God who lives a comprehensive human life, and so it is the Son who, as man, experiences all facets of this human life, including suffering and death.'[66]

But Calvin, on the other hand, says this:

Surely God does not have blood, does not suffer, cannot be touched with hands. But since Christ, who was true God and also true man, was crucified and shed his blood for us, the things that he carried out in his human nature are transferred improperly, although not without reason, to his divinity.[67]

Calvin denies that God as man could suffer, thinking that this is 'improper'; rather he suffered in his human nature. This is because 'God' refers to God in an unqualified way. This is why we find him only rarely using reduplicative expressions. For example commenting on John 3: 13 he says:

[W]hen Christ, still living on earth, said: 'No one has ascended into heaven but the Son of man who was in heaven' [John 3: 13], surely then, as man, in the flesh that he had taken upon himself, he was not in heaven. But because the selfsame one was both God and man, for the sake of the union of both natures he gave to the one what belonged to the other.[68]

Calvin seems to be saying that Christ's human nature cannot have the property of being in heaven, that is, of being ubiquitous. Therefore this quotation's expression 'as man' should be understood as 'in respect of the

---

[64] *Calvin's Catholic Christology*, 67.

[65] *Does God Suffer?* 201. Aquinas also has a discussion of reduplicative expressions, the use of which is governed by the following thought or rule—if the reduplicative expression 'as man' concerns the *suppositum* of human nature in union with the Word, then such a reduplicative expression is legitimate; if not, if it is considered as an expression of human nature per se, then it is not legitimate. Likewise (in the 11th article) the expression 'Christ as man is God' is permitted if the 'as man' refers to the *suppositum* of human nature in union with the Word, but not otherwise. So what is crucial to Thomas's treatment of these issues is the distinction between the concrete—in either the *suppositum* of the human nature ('Christ as man is a creature, Christ as man is God') or in the concrete hypostasis of the God–man—and the abstract as well as an awareness of the fact that even in the union the natures remain distinct, (*Summa Theologiae*, 3a, 16. 10–12).

[66] *Does God Suffer?* 201.   [67] *Inst.* II. 14. 2   [68] *Inst.* II. 14. 2

Mediator's human nature'. For Weinandy, orthodox use of the *communicatio* is always 'proper' and never 'figurative', always cryptic literal truth that is made true by the appropriate use of reduplicative expressions. It is literally true that God as man could suffer. For Calvin, the *communicatio* is always 'improper' when taken literally; it is a 'figure of speech' justified only by the fact of the union of human and divine natures in Christ.

THE SOUL–BODY ANALOGY

Richard Cross suggests that not only Scotus and Aquinas but also Calvin and Zwingli take a 'parts' model of the Incarnation—modelled on the human person being composed of the parts of soul and body—as their basic Christological pattern. The medievals denied the principle that predicates are literally ascribed to a whole only if they can be ascribed to all of its parts. As we have just seen Calvin thinks of the soul and the body as constituting 'parts' of a person, and holds that this is a most 'apposite parallel' to the Incarnation. Calvin's certainly seems to be a 'parts' Christology.

Insofar as Calvin offers a metaphysical basis for the Incarnation it is to be found in places such as *Inst.* II. 12. 3, in the assertion that Christ 'took the person and the name of Adam'. According to Heiko Oberman this amounts to the claim that the joining of the two natures of Christ takes place exactly in the Person, implying that he rejected an account of the Incarnation as a union of the divine hypostasis and a *suppositum* of human nature.[69] But in this passage Calvin does not say as much as this, but simply that the Lord 'coupled human nature with the divine' (*humanum naturam cum divina sociavit*). And he writes further of our common nature with Christ (*communem naturam*). Calvin is in general averse to asking 'How was it possible?' questions about the Incarnation. He rejected the scholastic question of whether the Son of God might have incarnated himself in a donkey not because he rejected the doctrine of the *suppositum* which warrants such a question but because of the speculative temper that such questions reveal, a temper which he abhorred.[70]

Calvin, following Augustine, certainly uses the analogy of the soul and body as a 'most apposite parallel' of the union of the natures in the Incarnation.

[T]he characteristics of the mind are [sometimes] transferred to the body, and those of the body to the soul. Yet he who consists of these parts is one man, not many. Such

---

[69] Oberman, *The Dawn of the Reformation*, 253.

[70] On this, see Oberman's interesting remarks on Ockham's 'asinine theology' in *The Harvest of Medieval Theology*, 255f.

expressions signify both that there is one person in man composed of two elements joined together, and that there are two diverse underlying natures that make up this person. Thus, also, the Scriptures speak of Christ: they sometimes attribute to him what must be referred solely to his humanity, sometimes what belongs uniquely to his divinity; and sometimes what embraces both natures but fits neither alone. And they so earnestly express this union of the two natures that is in Christ as sometimes to interchange them. This figure of speech is called by the ancient writers 'the communicating of properties'.[71]

On a pronounced substance-dualist understanding of the human person such as Calvin's it is possible to say that Jones was buried, or that he weighs 150 pounds, when what is strictly meant is that Jones's *body* was buried or that it weighs 150 pounds. Jones may say 'I am cold' when strictly speaking it is his body that is cold, and so on. For a substance-dualist, it is thus permissible to ascribe physical properties to the spiritual substance who is the person Jones—physical properties that the spiritual substance cannot have—and to ascribe spiritual properties to Jones the man (such as being vain, or God-fearing) that are not and cannot be properties of Jones's body. Similarly, to say that Jones is a thief is not to say that his body is a thief, or that his soul is a thief, but that Jones the human being is a thief. What makes such expressions permissible?

Calvin answers that they are made permissible by something like a principle of economy. Dualists may tolerate these things being said to avoid pedantry, and in view of the closeness of the union of body and soul there is a naturalness in doing so, even though what is said may not only be false but necessarily false. By the same token, the unity of the human person is shown by there being facts about a person that are not facts about his body per se or about his soul per se.

Occasionally, Calvin draws attention to what he thinks are mistaken uses of the body–soul analogy, as in his comment on John 2: 9:

The argument of Nestorius, who abused this passage to prove that it is not one and the same Christ who is God and man, may be easily refuted. He reasoned thus: the Son of God dwelt in the flesh, as in a *temple*; therefore the natures are distinct, so that the same person was not God and man. But this argument might be applied to men; for it will follow that it is not one man whose soul dwells in the body as in a tabernacle; and, therefore, it is folly to torture this form of expression for the purpose of taking away the unity of Person in Christ.[72]

Thomas Aquinas is one schoolman who, though a less pronounced dualist than Calvin, thinks that the analogy is in one respect apposite, but in another respect not. Exploring the nature of the union of the human and divine in

---

[71] *Inst.* II. 14. 1.   [72] *Commentary on the Gospel According to John*, I. 97–8.

Christ, he thinks that the 'two realities'—body and soul—that compose a man are not 'complete things' and so this type of union

cannot apply to the mystery of the Incarnation. First of all, because each nature, divine and human, holds its own complete meaning. Secondly, the divine and human natures cannot constitute something as quantitative parts in the way that members constitute a body, for the divine nature is incorporeal. Nor can they be related as matter and form, for the divine nature cannot be the form of anything, least of all of anything corporeal. It would also follow that the species resulting from such a union would be communicable to many, and thus there could be many Christs. Thirdly, Christ would exist neither in divine nor in human nature, for any difference added to a nature changes the species, even as each added unit varies a number, as Aristotle notes.[73]

However, if we think of the union of body and soul as constituting not a unity of nature, which it is, but as a unity of person, which it also is, we can perceive 'a similarity from the fact that the one Christ subsists in divine and in human nature'.[74]

Weinandy says that we must distinguish between using the body–soul union as a loose analogy, and using it as an instance of the union of two natures of which the Incarnation is another instance.[75] In fact Calvin's reverential agnosticism regarding the how of the Incarnation keeps him from seeking any worked-out metaphysical basis of it. The basis of the Incarnation is to be found simply in a general recognition of the closeness of the union of the divine and the human in Christ, a closeness which, he thinks, the language of the *communicatio* in Scripture strikingly testifies. As Oberman goes on to say, Calvin favours an understanding of Christology in terms of the fact that Christ is one mediator who executes the role in a variety of offices. The focus of his attention is on soteriology, not on metaphysics.

Whether Calvin's use of the body–soul analogy by itself commits him to a 'parts' Christology in a way that is carefully worked out is a moot point. Does he think that Christ's human nature is a 'part' of Christ? Does he think that his divine nature is? Can something that is metaphysically simple, such as Calvin thinks that Christ's divine person is, come to have a part? Certainly he says that Christ is a union of person and nature in a parallel way to that in which (he thinks) a human being is composed of two substances. But can natures be parts of other natures, substances parts of other substances? Although Calvin's use of the body–soul analogy is worked out in the sense that he sees a number of clear parallels between the two (and seems not to offer any points of disanalogy) it is fair to say that he does not get himself involved in mereological niceties.

---

[73] *Summa Theologiae*, 3a, 2. 2.   [74] *Summa Theologiae*, 3a, 2. 2.
[75] *Does God Suffer?* 182f.

It may be, as Weinandy suggests, that Calvin's use of the parallel of mind–body dualism leads him to emphasize the distinctness of the two natures of Christ, and so to assert the strict impropriety of the *communicatio*.[76] But it is much more likely that Calvin is motivated by two concerns. The first is to maintain the full, unqualified deity of the Son. The second is his refusal to speculate on the details of the union of the divine and human natures in Christ. However, on further examination he seems to use the soul–body analogy in a more restricted way than these motives would warrant, simply to make the point that the two natures, the human and the divine, are not so mingled with each other as not to retain their distinctive natures.[77] So Calvin is not one of those who claim, in using the analogy, that the Incarnation is the coming into being of a new composite, fused, hybrid nature,[78] neither fully man nor fully God; in fact, as we have seen, he repudiates any idea of the mixing of the natures. Nor, as we have seen, does Calvin say, on the basis of the mind–body analogy, that divine and human attributes are predicable of each other, except 'improperly'.

Perhaps what Weinandy's discussion of Calvin lacks is an appreciation of the varieties of dualism. No doubt some forms of dualism think of human beings as an ontological union, a mind–body hybrid. And there are Aristotelian types of dualism, as we noted in Thomas. But in those kinds of dualism that are attractive to Christians like Calvin a certain ontological primacy is given to the soul as the bearer of personal identity, since it is the soul that endures after the body's death. There cannot be a hybridization of soul and body that cannot be unscrambled at death. Calvin's dualism is rather pronounced, from his early writing denying the doctrine of soul-sleep, *Psychopannychia* (1534/42), to the mature edition of the *Institutes*:

Our controversy, then, relates to THE HUMAN SOUL. Some, while admitting it to have a real existence, imagine that it sleeps in a state of insensibility from Death to The Judgment-day, when it will awake from its sleep; while others will sooner admit anything than its real existence, maintaining that it is merely a vital power which is derived from arterial spirit on the action of the lungs, and being unable to exist without body, perishes along with the body, and vanishes away and becomes evanescent till the period when the whole man shall be raised again. We, on the other hand, maintain both that it is a substance, and after the death of the body truly lives, being endued both with sense and understanding. Both these points we undertake to prove by clear passages of Scripture. Here let human wisdom give place; for though it thinks much about the soul it perceives no certainty with regard to it. Here, too, let Philosophers give place, since on almost all subjects their regular practice is to put neither end nor measure to their dissensions, while on this subject in particular they quarrel, so that you will scarcely find two of them agreed on any single point! Plato,

---

[76] *Does God Suffer?* 187–8.　　　　[77] *Inst.* II. 14. 1.　　　　[78] *Does God Suffer?* 184.

in some passages, talks nobly of the faculties of the soul; and Aristotle, in discoursing of it, has surpassed all in acuteness. But what the soul is, and whence it is, it is vain to ask at them, or indeed at the whole body of Sages, though they certainly thought more purely and wisely on the subject than some amongst ourselves, who boast that they are the disciples of Christ.[79]

The difference between Calvin's and Weinandy's approaches to the use of the mind–body analogy might be put like this: If we think of the mind and body in union as forming an 'ontological union, this gives rise to a new and third reality called man',[80] then we will be wary of pressing the body–soul analogy onto Christological reflections for fear of thinking of the incarnate Son as a *tertium quid*, something neither divine nor human, or something whose identity consists in divine nature having a human form. But if, on the other hand, we think of a human being as a duality, a person in close union with a body, then there is less danger of a *tertium quid*, and consequently a more apposite analogy for the union of the divine person with human nature in the Incarnation.

As we noted earlier, in setting out the body–soul relationship as a 'parallel' to the union of divine and human nature in the Incarnation in *Institutes* II. 14. 1 Calvin emphasizes both that the characteristics of the mind are sometimes transferred to the body, and those of the body to the mind. What cases does he cite of divine properties being ascribed to Christ's human nature? As far as I can see he gives only one example. We have already noted a reference to the Son of Man ascending to heaven (John 3: 13).

Again, when Christ, still living on earth, said: 'No one has ascended into heaven but the Son of man who was in heaven' [John 3: 13], surely then, as man, in the flesh he had taken upon himself, he was not in heaven. But because the selfsame one was both God and man, for the sake of the union of both natures he gave to the one what belonged to the other.[81]

Following the consensus of the Fathers, and along with the other Reformers, Calvin took the phrase 'the Son of Man' to be an exclusive reference to Christ's humanity. And so it was natural for him to interpret John 3: 13 in the way he did. But if this is a mistaken view, as most modern commentators hold,[82] then while Calvin thinks there is a two-way *communicatio idiomatum*

---

[79] *Psychopannychia*, trans. Henry Beveridge in *Selected Works of John Calvin, Tracts and Treatises*, ed. Henry Beveridge and Jules Bonnet (Edinburgh, 1844, Philadelphia, 1858; repr. Grand Rapids, Mich.: Baker, 1983), iii., 419–20.   [80] *Does God Suffer?* 184.

[81] *Inst.* II. 14. 2. Again, it is important to bear in mind that for Calvin being in heaven is equivalent to being ubiquitous. See Calvin's comments on 'Our Father, which art in heaven' later on in this chapter.

[82] Delbert Burkett, *The Son of Man Debate: A History and Evaluation* (Cambridge: Cambridge University Press, 1999). See ch. 2 for the Patristic and Reformation understandings. I am indebted to my former colleague Eddie Adams for this reference.

there is scant, if any, New Testament evidence for divine properties being ascribed to Christ's human nature.

Joseph Tylenda, in his careful treatment of Calvin's understanding of the *communicatio idiomatum*, cites only John 3: 13 as an example of the communication of the divine to the human. Tylenda says:

> In all of Calvin's five examples [of the *communicatio*], the divine or human property is said of a subject, a person (Jesus Christ), and that subject is designated either in function of his divine nature as 'God', or 'Lord of glory', or in function of his human nature as 'Son of Man'. In none of the examples is the property of one nature applied to the other *nature as such*; it is always applied to a *subject possessing that nature*. It is true that Calvin writes 'a property of humanity is shared with the other nature'[83] and that the Scriptures 'assign to the divinity that which is proper to the humanity, and to the humanity that which concerns the divinity'[84] but these statements should be interpreted in accordance with Calvin's mind and examples.[85]

This interpretation of Calvin reads into his words something that is not there. For as we have seen, Calvin does not take 'God' in 'God purchased the church with his own blood' as a reference to Christ's divine nature, but to God in an unqualified sense. Hence the strict impropriety (though permissibility) of such language.

Presumably, the reason why there are few, if any, instances of divine properties being ascribed to Christ's human nature is that at no time is there a separately existing concrete human subject to which divine properties may be ascribed because there is no time when the human nature of Jesus Christ existed while not in union with the divine person of the Son. For although the Son of God has a nature that is ontologically independent from the human nature to which he was in union, the fact that that union was a matter of contingent free choice means that the human nature that the Son of God was in union with did not have a similar separate ontological existence but only existed as that which was created for the Son of God to be voluntarily united to. Only in adoptionist Christologies may the *communicatio* freely go both ways.

WHAT IS WARRANTED BY THE *COMMUNICATIO*?

What exactly is and is not warranted by the *communicatio idiomatum*, or is this 'rule' a purely ad hoc device with no rationale? Calvin appears to want to say that if Jesus makes atonement, then God makes atonement, but that if

---

[83] *Inst.* II. 14. 2.

[84] *Institutes* (1536), ch. 2 (Eng. trans. Ford Lewis Battles; Atlanta: John Knox Press, 1975), 70.

[85] Tylenda, 'Calvin's Understanding of the Communication of Properties', 59. Emphasis in original.

Jesus shed his blood, then God shed his blood only in an 'improper' fashion. God cannot literally shed his blood; it is only by the licence afforded by the *communicatio* that we can say that God shed his blood when Jesus did. On the other hand, God can literally make atonement, so that we do not need to appeal to the *communicatio* when we say that when Jesus makes atonement God makes atonement. But why are the different ways of treating these inferences not arbitrary and ad hoc? Why in the case of some of Christ's actions is there no need for the *communicatio* to be invoked—indeed good reason for it not to be invoked—whereas in the case of other actions invoking the *communicatio* is necessary to avoid incoherence and absurdity?

Calvin might respond to this in either of two ways. First, by saying that what warrants the inference 'Jesus made atonement, therefore God made atonement' is that there is separate scriptural warrant for the use of the conclusion of this argument. In the Old Testament and elsewhere God makes atonement; there is nothing incoherent in the supposition, indeed it is entirely appropriate. But there is no similar scriptural warrant to the effect that God is capable of being handled, or of being crucified, and such an idea is in any case incoherent.

Secondly, he might make a more formal metaphysical distinction between what later Reformed theologians (but not Calvin, in so many words) referred to as the communicable and incommunicable attributes of God. Attributes like immensity, eternity, omnipotence, and omnipresence are not communicable (or transferable) to the creature. But God has, in addition, communicable properties, such as holiness, mercy, etc., that can be transferred. Thus it makes sense for the Lord to say 'be ye holy, for I am holy' but not 'be ye omnipresent, for I am omnipresent'.

As part of his overall view of the *communicatio idiomatum* one of Calvin's theological successors in Geneva, Francis Turretin, expressly explains what he takes to be its correct sense in terms of the incommunicable divine properties. In the case of the communicable attributes, 'God produces in creatures . . . effects analogous to his own properties.' In the case of incommunicable properties, nothing analogous is found in the creature. However, 'This distinction cannot favor the error of those who maintain that the divine properties were communicated to the human nature of Christ. As will be seen in the proper place, communication in the concrete, as to the person (which we acknowledge in Christ) differs from communication in the abstract, as to nature (which we deny).'[86] Although Calvin does not make an appeal to the distinction between communicable and incommunicable properties in so many words, an examination of the places

---

[86] Turretin, *Institutes of Elenctic Theology*, III. vi.vii.

where he invokes the *communicatio* shows that it is some such distinction as this that he has in mind. Thus in *Institutes* II. 13. 4 he refers to the 'immeasurable essence' of the Word and the impossibility of the Word being confined within the limits of a human person. And in *Institutes* IV. 17. 30 he argues that the ubiquity of the Word does not imply the ubiquity of the flesh with which it is conjoined. Ubiquity and immensity are each examples of incommunicable attributes of God.

There is in fact more than a hint of this distinction in what Calvin says in a more formal way about the attributes of God in *Institutes* I. 10. 2, where he distinguishes between God's power and existence, on the one hand, and the powers by which he is 'toward us'—kindness, goodness, mercy, justice, judgement, and truth—on the other hand.

He is very emphatic on the incommunicable nature of God. Explaining the phrase, 'Our Father, who art in heaven' he says that God

is not confined to any particular region but is diffused through all things. But our minds, so crass are they, could not have conceived his unspeakable glory otherwise. Consequently, it has been signified to us by 'heaven', for we can behold nothing more sublime or majestic than this. While, therefore, wherever our senses comprehend anything they commonly attach it to that place, God is set beyond all place, so that when we would seek him we must rise above all perception of body and soul. Secondly, by this expression he is lifted above all chance of either corruption or change. Finally, it signifies that he embraces and holds together the entire universe and controls it by his might. Therefore it is as if he had been said to be of infinite greatness or loftiness, of incomprehensible essence, of boundless might, and of everlasting immortality.[87]

ASSESSMENT

What Calvin's approach to the *communicatio idiomatum* suggests is a kind of decision procedure with respect to the interpretation of texts that have to do with the Incarnation that goes something like this:

Does the text specify the two natures of Christ?
Yes: then respect the two natures
No
Does it impute what is human to what is divine?
Yes: then understand the text as a case of *communicatio idiomatum*
No
Does it refer to the one person of the mediator?

---

[87] *Inst.* III. 20. 40.

Yes: then respect that unity and do not assign the office of mediator to the one or the other nature separately.

By appealing to and endorsing the *extra* Calvin is claiming, in a particularly forthright and vivid way, that the expression 'Jesus Christ is God' cannot be an expression of identity. Otherwise, whatever is true of God must be true of Jesus Christ and vice versa; for, after all, in asserting that the one *is* the other we are saying that there are not two things, but one thing. The expression 'Jesus Christ is God' cannot mean that Jesus Christ is nothing but God, because he possessed a human nature. It is short for 'Jesus Christ is God in union with human nature'. Jesus Christ is divine and human; he has the properties of divinity and humanity. The Son of God, in becoming incarnate, came to have the properties of being (fully) human as well as of being divine.

Calvin's approach to the *communicatio idiomatum* as a way of defending and explaining his Chalcedonian Christology seems entirely consistent, but at least part of his motivation for his approach is probably found in his controversies with the Lutherans over the Supper. Calvin's fellow Reformer Zwingli adopted a similar line (as far as one can tell, quite independently of Calvin), within the context of controversy with the Lutherans. Richard Cross has shown that for Zwingli propositions where terms referring to human properties are predicated of the whole Christ and propositions where properties of one of the natures of Christ is predicated of the other are figuratively and not literally true.[88] Thus Zwingli says 'In Holy Scripture all the references to Christ are said of the whole and undivided Christ, even when it can easily be seen to which nature what is said should be referred'.[89] Since, then, 'Christ' refers to one who has both divine and human natures, saying 'Christ suffered' is not to claim that it is literally true that the divine nature of Christ suffered. Hence, 'Christ suffered' is not literally true. Again, in Christological contexts sometimes statements about one of the natures is applied to the other. This is warranted not by the fact that the divine nature is the human nature but because Christ possesses two natures.

These hermeneutical remarks about how to interpret the language of the New Testament are then used to offer criticism of Luther's hermeneutics, arguing that Luther confusedly attributes to the humanity of Christ those properties that are proper to his divinity. So both Calvin and Zwingli see certain biblical expressions as rhetorical. And each uses this point against Luther and the Lutherans.

---

[88] '*Alloiosis* in the Christology of Zwingli'.

[89] Quoted by Cross, '*Alloiosis* in the Christology of Zwingli', 116.

However, the extent to which controversy with the Lutherans motivated Calvin's approach ought not to be exaggerated. For he could equally well be said to be following the example of his mentor, Augustine.

For He was crucified after the form of a servant, and yet 'the Lord of glory' was crucified. For that 'taking' [taking the form of a servant] was such as to make God man, and man God. Yet what is said on account of what, and what according to what, the thoughtful, diligent, and pious reader discerns for himself, the Lord being his helper. For instance, we have said that He glorifies His own, as being God, and certainly then as being the Lord of glory; and yet the Lord of glory was crucified, because even God is rightly said to have been crucified, not after the power of the divinity, but after the weakness of the flesh.[90]

[90] *On the Trinity*, book I, ch. xiii, trans. A. W. Haddan.

4

Providence and Evil

CALVIN would not have recognized the 'problem of evil' as it is usually discussed today. Today, the argument from evil challenges God's existence. It is an 'atheological' argument, a product of the religious scepticism of the Enlightenment, claiming that since evil is prima facie incompatible with the existence of an all-good, all-powerful God, and evil manifestly exists, then prima facie God does not exist.

Calvin's approach, as a self-conscious exponent of the Christian tradition, takes as its chief premiss: God, our righteous Creator and Lord, exists. There is evil in the world that God originally created good. So there must be some way of reconciling with the original goodness of the creation and with God's immaculate righteousness both evil's entrance and its continuance. For God cannot be the author of sin; not the author of the first sin or of any subsequent sin. The issues raised by the modern 'problem of evil' and Calvin's discussion of providence and evil are, then, different. This is not to say that there isn't any overlap; there is, as we shall occasionally see.

A further important difference is that the modern debate is sparked by considering that the triad of propositions: (1) God is all-powerful, (2) God is all-good, and (3) There is evil, has as one of its unspoken premisses the belief that no one ought to suffer from evil, or that everyone has a right to receive the good that an all-powerful, all-good God is able to provide. But Calvin, along with the mainstream Christian tradition, emphatically denied this premiss. He held that the race is under a divine curse, and that much evil, perhaps most evil, although not all evil, owes its existence to the sinful actions of a cursed race or to divine retribution on such evil or to divine chastisement for it.

The issue of God and evil is made more acute for Calvin and for all who hold to what is currently called meticulous or risk-free or absolute providence, since for them there is a sense in which God wills everything that happens, including evil events and actions. According to Calvin, God not only created the universe, he also rules or governs it, including ruling or governing evil events and actions. And he rules the creation order teleologically, for an end or ends. Those events that are evil and that apparently thwart his will are in fact made to serve his will; God 'willingly permits' evil and so all actions, including evil actions, are decreed by him. God's providence is thus all-embracing.

> [A]nyone who has been taught by Christ's lips that all the hairs of his head are numbered [Matt. 10: 30] will look farther afield for a cause [for seemingly chance events], and will consider that all events are governed by God's secret plan. And concerning inanimate objects we ought to hold that, although each one has by nature been endowed with its own property, yet it does not exercise its own power except in so far as it is directed by God's ever-present hand. These are, thus, nothing but instruments to which God continually imparts as much effectiveness as he wills, and according to his own purpose bends and turns them to either one action or another.[1]

Of course, it is a considerable step from arguing that nothing evil falls outside God's plan to claiming that there are no chance events at all or that all chance events form part of God's plan. Perhaps on Calvin's view there are events which are so trivial that their chanciness (if they are chancy) would be neutral as regards the fulfilling of the divine purpose. For example, even on Calvin's view, although God may have a reason for A happening at t_1 and a reason for B happening at t_1, and so A happens when B happens, it may not follow that God has a reason for A happening when B happens. Again, the exact configuration of coffee grounds in the scoop as I place it in the filter may be of no consequence to me or to any other human being, and therefore (perhaps) of no consequence to God. By no consequence here I mean no causal importance for God's life or for any other form of intelligent life. This is a view that is consistent with much of what Calvin says, but there is not much evidence that it is his position.[2] If we suppose that the coffee grounds might arrange themselves randomly, then the random rearrangement of grounds in the coffee jar may be of consequence for me in that I delight to contemplate them, or the idea of them, but the movements in the jar nonetheless do not cause changes in me directly. No doubt more refinement is needed here, but the basic distinction is clear enough. Perhaps, then, the molecules could be permitted to arrange and rearrange themselves purely randomly and the effect of that randomness be confined to the coffee jar. And perhaps, for all Calvin says to the contrary, this could be his view also. If so, then the exact configuration of coffee grounds in that jar now is not a part of the divine plan. And similarly with the chanciness of quantum mechanics insofar as such events are of no consequence for human beings.

So perhaps there are chancy and coincidental events which are of no consequence to any created intelligent being, and perhaps God's providen-

---

[1] *Inst.* 1. 16. 2.
[2] There is some, for example, to Calvin's singling out 'human affairs' in *Inst.* 1. 16. 8.

tial rule concerns only what is of some consequence to created intelligent beings. But we stick closer both to the spirit and the letter of Calvin if we think of providence as the fulfilling of God's plan for the entire creation, and particularly for the human race, and of whatever is embraced by that plan.

In defending such a no-risk position Calvin was not introducing a novelty, even though his account of providence is perhaps unmatched in its trenchancy. His view is the standard Christian view. Thus, Thomas Aquinas affirms that everything is subject to divine providence.

Now the causality of God, who is the first efficient cause, covers all existing things, immortal and mortal alike, and not only their specific principles but also the source of their singularity. Hence everything that is real in any way whatsoever is bound to be directed by God to an end; as the Apostle remarks, *The things that are of God are well-ordered* (Rom. 13: 1). Since his Providence is naught else than the idea whereby all things are planned to an end, as we have said, we conclude quite strictly that all things in so far as they are real come under divine Providence.[3]

God provides for all things immediately and directly. His mind holds the reason for each of them, even the very least, and whatsoever the causes he appoints for effects, he it is who gives them the power to produce those effects. Consequently the whole of their design down to every detail is anticipated in his mind.[4]

For Thomas, God's providence is not only meticulous, like Calvin he also emphasizes that it is 'secret' in the sense that the reasons that God has for doing and permitting what he does are (for the most part) hidden from us:

[S]ince the order, reason, end, and necessity of those things which happen for the most part lie hidden in God's purpose, and are not apprehended by human opinion, those things, which it is certain take place by God's will, are in a sense fortuitous. For they bear on the face of them no other appearance, whether they are considered in their own nature or weighed according to our knowledge and judgment. . . . The same reckoning applies to the contingency of future events. As all future events are uncertain to us, so we hold them in suspense, as if they might incline to one side or the other. Yet in our hearts it nonetheless remains fixed that nothing will take place that the Lord has not previously foreseen.[5]

In this chapter we shall continue our account of Calvin's idea of God by considering his views on divine providence, especially as these are found in his disputation, *A Defence of the Secret Providence of God.*

Scholarly accounts of Calvin's doctrine of providence are mainly of two sorts. On the one hand, attention has been paid to the extra-scriptural sources of Calvin's views, particularly their agreement and disagreement with Stoic ideas of natural law and of fate. Calvin is seen as siding with the

---

[3] *Summa Theologiae*, 1a, 22. 2, trans. Thomas Gilby.
[4] *Summa Theologiae*, 1a, 22. 3.
[5] *Inst.* I. 16. 9.

Stoics in his endorsement of *apatheia*, for example, while stressing against fatalism that Christian providence is the personal governance of God.[6]

On the other hand, there is some interest in the way that Calvin's account of providence relates to other aspects of his thought. Susan E. Schreiner[7] argues for the focal importance of Calvin's views on providence in his account of nature's orderliness and as providing evidence of God's faithfulness. Yet apart from Schreiner's work, while considerable scholarly effort has been expended on the question of where predestination fits into Calvin's overall theological system, much less interest has been shown in the parallel question about providence.

If, as Hans Emil Weber stated, Calvin's system was the system of predestinarianism,[8] then we might expect Calvin to discuss predestination early in the *Institutes*. But of course he does not. His discussion moves about in the various editions of the *Institutes*. It started in 1536 as part of his discussion of the church, then became in 1539 part of his treatment of providence, until it finally found rest as part of Calvin's soteriology in 1559. This may seem surprising because, as we are about to see, it can be argued that Calvin's handling of predestination affords more than a clue to his estimate of providence and, consequently, should (it may seem) come either with it or before it.

The placement of predestination in the *Institutes* has been used as an argument for the fact that Calvin was not a scholastic in theological method, although Richard Muller helpfully reminds us of the pluriformity of even overtly scholastic treatments of the locus of predestination among Reformed theologians.[9]

What, precisely, have these reflections on predestination got to do with providence? First, for Calvin predestination is one aspect of providence, that aspect of God's governance of all things that concerns the destiny of the elect and of the reprobate. Secondly, the locus on providence *is* placed appropriately early in the final edition of the *Institutes* and it is also noticeably predestinarian in character. There Calvin claims that all events are governed by God's secret plan and that nothing takes place without his deliberation. God so attends the regulation of individual events, and they all so proceed from his set plan, that nothing takes place by chance.[10]

---

[6] See, for example, P. H. Reardon, 'Calvin on Providence: The Development of an Insight', *Scottish Journal of Theology* (1975).

[7] Susan E. Schreiner, *The Theater of His Glory* (Durham, NC: Labyrinth Press, 1991). Her treatment of Calvin's doctrine and its sources in ch. 1 provides valuable background to the issues discussed in this chapter.

[8] Quoted in Richard A. Muller, *God, Creation and Providence in the Thought of Jacobus Arminius* (Grand Rapids, Mich.: Baker, 1991), 9.   [9] Muller, *Christ and the Decree*.

[10] I am not offering this as evidence for the view that providence/predestination is the 'central dogma' of Calvin's thought.

Whence it follows that providence is lodged in the act; for many babble too ignorantly of bare foreknowledge. Not so crass is the error of those who attribute a governance to God, but of a confused and mixed sort, as I have said, namely, one that by a general motion revolves and drives the system of the universe, with its several parts, but which does not specifically direct the action of individual creatures. Yet this error, also, is not tolerable; for by this providence which they call universal, they teach that nothing hinders all creatures from being contingently moved, or man from turning himself hither and thither by the free choice of his will. And they so apportion things between God and man that God by His power inspires in man a movement by which he can act in accordance with the nature implanted in him, but He regulates His own actions by the plan of His will. Briefly, they mean that the universe, men's affairs, and men themselves are governed by God's might but not by His determination.[11]

In his treatment of providence and particularly in his application of the doctrine Calvin also cannot forbear to refer to the church, for God has a special care for his church which he deigns to watch more closely, and in any case it is only the believer who can make the proper use of this doctrine.[12] Predestination, then, is implied not only by the doctrine of providence itself but also by the proper use of that doctrine.

Whence Christ, when he declared that not even a tiny sparrow of little worth falls to earth without the Father's will [Matt. 10: 29], immediately applies it in this way: that since we are of greater value than sparrows, we ought to realize that God watches over us with all the closer care [Matt. 10: 31]; and he extends it so far that we may trust that the hairs of our head are numbered [Matt. 10: 30]. What else can we wish for ourselves, if not even one hair can fall from our head without his will? I speak not only concerning mankind; but, because God has chosen the church to be his dwelling place, there is no doubt that he shows by singular proofs his fatherly care in ruling it.[13]

This interweaving of the themes of providence and predestination in Calvin's treatment of providence suggests that the sometimes laboured and tortuous debates about why Calvin placed his discussion of providence in

---

[11] *Inst.* I. 16. 4. Cf. *Inst.* III. 23. 6 'If God only foresaw human events, and did not also dispose and determine them by his decision, then there would be some point in raising this question: whether his foreseeing had anything to do with their necessity. But since he foresees future events only by reason of the fact that he decreed that they take place, they vainly raise a quarrel over foreknowledge, when it is clear that all things take place rather by his determination and bidding.'

[12] *Inst.* I. 17. Wendel points out that the interweaving of providence and predestination in Calvin can be seen in the fact that God's providence extends over the wicked. Providence presupposes the distinction between elect and reprobate and is the outworking in time of the one eternal decree respecting each (F. Wendel, *Calvin: The Origins and Development of His Religious Thought*, 182).

[13] *Inst.* I. 17. 6.

book I and his discussion of predestination in book III in the final edition of the *Institutes* are, ultimately, somewhat forced and driven by ideology rather than by careful attention to the substance of each doctrine.

As Charles Partee reminds us, for Calvin providence is not exhausted by the idea of general providence, some general governance of the universe, perhaps equivalent to God's common grace, but includes and stresses particular providence where the whole of the creation in all its detail (whatever in Calvin's eyes its ultimate destiny may be) is subject to his decree and sovereign control.[14] Consequently, given its theological character and its position in the structure of the *Institutes*, providence/predestination *could* have functioned as a single theological axiom from which Calvin *could* have attempted to derive all other doctrines *more geometrico*, had he so chosen. Nothing in the place that Calvin gives to the discussion of providence/ predestination prevents this.

Yet those who sometimes claim for Calvin (or for Beza or whomever) such a geometrical theological method never actually show what such a theology, derived from a single axiom, would look like or discuss whether it would be recognizably Christian or not. Even those who, like Alister McGrath, cite Beza's celebrated diagram of the *ordo salutis* and call it a representation of the logical sequence of human redemption[15] do not succeed in showing anything other than that in Beza's view each phase of the execution of the decree is intelligible only in the light of what is immediately prior to it. They do not show, nor could they, that any stage in the execution in time of the eternal decree of salvation is logically *deducible* from the immediately prior stage or even from the conjunction of all prior stages. In other words, they confuse *consistency* with *deducibility*.

For even if it is (quite reasonably) supposed that the eternal divine decree comprehends within it all that is decreed, there may well be contingent connections among some if not all of these elements; and consequently, for Calvin or any later Calvinist, what has in fact been decreed can only be known, insofar as it can be known at all, from Scripture by an induction of its data, or known after the event.[16] The so-called axiom, therefore, could only

---

[14] Charles Partee, 'Calvin on Universal and Particular Providence', in Donald K. McKim (ed.), *Readings in Calvin's Theology* (Grand Rapids, Mich.: Baker, 1984), 74.

[15] Alister McGrath, *A Life of John Calvin* (Oxford: Blackwell, 1990), 215. This represents an older line of scholarship about Beza. Writers such as Jill Raitt and Richard Muller place much less emphasis upon the systematic impact of Beza's *Tabula Praedestinationis*. See e.g. Richard A Muller, 'The Myth of "Decretal Theology" ', *Calvin Theological Journal* (1995).

[16] It is then a gross distortion to say, with McGrath, that 'later Reformed writers are better described as philosophical, rather than biblical, theologians . . . concerned with metaphysical and speculative questions' (*A Life of John Calvin*, 212).

be a proposition or set of propositions summarizing such data. Such an axiom, the assertion of God's providence over all, would be ontologically basic, but not epistemologically so; and so it could not function in the fashion of an axiom, as axioms are usually understood. For an axiom, if it is not a proposition that is assumed for the sake of the argument, must be both logically basic and self-evidently or fairly obviously true.

Calvin's views on providence cannot be separated from his views of creation, for God is not a 'momentary creator' and so we do not understand what it is to say that God is the Creator unless we consider his providence.[17] A word or two on creation and its relation to providence is then in order.

Calvin holds that the universe is created by God *ex nihilo*. In common with many in the medieval period, he considered Aristotle's view that the world is without beginning to be incompatible with the biblical teaching about creation.[18] Some think that Calvin's emphasis on divine sovereignty and power over the whole creation has a flattening effect to the extent that Calvin sees the physical order as passive and plastic. This may seem to be reinforced by his emphasis on the idea of *creatio continua*, 'the universal activity of God whereby all creatures, as they are sustained, thus derive the energy to do anything at all'.[19] They also see in this idea of passivity an intellectual precondition of the rise of modern science because they see it to run against the Aristotelian notion of essences and fixed kinds. But such conclusions do not seem to be fully warranted in the light of what Calvin himself actually says. Creation, for Calvin, is of different kinds of things, for God 'endowed each kind with its own nature, assigned functions, [and] appointed places and stations',[20] kinds of things that have different and distinctive sets of powers, such as the power to propagate. Moreover, these 'several kinds of things are moved by a secret impulse of nature, as if they obeyed God's eternal command, and what God has once determined flows on by itself'.[21]

As with Aquinas, for Calvin the powers that created things possess involve efficient causality. God's eternal decree is also a case of efficient causality, indeed the prime case, even when it involves the permission of evil, for such permission is a 'willing permission', as we shall see, a permission that is causally sufficient for the occurrence of what is permitted. So, for example, every human action involves at least two sets of efficient causality, the power immanent in the created agent or agents, and the power of the transcendent Creator and Lord. With intelligent agents, there may then be two or more diverse intentions, and the intention of God and the intention of the

[17] *Inst.* I. 16. 1.

[18] For an explicit reference to Aristotle in this connection, see *Sermons on Job*, trans. Arthur Golding, 685.

[19] *Inst.* II. 4. 2.

[20] *Inst.* I. 14. 20.

[21] *Inst.* I. 16. 4.

creaturely agent may be at odds.[22] The idea of a hierarchy of causes was familiar enough in medieval theology. Aquinas, for example, distinguished between God the universal cause, and the particular causes within the creation.

> The universal cause is one thing, a particular cause another. An effect can be haphazard with respect to the plan of the second, but not of the first. For an effect is not taken out of the scope of one particular cause save by another particular cause which prevents it, as when wood dowsed with water will not catch fire. The first cause, however, cannot have a random effect in its own order, since all particular causes are comprehended in its causality. When an effect does escape from a system of particular causality, we speak of it as fortuitous or a chance happening, but this is with reference to a particular cause; it cannot stray outside the sway of the universal cause, and with reference to this we speak of it as foreseen.[23]

It is a linchpin of Calvin's account of the relation of providence and evil that there is 'diversity of purpose' in providence; in the one event, a human agent, Satan and the Lord may each have different purposes. He works this out in some detail in the *Institutes*.

> How may we attribute the same work to God, to Satan and to man as author, without either excusing Satan as associated with God, or making God the author of evil? Easily, if we consider first the end, and then the manner of acting. The Lord's purpose is to exercise the patience of His servant by calamity; Satan endeavors to drive him to desperation; the Chaldeans strive to acquire gain from another's property contrary to law and right. So great is the diversity of purpose that already strongly marks the deed. There is no less difference in the manner. The Lord permits Satan to afflict His servant; he hands the Chaldeans over to be impelled by Satan, having chosen them as His ministers for this task. Satan with his poison darts arouses the wicked minds of the Chaldeans to execute that evil deed. They dash madly into injustice, and they render all their members guilty and befoul them by the crime. Satan is properly said, therefore, to act in the reprobate over whom he exercises his reign, that is, the reign of wickedness. God is also said to act in His own manner, in that Satan himself, since he is the instrument of God's wrath, bends himself hither and thither at His beck and command to execute His just judgments.[24]

---

[22] See also his references to principal and secondary causation in *Inst.* I. 17. 6 and I. 17. 9 (in reference to providence) and II. 17. 2 (in reference to the work of Christ).

[23] *Summa Theologiae*, Ia, 22. 2.

[24] *Inst.* II. 4. 2. Cf. this quotation from Augustine, 'When the Father gave up the Son, when the Lord gave up His own body, when Judas delivered up the Lord, how was it that, in this one same "delivering up", God was righteous and man guilty? The reason was that, in this one same thing which God and man did, the *motive* was not the same from which God and man *acted.*' (*A Defence of the Secret Providence of God*, trans. Henry Cole (London: Sovereign Grace Union, 1927), 299–30.) *A Defence of the Secret Providence of God* was first published in 1558 in reply to the criticisms of Sebastian Castellio and to a lesser extent those of Albertus Pighius. The defence of providence, together with that on predestination, and

Furthermore, 'the several kinds of things are moved by a secret impulse of nature'.[25] There is not then necessarily a denial of Aristotelian or of some other kind of essentialism here, even though there is an emphasis upon God as the ultimate origin of all that there is.

Although Calvin here thinks that it is easy to attribute the same work to God, to Satan, and to man, he makes matters easier than they would be by not pressing the point that whatever the differences between these levels of agency action at each level is willed by God. So that while this idea of different levels may be necessary in order not to excuse Satan or to make God the author of evil, it would seem to be hardly sufficient. We shall return to this point later.

So while God is the first cause and the upholder of all that he has created and his governance of the universe is not enclosed 'within the stream of nature' nor borne along by a 'universal law of nature',[26] there are neverthe-less different kinds of secondary causes operating in the creation. Calvin is not an occasionalist.[27] This emphasis on sovereignty need not and does not express a modern anti-Aristotelian rather than a medieval sentiment because divine providence is a teleological arrangement for Calvin. Features of an Aristotelian teleology would seem to be at home in this framework because the natural ends of the various orders of creation can be sub-ordinated to the ultimate divine end. However difficult it is to do so, Calvin certainly endeavours to balance a concern with divine sovereignty with an emphasis upon creation's variety and fecundity. Yet at the same time any Aristotelianism that is present is muted and subordinated to Calvin's overriding theological concerns, as well as to his conviction that the Bible does not teach science.[28]

Calvin's short reply to Sebastian Castellio's views on predestination, 'Brief Reply in refutation of the calumnies of a certain worthless person in which he attempted to pollute the Doctrine of the Eternal Predestination of God', were translated into English by Henry Cole. They were published together, London 1856–7, though not as part of the Calvin Translation Society's edition of Calvin's writings, and reprinted in 1927 as *Calvin's Calvinism*. All page references occurring in the main text of the remainder of this chapter are to this reprinting. Calvin's *Concerning the Eternal Predestination of God* has been more recently translated by J. K. S. Reid (London: James Clarke, 1961), and Reid has also translated the *Brief Reply* in *Calvin: Theological Treatises* (London: S. C. M. Press, 1954).

[25] *Inst.* I. 16. 4. [26] *Inst.* I. 16. 3.

[27] Occasionalism is the view that no created being can causally affect any other created being. So-called causes are only 'occasions' of their so-called effects. God is the only efficient cause. Although it originated earlier, occasionalism became prominent in post-Cartesian philosophy especially through the influence of Nicholas Malebranche (1638–1715).

[28] For a brief discussion on the alleged anti-Aristotelian implications of Calvin's views on divine causality, see Reijo Työrinoja, 'God, Causality and Nature: Some Problems of Causality in Medieval Theology', in Eeva Martikainen (ed.), *Infinity, Causality, and Determinism* (Frankfurt am Main: Peter Lang, 2002), 57–8.

CALVIN'S DEFENCE OF THE SECRET PROVIDENCE OF GOD: TEN ARGUMENTS

We shall now investigate how Calvin's understanding of providence actually functions in his thought in order to show, inter alia, that it is not intended any more than is the doctrine of predestination with which it is intertwined, to function axiomatically in his system. It seems best to do this by examining a place where Calvin's doctrine is put under pressure namely, in his *Defence of the Secret Providence of God* and particularly in his case-by-case rebuttal of Castellio's arguments.[29] In showing that these doctrines do not function axiomatically for Calvin, several of the positive and distinctive features of his treatment of providence will emerge. In the Introduction I said that my treatment of Calvin's ideas would contain no account of his doctrine of predestination; this is the nearest I come to breaking that promise.

The *Defence* is rarely referred to when Calvin scholars treat his doctrine of providence. Their chief sources are Calvin's *Commentary on Seneca's De Clementia*, the relevant parts of the *Institutes*, the *Sermons on Job*, and his tract *Against the Libertines*. This omission is surprising given Calvin's detailed defence of the doctrine there. Calvin's text will be examined in a fairly ahistorical manner, his arguments considered as a contemporary philosopher might look at the arguments of Aristotle or Descartes without tracing their provenance (although Calvin clearly relies greatly on Augustine). The bulk of the remainder of this chapter will be devoted to examining a number of the arguments by which Calvin defends the doctrine of the secret providence of God against its detractors, on the assumption that unless a person's defence of his views is entirely *ad hominem*, it should reveal something of the place that the doctrine he is defending has in his overall scheme of things.

Calvin's defence of providence reveals a distinctive blend of scriptural appeal, rational argument, and reverential agnosticism. I shall not discuss the soundness of any of the appeals and arguments that Calvin employs but simply set them out as clearly as possible and then follow each with a short commentary. After making some concluding remarks about Calvin's view of providence and predestination, we shall look briefly at Zwingli's famous sermon on providence as an example of a Reformer whose views on divine providence, as he develops and defends them, could more reasonably be said to be geometrical or at least a priori in character. Finally, we shall inquire

---

[29] This sentence corrects the historical inaccuracies in Paul Helm, 'Calvin (and Zwingli) on the Providence of God', *Calvin Theological Journal* (1994). However, one oddity is that while Calvin mentions Pighius several times he never refers to Castellio by name, though he does say enough to identify him (*A Defence of the Secret Providence of God*, 259).

whether Calvin's view of providence entails determinism; and if so, what kind. In attempting to offer an answer to these quesions we shall consider not only his doctrine of providence but also his response to Libertinism.

In its English translation, Calvin's *A Defence of the Secret Providence of God*, which takes the form of a medieval disputation, includes an introduction by Calvin giving a short overview of his doctrine (34 pages in translation). The introduction is followed by a Calumniator's Preface and Calvin's reply to that preface, and then follow fourteen short Articles (or 'Calumnies'), ostensibly drawn from Calvin's writings,[30] generally followed by Castellio's brief observations and then by Calvin's much longer replies. Calvin's replies make up the bulk of the work (almost one hundred pages in translation); and it is to them that we will chiefly direct our attention.

Of the ten arguments to be discussed, the first four are from Calvin's replies to the preface and to Castellio's remarks on the first Calumny. The *Defence*'s indebtedness to scholastic forms of argument, a *quaestio* followed by 'on the one hand' and 'on the other hand' and then a judicious conclusion is hardly beneath the surface. Calvin does not hesitate to call his replies to Castellio's objections to his doctrine *arguments* (273), which is why I transcribe them as I do. It may be true, as Richard Muller suggests, that Calvin's Renaissance background leads him to prefer *persuasio* over *demonstratio*.[31] Nevertheless, there are places, with the *Defence* being one of them, where Calvin presents sustained arguments for his positions. These arguments are interspersed in the text with a good deal of heartfelt biblical exegesis (as well as personal abuse directed towards Castellio, just as Castellio directed a lot of it towards him).

In one of his writings on the Supper Calvin distinguishes among three kinds of reason.[32] First, there is reason as it is naturally implanted in us. This kind of reason cannot be condemned without insult to God. Secondly, there is the reason that subjects divine things to judgement. Such reason must 'retire' when faced with the heavenly mysteries. Thirdly, there is a kind of reason, sanctioned by Scripture, which cuts across earthly wisdom and the senses.[33] Calvin's *Defence* shows these distinctions at work because while he defends his understanding of divine providence by the use of reason, vindicating it from the charge of being self-contradictory or paradoxical (233) with arguments, he stops short of a rationalistic defence of providence,

---

[30] Calvin complains about them as being 'partly false and partly mutilated' (*A Defence of the Secret Providence of God*, 262).   [31] *The Unaccommodated Calvin*, 29.

[32] *The Clear Explanation of Sound Doctrine Concerning the True Partaking of the Flesh and Blood of Christ in the Holy Supper* (1561), in *Calvin: Theological Treatises*, 272.

[33] For discussion of some of these issues, see Paul Helm, *Faith and Understanding*, (Edinburgh: Edinburgh University Press, 1997), chs. 1 and 2.

and he warns against resisting the counsels of God when they do not harmonize with our reason, that is, with a set of a priori assumptions that we bring to our understanding of the providence of God as it is laid out in Scripture. The first kind of reason involves natural reasoning processes about all sorts of matters while the third, which may be involved in the first, is cautious about making assumptions in the name of reason.

In the *Defence*'s eloquent and stylish introduction Calvin gives a fairly lengthy summary of what he calls his 'arguments' concerning providence in the *Institutes*. Providence is God's ceaseless, meticulous care for and control of not only the forces and powers of the natural order but also of the various orders of his creatures, and especially of mankind, 'the noblest work of God', and, within the human race, especially of his church.

> For though God thus shows Himself the Father and the Judge of the whole human race, yet, as the Church is His sanctuary in which He resides, He there manifests His presence by clearer and brighter proofs; He there shows Himself as the Father of his family, and condescends to grant a nearer view of Himself, if I may so speak. (226)

Calvin then emphasizes the use to which the doctrine of providence ought to be put; namely, that those convinced of it should view their life and the lives of others not only in terms of secondary causes, which he here calls 'means', but in terms of God's will, the primary cause. In other words, the proper response to such providence is not to bridle at it, but to submit to it with awe and wonder, with a combination of fear and of confidence. Past success is to be attributed to God, the first cause; we are not to focus exclusively on secondary causes, but to pass through the 'veil' of secondary causes to the hand of God. Past sin is to be attributed to ourselves. Our attitude to the future is to be governed by the promises of God, 'the omnipotence of God, as seen in the glass of His word' (231). Providence is seen most evidently when God acts contrary to means, performing the unexpected. Thus, unlike the Stoics, Calvin holds that secondary causes are all subject to God, not God to secondary causes.

Yet as we have seen, Calvin also emphasizes the role of secondary causes in order to distinguish his view from Stoic ideas of fate. God works by means. What will happen is not fated to happen but happens as the result of the use of means. If I am destined to post the letter, then I am destined to use the appropriate means to post it. This has, for Calvin, a consequence that may seem surprising. He says:

> Wherefore, with reference to the time future, since the events of things are, as yet, hidden and unknown, everyone ought to be as intent upon the performance of his duty as if nothing whatever had been decreed concerning the issue in each particular case. Or (to speak more properly) every man ought so to hope for success in all

things which he undertakes at the command of God, as to be freely prepared to reconcile every contingency with the sure and certain Providence of God. (236)

The providence of God with regard to the future is secret not only in the sense that it is in fact true that we don't know what God is going to do, but it is secret in a rather different sense, that in order to act effectively we must *believe* that it is secret, and our actions must be governed not by an attempt to divine God's secret will, but by obedience to his commands and reliance on his promises. Though I may be destined to post the letter, I ought not to believe that I am; rather in ordering my affairs I am to follow the command of God, as expressed in this case, perhaps, in behaving prudently, believing neither that God will grant me success in posting my letter, nor that he will deny success to me. Here is one of the crucial points at which the secret and the revealed will of God come together. We shall discuss this further in Chapter 11.

These remarks provide us with a clue to Calvin's attitude to future contingents. The issue of the relation between God's foreknowledge and future contingents has invited much theological and philosophical speculation both before and since Calvin's time.[34] In particular, thinkers have found it extremely difficult to offer a convincing account of how God's foreknowledge is consistent with human freedom where such freedom is understood in an indeterministic sense. So much so that comparatively little attention has been given to the question of how God's providential control can be consistent with such freedom.

Calvin does not enter directly or at any length into this tradition of debate. In the *Institutes* he confines his treatment to two shortish sections (*Inst.* 1. 26. 8, 9). First, as already indicated, following Augustine he distances his position from that of Stoic fate. Such fate is a theory about the causal structure of created things. But divine providence is not an impersonal, immanent arrangement, it is an expression of God's wisdom and power which extends over the whole of creation including the plans and intentions of men. So nothing happens by chance. Any expressions of chance must be wholly referred to divine providence.

Yet many things are fortuitous for us. How so? Not because God's providence does not reach them, but because we are ignorant of them.

But since the order, reason, end and necessity of those things which happen for the most part lie hidden in God's purpose, and are not apprehended by human opinion, those things, which it is certain take place by God's will, are in a sense fortuitous.[35]

---

[34] See, for example, William Lane Craig, *The Problem of Divine Foreknowledge and Future Contingents from Aristotle to Suarez* (Leiden: E. J. Brill, 1988), and J. M. Fischer, (ed.), *God, Foreknowledge and Freedom* (Stanford, Calif.: Stanford University Press, 1989).   [35] *Inst.* 1. 16. 9.

So we may, perhaps we must, think of many events as fortuitous, because of our ignorance.

As all future events are uncertain to us, so we hold them in suspense, as if they might incline to one side or the other. Yet in our hearts it nonetheless remains fixed that nothing will take place that the Lord has not previously foreseen.[36]

Such fortuitousness, contingency, is not in the nature of things but is due to our ignorance. Nothing is contingent for God. For any possibility is either decreed by God, in which case it has a probability of 1, or it is not decreed by him, in which case it has a probability of 0. But because we are ignorant of what he has in fact decreed we must ourselves assign probabilities to future contingents that lie between these extremes. In terms of the decisions we make we cannot but live as if the future is not decreed in every detail (even though, as faithful Christians, we believe that it is). Living in this way involves not merely being ignorant of the outcome of our actions, but ignorant of those actions themselves and of the decisions that give rise to them until we actually undertake them. And we best undertake them not by first trying to predict what our decisions will be, or what the outcomes of our actions will be, by divining such matters, but by attending to God's revealed will for us. Believers must 'inquire and learn from Scripture what is pleasing to God so that they may strive toward this under the Spirit's guidance'.[37] Here is another important context in which Calvin's distinction between the revealed and the secret will of God is important.

The Lord has inspired in men the arts of taking counsel and caution, by which to comply with his providence in the preservation of life itself. Just as, on the contrary, by neglect and slothfulness they bring upon themselves the ills that he has laid upon them. How does it happen that a provident man, while he takes care of himself, also disentangles himself from threatening evils, but a foolish man perishes from his own unconsidered rashness, unless folly and prudence are instruments of the divine dispensation in both cases? For this reason, God pleased to hide all future events from us, in order that we should resist them as doubtful, and not cease to oppose with ready remedies, until they are either overcome or pass beyond all care.[38]

One might wonder if what Calvin here presents as a matter of divine pleasure isn't a matter of divine necessity. Is it that God simply chooses not to reveal the future, or that he cannot do so if the future is to take the character that he has decreed? Calvin does not appear to wish to press the issue of our ignorance of future contingents further by raising such questions.

God's providential decree imposes a necessity on what is decreed. Viewed apart from the decree, it is possible that Christ's bones, like anyone's bones,

---

[36] *Inst.* I. 16. 9.   [37] *Inst.* I. 17. 3.   [38] *Inst.* I. 17. 4.

be broken. But given that God has decreed that not one of them shall be broken 'it was necessary that all the parts of His body should remain whole, unbroken and uninjured'. Calvin thinks this distinction between what could happen, apart from God's decree, and what cannot happen, given his decree, preserves an acceptable sense of contingency in events and that it is more easily grasped than the distinction between *the necessity of the consequent* and *the necessity of the consequence* (231)[39] although he does not wholly object to these forms of expression.

Finally, Calvin gives attention to the 'greater difficulty of argument and judgment' (237) that arises when we consider the relation of divine providence to human desires and purposes. These matters will preoccupy him in the body of his *Defence*. Whatever the difficulties, he insists both that men act of their own volition and are therefore responsible for what they do and nevertheless, in spite of themselves, God governs them. In their own folly and madness they accomplish God's work. So God does not merely permit evil but ordains it. The 'one and simple' (256) will of God, moved by the highest of reasons, is the first cause of all things in heaven and earth, without God being the author of evil. Or to say it better, by adopting a distinction 'which formerly prevailed in the schools, and is now everywhere current, is perfectly true, provided it be rightly understood—"that the evil of the punishment, but not the evil of the fault, proceeds from God"' (248). It is because the universe is fallen and guilty and so under the judgement of God that for Calvin the judgement of God in ordaining evil as a punishment for evil figures so prominently in his thought at points such as these.

What follows are ten separate arguments by means of which Calvin defends his view of the secret providence of God against Castellio. These are not his only arguments but they are his chief ones. I shall state and comment on each of them, using as far as possible the words of the English translation, in the order in which they appear in the text.

ARGUMENT 1

After a preliminary skirmish over whether Calvin's doctrine of providence is equivalent to fate, a suggestion that Calvin rebuts in thoroughly Augustinian fashion,[40] Calvin addresses the first 'calumny', 'that God of his pure and mere will created the greatest part of the world to perdition' (264) with the following argument:

1. God decreed from the beginning everything that should befall the race of man (266).

---

[39] That is, the necessity of something that cannot be other than it is as distinct from the necessity of what is conditioned by a prior contingent act, in this case the act of God's prior decree.

[40] Cf. Augustine, *City of God* v. ix. Cf. *Inst.* I. 16. 8.

2. God can decree nothing but what is wise and holy and just, even though the reasons for God's decrees are sometimes hidden from us (266).
3. Therefore, there is no separation between God's will and his wisdom, holiness, and justice (266).
4. Therefore, God is not pure will (267).
5. Therefore, a fortiori, God cannot by his pure and mere will have created the greatest part of the world to perdition.

Although he is ostensibly attacking Calvin's doctrine of divine providence here, Castellio is in fact addressing predestination. In his reply, Calvin is happy to consider the fall of Adam and the choice of Jacob over Esau as falling under the order of providence. Calvin never says, Look, Castellio, you are changing the subject. You cannot attack providence by attacking predestination because the two are different and are to be defended differently.

In this first argument Calvin shows himself fully familiar with the move that separates God's will from his moral character, and rejects it: 'Therefore, with reference to the sentiments of the schoolmen concerning the absolute, or tyrannical, will of God, I not only repudiate, but abhor them all, because they separate the justice of God from His ruling power' (266). We shall consider the significance of Calvin's refusal to make such a separation more fully in Chapter 11.

ARGUMENT 2

Castellio argued by analogy that since God is the Creator of all animals and causes them to love their own offspring, he himself loves all men, who are his own offspring. Therefore, God did not create anyone to perdition (264). To this, Calvin replied:

1. Every animal naturally loves its offspring (267).
2. God loves the whole human race (268).
3. God is not bound by laws governing animals, since some of those laws (e.g. about propagation) are manifestly inapplicable to God (267).
4. So it does not follow that God ought to love all mankind equally (268).

Throughout his *Defence*, Calvin resolutely refuses to use analogies, such as the analogy of the love of an animal for its offspring (267, 269), if those analogies subvert Scripture. This is part of his general argument against the use of common sense and human reason in the sense of what appears reasonable to the average person, an instance of the second kind of reason in theological argument that was distinguished by Calvin and noted earlier (see, e.g. 296). In argument against Castellio, Calvin is not averse to appealing to empirical evidence, such as the marked differences that occur in the condition of human beings; yet his chief source of disanalogies for rebutting

Castellio is Scripture. His hermeneutical principle would appear to be: If an analogy conflicts with a scriptural analogy, it must be rejected.[41]

This involves a much more negative attitude to the use of analogy in theological argument than Calvin manifests elsewhere, especially with the Incarnation where, as we saw in the last chapter, in order to elucidate the Incarnation Calvin relied fairly heavily on the analogy between the union of God and man in the Incarnation and that of soul and body in a human being. (Unless one holds, as Calvin presumably did, that body–soul dualism is divinely revealed.)

ARGUMENT 3

Calvin thinks that Castellio may be inclined to grant that God foreknows evils but then would argue that God's foreknowledge is not the cause of evils. Here is Calvin's counter-argument:

1. Suppose God did not decree the Fall (272).
2. Yet, even if (1), God foresaw the Fall (272).
3. If God foresaw the Fall, then he could have preserved mankind by not permitting it (272).
4. God did not preserve mankind but permitted its ruin (272).

Calvin is not altogether happy with the idea of permission but uses it here as a concession to Castellio. (He is much happier with the phrase 'willing permission' as his use of it in the *Institutes* testifies.[42]) We shall return to this topic, and to the source of his unhappiness, later. Yet Calvin's concession makes this argument *ad hominem*, designed to show that if we suppose that God foresaw but did not decree the Fall, then he could have prevented what took place. But we must suppose that he chose not to prevent it and thus, by omitting to intervene, in permitting the Fall willed it. Calvin, in making this concession, distinguishes on this occasion between the foreknowledge and the foreordination of God, although he, along with the bulk of the medievals,[43] was unhappy to do so. Here, however, he allows it for dialectical purposes. He does not consider an obvious objection to (3), that if God foresaw the Fall, then the Fall would take place because God foresaw it. In Calvin's view, for God not to permit the Fall is for him not to have foreseen it.

---

[41] 'But if you are determined to make God subject to the laws of nature, you must necessarily accuse and condemn Him of injustice...' (269). 'You accuse God of injustice; nay, you declare him to be nothing above a monster, if He dares to decree anything concerning men otherwise than we ourselves should determine concerning our own children. If so, how shall we account for God's creating some dull of comprehension, others of greater incapacity, others quite idiots?' (271).

[42] e.g. *Inst.* I. 8. 1 and III. 23. 8. Calvin uses the phrase 'willing permission' in connection with the work of Satan, *Inst.* I. 14. 17. See also *Inst.* I. 16. 8 and I. 18. 2 and 3, where he states that everything happens either by God's command or permission.   [43] *Inst.* I. 16. 4.

Strictly speaking, then, premiss (2) should read: Yet, even if (1), God foresaw that the Fall would occur were he not to prevent it.

ARGUMENT 4

Castellio argues that God created all men for a happy life, for all were created in Adam who was placed by God in Paradise, which [was] a life of happiness (265). Calvin responds:

1. The original creation was good, including man's creation in rectitude and yet 'weak, frail and liable to fall' (274).
2. Man perished by his own infirmity and sin (274).
3. Nevertheless, the perishing of man by his own sin and fault was predestined by God (274).
4. So God predestined at least one sinful action.

John Hick has claimed that the Augustinian–Calvinist doctrine of the Fall is incoherent.

There is a basic and fatal incoherence at the heart of any theodicy based 'solution' [to the presence of evil]. The Creator is preserved from any responsibility for the existence of evil by the claim that He made men (or angels) as free and finitely perfect creatures, happy in the knowledge of Himself, and subject to no strains or temptations, but that they themselves inexplicably and inexcusably rebelled against Him. But this suggestion amounts to a sheer self-contradiction. It is impossible to conceive of wholly good beings in a wholly good world becoming sinful.[44]

Calvin's description of man as originally created (*quae fluxa et caduca erat*) is interesting and rather surprising.[45] But it would appear to give him the resources to reject this claim of Hick's that there is a self-contradiction in the idea that God both created mankind all good and yet they fell. To create something good is not to create it as good as could be.

This argument shows that in Calvin's view, though the Fall was predestined, yet mankind fell by its own fault. Calvin indicates that he will show hereafter how (2) and (3) harmonize. The remainder of Calvin's reply to Calumny 1 is taken up with arguing why salvation is not universal. It is noteworthy that in this and most of the subsequent arguments the soteric (i.e. predestinarian) aspects of God's providence are prominent in the discussion.

ARGUMENT 5

In his comments on the second Calumny, Castellio accuses Calvin of holding that God not only predestined Adam to damnation but to the causes of that

---

[44] John Hick, *Evil and the God of Love* (London: Macmillan, 1966), 285–6.

[45] Compare the *Inst.* I. 15. 8: 'Therefore Adam could have stood if he wished, seeing that he fell solely by his own will. But it was because his will was capable of being bent to one side or the other, and was not given the constancy to persevere, that he fell so easily.'

damnation, which is 'the doctrine of the devil', as Castellio calls it (279). Calvin brushes this charge aside, responding with an argument not in terms of God's relation to secondary causes but to his secret ordination of Adam's Fall.

1. God's foreknowledge and power are inseparable (281).
2. God did not prevent the Fall of Adam (281).
3. Had God willed to prevent the Fall, it would have been prevented by giving Adam fortitude and constancy to persevere (281).
4. Had God merely permitted the Fall, then the Fall would have occurred against his will (282).
5. But nothing occurs against God's will (283).
6. We cannot know at present why God willed the Fall (282).
7. But we know that God is necessarily righteous (283).
8. Therefore, the willing of the Fall was a righteous action (283).

Calvin has two goals with this argument.[46] First, to clarify his opposition to the idea that the Fall occurred by the mere permission of God; for such permission implies, in his view, that what is permitted is not fully in accord with the will of the one who permits it; and this cannot be true of God. With Augustine, whom he cites, Calvin holds that nothing could have happened had God not willed it to happen. Secondly, he wants to vindicate God's character as just. 'His eternal will, though it depends on none and on nothing but Himself, nor has any prior cause to influence it, is nevertheless founded in the highest reason and in the highest equity. . . . His will is the highest rule of the highest equity' (283). Again, Calvin permits no separation between God's moral character and his will, even though how what God wills is a true expression of God's moral character is often inscrutable to the human mind.

ARGUMENT 6

This argument is taken from Calvin's reply to Castellio's comments on the third Calumny. This charges Calvin with denying that, as far as sinful acts are concerned, there is any difference between the permission and the will of God.

1. There are numerous instances of God willing sin, e.g. Ezekiel 14: 9, 1 Kings 22, Job 1 (287–8).
2. Therefore there is no moral objection to believing that every sin is willed by God in a stronger sense than mere permission.

---

[46] In this argument (of those being considered here) Calvin comes closest to engaging with the bulk of modern philosophical discussion on the problem of evil. Calvin's commitment to (3) in this argument shows that he did not favour what has come to be known as the free will defence. For a representative set of modern discussions on this problem see Marilyn McCord Adams and Robert Merrihew Adams (eds.), *The Problem of Evil*, (Oxford: Oxford University Press, 1990). For further comment, see Chapter 6.

3. Nevertheless, God is not the author of sin (289).
4. (2) and (3) are not contradictory but express mysteries which at present surpass our comprehension (289).

In many respects, this argument brings us to the heart of Calvin's position. Several things are worth noting. First, the previous argument concluded that God does not merely permit sinful actions, but this one claims that sinful actions are due to the mere will of God. Second, the argument clarifies what Calvin would say about the distinction between sinful actions that are punitive, that is, divine punishment for other sins, and sinful actions that are not. He would recognize the distinction but regard it as irrelevant here. For if God wills sin punitively, he nonetheless wills sin, although he does not will sinfully; that is, in willing sin, his motive and intention are not and cannot be sinful, any more than a physician, in prescribing the emetic, wills pain for its own sake. Nevertheless, Calvin focuses attention on the relation between God and an evil action, not on any further reason or end why God might will such an evil. Secondly, Calvin makes a fine but for him a crucial distinction between God willing evil and God being the author of sin. According to Calvin, the former does not entail the latter; for God to be the author of sin he would himself have to be personally culpable or sinful; he would have to be a sinner. He cannot be, not because God is *ex legis*, but because he is essentially good, his will being the rule of the highest equity, as Calvin puts it earlier (283). Finally, in making these distinctions Calvin readily acknowledges that he does not purport fully to grasp or to be able to explain the differences; hence his appeal to the comprehension-surpassing reasons that God has. Calvin believes that when we see God face-to-face these matters will become clear. This makes it evident that for him the problem is an epistemological one, ignorance that arises from our 'epistemic distance' and not one that arises in the nature of things.

ARGUMENT 7

This argument is drawn from Calvin's reply to Calumny 4, which charges Calvin with asserting that 'All the crimes that are committed by any man whatsoever are, by the operation of God, good and just' (297). Castellio observes, in effect, that if this is so then the distinction between good and evil is obliterated. As is often his practice, Calvin replies to a general objection by citing and discussing a biblical case, in this instance the case of Job.

1. Job's goods were spoiled by robbers, by Satan and by God (298).
2. The robbers and Satan were guilty of the spoliation (298).
3. If God had been guilty of spoliation, then had Job blamed God, he would have been justified in doing so (298).

4. But Job did not blame God (298).
5. Therefore, though the spoliation is the work of God he is not morally guilty (298).

Here Calvin makes use of a tacit premiss about Job's uprightness to the effect that if upright Job, acting under none other influence than the inspiration of the Holy Spirit (298) did not blame God, then no one is justified in blaming him. (Calvin also mentions the case of Joseph being sold by his brothers to the Ishmaelites as well as incidents in the lives of Isaiah and Jeremiah and God the Father's delivering up of the Son for crucifixion.)

This is an interesting appeal to Scripture, embodying the equally interesting hermeneutical principle that whenever a saint or godly man is recorded in Scripture as vindicating God's character in a situation where the occurrence of personally damaging evil gives the person a strong prima-facie reason not to do so, this provides us with sufficient reason to conclude that God is not the author of sin even though he ordained the evil. This sort of case also provides Calvin with a reason why the divine willing of evil is not a mere permission. God's use of the wicked for holy ends, as in the crucifixion of his Son, underlines Calvin's aversion to speaking of the mere permission by God of evil. As we have already noted, for Calvin mere permission implies less than full willingness; but in ordaining evil for a holy end God wholly wills the evil; his will is sufficient for the occurrence of the evil, including the occurrence of all the secondary causes that are necessary and sufficient for it to happen. Calvin emphasizes *that* God acts in this way, and has little to say either about *how* God does so or *why* he does so. For instance, it becomes our sobriety and modesty of mind to remain willingly ignorant of how God can at the same time decree that men commit evil and nevertheless command them to continue in the right way (294). Calvin is adamant that no explanation that relies in any way upon common sense is acceptable (295–6). God's accommodation of his ways through anthropomorphic and symbolic utterances is vastly different from God's accommodating himself to common sense. Common sense, that is, natural, unregenerate reason is an unacceptable norm for interpreting Scripture, whereas the varied language that Scripture uses about God provides us with normative theological models, ways in which God has chosen to accommodate himself to human understanding (295).

ARGUMENT 8

This argument is taken from Calvin's reply to Calumnies 5 and 6. 'No adultery, theft, or murder is committed without the intervention of the will of God' and 'The Scripture openly testifies that evil doings are designed, not only by the will, but by the authority, of God' (300–1), and Castellio's observations on them. Again, Calvin considers Job's case.

1. God's motives and ends in Job's spoliation were different from those of the robbers (303).
2. Therefore, in Job's spoliation God is in a different moral position than the robbers (302–3).
3. Therefore, God's action and the robbers' action cannot be the same act (303).

Here Calvin appeals to what would nowadays be called the 'description under which' God ordains Job's distress. God ordains that action with a pure motive for a good end, whereas the robbers' act can only be described as a bad action done from an evil motive. His response also makes use of the principle, prominent in pre-Reformation theology, that God (as well as his motives and ends) is hierarchically related to his creation. 'God, who makes sovereign use of their wickedness [the wickedness of thieves and murderers], stands in an infinitely different, and in an all-high position above all men, and acts, and things' (303). This is a metaphysical and not a moral thesis; Calvin is not saying that human moral terms do not apply to God: Indeed, 'God never deviates in the remotest degree from His own nature; that is, from His own infinitely perfect rectitude' (303), but rather that human motives and divine motives are ontologically distinct and that the divine motives may incorporate the human, though not of course vice versa.

ARGUMENT 9

This argument is part of Calvin's reply to Calumny 7, 'Whatsoever men do when and while they sin, they do according to the will of God, seeing that the will of God often conflicts with his precept' (305). Here he says more about the distinction between what God reveals to be his will and what he secretly ordains.

1. The will of God, comprising his secret counsel and openly revealed voice, is simple and uniform (307).
2. God wills one end but frequently by different means (307).
3. God's will as set forth in the Law shows that he delights in righteousness and hates iniquity (308).
4. Yet God may secretly will that to be done which he forbids in the Law (308, 310–11).
5. The explanation of how God is able to do this is right now beyond our capacities (308).
6. Nevertheless, God's motives are wholly pure (310).

Calvin has difficulty, as did the medievals, in reconciling the oneness of God's will with the fact that God commands what he does not ordain to come to pass.[47] For instance, God commands honesty and yet decrees (or ordains) theft. We shall examine this tension further in Chapter 11. Here Calvin makes two points. First, in asserting the most perfect, divine, and consummate harmony (307) between God's commands and decrees, he had in view the one end of those two wills. The goal of God's hidden counsel and revealed voice is the same; hence there is actually only one will in God. And, secondly, it is characteristic for Calvin that God's decreeing will, as that which determines what shall come to pass, is mostly secret. This is what God determines to do as distinct from what he commands so that he may accomplish his purposes.

Calvin links the fact that God has only one will, although he may appear to have two, with the hierarchical considerations mentioned above. Because God's motives and ends are different in decreeing an act of adultery from the adulterer's own motives and ends, he, as the first cause, ordains it from pure motives and for pure ends; Calvin must maintain that God's motive in ordaining the adulterer's motive is different from the adulterer's motive.

God wills that adultery should not be committed, in as far as it is a pollution and violation of the holy bond of matrimony, and a great transgression of His righteous law. But, in as far as God uses adulteries, as well as other wicked doings of men, to execute His own acts of vengeance on the sins of men, He certainly executes the office and performs the sacred duty of a *Judge*, not unwillingly, but willingly! (309)

This does not imply that the evil of adultery is solely a matter of intention. But this discussion shows that, while Calvin is far from providing rationalizing explanations of God's ways, he does wish to remove any irreconcilable inconsistency (311) in the scriptural testimony and thus fulfil his earlier promise to defend the harmony of these matters (274–5). Calvin affirms that God's will is one but once again offers no theories about *why* or *how* this is so (312). For Calvin, harmonizing a set of propositions does not involve demonstrating its consistency (except its consistency with Scripture) but rebutting charges of logical inconsistency.

ARGUMENT 10

The last argument that we shall consider is taken from Calvin's reply to Calumnies 8 and 9, which concern God's relation to the hardening of Pharaoh's heart (e.g. Exod. 4: 21) and to hardness of heart in general. This is a special case of the general issue of the relation of God's will to human wickedness.

---

[47] See, for example, Aquinas, *Summa Theologiae*, 1a, 19. 6, 'Is God's will always fulfilled?'

1. God hardens men by giving them over to the Devil (319).
2. God by his secret counsel overrules so that those who are hardened do only what he has decreed (319).
3. Therefore, those who are hardened are the cause of their own hardening (319).

This argument appears to assume that God hardens men by not preventing their natural tendencies to hardness of heart from manifesting themselves (318). Thus there is an asymmetry between hardening and regenerating. In hardening, God leaves men; and so, Calvin says, they and not God are the cause of the hardening (319). In regenerating, God acts by imparting the influences of his secret Spirit (319).

Calvin is at some pains here, also, to remove from the scriptural data the appearance of contradiction (310). As noted, this provides an important clue as to the extent to which he may be said to be rational or rationalistic in his theological method; more on this shortly. Here also, as elsewhere, he refers to God's secret counsel or predestination. The adjective has at least a twofold importance. First, the providence of God is secret in that the *raison d'être* of many of God's providential workings, and particularly those that embrace evil acts, may be unknown and at present unknowable to us (228, 254). As we saw in the first chapter, for Calvin God has a mind of his own and chooses either to reveal or not to reveal a matter to his creatures as he sees fit. What he chooses not to reveal about what he nevertheless wills to come to pass is 'secret' or unknown. It is in this sense, but now emphasizing unknowability, that Calvin uses the phrase 'secret Spirit' (319) to refer to the Spirit's work in conversion. The Spirit works in conversion in a way that surpasses our present understanding. Secondly, God's providential workings are not in general knowable in advance but only in the event, and for this reason (among others) they are never to be thought of as the rule of our duty.

This completes our review of Calvin's arguments. These ten are not the only arguments that can be distilled from the text of his replies to Castellio, perhaps, but they certainly are the chief ones.

CALVIN'S SCHOLASTIC AND SCRIPTURAL METHOD

What can we glean about Calvin's general theological method from reviewing these arguments?

One lesson is that, when he is put under pressure by controversy, Calvin is not averse to deploying some of the standard conceptual distinctions of medieval scholasticism. In this short work, it is possible to identify at least four of these. First, he distinguishes between God as primary cause and the order of secondary causes (246–7), where every event in creation has both a primary and a secondary cause (230–1) and no secondary cause can influence the primary cause.[48] Secondly, he is fully familiar with the scholastic distinction between the necessity of the consequent and the necessity of the consequence (235), using it to show that while what God ordains necessarily comes to pass, what comes to pass is not of itself necessitated but only necessitated in virtue of his will.[49] Thirdly, Calvin repeatedly denies that his view of providence requires that God be understood, in accordance with that 'Sarbonic dogma', as pure will (248); rather, in God will and wisdom are inseparably united in one simple essence. Fourthly, he deems the scholastic distinction between the evil of punishment and the evil of fault to be perfectly true (248).

To complete the picture, Calvin demurs from Augustine's account of evil as a privation because it is 'an acuteness of argument which, to many, may not be satisfactory' (233).[50] In defending his own view against the charge that it denies contingency, he says, 'But to take contingency out of the world altogether would be absurd. I omit to notice here those various distinctions which are made in the schools. That which I shall adduce shall be simple, in my judgement, and not strained; and also, that which shall be profitable for the conduct of life' (234). An event is contingent, for Calvin, as long as its opposite could have occurred had God decreed it. Bones are naturally frangible. But if God decrees that some bone, though it could be broken, will not be, then necessarily it won't be.

> But if we look at the decree of God, which was fulfilled in its time, the bones of Christ's body were no more subject to fracture than the angels are subject to human sorrows. In this case, therefore, when we are required to look into the law and order of nature as appointed of God, I by no means reject the contingency involved, in my sense and meaning of such contingency. (235)

So Calvin was fully familiar with a range of scholastic distinctions, and he was prepared to use them on occasion, perhaps more frequently than is

---

[48] Calvin does not use the language of God's being the author of sin on this page, although what he does say is equivalent to denying that God is the author of sin. For his explicit use of such language, see *Inst.* II. 4. 2, where he cites Job 1 in making the appropriate distinctions, just as he does on 288f. of our text. See also 233, where he says 'that the will of God is the great cause of all things that are done in the whole world; and yet that God is not the author of the evils that are done therein'.

[49] For further recognition of these distinctions see *Inst.* I. 16. 9 and III. 23. 8.

[50] Though it seems to have been satisfactory for his fellow Reformer Peter Martyr Vermigli: 'I will say something about evil, the genus under which sin is included. Evil is a lack [*privatio*], I mean of goodness; not of all goodness but of such a good as is required for the perfection of the creature.... As a privation, evil cannot exist without good, for it must have a subject. Since a subject is a substance [*natura*], it is good; so evil can exist only in some good; blindness is a deprivation of sight; it does not hang in the air, but stays in the eye' ('Whether God is the Author of Sin', Scholium on 2 Sam. 16, in *The Peter Martyr Library*, vol. 4: *The Philosophical Works*, trans. Joseph C. McClelland (Kirkville, Mo.: Sixteenth Century Essays and Studies, 1996) 223).

generally realized, and even to claim that at least some of them are indispensable (251). Yet he drew the line when he believed that such distinctions were strained and were not readily useful in the elucidation of doctrine.

Facts such as these, as well as the formal structure of the *Defence*, as mentioned earlier, should be kept in mind when efforts are made to separate Calvin both from medieval scholasticism and from Reformed and Puritan scholasticism. Although the evidence suggests that he was not trained in scholastic theology, as some early Reformed theologians such as Peter Martyr Vermigli were, Calvin's willingness to use scholastic terminology was no doubt noted by later Reformed systematizers, who would have reckoned his use of it to warrant their use of it.

The arguments we have surveyed underline our earlier contention that, while Calvin propounds his doctrine of providence with utter confidence, it does not function axiomatically in his system. While in his view providence is plainly revealed in Scripture, it is nevertheless 'secret', 'mysterious', 'a great abyss', and so forth. These are not the marks of an axiom, which has its status because it is self-evident or obvious or perhaps because it is stipulated. Axioms function by having other propositions deduced from them. Does predestination/providence function like this in Calvin's thought? Clearly not. Nowhere in his defence of God's secret providence against Castellio does Calvin attempt to deduce other Christian doctrines from the idea of providence, or from particular instances of divine providence, nor does he defend providence by asserting that it is an indispensable theological first principle. He defends it because he believes it to be scriptural.

In virtue of what the doctrine of providence/predestination states, providence has a logical priority because it is in virtue of God's providential ordering that everything that happens in the universe comes to pass. But, Calvin would say, it does not follow from this that the doctrine of providence functions as an epistemological axiom, as a basic item of human knowledge from which, with the aid of logic, we can deduce other Christian doctrines.

In any case, although Calvin employs logical argumentation, he does not use logic 'remorselessly'. His willingness to draw an inference is constrained by the data of revelation. Yet while he does not use remorseless logic to deduce other Christian doctrines from divine providence, he does fairly remorselessly present arguments for its defence. Some may see in Calvin's willingness to resort to such arguments a concession in the direction of the natural knowledge of God. Yet however much Calvin relies upon such knowledge, it is likely that he would see things differently. These arguments are not for Calvin another *source* of the knowledge of God but merely a *means* of articulating that knowledge while keeping within what he regarded as the proper limits in doing so. As such, the logic employed in such arguments is for Calvin simply an extension of scriptural exposition, which also depends upon the knowledge of the languages used by the biblical writers.

That Calvin is suspicious of axiomatic theology of any kind appears from his almost universal suspicion of human reason or common sense as a source of theological knowledge. In Calvin's book, theological appeals like these are bound to be suspect and ought to fail. They ought to fail because they almost invariably take us away from the text of Scripture. Castellio's appeal to common sense is for Calvin the unbiblical reasoning of the natural man. Yet Calvin is certainly prepared to use argument and scholastic distinctions to protect the scriptural testimony about providence/predestination from false inferences and especially to maintain the consistency of biblical teaching. This appears most vividly in his discussion of what God commands as contrasted with what he ordains, by which he upholds the unity and consistency of the divine will (255).

Calvin has a great regard for consistency in theology. In his *Defence of the Secret Providence of God* as elsewhere he is very sensitive to the possibility of self-contradiction in his thought. But he does not go so far as to attempt to demonstrate consistency. Instead he argues from the principle that if two propositions are taught as true in the word of God they cannot be inconsistent. What might at first sight seem paradoxical or self-contradictory cannot be so if the 'glass' of Scripture reveals it (233). Similarly,

> This appearance of contradiction is that which dazzles and blinds your eyes. But God Himself, who well knoweth in Himself how it is that He willeth that same thing in one sense which is contrary to his will in another, pays no regard whatever to your dullness of understanding and stupidity... That there should be a conflict, therefore, between the true and false prophets, was inevitable. But God did not therefore contend with or contradict Himself, though He willed that both these true and these false prophets should come forth. (287)[51]

But if providence/predestination does not figure as an axiom in Calvin's system, neither is it simply to be regarded as an a posteriori reflection upon the data of human experience.[52] For as our analysis of Calvin's arguments has shown, there is little or nothing in them that amounts to an appeal to human experience interpreted in the light of Scripture. Rather Calvin appeals directly to Scripture's teaching, including of course the experience of such people as Job as well as the unequal distribution of both saving and non-saving grace revealed in Scripture. It is not our construction, our theorizing about this inequality, that affords us the doctrine of providence/

---

[51] See also *A Defence of the Secret Providence of God*, 311, 312, 319 for further references to self-contradiction and the need to avoid it.   [52] As is claimed by McGrath, *A Life of John Calvin*, 167.

predestination but the direct scriptural teaching about the source from which this inequality springs.

CALVIN AND ZWINGLI

To provide a point of comparison with Calvin's approach to predestination, it is worth glancing at Ulrich Zwingli's famous sermon on providence (1530).[53] Zwingli (1485–1531) deduces the idea of providence from the ideas of divine supremacy and truth. What is supremely good must be true[54] and what is supremely good and true 'must first of all know and understand all things' and 'must also have power over all things'.[55]

Hence I conclude, if the Supreme Divinity is the supreme good, and truth belongs to the nature of the good, so that the supreme good cannot be such unless it is true and indeed truth itself, I conclude, I say, that the supremely true is also supreme power and might. Let us now join these three and with the understanding of faith weld together the Supreme Divinity, that is, supreme power and might, secondly the supreme good, that is, the whole sum and essence of the good, finally essential truth, that is, simplicity, purity, light, genuineness and unchangeableness.[56]

As a result of this procedure Zwingli claims that we shall see both that Providence must exist and that it cares for and regulates all things.

From this piece of a priori reasoning, via a definition of providence as 'the enduring and unchangeable rule over and direction of all things in the universe',[57] Zwingli proceeds, in his third chapter, to deny the reality of secondary causes. He demonstrates this first in the case of the subhuman creation. Zwingli quotes Plato, Seneca, and other non-biblical writers equally with Paul, justifying this as follows: 'If, then, you find in Plato or Pythagoras what you scent as flowing from the foundation of the divine

---

[53] English trans. in Ulrich Zwingli, *On Providence and Other Essays*, ed. William John Hinke for Samuel Macauley Jackson (1922; repr. Durham, NC: Labyrinth Press, 1983). Page references in the text are to this translation. I am not suggesting that every feature of Zwingli's view of providence may be detected in this sermon. The view of Zwingli as a strong determinist who denied the efficacy of secondary causes can be found in older treatments, e.g. the discussion in Philip Schaff, *The Creeds of Christendom*, ii. 370, and in Reinhold Seeberg and Charles E. Hay, *Textbook of the History of Doctrines*, (Philadelphia: Lutheran Publications Society, 1905), ii 313. In *The Theology of Huldrych Zwingli* (Oxford: Clarendon Press, 1986), W. P. Stephens points to other, more biblical, contours of Zwingli's doctrine (86–97). Nonetheless, the contrast in method between Zwingli's *On Providence* and Calvin's *Secret Providence* stands out starkly.

[54] *On Providence and Other Essays*, 131.

[55] *On Providence and Other Essays*, 132. Stephens (*Theology of Huldrych Zwingli*, 93 n. 56) suggests that Zwingli's treatment of providence may be aimed at counteracting Renaissance views of chance. But the same might be said of Calvin's very different approach to providence.

[56] *On Providence and Other Essays*, 132.   [57] *On Providence and Other Essays*, 136.

mind, this is not to be disregarded because a mortal embraced it in his records . . . '[58]

What of mankind? He

also was created from matter and is a type of the whole universe so that as that is ruled and regulated by God, so is he by the soul, not by a soul that is different from God or exists of itself, but one which is subject to and dependent upon God, is inspired, fostered, ruled and fed by God, consisting of the Spirit of God; He *is*. the love which is commanded of us.[59]

Zwingli then proceeds to deny the reality of secondary causes in nature, and also in the cause of human actions. 'Whatever means and instruments, therefore, are called causes, are not properly so called, but by metonymy, that is, derivatively from that one first cause of all that is.'[60] God gives mankind his law, which is the will and nature of Deity; but because he is the Supreme Creator, no one being above him, what is law to us is not law to God. 'He is above the law, we are under the law.'[61]

Zwingli here clearly exemplifies the a priori theologian who attempts to deduce a Christian metaphysic about the nature of God and the creation, the law, the nature of sin and so on, from a doctrine of God as the Supreme Being that has been gained from a philosophical conglomerate extracted from Plato, Pythagoras, and others, and not by induction from Scripture. Yet it should be noted that not even Zwingli attempts to deduce the whole of Christian theology from the idea of a supreme being. Nevertheless his method stands in sharp contrast to Calvin's, who at every point believes that his doctrine of providence is taken from and shaped by Scripture. Calvin's arguments are intended to preserve the contours of this biblical view and nothing more.

This difference is starkly illustrated by their respective attitudes to the distinction between primary and secondary causes. As we have seen, Calvin (with the aid of the scholastics) defends that distinction because he believes it preserves the biblical testimony that God is both holy and the willing permitter of sinful actions. But in Zwingli's case, God's power must, for a priori reasons, be so supreme that the idea of there being any distinct causal agency apart from his disappears altogether.

Calvin and Zwingli each aim to establish the same conclusion; namely, that God decrees every event that comes to pass. But whereas Zwingli argues this by deduction from divine sovereignty abstractly considered and so is unable to maintain the distinction between primary and secondary causes, Calvin keeps this distinction while frankly recognizing his inability at present

---

[58] *On Providence and Other Essays*, 151.

[59] *On Providence and Other Essays*, 154.

[60] *On Providence and Other Essays*, 155.

[61] *On Providence and Other Essays*, 169.

to prove that these really are two kinds of causation operating at different ontological levels. Perhaps Calvin was referring to Zwingli's sermon on providence when, corresponding with Johann Heinrich Bullinger in 1552, he said:

Indeed I was astounded, on finding from your letter, that the kind of teaching which I employ is displeasing to many good men, just as Jerome [Bolsec] is offended by that of Zwingli. Wherein, I beseech you, lies the similarity? For Zwingli's book, to speak confidentially, is crammed with such knotty paradoxes, as to be very different, indeed, in point of moderation, from what I hold. You are wrong in inferring that I have promised a new work, in which I undertake to demonstrate that God is not the author of sin.[62]

If anyone among the Reformers can be said to have developed a doctrine of providence/predestination in axiomatic fashion and in an a priori and abstract way, then Zwingli is a more likely candidate for this dubious honour than is John Calvin.

WAS CALVIN A DETERMINIST?

One way to approach an answer to this question is to ask; what account of human choice provides what is necessary for what Calvin wants to say about human responsibility? In the *Institutes* Calvin emphasizes that any account of providence has to preserve a twofold sense of human responsibility. In the first of these Calvin, following Augustine, has in mind ancient views of fate. Providence is not fate, and does not absolve us from planning in an intelligent means–end way for the future and for our own place in it. Some of Calvin's language suggests a strong view of the power of human agency.

For he who has set the limits to our life has at the same time entrusted to us its care; he has provided means and helps to preserve it; he has also made us able to foresee dangers; that they may not overwhelm us unaware, he has offered precautions and remedies. Now it is very clear what our duty is: thus, if the Lord has committed to us the protection of our life, our duty is to protect it; if he offers helps, to use them; if he forewarns us of dangers, not to plunge headlong; if he makes remedies available, not to neglect them.[63]

We are not fated to do what we do, willy-nilly. But the course of our lives is largely the result of outcomes that result from planning and deliberation. And secondly, men and women are responsible for their actions that are the outcome of evil inclinations.

---

[62] John Calvin, *Letters*, ed. Jules Bonnet, in *Selected Works of John Calvin*, v., 333–4. See also the reference in *Inst.* III. 21. 1 to 'certain men not otherwise bad', that has been reckoned to refer to Zwingli.

[63] *Inst.* I. 17. 4.

Bearing in mind this strong emphasis upon human responsibility there are in principle two ways forward for Calvin. To affirm whatever theory of human action he believes to be necessary for responsibility in these senses, perhaps a version of indeterministic freedom. Such an appeal to free will might be supported by the consideration that immediately before launching into a discussion of providence he has concluded[64] that Adam sinned by the exercise of his free will. If Calvin took this strategy he would then have to attempt to reconcile such a view of freedom with his view of the meticulousness of providence, and there is no evidence of this in his *A Defence of the Secret Providence of God* or elsewhere in his treatment of providence. But in fact there is a good deal of circumstantial evidence that Calvin favoured an Aristotelian account of human responsibility based on the criteria of freedom from compulsion and action done with the awareness of the circumstances. Hence Calvin's focus on freedom as the absence of compulsion which we shall consider in Chapter 6.

The alternative strategy is not to opt for a theory of indeterministic freedom, but rather to emphasize the mysteriousness of the arrangement whereby God exercises particular providence over all the actions of men and women and yet these actions are not fated to take place but rather men and women, beginning with Adam and Eve, are responsible for their actions, and particularly for their evil actions. This is the strategy that Calvin favours. For Calvin is convinced that his view of providence is scriptural, and that it is of great importance, thus he takes it to the centre of the stage. In other words, Calvin does not 'suspend' his account of providence in order to make a space for indeterministic human freedom. And in any case, there are other reasons that Calvin has for not going down this route. We shall see that this provisional conclusion is borne out in Chapter 6 when we consider Calvin's views on free will.

So Calvin's views of providence (and of course of predestination) clearly tend towards determinism. Is Calvin in fact a determinist? In responding to this question I will not attempt to offer a definitive answer to it. Instead, I will offer an answer to the related question: If Calvin's views tend towards determinism, what kind of determinism would this be? Approaching this issue in this way should raise the level of debate. Given the varieties of determinism, simply to label Calvin a determinist or to refuse him the label is not very enlightening.

Modern discussion of determinism concerning human action is heavily influenced by science. This results in determinism being regarded as a reductionist thesis, part of a naturalistic or physicalistic monism, an account

---

[64] *Inst.* I. 15. 8.

of things in terms of neuro-physiology or of genetic evolution by natural selection. Most would agree that it would be anachronistic to attribute such views to Calvin, although some may be inclined to say that Calvin's emphasis on the all-embracing divine decree has a similar reductionistic, flattening effect. Just as a modern naturalist might say that thoughts, intentions and desires are nothing other than neural discharges, so (it might be thought) what Calvin holds is that thoughts, intentions, and desires are nothing but God's activity.

But of course Calvin is not an occasionalist, as we have seen. Whatever the theoretical difficulties of holding to two sets of necessary and sufficient causal conditions for the occurrence of some event, conditions of the primary cause, God, and of the relevant secondary causes, his clear commitment to secondary or 'inferior' causation implies that he does not think that God is the only causal agent. The activities of secondary causal agents may be *due to* the activity of God, their causal powers may be endowed and upheld by God, but that's a different matter.

And though Calvin does appeal to the mystery, the wonder and ineffability[65] of the fact that God's providence extends over all and yet men and women are not fated and are responsible for their actions, he does not *only* appeal to this. First, as we have seen, he holds that there are different orders of being. God has created the inanimate world, non-human animals, mankind, and the angels. It is characteristic of those orders that are endowed with will that the will is by definition non-coercible. And as we shall see in the next two chapters, Calvin frequently distinguishes acting freely from acting under coercion, although even when discussing free will he does not enter into much discussion of the complexities and subtleties of voluntary action or the variety of ways in which action may be coerced. For Calvin mankind, even though fallen, possesses reason, and although we are like the animals in certain respects, in other respects we differ from them. Of course, the way in which the movements of leaves blowing in the wind, or the wanderings of animals, are determined is different from the way in which the will is determined, even if it is. The will is determined 'from the front', by the agent's beliefs about what the world is like and is going to be like, as well as by his desires, and especially by his intentions to change the world in certain respects, or not to change it.

Further, as we saw earlier Calvin thinks that by appealing to various levels of agency, to man, to Satan, and to God, he is able to reject arguments of the form: since God has willed an evil, those who do the evil are excused from responsibility for it. He makes a particularly scathing application of this

---

[65] *Inst.* 1. 18. 3.

argument in his writings against the Libertines, as we shall shortly see. In such passages Calvin's emphasis is not on God causing evil, nor on planting evil, but on him 'finding' it, and on using what he finds for his own holy ends. In other words Calvin seems in passages such as this to attribute intrinsic powers to the various levels of agency, powers which agents at a higher level may utilize but which in doing so they do not obliterate.

The appeal to different levels is not only non-reductionist in Calvin's way of thinking, it also seems to be hierarchical, although Calvin does not spell this out explicitly as far as I am aware. Perhaps it appears so obvious that he does not see the need to. God, Satan, and mankind are on different levels not only in that Satan is employed in the 'Lord's work', and Job is employed in Satan's work, but in the further sense that the reverse cannot happen. Job can use neither Satan nor God, nor can Satan use God. This is not for moral reasons, but it seems to have a basis in the nature of things. It is an aspect of what might be called Calvin's *hierarchical essentialism*. This reinforces the impression that Calvin's determinism is non-reductionist.

So Calvin's determinism, if that is what it is, is pluralistic rather than monistic and reductionistic. God's providence meticulously upholds and governs creatures of various kinds, each capable of producing different kinds of secondary causes. In this sense, God 'respects' the structures and the powers of what he has created.

The other way in which Calvin's thought is resistant to the idea of a determinism that 'flattens' everything because of the all-encompassing divine decree is in his accepting the distinction, which he finds in Augustine, between what God does and what he permits. As we have noted from our discussion of his views of providence, acceptance of this distinction must almost be wrung from him. His disinclination to invoke the distinction between what God wills and what he permits has partly to do with his concern about potential misunderstandings of permission. But it has also to do with his sense that the whole human race is under divine judgement because of their sin, and thus very many evils can be interpreted in terms either of divine retributive punishment or of fatherly chastisement. Yet not all evils, and certainly not the first human evil, the fall into sin, can be so interpreted.

Because the divine decree is the decree of an intelligent being and not the determinism of impersonal forces, God can take up distinct intentional stances with respect to different kinds of occurrences. So God decrees to bring about specific things while he decrees to permit others. Nonetheless, his permission is a willing permission, and so it is causally sufficient for the occurrence of what he willingly permits; and yet God is not the author of sin, especially not in the sense that in permitting evil his desires and intentions are themselves evil.

All of this reminds us that insofar as Calvin is a determinist as a result of holding his view of providence, he does not avow determinism, any more than he avows providence, for theoretical reasons. Calvin does not adopt his view of meticulous providence because he thinks that it solves philosophical problems. Undoubtedly, his doctrine of primary and secondary causes (taken from the medieval tradition) and his distinction between doing and willingly permitting (taken from Augustine) involve theoretical, philosophical difficulties. Calvin acknowledges as much when he stresses the mysterious character of these doctrines. Yet he adopts these views with their attendant difficulties because he believes that other views involve an even greater difficulty; namely, the difficulty of not doing as much justice to the scriptural data as his own view.

Whether Calvin thinks that appeal to a hierarchy of agents, and his utilizing of the distinction between doing and willingly permitting, is sufficient to *explain* God's relation to sin, is doubtful. One reason to doubt this is that, as mentioned earlier, Calvin frequently appeals to the 'modesty and sobriety' of his immediate readership to ward off what he regards as invalid inferences, inferences of both a theoretical and a practical kind. If someone draws the inference that because he is an instrument of divine providence then he is not to be blamed for his evil Calvin regards this as a serious mistake not because he can provide a convincing argument to the contrary, but (as, he believes, his Christian readers will readily concur) such a proposal is immodest. Why should someone think of making it except to further express and to safeguard their wickedness?[66] To objections of a more theoretical kind that don't express such an antinomian tendency but focus instead on Calvin's failure to demonstrate his position, he would I suspect be more accommodating. But because he is ultimately concerned to foster the correct practical religious responses to the doctrine of providence rather than offer an explanation of it, the fact is that he is less interested in the theoretical issues. His confidence in his position does not arise from a belief that he has explained it, or answered all objections to it, but because he is persuaded that this is what Scripture teaches.

For our wisdom ought to be nothing else than to embrace with humble teachableness, and at least without finding fault, whatever is taught in Sacred Scripture. Those who too insolently scoff, even though it is clear enough that they are prating against God, are not worthy of a longer refutation.[67]

Here as elsewhere, Calvin's first aim is *persuasio* rather than *demonstratio*.

---

[66] See the objection Calvin considers in *Inst.* 1. 17. 5 and his reply in 1. 17. 6.

[67] *Inst.* 1. 18. 4.

DETERMINISM AND THE LIBERTINES

Calvin, like medieval theologians such as Aquinas, thinks in terms of a hierarchy of created causal powers, and particularly in terms of a class of beings who have intelligence, foresight, will, and opportunity to act, such as angels and those created in God's image. Agents with such powers do not act with necessity; they have the power of choice. Further evidence that some at least of the implications of 'determinism' used in the modern sense may be avoided if one thinks of such a non-reducible ontological hierarchy can be found in Calvin's reaction to some of the teachings of the Libertine sects, and in particular to their pantheism. This pantheism, at least as Calvin understands it, does have an unwelcome, reductionist effect. Whereas with at least some versions of physicalism every human action is nothing but physical motion, for the pantheist every human action is identical with the action of God. If physicalist reductionism is a downwards reduction, then pantheistic reduction offers an upwards reduction. So it obliterates the distinction between divine and human action, since every action is divine. This at least is how Calvin understood it.

After creating a single spirit among themselves, by means of which they destroy the nature of both the angels of heaven and the devils in hell, as well as human souls, the Libertines maintain that this single spirit constitutes everything. By this they do not mean what the Scripture means when it says that at the same time all creatures subsist in Him, are equally guided by Him, are subject to His providence, and serve His will, each according to its order. But they mean that everything in the world must be seen directly as his doing.[68]

The argument is that if there is only one agency, namely God's, then if that agency is good then those apparent agencies that are apparently evil are not in fact either agencies or evil. This is why Calvin goes on to say that those who uphold such teaching 'cast aside every distinction between good and evil'. The 'libertine' implications of such a doctrine are obvious enough. Alternatively, of course, the teaching makes God the author of sin, since if there are evil acts and God is the only agent then he must be evil. This line of argument shows how crucial for Calvin (and for the medievals) is the distinction between primary and secondary causation in vindicating God from the charge of being the author of sin. For, having upheld his characteristic view that whatever comes to pass does so by the will of God, Calvin continues:

---

[68] John Calvin, *Treatises Against the Anabaptists and Against the Libertines*, trans. and ed. B. W. Farley (Grand Rapids, Mich.: Baker, 1982), 238.

Satan and evildoers are not so effectively the instruments of God that they do not also act in their own behalf. For we must not suppose that God works in an iniquitous man as if he were a stone or a piece of wood, but He uses him as a thinking creature, according to the quality of his nature which He has given him. Thus when we say that God works in evil doers, that does not prevent them from working also in their own behalf.[69]

Calvin, at least, seems to think that this distinction is logically sufficient for this purpose, at least where the secondary causation in question is that of deliberative, intelligent, and unconstrained human action. And Calvin's use of this argument also indicates further evidence of what his likely reaction would be to any form of occasionalism even though he never seems to discuss it. Similarly, if, as has been suggested, one element in libertinism is Averroes' view of the universal intellect, then Calvin's opinion of this view is made abundantly clear.

Calvin has another argument against the Libertines that has to do with levels of intentionality, again echoing his earlier treatment of providence.

For the wicked man is motivated either by his avarice, or his ambition, or envy, or cruelty to do what he does, and he disregards any other end. Consequently, according to the root which motivates his heart and the end toward which he strives, his work is qualified and with good reason is judged bad.

But God's intention is completely different. For His aim is to exercise His justice for the salvation and preservation of good, to pour out His goodness and grace on His faithful, and to chastise those who need it. Hence that is how we ought to distinguish between God and men; by separating in the same work His justice, His goodness and His judgment from the evil of both the devil and the ungodly.[70]

Summing up the discussion of determinism in the last two sections of this chapter, I have argued that, at least in the context of Calvin's discussion of providence, there is reason to be cautious, and guarded, in describing Calvin as an unqualified determinist, though his views are certainly consistent with some versions of determinism. However, Calvin's anthropology may provide us with further evidence which would lead us to be less guarded in ranking Calvin among the determinists. It is to his anthropology that we now turn.

---

[69] *Against the Libertines*, 245.

[70] *Against the Libertines*, 246. Peter Martyr Vermigli concurs. 'God permits either willingly or unwillingly; certainly not unwillingly, for that would mean with regret, so that there would be a power greater than himself. If he consents with his will, permission is a kind of will. But you ask: if he wills at all, why does he forbid it? On the other hand I would inquire: if he did not desire it, how does it happen? For the will of God is invincible.' Scholium on 2 Sam. 16, *The Peter Martyr Library*, vol. 4: *The Philosophical Works*, trans. Joseph C. McClelland, 235.

5

The Soul

IN this chapter and the next we turn away, for the time being, from Calvin's idea of God—his metaphysics of theism—to consider some of the elements of his anthropology as these are found in the *Institutes*, particularly in book I, chapter 15, where he discusses human nature as created, and book II, chapter 2, where he treats fallen human nature. My ultimate aim in this chapter is to frame answers to the questions, 'Did Calvin think that the fall deprived mankind of reason and will?' and 'If not, in what sense do reason and will remain in the fallen?' Answering these questions will allow us to clarify Calvin's conceptions of the human person and of human nature and to estimate how important fallenness was for his epistemology. The next chapter will consider the idea of free will in greater detail. But first I shall make some more general remarks on Calvin's attitude to the soul's immortality.

THE IMMORTALITY OF THE SOUL

As we saw when discussing Calvin's Christology, Calvin is a substance dualist. He thought that among the philosophers only Plato had the right idea, linking the soul to the image of God and affirming its immortality. Almost all the other philosophers 'so attach the soul's powers and faculties to the present life that they leave nothing to it outside the body'.[1] The soul is an 'incorporeal substance', whose proper function is not only to animate the body but also to rule human life with respect to our duties both to other human beings and to God. Calvin's commitment to the idea of the 'seed of religion' (see below, Chapter 8) commits him to a doctrine of God-implanted innate ideas or innate tendencies. To act in accordance with these innate tendencies (insofar as they remain uncorrupted) is to act with reason. Calvin offers a brief definition of the soul: 'I understand by the term "soul" an immortal yet created essence.'[2] The endowments of the human mind proclaim that something divine has been engraved on it. The soul's immortality is conferred upon it by God who, following 1 Timothy 6: 15–16, is the only one

---

[1] *Inst.* I. 15. 6.   [2] *Inst.* I. 15. 1.

who has immortality properly or inherently. There is an interesting, brief discussion of this in his treatise on the *Bondage and Liberation of the Will*:

> ... we do not allow either that the soul is immortal of itself. Indeed Paul also teaches the same when he ascribes immortality to God alone. But we do not on that account acknowledge that the soul is by nature mortal, since we judge nature not from the initial character of its essence but from the permanent condition which God has imparted to his creatures. So although man had been created with the intention that he should never experience death or corruption, he brought death upon himself by his own fault. So when the apostle argues about the origin of death he does not ascribe it to nature but to sin. Accordingly, to have been free from the necessity to die was the wholeness of [man's] nature, but his present subjection to the judgment of death is a disease. This is the wholesome and simple philosophy which is violently overturned by those wandering, fleeting speculations of Pighius.[3]

Although liability to death may seem to be inconsistent with the soul's immortality, it is not in fact inconsistent because such immortality is a 'permanent condition' imparted by God to his creation that the body's death does not alter or negate.

It is not clear from the brief definition of the soul that Calvin provides in the *Institutes* whether or not he holds that reason can prove the soul's immortality, or whether reason by itself would lead us to conclude that the soul is not immortal and we believe that the soul is immortal only because it is revealed. The latter suggestion is probably too strong, given Calvin's sympathy with Plato at this point. He certainly offers arguments for the soul's immortality that do not depend upon divine revelation. For example, he thinks that the operation of the conscience

> is an undoubted sign of the immortal spirit. For how could a motion without essence penetrate to God's judgment seat, and inflict itself with dread at its own guilt? For the body is not affected by the fear of spiritual punishment, which falls upon the soul only; from this it follows that the soul is endowed with essence. Now the very knowledge of God sufficiently proves that souls, which transcend the world, are immortal, for no transient energy could penetrate to the fountain of life.[4]

The argument here appears to be: by the operation of conscience we have a sense of our guilt before God, which involves the knowledge of God. The source of such knowledge cannot be the body but must be the soul. So the soul is distinct from the body (i.e. it has 'essence'). And only what is not transient—that is, what once existing will not cease to exist—can have such knowledge. This argument's gaps are obvious enough. More interesting is whether Calvin sees such an argument as having premisses that do or do not

---

[3] *The Bondage and Liberation of the Will*, ed. A. N. S. Lane, trans. G. I. Davies (Grand Rapids, Mich.: Baker, 1996), 185.   [4] *Inst.* I. 15. 2.

depend upon Scripture. It is not very clear. At first sight, it seems that Calvin is simply appealing to the *sensus divinitatis*—to what later on, in Chapter 8, will be referred to as its 'moral component'. For Calvin is appealing to data that he finds in 'secular writers'.[5] But perhaps not; perhaps he is offering a theological interpretation of the data presented by the *sensus*, an interpretation that he believes is provided by Scripture.

In addition to this argument, Calvin refers to 'signs of divinity' and 'signs of immortality' in the soul, using these expressions interchangeably. The signs in question include the gifts and faculties of the soul, its 'nimbleness', the power of memory, human inventiveness, the soul's moral capacity, and the occurrence of dreams in sleep.[6] These gifts 'bear upon the face of them a divinity that does not allow itself readily to be hidden'.[7]

They [namely, 'men'] feel in many wonderful ways that God works in them; they are also taught, by the very use of these things, what a great variety of gifts they possess from his liberality. They are compelled to know—whether they will or not—that these are the signs of divinity; yet they conceal them within. Indeed, there is no need to go outside themselves, provided they do not, by claiming for themselves what has been given them from heaven, bury in the earth that which enlightens their minds to see God clearly.[8]

So there is sufficient evidence for an unprejudiced inquirer to conclude both that the soul has a 'divinity' and also that, presumably, it is on that account immortal.

Whatever Calvin thinks about what can and cannot now be proved about the soul by reason, he clearly affirms a platonized dualism, claiming that the soul dwells in the body 'as in a house',[9] a 'prison house'.[10] He also clearly has more confidence in the ability of some philosophers to reason to the soul's immortality than he has in their ability to reason to the form that that immortality will take in the post-mortem state; namely, in a resurrected body. 'It is difficult to believe that bodies, when consumed with rottenness, will at length be raised up in their season. Therefore, although many of the philosophers declared souls immortal, few approved the resurrection of the flesh.'[11]

Why is Calvin so committed to such dualism? This may be one theological area where Renaissance ideas, and especially the influence of Plato as mediated

[5] *Inst.* I. 15. 2.   [6] *Inst.* I. 15. 2.   [7] *Inst.* I. 5. 4.

[8] *Inst.* I. 5. 4.   [9] *Inst.* I. 15. 6.   [10] *Inst.* I. 15. 2.

[11] *Inst.* III. 25. 3. This reference to belief in the soul's immortality seems to be at odds with what Calvin says elsewhere about pagan views (e.g. *Inst.* I. 15. 6), that their interest in the soul is only with the present. Perhaps what Calvin means is that though many affirmed the soul's immortality they were nevertheless wholly preoccupied with this present phase of its life. At *Inst.* I. 15. 6 the 'many' is simply Plato ('hardly one, except Plato, has rightly affirmed its [the soul's] immortal substance').

through Augustine, dominate. He has little time for the Aristotelian view that the soul is the form of the body. Aquinas appropriated Aristotle's view, which then became the dominant outlook in the late medieval period and the baseline for all discussion. Where Calvin mentions this view, he does so only to dismiss it.

I take to task those given to fanciful subtleties who willingly drag forth in oblique fashion that frigid statement of Aristotle both to destroy the immortality of the soul and to deprive God of his right. For, since the soul has organic faculties, they by this pretext bind the soul to the body so that it may not subsist without it, and by praising nature they suppress God's name as far as they can.[12]

Behind this scathing reference to Aristotle there is a tradition of medieval debate as to whether Aristotle taught the soul's immortality or whether his views were compatible with the assertion of its immortality, as well as whether the soul's immortality could be established by reason, as a philosophical doctrine, or whether it was only derivable from divine revelation and was therefore an exclusively theological preserve. The need to have a view of human nature that manifestly entails the soul's immortality, however this is established, is clearly uppermost in Calvin's mind.[13]

We may glean a bit more about his attitude to reasoning about the soul from his early work *Psychopannychia*, written against Anabaptist ideas of soul sleep and soul death. There he argues that their positions are 'unsupported by reason and judgment'.[14] 'I will not hesitate to give a reason of my faith to all the good—not such a reason, perhaps, as may fully equip them both for defence and for carrying the war into the enemies' camp, but such a one as will not leave them altogether unarmed.'[15] Rather than attempt a rational proof of immortality, he argues from the key biblical idea that man was made in God's image. As God is a spirit so man, made in his image, is a spirit.[16] Whether or not Calvin thinks that it follows from this that consciousness is essential to the soul, he certainly holds that consciousness *is*

---

[12] *Inst.* 1. 5. 5. Calvin sometimes offers a more generalized condemnation not of Aristotle himself but of the excessive authority attributed to him. Thus he says that the Papists 'have not been afraid to give so great an authority to Aristotle, that the apostles and prophets were silent in their schools rather than he' (*Commentary on the Acts of the Apostles*, 17: 28).

[13] For an account of medieval approaches to death and resurrection see Marilyn McCord Adams, 'The Resurrection of the Body according to Three Medieval Aristotelians: Thomas Aquinas, John Duns Scotus, William Ockham', *Philosophical Topics* (1993).

[14] *Psychopannychia*, trans. Henry Beveridge, in *Selected Works of John Calvin* iii. 414. Although published in 1542, after the first edition of the *Institutes* (1536), the first version of *Psychopannychia* was written in 1534 but substantially recast. This earlier version is now lost. Calvin covers more or less the same ground in *Brief Instruction for Arming All the Good Faithful Against the Errors of the Common Sect of the Anabaptists* (1544), trans. B. W. Farley in *Treatises Against the Anabaptists and Against the Libertines*, ch. 6.

[15] *Psychopannychia*, 415.   [16] *Psychopannychia*, 424.

essential, so affirming the soul's sleep at death is equivalent to denying its continued existence. The perception of good and evil is also essential to the soul, at least the soul of a normal adult, and this perception survives the death of the body, and so death is not equivalent to the soul's annihilation.[17] As we have noted, Calvin emphasizes the soul's immortality by stressing in platonic fashion that the body is its prison; the soul's earthly condition is therefore a kind of fetter to it.[18] But while he does not here endeavour to prove the soul's immortality by reason, he certainly avails himself of platonic ideas, claiming, in a swipe against the Anabaptists, that the platonists 'certainly thought more purely and wisely on the subject than some amongst ourselves, who boast that they are the disciples of Christ'.[19]

Since the soul is immortal only in a derived and secondary sense, with the kind of immortality that God gives to a creature, it is as such subject to God's conserving agency. Man is 'supported by the kindness and power of God, since he alone has immortality, and . . . whatever life exists is from him'.[20] It is almost as if human immortality is a covenanted gift. So how does the soul's immortality differ from the continued existence of any other creaturely thing, since all creatures depend for their continued existence on God's conserving power? Calvin's answer might be that all that is needed for a soul's conservation is the divine will to sustain its existence, since, unlike a body in its fallen state, the soul does not suffer from a natural tendency to decay or dissolve.

THE SOUL'S FACULTIES

In the *Institutes* Calvin is somewhat ambivalent with respect to the value of philosophical discussions about the soul. On the one hand he characteristically wishes to avoid anything that is subtle or speculative, but on the other hand he does not think that philosophical discussions about the soul are worthless. Subtle questions are the province of the philosophers, yet they are not to be entirely repudiated.

But I leave it to the philosophers to discuss these faculties in their subtle way. For the upbuilding of godliness a simple definition [of the soul] will be enough for us. I, indeed, agree that the things they teach are true, not only enjoyable, but also profitable to learn, and skillfully assembled by them. And I do not forbid those who are desirous of learning to study them. Therefore I admit in the first place that there are five senses . . .[21]

---

[17] *Psychopannychia*, 453.

[18] *Psychopannychia*, 443.

[19] *Psychopannychia*, 420.

[20] *Psychopannychia*, 478.

[21] *Inst.* I. 15. 6. This underlines again Calvin's view that theology's importance does not imply that other sorts of study, such as philosophy, are worthless. So Arvin Vos's claim that Calvin 'rejects

Thus, despite his reservations about including philosophical discussion in the *Institutes*, he does nevertheless commit himself to certain philosophical conclusions. There are five senses. In addition, there is

fantasy, which distinguishes those things which have been apprehended by common sense; then reason, which embraces universal judgment; finally understanding, which in intent and quiet study contemplates what reason discursively ponders. Similarly, to understanding, reason, and fantasy (the three cognitive faculties of the soul) correspond three appetitive faculties: will, whose functions consist in striving after what understanding and reason present; the capacity for anger, which seizes upon what is offered to it by reason and fantasy; the capacity to desire inordinately, which apprehends what is set before it by fantasy and sense.[22]

This makes clear that despite his disavowal of a philosophical approach to the soul, Calvin endorses quite a complex picture of it; but he goes on to say that such complexity ought to be passed over in favour of a much simpler set of distinctions. He prefers a fairly simple account of the soul for a theological and practical reason—namely, the need to choose 'a division within the capacity of all'.[23] But he also has a deeper reason for dissenting from the philosophical view that reason is the faculty by which man governs himself properly—namely, such a view does not do justice to man's fallenness. The philosophers' optimistic view of the range of human powers proceeds from ignorance 'of the corruption of nature that originated from the penalty of man's defection'.[24] In other words, in Calvin's view 'the philosophers' have no true appreciation of the present depravity of human nature; they think that the present condition of mankind is the normal condition, whereas for Calvin it is radically abnormal. More to the point, they have a much rosier and more optimistic view of the soul's present powers than, Calvin believes, Scripture teaches.

Thus, according to Calvin, the philosophers characteristically account for moral conflict in the soul in terms of a clash between the senses, which incline to pleasure, and the understanding, which follows the good. The understanding is sometimes contemplative or theoretical, at other times active or practical. The appetite divides into will and concupiscence (that is, lust or excessive desire). Reason should govern the soul. When appetite follows reason, all is well; when appetite overthrows reason, the result is intemperance.[25] Philosophers regard the activity of both the senses and the understanding as 'normal', with moral failure put down to the clash between

philosophy as a whole' seems much too sweeping (*Aquinas, Calvin, and Contemporary Protestant Thought*, 122). Rather, he sees a division of labour and a difference of point of view and method between the philosopher and the theologian.

[22] *Inst.* I. 15. 6.   [23] *Inst.* I. 15. 6.   [24] *Inst.* I. 15. 7.   [25] *Inst.* I. 15. 6.

the two and nothing more. If appetite obeys the reason the result is virtuous action. But if it is subjected to the senses the result is vice. So conflict is not within the soul (as Calvin believes) but between the soul and what is baser, the bodily senses, as the will havers between the attractions of each. But the bodily senses can be subdued by the discipline of reason.[26] However, the idea that the choice between vices and virtues is within our power is too superficial an account for Calvin, as we shall see.

Calvin departed from this philosophical account both because he thought that the pagans were ignorant of the corruption of human nature[27] and because it is too complex. He prefers to think of the soul in terms that anyone can understand, simply as composed of understanding and will. The understanding distinguishes good from evil, what should be pursued and what should be avoided. The will endeavours to follow such proposed pursuits and avoidances.[28] But—and this qualification is the critical point as far as Calvin's relation to the philosophers is concerned—both understanding and will are corrupted by the Fall.

So, after a brief philosophical excursus in *Institutes* I. 15, Calvin settles for this simpler view of the human soul.[29] The understanding distinguishes between objects—that is, intentional objects—according to their worth; the will chooses and follows what the understanding approves of and rejects what it disapproves of. Thus the understanding leads and governs the soul, with the will following its judgement. (Calvin prefers the term 'will' to the philosophers' 'appetite'.) Sense is included in understanding. Does understanding include reason, for Calvin? Understanding in 'intent and quiet study contemplates what reason discursively ponders'.[30] Reason denotes the faculty which 'embraces universal judgment',[31] as well as the capacity to distinguish between good and evil.[32]

Endowment with reason and understanding distinguishes us from non-human animals.[33] Calvin affirms the tradition that sees humankind's being made in the image of God as our being given certain intellectual and moral endowments. He derides the Lutheran theologian Osiander's opinion that the image of God is to be found in the body (the body that was to be Christ's being the divine exemplar of all other human bodies) as well as in the soul. Calvin calls this view 'repugnant to all reason'.[34] We prove ourselves to be

---

[26] See Calvin's account of this conflict in *Inst.* II. 2. 2–3. One *locus classicus* of this view is Aristotle's account of what incontinence or weakness of will is in book VII of the *Nicomachean Ethics*. For a modern commentary see Sarah Broadie, *Ethics With Aristotle* (New York: Oxford University Press, 1991), ch. 5, who characterizes Aristotle's understanding of incontinence as 'giving in to physical appetite against one's better judgement' (268).

[27] *Inst.* I. 15. 7. [28] *Inst.* I. 15. 7. [29] *Inst.* I. 15. 7. [30] *Inst.* I. 15. 6.

[31] *Inst.* I. 15. 6. [32] *Inst.* II. 2. 12. [33] *Inst.* II. 1. 1. [34] *Inst.* I. 15. 3.

endowed with reason when we endeavour to approach God, but our reason is disturbed, often disagreeing with itself, due to its depravity.[35]

It is important to realize that, for Calvin, there is a sense in which the Fall has changed certain things and other things have remained the same. Before the Fall, man 'in his first condition excelled in these pre-eminent endowments, so that his reason, understanding, prudence, and judgment not only sufficed for the direction of his earthly life, but by them men mounted up even to God and eternal bliss'.[36] After the Fall, understanding and judgement remain, although in weakened and damaged states.

Since reason, therefore, by which man distinguishes between good and evil, and by which he understands and judges, is a natural gift, it could not be completely wiped out; but it was partly weakened and partly corrupted, so that its misshapen ruins appear.

For even though something of understanding and judgment remains as a residue along with the will, yet we shall not call a mind whole and sound that is both weak and plunged into deep darkness.

[I]n man's perverted and degenerate nature some sparks still gleam. These show him to be a rational being, differing from brute beasts, because he is endowed with understanding.[37]

The philosophers went astray because they 'were seeking in a ruin for a building, and in scattered fragments for a well-knit structure',[38] mistaking the abnormalities due to sin for the normal human condition and offering a superficial account of them.

By calling understanding 'a natural gift', Calvin means that it is part of the nature or essence of humanity, 'inseparable from man's nature',[39] and is such that it cannot disappear without our losing our nature and becoming bestial. Reason remains, as weakened but not obliterated, in two ways. First, not every human intention is depraved. Surprisingly, perhaps, Calvin does not subscribe to the view that all fallen actions proceed from an evil intention (although it must be borne in mind at this point that the *Institutes* is primarily a book addressed to Christians, to those whose natures have been regenerated): 'For we know all too well by experience how often we fall *despite our good intention*. Our reason is overwhelmed by so many forms of deceptions, is subject to so many errors, dashes against so many obstacles, is caught in so many difficulties, that it is far from directing us aright.'[40] There are some good intentions, but they are rendered inoperative by other factors. If, however, as this passage makes clear, certain things have remained despite

---

[35] *Inst.* I. 15. 6.   [36] *Inst.* I. 15. 8.

[37] *Inst.* II. 2. 12. I am quoting these passages out of sequence.   [38] *Inst.* I. 15. 8.

[39] *Inst.* II. 2. 12.   [40] *Inst.* II. 2. 25; my emphasis.

the Fall, certain things have also changed; reason is now partly weakened and partly corrupted. Reason once motivated unfallen humanity and now motivates the regenerate elect to the good (although it does not motivate the regenerate elect in all their actions, due to the sin remaining in them). Rather it motivates the unregenerate to evil, as a result of its corruption and weakness. Similarly, fallen man retains his will, though it too is depraved. One of the ways in which man is distinguished from non-human animals is that even in fallen human nature there is evidence of the desire to search out the truth, indeed human nature is captivated by love of truth which in fallen human nature lapses into dullness and vanity. 'The lack of this endowment in brute animals proves their nature gross and irrational.'[41]

Further, the understanding and will remain more fully operative in connection with what Calvin calls 'earthly things' or 'things below'.

[T]here is one kind of understanding of earthly things; another of heavenly. I call 'earthly things' those which do not pertain to God or his Kingdom, to true justice, or to the blessedness of the future life; but which have their significance and relationship with regard to the present life and are, in a sense, confined within its bounds. I call 'heavenly things' the pure knowledge of God, the nature of true righteousness, and the mysteries of the Heavenly Kingdom. The first class includes government, household management, all mechanical skills, and the liberal arts. In the second are the knowledge of God and of his will, and the rule by which we conform our lives to it.[42]

Part of Calvin's case for human accountability to God is that some knowledge and understanding of the right remains in fallen human nature,[43] particularly knowledge of the Law's Second Table.[44] (We shall look at this matter more closely in Chapter 12.) This gives Calvin the resources to develop a theory of agency that is distinctively human, even though mankind is fallen and therefore, in a sense, not fully or properly human.

This is Calvin's broad picture of human nature as fallen. Now I shall elaborate this picture, filling in some of its details, by arguing that three modern Calvin commentators have misunderstood him at various points. Each misinterpretation focuses on some features of the soul that Calvin thinks have arisen as a result of the Fall.

PINK ON CALVIN'S VIEW OF PRACTICAL REASON

Thomas Pink considers Calvin's account of the fallen self. As part of a broader survey of the obliteration of practical reason in the development of

---

[41] *Inst.* II. 2. 12.

[42] *Inst.* II. 2. 13. This connects with the themes of Calvin's understanding of the law, of common grace, and of 'civic righteousness'.   [43] *Inst.* II. 2. 22.   [44] *Inst.* II. 2. 24.

modern moral philosophy, he claims that in Calvin we find an 'outright denial'[45] of our practical rationality and that this is characteristic of anti-Pelagianism generally.

According to Pink, we find such practical rationality in Aquinas,[46] who regards such reasoning as characteristically human. Non-rational animals are motivated by non-rational appetite. Human beings have a rational appetite, a capacity for making decisions and forming intentions, a capacity that misfires when we act irrationally. The will, as rational appetite, chooses what practical reason apprehends as good. By contrast, according to Pink:

> For Calvin, it wasn't simply that the will was a rational capacity that was damaged, so that our will no longer reliably followed our reason. The reason of fallen humanity had, for Calvin, no motivational power whatsoever. Our rational judgments about how we should act no longer had any effect whatsoever on what actions we were motivated to perform. The human will was no longer a rational appetite at all.[47]

Consequently, Calvin developed an account of fallen agency as 'animal agency' that is no longer a rational appetite at all, no longer the exercise of a distinctive practical rationality.[48]

Pink argues that there is a historically discernible shift from what he calls practical-reason-based theories of human agency like Aquinas's to motivation-based theories of agency like Hobbes's and much modern action-theory. This shift involves the eclipse of belief in what Pink calls second-order agency, which is our capacity to remain motivated to perform particular first-order actions at a later date.[49] He thinks Calvin shares in this eclipse,[50] as evidenced by this passage from the *Institutes*:

> Since reason, therefore, by which man distinguishes between good and evil, and by which he understands and judges, is a natural gift, it could not be completely wiped out; but it was partly weakened and partly corrupted, so that its misshapen ruins appear. John speaks in this sense: 'The light still shines in the darkness, but the darkness comprehends it not' [John 1: 5]. In these words both facts are clearly expressed. First, in man's perverted and degenerate nature some sparks still gleam. These show him to be a rational being, differing from brute beasts, because he is endowed with understanding. Yet, secondly, they show this light choked with dense ignorance, so that it cannot come forth effectively.
>
> Similarly the will, because it is inseparable from man's nature, did not perish, but was so bound to wicked desires that it cannot strive after the right.[51]

---

[45] 'Reason and Agency', *Proceedings of the Aristotelian Society* (1996–7), 276.

[46] *Summa Theologiae*, 1a, 2. 6. 1.

[47] 'Reason and Agency', 276.

[48] 'Reason and Agency', 276.

[49] 'Reason and Agency', 268.

[50] 'Reason and Agency', 269 n. 13.

[51] *Inst.* II. 2. 12.

Pink believes that Calvin did not entirely abandon a practical-reason-based conception of human agency but that it is a conception that no longer has application, since the Fall has totally removed practical reason's motivational power.[52] Thus Pink is arguing, not that Calvin claims that practical reason has vanished from humanity but that the Fall has rendered it completely ineffective. Hence his word 'eclipsed'. The Fall has not resulted in a de-humanization of the race, so that it no longer possesses an essential feature of humanness—namely, practical rationality; humanity still possesses that feature, but it is inoperative.

Calvin's opening remarks of *Institutes* II. 2. 1. suggest that this may not be quite right. Even if it is true that no good thing remains in man's power, and that 'he is hedged about on all sides by most miserable necessity',[53] according to Calvin he should nonetheless 'be instructed to aspire to a good of which he is empty, to a freedom of which he has been deprived'. The capacity to receive instruction with regard to choices seems to be one aspect of such an aspiration. Calvin goes on to say that in fallen mankind 'something of understanding and judgment remains as a residue along with the will'.[54] Reason was not completely wiped out but it was partly weakened and partly corrupted, so that its misshapen ruins appear. 'In man's perverted and degenerate nature some sparks still gleam. These show him to be a rational being, differing from brute beasts, because he is endowed with understanding.'[55] 'We see implanted in human nature some sort of desire to search out the truth to which man would not at all aspire if he had not already savoured it. Human understanding then possesses some power of perception, since it is by nature captivated by love of truth. The lack of this endowment in brute animals proves their nature gross and irrational.'[56]

As we have noted, Calvin also makes a significant distinction between what he calls 'things below' or 'earthly things' and 'things above' or 'heavenly things'. So in the arrangement of this life no man is without the light of reason, and we reason about and motivate ourselves with regard to 'earthly things'. We shall see that while Pink's view of Calvin may be plausible in the case of heavenly things, it is less plausible in the case of the earthly.

Yet Pink's interpretation seems to be strengthened by what Calvin says in *Institutes* II. 2. 26, where he appears to be arguing that fallen man is no longer motivated by reason but by desire:

Now we must examine the will, upon which freedom of decision especially depends; for we have already seen that choice belongs to the sphere of the will rather than to that of the understanding. To begin with, the philosophers teach that all things seek

---

[52] 'Reason and Agency', 277.   [53] *Inst.* II. 2. 1.   [54] *Inst.* II. 2. 12.

[55] *Inst.* II. 2. 12.   [56] *Inst.* II. 2. 12.

good through a natural instinct, and this view is received with general consent. But that we may not suppose this doctrine to have anything to do with the uprightness of the human will, let us observe that the power of free choice is not to be sought in such an appetite, which arises from inclination of nature rather than from deliberation of mind. Even the Schoolmen admit that free will is active only when the reason considers alternative possibilities. By this they mean that the object of the appetite must be amenable to choice, and deliberation must go before to open the way to choice. And actually, if you consider the character of this natural desire of good in man, you will find that he has it in common with animals. For they also desire their own well-being; and when some sort of good that can move their sense appears, they follow it. But man does not choose by reason and pursue with zeal what is truly good for himself according to the excellence of his immortal nature; nor does he use his reason in deliberation or bend his mind to it. Rather, like an animal he follows the inclination of his nature, without reason, without deliberation. Therefore whether or not man is impelled to seek after good by an impulse of nature has no bearing upon freedom of the will. This instead is required: that he discern good by right reason; that knowing it he choose it; that having chosen it he follow it.[57]

First, we must note that the passage refers to 'heavenly things'. Nevertheless it looks like a straight denial of the claim that reason continues to motivate the fallen. Of course Calvin would not deny that sometimes human beings behave like animals, any more than Aquinas would. But on closer inspection Calvin is saying more than that. I think Calvin is arguing as follows:

1. The philosophers teach that all things seek good through a natural instinct. ('Seeking good' here means following after what a person believes furthers his own well-being and flourishing, whether or not what he seeks will actually do so. It may be that people follow 'some sort of good' without following the true good for themselves, that good which makes for a thing's own preservation, well-being, and flourishing.) But given that all things seek good in this fashion, by a natural instinct or inclination of nature, it does not follow that humans are in all respects like animals in doing so.
2. But free choice is a matter of mental deliberation, not of instinct, as even the Schoolmen agree.
3. Therefore, in creatures possessed of free choice the object of appetite is amenable to choice.
4. In common with other animals, man has an instinct for good.
5. But, because he has lost free will, man, though he may exercise rational choices with regard to 'heavenly things', does not follow through these choices. Calvin allows for the possibility that a person may discern good by right reason but not choose it nor follow it because of the disabling effects of sin.
6. Rather, regarding 'heavenly things' he now (like an animal) follows only instinct, unreflectively.

[57] *Inst.* II. 2. 26.

As we have seen, Calvin repeatedly maintains that fallen mankind *differs* from the beasts. When focusing on the difference he normally maintains that the Fall did not annihilate human nature. 'We see among all mankind that reason is proper to our nature; it distinguishes us from brute beasts, just as they by possessing feeling differ from inanimate things.'[58] In this 'we see . . . some remaining traces of the image of God, which distinguish the entire human race from the other creatures'.[59] Thus the passage from *Institutes* II. 2. 26 is concerned with similarity, not identity.

I offer two interpretations of what Calvin is saying at *Institutes* II. 2. 26. The first is more speculative and less securely based in what Calvin explicitly says, although it is incontrovertibly Calvinian in spirit. The second interpretation, consistent with the first, is more straightforward.

First, Calvin may be arguing that, having lost free will, man has no uncorrupted reason to deliberate between good and evil, as unfallen mankind could, but instead follows his natural inclinations like animals follow instinct, without deliberation. Yet we need to remember that, as Calvin sees things, the essential choice of rational appetite was already made by Adam—and by us in Adam. Consequently our present appetites are not, like animal appetites, appetites that preclude choice; rather, they are already chosen appetites, or appetites arising as a consequence of a choice. Yet since that choice (Calvin believes) was irrational or flew in the face of reason, it, and whatever follows from it, was not, and is not, a legitimate expression of a rational appetite. That choice is humanly irrecoverable, nothing we can do can undo it now, unless and until the power to choose the good is renewed by divine grace. So while fallen humans are like animals in following their appetites, they are also unlike the animals because their appetites are never chosen by them. Our present appetites have been chosen, irrevocably so, by us in Adam, and are irrecoverably what they are except for the intervention of divine grace.

Thus human reason, far from having no motivational power whatsoever, had and continues to have very great motivational power—motivational power to evil as a result of the primal choice. We are all motivated to perform our actions as a result of a primal irrational judgement; having decided by the abuse of reason to go through one door, the key to the other door has been taken off its key ring until it is put back on by God's grace. Human agency is still, for all Calvin may appear to say to the contrary, the exercise of a distinctive practical rationality; or, rather, it is the result of a practical rationality that was exercised and that we are now stuck with.

Putting this point in Pink's terminology, we could say that the Fall has resulted in our being motivated to do only evil actions, at least as regards

---

[58] *Inst.* II. 2. 17.   [59] *Inst.* II. 2. 17.

'heavenly things'; that is, Adam's choice is the primeval prior decision, a deliberate act of his reason that has left the race motivated to perform first-order evil acts unless and until this primeval decision is reversed by divine grace.

Secondly, we must bear in mind the restricted reference of the II. 2. 26 passage, a reference that is nonetheless of central importance for Calvin. He is clearly allowing that practical rationality in the sense of deliberation between alternatives still obtains in the case of what he calls 'things below'[60] and even, he says, the understanding 'is intelligent enough to taste something of things above, although it is more careless about investigating these'.[61]

In order to obtain a rounded picture of Calvin's position we must also attend to his statements on spiritual regeneration and on the nature of the knowledge of the 'heavenly things' from *Institutes* II. 2. 18 onwards. There Calvin both implies and says that human understanding is still present in the fallen race, as when he asserts that 'We must now analyze what human reason can discern with regard to God's Kingdom and to spiritual insight', thereby clearly implying the continued presence and activity of reason. Again, when he says that 'Human reason, therefore, neither approaches, nor strives toward, nor even takes a straight aim at, this truth: to understand who the true God is or what sort of God he wishes to be toward us',[62] he is harking back to his earlier discussion of human fallenness while making it clear that reason remains a human endowment that is active but in 'heavenly things' perversely and ignorantly so.

Institutes II. 2. 23–4 contains a particularly interesting passage where Calvin discusses and partly endorses Themistius' paraphrase of Aristotle[63] that the intellect understands that murder is evil, but when someone plots the death of an enemy he regards that particular murder as something good. The intellect lays down general principles that we often apply perversely in particular cases. Yet Calvin thinks that sometimes what is evil is done as evil, commenting that:

To my mind Aristotle has made a very shrewd distinction between incontinence and intemperance: 'Where incontinence reigns,' he says, 'the disturbed mental state or passion so deprives the mind of particular knowledge that it cannot mark the evil in its own misdeed which it generally discerns in like instances; when the perturbation subsides, repentance straightway returns. Intemperance, however, is not extinguished or shattered by the awareness of sin, but on the contrary, stubbornly persists in choosing its habitual evil.'[64]

---

[60] *Inst.* II. 2. 13. [61] *Inst.* II. 2. 13. [62] *Inst.* II. 2. 18.

[63] Themistius (*c.* AD 360) was one of the first commentators on Aristotle.

[64] *Inst.* II. 2. 23. The quotation is said by the editor to be from Aristotle's *Nicomachean Ethics* II. 1–3. 1145–7, but I have been unable to trace its exact source there.

Consequently,

> when you hear of a universal judgment discriminating between good and evil, do not consider it sound and whole in every respect. For if men's hearts have been imbued with the ability to distinguish just from unjust, solely that they should not pretend ignorance as an excuse, it is not at all a necessary consequence that truth should be discerned in individual instances. It is more than enough if their understanding extends so far that evasion becomes impossible for them, and they, convicted by the witness of their own conscience, begin even now to tremble at God's judgment seat.[65]

Such language suggests that nothing in Calvin's position requires him to dissent from Thomas Aquinas's model of agency, as described by Pink,[66] concerning whether we may deliberately get up in the morning! This is also true for the action-coordinating function of decisions, provided these are restricted to 'earthly things' in the case of the unregenerate, although they apply to both 'earthly' and 'heavenly' things in the case of the regenerate.

We might compare Calvin's position with what Immanuel Kant says in the opening paragraphs of *Religion Within the Limits of Reason Alone*, where he argues that the propensity to wickedness in human beings is a property of the will that belongs to it by nature. On the one hand, Kant wants to say that the disposition to adopt an evil maxim must be the result of free choice, but (abstracting from the idea of a historic Fall) not of a primeval free choice. On the other hand, he wants to say that such a disposition is part of human nature. It is a 'property of the will which belongs to it by nature (although actually the disposition is grounded in freedom)'.[67] A man, insofar as he is evil, acts out of evil maxims that are a part of his nature but that are also (in some strange way) chosen. For Calvin, by contrast, the evil maxims that human beings live arise out of a free choice made in time; a choice that, having once been made, cannot be made again or reversed apart from the freeing effects of divine grace.

According to Kant, man is evil *by nature*. That is, 'evil can be predicated of man as a species; not that such a quality can be inferred from the concept of his species (that is, of man in general)—for then it would be necessary'.[68] This parallels what Calvin says; it is not part of the essence of man that he is evil, but it is a feature of his (fallen) nature.

Summarizing, I have argued that Pink's case against Calvin, even on its bleakest interpretation, is not proven, since Calvin makes repeated distinctions between mankind and non-human animals, and ascribes reason to

---

[65] *Inst.* II. 2. 24. [66] 'Reason and Agency', 267.

[67] Immanuel Kant, *Religion Within the Limits of Reason Alone*, trans. T. M. Greene and H. H. Hudson (New York: Harper & Row, 1960), 21. [68] *Religion Within the Limits of Reason Alone*, 27.

fallen men and women. Secondly, even if this is discounted, Calvin's negative remarks about reason apply only to the non-regenerate, for in regenerate practical reason the reason-based power of deliberating over the good is restored. Calvin's negative remarks about reason apply in any case only to 'heavenly things' since with regard to 'earthly things' reason remains active even in fallenness and unregeneracy.

HOITENGA ON CALVIN'S CONTRADICTIONS

In chapter 2 of his *John Calvin and the Will*[69] Dewey Hoitenga claims that there is a basic inconsistency in Calvin (to which there is a parallel in Thomas Aquinas) between the 'intellectualist' account that he gives of unfallen humanity and the 'voluntarist' account that he gives of the Fall. In unfallen humanity the will was designed to follow the understanding and did in fact follow it, yet the Fall was nonetheless not caused by a defect in the understanding but by a defective will.

In fact, Hoitenga finds two inconsistencies: The first is that Calvin is an intellectualist on human nature as it was created, but a voluntarist on both its fallen and redeemed states.

Calvin forsakes his intellectualist account of our created state as soon as he describes the fall. He describes the fall, however, in the same chapter ([*Inst.*] 1. 15) in which he describes the created state. The result is that his intellectualist and voluntarist accounts of human nature as it was created occur in very close proximity to each other. Indeed, the inconsistency between them occurs within the one single chapter.[70]

Hoitenga quotes passages from *Institutes* 1. 15. 7 and 1. 15. 8 in support of Calvin's intellectualist account of the human mind as created and, from the very same place, his account of the Fall as attributable to an act of the will rather than an act of the intellect.

Therefore God provided man's soul with a mind, by which to distinguish good from evil, right from wrong; and, with the light of reason as guide, to distinguish what should be followed from what should be avoided. For this reason, the philosophers call this directing part τὸ ἡγεμονικόν. To this he joined will, under whose control is choice. Man in his first condition excelled in these pre-eminent endowments, so that his reason, understanding, prudence, and judgment not only sufficed for the direction of his earthly life, but by them men mounted up even to God and eternal bliss. Then was choice added, to direct the appetites and control all the organic motions, and thus make the will completely amenable to the guidance of the reason . . . Adam could have stood if he wished, seeing that he fell solely by his own will. But it was because his will was capable of being bent to one side or the other, and was not given the constancy to persevere, that he fell so easily. Yet his choice of good and evil was free, and not that alone, but the highest rectitude was in his mind and will, and all the organic parts were rightly composed to obedience, until in destroying himself he corrupted his own blessings.[71]

Hoitenga then claims that:

Calvin clearly undermines the intellectualist account he has just given, in the very same section. For he attributes the fall not to a failure of the intellect, but to the free choice of the will. That is, the will was free *not* 'always to be mindful of the bidding of the understanding' (to quote his earlier intellectualist language 1. 15. 7); *not* to be 'completely amenable to the guidance of reason' (1. 15. 8).[72]

The second inconsistency, a second conflict in his account of the will, is

a conflict between his description of the natural components or functions of the will as it was created and his description of these same components or functions in the fallen state.[73]

If we can provide a satisfactory explanation of the first inconsistency this will go a considerable way to providing an explanation of the second inconsistency.

Connecting this discussion with our previous discussion of Pink, Calvin's account of the dislocation due to the Fall is in respect of 'heavenly things'. So even if Hoitenga were correct in his account of Calvin, it would not necessarily apply to 'earthly things'. Calvin could, perfectly consistently, continue to offer an intellectualist account of mankind's relation to 'earthly things'.

Prima facie, one reason for thinking there is some way to establish the consistency of what Calvin is saying here—or, at least, that Calvin thought it was consistent—is the very rapidity of the alleged shift from intellectualism to voluntarism in Calvin's text. If this shift occurred in different books written by Calvin at widely separated times, then it might plausibly be supposed that any inconsistency might be explained by some change or development in Calvin's view. But the shift allegedly occurs over two paragraphs, written by a person of keen intelligence and in a work that was repeatedly revised for its successive editions. Were such a blatant inconsistency present, then we might think that either Calvin himself or one of his keen-eyed critics would have spotted it.

Is there an explanation for the apparent inconsistency? Yes. According to Calvin, the Fall is to be explained (insofar as it can be explained at all) by the disordering of the internal structure of mankind's created character. Following mankind's creation in the image of God, this structure was intellectualist in character. There would only be a contradiction of the sort that Hoitenga identifies if he could show that Calvin held that in unfallen humanity

---

[71] *Inst.* 1. 15. 8.　　　[72] *John Calvin and the Will*, 48–9.　　　[73] *John Calvin and the Will*, 69.

the will is *essentially* subordinated to the intellect. For then it would have been metaphysically impossible for intellectualism to be supplanted by voluntarism in the way that Calvin explains the Fall. But nothing suggests that Calvin held that intellectualism implies the intellect's essential superiority to the will. Rather, he claimed that the will is *normally* or *ideally* subject to the intellect, and that when there is a disruption of this normal order, as there was in the Fall (indeed, that was what the Fall was, for Calvin), human nature changes accidentally but not essentially. As Calvin says later on in the *Institutes*, mankind's corruption does not flow from nature, 'in order to indicate that it is an adventitious quality which comes upon man rather than a substantial property which has been implanted from the beginning'.[74]

The essential feature of human nature is that it has both intellectual and volitional components. As we saw in our discussion of Pink on practical rationality, for Calvin human nature retains its essence after the Fall, but there is a difference in that its components become disordered. Indeed, as we shall see in the next chapter, not only does Calvin hold that fallenness is an accidental or contingent aspect of human nature, he makes much of this fact in his polemic against Pighius. However, the basic question is not one of the subordination or superordination of each of a pair of faculties but of the respective roles played by faculties with inherently different capacities. For Calvin, the will was subordinate to the understanding as mankind was created, but it was, unlike the understanding, inherently unstable if left to itself. It *was* left to itself, and perversely and irrationally turned aside from its subordinate position.[75]

BRÜMMER ON CALVIN, BERNARD, AND THE WILL

In 'Calvin, Bernard and the Freedom of the Will'[76] Vincent Brümmer claims to have identified another inconsistency in Calvin's anthropology. He begins by pointing out that there are striking similarities between Bernard of

---

[74] *Inst.* II. 1. 11.

[75] For a similar explanation of Calvin's alleged inconsistency see Richard A. Muller, *The Unaccommodated Calvin*, 166. 'Under the terms of Calvin's ideal or philosophical definition, reason ought to announce the good and the will ought to follow the dictates of reason, albeit freely and of its own choice ... Reason itself, after the fall, only vaguely and indistinctly perceives the truth of God—like a distant lightning flash in the darkness, comments Calvin—and it never, of its own, either "approaches" or "strives toward" God ... Calvin thus moves toward a soteriological rather than a purely metaphysical or philosophical voluntarism.'

[76] *Religious Studies* (1994). See also Vincent Brümmer, 'On Not Confusing Necessity with Compulsion: A Reply to Paul Helm', *Religious Studies* (1995). The critique of Brümmer that follows is broadly endorsed by Anthony N. S. Lane, *Calvin and Bernard of Clairvaux* (Princeton: Princeton Theological Seminary, 1996), 36f.

Clairvaux and Calvin on the nature of free will, similarities which Calvin acknowledges in book II, chapter 2, of the *Institutes*. But later on in book II Calvin reverts to the traditional 'Calvinist' view that God's persevering grace granted to the elect is causally efficacious, so denying free will. Presumably, Calvin did not realize that he was at odds with himself any more here than in Hoitenga's case. So, according to Brümmer, in one comparatively short passage in his seminal work Calvin contradicts himself on what was for him a central concept, free will, first by affirming free will and then by denying it— or at least by saying things that entail its denial. But there is a way of making Calvin's views consistent, according to Brümmer, by noting, following John Lucas, that causal *importance* is not equivalent to causal *sufficiency*.

If Brümmer is correct, then this is (to say the least) surprising. For if he is correct, then Calvin must at this point be repudiating the Augustinianism of the anti-Pelagian writings, an outlook that was obviously crucially influential for him. Further, if Brümmer's interpretation of Calvin is on the right lines then it is astonishing that Calvin's many friendly and unfriendly commentators have never noticed such a manifest inconsistency. Had they done so, they would surely have made hay over it. But whatever the explanation may be for how Calvin got himself into this alleged tangle, Brümmer provides him with an easy way to straighten things out; Calvin has simply to deny the causal sufficiency of divine grace! Brümmer has misinterpreted Calvin and his proposed harmonizing interpretation is both unnecessary and unsuccessful, besides being utterly unappealing to Calvin himself.

Any discussion about 'free will' must necessarily state clearly in what sense or senses of that expression freedom is being affirmed or denied. So here is a crucial passage from the *Institutes* that provides the starting point for Brümmer's discussion:

[I]n the schools three kinds of freedom are distinguished: first from necessity, second from sin, third from misery. The first of these so inheres in man by nature that it cannot possibly be taken away, but the two others have been lost through sin. I willingly accept this distinction, except in so far as necessity is falsely confused with compulsion.[77]

This is part of chapter 2 of book II of the *Institutes*, entitled, 'Man Has Now Been Deprived of Freedom of Choice and Bound Over to Miserable Servitude'. As we noted previously, in the early sections of this chapter Calvin controverts the doctrine of 'the philosophers', particularly Plato and Aristotle. 'They say: If to do this or that depends upon our choice, so also does not to do it. Again, if not to do it, so also to do it. Now we seem to do what we do, and to shun what we shun, by free choice.' The Church Fathers also tend

---

[77] *Inst.* II. 2. 5.

to accept freedom of will in this sense; 'many of them have come far too close to the philosophers'. All the ancient fathers, 'save Augustine, so differ, waver, or speak confusedly on this subject, that almost nothing certain can be derived from their writings'. Later writers 'fell from bad to worse', offering various definitions of free will none of which Calvin finds satisfactory, except Augustine's, which 'did not exclude divine grace'. Lombard and the scholastics tended to follow Augustine's definition.[78]

These remarks—and particularly those on 'the philosophers'—provide fairly strong prima facie evidence that what Calvin was objecting to here was an indeterministic or libertarian view of human choice, and more specifically, to the view that we possess the power to choose indeterministically or indifferently between good or evil courses of action.

As Brümmer points out, Calvin takes over the distinctions among the three kinds of freedom from Lombard and Bernard, though Bernard is not actually referred to by Calvin in the text at this point. Both Calvin and Bernard argue that in one sense 'free will' was lost in the Fall, while in another sense it was retained despite the Fall. Let us call these, respectively, the *moral* sense of free will and the *metaphysical* sense. These senses correspond, roughly and respectively, to Calvin's second and first kinds. (The third kind, freedom from misery, can be set aside in this discussion, since it refers to the sort of freedom which the redeemed enjoy in heaven and is not at issue here.) The issue is over the precise understanding of the metaphysical sense of freedom, the kind of freedom that on Calvin's view is essential to human nature and so is not lost in the Fall.

Brümmer assumes that for Bernard (and for Calvin) this sense of freedom is what is usually referred to as indeterministic or libertarian freedom—the sort incompatible with causal determination. Having sketched Bernard's view, Brümmer says: '[T]he soul is "self-determining" in the sense that its actions are freely initiated by the will and are not the effects of some necessitating cause outside the will. This does not only exclude the effects of some external necessity, but also all forms of internal necessity beyond the will, such as reason or the mind.'[79] In the following I shall accept this interpretation of Bernard,[80] but investigate whether it is Calvin's view in *Institutes* II. 2. 5 and subsequently.

---

[78] *Inst.* II. 2. 3–4.   [79] 'Calvin, Bernard and the Freedom of the Will', 444.

[80] But see Anthony N. S. Lane, *Calvin and Bernard of Clairvaux*, and *John Calvin: Student of the Church Fathers*, ch. 4. For some evidence from the *Institutes* that Brümmer may not have interpreted Bernard correctly, note Calvin's appeal to Bernard (alongside Augustine) as one (of the few?) whom Calvin claims clearly understood the distinction between the outward call of the gospel and the inward, efficacious call at *Inst.* III. 22. 10.

First, note Calvin's reservation over the threefold distinction quoted earlier. He says 'I willingly accept this distinction, *except in so far as necessity is falsely confused with compulsion.*' What does this mean? Calvin is stating that freedom from necessity is often mistakenly confused with freedom from compulsion and that he is happy with this distinction provided this confusion is noted and avoided. This gives us an important clue to Calvin's position.

Lombard's views on free will are both approved of and censured by Calvin.

Lombard finally declares that we have free will, not in that we are equally capable of doing or thinking good and evil, but merely that we are freed from compulsion. According to Lombard, this freedom is not hindered, even if we be wicked and slaves of sin, and can do nothing but sin.[81]

Surely my readers will recognize that I am bringing forth nothing new, for it is something that Augustine taught of old with the agreement of all the godly, and it was still retained almost a thousand years later in monastic cloisters. But Lombard, since he did not know how to distinguish necessity from compulsion, gave occasion for a pernicious error.[82]

Whatever Lombard's overall view may have been, it is clear that in Calvin's mind the 'pernicious error' is to confuse freedom from compulsion and freedom from necessity. To confuse necessity with compulsion is to say that the two are identical and hence that to be free from compulsion is to be free from necessity. Calvin thinks this equation is false. Freedom from necessity may entail freedom from compulsion, but the reverse entailment does not hold, according to Calvin.

In *Institutes* II. 3. 5, Calvin argues that mankind is subject to the necessity of sinning and yet is not compelled to sin. The nature of fallen mankind is such that each member of the race cannot but sin, though each sins in an uncompelled way. And as we shall see at greater length in the next chapter, Calvin does not think that the power to do evil willingly is worth calling free will. Free will is willingly doing the good because it is good. What then does Calvin mean by freedom from compulsion, the freedom that he contrasts with the freedom of necessity and that he says is consistent with it? I suggest that what he does *not* mean is freedom from efficient causation—nor even freedom from all elements of psychological constraint.

Whatever a person finds to be psychologically constraining is not compelling in the relevant sense. For Calvin would surely not deny that there are elements of felt constraint in the spiritual life that fall short of compulsion. A person touched by a tender conscience, or by the fear of God,

---

[81] *Inst.* II. 2. 6.   [82] *Inst.* II. 3. 5.

may feel constrained to pay back what he has borrowed. It is not likely that Calvin would say that whoever acts for fear of his conscience is being compelled to act, anymore than he would say that the restlessness of Augustine's heart—restless until it found its rest in God—was a case of compulsion in his sense.

Nor can the distinction be put merely in terms of preference, saying that a person is compelled when he does what he would prefer not to do, for someone may prefer to have a sensitive than an insensitive conscience, even though he is continually troubled by its workings.

To get further, we need to distinguish between those matters that a person wishes to be identified with and those that he does not, as well as to distinguish between those states occurring in a person that he would reject and which thus become external to him and those that he would not reject and which thus remain internal to him. Someone with a sensitive conscience may not reject that conscience; he may prefer it over an insensitive conscience, although he may prefer even more to act effortlessly in accordance with his conscience.[83] Thus a person is free (although he may be necessitated) when, roughly speaking, he is exercising his choice in ways that he identifies with, even though such exercise may involve elements of psychological constraint.

What does Calvin mean by acting out of necessity, if not acting by external constraint? To understand this, we must bear in mind the intentionalist character of action for Calvin. Although not every action-type is either commanded or forbidden by God—there are *adiaphora*—nevertheless every action has a moral character that is a function of the motive from which the action is done. For Calvin, fallen and unregenerate human nature is such that no human action is performed for the right motive; the unconverted do not even want to have right motives—at least, they do not want to have right motives for the right reason. So whenever there is the prospect of action from objectively good motives and action from objectively bad ones, a fallen and unregenerate human person will invariably act from bad motives, while not of course regarding these motives as bad.

If we suppose that a life consists of a series of choices between alternatives, then to act out of necessity in Calvin's sense is to choose that series of alternatives that better furthers a person's sinful objectives, either by performing an action commanded by God, or one forbidden, or one neither commanded nor forbidden, but in each case from unrighteous motives 'with the most eager inclination'.[84]

---

[83] Those familiar with Harry Frankfurt's 'Identification and Externality', in *The Importance of What We Care About* (Cambridge: Cambridge University Press, 1988) will recognize how indebted these remarks are to that paper.   [84] *Inst.* II. 3. 5.

[M]an, as he was corrupted by the Fall, sinned willingly, not unwillingly or by compulsion; by the most eager inclination of his heart, not by forced compulsion; by the prompting of his own lust, not by compulsion from without. Yet so depraved is his nature that he can be moved or impelled only to evil. But if this is true, then it is clearly expressed that man is surely subject to the necessity of sinning.[85]

How strong a view of the necessity of sinning—*non posse non peccare*—Calvin has can be seen from the illustration he uses of God's goodness.

But suppose some blasphemer sneers that God deserves little praise for His own goodness, constrained as He is to preserve it. Will this not be a ready answer to him: not from violent impulsion, but from His boundless goodness comes God's inability to do evil? Therefore, if the fact that he must do good does not hinder God's free will in doing good; if the devil, who can do only evil, yet sins with his will—who shall say that man therefore sins less willingly because he is subject to the necessity of sinning?[86]

Of course, Calvin is not saying that the necessity of sinning is in every respect like the necessity God has to do good. But the two are alike in that in each case necessity is consistent with freedom from 'violent impulsion', even though God has his necessity necessarily and mankind has its contingently.

Now, when I say that the will bereft of freedom is of necessity either drawn or led into evil, it is a wonder if this seems a hard saying to anyone, since it has nothing incongruous or alien to the usage of holy men. But it offends those who know not how to distinguish between necessity and compulsion.[87]

Brümmer is exactly right when he says[88] that 'Bernard's "freedom from necessity" is what Calvin refers to as freedom from compulsion'. But these are not, as Brümmer thinks, simply two ways of referring to the same thing, mere stylistic variants with Bernard preferring 'necessity' and Calvin preferring 'compulsion'. It is therefore incorrect to say that 'Calvin's distinction between freedom from compulsion and freedom from necessity corresponds to Bernard's distinction between *liberum arbitrium* (or "freedom from necessity") and *liberum consilium* (or "freedom from sin")'.[89] This makes the very same conflation between necessity and compulsion that Calvin repeatedly criticizes Lombard for.

For Calvin, I suggest, *compulsion* is a psychological, and not a metaphysical, concept. (Thus he contrasts freedom with being forced, and refers to a voluntary disposition to do evil.[90]) To be free from compulsion is not, for Calvin, to be indeterministically free, but to be acting in accordance with one's preferences. Such freedom is consistent with either metaphysical

---

[85] *Inst.* II. 3. 5.   [86] *Inst.* II. 3. 5.   [87] *Inst.* II. 3. 5.

[88] 'Calvin, Bernard and the Freedom of the Will', 447.

[89] 'Calvin, Bernard and the Freedom of the Will', 450.   [90] *Inst.* II. 2. 7.

necessity or contingency, and Calvin opts for the former for reasons which we shall examine in the next chapter.

So in referring to Calvin's view of the freedom that fallen mankind enjoys, Brümmer is incorrect to conclude that 'this is the freedom of choice between alternative courses of action', understood indeterministically. The fact that we choose between alternative possibilities and that such choices are an inseparable feature of human nature does not, for Calvin, entail metaphysical indeterminism. Rather it entails freedom from compulsion, which is compatible with the necessity of causal determinism.

Man will then be spoken of as having this sort of free decision, not because he has free choice equally of good and evil, but because he acts wickedly by will, not by compulsion. . . . A noble freedom, indeed—for man not to be forced to serve sin, yet to be such a willing slave that his will is bound by the fetters of sin![91]

Once again it is noteworthy that the contrast Calvin here draws is not between freedom and causation, but between freedom and compulsion or force, even while still being bound by the fetters of sin.

Given that Brümmer holds that both Bernard and Calvin maintain an indeterministic view of human freedom and yet each also maintains that the Fall makes a necessity of sinning, he has to provide an explanation of how such indeterminism and necessity can coexist in the same person. He offers an explanation in terms of ignorance of God's will and/or of loss of strength: 'We cannot choose to do God's will because we do not know what it is, and even if we should know it, we lack the strength to realize it consistently.'[92]

Considered in isolation, the loss of strength that Brümmer appeals to would seem to inhibit what he regards as our basic indeterminism, because to the extent that a person is weak, to that extent he cannot exercise an indeterministic choice. Calvin's view is much more radical; it is that the loss of free will to do good is such that even when a person has the knowledge of God's will he does not will to do it.

Man is so indulgent toward himself that when he commits evil he readily averts his mind, as much as he can, from the feeling of sin. This is why Plato seems to have been compelled to consider (in his *Protagoras*) that we sin only out of ignorance. This might have been an appropriate statement if only human hypocrisy had covered up vices with sufficient skill to prevent the mind from being recognized as evil in God's sight. The sinner tries to evade his innate power to judge between good and evil.[93]

Yet this longing for truth, such as it is, languishes before it enters upon its race because it soon falls into vanity. Indeed, man's mind, because of its dullness, cannot

---

[91] *Inst.* II. 2. 7.   [92] 'Calvin, Bernard and the Freedom of the Will', 447.

[93] *Inst.* II. 2. 22.

hold to the right path, but wanders through various errors and stumbles repeatedly, as if it were groping in darkness, until it strays away and finally disappears. Thus it betrays how incapable it is of seeking and finding truth.[94]

In sum, it is crucial that Calvin's distinction between compulsion and necessity be carefully observed if we are to reach a correct understanding of his view of freedom. Employing the distinction it is possible, in his view, to hold both that a person sins of necessity and yet willingly, and also that only divine grace is causally sufficient for perseverance.

In his paper's final section, Brümmer argues that despite Calvin's agreement with Bernard on freedom from necessity, when he expounds his doctrine of perseverance in *Institutes* II. 3. 11, Calvin reneges on this agreement. For while, Brümmer claims, Calvin has previously maintained that we retain indeterministic freedom of choice despite sin, his account of perseverance in grace contradicts this because it is expressed in terms of the causal sufficiency of divine grace.

Because divine grace is effectual grace, it cannot depend upon the exercise of a human indeterministic choice for its efficacy. Given efficacious grace, Calvin, like any good Augustinian, cannot allow that 'our relationship with God remains fundamentally personal and non-deterministic',[95] although Calvin, no more than Augustine, would equate the personal with the indeterministic. Calvin would reject Brümmer's repeated contention that only indeterministically free agents are personal agents.[96]

But does Calvin's treatment of perseverance contradict his earlier claims? Certainly not. Rather, we find him continuing to uphold in a thoroughly consistent fashion his earlier distinction that, though man sins of necessity, yet he does not do so from compulsion. Throughout Calvin's treatment of perseverance we find a starkly monergistic account of grace. Because man sins of necessity, he can only be redeemed by conversion.

God begins his good work in us . . . by arousing love and desire and zeal for righteousness in our hearts; or, to speak more correctly, by bending, forming, and directing, our hearts to righteousness. He completes the work, moreover, by confirming us to perseverance.

What takes [the] place [of our own will in conversion] is wholly from God. I say that the [human] will is effaced; not in so far as it is will, for in man's conversion what belongs to his primal nature remains entire. I also say that it is created anew; not meaning that the will now begins to exist, but that it is changed from an evil to a good will. I affirm that this is wholly God's doing, for according to the testimony of the same apostle, 'we are not even capable of thinking' [II Cor. 3: 5].[97]

---

[94] *Inst.* II. 2. 12.
[95] 'Calvin, Bernard and the Freedom of the Will', 451.
[96] e.g. 'Calvin, Bernard and the Freedom of the Will', 451.
[97] *Inst.* II. 3. 6.

Conversion by such divine grace is continued by the granting of persevering grace. As is well known, 'conversion' for Calvin describes not only an initial act; it is a way of characterizing the entire life of faith.

'He does not move the will in such a manner as has been taught and believed for many ages—that it is afterward in our choice either to obey or resist the motion—but by disposing it efficaciously.'[98] This is a clear account of the causal necessity and sufficiency of divine grace. Yet Brümmer is mistaken in thinking that Calvin's account of perseverance 'is based above all on the "efficacious" compulsion of grace which eliminates our ability to reject it'.[99] Granted that Calvin, with Augustine, teaches that grace overcomes a person's ability to reject it, but this is done not by sheer (psychological) compulsion, but 'when we, who are by nature inclined to evil with our whole heart, begin to will good, we do so out of mere grace'.[100] It is grace alone that enables a person, in Frankfurt's terminology, to want to want to be righteous. We shall look at this more systematically in the following chapter.

Brümmer reveals just how flawed his understanding of Calvin is on this point when he equates efficacious grace with overriding compulsion.[101] Rather, Calvin argues that efficacious grace, though it is the product of divine causal sufficiency, does not necessarily register itself as psychological compulsion, and the two are most certainly not equivalent. It is because Calvin held that mankind sins by necessity but not by compulsion that the only way in which God's grace could be effective is by its being causally sufficient. Far from the later sections of book II of the *Institutes* being inconsistent with the earlier, the earlier sections require the later.

At the very end of his paper Brümmer offers a way of harmonizing Calvin's reasons for stressing the doctrine of perseverance with Bernard's libertarianism. Brümmer accuses Calvin of confusing the distribution of causal power and the distribution of moral responsibility.[102] He argues that there may be a set of necessary conditions that are jointly sufficient for the production of an event without responsibility for the event being similarly distributed; rather, responsibility is based on selecting one or more but never all of these necessary conditions. In the light of this, Brümmer claims, we can see why 'believers will always say *Soli Dei Gloria!* and give God all the credit for their own conversion or spiritual successes'.[103] In doing this, a believer is not denying that his indeterministically free will has played a necessary part in these events but he is recognizing that as soon as he says this he is saying

---

[98] *Inst.* II. 3. 10.   [99] 'Calvin, Bernard and the Freedom of the Will', 452.

[100] *Inst.* II. 3. 8. But note Calvin's reference elsewhere to the 'impulsion' of the Holy Spirit (*Inst.* II. 2. 26).

[101] 'Calvin, Bernard and the Freedom of the Will', 452.

[102] 'Calvin, Bernard and the Freedom of the Will', 454.

[103] 'Calvin, Bernard and the Freedom of the Will', 454.

too much and—here Brümmer is quoting from J. R. Lucas's *Freedom and Grace*[104]—

arrogating to himself a credit that is God's, and speaking as though he were of himself sufficient to obtain his own salvation: so he goes on to say at once 'Yet not I, but God in me', and attributes all to the grace of God rather than himself, meaning by the grace of God all those factors which he recognizes as having been at work in his own conversion and pilgrimage, apart from himself.

Brümmer argues further that perseverance is ensured because any other course of action is 'unthinkable' for the believer. Let us briefly consider these claims in turn.

The point about causation and responsibility is not altogether convincing, for it rests upon confusing causal responsibility and moral responsibility. If one cause of a tragic event is a natural occurrence, say the direction and strength of the wind, then that occurrence cannot be held *morally* responsible—and thus liable to praise or blame—for the accident that took place. In that situation, if we are investigating who is to blame for the accident, then we look for features of the situation that result from choice or that—in the case of culpable omissions—ought to have. (Of course, if the wind's strength is such as to make it physically impossible to execute a plan, then it alone is causally responsible but it is only blameworthy in the causal, not moral sense.) And even if human agency figures in a number of the necessary causal conditions, it does not follow that selecting one condition for particular attention is arbitrary.

Whether or not Brümmer's discussion of moral and causal responsibility is convincing it is hard to imagine Calvin being at all attracted by the suggestion that salvation *sola gratia* is due to a well-mannered human emphasis on what we should identify as being *the* cause and what we should not, and nothing more. For since Calvin regards sufficient causal power for conversion (including perseverance) to come from God alone, the responsibility and praise for that conversion must likewise be given to God alone. As Calvin puts it, 'The first part of a good work is will; the other, a strong effort to accomplish it; the author of both is God.'[105] Lucas, whom Brümmer cites at this point, must be mistaken in claiming that a Christian must believe in indeterministic freedom, since Calvin was a Christian and it is highly likely that he did not believe in such freedom. The question for Calvin is not whether a person will be well-mannered enough not to claim credit for his conversion if a necessary condition of it stems from himself, but whether, in such circumstances, he is *entitled to* claim credit. Since Calvin believed that credit for conversion is entirely God's because God's power is causally

[104] J. R. Lucas, *Freedom and Grace* (London: SPCK, 1976), 13.   [105] *Inst.* II. 3. 9.

sufficient for conversion, he is concerned not with the social mores governing a person's talk about his conversion but with what is the strict truth of the matter.[106]

Further, Brümmer's harmonization of Calvin with Bernard requires the idea that for a believer 'turning his back on God would be such an unreasonable thing to do that it is for the believer "unthinkable" '.[107] But Calvin's account of perseverance in grace does not require the truth of the following general proposition: 'No one in whom efficacious grace works ever thinks of forsaking God.' Rather, the very point about perseverance—what makes it *persevering grace*—is that, when those in whom God's efficacious grace is present think of forsaking God, that grace prevents the thought from fathering the deed.

This discussion of Brümmer, Bernard, and Calvin has prepared the way for a fuller enquiry into Calvin's views on the bondage of the human will.

[106] For a discussion of Lucas's views, see Paul Helm, 'On Grace and Causation', *Scottish Journal of Theology* (1979).

[107] 'Calvin, Bernard and the Freedom of the Will', 455.

6

Free Will

ALTHOUGH John Calvin was not primarily a philosopher the previous chapters have demonstrated that his work as a theologian was undertaken with considerable awareness of philosophical ideas and arguments. Sometimes Calvin consciously and deliberately distances himself from particular philosophers and at other times warns against the excesses of philosophical speculation.[1] But he never fails to see the influence and significance of philosophical concepts, and warmly endorses certain ideas and arguments that he finds, for example, in Cicero and in Plato.[2] Although he rarely, if ever, uses a philosopher as a primary source of ideas, he does appeal to them for confirmation,[3] thus falsifying the claim made by some theologians that Calvin was a purely scriptural thinker whose thought was uncontaminated by pagan influence even when that thought was mediated by the medieval tradition[4] and by Renaissance humanism.[5] While Calvin echoed some of the features of the Renaissance critique of scholasticism, his practice shows that in his case this critique did not amount to a blanket rejection of the medieval way of doing theology, with its characteristic interplay of philosophical and theological issues.

In placing a positive value on the best of pagan thought Calvin followed his mentor Augustine of Hippo, but as we noted in the previous chapter he also, like Augustine, regards such thought as seriously flawed in the moral power it ascribes to the human will.[6] In his controversy with the Pelagians, Augustine came to hold that no human being can presently motivate himself to perform actions which are morally good in the sense of being meritorious and pleasing to God. Nor can a person by his own effort of will turn himself to God. Indeed each thinker regarded the rejection of these two claims as

[1] *Inst.* I. 15. 6.

[2] *Inst.* I. 3. 1; I. 3. 3; I. 15. 6. Charles Partee, *Calvin and Classical Philosophy*, has a full survey of Calvin's philosophical connections.

[3] As in the case of Cicero, whose views in *The Nature of the Gods* Calvin cites as confirmation of his own view about the universality of the *sensus divinitatis* (*Inst.* I. 3. 2).

[4] As in *Inst.* II. 2. 5.

[5] Such a view surprisingly ignores the fact that Calvin's first published work was a commentary on Seneca's *De Clementia* (trans. and ed. as *Calvin's Commentary on Seneca's De Clementia* by F. L. Battles and A. M. Hugo (Leiden: Brill, 1969)).   [6] *Inst.* II. 2–3.

evidence of one of the more unfortunate and powerful influences of pagan thought on Christianity.[7]

So Calvin's views on the freedom and bondage of the will must be understood in the context of the long medieval tradition of debate about this complex of issues, and particularly in the light of the thought of one of the fountainheads of that tradition, Augustine of Hippo and (as we saw in the previous chapter) of Bernard of Clairvaux. Discussion and evaluation of his views on the bondage of the will provide us with further insight into his metaphysics of the human person.

This chapter focuses on Calvin's major work *The Bondage and Liberation of the Will.*[8] Published in 1543, it is a reply to the first six books of the Louvain theologian Albertus Pighius's *Ten Books on Human Free Choice and Divine Grace*, published in 1542, which were an attack on Calvin's views as these are expressed in the 1539 edition of the *Institutes*, particularly chapter 2, 'The Knowledge of Humanity and Free Choice'.[9] As part of the later Bolsec controversy Calvin responded to the last four books of Pighius's work nine years later, in his *Concerning the Eternal Predestination of God* (even though Pighius had in the meantime died).[10] *The Bondage and Liberation of the Will* can be regarded as an expansion and re-presentation of what Calvin says in the 1539 edition of the *Institutes*. A. N. S. Lane, in his excellent notes to the first English translation of the former work, never suggests that Calvin deviates from his teaching in the *Institutes* in his reply to Pighius, nor would he have been correct to do so.

Calvin would probably have been displeased with the title of this chapter for reasons I shall give. I shall then attempt to expound the main features of Calvin's views, and, in particular to separate carefully what Calvin himself called the 'two issues', the issues of God's providence over all, and the will's bondage, that he believes are liable to be confused together when human willing is discussed.[11] These issues are separate for Calvin because divine

---

[7] *Inst.* II. 2. 3.

[8] *The Bondage and Liberation of the Will*, ed. A. N. S. Lane, trans. G. I. Davies (Grand Rapids, Mich.: Baker, 1996).

[9] There is no published English translation of the 1539 edition of the *Institutes*, but the Battles translation of the definitive 1559 edition indicates which passages are parts of the 1539 edition, which are re-writes, and which are entirely new passages. In what follows I shall refer mainly to passages of the first type in giving Calvin's views.

[10] *Concerning the Eternal Predestination of God* (1552), trans. J. K. S. Reid (London: James Clarke, 1961).

[11] In view of Calvin's explicit and repeated concern to distinguish between 'two issues' it is surprising that it is sometimes said that it is because Calvin fails to distinguish different 'perspectives' that he fails to achieve a harmonious and consistent position on the question of free will. (See Marijn de Kroon, *The Honour of God and Human Salvation: Calvin's Theology According to his Institutes*, trans. J. Vriend and

providence is not temporally indexed, and providential control is indeed a necessary power of God. For Calvin cannot contemplate a world created by God in which he fails to have control over every event in that world. (He frequently contrasts his view of providence with that of the Epicureans.) By contrast, the bondage of the will to sin has been brought voluntarily by mankind on itself; it was not always thus.

No doubt there are two issues here. I shall argue, however, that Calvin cannot altogether avoid connecting them when dealing with the bondage and liberation of the will. But since my main aim is to try to understand what Calvin taught in *Bondage* rather than to engage in a critical discussion of it, or in a historical comparison or evaluation of it, the remainder of the chapter will be devoted to that.

'FREE WILL'

Calvin would have disliked this chapter's title because he did not like the adjective 'free' (*liberum*) being applied to the noun 'will' (*arbitrium*).

Now as far as the term ('freedom') is concerned I still maintain what I declared in my *Institutes*, that I am not so excessively concerned about words as to want to start an argument for that cause, provided that a sound understanding of the reality is retained. If freedom is opposed to coercion, I both acknowledge and consistently maintain that choice is free, and I hold anyone who thinks otherwise to be a heretic. If, I say, it were called free in the sense of not being coerced nor forcibly moved by an external impulse, but moving of its own accord, I have no objection. The reason I find this epithet unsatisfactory is that people commonly think of something quite different when they hear or read it being applied to the human will. Since in fact they take it to imply ability and power, one cannot prevent from entering the minds of most people, as soon as the will is called free, the illusion that it therefore has both good and evil within its power, so that it can by its own strength choose either one of them.[12]

Calvin believed that one effect of sin was to breed illusions in the human mind, and that no illusion was more pernicious than that of the supposed freedom of the will. So he continues:

Lyle D. Bierma (Edinburgh: T. & T. Clark, 2001), 46–7.) For Calvin clearly distinguishes between God's providence over all, and human fallenness, and in any case there does not seem to be an inconsistency between what he says about the nature of human action and the consequences of human fallenness.

[12] *Bondage*, 68. Unlike Calvin, Peter Martyr Vermigli seems to have been willing to permit the phrase *liberum arbitrium*, provided that it is not misunderstood. 'We are not to contend about the word, and may allow *liberum arbitrium* so long as it is the same as *voluntas*, and that freedom in spiritual matters is not attributed to it. We also take the will to be free only through grace; otherwise it is a slave.' 'Free Will', in *The Peter Martyr Library*, vol. 4: *The Philosophical Works*, trans. Joseph C. McClelland, 284.

But since Pighius is always craftily confusing coercion with necessity, when it is of the greatest importance for the issue under discussion that the distinction between them be maintained and carefully remembered, it is appropriate to note how the following four [claims] differ from one another: namely that the will is free, bound, self-determined, or coerced. People generally understand a free will to be one which has it in its power to choose good or evil, and Pighius also defines it in this way. There can be no such thing as a coerced will, since the two ideas are contradictory. But our responsibility as teachers requires that we say what it means, so that it may be understood what coercion is. Therefore we describe [as coerced] the will which does not incline this way or that of its own accord or by an internal movement of decision, but is forcibly driven by an external impulse. We say that it is self-determined when of itself it directs itself in the direction in which it is led, when it is not taken by force or dragged unwillingly. A bound will, finally, is one which because of its corruptness is held captive under the authority of evil desires, so that it can choose nothing but evil, even if it does so of its own accord and gladly, without being driven by any external impulse.[13]

These passages echo the following passage from the *Institutes*:

Indeed, I abhor contentions about words, with which the church is harassed to no purpose. But I have scrupulously resolved to avoid those words which signify something absurd, especially where pernicious error is involved. But how few men are there, I ask, who when they hear free will attributed to man do not immediately conceive him to be master of both his own mind and will, able of his own power to turn himself toward either good or evil?[14]

Calvin does not deny that a good sense may be given to the phrase 'free will'. It is the liberty to choose between alternatives, a characteristic of intelligent agents, the absence of which indicates psychological coercion or the application of external force. Yet he is convinced that even when we have been at pains to give it this sense when people hear 'free will' they will continue to think of a will that has unrestricted power to choose either good or evil courses of action. It is precisely in this sense that Calvin denies that men and women possess free will.

There is another complicating factor, though this is not brought out explicitly by Calvin. It is that he uses two words, *voluntas* and *arbitrium*, usually translated 'will' and 'choice' respectively, and another word for choice, *electio*. *Voluntas* has to do with the deep-seated 'set' of the will, its basic orientation, for Calvin its basic orientation either to the service of God or in rebellion against him. The words translated 'choice' refer to the occasions of choice between alternatives. One way of putting Calvin's basic points about free will is to say that the power to choose (*electio, arbitrium*) remains intact except where a person is compelled, but that it is misleading

---

[13] *Bondage*, 69   [14] *Inst.* II. 2. 7.

to call such a power of choice 'free will'. But as a result of the Fall the *voluntas* is not free, it is orientated to serve the creature rather than the Creator and can only be reorientated by God's grace. Because of this the choices that are the expression of the fallen *voluntas*, though they are genuine choices, can never be well-motivated choices of what is good, and so are not free. If it is true that Calvin did not put the point in this way himself, as it seems to be, then this is rather surprising.[15]

The sense of free will which Calvin denies to be possessed by men and women is, as philosophers nowadays would say, indexed in its character. Men and women do not 'naturally' possess free will (in this sense) *now*, in the present post-lapsarian state of the human race. The race once did possess it, in unfallen Adam, but the race having fallen, free will in this sense is gone, and is irrecoverable apart from divine grace.

So there is a short, sharp answer to the question 'Does Calvin believe in free will?' Yes, he believes that we have on appropriate occasions the power to choose between alternatives in a way which is uncoerced. No, he does not believe that we naturally possess free will in the sense of the power to choose what is good, at present; but yes, unfallen man had free will in that sense. We do not possess such free will now, and so Calvin's advice is that we had better not use the phrase about ourselves lest, by using it to affirm specific human powers that we do not possess, we flatter ourselves that we possess the power to choose either good or evil.

The distinction between power of free choice which we retain though fallen, the sense of 'free' which Calvin is reluctant to use because of its misleading connotations, and the sense of 'free' in which a person is freed by grace to do the good, is well brought out by Thomas Aquinas, even though he does not use the idea of freedom in so many words:

Man is the master of his acts, including those of willing and of not willing, because of the deliberative activity of his reason, which can be turned to one side or the other. But that he should deliberate or not deliberate, supposing that we were master of this too, would have to come about by a preceding deliberation. And since this may not proceed to infinity, one would finally have to reach the point at which man's free decision is moved by some external principle superior to the human mind, namely by God, as Aristotle himself demonstrated. Thus the mind even of a healthy man is not so much the master of its acts as not to need to be moved by God. Much more the

---

[15] In this connection it is a pity that in *Bondage* the terms *sponta* and *spontanea* are translated 'of its own accord' and 'self-determined' respectively, since in current philosophical usage 'self-determined' describes a version of indeterminism whereas 'liberty of spontaneity' (current in the 18th cent. and still occasionally used) refers to the sort of liberty that is compatible with determinism. To philosophical ears to translate *spontanea* as 'self-determined' tends to prejudge the question of whether or not Calvin is a determinist of some sort.

free decisions of a man become weak after sin, which the spoiling of nature hinders from the good.[16]

Calvin tirelessly insists on the fact, against Pighius but with Augustine, that our present lack of free will is not part of our nature, but is a corruption of our nature. Indeed, Calvin does not hesitate to make use of scholastic terminology to make the point; the loss of free will is, he says, not a loss of part of the essence of human nature, but it is an accident.[17] As he puts it in the *Institutes*, human corruption 'is an adventitious quality which comes upon man rather than a substantial property which has been implanted from the beginning'.[18]

Calvin denied that we have free will (in the sense of having power to choose both good and evil) but, as we can learn from the passages already cited, he equally emphatically affirmed that the absence of free will in this sense does not entail coercion. *Bondage* includes a short Excursus, 'Coercion versus Necessity', that establishes the difference.[19] One corollary of the denial of free will is that there is a sense in which what a person wills he wills necessarily; his lack of free will means he cannot but will evil. We shall try to see more clearly what this means shortly. Yet for Calvin it does not follow from the denial of free will that what a person chooses is the result of coercion. The importance of the distinction for Calvin is that while acting out of necessity is consistent with being held responsible for the action, and being praised or blamed for it, being coerced is inconsistent with such praise or blame. In his criterion of praise and blame he explicitly follows Aristotle.

When Aristotle distinguished what is voluntary from its opposite, he defines the latter as τὸ βίᾳ ἢ δι' ἄγνοιαν γιγνόμενον, that is, what happens by force or through ignorance. There he defines as forced what has its beginning elsewhere, something to which he who acts or is acted upon makes no contribution (*Ethic. Ni.* 3. 1).[20]

So normal human activity is not forced or coerced; insofar as it proceeds from fallen human nature it is not free because a person with a fallen nature does not have the power to choose what is good. Being fallen, his nature is modified and he chooses, and can choose, only what is evil.

How is this modification to be understood? Once more, in answer to this question, Calvin resorts to a scholastic distinction.

---

[16] *Summa Theologiae*, I. 2ae, 109. 3, trans. Cornelius Ernst.

[17] *Bondage*, 213.   [18] *Inst.* II. 1. 11.   [19] *Bondage*, 146–50. Cf. *Inst.* II. 2. 7.

[20] *Bondage*, 150. 'Those things, then, are thought involuntary, which take place by force or owing to ignorance; and that is compulsory of which the moving principle is outside, being a principle in which nothing is contributed by the person who acts—or rather is acted upon, e.g. if he were to be carried somewhere by a wind, or by men who had him in their power' (Aristotle, *Nicomachean Ethics*, trans. David Ross, revised by J. L. Ackrill and J. O. Urmson (Oxford University Press, 1980), 48).

Or is Pighius still so uneducated as not to recognise anything in between the substance of the will, or the faculty of willing, and its actions or its actual effects? He has certainly disappointed me enormously. For I thought that he was trained in at least the first principles of logic. Now I see that he is completely bereft of education and of common sense. Since no one is so unlearned as not to set habit in between. For what is the point of these forms of speech, 'someone of a good or evil mind', if not to indicate this quality? Nor indeed did I fail to mention this. For in relation to the present issue, following Bernard I proposed three things for consideration: to will per se, that is, simply to will; then to will badly; and [to will] well. The first is the faculty of willing or, if preferred, the substance. To will well and badly are qualities or opposed habits which belong to the power itself.[21]

The Fall thus resulted in the loss of the habit—or, in our terms, ability, to will well.

Pighius tried to force Calvin into the position of maintaining that if one supposes the absence of free will as Calvin did, then it is impossible for a person's reason and will to be changed 'unless the substance of the rational soul itself were also removed, and a new, different soul entered in its place';[22] that is, unless the person concerned became a numerically different person. But Pighius had overlooked the fact that though the soul's powers are essential to it, those powers can have accidental qualities. 'Our power of reasoning, which has its seat in the mind, and our ability to will, which resides in the heart, are both defective and corrupted by sin.'[23]

The point can be illustrated in the following way. It is part of a ferret's nature to climb through pipes and down holes, but it is not part of a greyhound's nature to do this. To be in bondage to sin is not a part of human nature in this sense. To be in bondage is, according to Calvin, an accident of human nature, brought about by the Fall, like a ferret being blinded and so not being able to locate pipes and holes even though his nature as a burrower remains.

The bondage of the will to sin consists precisely in the fact that the already chosen end cannot now be unchosen, since for Calvin (as we saw in the previous chapter) part of the penalty of having made a wrong choice about 'heavenly things' is that the capacity for making right choices about such things is taken away. We shall explore the nature of this incapacity later on.

So, in summary, Calvin denies that we now possess free will in the sense defined; nevertheless many of our actions are unforced, and all these unforced actions proceed from a sinful *habitus* of the soul, that (unlike the understanding and the will) is a contingent feature of the soul, possessed by all who are fallen, and which its possessors are unable to rid themselves of by their own unaided powers. We are to be blamed for those actions proceeding

---

[21] *Bondage*, 209. [22] *Bondage*, 213. [23] *Bondage*, 213.

from this evil *habitus*, as all our actions do prior to the onset of God's regenerating grace, which results in the creation of a new *habitus* of the soul.

Calvin and the modern debate about 'freedom'

Philosophical debate about human freedom since the time of Calvin has divided the conceptual cake somewhat differently. Emphasis has generally fallen on that sense (or those senses) having to do with coerced and un-coerced action, and the sense (or senses) in which the will is free from causal determinism, and not on moral senses of freedom. We must bear this in mind when the term 'freedom' is used in the next few paragraphs as we endeavour to match Calvin's views of coerced and uncoerced action (which he thought did not concern the real issue of 'free will'), with this subsequent discussion of freedom and determinism.

Particularly since the rise of modern science and of naturalistic views of the human person there has been an almost but not quite exclusive pre-occupation with freedom and causal determinism. Modern debate has centred around two different conceptions of human action; on one account, a free act is one where only necessary causal conditions are outside the self, and the agent himself is the cause. Freedom is then the liberty to do otherwise than one does in precisely the same circumstances. The other main account finds freedom to be consistent with determinism, because it is necessary and sufficient for an act being free that the person did it, and wanted to do it, even though there exists in principle a causally sufficient explanation of what was done.

It is perhaps anachronistic to attempt to place Calvin's views on coerced and uncoerced action exactly in the terms of this later debate; nevertheless, I shall attempt roughly to do this. We have already noted that his account of providence appears to commit Calvin to a pluralistic or hierarchical kind of determinism. I intend this to supplement that earlier discussion.

On its surface the evidence for whether Calvin favours a form of determin-ism looks inconclusive. On the one hand, Calvin speaks unreservedly of the self-determination of the will. 'We say that it is self-determined when of itself it directs itself in the direction in which it is led, when it is not taken by force or dragged unwillingly.'[24] Initially this language may seem to place Calvin in the libertarian or agent–causation camp. But Calvin would appear to be redefining the idea of self-determination at this point since the will is 'led', though in an uncoerced fashion. Indeed his favoured position is to speak of freedom (though not the sense of 'freedom' that he favours, as we have seen) as being the absence of coercion, and this appears to place him in the

---

[24] *Bondage*, 69.

compatibilist camp, where to act freely is to act according to your beliefs and desires, in an uncoerced way.

The evidence so far appears somewhat ambiguous. But there are two other strands of data that are relevant, and to which we must turn.

Calvin's language for regeneration

The first of these concerns the language that Calvin uses regarding the regenerating power of the Holy Spirit. He uniformly sees the Spirit working in regeneration as a causal agent, and more importantly, as an effective or causally sufficient agent who produces a new *habitus* of the soul, and so provides the ability to will and do the good, albeit imperfectly. Calvin emphatically rejected what he took to be the Pelagianizing theology of Pighius, arguing against Pighius that the Spirit produces not only necessary conditions for good action, conditions which we could prepare ourselves to receive, and cooperate with when they occurred, but sufficient conditions for action which we cannot prepare ourselves for, or make more likely to occur, or unaidedly cooperate with. Nevertheless, despite this causal sufficiency, the Spirit does not compel the will but renews it.

When the Lord says that he will cause us to walk in his precepts, he is not promising that he will merely render the heart capable of turning in either direction, so that it will be as ready and inclined to resist him as to obey. It is rather that, being entirely formed and prepared for obedience, it already has the righteousness of God impressed and engraved upon it. For no one is so dull-witted as not to see both Pighius's remarkable malice and his shameless and almost despairing rashness in restricting the grace of God here. The Lord says that he will cause us to serve him. [Pighius] renders it that he will make us able either to walk or not to walk [in his ways].[25]

And, again,

We do not shrink from the customary manner of speaking whereby people are said to run and to strive and to labour—provided that it is not denied to us that, for the struggle and for the race (or labour), both the desire and the strength are also bestowed on them by the grace of God. Or, if it is more pleasing for our meaning to be expressed in the words of a prophet, we willingly allow that people act, but it is because God causes them so to do.[26]

Here, once again, the language of causal sufficiency is used. God causes people to act, and yet such people, in performing such actions, act in a self-determined and voluntary manner. Indeed insofar as they do good they act freely in the further sense of 'free' which Calvin reserves for properly motivated actions. This language strongly suggests a compatibilist position

---

[25] *Bondage*, 211.   [26] *Bondage*, 236.

that argues that persons are free when they do what they want to do, even if their actions are caused by their desires and beliefs. For the Spirit produces a new *habitus* in the regenerate by producing new set of desires, (or of dispositions to desire) in them. Where men and women act prompted by such desires in Spirit-produced circumstances they 'own' their motives and the actions flowing from them in a significant and characteristic way.[27]

So far, then, the evidence inclines us to the view that although Calvin uses the language of self-determination he understands that language in a way that is consistent with the position known to modern philosophers as compatibilism, the compatibility of free will (in the sense that Calvin dislikes) with causal determinism.

Aquinas takes a position on free will that Calvin would generally endorse, despite the tendency of many modern commentators to place Aquinas in the indeterministic camp. Like Calvin, although he uses the language of self-determination (calling it 'free' in a way that Calvin would have disliked) what he says about freedom is hardly consistent with modern libertarianism.

Free decision spells self-determination because man by his free decision moves himself into action. Freedom does not require that a thing is its own first cause, just as in order to be the cause of something else a thing does not have to be its first cause. God is the first cause on which both natural and free agents depend. And just as his initiative does not prevent natural causes from being natural, so it does not prevent voluntary action from being voluntary but rather makes it be precisely this. For God works in each according to its nature.[28]

Like Calvin, Aquinas believes that the possession of free will is tested by the relevance of exhortations. 'Man has free will; other wise counsels, exhortations, commands, prohibitions . . . would be in vain.' Here also he appears to endorse a compatibilist view of human freedom.

Also like Calvin, Aquinas (following Bernard) distinguishes between free will as a power and as a habit. 'A power enables a man to act, while a habit disposes him to act well or ill.' Further, 'A man is said to lose his liberty of decision by sin, not in the sense that it takes away the liberty he has by nature,

---

[27] On the idea of 'ownership' see Harry G. Frankfurt, 'Identification and Wholeness', in *Necessity, Vision and Love* (Cambridge: Cambridge University Press, 1999).

[28] *Summa Theologiae*, I. 83. 1 (trans. Timothy Suttor). It is interesting to compare the wording of the *Westminster Confession of Faith* (1647): 'God from all eternity did by the most wise and holy counsel of his own will, freely and unchangeably ordain whatsoever comes to pass: yet so as thereby neither is God the author of sin, nor is violence offered to the will of the creature, nor is liberty or contingency of second causes taken away, but rather established' (III. 1); 'Although, in relation to the foreknowledge, and decree of God, the first cause, all things come to pass immutably and infallibly, yet, by the same providence, he ordereth them to fall out according to the nature of second causes, either necessarily, freely, or contingently' (v. 2) (*Documents of the English Reformation*, ed. Gerald Bray (Cambridge: James Clarke, 1994), 490, 491).

for only coercion does that, but in that it takes away his freedom from guilt and unhappiness.'[29] Calvin also contrasts liberty and coercion but he thinks that sin takes away more than freedom from guilt and unhappiness; it removes the ability to will the good.

It may seem that, contrary to Calvin, Aquinas is here arguing that free will is 'indifferent to good or evil choice', and so endorsing (despite his other remarks) an indeterministic liberty of indifference. But Aquinas is here discussing the relation between will and habit and arguing that habits are what dispose the will in either a good or a bad direction. Like Calvin, and unlike Pighius, he is arguing that bad or good habits are contingently related to the will, not an essential part of it. Habits dispose us in either a good or a bad direction. So the will, as a principle of choice, is indifferent to good and evil. Considered merely as a power, it may choose either. It in fact chooses as it is disposed, either by an evil or a good habit. For Aquinas, then, free will is a power that is affected by the habits which it possesses, which is a position very similar, if not identical to, the one that Calvin endorses against Pighius.

However, there is one further line of argument that, if it is convincing, would allow for Calvin being an incompatibilist. Suppose we distinguish between actions of a certain *type*, and particular occurrences of actions of that type, particular *tokens* of the type. A certain type of action would be an action of a certain description, say, giving to the poor for the glory of God. On Calvin's view, as we have seen, only the Spirit, in liberation of the will and the production of a new *habitus* of the soul, can give to a person the capacity to perform actions of that type. So the Spirit's work is the causally sufficient condition for the production of certain action-types. But perhaps the Spirit is only a necessary condition of the production of tokens of that type. Suppose that you are in a walled rose garden that you can't escape from, perhaps a garden that you don't want to escape from. Then there are types of action that you can't perform tokens of. For example, you can't visit the Eiffel Tower or swim in the sea. But there are other action tokens that, if you possess libertarian freedom, you can choose between; for example, the action token of picking this white rose now or of picking this red rose now.

Is there evidence in *Bondage* that Calvin might favour such a view? Some evidence superficially seems to support it, or at least to be consistent with it. After noting that Pighius claims that 'the fruits of good works are technically produced by us and by the life-giving force which is in us', which we have received from God, Calvin goes on to say that:

If [by this] he understands the will with which we will (which is implanted in us by nature), the judgment with which we choose, the power to endeavour with which

---

[29] *Summa Theologiae*, I. 83. 2.

we endeavour, I have no objection—provided that he allows at the same time that we acquire righteousness of will, judgment, and endeavour by grace alone.[30]

These remarks are compatible with the idea that God's grace extends to types of actions, but not to tokens of those types. In spite of this, however, Calvin seems generally to support the thesis that God's grace is necessary and sufficient for both action types and action tokens. For example, 'We do indeed teach that man is so acted upon by the grace of God that he nevertheless [also] acts at the same time, but he acts in such a way that the effectiveness of the action is and remains entirely in the control of the Spirit of God.'[31] Here Calvin seems to have both action types and action tokens in mind. And this is the point where (as we shall see shortly) the 'two issues' which Calvin endeavours to keep separate, the issue of divine providence and the issue of the bondage of the will to sin and its liberation, inevitably come together. As we saw in Chapter 4, Calvin believes in particular providence. God governs the occurrence of every action token. It is possible to combine a view making the grace of God necessary and sufficient for the production of any good action type but only necessary for the production of any good action token, with an act of indeterministically free choice being also necessary, but only if this is combined with a view of providence that does not extend God's providential control to every action token. But this cannot be Calvin's view, for on his view God does exercise providential control over every action token.[32]

THE 'TWO ISSUES'

The second and final strand of evidence in favour of a compatibilist understanding of human agency is from what Calvin calls the 'different issue'.

---

[30] *Bondage*, 230.

[31] *Bondage*, 172. Compare Peter Martyr Vermigli, 'Nor is it within our capacity to be content with what is set before us; they must be proposed with force, efficacy and power, so that the understanding may be affected with an uncommon light, and the will strengthened lest it submit to evil desires and temptations that call it away from spiritual things. When this is done it assents to the words and promises of God, and justification follows. The intellect is actively predisposed to such assent, willing and agreeing to what is proposed; but it remains passive toward that power of God, the force and efficacy which heals and converts it; for through him all this is received and comes about.' 'Free Will', in *Peter Martyr Vermigli, Philosophical Works*, trans. J. C. McClelland, 285.

[32] As we have noted, in developing his account of particular providence Calvin shows awareness of both Epicureanism, with its emphasis upon chance, and of Stoic fate, and develops his own view in a way which self-consciously mediates between these two extremes. On this, see Partee, *Calvin and Classical Philosophy*, part 3.

In at least two places in *Bondage* Calvin accuses Pighius of mixing up two different issues:

I could wish that I had an opponent who would attack me from every side but not rush at me in a blind and confused combat as this man does, for, having resolved to discuss two different issues separately, he now mixes them up together. He says: If even to think anything good or evil is in nobody's power, but everything happens by 'absolute necessity'. . . . But he has undertaken to deal with the providence of God, on which this necessity depends, elsewhere, and this is just what he does in the last four books of his work. Why then does he now mix up this issue with the other one? Let him say whatever he has to say, even if it is weak, even if it is worthless; if only he will stay in one place, I will let him say it.[33]

And later, 'As for the necessary or chance occurrence of events, I prefer not to touch on this at the present time, lest by entwining different topics I confuse the order of my discourse.'[34]

As we have seen, Calvin deliberately separates his reply to Pighius's first six books from his reply to the remaining four books, which is clear evidence that in Calvin's mind these two sections of the work deal with different issues.

In stressing the separateness of the 'two issues' Calvin may also have had in mind the thought that in his *The Bondage of the Will* Martin Luther had brought the two issues rather indiscriminately together. Part of Luther's cumulative case against Erasmus's view of the will's liberty was not only that the will was in bondage to sin but also that God's foreknowledge of all events necessitates the occurrence of those events. Luther had said: 'It is, then, fundamentally necessary and wholesome for Christians to know that God foreknows nothing contingently, but that He foresees, purposes and does all things according to His own immutable, eternal and infallible will. This bombshell knocks "free-will" flat, and utterly shatters it.'[35]

But there is reason to think that the relationship between the two Reformers has been misunderstood at this point. It is not obvious that Calvin wants to 'put clear water' between himself and Luther on this issue or that he was either annoyed or embarrassed by Luther's views.[36] For both Luther and Calvin refer to the scholastic distinction between the necessity of the consequent (*necessitas consequentis*) and the necessity of the consequence (*necessitas consequentiae*) in connection with the will of God. Luther, in

---

[33] *Bondage*, 35.   [34] *Bondage*, 172.

[35] Martin Luther, *The Bondage of the Will*, trans. J. I. Packer and O. R. Johnston (London: James Clarke, 1957), 80.

[36] These claims are made by A. N. S. Lane in his introduction to Calvin's *Bondage and the Liberation of the Will*, xxiii.

typical fashion, claims that as far as the will of God is concerned the distinction is one without a difference.

So their absurd formula, *all things take place by necessity of consequence, but not by necessity of the thing consequent*, amounts merely to this: everything takes place by necessity, but the things that take place are not God Himself. But what need was there to tell us that?—as though there were any fear of our claiming that things which happen are God, or possess a divine and necessarily existent nature! So our original proposition still stands and remains unshaken; all thing take place by necessity.[37]

That is, since no one wishes to affirm that everything that happens does so by metaphysical necessity, the distinction between the necessity of the consequent and the necessity of the consequence is inapplicable in this case. All things are necessary, but they are so in virtue of the will of God.

Whether or not Luther is justified in calling the distinction 'absurd' is another matter. Calvin certainly does not agree with him in this judgement. As we noted in the discussion of providence, Calvin is more respectful of the distinction between the two sorts of necessity itself, claiming that although he shrinks from the received forms of speech, and the distinction between absolute and consequential necessity, this is only so that 'no subtlety of reasoning might prevent the simplest reader from understanding and acknowledging the truth of what I testify'.[38] But each of the Reformers argues that the will of God necessitates things, each denies that God is subject to fate, and that the necessity of what occurs is a necessity unrelated to the will of God. The only material difference is that Calvin wishes to hold to the separateness of the 'two issues' while Luther combines them in his cumulative case for the bondage of the will. But his substantive position is the same as Luther's: nothing happens but by the will of God; hence the will of God necessitates everything. But the will of God is contingent, since 'to take contingency out of the world altogether would be absurd'.[39] He puts this clearly in the following remarks in the *Institutes*:

Not always does a like reason appear, but we ought undoubtedly to hold that whatever changes are discerned in the world are produced from the secret stirring of God's hand. But what God has determined must necessarily so take place, even though it is neither unconditionally, nor of its own peculiar nature necessary. A familiar example presents itself in the bones of Christ. When he took upon himself a body like our own, no sane man will deny that his bones were fragile; yet it was impossible to break them [John 19: 33, 36]. Whence again we see that distinctions concerning relative necessity and absolute necessity, likewise of consequent and

[37] Luther, *The Bondage of the Will*, 82.   [38] *The Secret Providence of God*, 235.
[39] *The Secret Providence of God*, 234.

consequence, were not recklessly invented in schools, when God subjected to fragility the bones of his Son, which he had exempted from being broken, and thus restricted to the necessity of his own plan what could have happened naturally.[40]

Bones do not break of necessity, yet it could have happened naturally that the bones of Christ broke, as it happened naturally that he ate and slept. But God had determined otherwise. And so in virtue of the will of God Christ's bones, though naturally fragile, were in fact incapable of being broken. So God's will is the 'highest and first cause of all things'. In this sense it is 'absolute'. But this does not mean that the things that occur do so with the necessity which God himself has. Calvin is at pains to stress that this is not the case. Further, it does not follow that because men and women in bondage to sin necessarily sin that this necessity is the same necessity as that by which all events fall under the will of God. Calvin generally wishes to reserve the discussion of this latter sense of necessity for when he discusses providence, in what he intended at that time to be a separate book discussing the last four chapters of Pighius's work.

For we do not say that the wicked sin of necessity in such a way as to imply that they sin without wilful and deliberate evil intent. The necessity comes from the fact that God accomplishes his work, which is sure and steadfast, through them. At the same time, however, the will and purpose to do evil which dwells within them makes them liable to censure. But, it is said, they are driven and forced to this by God. Indeed, but in such a way that in a single deed the action of God is one thing and their own action is another. For they gratify their evil and wicked desires, but God turns this wickedness so as to bring his judgments to execution. This subject is one that I am touching on lightly with, as it were, only a brief mention, since elsewhere it will have to be treated at greater length and with more attention.[41]

This brief discussion of his position, depending as it does for its articulation on the scholastic distinction between God the primary cause and human beings as secondary causes, makes it clear that Calvin's view of predestination (a corollary of his view of providence) may not from a strictly logical point of view require a compatibilist understanding of human freedom. For it is possible to hold both to predestination and to libertarian human freedom, providing one sufficiently emphasizes the inscrutability and incomprehensibility of such an arrangement. Nevertheless it is obvious that Calvin's view of providence and compatibilism go naturally together.

So, on balance, considering both Calvin's explicit statements about the nature of human bondage and liberation together with his view of providence and predestination, we may say that his view *favours* a compatibilist view of human action, even if it does not *entail* it, and that it would perhaps

---

[40] *Inst.* 1. 16. 9.   [41] *Bondage of the Will*, 37–8.

be anachronistic to press his texts too far in an attempt to answer questions that only developed later in western culture.

Yet while Calvin holds that God ordains all events and determines many of them, he does not hold that he determines all of them if to determine means to 'efficiently cause'. For God cannot efficiently cause evil actions, or, at least, he cannot cause evil actions for evil reasons, since God cannot do evil, and so a fortiori he cannot will evil; at least, not *as* evil.[42] In contrast with many scholastics, Calvin does not deploy the privative notion of evil at this point, because as we have seen he does not favour that notion.

THE BONDAGE OF THE WILL—HOW ARE WE TO UNDERSTAND IT?

So far we have focused on Calvin's teaching on the metaphysics of human action. While the preponderance of modern philosophical discussion on human freedom is concerned with the freedom–causal determinism issue, other discussions may throw light on what Calvin was saying on *Bondage*'s chief topic, the moral corruption of the human person and his liberation through grace. These discussions may provide us with tools that will enable us to clarify further what Calvin and his mentor Augustine of Hippo meant by the bondage of the will and its liberation.

Calvin rejects what might be called the 'pagan' or philosophical account of the bondage of the will as part of his general case against pagan ethics, which is that it presents too rosy a picture of human moral capabilities. With regard to moral and spiritual matters the philosophers are 'blinder than moles',[43] they regard the acquiring of virtue as a ground for pride,[44] they are ignorant of the new birth.[45] But Calvin's most basic criticism of pagan philosophers and those Christians unduly influenced by them, is that in their analysis of free will and virtue and vice 'they were seeking in a ruin for a building'.

Hence the great obscurity faced by the philosophers, for they were seeking in a ruin for a building, and in scattered fragments for a well-knit structure. They held this principle, that man would not be a rational animal unless he possessed free choice of good and evil; also it entered their minds that the distinction between virtues and vices would be obliterated if man did not order his life by his own planning. Well reasoned so far—if there had been no change in man. But since this was hidden from them, it is no wonder they mix up heaven and earth![46]

One consequence of this is that they have deficient views of human fallenness; not surprisingly, for they have no concept of a Fall. In *Inst.* II. 2. 2 Calvin

---

[42] Here is one important respect in which Calvin's determinism, if that is what it is, differs from modern naturalism in which the causes of our actions are mechanistic, not teleological.

[43] *Inst.* II. 2. 18.   [44] *Inst.* III. 7. 2.   [45] *Inst.* III. 7. 1.   [46] *Inst.* I. 15. 8.

repeatedly inveighs against 'the philosophers' (they are referred to five or six times in two short sections)[47] and their view of the 'bondage of the senses' (*servitutem sensus*). The philosophers in question seem to be Plato and Aristotle though he does not mention them by name. The bondage of the senses is the captivity of the understanding to the senses. On this account the appetite havers between obeying the reason and obeying the senses. If the appetite 'subjects itself to the bondage of the senses, it is so corrupted and perverted by the latter as to degenerate into lust'. But Calvin is particularly concerned at the way in which Christians such as Peter Lombard, who do have the concept of the Fall, have nevertheless adopted such a superficial view.

These philosophers consequently declare that the understanding is endowed with reason, the best ruling principle for the leading of a good and blessed life, provided it sustains itself within its own excellence and displays the strength bestowed upon it by nature. But they state that the lower impulse, called 'sense', by which man is drawn off into error and delusion is such that it can be tamed and gradually overcome by reason's rod.[48]

This is too superficial for Calvin because it places the source of 'bondage' in the senses alone, when for Calvin 'Not only did a lower appetite seduce him [Adam], but unspeakable impiety occupied the very citadel of his mind, and pride penetrated to the depths of his heart. Thus it is pointless and foolish to restrict the corruption that arises thence only to what are called the impulses of the senses.'[49] 'The whole man is overwhelmed—as by a deluge—from head to foot, so that no part is immune from sin and all that proceeds from him is to be imputed to sin.'[50]

So fallen humankind is in bondage to sin. I want to clarify the way in which, for Calvin, sin imposes restrictions on the range of a person's choice, restrictions of a kind that warrant his view that there are certain things a sinful person cannot do, even though that person is not compelled to do what he does. In other words, I want to do justice to what we might call the *modalities* of the action of the person who is in bondage to sin, while still maintaining Calvin's insistence that such actions are voluntary and not the result of external coercion. The bondage of which Calvin speaks is not like the bondage that results from physical imprisonment, nor is it a craving of a purely physical kind, like the craving for water or alcohol.

We might initially think that the bondage of the will consists in having desires of a certain intensity and strength, such that a person who is overcome by such desires cannot but fulfil them or cannot but fulfil them if physically unimpeded. We certainly use the language of force in describing

---

[47] *Inst.* II. 2. 2, 3.   [48] *Inst.* II. 2. 2.   [49] *Inst.* II. 1. 9.   [50] *Inst.* II. 1. 9.

the operation of such intense desires; a person may be overcome by a desire, and we may say that in the circumstances he could not help doing what he did.

Yet there are several problems with this attempt to identify the modality of bondage with psychological, felt intensity, one being that of identifying in a non-circular way what the strength of a desire is; and another being that a person may have a strong desire for something that is relatively trivial and inconsequential in his life. This is significant for Calvin because bondage to sin is not trivial or inconsequential. A person may have an intense desire for a non-trivial end that he also strongly disapproves of having. But the most important problem is that it would imply that all sinful actions are psychologically compelled.

Probably the best prospect of making progress here is to distinguish between what contemporary philosophers call first-order and second-order desires.[51] Not only do we, as persons, desire certain things with varying degrees of intensity, we are able to take up attitudes to, and to possess desires about, those desires. Thus a person might want another cream cake but not want to want the cake; alternatively, he may want another cake and want to want it! In taking up the issue in this way I am not arguing or implying that one can thereby bypass the traditional determinism–free will debate, as Harry Frankfurt has been taken to be claiming.[52] I am using it simply for the purposes of trying to be clear on the modalities of Calvin's view of the bondage of the will and its liberation.

What is the difference between these two cases? Following Harry Frankfurt, I suggest that the difference lies in whether or not such a person *owns* or *identifies with* a particular first-order desire or range of desires. I may have a desire for a cream cake and not 'own' or 'identify with' the desire, and so be ashamed of or rueful at the fact of my desire. In that case, my second-order desire is not to have that particular first-order desire. On

---

[51] I am adapting this from Harry Frankfurt's papers 'Freedom of the Will and the Concept of a Person', in *The Importance of What We Care About*, 23, and 'Identification and Wholeness in *Necessity, Volition and Love*'. In 'Sanctification, Hardening of the Heart, and Frankfurt's Concept of Free Will', *Journal of Philosophy* (1988). Eleonore Stump develops Frankfurt's distinction and adapts it to illuminate features of Christian conversion, though not in a way which would, I think, have met with Calvin's approval. And in her 'Augustine on Free Will', while offering a hierarchical, Frankfurt-type account of Augustine's view of the will, she struggles somewhat unsuccessfully to interpret Augustine as a libertarian (Eleonore Stump and Norman Kretzmann (eds.), *The Cambridge Companion to Augustine* (Cambridge: Cambridge University Press, 2001)). John M. Fischer and Mark Ravizza present a plausible case for the consistency of such a hierarchical view of the self with compatibilism in their *Responsibility and Control* (Cambridge: Cambridge University Press, 1998).

[52] For a collection of papers relevant to this debate see John Martin Fischer and Mark Ravizza (eds.), *Perspectives on Moral Responsibility* (Ithaca, NY: Cornell University Press, 1993).

the other hand, I may have a desire for a cream cake and 'own' the desire, experiencing no dissonance between my first-order and my second-order desires.

I suggest that for Calvin (and for Augustine, who was watching over Calvin's shoulder at points such as these) the voluntariness of the state of being in bondage to sin lies in this idea of ownership or identification, and not in the area of choice *ab initio*. On his view fallen men and women are born into the world already possessing a certain structure of desires that they then own; it is in their uncoerced and hence voluntary ownership of and identification with this structure that their responsibility before God, and their culpability, ultimately lie.

This is part of the picture. But, as I hope that my trivial example of the choosing of a cream cake indicates, for Calvin there is more to the will's bondage to sin than just this hierarchical structure. For one thing, the structure must cover matters of fundamental moral and spiritual import-ance. For Calvin, sin and righteousness concern the most central of issues, a person's relation to God. For another, what constitutes bondage is that the fundamental, non-trivial, second-order desires are stable and effective, that is, they carry through to willed courses of action. A person who is in bondage to sin is someone who owns and identifies with his desire to serve and worship the creature rather than the Creator and whose actions express this orientation appropriately. Let us look at each of these points in turn.

For Frankfurt a person is free if there is an alignment between what that person wants and what he wants to want. So that human freedom has a purely structural character. On Frankfurt's account Satan is free if his first- and second-order desires are in appropriate alignment. So for Calvin this point about structure can only be half the story. For the person in bondage to sin has his first- and second-order desires aligned, but because the desires are expressions of an unrighteous motive their alignment is not an expression of freedom but of bondage even though, as Calvin stresses, such a person does not recognize his bondage to sin for what it is. For Calvin one of the characteristics of such bondage is that it is self-deceiving. The course of life of a person in bondage seems right to him. This is the way he wants to go. He owns his second-order desire in the sense that it becomes a part of himself. But his course of action is in fact godless.

In the *Institutes* Calvin recognizes this in the following way. Commenting on a distinction made by Augustine he says:

The chief point of this distinction, then, must be that man, as he was corrupted by the Fall, sinned willingly, not unwillingly or by compulsion; by the most eager inclination of his heart, not by forced compulsion; by the prompting of his own lust, not by compulsion from without. Yet so depraved is his nature that he can be moved or impelled only to evil. But if this is true, then it is clearly expressed that man is surely subject to the necessity of sinning.[53]

The second element is implicit in the first but needs to be spelled out. In order for a person to be in bondage to sin, in Calvin's sense, he must not only want to have his desire to worship and serve the creature more than the Creator, but that second-order desire must be stable and strong, effective in making the corresponding first-order desire his will. It is not a second-order desire that is continually liable to frustration from competing second-order desires and which as a consequence only fitfully carries through to willed action.[54]

So the person in bondage to sin must be distinguished from the unwilling addict. The unwilling addict is in the grip of a physical craving such that his actions of a certain type are overdetermined. As a result of this over-determination, the addict's first-order desires for the drug are impervious to any change in his second-order desires to desist from its use. He may want not to want the cigarette but his craving for it prevails. So there is a mis-alignment of first and second orders due to the overbearing strength of the first-order desire. While what Calvin regards as the uniformly evil life of a person in bondage to sin proceeds from a second-order desire that is wholly set upon the creature rather than the Creator, such a person is not in the physical grip of anything, nor is his first-order desire overdetermined. Were sin like such a physical addiction then it could be described as coercive. Rather, the action of the person in bondage to sin is determined by the character of his second-order desire, by its stability and centrality and by the fact that the person 'owns' that desire. (From what we saw earlier, Calvin would call this a habit of mind.) It must also be distinguished from the case of a person who vacillates from day to day over what he wants to want. Here there are periods of alignment, but no stability. Should the stable, fundamental second-order desire change—or be changed—by becoming weaker, or fitful, say, then such a change would be sufficient to bring about appropriate changes in first-order desires.

In this state of bondage to sin a person could say, using Martin Luther's words, 'Here I stand. I can do no other.' He 'stands' in adherence to a course of action that is wholly evil because it proceeds from a wholly evil motivation, and these words are not an expression of passivity in the face of coercion (as in 'I couldn't help letting the hot plate fall to the floor') but

---

[53] *Inst.* II. 3. 5.

[54] Frankfurt calls effective second-order desires 'volitions' and does not deal much with ineffective second-order desires. The development of the distinction between effective and ineffective second-order desires is due to Eleonore Stump, 'Sanctification, Hardening of the Heart, and Frankfurt's Concept of Free Will'.

of a directed 'internal' activity, directed from the most basic level of his personality.

So the modality, the necessity that is characteristic of the bondage, refers not to passivity in the face of external necessity but to the inability of a man in bondage to sin (at this stage in his career) to alter his second-order desire to worship and serve the creature rather than the Creator. He authoritatively identifies himself with such a course of life. Had such a person been physically or in other ways compelled to do what is good, then his inner self would or could have repudiated this.

Let us now turn our attention to the liberation of the man who is in bondage to sin.

LIBERATION

How does the person in bondage to sin, with his firm effective second-order desire to want to serve the creature, effect the transition and identify himself with an effective second-order desire to want to want to serve the Creator? How does a fundamental, authoritative, second-order desire about such a fundamental matter, a desire which the person owns or identifies with, come to be replaced by a second-order desire of the same fundamental character, but which is a desire to serve the Creator?[55]

In trying to answer these questions we confront a more general difficulty. An account of a transition from possessing one fundamental, effective desire to possessing a similar desire of an opposite kind, must involve the exercise of a new capacity, the capacity to break the effectiveness of the second-order desire to serve the creature and then to own and identify with the contrary desire to serve the Creator. A person who shares the theological views of Pighius must explain the transition by denying that sin is a form of bondage in Calvin's sense and then by saying that by an act of the will, assisted by divine grace, a person may come to possess the capacity to serve the Creator. By the same token he had the power to resist the proffered divine assistance. And so even as fallen he must possess freedom of will in the sense heartily repudiated by Calvin—freedom to choose between good and evil.

Although we have seen that at one important place in his argument Calvin appeals approvingly to Aristotle, there are other places where he appears to be less than complimentary to The Philosopher. Debating about the hardness

---

[55] Here it might be inquired whether a person who has a second-order desire owns and identifies with it. If so, do we not need to posit a third-order desire, and then a fourth-order desire, and so on *ad infinitum*? Interesting responses to this question are to be found in Harry Frankfurt, 'Three Concepts of Free Action', in *The Importance of What We Care About*, and by Eleonore Stump in 'Sanctification, Hardening of the Heart, and Frankfurt's Concept of Free Will'.

of the human heart and the need for grace, Calvin states 'Pighius declares that the hardness was incurred through bad habit. Just as if one of the philosophers' crew should say that by evil living a person had become hardened or callous towards evil.' Calvin's (and Augustine's) view is at odds with the Aristotelian idea—the idea of the 'philosophers' crew'—that we become just by doing just acts, prudent by doing prudent acts, brave by doing brave acts. It may be true, as Richard Swinburne says,[56] that 'other things being equal, each time one does something, the more natural doing it becomes. Doing an action of a certain kind frequently gives one the character of one who is naturally inclined to do actions of that kind.' But if, for example, being just is not simply a matter of habitually or spontaneously doing what is objectively just but also a matter of having the right motives and dispositions in doing so—if, in other words, we take a motivational view of ethical goodness, as Calvin and Augustine do—then the question is how we do the just thing in the first place, how we come to be remotivated to love justice. Calvin's answer is that we can only do a just act in the first place by having the *habitus* of our minds redirected, a redirecting that, at least in its first stages, must be done for and to us rather than our doing it.

There is reason to think that Calvin is not being quite fair to Aristotle here, if indeed he had Aristotle clearly in view.[57] For Aristotle does not only say, 'This then, is the case with the virtues also; by doing the acts that we do in our transactions with other men we become just or unjust, and by doing the acts that we do in the presence of danger, and by being habituated to feel fear or confidence, we become brave or cowardly.'[58] He also says:

Again, the case of the arts and that of the virtues are not similar; for the products of the arts have their goodness in themselves, so that it is enough that they should have a certain character, but if the acts that are in accordance with the virtues have themselves a certain character it does not follow that they are done justly or temperately. The agent also must be in a certain condition when he does them; in the first place he must have knowledge, secondly he must choose the acts, and choose them for their own stakes, and thirdly his action must proceed from a firm and unchangeable character.[59]

There is plenty of scope here for Calvin to adapt Aristotle to his own view by claiming that a firm and unchangeable desire to be virtuous can only be brought about by the efficacious grace of God.

---

[56] *Atonement and Responsibility*, (Oxford: Clarendon Press, 1989), 32.

[57] He does not mention Aristotle by name and in the parallel treatment of the point in the *Institutes* the only philosopher he explicitly refers to is Cicero who Calvin believes thinks that we acquire virtue for ourselves and that we and not God are to be praised for it (*Inst.* ii. 2. 3). Yet Calvin takes Cicero's opinion to be that of all philosophers.   [58] *The Nichomachean Ethics*, 19.

[59] *The Nicomachean Ethics*, 34. I was reminded of this point by Harry Bunting.

To Calvin it is unclear how someone who holds Pighius's view can explain how a fundamental, effective second-order desire to serve the creature can be supplanted by an appropriately fundamental, effective second-order desire to serve the Creator other than by saying that the second-order desire of the person in bondage is rendered ineffective by divine grace, and grace produces an effective second-order desire of the opposite kind.

So Calvin holds that a new, effective second-order desire—a new accidental property of the *habitus* of the soul, as he would put it—is created by the immediate work of the Spirit. This work of the Spirit, which may be instantaneous, does not necessarily register itself instantaneously on the consciousness but may initiate a conscious process of discernible stages. Perhaps if he were asked to illustrate such a process at work Calvin would refer to what happened to Augustine in the garden.

In his treatment of these matters in the *Institutes* it is in his characterization of liberation from sin rather than in his discussion of bondage to sin that Calvin's hierarchical view of the self becomes explicit. Writing of 'vivification' (*vivificatio*), the enlivening of the soul by the Holy Spirit, he says that it means 'the desire to live in a holy and devoted manner, a desire arising from rebirth; as if it were said that man dies to himself that he may begin to live to God'.[60] If a person dies to himself his fundamental, effective second-order desires are replaced by other effective second-order desires. Similarly, repentance is a 'departing from ourselves' in which 'we turn to God, and having taken off our former mind, we put on a new'.[61] The soul 'puts off its old nature'.[62] 'It is a very hard and difficult thing to put off ourselves and to depart from our inborn disposition.'[63] Who is the 'we' who puts off 'ourselves'? In Frankfurtian terms, the second-order fundamental desires constitute in each of us a 'self'. Calvin might say that Frankfurt is formalizing language that is familiar to the Christian from the writings of Paul in Romans 7, Ephesians 4, and elsewhere.

Earlier we pointed out that Calvin uses different words for the will, *voluntas, arbitrium, electio*. *Voluntas* is typically translated as 'will', *electio* and *arbitrium* as 'choice' or 'decision'. This can be illustrated from the following section of the Battles translation:

Now we must examine the will [*voluntas*], upon which freedom of decision [*arbitrii libertas*] especially depends; for we have already seen that choice [*electionem*] belongs to the sphere of the will rather than to that of the understanding. To begin with, the philosophers teach that all things seek good through a natural instinct, and this view is received with general consent. But that we may not suppose this doctrine to have anything to do with the uprightness of the human will [*voluntas*], let us observe that the power of free choice [*liberi arbitrii*] is not to be sought in such an

---

[60] *Inst.* III. 3. 3.   [61] *Inst.* III. 3. 5.   [62] *Inst.* III. 3. 6.   [63] *Inst.* III. 3. 8.

appetite, which arises from inclination of nature rather than from deliberation of mind.[64]

Perhaps it is not too fanciful to think that in Calvin's thought the will (*voluntas*) operates at the second-order. In the language of the Battles translation we are free when our will is renewed by the Spirit to the point where it is effective in producing properly motivated choices or decisions which conform to the commands of God.

On Calvin's (and Augustine's) view of the matter it won't do to say that Christian sanctification is the process initiated by, say, a person's being strengthened by a prayer to God. For the desire to pray, or at least the properly motivated, effective desire to pray, is itself the gift of the Spirit, the first workings of liberation from bondage to sin. To suppose that God acts on a first-order desire, strengthening it only at the behest of human initiative— such as a prayer for God to do so, issuing from an appropriate second-order desire—appears to be semi-Pelagian in character and to violate Calvin's opposition to the claim that we can prepare ourselves for grace that he expresses throughout *Bondage* as well as in the *Institutes*. 'Now it is certain that the human heart always swells with pride and blind self-assurance until it is tamed and subdued by the Spirit of God and settles into humble submission. Nor indeed do we deny that man is prepared in this way to receive the gift of righteousness, but it is by the direction of the Holy Spirit, not by his own strength.'[65] So the way in which the transition from bondage to liberation is brought about is by God directly and efficaciously giving the person in bondage an effective second-order desire that is 'himself' while at the same time empowering him to disown the contrary second-order desires. This does not mean that the disowned second-order desires, and the appropriate first-order desires, are never active, but that they are never henceforth fundamental in the way they were before. When they are active then the conflict between flesh and spirit classically sketched by Paul in Romans 7 is instantiated. There is war between the centrally owned, effective second-order desires to serve the Creator and the still active but no longer fundamental nor fully effective second-order desire to serve the creature.

The last thing which vexes [Pighius] is my statement that after regeneration the faithful soul is divided into two parts. Every time he mentions this he says that I am imagining or dreaming it. For today the theology of the Romanists is to consider as incredible what ought to be the most familiar knowledge to a Christian. But seeing that such people have no more spiritual experience than do brute beasts, at least the authority of Paul should suffice to put a gag on Pighius. Since it ought not to

---

[64] *Inst.* II. 2. 26. The Latin originals in brackets have been added to the Battles translation.

[65] *Bondage*, 193.

be in doubt that in the seventh chapter of Romans he portrays a person who is regenerated, let us see whether he does not in that passage present in living form that very thing of which I speak. So then he bemoans the common bondage of the faithful in [speaking of] his own person. For while he wills and desires the good, he does not find the ability to accomplish this. With his mind he agrees with the law of God, but in his flesh with the law of sin, and so he does not do the good which he loves, but rather the evil which he hates. You will see his will agreeing with righteousness. Where then does the obstacle come from, which prevents the action from following? Surely only from a contrary desire. Where, next, does that desire come from, if not from the fact that remnants of the old man which struggle against the Spirit live on in him?[66]

Putting this in slightly different terms, on Calvin's view the person who is freed from bondage to sin does not at once experience a *complete* causal alignment between fundamental, effective second-order desires and the production of first-order desires. The new second-order desire is effective but not completely so, as is shown by the continuing operation of other second-order desires (the 'another law' referred to by Paul in Romans 7: 23) which are not fundamental and so in that sense are not 'me' but for which I am nonetheless responsible. Until there is complete alignment there remains an element of conflict within his person, one that is deeper than the conflict between duty and inclination or that engendered by the strife between competing goals.[67]

Although as far as I am aware Calvin does not discuss the question, there is no reason to think that he would deny that God could immediately remove the evil *habitus* of the soul as well as all its evil effects. He could do so, but he has a good reason not to do so, a reason not unconnected with what is sometimes referred to as 'soul-making'.

CALVIN, FREEDOM, AND THE FREE WILL DEFENCE

In this chapter I have tried to take a fresh look at Calvin's views on the bondage of the will to sin. We have seen that he tries, but not with complete success, to separate this issue from the 'other issue' of the particular providence of God over all things. We have also seen that although he makes statements that, on the surface, may seem to imply the opposite, overall the evidence is that Calvin favoured what is today called a compatibilist position on free will, holding that human responsibility is compatible with a form of

---

[66] *Bondage*, 179.

[67] For an interesting discussion of Thomas Aquinas's approach to Romans 7, see Norman Kretzmann, 'Warring Against the Law of My Mind: Aquinas on Romans 7', in T. V. Morris (ed.), *Philosophy and the Christian Faith* (Notre Dame: University of Notre Dame Press, 1988).

causal determinism. Finally, we have tried to elucidate the modalities of the will's bondage to sin, modalities which have frequently been confused with the metaphysical modalities of the nature of human action.

This allows us readily to see how Calvin would have responded to the modern claim that the existence of evil is consistent with the existence of an all-loving, all-powerful God because it is possible that God has endowed human beings with libertarian free will. This implies that although God could bring it about that human beings exist and never do what is evil he cannot bring it about that human beings exist *such that* they never do evil. Calvin would clearly not be disposed to respond to the problem of evil in these terms, even if he acknowledged the problem as currently discussed. For in his view God could have prevented human beings from doing evil in a way that is consistent with their freedom, for their freedom is a compatibilist freedom. He is quite explicit on this.

Now we need bear only this in mind: man was far different at the first creation from his whole posterity, who, deriving their origin from him in his corrupted state, have contracted from him a hereditary taint. For, the individual parts of his soul were formed to uprightness, the soundness of his mind stood firm, and his will was free to choose the good. If anyone objects that his will was placed in an insecure position because its power was weak, his status should have availed to remove any excuse; nor was it reasonable for God to be constrained by the necessity of making a man who either could not or would not sin at all. Such a nature would, indeed, have been more excellent. But to quarrel with God on this precise point, as if he ought to have conferred this upon man, is more than iniquitous, inasmuch as it was in his own choice to give whatever he pleased. But the reason he did not sustain man by the virtue of perseverance lies hidden in his plan; sobriety is for us the part of wisdom.[68]

Calvin is not prepared to entertain discussion of what the Lord ought to have done, but he is clear on what he could have done. The Lord in fact left the original pair to the liberty of their own will, and they defected. Why did he do so? It is here that Calvin would appeal once more to the 'epistemic gap' between our understanding and God's.

But we must so cherish moderation that we do not try to make God render account to us, but so reverence his secret judgments as to consider his will the truly just cause of all things. When dense clouds darken the sky, and a violent tempest arises, because a gloomy mist is cast over our eyes, thunder strikes our ears and all our senses are benumbed with fright, everything seems to us to be confused and mixed up; but all the while a constant quiet and serenity ever remain in heaven. So we must infer that, while the disturbances in the world deprive us of judgment, God out of the pure light of his justice and wisdom tempers and directs these very movements in the best-conceived order to a right end.[69]

[68] *Inst.* 1. 15. 8.   [69] *Inst.* 1. 17. 1.

Calvin's recognition of an epistemic gap between what human beings can possibly know and what God knows has cropped up more than once. This epistemic caution is one factor in accounting for the modesty of Calvin's metaphysical reflections on the relation between the nature and activity of God and our own activity. So it is appropriate that we next give consideration to a central, if not the central, epistemic idea in Calvin's thought.

7

Divine Accommodation

WE move from considering central aspects of Calvin's metaphysics to a central idea of his religious epistemology, the idea that much of our knowledge of God is due to God's gracious accommodation of himself to our straitened epistemic condition. This is one corollary of Calvin's acceptance of the 'epistemic gap' between God and ourselves which we first discussed in Chapter 1. Appealing to the gap is also central to Calvin's approach to evil, as we have seen.

Calvin holds that although the distinction between God as he is in himself and as he is towards us would operate no matter what the human noetic condition, God has more particularly accommodated himself to our creaturely ways of thinking in his speech to us in Scripture in order to make known to us his remedy for human fallenness. So Calvin prefaces his discussion of the Trinity with these comments:

> For who even of slight intelligence does not understand that, as nurses commonly do with infants, God is wont in a measure to 'lisp' in speaking to us? Thus such forms of speaking do not so much express clearly what God is like as accommodate the knowledge of him to our slight capacity (*tenuitati nostrae*). To do this he must descend far beneath his loftiness.[1]

However, before we examine such 'lisping' more closely we should note that accommodation is an idea which operates at various levels and in various contexts in Calvin's thought.

Stephen Benin has claimed that 'Since for Calvin all knowledge and truth were contained in Scripture, and since knowledge and truth could not be obtained by humans but had to be given them, then Scripture, in some way or other, had to be tempered to the human capacity. For Calvin, this meant that Scripture was accommodated to the human level.'[2] Recent work on Calvin has shown that his appeal to the idea of accommodation is more ramified than Stephen Benin allows, even granting that he says of Calvin that

---

[1] *Inst.* I. 13. 1.

[2] Stephen D. Benin, *The Footprints of God* (Albany, NY: SUNY Press, 1993), 189. See also Ford Lewis Battles, 'God was Accommodating Himself to Human Capacity', in Donald K. McKim (ed.), *Readings in Calvin's Theology* (Grand Rapids, Mich.: Baker, 1984).

he is the closest Christian rival to Chrysostom, who uses the idea of accommodation 'seemingly without end'.[3] It is possible to distinguish at least three different contexts in which Calvin makes use of the idea of accommodation.

First, the historical context. David F. Wright has drawn attention to remarkable passages in Calvin in which he argues that due to the hardness of heart of the people of Israel God accommodated himself to them over ethical issues. Let us call this the *morally indexed* sense of accommodation; such divine accommodation is always at a given time or epoch. For example, concerning laws governing the marrying of women taken captive (Deuteronomy 21: 10–13), Calvin writes:

> It was better, indeed, that they should altogether abstain from such marriages; yet it was difficult so to restrain their lust as that they should not decline from chastity in the least degree; and hence we learn how much license conquerors allow themselves in war, so that there is no room for perfect purity in them. Wherefore God so tempers His indulgence as that the Israelites, remembering the adoption wherewith He had honoured them, should not disgrace themselves, but in the very fervour of their lust should retain some religious affection.[4]

The word 'accommodation' does not often appear in such remarks, but the idea is clearly there. There is an interesting contrast in Calvin's thought highlighted by such passages. In general Calvin yields to no one in his insistence on divine sovereignty. Yet in these passages the sovereign God is shown to have another side. God limits himself in his relation to his Israel. He may even be said to be in thrall to the passions of his rude, primitive people; not only limiting himself, but being limited by them.[5] Yet Calvin's approach here is not entirely novel. He here seems to take a similar position to that of Duns Scotus, for example, who argued that in permitting Patriarchal bigamy God accommodated himself in order to preserve the good of procreation over the good of monogamy.[6]

---

[3] *The Footprints of God*, p. xix. Calvin read Chrysostom thoroughly, particularly in preparing his exegetical work, as Anthony N. S. Lane shows, *John Calvin: Student of the Church Fathers*.

[4] John Calvin, *Commentaries on the Four Last Books of Moses arranged in the Form of a Harmony*, II. 71. David Wright has explored various aspects of divine accommodation in a number of papers: See 'Calvin's Pentateuchal Criticism: Equity, Hardness of Heart and Divine Accommodation in the Mosaic Harmony Commentary', *Calvin Theological Journal* (1986); 'Accommodation and Barbarity in Calvin's Old Testament Commentaries', in A. G. Auld (ed.), *Understanding Poets and Prophets: Essays in Honour of George Wishart Anderson* (JSOT Supplement Series 152; Sheffield: JSOT, 1993); 'Calvin's "Accommodation" Revisited', in P. De Klerk (ed.), *Calvin as Exegete* (Grand Rapids, Mich.: Calvin Studies Society, 1995); 'Calvin's Accommodating God', in W. H. Neuser (ed.), *Calvinus Sincerioris Religionis Vindex* (Kirksville: Sixteenth Century Journal Publisher, 1996/7).

[5] For discussion of this point, see Wright, 'Calvin's Pentateuchal Criticism', 45f.

[6] See *Duns Scotus on the Will and Morality*, ed. Allan B. Wolter (Washington: Catholic University of America Press, 1986), 291–3.

Second, there is a sense in which the accommodation works the other way. According to Calvin we must accommodate ourselves to God. 'Thus once we begin to conceive of God as he truly is, that is, in his justice, integrity and righteousness, we will only want to accommodate ourselves to him.'[7] Let us call this *human* accommodation.

Finally there is the sense for which Calvin is best known, the primary sense, in which according to him God accommodates himself to us in speaking of himself. The need for such accommodation is a permanent feature of our relationship to God and so we may call this the *revelational* sense of accommodation.

Calvin's view of God's accommodation of himself in this more fundamental way is to be distinguished from the use of that term by later, Enlightenment, thinkers. In what might be called the first phase of the Enlightenment the idea of accommodation was used to account for what were taken to be errors and other discrepancies in the text of Scripture, including Jesus' own accommodation to the errors of the people of his day. But the idea of textual error in the Bible, or of Jesus including erroneous material in his teaching for pedagogic purposes, would have been abhorrent to Calvin.[8]

In later phases of the Enlightenment there was a more thoroughgoing disparagement of revelation as a source of knowledge of God, and the very idea of revelation came to be thought of as an accommodation to more primitive periods of reasoning than the present. So that, for example, the idea of an atonement for sin, the language about angels and the devil, as well as of heaven and hell (all of which were drawn from scriptural revelation) were said to be accommodations to popular ideas and so to be an approximation to what is true, and incidental to what God in fact wants us to know. For Calvin accommodation is a way of presenting what is true, particularly what is true of God. For the Enlightenment it is a transposition of what is true into a pre-modern form because of the limited capacity of the popular, primitive mind to assimilate ideas that only a 'modern', informed and cultured intellect could appreciate in its unaccommodated form.

The closest that Calvin comes to this later position is in his hermeneutical principle that the language of Scripture is the language of everyday appear-

---

[7] Calvin, sermon on Deuteronomy 5: 8–10, quoted by Guenther Haas, *The Concept of Equity in Calvin's Ethics* (Carlisle: Paternoster Press, 1997), 57.

[8] For an interesting discussion of the change in the use of 'accommodation' within the Reformed tradition, and the influence of Faustus Socinius on that change, see Martin I. Klauber and Glenn S. Sunshine, 'Jean-Alphonse Turretini on Biblical Accommodation: Calvinist or Socinian?', *Calvin Theological Journal* (1990). For further discussion of this sense of 'accommodation' see Stephen D. Benin, *The Footprints of God*, ch. 8.

ance, not of scientific exactness. As he puts it in his sermon on Job 9: 7 f., 'God speaketh unto us of these things, [the planets and stars] according to our perceyving of them, and not according as they be.'[9] However, Calvin does not seem to use the term 'accommodation' in this connection, although the idea that he expresses clearly involves an accommodation of sorts.

But he does not invoke this hermeneutical principle as frequently as he might have done. Calvin's pre-Enlightenment approach is perhaps most vividly seen in his failure to appeal to accommodation as a way of escaping hermeneutical difficulties, where doing so might be expected to have provided him with some relief. He never appeals to accommodation to remove possible scientific difficulties raised by the Bible, though as we have seen he does not think that the Bible is a scientific textbook. Take, for example, the story of Joshua's long day, when by divine power Joshua made the sun and the moon stand still (Joshua 10: 12, 13). Given his fondness for invoking the idea of accommodation, one might have expected Calvin to interpret the standing still of the sun in phenomenal rather than real terms; this is how it appeared, not how it really was, and so it was a case of God accommodating himself to the needs of his people. But in fact his interpretation of the long day is unremitting in its literalness.

When, without hesitation, he [i.e. Joshua] opens his mouth and tells the sun and the moon to deviate from the perpetual law of nature, it is just as if he had adjured them by the boundless power of God with which he was invested. Here, too, the Lord gives a bright display of his singular favour toward his Church. As in kindness to the human race he divides the day from the night by the daily course of the sun, and constantly whirls the immense orb with indefatigable swiftness, so he was pleased that it should halt for a short time till the enemies of Israel were destroyed.[10]

So, fond though Calvin was of the idea of accommodation, he did not use it as a cure-all for any problem of understanding which the text of Scripture might present. Rather he seems to have appealed to accommodation princi-pally in connection with our understanding of the activity of God himself. It is this pre-Enlightenment sense of accommodation which is expressed in the following paragraph from the *Institutes*:

What, therefore, does the word 'repentance' mean? Surely its meaning is like that of all other modes of speaking that describe God to us in human terms. For because our weakness does not attain to his exalted state, the description of him that is given to us must be accommodated to our capacity (*ad captum*) so that we may understand it. Now the mode of accommodation is for him to represent himself to us not as he is in himself, but as he seems to us. Although he is beyond all disturbance of mind, yet he testifies that he is angry towards sinners. Therefore whenever we hear that God is

---

[9] *Sermons on Job*, 157.   [10] *Commentary on Joshua*, 10. 12.

angered, we ought not to imagine any emotion in him, but rather to consider that this expression has been taken from our own human experience; because God, whenever he is exercising judgment, exhibits the appearance of one kindled and angered. So we ought not to understand anything else under the word 'repentance' than change of action, because men are wont by changing their action to testify that they are displeased with themselves. Therefore, since every change among men is a correction of what displeases them, but that correction arises out of repentance, then by the word 'repentance' is meant the fact that God changes with respect to his actions. Meanwhile neither God's plan nor his will is reversed, nor his volition altered; but what he had from eternity foreseen, approved, and decreed, he pursues in uninterrupted tenor, however sudden the variation may appear in men's eyes.[11]

This paragraph forms the conclusion of Calvin's answer to an objection to his account of divine providence. The objection is that his account is not consistent with the scriptural teaching about divine repentance. The language of 'repentance' suggests that 'the plan of God does not stand firm and sure, but is subject to change in response to the disposition of things below'.[12] Calvin argues that when repentance is ascribed to God it does not imply disturbance of mind, and that the fact that Scripture also says that God does not repent and is unchangeable shows that repentance can only be figuratively ascribed to God. Thus for Calvin texts such as 1 Samuel 15: 29 and Numbers 23: 19 take precedence over those such as Genesis 6: 6 or 1 Samuel 15: 11 because they tell us what God is, not merely what he is like. Calvin then proceeds to provide what in his view is the *raison d'être* of such language, namely that through it God accommodates himself to us.

This theme of divine accommodation in Calvin, which is evident both in his sermons and in his theological writings, has been discussed from various angles. In this chapter I wish to consider Calvin's remarks, of which the paragraph cited above is a typical and central example, as contributions to theological language, even though as we have seen not all of Calvin's cases of accommodation concern language.

As we saw in Chapter 1, and as is apparent in the passage just cited, Calvin distinguishes between God 'as he is in himself' and 'as he seems to us', a distinction that corresponds to the medieval distinction between God *in se* and *quoad nos*. According to Calvin, God as he is in himself has an unaltered and an unalterable plan formed in eternity. God as he seems to us 'repents'. So in order to understand such divine repentance in a way that is consistent with God having an unaltered plan it must be purged of its usual associations of displeasure, especially displeasure with the self, of fluctuation in mood or

---

[11] *Inst.* 1. 17. 13. See also, for example, his *Commentaries* on Genesis 1: 16, 3: 21. Psalm 10: 1, and Matthew 23: 27. Other references are to be found in Battles, 'God was Accommodating Himself'.

[12] *Inst.* 1. 17. 12.

temper, and of ignorance that are intrinsic features of human repentance. The word 'repentance' is nevertheless appropriately used, according to Calvin, because God's actions change over time. He does A at one time and not-A at a later time, but in doing so he does not change his mind. So when the language of repentance is ascribed to God it is not ascribed with full literalness. In other words, the language of repentance when ascribed to God does not carry with it exactly the same semantic value that it has when ascribed to human beings, but it is nevertheless appropriate language to use of God because it carries some of that value. In God's case the meaning of such terms is controlled or modified by a core of metaphysical truths about God, such as his immutability and his omniscience, which comprise his unchangeable nature and will.

LANGUAGE ABOUT GOD

A central issue in religious language concerns the degree to which language about God must be qualified, non-literal language. Some prominent theologians and philosophers have maintained what we might call literalism or univocalism, the view that while not all language about God is literal, much of it must be. A good example is the eighteenth-century Anglican bishop, George Berkeley (1685–1753). In his study against deism, *Alciphron*, Berkeley denies that words such as knowledge, wisdom, and goodness, when spoken of God, have a different sense from when they are spoken of people. Hence the problems raised by, say, the apparent incompatibility of divine foreknowledge and human freedom cannot be solved by maintaining that 'knowledge' in God means something quite different from what it means for men. 'But all men who think must needs see this is cutting knots and not untying them. For, how are things reconciled with the Divine attributes when these attributes are in every intelligible sense denied; and, consequently, the very notion of God taken away, and nothing left but the name without any meaning annexed to it?'[13] So it must be literally and unqualifiedly true that God is wise, that God knows, and so on. Among contemporary philosophers of religion, William Alston is a stout defender of the view that some terms may be ascribed literally to God.

Suppose that 'comfort H' or 'forgive H', or 'command H to do A', as applied to human beings, does mean something like 'bring about effect E by some movements

---

[13] George Berkeley, *Alciphron* (1734), IV. 17. But it needs to be borne in mind that in Berkeley's case this univocalism about language about God was coupled with an emotive theory of language to cover religious 'mysteries' such as grace, the Trinity, original sin, and a future state. See David Berman, 'Cognitive Theology and Emotive Mysteries in Berkeley's *Alciphron*', in *George Berkeley, Alciphron in Focus* (London: Routledge, 1993).

of one's body'. In that case we cannot use any of these terms of God in just that sense. But not to worry. We can simply lop off the requirement of the effect's being brought about by movements of the agent's body, thereby constructing a less specific derivative sense: *produce effect E in some way or other*. The term with that sense, which is surely intelligible if the original sense was, can then be applied univocally to God and man.[14]

Others take the view that all language about God is metaphorical,[15] while still others have held a thesis that does not seem to lie on the continuum of views just cited, namely, that all our language about God should be negative. Moses Maimonides (1135–1204), the Jewish philosopher, is a good example of this.

As everyone is aware that it is not possible, except through negation, to achieve an apprehension of that which is in our power to apprehend and that, on the other hand, negation does not give knowledge in any respect of the true reality with regard to which the particular matter in question has been negated—all men, those of the past and those of the future, affirm clearly that God, may he be exalted, cannot be apprehended by the intellects, and that none but He Himself can apprehend what He is, and that apprehension of Him consists in the inability to attain the ultimate term in apprehending him.[16]

Calvin's references to divine incomprehensibility and inscrutability naturally predispose him to the *via negativa* even though, as we shall see, he can by no means be called a negative theologian.

However, few reflective theologians have maintained that *all* language used about God is used literally, or negatively, or metaphorically. It is usually reckoned that metaphor, analogy, simile, and symbol each have an important place in any fully developed account of theological language, but that such language about God must be 'anchored' in a core of univocally true expressions. Even Aquinas, who is usually cited as the classical source for the view that language about God is analogical, is at pains to point out that some language about God is literal or univocal.

Some words that signify what has come forth from God to creatures do so in such a way that part of the meaning of the word is the imperfect way in which the creature shares in the divine perfection. Thus, it is part of the meaning of 'rock' that it has its

---

[14] 'How to Think About Divine Action', in Brian Hebblethwaite and Edward Henderson (eds.), *Divine Action: Studies Inspired by the Philosophical Theology of Austin Farrer* (Edinburgh: T. & T. Clark, 1990), 67. See also the articles in part 1 of William Alston, *Divine Nature and Human Language. Essays in Philosophical Theology*, (Ithaca: Cornell University Press, 1989).

[15] Sallie McFague, *Metaphorical Theology: Models of God in Religious Language* (Philadelphia: Fortress Press, 1982).

[16] Moses Maimonides, *Guide of the Perplexed*, trans. with an introd. and notes by Shlomo Pines, with an introductory essay by Leo Strauss (Chicago: University of Chicago Press, 1963), I. 59.

being in a merely material way. Such words can be used of God only metaphorically. There are other words, however, that simply mean certain perfections without any indication of how these perfections are possessed—words, for example, like 'being', 'good', 'living' and so on. These words can be used literally of God.[17]

One of Thomas Aquinas's reasons for his analogical theory of predication of terms for God concerns his view of how language is acquired. We learn the meaning of terms through our mundane experience. When words are transferred to the supermundane, to the transcendent God, some alteration in meaning is called for, and so this is the element of equivocation that inevitably affects theological predication. Alongside it Aquinas holds the complementary thesis, not that the meaning of terms for God is derived from human experience, but that it is derived from God, that God is not metaphorically a king, but that human kings are. He is the paradigm king of which earthly kings are but faint replicas. Thus human fatherhood or kingship is to be understood by analogy from divine fatherhood, rather than the reverse.

We have to consider two things, therefore, in the words we use to attribute perfections to God, firstly the perfections themselves that are signified—goodness, life and the like—and secondly the way in which they are signified. So far as the perfections signified are concerned the words are used literally of God, and in fact more appropriately than they are of creatures, for these perfections belong primarily to God and only secondarily to others.[18]

Roger White concludes an interesting discussion of this view by saying:

I argued that, contrary to many of our immediate intuitions, the primary sense of a large number of the words we use predicatively is not to be found in their use in making predications about everyday empirical objects, but rather in their use to allude to an idea or standard of comparison to which those objects in some way approximate. I suggested that this was in particular true of almost all the words at stake in the doctrine of the divine attributes, and further that there it was true that it was by no means a necessary condition of our having understood the sense of the word that we should be able to spell out what in fact such an ideal would be like.[19]

The direction of fit goes from the divine to the human. But this suggestion does not solve all our problems. For even so we need to know what it is about divine fatherhood which makes human fatherhood a faint imitation of it,

---

[17] *Summa Theologiae*, 1a, 13. 3.

[18] *Summa Theologiae*, 1a, 13. 3, trans. Herbert McCabe. See also 1a, 13. 6.

[19] See the remarks of Roger White in 'Notes on Analogical Predication and Speaking about God', in Brian Hebblethwaite and Stewart Sutherland (eds.), *The Philosophical Frontiers of Christian Theology. Essays presented to D. M. Mackinnon* (Cambridge: Cambridge University Press, 1982), 221–2. Besides Aquinas, White finds such a view in Karl Barth.

though White argues that we need to look no further than the Gospels for help with this problem.[20]

The view that all language about God is non-literal courts self-refutation. For if all language about God is non-literal then that claim itself, being a claim about God, is likewise non-literal. Perhaps such an unwelcome consequence could be avoided by distinguishing between first- and second-order language about God, though it is not easy to see why, if some second-order language about God is literal, no first-order language can be.

The reasons given for adopting the view that all language about God is non-literal, which William Alston calls 'panmetaphoricism',[21] are various. Sometimes it is that the human mind is necessarily limited in its knowledge of God; at other times it is that human language is essentially non-literal; and at still other times that literal language is religiously defective. Sallie McFague, for example, holds that all language about God is or ought to be treated as non-literal, because otherwise idolatry ensues.

THE LANGUAGE OF ACCOMMODATION

Where, in this welter of views, do Calvin's various remarks about language about God, and particularly his remarks about God's accommodation, lie? We have already seen that Calvin's views about the language used of the Trinity is somewhat cautious and reserved. God is literally three-in-one, but he is not literally three persons in the sense of 'person' in which Calvin himself is a person; yet God is in some sense a person. God literally exists, he is literally one, he is literally three-in-one, he is literally wise, and good, and truthful. In discussing his views on providence we have noted his reluctance to use 'models' of God, at least where these models are drawn from non-scriptural sources. Though we cannot fully 'comprehend' God's essence, we can 'apprehend' it through his self-revelation. Calvin is clearly not a 'panmetaphoricist'.

The appeal to accommodation is another strand in Calvin's overall understanding of theological language, and one that is more characteristic of him, though not unique to him. His idea of divine accommodation governs the use of anthropomorphic and anthropopathic language in Scripture to characterize God. Such accommodated language is 'controlled' by literal truths about God's nature. So in highlighting the place of divine

---

[20] This is Calvin's position too. 'Therefore this honor of being called Father properly belongs to God alone and can only apply to men when it pleases him to confer it on them', *John Calvin's Sermons on the Ten Commandments*, trans. B. W. Farley (Grand Rapids, Mich.: Baker, 1980), 138. I owe this reference to Mark Talbot.

[21] William Alston, 'Irreducible Metaphors in Theology', in *Divine Nature and Human Language*.

accommodation Calvin is not claiming that we will not be able to speak of or understand God at all unless he accommodates himself to our understanding and refers to himself in ways which imply change as he interacts with his people. Calvin's view accords with that of Aquinas in holding that some human language about God is exact. Unlike metaphorical or analogical expressions, such exact language does not require radical qualification, though it does require *some* qualification.

There is considerable evidence to show that Calvin held that much human language is unqualifiedly true of God. Thus in the paragraph from the *Institutes* I. 17. 13 quoted earlier in this chapter, Calvin refers to what God had from eternity foreseen, approved, and decreed, and while this language is being used in contrast to the language of divine repentance, there is no suggestion that we have difficulty in understanding what it means to assert that God eternally foresees what will happen, or that it needs qualifying in order to make it intelligible. It is true that such language can be made even more precise, though those who use it rarely see the need for such precision. God foresees even though he does not have eyes; he knows immediately. And if his eternal knowledge is a timelessly eternal knowledge then he does not, strictly speaking *fore*know. One reason why Calvin thought that language about divine repentance is an accommodation to our understanding but that of God foreseeing is not is that such foreseeing coheres with his 'core theism', particularly his emphasis upon God's eternity and immutability, whereas the ascription of repentance to God doesn't. Further, the very fact that we can recognize certain expressions as divine accommodations to our human understanding implies that it is possible to think of God in unqualified or literal ways, though (as we have seen) to say that we can do so does not mean that we can fully comprehend the meaning of such expressions when applied to God.[22]

So it would be wrong to think of Calvin's remarks about accommodation as signalling a reductionist thesis, as if all expressions about God must be translated into anthropomorphic terms before they can be understood. (In any case would we not have to possess some understanding of them in order to be able to make the translations?) Similarly, as we saw in Chapter 1, it would be inaccurate to read into Calvin's remarks about God as he is in himself the theological agnosticism of much post-Kantian Protestant theology. For Calvin, God is not an unknowable *noumenon* or substrate. Indeed, the reasons that Calvin gives for the language of accommodation has surprisingly little to do with the limitations of human knowledge. They have

---

[22] Failure to observe that Calvin clearly distinguishes accommodated from non-accommodated language mars John Sanders's discussion of Calvin's views (John Sanders, *The God Who Risks* (Downer's Grove, Ill.: Inter Varsity Press, 1998), 68.)

at least as much to do with what Calvin considers to be the 'torpor' of the human mind, and particularly with the need for God to achieve certain ends in the lives of those to whom he makes himself known in these ways.

The reason that Calvin cannot be an agnostic or a reductionist about God's nature is that he believed that God has revealed much about himself in Scripture. As we have seen, Calvin held that God has revealed that he does not (literally) repent but that he (literally) foreknows, approves, and decrees. Believing this, Calvin could hardly be committed to the Kantian thesis that it is a necessary feature of the human mind that it cannot know any of what exists beyond space and time. Calvin held that God cannot be fathomed by the human mind, he is unsearchable; nevertheless, though full or comprehensive knowledge of God is not possible, limited but accurate knowledge is. Even where God has not accommodated himself to us, where language about God is to be taken literally, we cannot fully comprehend the meaning of such terms.

Reductionism is one extreme to be avoided in the interpretation of Calvin's remarks about accommodation. The other extreme is to think that for Calvin the appeal to divine accommodation is a mere teaching tool, holding that it is pedagogically useful for us to have God represented to us in these human ways, and that there is nothing more to accommodation than that. Calvin does stress this pedagogical aspect. God, he says, lisps like a nurse; he speaks of himself in human terms to stir us from our natural torpor, for the language of accommodation is vivid and immediate. But this is not all that he has to say in explaining and defending the idea of accommodation.

If each of these two extremes is to be avoided or qualified, what is Calvin saying? His overall position seems to be something like this: Given that God, the eternal God, has not only decreed the course of history but has himself acted in history, in particular in dialogue with his ancient people Israel, such divine actions can only be understood and, more particularly, can only be responded to, when they are taken to be the actions of a person who is himself in time and who therefore appears to change or vary in his action. More than this, if men and women who are themselves in time are to respond to God, then he must represent himself to them as one to whom response is possible, as one who acts and reacts in time. Further still, if God is going to put people to the test by what he reveals to them in time then he cannot reveal to them the outcome of the test, even though he knows what that outcome is, for otherwise the test would not be a real test for them. For Calvin, only on such an understanding of divine activity is the divine–human interaction that is at the heart of biblical revelation, and particularly at the heart of the Old Testament narrative passages, possible.

So it is a logical point, rather than a pragmatic or pedagogic point, that is at the centre of Calvin's remarks about divine accommodation. A logically necessary condition of dialogue between people, or between God and humankind, is that the partners in the dialogue should act and react in time, or appear to do so. If dialogue with God is to be real dialogue, then God's language about himself cannot be restricted to characterizing himself as eternal and immutable, even though his nature and purposes are eternal and immutable, but he must accommodate himself to speak in ways that are characteristic of and essential to persons in dialogue with each other.

So Calvin treats the language about divine repentance as figurative, non-literal language, as did his medieval forebears such as Aquinas. Aquinas is equally emphatic that God's will is unchangeable. And so, words ascribing change to God, or words ascribed to God that entail change,

have a metaphorical turn according to a human figure of speech. When we regret what we have made we throw it away. Yet this does not always argue second thoughts or a change of will, for we may intend in the first place to make a thing and scrap it afterwards. By similitude with such a procedure we refer to God having regrets, for instance in the account of the Flood, when he washed off the face of the earth the men whom he had made . . . to speak of God as repenting is to use the language of metaphor . . . the conclusion to this argument is not that God's will changes, but that he wills change.[23]

This account of divine repentance as metaphor, and the endorsement of the Augustinian distinction between willing a change and changing a will, is characteristic of Aquinas, and in passages such as that just cited he is beginning to explain why such language is warranted. But I suspect that there is a kind of inertness to his account of metaphor. Granted that the language of divine repentance is metaphorical, that God does not literally and un-qualifiedly repent, this seems to lay to rest our qualms as regards the consistency of using such language about God alongside the use of literal terms. But this does not begin to explain why there is metaphorical language about God in the first place. Aquinas simply says: Given that there is such language, it must, in virtue of divine immutability, be treated by us as metaphorical.

In Calvin, I believe, we find at least the elements of a theory of non-literal language about God that justifies and vindicates its use. While Calvin moves beyond Thomas in the account he gives of theological language—as I shall try to show shortly— he nevertheless bases his view on the familiar scholastic contrast between what God is in himself and what he is to us, as we have seen. There cannot be knowledge of God in his essence apart from knowledge of

---

[23] *Summa Theologiae*, 1a, 19. 7. trans. Thomas Gilby. Earlier in this section Aquinas argues that a person must 'accommodate' himself to a fresh situation.

the divine nature as this is revealed to us. All our knowledge of God is a posteriori and not the result of a priori human speculation.[24] The language of the divine attributes is not nominal, but real; it gives us real knowledge of God, but it is folly to attempt to go behind or beyond these attributes to know God as he is in himself. For only God himself can know himself.

How does Calvin go beyond Aquinas? By not being content, in what we might call his overall account of theological language, simply to say that we can give a consistent account of such language by recognizing that some expressions attributed to God are metaphorical or analogical. He emphasizes that at least some of the language that we use of God is language that God uses of himself, and language which God gives us to use of him. The direction of fit, so to speak, is not from ourselves to God (as it tends to be with Aquinas, and more so with Maimonides, even when dealing with the very same issue of the non-literal use of language that Calvin deals with) but from God to ourselves. Divine accommodation, as Calvin treats it, is not primarily *our* theory about theological language, it is an account of some of the conditions under which God chooses to say and *must* say certain things about himself in order to achieve certain ends. It is an integral feature of his gracious self-revelation.

Calvin's approach to God's accommodation to us is in sharp contrast to his attitude to human attempts to accommodate God, to idolatry. God accommodates himself to us: we do not accommodate God to ourselves. The language he uses both to commend divine accommodation and condemn idolatry is very similar and must be deliberate. Man's nature 'is a perpetual factory of idols' and 'Man's mind, full as it is of pride and boldness, dares to imagine a god according to its own capacity (*pro captu*); as it sluggishly plods, indeed is overwhelmed with the crassest ignorance, it conceives an unreality and an empty appearance as God.'[25] The only warrant we have for coming to God is his gracious accommodation of himself 'to our capacity' in Scripture. Calvin argues that the strength of divine opposition to idolatry is seen in the fact that though Scripture often speaks 'in the manner of the common folk',[26] where idols are concerned, far from them being regarded as 'helps', the true God is everywhere in Scripture contrasted with idols.[27] However, Scripture's principled rejection of human attempts to paint or sculpt gods, or likenesses of the true God, does not imply a root and branch opposition to sculpture and painting, which are gifts of God, but which should only be employed to depict what is visible, not the invisible God.[28]

So Calvin's account of non-literal language about God is expressed in terms that are more dynamic and theocentric, and even more distinctively

---

[24] Cf. *Summa Theologiae*, 1a, 12. 12.   [25] *Inst*. I. 11. 8.   [26] *Inst*. I. 11. 1.
[27] *Inst*. I. 11. 8.   [28] *Inst*. I. 11. 12.

Christian, than Aquinas's. Accommodation is a divine activity, and since the ends that God seeks to secure by the use of such language are ultimately soteric in character, we must see the idea of God's accommodation of himself in his language about himself as integral to his grace, an accommodation that has its end-point in the accommodation of God the Son in the Incarnation, although Calvin does not seem to use the term in developing his account of the Incarnation. Given our previous discussions of Calvin's Christology it is easy to see how this kind of accommodation fits in with the Incarnation. For although the Word clothed himself in our flesh, he nevertheless remained what he was, fully divine.

In order that we may see more clearly Calvin's positive use of this idea of accommodation here is part of his treatment of a particularly hard case for him, the case of Hezekiah, who was told by the Lord that he would die, and who then prayed for a longer life, which moved God to remit his death sentence by fifteen years.

But it may be thought strange that God, having uttered a sentence, should soon afterwards be moved, as it were, by repentance to reverse it; for nothing is more at variance with his nature than a change of purpose. I reply, while death was threatened against Hezekiah, still God had not decreed it, but determined in this manner to put to the test the faith of Hezekiah. We must, therefore, suppose a condition to be implied in that threatening; for otherwise Hezekiah would not have altered, by repentance or prayer, the irreversible decree of God . . . And thus we must suppose an implied condition to have been understood . . . Nor are we at liberty to infer from it that God used dissimulation by accommodating his discourse to the capacity and attainments of man . . . In order to prepare Hezekiah by a spiritual resemblance of death, and gradually form him to a new life, he keeps back a part of the discourse.[29]

Having earlier distanced Calvin's approach to the divine nature from that of Kant and various post-Kantian theologies, we can nonetheless begin to understand Calvin's position further by noting something further about Kant's epistemology. For all Kant may say to the contrary, there is a contingent connection between his view that human beings are necessarily time-bound and space-bound, and his principled agnosticism about God. So in his remarks about divine accommodation we might see Calvin giving due recognition to our time- and space-bound existence while denying that this entails a fundamental agnosticism about God's attributes. It is surely a necessary truth about any embodied person that she occupies space and endures through time. The necessities of these relations to time and space generate further necessary truths about us, truths that are true in every

---

[29] *Commentary on Isaiah*, 38: 4.

possible world in which we exist as embodied agents. For example, the truth of *if X begins to exist before Y then X can never begin to exist later than Y*. In revealing matters to space- and time-bound people like us, and particularly in seeking to elicit responses from us, God must accommodate himself to our metaphysical and epistemic situation.

This is how Calvin sees God acting in the case of Hezekiah. The incident as a whole is a test of Hezekiah's faith. God tests him by announcing his death, so eliciting a responsive prayer from him. In response to the prayer God grants to Hezekiah an additional lease of life.

Does Hezekiah then have to believe what is false, namely that God is capable of changing his mind? Does he have to believe that God believes what he announces, that Hezekiah will die? No, there would be nothing to stop Hezekiah from believing 'Either God has eternally decreed my death or he has eternally decreed that I will live for I don't know how many further years, if I pray to him and mend my ways'. And because Hezekiah does not know which possible outcome God has decreed, and (naturally enough) wishes to live longer, he prays accordingly. What Hezekiah's story does require, however, is that he believes that God genuinely asserts what he states on a given occasion but that statement is not necessarily a full account of what he has decreed. Perhaps he also believes that one rationale for such a partial disclosure is that God wishes to bring about certain changes in Hezekiah himself. God cannot genuinely test Hezekiah if he announces the results of the test in advance. So Hezekiah does not need to believe that God has changed but only that there is or that there may be a certain dislocation between what God has willed in total about his life and death, and what he begins to reveal of what he has willed on some particular occasion, and that there may be a good reason for this dislocation, such as God's desire to test Hezekiah in order to draw out his faith.

Hezekiah may well recognize that some language about God implies change even when (as Calvin believes, and as he believes that Hezekiah believes) God does not and indeed cannot change. Here is one possible reason why and how it is that sometimes our language about God is necessarily changeful even if God is necessarily changeless. Suppose that God does A at t1, which X notices at t1 and then God does not-A at t2, which X notices at t2. From X's point of view this appears as a change, in precisely the same way as a human person may be said to have changed his mind if he does A at t1 and then does not-A at t2. That is, God is perceived to have willed what, were it to be or have been a human action, might constitute a real change of will in a human. And this is because what God has willed is truly although perhaps rather loosely expressible in contrary or contradictory terms. It is *loosely* expressible in such ways because these ways omit the temporal indexing of God's actions. We can temporally index God's actions, just as we can human actions, and so account for divine 'change' over time as the possession of different temporally ordered properties. By temporally indexing, we can see that eternally willing that A occur at t1 and eternally willing that not-A occur at t2 is not necessarily contradictory. Furthermore by coming to see that God might eternally will both A at t1 and not-A at t2 we can see that such non-contradictory actions do not even require a real change in the will of God.

So if God eternally decreed to announce at t1 Hezekiah's death and then to announce at t2 his recovery, then God may not have changed (if his eternal will was to bring about Hezekiah's recovery) and his announcement that Hezekiah will die and then that he will live can be expressed as component parts of one eternal will. Putting the point even more fully, what God in fact decreed was not Hezekiah's recovery, but the recovery of Hezekiah *upon request*, with the request being a component part of the entire decree. And at least part of the purpose may be to elicit this request. (Note Calvin's reference to an 'implied condition' in the quoted passage.) The original sentence of death was announced to elicit this request. And, in spite of what I have said about Hezekiah's not having to believe anything false, God may nonetheless be thought of by Hezekiah as having changed because it is most natural to do this, since someone rarely has the time or makes the effort to think in the fashion that we have been laying out. So, as Calvin interprets the passage, it is a unit, and one does not do justice to its meaning by treating each phrase separately with an unnatural literalness. So another though subsidiary part of the explanation for the language of accommodation is the desire for economy of expression. Perhaps the prominence that Calvin gives to this side of things, and his sympathy for it, reflect his own humanist leanings.

Can we say that in such circumstances not only *may* God be thought of as having changed, but that he *must* be thought of in this way? Perhaps we can. For when we are agents, as Hezekiah was, we cannot but think of time in terms of the past, the present time, and time that is future to us. Perhaps thinking in this fashion does not tell us what the world is like, just as thinking of God as changing does not tell us what God is like; nevertheless as agents we cannot avoid thinking in such a fashion.

This is because it is an intrinsic part of human agency to face the future as the future and not simply as a later time. In the context of our own undertakings we must inevitably think of what we know and will now, in the present, and what we undertake in the future. If we could not do that, then it would be impossible for us to intend to act at a certain time and so impossible for us to act at all. Perhaps thinking of our action in such ways is more like a case of 'knowing how' than of 'knowing that' about time, and perhaps thinking about God as changeful is necessary if people are to know how to regulate their lives appropriately with respect to him. This is not pure pragmatism, not even the pragmatism of good pedagogy; it is a practical stance which necessarily arises out of the metaphysical position that human beings occupy; it has about it, therefore, a kind of inevitability.

This, then, is the point of logic—or of metaphysics—that is at the heart of Calvin's view, though he is rarely if ever explicit on the point. It is a logically necessary condition of dialogue between people, or between God and mankind, that the partners in the dialogue should appear to act and react in time. If dialogue with God is to be real dialogue, then God's language about himself cannot be restricted to characterising himself as eternal and immutable, but he must accommodate himself to speak in ways that are characteristic of and essential to, persons in dialogue with each other. In such a way Calvin can be said to *work with* the idea of divine accommodation in a way that goes beyond Aquinas's appeal to metaphor.

Some Implications

I have raised the question of whether, according to Calvin, God's repentance is a real repentance and now I shall need to consider in more detail some of the implications of this last paragraph, in particular, to ask whether, according to Calvin's doctrine of divine accommodation, God *really* engages in dialogue with humanity, or only merely appears to do so. If the sense of 'repentance' is qualified, may not the sense of 'dialogue' also be qualified? If God only appears to enter into dialogue, and does not really do so, or does so in only a qualified sense, does this matter? Would it be fatal to Calvin's understanding of such passages as Hezekiah's testing?

As we saw in Chapter 2, Calvin holds that God exists in an immutable, timelessly eternal fashion. For God there is no earlier and later; everything is immediately present to him. In this he follows Boethius, Augustine, Anselm, Aquinas, and a host of other Christian theologians. It follows from God's timeless eternity that he is immutable; he cannot change or be changed, since to change or to be changed implies existence in time, and God is not in time. If God cannot change, then although he may be able to act in time, it does not appear that he can react to what occurs in time. For such a reaction would suppose that God was in time. He can timelessly decree an action the effect of which occurs in time at a particular date. For instance, God can eternally decree that the sun rises at 7: 47 on a particular morning and at a particular place, and he can timelessly decree to react to what he knows will occur in time. But he cannot decree in time to do anything in time, including to decree something in time, since to decree in time is to be in time. That is, God cannot decree in real time to react, say, to a prayer, since any such decree would have to occur at a time either before or after the prayer, and this would require God to be in time.

Or can he? William Alston has pursued the question of whether a God who exists in timelessly eternal fashion can *respond*, which is essentially the same question.[30] It will be instructive to reflect upon Alston's argument, to try to get clearer on what Calvin is saying and on what it implies.

Under normal circumstances conversational dialogue between people obviously entails the need to be able to reply to what has been said. But can a timeless God react by making a reply to what has been said to him? An obvious objection is that if God is timeless, he cannot believe anything that requires for its sense and appropriateness the occurrence of an event before the formation of the belief. If God literally replies to something that is uttered, his reply will have to occur after what it is a reply to. Or so it may seem. But Alston argues that the need for a reply to come after what is replied to is a contingent or accidental feature of replies. In his view something would be equally well a reply if it were contemporary with what it were a reply to. 'If I could be so closely tied to you as to apprehend your cry while you are in the act of producing it, and if I were able to offer my consolation (or at least do the most immediate part of this, the volition) at that very same moment of apprehension, would I not still be responding to your cry?'[31] Perhaps this is correct, provided that we are warranted in thinking of the relation between a timeless God and his creation as one of simultaneity. Whether we are warranted in doing this is a large question and thankfully we may let it pass here.[32]

Supposing that there is nothing odd about a timeless reply, Alston then divides the question of whether a timeless deity could say something as a reply to a human utterance into two sub-questions.[33] One question is, could an omnidetermining, timeless deity, a God who decides every detail of his creation, reply, for instance, to a question from Moses? It is a rather puzzling feature of Calvin's approach to the Hezekiah passage and to similar passages that he does not raise such a question, nor find it necessary to say anything about the issue. If God accommodates himself, is the dialogue itself part of the accommodation? Calvin does not say. What is of particular interest to us is that it is widely held that Calvin viewed God as omnidetermining and as we have seen there is some plausibility to this view, and so Alston's discussion is

---

[30] 'Divine–Human Dialogue and the Nature of God', in his *Divine Nature and Human Language*.

[31] 'Divine–Human Dialogue', 155.

[32] On this see e.g. Paul Helm, *Eternal God: A Study of God without Time* (Oxford: Clarendon Press, 1988), and Brian Leftow, *Time and Eternity* (Ithaca: Cornell University Press, 1991).

[33] 'Divine–Human Dialogue', 157.

pertinent. Alston's second sub-question is, could a timeless deity who is not omnidetermining reply to a question from Moses? In trying to understand Calvin's ideas we have more interest in Alston's answer to the first question than in his answer to the second; but his answer to the second question is not without interest.

To the first question Alston answers—in a sense, yes. God's utterance could be performed as a reply to Moses, but not as a piece of genuine dialogue, for a genuine dialogue requires that the question replied to,

'stands over against' God as something independent of His will, something introduced into the situation by the initiative of another, something to which He has to adjust His conduct, something that requires a special ad hoc 'response' on His part. . . . Thus if the *uttered as a reply* condition is to be sufficient for genuine dialogue, we must specify that the [question asked] is, to some degree, independent of S's will.[34]

What of the second case? Could an immutable timeless, omniscient God, but one who does not determine every detail of his creation enter into genuine dialogue? Alston claims that he could. Given that the divine response to a free human action could be simultaneous with that action 'there is no bar to the awareness of each and every free act, along with the responses thereto, occupying the one eternal now'.[35]

Let us for the moment concentrate on the case of the non-omnidetermining God. It is plausible to suppose that such a God can no more or less enter into dialogue than can a timeless, omnidetermining God and that if the conditions for dialogue do not exist in the omnidetermining case, then they do not exist in the other case either. In attempting to show this, I shall make one assumption: namely that the human participant in this dialogue has some understanding of what it is for God to be timeless and omniscient with regard to the future and believes that his divine interlocutor is both timeless and omniscient.

If what Alston says about timelessness and dialogue is correct, and assuming that divine omniscience reaches to the future, then to every piece of human dialogue there timelessly exists in the divine mind a specification of the reply. The reply does not exist until it is uttered as a reply, but the specification of the reply exists timelessly. What the timeless deity does in entering into dialogue is not to formulate a new reply upon learning of the human utterance, but to utter in time what is timelessly true because timelessly known by him.

Let us now turn our attention to the human partner in this dialogue. Either such a person is entitled to believe that a specification of the prop-

[34] 'Divine–Human Dialogue', 158.　　　　　　　　　[35] 'Divine–Human Dialogue', 159.

osition that he is about to conceive and to utter, and the reply to it, exist timelessly in the divine mind, or he is not entitled to believe this. If he is not entitled to believe this, then a reason must be provided why a person may not believe what, given that divine omniscience reaches to the future, is presumably true. But what could that reason be? And if the person is entitled to believe that there exists a specification of one proposition in the divine mind, then is he not entitled to believe that there is such a specification of many such propositions which express truths future to him and which involve him?

So suppose that a person such as Hezekiah does believe that such a specification exists. Of course he does not know what the specification is. Nevertheless, the fact that he believes that there is such a specification means that he believes something which is not a normal condition of inter-human dialogue. Imagine a conversation between Smith and Jones. It is a normal condition of such a conversation, of its 'openness', that Smith does not know (even though he may have a shrewd idea) what Jones will say until Jones forms and expresses his thought and that Jones forms and expresses his thought believing that Smith does not already possess a specification of it.

Given these commonplace features of human conversation it follows that if God's omniscience includes the future then 'dialogue' in the divine–human case has become somewhat stretched in meaning from that which obtains in its usual, interpersonal setting, whether or not we regard God, in Calvin's way, as an omnideterminer. For dialogue in the divine–human case contains the important feature that in virtue of divine knowledge of what is future, the human partner in the dialogue may reasonably believe that God timelessly knows what has not yet come into his own mind. And this is sufficient to upset the mutuality that is a normal feature of human conversation and which Alston seeks to preserve in any acceptable account of divine–human dialogue.[36]

So we must conclude that dialogue or conversation between an omniscient, timelessly eternal God, and a human partner contains features that are absent from everyday human conversations. But is this so surprising? Ought we not to expect that the conditions of divine–human dialogue could not exactly parallel dialogue between two humans? And perhaps we ought to conclude that 'dialogue' differs somewhat in meaning in the two cases. But does this mean that an omnidetermining God does not really engage in dialogue with men and women? Why would this follow?

If by the persuasiveness of some argument that we have not considered it does follow that an omnidetermining God cannot enter into genuine

---

[36] 'Divine–Human Dialogue', 153.

dialogue with his creatures, there would seem to be equally good reason to suppose that a timelessly eternal God who is *not* omnidetermining does not enter into genuine dialogue with men and women either. For what creates the crucial objection to understanding such 'dialogue' literally is not the question of whether or not God is omnidetermining, but the assumptions that he is timelessly eternal and omniscient with respect to our future.[37]

There is one other factor that bears on the case. If this argument is sound, not only may Calvin not be embarrassed by the thought that in the Hezekiah story and other similar stories the idea of dialogue is being stretched, he would in all likelihood dissent from the assumption that in considering the issue of dialogue with God the default position is that there is parity between the partners in dialogue. As we have seen, he thinks that Hezekiah's Lord is putting him to the test, something which he has a perfect right to do. Calvin would have been horrified to suppose that Hezekiah and the Lord were equal dialogue partners and that firm guidance in understanding their relationship can be gained from exploring the dynamics of human inter-personal relationships. Perhaps Calvin might also have pointed out that parity among humans in dialogue is also rarely attained, and is perhaps not always desirable as an ideal.

CHANGE

The final matter to be considered is the sense in which, according to Calvin, God may be said to change. Calvin says that when the language of repentance is ascribed to God it signifies change of action on God's part although not a correction, and that such a change carries with it no suggestion of remorse or compunction on God's part. At the same time, neither God's plan nor his will is reversed, nor is his volition altered. So Calvin wishes to claim both that God changes his action and yet his plan and volition is unchanged. Is it possible to hold such a position consistently, as Calvin clearly would wish?

There are certain kinds of change that present no problems of consistency and that are required by any reasonably well-worked-out account of provi-dence. For example, if God decrees that the sun will rise, and that it will set, has he changed? The relation of the sun to planet earth has changed, but has God changed? Clearly not; the sun's rising at one time and setting at another can be part of one eternal decree; otherwise, God could not decree the regular variation of anything. As we saw earlier, Augustine and Aquinas distinguished between change of will and willing a change, a distinction

---

[37] I have discussed Alston's views on dialogue in more detail in 'The Problem of Dialogue', in G. E. Ganssle and D. M. Woodruff (eds), *God and Time: Essays on the Divine Nature* (New York: Oxford University Press, 2002).

which Calvin approves of, though there is no instance that I know of where Calvin uses this precise expression.

But what about God's commands? Suppose that at one time God permits polygamy, while at another time he forbids it. Has he changed? Has his mind changed? Augustine also considers this kind of case: 'I also did not know that true inward justice which judges not by custom but by the most righteous law of almighty God. By this law the moral customs of different regions and periods were adapted to their places and times, while that law itself remains unaltered everywhere and always.'[38] Augustine has in mind a situation where a father may at first forbid his child to do something—e.g. possess matches— and then permit what he previously forbade. Has the father changed in his policy towards the child? Not necessarily. For what the father does at different times may be different phases of implementing the same policy. And perhaps 'change' of this kind is necessary precisely in order to carry out one unchanging policy consistently over time, one benevolent policy towards the child as she grows and matures.

The fundamental point is that such language is not dispensable but necessary, and not necessary only for a parent but necessary for us all in view of our moral and metaphysical position vis-à-vis God. If a timelessly eternal God is to communicate to embodied intelligent creatures who exist in space and time, and if he is to bring about his purposes through them, and in particular to gain certain kinds of responses from them, then he must do so by representing himself to them in ways that are not literally true. This seems to be the essence of Calvin's position. How could God put Hezekiah to the test apart from testing him step by step and so appearing to change his mind? So the impression we may form, while reading the biblical narra- tives, that God changes is an illusion that arises because we only learn of God's purposes for the actors in the narrative (and perhaps for others) bit by bit.

On Calvin's view of divine accommodation statements such as 'God repented' are false, if taken literally, because God does not literally repent and cannot do so. But although they are literally false, some truth about God may nevertheless be conveyed by them. Someone who upholds the principle of non-contradiction in logic nevertheless may, when asked if it is raining, say 'It is and it isn't'. A person who says 'I'm not myself this morning' may be perfectly understood. Such speakers in uttering what is literally self- contradictory do not believe that they have actually flouted the principle by asserting something that is literally impossible. Rather they succeed in conveying something intelligible and perhaps true using language that,

---

[38] *Confessions*, III. vii, trans. Henry Chadwick (Oxford: Oxford University Press, 1992), 44.

strictly speaking, is incoherent. Similarly, a tautology such as 'a rule is a rule' may, when uttered, nonetheless perform a clear cognitive function just as someone who denies geocentricism as a theory about the heavenly bodies may nevertheless say 'It's warmer in the garden now that the sun has come out from behind the clouds'.[39]

Each of these sentences, given a suitable context, may be taken to convey contingent truth. Sometimes looseness in speech signifies waffle and incoherence. But at other times language may be loose (when judged from some particular standpoint) but economical, and thus the very opposite of waffle. It is hard to believe that language which accommodates God's activity to our situation is typically misleading or wrong any more than it is misleading to say that it is and it isn't raining. Such language may record how things are in an unpedantic and vivid way.

But what if God announces that he will do such and such a thing and then shortly afterwards announces that he will not? He announces the destruction of mankind, and then repents (Genesis 6: 6); he establishes the kingship of Saul, and then repents, rejecting Saul (I Samuel 15: 26–8); he commands the overthrow of Nineveh, and then relents (Jonah 3: 4); he announces the death of Hezekiah, and then defers his death (Isaiah 38). In these cases does God change? Does the use of such language involve God in insincerity? Not necessarily. What is sincere is, say, his intention to test Hezekiah and also his intention that he pass the test. As we have seen earlier, in order for this sincere intention to be carried out it does not follow that each separate element in his dialogue with Moses, when isolated from all the other components, should take the form of a sincerely uttered truth, but that the entire testing should be sincerely intended.

In each of the examples we have cited there are significant changes between the time when God announces his first intention and later announces his second. For example, between the time when God establishes Saul as king and rejects him, Saul enters on a course of disobedience to God. It is in the light of these changes that the second, countermanding decree is announced. Why is this any different from the case of the parent who, on judging that a child is sufficiently mature, permits what he had at an earlier time forbidden?

Of course, since Calvin believes that God ordains the future he may reasonably suppose that he willingly permitted Saul's moral deterioration, and willed that Hezekiah would pray to him for a longer life. Consistently with this, Calvin holds that God has one eternal will with respect to Saul, for

---

[39] For this example, see Peter van Inwagen, *Material Beings* (Ithaca: Cornell University Press, 1990), 101.

example: first to establish him as king and then in the light of his willingly permitted deterioration to reject him as king.

A second way of arguing that God does not change even when he is said to repent is to suppose that the first decree has a tacitly conditional form. Calvin seems to prefer this way of arguing, at least in his account of Hezekiah's prayer. So, in the case of Saul, God decrees his kingship on the understanding that he will be an honourable and obedient king. A parent may say to his child 'Provided that you will not misuse them, you may have matches'. Neither God nor the parent changes if Saul or the child is disobedient and then Saul is deprived of the kingship or the child of the matches. One can imagine that Calvin might have believed that a defence of God's change-lessness in these terms might find support from what the Bible represents as the covenant character of his promises.[40]

PHILOSOPHY AND FAITH

A recurring theme in western philosophy, going back at least to Plato, has been that philosophers have an insight into the nature of things that is denied to those who are not philosophers; the contrast, if you like, between appearance and reality. Most folk live in a world of appearance; the phil-osopher, and only he, has access to the world of reality, to the world as it really is. The Jewish medieval philosopher Maimonides, for example, held that the philosopher gains flashes of truth as when the whole landscape is lit up for a moment in a flash of lightning. According to Maimonides some, like Moses, have continuously repeated flashes of lighting; for others the lightning flashes only once; some only see in the way in which light is reflected in a polished stone. But then there are those who never even once see a light, but grope about in their night. 'They are the vulgar among the people. There is then no occasion to mention them here in this Treatise.'[41] Maimonides' hyper-intellectualism, as I shall call this attitude, comes out again in his account of divine providence. According to what he says about providence, it is primarily concerned with the preservation of the intellect. God's providential care for a person is, it seems, in direct proportion to that person's intellectual power or capacity.[42] And as Maimonides tells us in the final chapter of the *Guide*, the true perfection of man is equated with the holding of 'true opinions concerning the divine things. This is in true reality the ultimate end; this is what gives the individual true perfection belonging

---

[40] I have tried to develop this point more fully in 'Omnipotence and Change', *Philosophy* (1976), 454–61.

[41] *The Guide of the Perplexed*, I. 8.   [42] *Guide*, III. 17; II. 12; III. 51.

to him alone; and it gives him permanent perdurance; through it man is man.'[43]

With Calvin, although he sometimes uses language that is strikingly similar to that used by Maimonides, there is the reverse approach, and a much more egalitarian temper.

Certainly I do not deny that one can read competent and apt statements about God here and there in the philosophers, but these always show a certain giddy imagination. As was stated above, the Lord indeed gave them a slight taste of his divinity that they might not hide their impiety under a cloak of ignorance. And sometimes he impelled them to make certain utterances by the confession of which they would themselves be corrected. But they saw things in such a way that their seeing did not direct them to the truth, much less enable them to attain it! They are like a traveler passing through a field at night who in a momentary lightning flash sees far and wide, but the sight vanishes so swiftly that he is plunged again into the darkness of the night before he can take even a step—let alone be directed on his way by its help.[44]

For Calvin the lightning lights up revealed truth, truth that is available without any special intellectual preconditions, whereas for Maimonides the lightning illuminates truths available only to the prophets and philosophers. For Calvin neither the philosophers nor the theologians occupy a privileged position with regard to thought and language about God. God 'lisps' or 'accommodates' himself not only to children in the nursery, or to those who have no particular intellectual aptitude for metaphysical reflection. He speaks in this way to us all, condescending from his loftiness to make himself known to us in familiar terms, to enter into dialogue with us, and to become incarnate for us. This is because according to Calvin the similarities of the human metaphysical and moral position—that of sinful creatures living in space and time—far outweigh any differences in intellect or aptitude there may be among us. And according to Calvin, God's providence extends over all men and women, not to a privileged subset. Finally, the vision of God which beckons us is not a purely intellectual vision, available only to an intellectual elite, but a vision which is the gift divine grace granted to men and women of all types and stripes who will walk the streets and enjoy the sights of the New Jerusalem.

---

[43] *Guide*, III. 54. I am indebted for some of these references to Maimonides' hyper-intellectualism to David Burrell, *Knowing the Unknowable God: Ibn-Sina, Maimonides, Aquinas* (Notre Dame, Ind.: University of Notre Dame Press, 1986), 65, 84.   [44] *Inst.* II. 2. 18.

8

Natural Theology and the *Sensus Divinitatis*

In the first six chapters we have looked at some central metaphysical claims of Calvin; about the essence and will of God, the Trinity and the Person of Christ, the nature of the human person, and free will. In the last chapter we looked at one prominent way in which, in Calvin's view, God facilitates the knowledge of himself. When necessary, God accommodates himself to our human epistemic situation, particularly to our situation in time. We shall now look at how, according to Calvin, despite this gracious accommodation, the knowledge of God is hindered if not entirely subverted. So in this chapter we shall be concerned with central features of Calvin's natural theology, its character and its limitations.

INTRODUCTION

Every student of Calvin knows of the controversy which surrounds the question of his attitude to natural theology in the *Institutes*. At one extreme is the opinion that Calvin was a natural theologian without qualification, which is the view, for example, of B. B. Warfield.[1] In support of this view are, for example, the brief references in the early parts of book I of the *Institutes* to 'common proofs' and the way in which Calvin appeals to 'external proofs' of the divinity of Holy Scripture, albeit giving them a secondary place to that of the internal testimony of the Holy Spirit in attesting to the divinity and authority of Holy Scripture. Even though the direct references to natural theology may be somewhat muted, it could be argued that in the light of Calvin's enthusiasm for such 'external proofs' of the authenticity of Scripture the reason why he did not devote attention to natural theology in the *Institutes* is not because he did not believe in it, but because it was not an issue in the church of the Reformation period, as the sufficiency of Scripture (for example) was. We shall develop these points in due course.

At the other extreme is the view that Calvin repudiated any appeal to natural theology or natural reason in formulating his theological system, but

[1] B. B. Warfield, 'Calvin's Doctrine of the Knowledge of God', in *Calvin and Calvinism*. Though it should be noted that Warfield does not suggest that natural theology is a strong or dominant feature of Calvin's theology. See also Edward A. Dowey, *The Knowledge of God in Calvin's Theology*.

rather that he saw himself as a theologian of the word, even a theologian of crisis in the Barthian manner.[2] (Perhaps there is an element of wishful thinking in Barth's attitude to Calvin, more a question of what Calvin ought to have believed rather than what he did believe.) Somewhere in the middle is the view, given eloquent contemporary expression by Alvin Plantinga and others, that Calvin believed that there is an innate natural knowledge of God, and that the beliefs which express this innate *sensus divinitatis* are properly basic, beliefs that a person is rationally entitled to hold.[3]

As background to attempting to estimate what Calvin's attitude to natural theology was, it has to be borne in mind that there is an increasing trend in current scholarship to distinguish between medieval natural theology, and the evidentialist natural theology of the Enlightenment and post-Enlightenment periods. Thomas Aquinas is no longer automatically read through Enlightenment eyes. Instead, his natural theology is regarded as being internal to his Christian theology, a case of faith seeking and gaining understanding, rather than a necessary prolegomenon to faith. Natural theology is possible but not necessary for the rationality and certainty of faith.

CALVIN ON PAUL'S PREACHING

One way of approaching this spectrum of interpretations of Calvin and of forming some sort of overall assessment of where Calvin's view of natural religion and natural theology actually falls within it, is to examine other places in Calvin's corpus than the much-traversed passages in the *Institutes*. There are places in his Commentaries where his attitude to natural theology and natural religion might be expected to be revealed. One of these loci is Calvin's treatment of parts of Acts 14 and of Acts 17. So before revisiting what Calvin says in the *Institutes* we shall consider his treatment of these passages.

If it is true that Karl Barth nowhere provided a full-length exegesis of Acts 17 (as James Barr asserts),[4] the same cannot be said of Calvin. He preached through Acts, though his sermons on Acts 14 and 17 are now sadly lost, only those preached on Acts 1–7 (44 sermons) surviving of this series. But he included extensive remarks on the two chapters in his *Commentary on the Acts of the Apostles* (1552–4).

---

[2] Karl Barth and Emil Brunner, *Natural Theology*, trans. Peter Fraenkel (London: Geoffrey Bles, 1946). Assessment of this debate is hampered by the fact that both protagonists contend over whether or not there is a 'point of contact' between fallen mankind and God without seriously attempting to say what that expression implies.

[3] Alvin Plantinga, 'Reason and Belief in God', in *Faith and Rationality*.

[4] *Biblical Faith and Natural Theology*, (Oxford: Clarendon Press, 1993), 26.

Acts 14: 15–18

We shall look first at Acts 14, and focus on Calvin's remarks on v. 17 ('Though he left not himself without witness . . . ').[5] Calvin highlights Paul's use of the Romans 1 point (as Calvin sees it) regarding the inexcusability of men due to their natural knowledge of God. 'This kind of testimony, whereof mention is made, was such as that it made men without excuse, and yet was it not sufficient to salvation.'[6] What follows is a summary of Calvin's main observations on this passage.

According to Calvin, Paul and Barnabas say that God is 'showed' by natural arguments (evidences). The Apostles do not speak in a subtle way of the natural order, nevertheless 'they take this principle, that in the order of nature there is a certain and evident manifestation[7] of God, and of his providence, in that the earth is watered by rain . . .'.[8] Calvin also uses this as an argument against the eternity of the world or rather he claims that arguments for the eternity of the world are inconsistent with what those who offer them really thought, which is that the world is created and providentially governed by God.

It appears that for Calvin the 'manifestation' is not so much a formal proof proceeding from indubitable premisses, but a display of power and skill, as when a weightlifter demonstrates his prowess by lifting great weights. Nevertheless, because (unlike in the weightlifter example) the one whose power is demonstrated (or manifested) is not a visible part of the demonstration, one may, without straining things much, or even at all, think of Calvin's mind moving in an area adjacent to that occupied by cosmological proofs of the existence of God.[9] That is, that the evidence provided by the watering of the earth by rain may provide the basis of an inference to the existence of God, and thus to a demonstration of his existence in a more discursive way. So it is not at all obvious, on the basis of what Calvin says here, that he would have violently disagreed with Thomas Aquinas's view that in Romans 1 (and therefore in Acts 14) Paul has cosmological proofs in mind.

Nevertheless, Calvin also stresses that Paul is speaking to an 'unlearned multitude'. So we are not to suppose that Paul was arguing subtly, 'after the manner of the philosophers'.[10] However, there is clearly some ambivalence

---

[5] *Commentary on the Acts of the Apostles*, II. 18ff.

[6] *Commentary on the Acts of the Apostles*, II. 19.

[7] *manifestio*, translated as 'demonstration' by John W. Fraser in *Calvin's Commentary on Acts*, (Edinburgh: Oliver & Boyd, 1966), 3.   [8] *Commentary on the Acts of the Apostles*, II. 19–20.

[9] For another example of this, see Calvin's *Commentary* on Psalm 19: 1 'When a man, from beholding and contemplating the heavens, has been brought to acknowledge God . . .'. Richard Muller may well be correct when he says that Calvin typically prefers to express such arguments in a rhetorical rather than a formally demonstrative fashion (*Post-Reformation Reformed Dogmatics*, III. 173–4).

[10] *Commentary on the Acts of the Apostles*, II. 19.

in Calvin at this point, for while making reference to the unlearned multitude, he at the same time implies that the words of Paul were sufficiently nuanced to be making a point against a central feature of Classical metaphysics, the necessity of the world. Calvin thinks that Paul here refutes that view by his appeal to God as creator and sustainer of the world, and that those to whom he spoke acknowledged this by speaking not as they thought[11] (namely that there is a God) but by being maliciously and barbarously unthankful. So (he seems to imply) anyone who affirms the eternity (and therefore the necessity) of the world does so in the face of demonstrable evidence to the contrary, evidence of a divine creator and sustainer of the world. It is in this dislocation between what such people knew, and their unthankfulness to God, that their culpability lies.

Calvin appears to deviate from a standard medieval position on the necessity of the world, that it is neither provable nor refutable by reason, but that it can be established only by appeal to revelation.[12] For he seems to say that there is evidence of the world's createdness from nature independently of revelation.

Acts 17: 16–33

Calvin's treatment of this more famous and lengthier passage is correspondingly more elaborate. In general terms, one finds here the same ambivalence towards philosophy that we have earlier noted in the *Institutes*. On the one hand, Athens is a vivid illustration of the 'vanity of man's wisdom',[13] where the name of God is wickedly profaned.[14] The men of Athens crave novelties, and are full of talk; both are the fruits of idleness.[15] On the other hand, 'though the philosophers do not reason purely, yet they say somewhat. Yea, they speak much concerning eternal life and the immortality of the soul; but as touching faith . . . not a word.'[16] Later, he endorses the view of 'certain of the philosophers' that man is a microcosm of the world 'because he is above all other creatures a token of God's glory, replenished with infinite miracles'.[17] The Epicureans are judged for being despisers and open enemies of liberal arts.[18]

---

[11] 'According to the understanding of their minds' (Fraser, 13).

[12] For this medieval view see, for example, Thomas Aquinas, 'On the Eternity of the World' (1271), in *Thomas Aquinas: Selected Writings*, trans. Ralph McInerny (London: Penguin Books, 1998).

[13] *Commentary on the Acts of the Apostles*, II. 146.

[14] *Commentary on the Acts of the Apostles*, II. 147.

[15] *Commentary on the Acts of the Apostles*, II. 153.

[16] *Commentary on the Acts of the Apostles*, II. 152.

[17] *Commentary on the Acts of the Apostles*, II. 167 (cf. *Inst.* I. 1. 2).

[18] *Commentary on the Acts of the Apostles*, II. 149.

I hope that it is not reading into what Calvin writes to offer the suggestion of a two-phase appreciation of pagan thought; in the face of the gospel that Paul preached it reveals its bankruptcy, but it sometimes speaks the truth in more general matters.

It is also interesting that Calvin relies on pagan history and literature for his picture of Athens, which in his view faithfully corroborates Luke's account. So Horace is quoted: 'Fly a demander of questions, for the same is also a blab', and Cicero is referred to with approval (on the decay of Athens); more generally 'surely that which Luke saith here is witnessed by all writers, both Greek and Latin, that there was nothing more light, covetous, or froward than that people'.[19] Persius is quoted with approval, at length.[20] So if one is to form an overall estimate of Calvin's view of natural religion one has to include not only an understanding of the expressions of the religion itself (as in what Paul and Barnabas encountered in Athens) but also the views of those pagan writers who had a negative opinion of the religion of Athens and who formed their opinions without the help of the supernatural light of the Christian gospel.

A key to Calvin's analysis of the Athenian religion is his view that there can be no true worship without the knowledge of God, and that that knowledge brings certainty and contentment. So the Athenians' worship of many gods is an expression of their deep though not total ignorance of God, and their restlessness follows as a consequence. Paul's strategy, according to Calvin, having unmasked the self-deception of the Athenians, is to 'insinuate himself and . . . purchase favour for his doctrine'[21] by not rejecting their 'unknown God' out of hand, but by inviting them to know him. 'Thus doth Paul return again to that principle, that God cannot be worshipped rightly unless he be first made known.'[22] Paul does not in any way endorse the worship of the unknown God, or regard it as an instance of true though uninformed worship, but uses the Athenians' 'corrupt affection' as a teaching aid.

It is hard to accept that Calvin is altogether consistent at this point. If someone knows that God exists, and possesses sufficient knowledge to make him inexcusable for the bad use that he makes of it (as Calvin goes on to argue), then surely he knows something, his belief has some cognitive content, however much it may be accompanied by falsity. Yet Calvin appears to deny this. But if he does deny it, then how is he warranted in due course in moving from the question of God's existence to what he calls the 'second point', the question of what God is like? One suggestion is that he thinks that

[19] *Commentary on the Acts of the Apostles,* II. 153.
[20] *Commentary on the Acts of the Apostles,* II. 162.
[21] *Commentary on the Acts of the Apostles,* II. 157.
[22] *Commentary on the Acts of the Apostles,* II. 157.

people in such a position do not have true knowledge of God, that which has appropriate moral and affective components, but only that knowledge which 'flits in the brain'. However that may be, it appears that Calvin is willing to recognize a 'point of contact' here, an overlap in cognitive content between pagan and Christian beliefs about God.

The Athenians were already persuaded that there was some divinity, but their ignorance of the true God led them astray. So Paul starts not from the 'first point' 'that there is some divine power or godhead which men ought to worship', because the Athenians were already persuaded of that. So why does this not show that they have some knowledge of God, albeit rudimentary and confused? Because if you know that there is a god, but not what he is like, then you don't know what God is. Rather 'Paul descendeth unto the second point, that the true God must be distinguished from all vain inventions'.[23] Not that there is a God, but what that God is. Calvin places emphasis on God's transcendence, that unlike the pagan gods he is apart from the creation, and on the obligation to the worship of God, that is, the worship of God as Spirit.[24]

So according to Calvin, Paul does not say that the Athenians were worshipping the true God despite themselves (though Paul's words certainly seem capable of bearing that interpretation), for this would flout Calvin's principle that there can be no true worship without knowledge. Instead in his view Paul uses their worship of the unknown god as a launching pad for the preaching of the true God. Whatever they were the Athenians were not, in Calvin's eyes, anonymous Christians! Paul's first positive task is to preach what God is. So what strategy does Paul adopt? Here Calvin is very clear. Paul adapts his preaching to his audience; 'he draweth proofs [of who God is] from nature itself; for in vain should he have cited testimonies of Scripture'.[25]

Calvin does not suggest that Paul starts where he does in his presentation of the gospel to the Athenians for purely rhetorical reasons, in order to produce a more effective *persuasio*. Rather, his reference to the 'two points' suggests that he has in mind the more formalized, logical ordering of a *demonstratio* of the being and nature of God to pagans. However, as we suggested earlier, when Calvin uses the term 'demonstration',[26] he may not have in mind a discursive proof (or proofs) of God's being, but rather an account of the manifestation of the existence and power of God, of what God is, in the creation.

[23] *Commentary on the Acts of the Apostles*, ii. 158.

[24] *Commentary on the Acts of the Apostles*, ii. 161.

[25] *Commentary on the Acts of the Apostles*, ii. 158.

[26] *Commentary on the Acts of the Apostles*, ii. 159, 'demonstration' (Fraser, 113). (But see Calvin's comments on v. 27 (*Commentary on the Acts of the Apostles*, ii. 166).)

What is interestingly downplayed in his account, despite the rough reception which Calvin recognizes that Paul receives, is the Romans 1 point, the thought that God demonstrates[27] his being and his excellencies in order to leave men without excuse. In discussing Acts 17: 27 Calvin raises the interesting question, 'whether men can naturally come unto the true and merciful knowledge of God'.[28] Given that Paul says that it is sluggishness that prevents men from recognizing the presence of God, does this mean that if men were not sluggish they would perceive his presence? It may seem so. But Calvin answers that 'having nature only for our guide' we cannot know what only the illumination of the Spirit can give us.[29] So Paul, by appealing to the works of God (and not to his secret substance/essence), shows that God is the Creator and Lord of the world. God created the world, so he cannot be confined to a space in the world ('It followeth, that he can be included and shut up within no space of place').[30]

There is another logical oddity or curiosity at this point. On the one hand, according to Calvin mankind's knowledge of God, rudimentary and suppressed from consciousness though much of it is, leaves people without excuse before God. (This, he believes, is Paul's teaching in Romans 1.) What are they responsible for? Presumably, for not responding appropriately to what they know. So they must have some knowledge of God. Suppose, on the other hand, that they *were* to respond to what they know, what would the consequence be? It would not be, for Calvin, that they then enjoyed salvation. So they are in something of a dilemma: damned if they don't respond, and damned if they do! Perhaps Calvin would regard a question about what the consequences would be if men and women did respond favourably to the knowledge given to them as being speculative. For all people respond negatively. Or perhaps he would say that if there were those who respond positively they would be given more light and grace on the principle of 'to him that has shall be given'. It is not easy to say, given that all Calvin tells us about is the 'primal and simple knowledge to which the very order of nature would have led us if Adam had remained upright'.[31]

What are we to make of this? Perhaps the way to approach this issue which is most sympathetic to Calvin is to connect it with the use of the law to

---

[27] 'This clearly proves how much men gain from this demonstration of the existence of God, viz. an utter incapacity to bring any defence to prevent them from being justly accused before the judgment-seat of God. We must, therefore, make this distinction, that the manifestation of God by which He makes His glory known among His creatures is sufficiently clear as far as its own light is concerned.' (*Calvin's Commentary on Romans*, trans. Ross Mackenzie (Edinburgh: Oliver & Boyd, 1961), 31.)

[28] *Commentary on the Acts of the Apostles*, II. 166.

[29] *Commentary on the Acts of the Apostles*, II. 167.

[30] *Commentary on the Acts of the Apostles*, II. 159.   [31] *Inst.* I. 2. 1.

convince people of their sins. The function of God's continuing natural revelation in a fallen world is not to place people on the first rung of the ladder which leads to the true knowledge of God, but to show them their bankruptcy. If this suggestion is cogent it is not only the revealed law of Moses which may have this function, the law written on the heart may also have it. More will be said about Calvin's view of the natural law in Chapter 12.

It is not clear whether Calvin thinks that v. 26 onward is a continuation of what Paul teaches of the extent of what we can, by natural means, know of God, or whether this is a further commentary of Paul's on what he had already said, a commentary on man's natural knowledge of God, but one that is informed by what Paul knows from God's revelation in the gospel. So when Paul says (v. 26) that God 'hath appointed the times before determined, and the bounds of their habitation' (which Calvin takes to be a reference to the all-encompassing providence of God[32]), is this an inference drawn from something about God known naturally, or is it a commentary (informed by 'special revelation') on what is known naturally about God? It is not clear.

What of the 'half a verse' which Paul quotes out of Aratus (v. 28)? Calvin has an interesting exegetical comment on the emphasis on 'life' in v. 28. He says, in effect, that it is an argument of Paul's from the greater to the less. If the human race has life in God, then a fortiori everything else is in God. This is because, in Calvin's view, there is a hierarchical arrangement in the existence of things, somewhat as follows:

life

is more excellent than

motion

which is more excellent than

existence.

And so 'We have not only no life but in God, but not so much as moving; yea, no being, which is inferior to both.'[33]

What Aratus knows comes 'from no other foundation save only from nature and common reason'. 'It is not to be doubted but that Aratus spake of Jupiter.'[34] Paul does not take what was applied to Jupiter and apply it to the true God, according to Calvin. Rather, what Aratus says of Jupiter is testimony to his being imbued with some knowledge of God, even though he wrongly appropriates that to Jupiter, who is no god. 'The first general

---

[32] *Commentary on the Acts of the Apostles*, II. 165.

[33] *Commentary on the Acts of the Apostles*, II. 168.

[34] *Commentary on the Acts of the Apostles*, II. 169.

knowledge of God [namely, that there is a God] doth nevertheless remain still in them.'[35] Calvin further illustrates from Virgil. When Virgil says 'all things are full of Jove', according to Calvin he expressed the power of God, but 'through error he put in the wrong name'.[36]

So what (according to Calvin) Paul is doing in quoting from Aratus is appropriating from him (despite or notwithstanding what Aratus himself meant by these words) a 'true maxim'.[37] So Aratus' words can be taken in a true sense, though not in a 'contrary sense'.[38] It almost seems that Calvin is operating with a sort of *sensus plenior* here. It is not that Aratus intended more than he knew, however, but that he gave a wrong expression of the 'true principles' about God which all men are imbued with, the 'first general knowledge of God doth nevertheless remain still in them'. (This is a reference to the *sensus divinitatis*, presumably, though Calvin does not mention the term explicitly.) For 'it may be that Aratus did imagine that there was some parcel of the divinity in men's minds, as the Manichees did say, that the souls of men are of the nature of God'.[39] And what, according to Calvin, Paul is doing in appropriating Aratus' words is attempting to bring the Athenians back on track from the 'wicked inventions' which the natural knowledge of God gives rise to as soon as the likes of Aratus 'begin to think upon God'.[40] This is in rather the same way in which Virgil is said to invent things about the Spirit. Thus (in the case of Aratus) he did not knowingly and intentionally speak the truth, but the words he spoke in speaking error can nevertheless be understood in a way that is consistent with the truth about God's relation to the world.

So there is a certain ambivalence in Calvin's understanding of what Paul is doing in Acts 17. On the one hand, the Athenians believe that there is a god, and Aratus believes that we live and move and have our being in him. So one might gather from this that the Athenians were not totally ignorant, and that Paul had some common ground with them. And indeed he seems to, for he has no need, according to Calvin, to spend time on the 'first point', on trying to establish God's existence by argument. But on the other hand, the Athenians are totally ignorant of what God is like, and so cannot offer acceptable worship of God. They don't intend to refer to the true God and don't succeed in doing so despite themselves. Nevertheless it seems clear that according to Calvin, Paul legitimately resorts to forms of natural argument,

---

[35] *Commentary on the Acts of the Apostles*, II. 170.
[36] *Commentary on the Acts of the Apostles*, II. 170.
[37] *Commentary on the Acts of the Apostles*, II. 170.
[38] *Commentary on the Acts of the Apostles*, II. 169.
[39] *Commentary on the Acts of the Apostles*, II. 170.
[40] *Commentary on the Acts of the Apostles*, II. 169.

and this would seem to support the view that Calvin himself was not flatly opposed to all forms of such argument.

One possible conclusion is that Calvin thought that natural theology was possible but not necessary for *ab initio* knowledge of God, but that it was sometimes usable as an apologetic tactic in the way that, he might argue, Paul used it at the Areopagus.

THE *SENSUS DIVINITATIS* IN THE *INSTITUTES*

We now turn to Calvin's discussion of the natural knowledge of God as this is found in the *Institutes*. Whatever may have been Calvin's attitude to discursive natural theology, it is incontestable that central to his treatment of the natural knowledge of God is his endorsement of a universal *sensus divinitatis* (henceforward SD).

Besides being of historical and theological interest Calvin's views on the *sensus divinitatis* have also aroused considerable philosophical interest in recent years in connection with the articulation of 'Reformed' epistemology. Part of that articulation has had to do with the critique of strong foundationalism that is intrinsic to Reformed epistemology, a critique of the idea that all human knowledge, including the knowledge that we may have of God, is derived or ought to be derived by inference from universal self-evident truths if such beliefs are to be rational. What is characteristic of 'Reformed' epistemology, in its first expression, is a version of weak foundationalism, propositions that one is entitled to hold which are not self-evident to everyone.[41] For it has been argued that not only is strong foundationalism referentially incoherent, and weak foundationalism permissible, but that a person is within his epistemic rights to take the proposition 'God exists' as part of the foundations of his noetic structure, even though it is not self-evident, that is, evident to any rational person, that God exists. This entitlement holds good even though one may not be able to prove that God exists by using steps that are self-evident, from premises that are self-evident. It is sufficient for such an entitlement that that belief be part of an individual person's properly basic noetic structure.

More recently, 'Reformed' epistemologists have seen in the SD not only a case for belief in God being in the foundations of a person's noetic structure, and so properly basic for that person, but rather as a mechanism which, when properly functioning, and in a propitious environment, produces true beliefs, foremost among which is the true belief that God exists. So Alvin Plantinga says that 'Calvin's basic claim is that there is a sort of instinct, a

---

[41] See, for example, Alvin Plantinga 'Reason and Belief in God', in *Faith and Rationality*.

natural human tendency, a disposition, a nisus to form beliefs about God under a variety of conditions and in a variety of situations'.[42]

The basic idea, I think, is that there is a kind of faculty or a cognitive mechanism, what Calvin calls a *sensus divinitatis* or sense of divinity, which in a wide variety of circumstances produces in us beliefs about God. These circumstances, we might say, trigger the disposition to form the beliefs in question; they form the occasion on which those beliefs arise. Under these circumstances, we develop or form theistic beliefs—or, rather, these beliefs are formed in us; in the typical case we don't consciously choose to have those beliefs. Instead, we find ourselves with them, just as we find ourselves with perceptual and memory beliefs.[43]

Either way, whether the SD is thought of as providing evidence which entitles us to form beliefs in God without argument or inference, or as a mechanism for forming such beliefs in the right circumstances, 'Reformed' epistemology takes encouragement from the belief that in Calvin one finds very little attention given to the proofs of God's existence in either the Thomist or the Enlightenment senses. There is little interest in developing a natural theology, and no requirement that a person ought to be able to prove that God exists, or to have that proof made by another on his behalf, in order for his belief in God's existence to be rational.

There may be reasons for Calvin's relative disinterest in these questions other than a rejection of the indispensability of natural theology. Calvin does not use his espousal of the SD to repudiate the project of natural theology, and the reason for this may be that he accepts both the propriety and validity of such arguments, and that since in any case natural theology was not rejected as a matter of principle in his day he did not feel the need to address the issue any more than he addressed the issue of *creatio ex nihilo*, say, or the relation of universals to the mind of God, or divine simplicity. Besides, there are at least two places, early on in the *Institutes*, where Calvin seems briefly to endorse some kind of cosmological proof of God's existence.

Having referred to the 'praises of God's power' to be found in Job and Isaiah, Calvin says:

These I now intentionally pass over, for they will find a more appropriate place where I shall discuss from the Scriptures the creation of the universe. Now I have only wanted to touch upon the fact that this way of seeking God is common both to strangers and to those of his household, if they trace the outlines that above and below sketch a living likeness of him. This very might leads us to ponder his eternity; for he from whom all things draw their origin must be eternal and have beginning from himself. Furthermore, if the cause is sought by which he was led once to create

---

[42] Alvin Plantinga, *Warranted Christian Belief*, 171. Plantinga cites *Inst.* 1. 3. 1.

[43] *Warranted Christian Belief*, 172–3.

all these things, and is now moved to preserve them, we shall find that it is his goodness alone.[44]

Here Calvin clearly envisages a type of argument, independent of special revelation, which leads from features of the world to God. Perhaps this is more the endorsement of a theology of nature than of a natural theology; it is not so much that there must be a God because the world has such and such features as that since the world has these features (and given that God exists) then he must have such and such features. However this may be, writing of the need for Scripture in order that we may receive a much fuller and clearer revelation of God he says:

This, therefore, is a special gift, where God, to instruct the church, not merely uses mute teachers but also opens his own most hallowed lips. Not only does he teach the elect to look upon a god, but also shows himself as the God upon whom they are to look. He has from the beginning maintained this plan for his church, so that besides these common proofs he also put forth his Word, which is a more direct and more certain mark whereby he is to be recognized.[45]

Here Calvin thinks of the Word of God supplementing and even in some sense supplanting 'common proofs', proofs available to all, that there is a god.

So we may plausibly surmise that in addition to this modest but significant appeal to natural theology, Calvin took the view, characteristic of the medievals, that natural theology is possible but not necessary for genuine religious belief.[46] 'We see that no long or toilsome proof is needed to elicit evidences that serve to illuminate and affirm the divine majesty.'[47] Such proofs may be possible, but they are not needed. We have seen that Calvin often takes the view that much in the medieval outlook can be taken for granted. Natural theology may be a case in point. This argument from silence, or from relative silence, is of course of limited value. It might go either way. But whichever way we take it, the relative silence does not suggest a rooted antipathy to natural theology on Calvin's part, and this is borne out by what we found in our earlier discussion of his comments on Acts 14 and Acts 17.

Further, although Calvin does not say a great deal directly about natural theology, there is good reason to think that his attitude to it may be inferred from what he says, in parallel fashion, about proofs of the divinity of Holy Scripture. He devotes the eighth chapter of the first book of the *Institutes* to a discussion of the external *indicia* of Holy Scripture. He argues that they can

---

[44] *Inst.* 1. 5. 6.

[45] *Inst.* 1. 6. 1. Note also Muller's reference to Calvin's endorsement of natural theology in his commentary on Psalm 104 (*The Unaccommodated Calvin*, 115).

[46] Besides appealing to Calvin, Plantinga cites Aquinas, 'To know in a general and confused way that God exists is implanted in us by nature' (*Summa Theologiae*, 1a, 2ae, 1. 1).   [47] *Inst.* 1. 5. 9.

never establish the divinity of Holy Scripture with full certainty; that they are nevertheless useful for rebutting objections to the divine authorship of Holy Scripture, and they can be used to form positive opinions about Scripture. One could easily imagine Calvin taking a parallel attitude to the 'common proofs'; that though they are religiously inadequate, they are nevertheless useful for bringing men and women to hold the opinion that there is a God, or even demonstrating the existence of God, besides rendering them inexcusable. We shall take up Calvin's attitude to God's revelation in Scripture more fully in the next chapter.

What is clear is that Calvin shows little or no interest in the *rationality* of religious belief as such or in what constitutes warrant for a theistic belief. As we have seen, his appeal to the SD has been taken by 'Reformed' epistemologists as either a piece of internalist epistemology, as offering an account of epistemic justification or warrant in terms of providing grounds or evidence for belief, or as offering an account of epistemic justification in terms of a causal condition or a set of such conditions. Not surprisingly, Calvin does not take a position on the debate between foundationalists and non-foundationalists regarding the foundations of knowledge. It is thus somewhat anachronistic to impute to Calvin a particular response to a set of issues having to do with the rationality of religious belief which were only addressed in the Enlightenment and subsequently. One consequence of the doubt cast on strong foundationalism has been the encouragement of one kind or another of epistemological pluralism. This has led epistemologists, including 'Reformed' epistemologists, to focus in the first instance upon internalism and particularly on the ethics of belief-formation, and latterly on externalism, on the operation of belief-forming mechanisms which, when they function properly in a propitious environment, issue in the knowledge of God if it is true that God exists. But Calvin's stress is not on the rationality of believing in God, nor on its non-rationality, nor on cognitive mechanisms for the production of knowledge, but on human accountability for the knowledge of God, for either the fact of that knowledge, or for the proper use of the capacity for such knowledge that, as a matter of brute fact, each of us possesses in virtue of the SD. The reason for this stress will become clear in what follows.

Nonetheless Calvin does have what might loosely be called a religious epistemology that is grounded in the *sensus divinitatis*. According to him, in virtue of the fact that we all possess this sense, God's existence does not have to be argued for in order for it to be known that God exists. Nor does any appeal need to be made to considerations of a general kind in order to establish that God is universally known. The most that is needed is for us to be aware of certain matters of fact. Calvin's use of the term 'sense' signals that in his view the knowledge of God is a common human endowment; mankind is created not only as capable of knowing God, but as actually knowing him. By appealing to the SD Calvin implicitly rejects the view that unbelief or agnosticism are the natural human conditions, or that it is rational to presume atheism, but implies that belief in God is natural in the sense of being part of man's original condition, part of what it means to be really or fully human.

The SD, the awareness of divinity and the capacity for such an awareness, is central to Calvin's religious epistemology even though he uses the term 'know' in a way that is richer than the merely epistemic. On the merely epistemic view, one may know that *p*, or know A, while at the same time viewing *p* or A with distaste or repugnance. But for Calvin, to know in the full sense is to be not only in the appropriate epistemic condition, but also in a positive affective and conative condition towards the one whom one knows. 'Now, the knowledge of God, as I understand it, is that by which we not only conceive that there is a God but also grasp what befits us and is proper to his glory, in fine, what is to our advantage to know of him. Indeed, we shall not say that, properly speaking, God is known where there is no religion or piety.'[48] The consequences of this view of what the knowledge of God comprises will become apparent later.

The exposition which follows will involve us in a discussion in three phases. The first phase summarizes Calvin's basic position on the *sensus*; the second phase goes into what Calvin thought the SD was in its pristine condition; while the third phase looks at what he takes to be the effects of sin upon it. However, we shall find it difficult to keep these later two final phases completely separate, as Calvin himself finds it difficult to do so. Having looked at the two aspects of the *sensus*, unfallen and fallen, we shall then try to form a view about what Calvin means or may mean by the noetic effects of sin, the effects of sin upon the mind of man, including its effects upon this basic endowment.

So first to the main elements of Calvin's views on these two conditions of the SD, the pristine and the fallen, as they are found in the opening pages of the *Institutes*.

THE *SENSUS*: THE BASIC POSITION

In the *Institutes* Calvin has this to say about the SD:

There is within the human mind, and indeed by natural instinct, an awareness of divinity. This we take to be beyond controversy. To prevent anyone from taking

---

[48] *Inst.* I. 2. 1. This is one of the reasons why Calvin does not believe that the Athenians, or Aratus, for example, have knowledge of the true God.

refuge in the pretense of ignorance, God himself has implanted in all men a certain understanding of his divine majesty. Ever renewing its memory, he repeatedly sheds fresh drops. Since, therefore, men one and all perceive that there is a God and that he is their Maker, they are condemned by their own testimony because they have failed to honor him and to consecrate their lives to his will. If ignorance of God is to be looked for anywhere, surely one is most likely to find an example of it among the more backward folk and those more remote from civilization. Yet there is, as the eminent pagan says, no nation so barbarous, no people so savage, that they have not a deep-seated conviction that there is a God. And they who in other aspects of life seem least to differ from brutes still continue to retain some seed of religion. So deeply does the common conception occupy the minds of all, so tenaciously does it inhere in the hearts of all! Therefore, since from the beginning of the world there has been no region, no city, in short, no household, that could do without religion, there lies in this a tacit confession of a sense of deity inscribed in the hearts of all.[49]

While Calvin is here ostensibly setting out the nature of the *sensus* in its unfallen condition, it is noticeable that he does not strictly separate the treatment of the *sensus* as unfallen from that as fallen; savage and barbarous nations, nations that are savage and barbarous because (presumably) they experience the effects of the Fall, nonetheless give evidence of the universality of the *sensus*. One reason for not clearly separating the *sensus* fallen from the *sensus* unfallen is that there is a strong empirical element in Calvin's view; in effect he says that we can see now, by looking around, that the *sensus* is universally distributed and is therefore, in one important sense of the term 'natural', natural to mankind. There is also a kind of a fortiori argument implied in Calvin at this point; if the *sensus* is universally distributed in the post-lapsarian present, then a fortiori it must have been originally natural.

This is one aspect of Calvin's teaching. The claim is that the sense of God is universal, and that it is capable of finding expression in a variety of theologies; polytheism in religion, for example, is for Calvin evidence of the operation of the *sensus* (though of its malfunctioning) equally as much as is monotheism. We shall return to this important point later. But Calvin also goes on, in the next chapter of the *Institutes*, to claim that this knowledge of God is either smothered or corrupted.

Experience teaches that the seed of religion has been divinely planted in all men. But barely one man in a hundred can be found who nourishes in his own heart what he has conceived; and not even one in whom it matures, much less bears fruit in its season [cf. Ps. 1: 3]. Now some lose themselves in their own superstition, while others of their own evil intention revolt from God, yet all fall away from the true knowledge of him.[50]

---

[49] *Inst.* I. 3. 1. The 'eminent pagan' is Cicero.   [50] *Inst.* I. 4. 1.

Calvin, of course, holds that we are all fallen, and remain fallen. He provides no place for epistemic perfectionism, any more than he does for moral perfectionism. Each of us (even those who enjoy the knowledge of Christ the Redeemer) continue to have a warped or corrupted *sensus divinitatis*, just as the epistemic gap between the knowledge that the Creator has and that which his creatures can have remains. So the basic position is that all mankind have the *sensus* in virtue of their humanity, presumably in virtue of their being created in the image of God, and this *sensus* has not been eradicated by the Fall, but it continues to function, or rather to malfunction, to the same universal extent.

Let us now consider each of these phases in the history of the *sensus* in more detail.

THE PRISTINE SENSUS

Several things are clear about the SD in its original form from the extracts given above, and several things are not so clear.

In the first place, by the knowledge of God which the SD conveys Calvin appears to mean two things, or we might say that the knowledge conveyed has two aspects. It is 'that by which we . . . conceive that there is a God' and further, it is that by which we 'grasp what befits us and is proper to his glory, in fine, what is to our advantage to know of him'.[51] That is, the knowledge of God given in the SD has both what I shall call metaphysical-cognitive and moral-cognitive components[52] which Calvin covers by the umbrella term 'knowledge'; the knowledge that the SD gives us of God leads us, or ought to lead us, to worship and serve him. Let us look at these two components in turn.

The metaphysical-cognitive component Calvin states briefly as 'that by which we . . . conceive that there is a God'. The SD is 'an awareness of divinity'; by it men 'perceive that there is a God and that he is their Maker'.[53] These expressions confirm Calvin's relative lack of interest in the *Institutes* in discursive proofs of God's existence as the basis for religious epistemology. There is a directness, an immediacy about the sort of knowledge of God that Calvin wishes to focus on. But it is necessary to note something else that Calvin does not say in these expressions. He is not claiming that by virtue of the SD all men conceive of God; that is, he is not claiming that there is direct comprehension (or even apprehension) of God's essence. Indeed we know from what Calvin writes elsewhere about the incomprehensibility of God

---

[51] *Inst.* 1. 2. 1.

[52] The use of these terms is not intended to deny that for Calvin moral values have a metaphysical component.   [53] *Inst.* 1. 3. 1.

that he would be vehemently opposed to such an idea. He writes, for example, that 'his essence is incomprehensible; hence, his divineness far escapes all human perception'.[54]

Much less is Calvin saying that all men have a direct experience of God. The sentences that we are discussing do not amount to an appeal to religious experience either as a mystical 'encounter' with the divine or as some other kind of direct awareness of God. The idea of an experience of God does not enter into any of the terminology that Calvin uses to characterize the SD.[55]

Rather by the SD all men conceive (or perceive) *that there is a God*; that is, there is recognition by all men of the fact that there is a God. This basic knowledge of God is propositional in content rather than a person to person awareness of God. Granted that this knowledge has the form of a judgement that there is a God, we may go on to ask, is such a judgement immediate, or is it the result of an inference? It seems to have two aspects. There is, in the first place, the *sensus*, a human disposition to interpret certain data in certain ways. It is this disposition that is innate, and Calvin says that whatever it is that this faculty grasps, it is able to be remembered by the one who grasps it, and to have that memory renewed by new daily experiences.

'God himself has implanted in all men a certain understanding of his divine majesty. Ever renewing its memory, he repeatedly sheds fresh drops.'[56] This, what the *sensus* senses, is the second aspect. So the *sensus* is like a memory which is kept fresh by continual reminders of what has been remembered, or like a skill which is kept up by daily practice. A person may continue to have a vivid memory of a dead loved one, by often looking at photographs, by playing videotapes, and the like. A person may have the ability to ride a bicycle, but only so long as she keeps in practice. If she does not practise, then she loses the skill, though perhaps she retains the disposition to regain it. A person may have the disposition to identify and name trees, or birds, but the actual ability to identify is lost or worsened if it is not kept up. In a similar way, mankind in its original condition had the innate disposition to conceive that God exists, a disposition which did not in any way jar with, but was confirmed by, its daily experience.

So the SD has two aspects. Each of these aspects is necessary for the proper functioning of the SD and together they are sufficient. The SD might exist for a time without the awareness of features of the external world which daily renews it. Without that repeated triggering, Calvin seems to imply, the sense of God would peter out because the knowledge conveyed by the *sensus* would

---

[54] *Inst.* 1. 5. 1. See also *Inst.* 1. 3. 1 and 1. 13. 1.

[55] This interpretation contrasts with that of Dewey Hoitenga, *Faith and Reason from Plato to Plantinga* (Albany, NY: SUNY Press, 1991), 150, who interprets the immediacy as parallel to the direct sensory acquaintance with physical objects.   [56] *Inst.* 1. 3. 1.

not be sustained by appropriate features of the environment discerned a posteriori. Likewise, without the knowledge to begin with the data supplied by daily experience would be insufficient to sustain the knowledge of God. So by the SD and a triggering environment we gain and retain the knowledge of God. The *sensus* is thus not merely a sense for knowing God, when it is working properly in the right conditions it is a sense that tells us that there is a God.

Michael Sudduth has taken this a step further.[57] He has suggested that what Calvin says is compatible with the position he calls 'mediate natural theology'. In recognizing that the awareness of God provided by the SD is immediate one should distinguish between psychological and epistemological immediacy. There may be no awareness of an inference or inferences being drawn and so the awareness that there is a God may be immediate. And yet there may be inferences at work, for the premiss or premisses of the inference may be held unconsciously and there may be no psychologically identifiable process of inferring. Sudduth sees support for this in what Calvin says about the evidence around us being compelling evidence that there is a God even though men then go on to conceal it.[58]

With this distinction before us he suggests that we may see more clearly that Calvin has in mind two different ways in which a person may arrive at a natural knowledge of God. The sense of divinity gives knowledge by itself, but there is in addition knowledge that there is a God to be had from the way in which he 'daily discloses himself in the whole workmanship of the universe',[59] these two ways corresponding to the arguments of *Institutes* I. 4 and I. 5 respectively. People may already possess the belief, held dispositionally, that if there was evidence of such and such a degree and kind they would believe that there is a God, be presented with such evidence, and then believe that there is a God, with no consciously held steps of inference being involved.

So is Calvin referring to one kind of knowledge which is sustained and renewed in various ways? Or is he referring to two separate sources of knowledge, one immediate and one inferential? In attempting to answer these questions there is the obvious danger that in fine-tuning Calvin's words we shall go beyond his own ideas, what he thought, to consider what sense his words, taken more abstractly, may bear. Nevertheless these suggestions are both interesting and plausible.

Whether or not we press this distinction the SD is not a case of immediate experience of God, as the experience of a patch of blue may be immediate;

---

[57] Michael L. Czapkay Sudduth, 'The Prospects for Mediate Natural Theology in John Calvin', *Religious Studies* (1995).   [58] *Inst.* I. 5. 4.   [59] *Inst.* I. 5. 1.

rather it is a judgement of a highly un-self-conscious and automatic kind, 'natural' in yet another sense of that term, based upon the SD itself or on an experience of certain features of the physical world, upon its beauty and orderliness and other features. This judgement is accompanied by a feeling of obviousness or naturalness in the way in which it is natural for us to believe that there has been a past, or that there are minds other than our own minds, or that $2 + 2 = 4$. One might even say that the judgement or awareness that there is a God supervenes upon experiences of the natural world in that whoever has a properly functioning SD would, when brought to experience data of a certain kind, immediately, without the need for conscious ratiocination, form the belief that there is a God, or have that belief sustained or reinforced.

There is a principle of universalizability at work, or in the background, here. If A has a properly working SD, and has the knowledge that there is a God renewed by data $D_1 \ldots D_5$, then anyone else with a properly working SD, with the knowledge of data $D_1 \ldots D_5$, would have the knowledge that there is a God renewed. This is another justification for Calvin's use of the term *sensus*.

So much, for the moment, for the metaphysical-cognitive aspect of the SD, though some of the distinctions we have been considering may equally apply to the other aspect of the SD, the moral-cognitive component. This concerns the awareness of certain obligations arising out of the knowledge of the fact that God is the source of all goodness.

This I take to mean that not only does he sustain this universe (as he once founded it) by his boundless might, regulate it by his wisdom, preserve it by his goodness, and especially rule mankind by his righteousness and judgment, bear with it in his mercy, watch over it by his protection; but also that no drop will be found either of wisdom and light, or of righteousness or power or rectitude, or of genuine truth, which does not flow from him, and of which he is not the cause.[60]

This is corroborated by Calvin's later claim that the knowledge of God is sufficient to convey a sense of obligation.[61]

What this means appears to be something like the following: that given a properly working SD the natural awareness of the world around us, and of ourselves, activates or sustains the belief not simply that God exists, but that God has created and is sustaining all that one is aware of. So the cognitive content of the *sensus* is not merely that God exists, but that God the Creator exists. This awareness, that oneself and all that one sees is the creation of God, in turn triggers beliefs and feelings of awe, respect, gratitude, and obligation to the benefactor of the whole, beliefs and feelings which are

---

[60] *Inst.* I. 2. 1.   [61] *Inst.* I. 2. 2.

entirely appropriate given the knowledge of the Creator that men possess, and commitment to a moral principle such as: *Benefactors ought to be loved and respected.*

That is, a component part of the SD is a moral faculty capable of reasoning as follows: I ought to love and respect whoever has created and sustains me, if anyone has; I am naturally aware that God has created and sustains me; therefore, I ought to love and respect God. But although the moral faculty must be capable of reasoning in this fashion, it need not actually reason like this; the moral judgement that God is to be loved and obeyed may be automatically formed. And because in the unfallen state there was no weakness of will or failure of any other kind, then those who reasoned in this fashion did love and obey God, did 'consecrate their lives to his will'.[62] Using Immanuel Kant's terminology we might say that each person with a properly working SD in a properly working environment has a 'holy will', a will that loves and respects God, and which willingly meets obligations to do so, while not recognizing these *as* obligations.

Despite the earlier reservations we expressed as to Calvin's interest in discursive proofs of God's existence, he may nevertheless quite properly be said to have a natural theology, so long as one bears in mind the diverse meanings of that expression. His natural theology is not one that is primarily based upon discursive proofs (though we have noted evidence that suggests that Calvin is not entirely hostile to such proofs) but upon innate, properly functioning capacities common (i.e. natural) to all people, which when brought to bear on the common world of sense experience, the natural world, yield a grasp that there is one God and creator of this entire world who is to be worshipped and served. There is a sense in which for Calvin the universality of the SD is a more radical and powerful kind of natural knowledge than that afforded by the proofs. For discursive proofs of God's existence can only be understood by a few (as Aquinas himself recognized), whereas by the SD all are aware of the existence of God and are accountable for that knowledge.

Because of this emphasis upon the natural knowledge of God, Calvin would be strongly averse to the thought that the only knowledge of God that people have, or may have, is the knowledge of God's redeeming grace in Christ. While apparently not giving much support to the reliance of a theologian such as Aquinas on natural theology, Calvin would nonetheless have agreed with the medieval and scholastic emphasis that redemptive grace builds upon nature (the effects of the innate, universally distributed *sensus*). It does not subvert it, though it does renew it. However, to say this is to

---

[62] *Inst.* I. 3. 1.

anticipate an aspect of our later discussion of Calvin's view of the *sensus* as fallen.

So the SD is a universal phenomenon. And one important point that arises from Calvin's description of this awareness that there is a God as a *sense* is precisely to draw attention to its universal, 'natural' character. The SD is not of course a sense in the way in which the five senses are. But as the five senses are universal human capacities to discriminate sounds and tastes and so forth which arise in our environment, and are the proper endowment of any normal human being, so the SD is a universal (and original) capacity, distinct from the five senses but not wholly unrelated to their operation, as we have seen. Thus it is a natural capacity, a capacity to know that there is a God, a capacity which is activated or actualized when proper attention is given to the world that we inhabit as, in an unfallen world, it invariably would be.

So it is not accurate to say that Calvin's account of the SD is of an innate idea of God. As we saw from his interpretation of Paul's preaching he is not committed to the position that all men and women are born with a fully formed concept of God. Had he known of John Locke's critique of innate ideas, including the innate idea of God, Calvin could or would have concurred.[63]

Locke famously believed that the idea of God has the best chance of any of our ideas of being innate, but argued that the evidence for its innateness, as for that of all ideas, is consistent with and better explained by the non-innateness hypothesis. If the universality of the idea of God proves its innateness, then the universality of the idea of fire may as well prove its innateness. Furthermore,

I grant that *if* there were *any ideas* to be found *imprinted* on the minds of men, we have reason to expect *it should be the notion of his maker*, as a mark GOD set on his own workmanship, to mind man of his dependence and duty; and that herein should appear the first instances of human knowledge. But how late is it before any such notion is discoverable in children? And when we find it there, how much more does it resemble the opinion and notion of the teacher than represent the true God?[64]

Further,

Can it be thought that the *ideas* men have of God are the characters and marks of himself, engraven in their minds by his own finger, when we see that, in the same country, under one and the same name, *men have far different*, nay often *contrary and inconsistent ideas* and concepts *of him*? Their agreeing in a name, or sound, will scarce prove an innate notion of him.[65]

---

[63] John Locke, *An Essay Concerning Human Understanding*, ed. J. Yolton (London: Dent, 1961), book I.

[64] *An Essay Concerning Human Understanding*, I. 4. 13.

[65] *An Essay Concerning Human Understanding*, I. 4. 14.

Hence, on the grounds of explanatory simplicity, the non-innateness hypothesis ought to be preferred. It accounts better than does the innateness hypothesis for the fact that people have a similar conception of God to their teachers, and different conceptions of God, where they occur, tend to disprove the innateness hypothesis. The most that appeal to innateness might prove, according to Locke, is an innate idea of the name of God.

Calvin, no more than Locke, claims that we each have an innate idea of God, nor even an innate idea of some god or other. Rather, as we have seen, according to Calvin the SD is an innate endowment triggered by factors which are not innate, namely the features of the external world and of ourselves. It would have come as no surprise to him to be told that where two people occupy different environments, for example where they have teachers with different ideas of God, then the ideas of God which they form will also be different. Were Calvin to have addressed the very un-Calvinian counter-factual question, 'What would the original condition of mankind have been had mankind not been placed in the environment they were in fact placed in but in some chaotic environment?' consistently with his position he ought to have said: the SD would not have been fully or properly activated, and despite possessing the pristine *sensus*, such people would not have had the knowledge of God. At the same time, Calvin does not endorse the *tabula rasa* of the empiricist. For there are innate dispositions to believe that there is a god.

How does Calvin arrive at conclusions similar to those of Locke? Calvin claims that the knowledge that he, John Calvin (together with, he believes, his readers), has that all men and women have the SD is a posteriori in character: 'Experience teaches that the seed of religion has been divinely planted in all men.'[66] He does not say that the knowledge that all people are endowed with the SD is known through reason, nor (for all his emphasis upon the supreme authority of the Bible) through the Scriptures, but through daily experience. It is how people behave that, so to speak, gives them away, and it is our knowledge of this behaviour in ourselves and in others that makes the universal possession of the SD evident.

Being an empirical claim, the claim that all people possess a SD is presumably in principle open to empirical refutation. But what would count as an actual refutation of it? It is hard to say. As we have already seen, because Calvin believes that the SD, though possessed by everyone, is perverted in everyone by sin (a factor that we shall come to discuss later on), he is not surprised by the existence of what he regards as false belief, idolatry, and such like, among the 'barbarous' nations. So the fact that there are polytheists, or animists, or dry as dust deists, does not for Calvin refute his claim as to the

---

[66] *Inst.* I. 4. 1.

universality of SD; rather he takes it to confirm that claim, for such religious beliefs and expressions of belief are evidence of the perversion of the SD in human beings; and it is impossible to pervert what does not exist. What would refute his claim about the universal distribution of the *sensus* would be the existence of a person who gave no glimmer of concern, at any point in her life, whether or not God exists, or whether or not she has a conscience.

Calvin is not saying that the belief and behaviour that he draws attention to is conclusive evidence that God exists, but it is evidence for the conclusion that the sense of God is universal. It is worth dwelling on this distinction for a moment or two.

It is well known that Calvin refers to the views of Cicero in articulating his view of the SD, and also that Cicero's *The Nature of the Gods* is one of the main ancient sources for what is known as the Argument from Universal Consent for the existence of God. 'The crux of the matter is known to all men everywhere. From their birth it is inscribed upon their minds that gods exist.'[67] Similar words are found in Seneca's *Epistulae Moralis.* 'We are accustomed to attach great importance to the universal belief of mankind. It is accepted by us as a convincing argument. That there are gods we infer from the sentiment engrafted in the human mind; nor has any nation ever been found, so far beyond the pale of law and civilization as to deny their existence.'[68] Calvin appeals not only to the universality of belief in God, but also to its 'proleptic' character. This universal belief in God is not acquired, but it is a preconception, a disposition to believe in God from which it arises naturally. It is a 'common notion'. Calvin no doubt derived this language from the Stoics, mediated by Cicero's *The Nature of the Gods.*[69] But it is doubtful whether he himself believed that he took the very idea from such sources, for it is surely more likely that he believed that the Apostle Paul taught it in the first two chapters of his letter to the Romans.

But what is Calvin's estimate of the idea that this view of the proleptic character of belief in God is accompanied by the argument for the existence of God from universal consent? Are we to conclude that Calvin subscribes to a version of the argument from consent, and that the appeal to the SD encapsulates such an argument?

---

[67] Cicero, *The Nature of the Gods,* trans. Horace. C. P. McGregor (London: Penguin Books, 1972), 128.

[68] Cited in Paul Edwards, 'Common Consent Arguments for the Existence of God', in Paul Edwards (ed.), *The Encyclopaedia of Philosophy* (London: Macmillan, 1967), II. 147–55.

[69] There is a useful brief account of *prolepsis* in Edward Adams, 'Calvin's View of Natural Knowledge of God', *International Journal of Systematic Theology* (2001). See also M. Schofield, 'Preconception, Argument and God', in M. Schofield, M. Burnyeat, and J. Barnes (eds.), *Doubt and Dogmatism: Studies in Hellenistic Epistemology* (Oxford: Clarendon Press, 1978), and E. Grislis, 'Calvin's Use of Cicero in the Institutes I: 1–5 — A Case Study in Theological Method', *Archiv für Reformationsgeschichte* (1971).

Despite the allusions to Cicero, this would be a rather hasty conclusion to draw. In fact there is more reason to think that Calvin subscribes to what one might call an inverted form of the argument from consent. For he writes the *Institutes* as a Christian man and theologian. For him (and, he trusts, for his readers) it is a fundamental fact that God exists, for this is known through their own experience and is affirmed by the self-authenticating character of Scripture. One gains the impression reading the *Institutes* that Calvin would not have been greatly ruffled in his faith were, say, out-and-out atheism to have been widespread. But in that case why does he insist upon the fact of the universal *sensus divinitatis*? Is it simply because he believes that the Apostle Paul teaches so?

There is a further reason why Calvin appeals to Cicero and to what might reasonably be called 'empirical sources' in general to support his belief that there is a universal or near-universal *sensus divinitatis*, because Cicero's is independent evidence. Calvin held that the presence of such a sense is clearly taught by Paul in the first two chapters of the letter to the Romans. For example, in commenting on Romans 2: 14 Calvin claims that 'there appeared in the Gentiles a natural light of justice which did supply the place of the law . . . a certain discretion and judgment . . . certain seeds of justice abiding in their wit'. He goes on: 'It is not to our purpose to inquire what sort of God they imagined him to be, or how many gods they devised; it is enough to know, that they thought that there is a God, and that honour and worship are due to him.'[70] That is, they possess a *sensus divinitatis*. It might be thought that to cite such passages would be sufficient for Calvin to establish the fact. But this procedure would be self-defeating, because it would (in effect) be an appeal to special revelation to ground the reality of general revelation. Such an appeal would clearly nullify such a grounding. So Calvin does not believe in the universality of the *sensus divinitatis* only (or perhaps primarily) because it is taught by Paul, but because there is, as a matter of plain observation, a universal *sensus divinitatis*, as Cicero and other informed writers from outside the circle of special revelation testify.[71] To retain the integrity of this appeal Calvin must make it a matter of direct report, not a report mediated by Scripture. Though it could, consistently with his position, be endorsed by Scripture. Indeed, if the presence of the *sensus divinitatis* is universal, one

---

[70] *Commentary on Romans* 2: 14–15.

[71] T. H. L. Parker makes a similar point. 'Calvin's argument is that all men have this innate knowledge of God's existence. If that is so, then the heathen philosophers must also have such a knowledge and express it in their writings. Hence, merely to be able to make legitimate use of these writings is a confirmation of the argument' (*Calvin's Doctrine of the Knowledge of God*, 2nd edn. (Edinburgh: Oliver & Boyd, 1969), 35).

would expect (as part of this universal testimony) writers such as Paul to endorse it, as indeed (according to Calvin) they do.

The widespread, near-universal belief in God or the gods is offered by Calvin as empirical support for the thesis that God is known to all men, a proposition which he believes is taught in the Bible. It is not that Calvin argues (in the manner of the argument from universal consent) that there is widespread or universal belief that God exists, therefore God exists, but the opposite. Given that he, John Calvin, knows that God exists, experience confirms that this knowledge is universal, though universally corrupted. Calvin appeals to Cicero, it is true, but he turns Cicero's argument from consent upside down; he uses it not to establish that God exists *ab initio*, but to provide confirmatory evidence for what he already knows. We shall shortly discuss his reason for doing so.

There is one other matter that calls for general comment. What exactly is 'the divine' that all men have a sense of? What is the sense and reference of this term? As we have seen in discussing his comments on Acts 14 and 17 Calvin is clearly not saying that all those who have a sense of God have a sense of the same God. Those whose sense of God finds expression in polytheism, for example, have a different and incompatible sense of God or the gods from those whose sense of God finds expression in monotheism. But do all who give different senses to 'God' or 'the gods' in fact refer to the same God? As we have seen from Calvin's comments on Acts 17 it is not plausible to suppose that he is offering some early version of John Hick's *An Interpretation of Religion*, believing that though the senses which different religionists attach to 'the divine' are different, all these senses have a common referent. And yet, as we have also noted, Calvin thinks that Aratus and company have *some* knowledge of God.

It is just possible that Calvin may be best interpreted as arguing that the SD gives to all men a confused knowledge of the true God. Even the atheist, according to Calvin, is able to distinguish right from wrong and may believe that there is something which enables us to make these discriminations. Calvin himself holds that what enables us to distinguish right from wrong is God himself, while the atheist, of course, denies this. Thus for Calvin 'that which enables us to distinguish right from wrong' is a true description of God, so that even the atheist in believing that there is something which enables us to distinguish right from wrong (say) may be said to have a true *de re* belief about God. But though this may be implied by Calvin's position such an interpretation surely goes beyond what Calvin actually had in mind.[72]

---

[72] For discussion of this point, see Plantinga, *Warranted Christian Belief*, 176–7.

It is more accurate to suppose that for Calvin the divine of which all men have a sense is more like the recognition of a category of things than of some thing or things within a category. What Calvin is therefore saying is perhaps something like this; that all men have an awareness of something (or things) that performs a unique categorical function; just as 'material object' plays a unique categorical function, namely that of referring to a class of three-dimensional physical objects existing in space and time, though different people have conflicting beliefs about what material objects there are, and 'joke' plays a unique categorical function, though people differ about what is funny, so 'the divine' plays such a function, though different people have conflicting beliefs about the character of the divine, about what God or gods there are. Some are monotheists, some are polytheists, some are animists, and so on; some believe that the fact of the existence of a God or gods places certain obligations on us, others who believe in God believe that they have other obligations, or perhaps no obligations at all. The functioning of the SD consists in the awareness of the categorical function performed by 'the divine', something like 'object of worship', or 'that from whom all things have come', together with a disposition to believe in and respect whoever is judged to perform this function.

THE PERVERTED *SENSUS*

Let us now turn our attention to the other side of the coin, to Calvin's belief that the human race is fallen, and its consequences for the SD. Some writers believe that Calvin's recognition of the perversion of the SD rules out any prospect of natural theology. So T. H. L. Parker maintains that 'The image of God has been corrupted in such a way that God can now be known only by the special, redemptive illumination of the soul by the Word and the Spirit. Man, being out of harmony with God and with His creation, can no longer perceive the revelation of God which is the true meaning of the universe.'[73] Parker is, however, forced into a retreat from this position by noting what Calvin himself says. He notes that fallen mankind has some awareness of God which has not been rightly used, and interprets Calvin on Romans 1: 21 as saying that God had so shown himself (*se demonstrasse*) by his works that men could not help seeing.[74] These may be references to the SD but they hardly rule out the possibility of natural theology, as we noted earlier.

We have already touched on what Calvin has to say about the perverted SD in discussing his treatment of the unfallen SD, and this is not surprising,

---

[73] *Calvin's Doctrine of the Knowledge of God* (2nd edn. 1969), 48. Any attempt to make Calvin a natural theologian is 'destroyed' (53).

[74] *Calvin's Doctrine of the Knowledge of God*, 69.

for so impressed is he by the lapsed character of the SD that he refers to this, as it is expressed, for example, in the idolatry of the 'barbarous', even when ostensibly discussing the SD in its unfallen condition. But it is interesting that for all his stress on the dramatic and deep effects of the Fall, Calvin does not say that the Fall has completely eradicated the *sensus*.

Nor does Calvin entertain what one might call a doctrine of suppression. There is no evidence that he thinks that all men and women have a sense of the true God in their religious subconscious which they then suppress or transmute into an animistic or polytheistic variant of that. Calvin does not employ the idea of levels of consciousness, and say that although men and women may profess to be polytheists, or animists, deep down they are monotheists of the sort that Calvin himself was. He is not saying that polytheism is a mere surface expression of belief, an attempt to escape what deep in their hearts polytheists know to be true, that there is one God. Nor, even, does Calvin explain the diversity of religious belief and practice by invoking something akin to the idea of false consciousness as employed by Marx and the Marxists to explain away religious belief. By his account of the noetic effects of sin he may be committed to something akin to a doctrine of false consciousness, a kind of self-deception, but if so it does not, he believes, work successfully to eradicate belief in God in those who are under its sway.

At first glance it is rather surprising that Calvin does not make more of the idea of self-deception in offering an account of the effects of sin. There is, to be sure, some reference to one effect of sin being that we flatter ourselves (*Inst.* II. 1. 2) and give expression to blind self-love, and there is clearly here a reference to the self-deceiving character of sin. Certainly as we shall shortly see he does not appeal to self-deception in giving his brief account of atheism. Rather the atheist is one who wants not to believe in God but occasionally events force him to.

Why is this? Why does not Calvin invoke self-deception as an important feature if not the most important feature of the noetic effects of sin? The reason is that (as we saw earlier) he adopts the broadly Aristotelian view that a person is responsible for their action when they are not compelled to act and when they act in knowledge of the circumstances. Hence whatever sin does it cannot be thought to entirely remove the knowledge of God afforded by the SD otherwise people would not be responsible for what they do. In support of this Calvin explicitly rejects Plato's view that we sin only out of ignorance and endorses Aristotle's view of sin as intemperance, as knowingly and stubbornly, without regret, persisting in choosing evil.[75] So for Calvin

---

[75] *Inst.* II. 2. 22–3. Aristotle's accounts of the conditions of responsibility and of the relation between incontinence and intemperance are to be found in *Nichomachean Ethics*, books III and VII respectively.

sinfulness is not to be understood as due to a state of ignorance or false-consciousness brought about by self-deception even though self-deception is an aspect of sin.

However, there is *some* similarity between the approach of writers such as Marx and Freud, and Calvin. To see this, let us briefly consider an aspect of Calvin's theory of error. What is error about God due to? According to Calvin it is not due, basically, to a lack of information. Error is not mainly due to ignorance. Nor is it due to mere weakness. Nor is it due to the influence of the environment; nor to a combination of these factors. In fact, it is rather surprising that Calvin seems to pay little or no attention to the fact that the environment now bears the marks of the Fall, and might be expected to affect the triggering of the *sensus*. Rather in chapter 5 of book 1 of the *Institutes* he stresses that the natural world continues to provide clear and inexcusable evidence that it is the creation of God, for 'men cannot open their eyes without being compelled to see him'.[76]

As we saw in our discussion of Calvin's understanding of the Fall in Chapter 5, error is due to the perversity or wilfulness of the human self, a perversity that is often, but not always or necessarily accompanied by, and made possible by, self-deception. Because the issue of God's existence is of considerable importance for men and women, that is, it is not a mere theoretical or trivial issue, sin leads, via a mechanism of self-deceiving wilfulness, to the true God being displaced from within the category of the divine by belief in many gods; or else there may be a mere theoretical acceptance of the reality of the true God; God is not known, in Calvin's sense of that term.

It may be plausible to construe Calvin as holding that the varieties of religious belief are perversions of the one true belief which all people are disposed to hold if they are true to their nature as human beings. Such diverse religious beliefs would thus provide both strong empirical confirmation of Calvin's thesis as well as evidence that the original endowment had been perverted. But what would Calvin say of out and out atheism? Does not such atheism provide empirical refutation of his claim about the universality of the *sensus*?

Calvin does in fact consider atheism, in the following terms:

If, indeed, there were some in the past, and today not a few appear, who deny that God exists, yet willy-nilly they from time to time feel an inkling of what they desire not to believe. One reads of no one who burst forth into bolder or more unbridled contempt of deity than Gaius Caligula; yet no one trembled more miserably when any sign of God's wrath manifested itself; thus—albeit unwillingly—he shuddered at the God whom he professedly sought to despise.[77]

<hr/>

[76] *Inst.* 1. 5. 1.   [77] *Inst.* 1. 3. 2.

Calvin seems to be saying the following; that the fact that atheists may occasionally feel the pull of theism, or of some other religious belief which entails theism, is evidence of the SD. More particularly he claims that the evidence of the SD is seen, in the case of those who are avowed atheists, in the moral rather than the metaphysical aspect of the SD. For Calvin goes on:

Indeed, they seek out every subterfuge to hide themselves from the Lord's presence, and to efface it again from their minds. But in spite of themselves they are always entrapped. Although it may sometimes seem to vanish for a moment, it returns at once and rushes in with new force. If for these there is any respite from anxiety of conscience, it is not much different from the sleep of drunken or frenzied persons, who do not rest peacefully even while sleeping because they are continually troubled with dire and dreadful dreams. The impious themselves therefore exemplify the fact that some conception of God is ever alive in all men's minds.[78]

That it is chiefly the moral rather than the metaphysical aspect of the *sensus* that remains in evidence in the case of the avowed atheist is borne out by these further remarks: 'Although Diagoras and his like may jest at whatever has been believed in every age concerning religion, and Dionysius may mock the heavenly judgment, this is sardonic laughter, for the worm of conscience, sharper than any cauterizing iron, gnaws away within.'[79] That is, however men may attempt to harden their hearts they cannot eradicate or smother the voice of conscience. Where the existence of God is explicitly denied the influence of the SD may still make itself felt in the production of certain kinds of moral awareness. We shall look in more detail at the moral aspect of Calvin's natural knowledge of God in Chapter 12.

THE NOETIC EFFECTS OF SIN

So perhaps, despite what was said earlier, it is helpful to think that Calvin believes the SD to operate at different levels, or at least in different ways in different people. In some it operates epistemically and evidentially, in the recognition they give to the existence of God or the gods; while in others it operates morally, via their conscience, as they recognize, however fitfully, that they have obligations which they fail to keep and are, despite themselves, troubled by such failure.

Can we get any closer to understanding what mechanisms are involved in what Calvin sees as the intellectual and moral degeneration that has taken place in our knowledge of God as a result of the Fall? Perhaps we can, in the following way. We have already noted that according to Calvin the original SD has both a metaphysical and a moral component. As Calvin understands

[78] *Inst.* I. 3. 2.   [79] *Inst.* I. 3. 3.

the original creation, it is something which bears the marks of the goodness of the creator. The creation is not only the result of God's power, but of his character as the supreme benefactor. God is good, and his creation is good. And mankind, chief among the products of God's creation, is also created good.

The Fall is a moral rupture between the Creator and mankind. It is mysteriously brought about by the subverting of the intellect by wilfulness and has (among other things) dire noetic consequences. These consequences are not such that, being fallen, a person is unable to count, or to reason, though perhaps human abilities to do these things are reduced. Perhaps in an unfallen human being the capacity to do mental arithmetic or formal logic is indescribably greater than anyone's at present. Perhaps after the Fall even the best formal logicians fall below a threshold which the worst unfallen formal logician could attain to. Such speculation, although rather un-Calvinian in spirit, is not ruled out by anything that Calvin says. Nevertheless, the way in which the lapse has ruptured the relationship with God and has noetic consequences might be something like the following.

It is a well-known fact that different conceptions, or perhaps different varieties of self-interest lead to different interpretations of the facts, and even to a denial of facts. Through the intrusion of self-interest we misinterpret evidence, hide from evidence, are a prey to imagination, uncritically accept common opinion, follow fashion, and the like. In a similar way, Calvin would argue that the Fall has brought about misguided conceptions of self-interest. A person does not now believe that his self-interest is bound up with the knowledge and service of God, but in other ways. And as a result of this, he misinterprets relevant evidence, he suppresses evidence, he accepts common opinion, and so on.[80]

So Calvin would wish to distinguish the evidence that there is a God from the conditions for its true recognition. Nothing that has been said about the ways in which, according to Calvin, the SD is perverted, ought to be taken as suggesting that Calvin was a subjectivist or relativist about matters of fact. The facts of the creation are what they are, in virtue of the one creative act of God. But Calvin would also emphasize a kind of correlation between such objective facts and the character and powers of the cognizers of those facts. Knowledge or true understanding of the facts is thus a function not only of what the facts are, but also of the nature of those who are apprehenders or would-be apprehenders of the facts.

---

[80] For discussion of this theme see William Wainwright, 'The Nature of Reason: Locke, Swinburne and Edwards', in Alan G. Padgett (ed.), *Reason and the Christian Religion* (Oxford: Clarendon Press, 1994), and William Wainwright, *Reason and the Heart* (Ithaca: Cornell University Press, 1995).

The fact that human beings cannot hear sounds beyond a certain frequency range, but bats can, is a fact about one limitation of human nature. The nature of human nature conditions the sort of world we shall perceive. There are sounds created in the world such that they cannot be heard by normal human beings. A bat occupies a very different sensory environment from a human being. In a similar way, Calvin would say, there is evidence to be gained from the world, evidence which reinforces and sustains the belief that there is a God, in those who are properly equipped to receive it. This equipment does not consist in the existence of a sixth sense, nor in one of the five senses suitably augmented, nor even of a moral sense of the Hutchesonian kind (a sense which intuits non-natural values), but in a set of moral and emotional preconditions for evaluating evidence, including moral evidence, correctly.[81]

Here I am reading Calvin as an evidentialist;[82] he is not claiming in the vein of William James that our moral and passional nature is such that in certain circumstances we are justified in believing what there is insufficient evidence for. But appreciating the evidence, its range and pertinence, is a function not merely of the senses, or the reason, or of some combination of these, but also—since the universe has a moral character—of the cognizer's moral character as well, his powers of moral appreciation, and particularly his appreciation of himself as a moral being.

The fallen investigator, according to Calvin on this interpretation, has certain wants and interests; in an unfallen condition, these wants and interests are natural in the sense that they are part of the original God-imparted endowment. So it is in terms of these interests affected by the Fall that the strength of the evidence for God's existence is assessed. (Calvin would have had no truck with the idea that there is an intrinsic ambiguity in the evidence such that in principle the same event might be 'seen as' the hand of God, or 'seen as' the product of purely naturalistic forces. He would not possess the anxiety of many modern religious epistemologists to preserve human indeterministic freedom by invoking an intrinsic 'epistemic distance'. For Calvin, such distance, where it exists, is a loss, not a gain.)[83]

---

[81] Merold Westphal, 'On Taking St. Paul Seriously: Sin as an Epistemological Category', in T. Flint (ed.), *Christian Philosophy* (Notre Dame: University of Notre Dame Press, 1990).

[82] For other discussions of Calvin in relation to 'Reformed' epistemology, see Derek S. Jeffreys, 'How Reformed is Reformed Epistemology? Alvin Plantinga and Calvin's "Sensus Divinitatis" ', *Religious Studies* (1997); John Beversluis, 'Reforming the "Reformed" Objection to Natural Theology', *Faith and Philosophy* (1995). We shall look at Beversluis's views more closely in ch. 9.

[83] For the idea of epistemic distance in this sense, see John Hick, *Faith and Knowledge*, (London: Macmillan, 1966), and 'Religious Faith as Experiencing-As', in G. N. A.Vesey (ed.), *Talk of God* (London: Macmillan, 1969).

The idea of there being an intrinsic ambiguity in the evidence, a view which Calvin does not in my view favour, ought not to be confused with the idea of an epistemic distance, discussed earlier, in Chapter 1 for example. The creature's epistemic distance arises from the respective cognitive and intellectual powers of Creator and creature. It is just because what God says is clear and unambiguous that it is recognized by the created intellect as unfathomable.

Behind this understanding of what may be involved in the appreciation of certain data is a view of human nature rather different from that to which we have become accustomed since the Enlightenment. Human nature is not to be understood exclusively in ratiocinative and sensory-evidential powers, with human values being relegated to 'the passions'. Human nature also includes moral and affective powers as well. It does not follow that disinterested impartiality is the sole or even the chief intellectual virtue, though things very like it, the virtue of reconsidering one's position, paying attention to criticism, revising one's belief in the light of new information, are among the virtues. This aspect of Calvin's epistemology is perhaps closer to the aesthetic and moral appreciation of a work of art than it is to the sort of understanding that operates in the natural sciences.

CALVIN AND 'REFORMED' EPISTEMOLOGY

Earlier we noted that Calvin has a great interest in the place that the SD plays in moral accountability, little or no interest in rationality. Perhaps in his remarks about the SD Calvin is not providing us with the materials for constructing an alternative epistemology to strong foundationalism nor consciously alluding to mechanisms of belief formation. His claim is not that strong foundationalism is wrong. It is more radical than that: that the noetic effects of sin are universal and, humanly speaking, are ineradicable; the recommended remedy is not the development of an alternative epistemology, but the knowledge of God the Redeemer freely given to us in Christ.

This discussion of the SD took as one of its starting points the anti-strong foundationalist turn in modern epistemology, some of which, it has been claimed by the 'Reformed' epistemologists, finds precedent and warrant in Calvin's views of the SD. Some philosophers of such a turn see Calvin's disinterest in natural theology as an anticipatory repudiation of the strong foundationalism of the Enlightenment and as a form of weak foundationalism. Calvin is the case of a Christian thinker who does not scruple to place the proposition that God exists (and many similar theistic propositions) in the foundations of his noetic structure, and to affirm that all men, despite their fallenness, ought to place them there as well. For someone who, following Calvin's example, adopts this 'Reformed' epistemology, a convincing natural theology is not necessary to establish the rationality of religious belief, even though it may be sufficient for it.

But is Calvin in fact a foundationalist in any sense? In 'Reason and Belief in God' Alvin Plantinga cites various passages from the *Institutes* regarding the SD, including this one:

Lest anyone, then be excluded from access to happiness, he not only sowed in men's minds that seed of religion of which we have spoken but revealed himself and daily discloses himself in the whole workmanship of the universe. As a consequence, men cannot open their eyes without being compelled to see him.[84]

And then draws the following conclusion:

Calvin's claim is that one who accedes to this tendency and in these circumstances accepts the belief that God has created the world—perhaps upon beholding the starry heavens, or the splendid majesty of the mountains, or the intricate, articulate beauty of a tiny flower—is entirely within his epistemic rights in doing so. It is not that such a person is justified or rational in so believing by virtue of having an implicit argument—some version of the teleological argument, say. No; he does not need any argument for justification or rationality. His belief need not be based on any other propositions at all; under these conditions he is perfectly rational in accepting belief in God in the utter absence of any argument, deductive or inductive. Indeed, a person in these conditions, says Calvin, *knows* that God exists.[85]

And more recently, as we have seen, Plantinga has appealed to the SD as a cognitive mechanism which when it functions properly in a favourable environment produces in us true beliefs about a God, even the knowledge that there is a God.

Merold Westphal claims that Plantinga's appeal to Calvin as one who has anticipated the foundationalist-evidentialist objection to theistic belief and given the outlines of an alternative account of religious knowledge is right as far as it goes, but that it does not go far enough. Commenting on Plantinga's account of the effect of sin on the SD, 'Although this disposition to believe in God is partially suppressed, it is nonetheless universally present', Westphal says:

Calvin would have put that last part rather differently, I suspect. In order to remind us that none of us come *naturally* to a proper knowledge of God, he would have said that while the tendency to believe is present, it is nevertheless suppressed, reversing Plantinga's order and emphasis. And in order to remind us that *none* of us comes naturally to a proper knowledge of God, he would have said that while the tendency to believe is universally present, it is *universally*, and not just partially, suppressed. Both terms are ambiguous and might miss his meaning. Universal suppression

---

[84] *Inst.* 1. 5. 1.   [85] Alvin Plantinga, 'Reason and Belief in God', in *Faith and Rationality*, 67.

might be construed as degree rather than extension, suggesting that creation is entirely obliterated rather than that none of us is exempt from the distorting effects of sin. Partial suppression might be construed as extension rather than degree, suggesting that some of us are exempt rather than that our natural tendency to believe in God has been distorted but not obliterated. I do not doubt that Calvin would rather risk overstating the damage by speaking of universal suppression than risk suggesting that some are exempt from the noetic effects of sin by speaking of a partial suppression.[86]

Perhaps Plantinga's earlier appeal to Calvin, his appeal to the SD as an instance of a rational belief in the absence of argument, at most amounts to this, that Calvin offers what is an enthymematic argument from the premiss that there are people who without argument have the belief that God exists, to the conclusion that they are entitled to such a belief. The suppressed premiss is something like:

(S) It is rational to believe in God's existence without argument.

But is this a reasonable conclusion to draw from Calvin? There is reason to think that it is not. For one thing, as we have noted there is no evidence from the passages cited (or from any similar passages) that Calvin has in mind the rationality of religious belief.

Plantinga also quotes remarks of Calvin's about the fact that the authority of Scripture is based not on 'rational proofs' but the conviction that the Bible is the word of God ought to rest 'in a higher place than human reasons, judgements, or conjectures, that is, in the secret testimony of the Spirit'.[87]

It is true that there is a kind of parallel between Calvin's remarks here and the denial of strong foundationalism; according to Calvin, in the case of the knowledge of God men do not have reasons for believing that there is a God, while in the case of the authority of Scripture men do not *need* reasons for accepting the Bible as God's word; no reasons, that is, that are grounded in what is only outside the Bible. But there is a significant lack of parallel also, for in discussing the authority of the Bible, Calvin is making a normative claim, a claim about where we *ought* to ground our conviction that the Bible is the word of God. But it is not at all clear that in Calvin's mind these remarks about the self-authenticating character of the Bible apply in a parallel way to belief in God's existence. We shall consider Calvin's appeal to the self-authenticating character of Scripture in the next chapter.

What we have found in Calvin is little or no interest in the rationality of religious belief or in cognitive mechanisms producing warrant. (Rationality

---

[86] 'On Taking St. Paul Seriously', 213.

[87] Plantinga, 'Reason and Belief in God', 67. See Plantinga, *Warranted Christian Belief*, ch. 8 for an extended treatment of this aspect of Calvin's thought.

in this sense is perhaps as much a child of the Enlightenment as is strong foundationalism; certainly one struggles to find any interest in such an issue in Calvin.) Rather, Calvin's interest in knowledge is not in the rational grounds for theistic belief, or in rational entitlement, but in establishing that since all men and women have some knowledge of God, they are culpable when they do not form their lives in a way that is appropriate to such knowledge.

For how can the thought of God penetrate your mind without your realizing immediately that, since you are his handiwork, you have been made over and bound to his command by right of creation, that you owe your life to him?—that whatever you undertake, whatever you do, ought to be ascribed to him?[88]

Since, therefore, men one and all perceive that there is a God and that he is their Maker, they are condemned by their own testimony because they have failed to honor him and to consecrate their lives to his will.[89]

But can what Calvin says be used for other purposes? Could one argue that the fact of the universality of the seed of religion proves the rationality of religious belief, or renders it unnecessary? Can one rationally reconstruct Calvin to yield the distinctive tenets of 'Reformed' epistemology?

Perhaps one can. Perhaps what Plantinga has in mind in appealing to Calvin is an argument that is something like the following:

(1) The original epistemic condition of mankind was such that every human belief held then was fully rationally justified.
(2) Originally, mankind believed in God without needing any reasons for doing so.
(3) It is rational to believe whatever propositions remain of the original epistemic condition.
(4) For any present belief, if that belief is identical with a belief that was part of the original human condition, then that belief is rational.
(5) Some people presently believe in God without having any reasons for doing so.
(6) Such a belief is part of the original epistemic condition.
(7) Therefore, those who presently believe in God without reasons for doing so are rational.[90]

This seems to me to be much more plausible an account of the argument implicit in the passages from Calvin like those cited. However, in this reconstruction there is still an emphasis upon issues of rationality that is not

[88] *Inst.* I. 2. 2.

[89] *Inst.* I. 3. 1.

[90] The argument requires further refinement to distinguish between those propositions which are identical in cognitive content with part of the initial endowment but which are newly believed, and those which remain from the endowment. But as it stands it serves for present purposes.

present in Calvin. For in asserting the universality of the SD Calvin is making a broad factual claim, that as a matter of fact everyone has in them the seed of religion. And, following Paul in Romans 1, he is more concerned with using this fact about knowledge to establish the *responsibility* of all people in the sight of God for the use to which they put this knowledge than he is about saying anything about *rationality* or warrant. The point about foundationalism, whether weak or strong, is as Plantinga says, a point about epistemic entitlement; but as we have seen Calvin says nothing about this, and he may imply nothing about it either.

Another attempt at harnessing Calvin to 'Reformed' epistemology might be made by using the approach of another such epistemologist, Nicholas Wolterstorff. Wolterstorff distinguishes between ineluctable beliefs, propositions we could not have refrained from believing, and eluctable beliefs, which we could have refrained from believing.[91] In the case of propositions ineluctably believed we are rational in continuing to hold such beliefs in the absence of adequate reasons to cease from believing them. Ineluctable believing is innocent until it is proved guilty. And so, Wolterstorff claims, someone who comes to belief in God immediately, without reasons, might nonetheless be justified in having and holding such a belief.[92] Wolterstorff does not offer this as a gloss on Calvin, but could it be taken to be such? It is hard to see how. For Calvin does not seem to pay much attention to the question of whether someone who, as the result of the working of the SD, believes in God or the gods, could have refrained from so believing.

If all men and women believed in God, then there would (in one sense) be no need to establish the existence of God rationally, but (in another sense) this universality would not settle anything. But in any case Calvin does not say that all men believe in God; he says that all men have the seed of religion, the disposition to believe in God.

Those who look to Calvin as the *origo* of 'Reformed' epistemology are in something of a dilemma at this point. If they appeal to him to provide a premiss of a factual kind about the seed of religion working in all people, then they will certainly find evidence for this in Calvin, as we have seen. But it does not follow from Calvin's remarks about the seed of religion that a person is entitled to believe in God reasonlessly, nor does Calvin say that it does. He does not say that it does, nor does he deny that it does. If on the other hand they appeal to a normative proposition as a premiss, a proposition about what men and women ought to believe, which they would find warrant for in Calvin's remarks about the responsibility of all men

---

[91] Wolterstorff, 'Can Belief in God be Rational If It Has No Foundations?', in Alvin Plantinga and Nicholas Wolterstorff, *Faith and Rationality*, 162.

[92] Wolterstorff, 'Can Belief in God be Rational If It Has No Foundations?', 176.

and women before God, it is surely implausible to suppose that such a proposition is acceptable without reason or argument.

The problem with appealing to Calvin is that his remarks about the SD are first-order observations. He does not theorize about what he takes to be matters of fact; and where he does theorize, as in his brief remarks about the grounds for accepting the authority of Scripture, these remarks do not seem to be directly applicable to questions about the rationality of belief in God.

9

Revelation

In this chapter we continue an examination of Calvin's epistemology by looking at what he says about God's revelation in the Bible, and in particular about how a person may know that this book is indeed God's revelation. Calvin does not often use 'revelation' or 'reveal' in connection with Scripture, but employs a variety of expressions such as 'made manifest'[1] and refers to the Bible as 'oracles'.[2] We have already seen that Calvin uses such terms as 'reveal', 'manifest', and 'disclose' in a wider sense, to refer to what God continuously discloses about himself in the world at large. God has 'revealed himself and daily discloses himself in the whole workmanship of the universe'.[3] Here we shall be concerned with what he says about revelation in what is for him a deeper and fuller sense, God's disclosure of himself through prophets and apostles, and supremely in Christ. Our concern will be with Calvin's understanding of the epistemology of such disclosure.

Calvin's main treatment of these issues comes early on in the *Institutes*, in chapters 6–8 of book I, which follow on immediately after his treatment of God's disclosure of himself in nature and of the *sensus divinitatis*, though further important elements come later, in his discussion of the work of the Holy Spirit in producing assured faith in God's elect, in *Institutes* III. 2. In fact Calvin sees these as forming one discussion. We shall look at Calvin's view of the assurance of faith later on in the chapter.

Calvin says that if we are to come to God, as distinct from having merely hazy ideas of God drawn from nature, then we need 'the light of his Word'.[4] For the Bible gathers together these confused notions we have of God and clearly shows us the true God. So 'besides the common proofs[5] he also put forth his Word, which is a more direct and more certain mark whereby he

---

[1] *Inst.* I. 6. 1.

[2] Calvin's attitude to 'errors' in the text of Scripture, and his views of divine inspiration, have been widely discussed in work that has often been ideologically driven. See, for example, J. K. S. Reid, *The Authority of the Bible* (London: Methuen, 1957) and John Murray, *Calvin on Scripture and Divine Sovereignty* (Grand Rapids, Mich.: Baker, 1960).

[3] *Inst.* I. 5. 1.   [4] *Inst.* I. 6. 1.

[5] As we noted earlier, it is plausible to read this as a reference to natural theology.

is to be recognized'.[6] For Calvin doctrine is essential to religion, and true doctrine is to be found in Scripture.

According to Calvin the epistemology of the manifestation of God in Scripture is intimately bound up with the idea of scriptural authority. In setting out his understanding of revelation and of its epistemology he is in effect (as part of the Reformation conflict) asking and answering the question of where ultimate religious authority is located. His answer is: not in the idea of God derived from the *sensus divinitatis*, nor from God's daily disclosure of himself, for that evidence, though universally dispersed, is ambiguous and inconsistent (though perhaps not inherently so). The Bible's authoritativeness does not derive in *two* steps from the endorsement of some higher human authority, such as the Fathers or the Councils of the Church, which are reckoned to be in a more privileged epistemic position than we are and which validate the word of God as authoritative. Rather, it derives in *one* step from God himself, for God manifests himself.

Calvin typically contrasts the authentic revelation which is certain with what is doubtful or controversial. What is at stake is whether the Scripture has the authority of God or not. If it has God's authority then, since God is infallible, that fact will transfer to his word. So authority is at least partly an epistemic notion. 'Scripture exhibits fully as clear evidence of its own truth as white and black things do of their color, or sweet and bitter things do of their taste.'[7] Recognizing the authority of the Bible is like recognizing a colour or a taste for oneself; each is a one-step procedure not involving inference, or only involving it in a minimal fashion. What others tell you about a pineapple is no substitute for tasting one. This is at the core of what Calvin refers to as the self-authenticating or self-witnessing character of Scripture.

Self-authentication is an epistemological consequence or corollary of the Reformation emphasis that only God can witness to God. Only if God witnesses to God in this direct fashion is that witness thoroughly trustworthy. Calvin does not for one moment deny that God's fuller knowledge of himself is mediated by Scripture, or that it requires the illumination of the Holy Spirit to be properly understood and appreciated. It is direct in that no distinct human endorsement is necessary. This is why Calvin believes that he is warranted in using verbs such as 'witness', 'disclose', and 'speak'.

If I am immediately aware of feeling a coin in my pocket, this is possible because, in addition to having the appropriate sensory apparatus, and having certain sensations, I already know what a coin feels like. Perhaps one strand in Calvin's idea of self-authentication is that it provides a fuller awareness of what the divine is like, fuller than the SD and than God's witness to himself in

---

[6] *Inst.* I. 6. 1.   [7] *Inst.* I. 7. 2.

nature. We already have such a sense in virtue either of our creation in God's image, or the operation (however flawed) of the *sensus divinitatis*, or of both. What Scripture provides is a deeper or more genuine or fuller case of that divinity of which we already have a dim sense. It is 'another and better help' to direct our attention to God the creator.[8] In Scripture we know both what we may expect from God and we actually receive it.

The key to understanding Calvin's view of how God's disclosure of himself in Scripture is authenticated to us is that he believes that God himself directly or immediately authenticates and endorses his Word in the minds and consciences of men and women as they read or reflect on some part of it. For Calvin only such a direct, one-step endorsement can provide the necessary assurance and certainty about the matters which the oracles reveal.

However, adopting a procedure which is at first sight at odds with this, besides this appeal to the self-authenticating character of the Bible in *Institutes* I. 7 he provides a much lengthier treatment of what he calls 'proofs of the credibility of Scripture', in *Institutes* I. 8. In considering the arguments of both these chapters we shall reverse Calvin's order. The external proofs play a subordinate role to the appeal to the self-authenticating character of Scripture. They are not prolegomena to it, nor do they supplant it. Further, what these proofs deliver is for Calvin much inferior to the one-step testimony of the Spirit. Nevertheless, Calvin devotes a good deal of attention to them. For ease, let us refer to these proofs as the 'external' proofs and the testimony of the Spirit as the 'internal' proofs of the divinity of Scripture.

EXTERNAL PROOFS

In making this distinction between internal and external proofs, and in the relative value which he places on each, Calvin shows himself to be in line with the medieval treatment of God's special revelation. In discussing whether Christian theology is a science Thomas discusses the distinctive basis of Christian theology and how that basis is established. 'The premises of other sciences are either self-evident, in which case they cannot be proved, or they are proved through some natural evidence in some other science. What is exclusive to this science's [theology's] knowledge is that it is about truth which comes through revelation, not through natural reasoning.'[9] And how is the judgement that what the science of theology is based on is revelation to be made? Aquinas says that in general there are two kinds of wisdom corresponding to two ways of passing judgement; from an internal bent or habit or sympathy, or through a cognitive process. Each of these is exemplified in the case of judging revelation.

---

[8] *Inst.* I. 6. 1.   [9] *Summa Theologiae*, 1a, 1. 6 (trans. Thomas Gilby).

The first way of judging divine things belongs to that wisdom which is classed among the Gifts of the Holy Ghost; so St. Paul says, *The spiritual man judges all things*, and Dionysius speaks about *Hierotheus being taught by the experience of undergoing divine things, not only by learning about them*. The second way of judging is taken by sacred doctrine to the extent that it can be gained by study; even so the premises are held from revelation.[10]

So the authority of the revelation which forms the basis of Christian theology is principally formed by the possession of an inner sympathy or bent which is a gift of the Holy Spirit. Even what is gained by study depends on this. This is Aquinas's 'inner' proof; it obviously bears a close resemblance to what Calvin says about the inner testimony of the Holy Spirit. Consequently, 'As the other sciences do not argue to prove their premises, but work from them to bring out other things in their field of inquiry, so this teaching does not argue to establish its premises, which are the articles of faith, but advances from them to make something known, as when St. Paul adduces the resurrection of Christ to provide the resurrection of us all.' But what when someone opposes this teaching, believing nothing of what is divinely revealed?

If, however, an opponent believes nothing of what has been divinely revealed, then no way lies open for making the articles of faith reasonably credible; all that can be done is to solve the difficulties against faith that he may bring up. For since faith rests on unfailing truth, and the contrary of truth cannot really be demonstrated, it is clear that alleged proofs against faith are not demonstrations, but charges that can be refuted.[11]

May Christian theology not also use human reasoning? May it not appeal to the authority of the philosophers? Yes it may.

Yet sacred doctrine employs such authorities only in order to provide as it were extraneous arguments from probability. Its own proper authorities are those of canonical Scripture, and these it applied with convincing force. It has other proper authorities, the doctors of the Church, and these it looks to as its own, but for arguments that carry no more than probability.[12]

In the *Summa Contra Gentiles* Aquinas gives examples of such extraneous or external arguments for the authority of canonical Scripture.

Those who place their faith in this truth [namely, revealed truth], however, 'for which the human reason offers no experimental evidence' (St. Gregory, *Homiliae in evangelia*, II hom. 26. i) do not believe foolishly, as though 'following artificial fables' (II Peter 1: 16). For these 'secrets of divine Wisdom' (Job 11: 6) the divine Wisdom itself, which knows all things to the full, has deigned to reveal to men. It reveals its

---

[10] *Summa Theologiae*, 1a, 1. 6.   [11] *Summa Theologiae*, 1a, 1. 8.

[12] *Summa Theologiae*, 1a, 1. 8.

own presence, as well as the truth of its teaching and inspiration, by fitting arguments; and in order to confirm those truths that exceed natural knowledge, it gives visible manifestation to works that surpass the ability of all nature. Thus, there are the wonderful cures of illnesses, there is the raising of the dead, and the wonderful immutation in the heavenly bodies; and what is more wonderful, there is the inspiration given to human minds, so that simple and untutored persons, filled with the gift of the Holy Spirit, come to possess instantaneously the highest wisdom and the readiest eloquence.[13]

There are three clear points of correspondence between Aquinas's procedure and Calvin's: first, the contrast between external (or 'extraneous') and internal proofs of revelation; secondly, the claim that external proofs cannot establish the faith with certainty, they can only serve to rebut objections to it; and thirdly, the connected point that the belief that external proofs offer only probability, opinion, whereas internal proofs offer certainty. Let us look at these in turn as Calvin discusses them.

Calvin makes a clear contrast between the external and internal proofs. The external proofs have a subsidiary role, they are 'aids' in fortifying the authority of Scripture by arguments.[14] But not all these data are strictly speaking 'external', since Calvin first points to certain phenomena that are internal to the text of Scripture. Among these are its truthfulness as seen in the frankness of the writers, who often testify against themselves, to their own disadvantage. Calvin treats Moses as something of a paradigm; just as his own word was confirmed by publicly witnessed miracles, so is Scripture more generally. Prophecies prove their genuineness by being against expectations. Prophecies have been fulfilled. The Law and the Prophets have been preserved. The style of the evangelists, and Paul's remarkable conversion, testify to the genuineness and authority of the New Testament. Such data, Calvin thinks, offer cumulative evidence attesting the credibility of Scripture.

En passant, amongst some weak, though traditional arguments, Calvin introduces other interesting arguments without developing them. 'Human writings' may captivate us, Scripture more so.

Read Demosthenes or Cicero; read Plato, Aristotle, and others of that tribe. They will, I admit, allure you, delight you, move you, enrapture you in wonderful

---

[13] *Summa Contra Gentiles*, 1. 6. 1, trans. Anton C. Pegis (Garden City, NY: Image Books, 1955). For further discussion of the similarity between Aquinas and Calvin, see Arvin Vos, *Aquinas, Calvin, and Contemporary Protestant Thought*, ch. 1.

[14] Calvin is here endorsing a long tradition. For example, Duns Scotus offers some of the very same arguments which Calvin uses, e.g. the internal concordance or consistency of Scripture, and the fact that Scripture contains divinely attested miracles. Like Calvin, he thinks that such arguments are rationally compelling, but that they fall short of a proof. (On this, see Richard Cross, *Duns Scotus* (New York: Oxford University Press, 1999), 12.)

measure. But betake yourself from them to this sacred reading. Then, in spite of yourself, so deeply will it affect you, so penetrate your heart, so fix itself in your very marrow, that, compared with its deep impression, such vigor as the orators and philosophers have will nearly vanish.[15]

To the sceptical claim that perhaps Moses never even existed, Calvin retorts, 'Yet if anyone were to call in doubt whether there ever was a Plato, an Aristotle, or a Cicero, who would not say that such folly ought to be chastised with the fist or the lash?'[16] Among the external proofs properly so-called, Calvin appeals to the consent of the church, the universal impact of the Scriptures, and the fidelity of the martyrs.[17]

What is the epistemic value of these various appeals, which Calvin says is a mere selection of the many others that could be given? They have a confirmatory role for the believer, but more importantly they 'vindicate' Scripture against its disparagers. But even considered cumulatively, such 'proofs' are insufficient to produce faith 'until our heavenly Father, revealing his majesty there, lifts reverence for Scripture beyond the realm of controversy . . . those who wish to prove to unbelievers that Scripture is the Word of God are acting foolishly, for only by faith can this be known'.[18] Like Thomas, Calvin held that the external proofs can at best offer confirmation of a faith already held, and provide arguments that may disarm the critic. This is because such proofs yield only probability, falling short of the certainty that is characteristic of belief in articles of the faith.

So Calvin believes that there is a significant asymmetry in establishing the authority of God speaking in Scripture in this way. It is possible, he thinks, to provide reasons for Scripture's authoritativeness, using them to meet the objections and cavils of opponents to it. He thinks that one might by reasoning in this way rebut objections to the authority of Scripture. But the possibility of doing this, and the reasons that may be adduced in doing so, are not themselves sufficient to establish with full certainty the divine authority of Scripture. That debate remains at the level of opinion. Only God can establish the divine authority directly for himself. And so to successfully rebut objections to Scripture is not sufficient to establish its full authority.

For my part, although I do not excel either in great dexterity or eloquence, if I were struggling against the most crafty sort of despisers of God, who seek to appear shrewd and witty in disparaging Scripture, I am confident it would not be difficult for me to silence their clamorous voices. And if it were a useful labor to refute their cavils, I would with no great trouble shatter the boasts they mutter in their lurking places. But even if anyone clears God's Sacred Word from man's evil speaking, he

---

[15] *Inst.* I. 8. 1. It is hard not to think that such statements are partly autobiographical.

[16] *Inst.* I. 8. 9.   [17] *Inst.* I. 8. 12, 13.   [18] *Inst.* I. 8. 13.

will not at once imprint upon their hearts that certainty which piety requires. Since for unbelieving men religion seems to stand by opinion alone, they, in order not to believe anything foolishly or lightly, both wish and demand rational proof that Moses and the prophets spoke divinely. But I reply: the testimony of the Spirit is more eloquent than all reason.[19]

To say that such proofs cannot convince people that Scripture is the Word of God is to say that they will not bring certainty. To satisfactorily meet objections to faith is not equivalent to proving what is believed, for in responding to 'cavils' one is still in the realm of 'opinion'. Throughout the discussion of the authority of Scripture Calvin repeatedly contrasts 'opinion' with 'certainty'.[20] In doing so he was simply taking up and endorsing the medieval view that revealed theology has Scripture as its first principles and both its certainty and scientific character derive from this fact.

INTERNAL PROOFS

Let us now consider what for Calvin is the heart of the matter, the proof which Scripture itself gives of its divine authority via the self-authenticating work of the Holy Spirit. It is the Spirit who causes the divinely-authored Word and therefore the authority of Scripture, that which it has inherently, to shine in a way which, because of our darkened minds, it otherwise would not. In this activity the Spirit does not produce the authority, he witnesses to it. Calvin sees the production of this recognition of authority in strongly personal terms. It is the result of the activity of God the Holy Spirit on the soul, and it is an integral part of God's redemptive grace to sinners. This is something which the medievals did not deny, but which he brings to the forefront and stresses.

For Calvin, recognizing the authority of the Word of God is quite different from conferring authority on it. Such recognition is primarily a cognitive affair, but one which brings with it certain normative consequences when it is successful. He insists that such recognition of Scripture prompted by the cooperation of Spirit and Word is a one-step affair. As we have noted, Calvin thinks that a two-step authenticating of Scripture, in which human authorities or 'external proofs' play a crucial part, while it is of value, is nevertheless epistemically inferior, and has a strong tendency to endow the human authorities with a privileged role in conferring authority on the Bible. The person who benefits from the one-step process receives immediate testimony to the divinity of the Word of God, and as a consequence gives

---

[19] *Inst.* 1. 7. 4. Here is one of the few places where Calvin appears to be concerned with rational proof, with 'disputation', but it is clearly a reference forward to the discussion of the various external proofs undertaken in his following chapter. [20] e.g. *Inst.* 1. 7. 4.

immediate recognition to it. It is a one-step process as compared to the appeal to the external proofs, or to Church Councils. This one-step process itself has distinct elements, as we shall see. So it is that in grounding the authority of the Word of God, Calvin makes appeal to what he calls 'the testimony of the [Holy] Spirit', a direct activity of God himself on the human spirit.

If we desire to provide in the best way for our consciences—that they may not be perpetually beset by the instability of doubt or vacillation, and that they may not also boggle at the smallest quibbles—we ought to seek our conviction in a higher place than human reasons, judgments, or conjectures, that is, in the secret testimony of the Spirit.[21]

Calvin is not endorsing illuminism. Far from it. The conviction which, according to him, the Spirit confers, is a conviction about the truth of something distinct both from the Spirit and the person to whom the Spirit testifies. It is the conviction that (as Calvin puts it) God speaks in Scripture, a conviction conferred by the Spirit through a person's awareness of the cognitive and other content of the Word of God.

Calvin is not here saying that the activity of the Spirit which is sufficient to establish the authority of the Word of God is unreasonable or irrational or non-rational in character. How could that be, when the Spirit is the Spirit of the most wise and all-knowing God? Nor is the Spirit's work a purely subjective persuasion, a groundless feeling of conviction. It is rather that what the Spirit testifies to or illumines are certain features of the objectively true character of Scripture, and such illumination, providing the certainty 'which piety requires' does not need any rational or empirical considerations external to Scripture to add further support to it. So Calvin's idea of the testimony of the Holy Spirit (despite the use of the word 'testimony') is modelled on direct sense perception rather than on an inferential process using the data of Scripture, or data external to Scripture, as premisses. His position is something like:

(1) If S by the illumination of the Spirit comes to believe that what the Scriptures teach are God's word then he is fully convinced that this is so.

By contrast with:

(2) If S's cavils against the authority of the Word of God are satisfactorily rebutted, then S cannot as a consequence of this be fully convinced that the Scriptures are God's word.

It is an interesting fact that Calvin brackets together self-authentication and certainty, and contrasts (in terms of certainty) the self-authentication of

<hr>

[21] *Inst.* I. 7. 4.

Scripture (which, he says, is 'utterly certain' (*certio certius*))[22] and the external validation of Scripture (which, he says, is a matter of opinion). For there is no necessary connection between a self-authenticating experience of something, and the utter certainty of the presence or the truth of that thing. Thus, to use a mundane example, a stick of cinnamon can be authenticated (externally) by a shipper's bill or by a supermarket receipt. By contrast, it immediately authenticates itself to our olfactory machinery by its distinctive smell. But that smell can be less or more distinct (as when the children have just played with the spice jars), and it can be a matter of doubt or debate (based on smell alone) as to whether or not one of those jars contained cinnamon sticks. And in a similar fashion one could easily envisage a case of someone who experienced the self-authenticating testimony of the Spirit, but for whom that testimony was almost crowded out by the presence of other immediate or direct experiences, or indirectly acquired beliefs. There is no doubt a good reason (in terms of the Reformation conflict) why Calvin makes the link between the self-authenticating character of Scripture and certainty. No doubt he wants to ground the divine authority in Scripture itself, and not in the external authority of unaided human reason or (most important of all for him) in the unreformed Catholic Church. Nevertheless, there is no necessary connection between the self-authentication and absolute certainty, and later on we shall see that Calvin admits as much. So that we shall find that Calvin's final position is more like:

> (1a) If S by the illumination of the Spirit comes to believe that what the Scriptures teach is God's word then he ought ideally to be fully convinced that this is so, and may in fact be fully convinced.

When God himself testifies to what he has revealed, such testimony is sufficient to carry the fullest degree of conviction that it is necessary for a human being to have. We must shortly ask what this fullest degree of conviction is.

Let this point therefore stand: that those whom the Holy Spirit has inwardly taught truly rest upon Scripture, and that Scripture indeed is self-authenticated [*autopiston*]; hence, it is not right to subject it to proof and reasoning. And the certainty it deserves with us, it attains by the testimony of the Spirit . . . Therefore, illumined by his power, we believe neither by our own nor by any one else's judgment that Scripture is from God; but above all human judgment we affirm with utter certainty (just as if we were gazing upon the very majesty of God himself) that it has flowed to us from the very mouth of God by the ministry of men. We seek no proofs, no marks of genuineness upon which our judgment may lean; but we subject our judgment and wit to it as to a thing far beyond any guesswork! This we do, not as persons accustomed to seize upon some unknown thing, which, under closer

---

[22] *Inst.* 1. 8. 5.

scrutiny, displeases them, but fully conscious that we hold the unassailable truth! Nor do we do this as those miserable men who habitually bind over their minds to the thralldom of superstition; but we feel that the undoubted power of his divine majesty lives and breathes there. By this power we are drawn and inflamed, knowingly and willingly, to obey him, yet also more vitally and more effectively than by mere human willing or knowing![23]

Clearly enough this is not the language of analytic epistemology, but it is nevertheless possible to distil from it epistemological ideas and claims of some interest. There is first the idea of self-authentication; and then the contrast which Calvin draws between human judgements (which are opinions) and the 'utter certainty' which the Spirit's testimony brings, a testimony 'above all human judgment'. We must consider more fully the idea of self-authentication, and then the quality of the certainty that Calvin claims for it (let's call this HSC, Holy Spirit Certainty); then what Calvin calls the 'assurance of faith', and finally the nature of the evidential character of that to which the Holy Spirit testifies.

SELF-AUTHENTICATION

Calvin's ideas about how the certainty of the revelation is established are foundationalistic—'unless this foundation is laid, its authority will always remain in doubt'.[24] To the attuned philosophical ear, 'foundationalism' suggests a noetic structure according to which there are certain basic, perhaps self-evident or incorrigible foundational propositions, or propositions otherwise 'properly basic', which provide the rational basis for all other warranted beliefs. Does Calvin's idea of self-authentication play the role taken by incorrigibility in classical foundationalism? It is not clear that it does. To begin with, as we have noted, the idea of self-authentication, when used in a theological context at the time of the Reformation, partly functioned negatively, to block off other possible sources of Christian theological authority. For another, it would be anachronistic to suppose that Calvin was using 'foundation' in a way that coincides with modern epistemological usage. So it is not likely that for Calvin 'self-authenticating' means 'incorrigible' (i.e. being logically impossible to be in error, or being impossible to override or correct) or something equivalent to it. There are several further reasons for thinking this.

For one thing, self-authentication for Calvin is a function of the meaning or perceived meaning of a text. The sort of interpretation that is a necessary feature for the understanding of any document is thus a necessary condition

---

[23] *Inst.* I. 7. 5.   [24] *Inst.* I. 8. 1.

for getting at the meaning of the Bible—vocabulary, syntax, the nuances of natural languages, the need for general knowledge as background, and so forth. Data afforded by these skills are all corrigible; hence if some knowledge of them is necessary for the interpretation of the Bible, as seems reasonable, then the Bible cannot be self-authenticating in any way which implies incorrigibility, since the use of corrigible ('fallible' would be a more Calvinian term) helps is necessary for understanding it. That the Bible cannot be self-authenticating in this strict sense is shown by the fact that it has to be treated like any other book in discerning the historical provenance of its constituent documents, their date, the grammar and vocabulary employed in them, and the use of various canons of interpretation. Nowhere does Calvin suggest that the Holy Spirit overrides these, or that he confers his own meaning of the text. These helps are needed not in order to prove its authenticity but to gather its meaning. That Calvin endorsed such an approach is made abundantly clear by his voluminous commentaries on almost every book of Scripture and by his interesting remarks on implicit faith, to which we shall come. If each verse of the Bible bore its meaning on its face, and if knowing that meaning led immediately to a conviction about the God-givenness of the verse, what need would there be of commentaries?

So there is an inbuilt indirectness involved in getting at the meaning of the Bible; hence self-authentication, though a one-step process, cannot be equivalent to the incorrigibility of modern epistemology. If this is a reasonable conclusion, then we need to be clear on how self-authentication is a one-step approach to scriptural authority. Calvin recognizes the need for external human assistance in understanding and accepting Scripture, just as he recognizes the place of external proof in establishing the Bible's authority. The process of self-authentication uses the fruits of such assistance, hence the need for a learned Christian ministry, for creeds, confessions of faith, and biblical commentaries. One problem for Calvin is thus: how could some statement in Scripture present itself convincingly as the Word of God when, as happens, a person is unsure of the meaning of that statement? We shall look at what Calvin says on this later on. Could he perhaps hold that one-step self-authentication applies to certain core affirmations of Scripture, and that a faithful interpreter should interpret the non-core affirmations in a way that is consistent with the core; the so-called 'analogy of faith'?

If it is correct to interpret Calvin in terms of an implied distinction between core and non-core scriptural statements, then there is a sense in which the core statements, being immediately convincing, are incorrigible: to know what they mean is to be convinced of their truth, just as to know what $2 + 2 = 4$ means is to be convinced of its truth, or to know that if I am aware of a sensation of red then I cannot be mistaken, though I could be mistaken that what I sense is a pillar box. This implies that understanding the meaning of the core expressions is easy or fairly easy; their meaning is clear and indisputable. And anything that is self-authentic in this sense may be 'properly basic' in the sense given currency by present-day 'Reformed' epistemologists.[25] More on all this shortly.

CERTAINTY

So at first sight it is not clear how the sense of the self-authentication of Scripture which covers both core and non-core statements could be equivalent to incorrigibility in the modern epistemological usage. Yet as we have also seen, for Calvin the certainty conveyed in HSC is not mere subjective certainty, a feeling of confidence that is otherwise ungrounded. Indeed, Calvin holds that what HSC conveys may be, though it is not necessarily, a case of knowledge, *notitia*, not *scientia*. Here are some of his strong expressions on this point: 'Credibility of doctrine is not established until we are persuaded beyond doubt (*indubie*) that God is its [i.e. Scripture's] author.'[26] 'We affirm with utter certainty (just as if we were gazing upon the majesty of God himself), that it [Scripture] has flowed to us from the very mouth of God by the ministry of men . . . we hold the unassailable truth!'[27] 'Such, then, is a conviction [*persuasio*] that requires no reasons; such a knowledge [*notitia*] with which the best reason agrees—in which the mind truly reposes more securely and constantly than in any reasons.'[28]

When we find Calvin using the word 'knowledge' we need to use a little caution. His usage is to be distinguished from the modern epistemological usage, according to which knowledge is justified true belief, or what warrant yields if what is warranted is true. So when Calvin says that knowledge is supported by reasons, as in the passage just quoted, he is not to be taken either as affirming or denying the modern sense. And of course *notitia* has a different set of criteria from *scientia*. For *scientia*, demonstrative knowledge, is knowledge which is gained by discursive proofs from indubitable premisses. As we have seen, Calvin thinks that Scripture is indubitable to those who have been granted HSC, but this cannot be proved generally, though external reasons can provide some grounds for holding the opinion that the Bible is God's Word. He uses the word 'knowledge' because of its

---

[25] See e.g. Alvin Plantinga, 'Reason and Belief in God', in *Faith and Rationality*.

[26] *Inst.* 1.7.4.   [27] *Inst.* 1.7.5.

[28] *Inst.* 1.7.5. This echoes the point noted earlier in our discussion of Calvin's account of the Trinity, that the teaching of Scripture, though above reason, is not contrary to reason. Cf. Aquinas, *Summa Contra Gentiles*, 1.5.

connotations of certainty and finality, but he is usually careful to qualify it. Thus:

> When we call faith 'knowledge' [*cognitionem*] we do not mean comprehension of the sort that is commonly concerned with those things which fall under human sense perception. For faith is so far above sense that man's mind has to go beyond and rise above itself in order to attain it. Even where the mind has attained, it does not comprehend what it feels. But while it is persuaded of what it does not grasp, by the very certainty of its persuasion it understands more than if it perceived anything human by its own capacity.[29]

At the same time faith is more than opinion.

> But now we ought to examine what this faith ought to be like, through which those adopted by God as his children come to possess the Heavenly Kingdom, since it is certain that no mere opinion [*opinionem*] or even persuasion [*persuasionem*] is capable of bringing so great a thing to pass.[30]

We note here a shift from the descriptive to the normative; not what faith in fact is, so much as what it ought to be. We see Calvin clearly echoing the medieval contrast between *scientia*, opinion, and faith, with faith having the certainty of *scientia* but not having the comprehension that is intrinsic to it. Calvin shows little interest in knowledge as *scientia*, demonstrative proof, perhaps because of his relative lack of interest in natural theology, or because he thought that natural theology falls within the province of philosophy, or because of his awareness that even for medievals such as Aquinas theology is a case of *scientia* in only a subordinate sense.[31] We shall return to this contrast later. But perhaps *scientia* is part of what he means by 'comprehension' at least in some of its applications.

We are now in a position to reflect a little further on the degree and kind of certainty which Calvin believes self-authentication delivers. As we have seen, it would be unwise to jump to the conclusion that in affirming that the Holy Spirit conveys the divine authority of Scripture with full certainty Calvin has

---

[29] *Inst.* III. 2. 14. This passage, and others to follow, are taken from Calvin's treatment of faith in book III of the *Institutes*. Faith for him is what the Holy Spirit produces in the mind of the Christian, and HSC is an aspect of this.   [30] *Inst.* III. 2. 1.

[31] Aquinas, of course, draws a sharp contrast between knowledge as *scientia* and the certainty of faith. Nevertheless for Aquinas theology is a science which does not derive from self-evident principles but from principles which are from God and not immediately known to us. The certainty derives from revelation. Christian theology is a science 'for it flows from founts recognized in the light of a higher science, namely God's very own which he shares with the blessed. Hence, rather as harmony credits its principles which are taken from arithmetic, Christian theology takes on faith its principles revealed by God' (*Summa Theologiae*, 1a, 1. 2, trans. Thomas Gilby). Arvin Vos has an illuminating discussion of the relation between Aquinas and Calvin on these issues, *Aquinas, Calvin and Contemporary Protestant Thought*, chs. 1, 4, and 5.

in mind some kind of Cartesian certainty that is immune from doubt. Besides the qualified way in which medieval theology referred to theology as *scientia* there is a long tradition in the history of theology which regards it not as a theoretical but a practical discipline, as *sapientia*, the wisdom of which enables us to come to God and to keep us, as *viatores*, on the true path. Here we may recall the opening words of the *Institutes*. 'Nearly all the wisdom we possess, that is to say, true and sound wisdom, consists of two parts: the knowledge (*cognitione*) of God and of ourselves.'[32]

On this view the sources of the knowledge of God have a practical function; God's revelation is more like a handbook or recipe book than a theoretical treatise. So when Calvin says of the certainty of faith that it 'requires full and fixed certainty (*plenum et fixam certitudinem*) such as men are wont to have from things experienced and proved',[33] he might seem to be arguing that such certainty is not superior to certainty about mundane matters, but is in the same class, and that it has to be understood by reference to the sort of certainty which obtains in such cases. It might be thought that Calvin's 'Scotist' stress (if that is indeed what it is) on theology as wisdom derived from reliance on divine testimony might allow him to manage with a degree of certainty that is more like know-how than knowing that. But this would also be a mistake. For theology when it is true to itself is a matter of resting on God's true testimony to himself, it is not merely a set of skills.

However, Calvin does not say, or imply, that HSC is greater than any degree of certainty a person may have about anything else. Among the things that have high degrees of certainty are claims (made under the appropriate conditions) such as: 'I have two hands', $2 + 2 = 4$, 'I have a headache', and (if we are English-speakers) that 'tree' is the English word for a tree. We also have high degrees of certainty about a host of vague propositions such as: 'There is something green out there.' It is not clear that Calvin is saying that HSC is as great or is greater than the degree of certainty I have that I have two hands.

Rather his discussion is focused on the contrast between one degree of certainty (drawn from one source) about the Bible and another degree of certainty (drawn from another source) about the Bible. Perhaps what Calvin is doing is making a comparative judgement between the degree of certainty produced by the internal testimony of the Holy Spirit and that provided by the external *indicia*. It may be obvious that a proposition might be more certain than all its competitors without being maximally certain. So the Bible may be more certain to a person, as a result of the Holy Spirit's work, than if it were backed merely by the testimony of the Councils or the

---

[32] *Inst.* I. 1. 1.   [33] *Inst.* III. 2. 15.

'external' marks of its certainty. On this view, for *p* to be self-authenticating it is not necessary that it is inconceivable that there be nothing more certain than it, only that it passes a threshold of certitude. For example, if one is certain of *p* with that degree of certainty which the Holy Spirit conveys then one places confidence in *p* without reserve. We shall return to this point later on.

There is a variety of reasons, then, to think that HSC as Calvin uses it is to be distinguished from such technical terms as 'incorrigible', 'self-verifying', 'self-validating', 'indubitable', or 'infallible', as these are standardly used in classical foundationalist writings and in modern epistemology more generally, even though some of his uses may approach these.[34]

It must also be borne in mind that for Calvin there is no general phenomenon of HSC possessed by documents or sources of information of different kinds, of which the self-authentication of Scripture is an instance or special case. Only Scripture may now have HSC, though no doubt Calvin would hold that to his first disciples the very words of Christ came to have that character. This is another way of noting the difference between HSC as it relates to Scripture and the incorrigibility of strong foundationalism. For according to strong foundationalism there may be beliefs about very different matters that each have the property or quality of being incorrigible. Incorrigibility is thus a formal or general property, whereas for Calvin self-authentication is a property possessed by the content of the Scriptures, by whatever expresses the meaning of Scripture, and by nothing else.

Calvin does not seem exercised over the problem of circularity that may appear to occur at such points as these, that which arises out of the fact that Scripture alone teaches about the work of the Holy Spirit and the Holy Spirit is necessary for the authentication of Scripture. It seems that the Holy Spirit is validated by the Scripture, and yet Scripture is validated by Spirit. Had he been pressed on the question he might have dissolved the circle in the manner of Francis Turretin: 'For here the question is diverse and the means or kind of cause is different. We prove the Scriptures by the Spirit as the efficient cause by which we believe. But we prove the Spirit from the Scriptures as the object and argument on account of which we believe.'[35] In a parallel way Calvin thinks of Christian faith not so much as a species of

---

[34] As we noted, Calvin does occasionally use the term *sponte sese* (translated by Battles as 'self-evident'). Thus the wisdom, power, and goodness of the Creator is self-evident to anyone who seriously thinks about the natural order (*Inst.* I. 16. 1).

[35] *Institutes of Elenctic Theology*, II. VI. xxiv. This argument is congenial to what we shall see later on is Calvin's 'externalist' understanding of the work of the Spirit in self-authenticating Scripture. The Spirit acts as the 'efficient cause', not as the ground or evidence of the Scripture's God-givenness.

faith considered more generally, nor even as a species of religious faith (though no doubt it is that), but as unique; it has a distinctive intentional object. It is conceptually or internally related to the Word of God, and in particular to Christ. 'There is a permanent relationship between faith and the Word. He could not separate one from the other any more than we could separate the rays from the sun from which they come.'[36] So it is to faith, the subjective pole of the believer's relationship with the word of God, that we now turn.

THE ASSURANCE OF FAITH[37]

Earlier we touched on the question of whether Calvin's remarks on faith are to be taken as descriptive or normative. Raising these alternatives suggests one more thing that Calvin may have in mind in what he is saying. What he is setting forth in his account of self-authentication and its certainty is an ideal position. So a recognition of the divine character of what the Scriptures contain is not a position every Christian starts from, but it is typical, or ideal, or what is tacitly revealed in practice. Calvin is saying that this is how, ideally, it ought to be, and that sometimes (or often) this ideal is realized or achieved. The clue to the thought that Calvin's remarks on self-authentication represent an epistemic ideal, attainable but not always attained, lies in his remarks on faith in book III of the *Institutes* which intentionally continue and fill out discussion of self-authentication in book I. In opening the discussion there, he writes that 'now we ought to examine what this faith ought to be like'.[38] For Calvin faith is closely allied to the internal testimony of the Holy Spirit.[39] Faith rests upon God's word,[40] 'It is the function of faith to subscribe to God's truth whenever and whatever and however it speaks';[41] 'and faith results from the work of the Spirit'.[42] When he comes to offer a 'right definition' of faith Calvin focuses it more narrowly on (but does not confine it to) God's benevolence. 'Now we shall possess a right definition of faith if we call it a firm and certain knowledge [*firmam certamque cognitionem*] of God's benevolence toward us, founded upon the truth of the freely given promise in Christ, both revealed to our minds and sealed upon our hearts through the Holy Spirit.'[43] But while Calvin provides this

---

[36] *Inst.* III. 2. 6.

[37] Calvin invariably uses this phrase with respect to the ground or object of faith, the Word of God and the promise of Christ. He does not use the phrase reflexively, with respect to the question of whether the one who has faith is assured that he has it, though he does concern himself with the danger of presumption and with the need for self-examination. We shall follow Calvin in this usage.

[38] *Inst.* III. 2. 1.   [39] *Inst.* III. 2. 33f.

[40] *Inst.* III. 2. 6, 'it is a knowledge of God's will toward us, perceived from his Word'.

[41] *Inst.* III. 2. 7.   [42] *Inst.* III. 1. 4.   [43] *Inst.* III. 2. 7.

definition of faith it is not a definition in the sense of a set of necessary and sufficient conditions for the presence of faith to any degree, but it is a definition of an ideal, of what faith ought to be like, of what at its best it is. This is clear from what he goes on to say. On the one hand he stresses faith's certainty,[44] yet both before giving the definition of faith Calvin says that it is surrounded by error and unbelief,[45] and after giving it he says that even weak faith is real faith.[46]

It is not fanciful to think that having weak faith is parallel to coming across an obscure passage of Scripture.[47] If a person doesn't know what that passage really means, how can he have faith in it, if faith implies knowledge? Calvin's answer is that in these instances the believer has implicit faith, faith (presumably) of the form: whatever the true meaning of this obscure passage turns out to be, I now have faith in it. 'We certainly admit that so long as we dwell as strangers in the world there is such a thing as implicit faith; not only because many things are as yet hidden from us, but because surrounded by many clouds of errors we do not comprehend everything.'[48] However, despite this affirmation Calvin is not in general well disposed to the idea of implicit faith and is emphatic (in his critique of other views of implicit faith) that it is parasitic on the cases where faith is not implicit. Writing about the first disciples he says:

But although they had faith in the words of him whom they knew to be truthful, the ignorance that as yet occupied their minds so enveloped their faith in darkness that they were almost dumfounded. Hence, also, it said that they finally believed after they themselves had discovered the truth of Christ's words through the very fact of his resurrection. Not that they then began to believe, but because the seed of hidden faith—which had been dead, as it were, in their hearts—at that time burst through with renewed vigor! For there was in them a true but implicit faith because they had reverently embraced Christ as their sole teacher. Then, taught by him, they were convinced he was the author of their salvation.[49]

And as regards weak faith:

So we see that the mind, illumined by the knowledge of God, is at first wrapped up in much ignorance, which is gradually dispelled. Yet, by being ignorant of certain things, or by rather obscurely discerning what it does discern, the mind is not hindered from enjoying a clear knowledge of the divine will toward itself. For what it discerns comprises the first and principal parts in faith. It is like a man who, shut up in a prison into which the sun's rays shine obliquely and half obscured through a rather narrow window, is indeed deprived of the full sight of the sun. Yet his eyes dwell on its steadfast brightness, and he receives its benefits.[50]

---

[44] *Inst.* III. 2. 15.   [45] *Inst.* III. 2. 4.   [46] *Inst.* III. 2. 15.

[47] Calvin considers such a case in *Inst.* III. 2. 4.   [48] *Inst.* III. 2. 4.

[49] *Inst.* III. 2. 4.   [50] *Inst.* III. 2. 19.

These remarks about the certainty of faith, implying that the 'right definition' which Calvin gives is a definition of faith in its ideal form, strongly suggest that Calvin would favour a similar approach in regard to HSC, for as we have seen for Calvin the internal testimony of the Holy Sprit and the Spirit's work in producing faith in God's elect are all of a piece. They also suggest that coming to accept the self-authenticating character of Scripture may in some cases take time. And so what Calvin is setting forth is not so much an empirical claim in the form of a reportive definition, but an account of an attainable ideal. Ideally, the internal testimony of the Holy Spirit brings the highest degree of certainty. But prejudice and ignorance may get in the way, and in the presence of these obstacles the Spirit may convey a degree of certainty less than the highest, but even in the case of weak faith the Spirit may be operating authentically.

What Calvin is saying here can be expressed in terms of degrees of belief. However such degrees are to be measured, it is clear that we believe some things more strongly than others. Perhaps Calvin is simply conceding that while the believer may have a strong belief about some matters of his faith, he may have a much weaker belief about other matters, and may even, due to his 'ignorance', believe what is inconsistent. How else would he account for the presence of incompatible beliefs among equally well-intentioned and well-motivated believers? For while Calvin appears to take an infallibilist position regarding the central matters which Scripture affirms, he never claims that the process of submitting to the teaching of Holy Scripture may not in fact lead to someone holding inconsistent beliefs, and quite understandably he would not attribute such inconsistencies to the work of the Holy Spirit.

EVIDENCE

In the main part of this section we shall try to explore the nature of Calvin's evidentialism as regards revelation. For Calvin insists that the Bible authenticates itself with HSC by evidencing itself to us. Calvin does not seem to refer to 'self-evidence' in this connection, nor even to 'evidence', but uses equivalents such as 'manifest signs'. Yet it is clear, from the structure of Calvin's discussion in *Institutes* I. 6–9, that he is all the time eager to focus on the content of Scripture. It is this content of Scripture, its redemptive-historical 'message', that manifests itself, not Scripture considered formally as a library of sixty-six books each of which shares certain distinguishing features. We have already seen that he thinks that 'external' proofs have limited value. In addition he is scathing in his denunciation of the Libertines who endeavour to separate the Spirit from the Word.

In an interesting discussion of faith as it was thought of in the circle of John Mair (or Major)[51] Alexander Broadie considers how this circle saw the relation of faith and evidence.[52] The similarities with Calvin, and also the dissimilarities, are striking.

The basic contrast is between what Broadie calls evident and inevident assent. Evident assent is one which is true, unhesitating, in assenting to which the intellect cannot be deceived.[53] For example, the proposition that I am now typing this sentence is one to which I give evident assent. The will has no place in the making or giving of such an assent. Inevident assent is, surprisingly perhaps, also an assent which is certain, offered without hesitation. The difference is that such assent cannot be caused in the human intellect without a command of the will. It is this kind of assent, willed assent rather than inevitable assent, which according to Mair and his circle is intrinsic to faith, because the propositions of faith are not evidently true, but they are certain, and as such are assented to by an act of the will. So faith falls between evident assent and opinion, for opinion unlike evident assent is susceptible to uncertainty, self-deception, and hesitation.[54] The prominence given to the will in faith is no doubt linked to medieval ideas of human merit, the possibility of which Calvin repudiated (as we shall see in the next chapter), just as he thought the idea of faith as mere assent unsatisfactory.[55] He would also have been repelled by the discussions in Mair's circle about whether God could, by his *potentia absoluta*, deceive us, and in what circumstances. We shall discuss Calvin's attitude to *potentia absoluta* in Chapter 11.

These are significant differences between Calvin's own position and the Mairite view. But the similarities are equally striking, one in particular. One is that faith is certain, assured, unhesitating, and not mere opinion (though one cannot help feeling that the Mairites, just as much as Calvin, had ideal faith in view here). Another is that faith depends on authority and testimony.[56] Authoritative testimony provides the grounds for the assent, but it does not necessitate or guarantee assent. What more is needed, for a Mairite, is an act of assent; Calvin, also thinks that assent is involved, but more. Both the assent and whatever else is needed are brought about by the work of the Holy Spirit, 'revealed to our minds and sealed upon our hearts

---

[51] John Mair/Major (1467/8–1550) was a Scotist (and a Scottish) theologian. What makes this comparison additionally interesting is that it has been hazarded that the young Calvin received instruction from John Major in Paris. Discussion of Major's possible influence on Calvin is assessed by A. N. S. Lane, *John Calvin: Student of the Church Fathers* (16ff.) We shall consider Calvin's 'Scotism' in ch. 10.

[52] Alexander Broadie, *The Shadow of Scotus* (Edinburgh: T. & T. Clark, 1995), lecture 5.

[53] *The Shadow of Scotus*, 73.   [54] *The Shadow of Scotus*, 79.

[55] *Inst.* III. 2. 1, 'Indeed most people, when they hear this term ["faith"], understand nothing deeper than a common assent to the gospel history'.   [56] *The Shadow of Scotus*, 81.

through the Holy Spirit'.[57] Yet Calvin does not investigate too closely the source of assent in faith and the part that the will plays, though the will undoubtedly does play an important part in faith. He is more interested in its fiducial character, its reliance on the 'freely given promise in Christ' and he inveighs against the Catholic view of faith as mere (and implicit) assent.[58] Nothing illustrates more emphatically that John Mair and John Calvin, for all their nearness in space and time, are separated by the figure of Martin Luther.

Let us now consider more closely the evidential component of faith in Calvin's view. By ascribing evidentialism to Calvin I mean the view that (in the context of the idea of self-authentication) the firm belief in the divinity of the Scriptures is formed by the acceptance of evidence which the Scripture itself presents; the person thus convinced has the belief on the basis of that evidence. The internal testimony of the Holy Spirit makes available to the minds of men and women, the grounds, the *indicia*, internal to Scripture itself, and the acceptance of these grounds is what provides the evidence of its being God's word. The Spirit does this by so presenting that evidence that according to Calvin the belief is held (ideally, as we have seen) with utter certainty. On this understanding the belief is formed in a way that has by modern epistemologists come to be called 'internalist', that is, the belief is grounded on the evidence which the person himself possesses. However, this internalist interpretation will have to be refined somewhat in what follows.

An Externalist Calvin?

In his major work on religious epistemology *Warranted Christian Belief*, Alvin Plantinga has appropriated Calvin's doctrine of the internal testimony of the Holy Spirit (and what Thomas Aquinas has to say about the 'instigation' or 'instinct' of the Holy Spirit),[59] seeing this as a forerunner or an exemplar of his own defence of the warranted belief that the Scriptures are the word of God. We saw in Chapter 8 that for Plantinga belief in God may be properly basic, that is, a person may be entitled to believe that God exists without evidence or argument, in rather the way in which we believe that there is a past, or that there are minds other than our own mind.[60] He finds warrant or precedent for this view in what Calvin says about the *sensus*

---

[57] *Inst.* III. 2. 7.   [58] *Inst.* III. 2. 1.

[59] Aquinas, *Summa Theologiae*, 2a, 2ae, 2. 9, 'One who believes does have a sufficient motive for believing, namely the authority of God's teaching, confirmed by miracles and—what is greater—the inner inspiration of God inviting him to believe. Thus he does not *give credit lightly*.' This passage is quoted by Plantinga, *Warranted Christian Belief*, 249 n. 18.   [60] *Warranted Christian Belief*, 175.

divinitatis. In a parallel way Plantinga holds that belief that the Scriptures are the word of God may be immediately formed in the mind.

What is required for *knowledge* is that a belief be produced by cognitive faculties or processes that are working properly, in an appropriate epistemic environment . . . according to a design plan that is aimed at truth, and is furthermore *successfully* aimed at truth. But according to this model [the 'Extended Aquinas/Calvin model'] what one believes by faith (the beliefs that constitute faith) meets these four conditions.

First, when these beliefs are accepted by faith and result from the internal instigation of the Holy Spirit, they are produced by cognitive processes working properly; they are not produced by way of some cognitive malfunction. Faith, the whole process that produces them, is specifically designed by God himself to produce this very effect—just as vision, say, is designed by God to produce a certain kind of perceptual beliefs. When it does produce this effect, therefore, it is working properly; thus the beliefs in question satisfy the external rationality condition, which is also the first condition of warrant. Second, according to the model, the maxi-environment in which we find ourselves, including the cognitive contamination produced by sin, is precisely the cognitive environment for which this process is designed. The typical minienvironment is also favorable. Third, the process is designed to produce *true* beliefs; and fourth, the beliefs it produces—belief in the great things of the gospel—are in fact true; faith is a reliable belief-producing process, so that the process in question is *successfully* aimed at the production of true beliefs.[61]

There is this important difference between the case of the *sensus divinitatis* and that of the internal testimony of the Holy Spirit, however. A properly basic belief in the existence of God is according to Plantinga (and Calvin) a universal endowment of the human race, something which is innate or concreated, though universally perverted by sin. The basic belief that the Scriptures are the word of God is a particular endowment, given only to some, and is the result of the intrusion of the Holy Spirit into the mind, when that mind is aware of some central aspect of the Christian revelation, the articles of the faith. So it is an intrusion into the exercise of the cognitive capacities of certain men and women.[62]

---

[61] Plantinga, *Warranted Christian Belief*, 256–7. Note that Plantinga's account presupposes the thoroughly Calvinian idea that faith is a form of knowledge.

[62] This particularism is only a contingent fact, however. There is nothing to prevent God giving everyone the benefit of the internal testimony of the Holy Spirit. Plantinga thinks that many people (perhaps himself included) have formed the belief that God exists in a properly basic fashion. Or if they have not formed the belief in this way, they are entitled to hold the belief thus, without having reasons or evidence. How many do this is of course an empirical question. But one may wonder whether the formation of such basic beliefs about God is not in fact helped along, perhaps necessarily helped along, by the person in question already having a developed theism. (On this, see Merold Westphal, 'On Taking St. Paul Seriously: Sin as an Epistemological Category'.)

My Christian belief can have warrant, and warrant sufficient for knowledge, even if I don't know of and cannot make a good historical case for the reliability of the biblical writers or for what they teach. I don't *need* a good historical case for the truth of the central teachings of the gospel to be warranted in accepting them . . . On the model, the warrant for Christian belief doesn't require that I or anyone else have this kind of historical information; the warrant floats free of such questions. It doesn't require to be validated or proved by some source of belief *other* than faith, such as historical investigation.[63]

Here Plantinga echoes Calvin's (and Aquinas's) estimate of the external proofs of the authenticity of Scripture as God's revelation that we discussed earlier. Plantinga cites Calvin in support of his belief that Scripture (through the work of the Holy Spirit) carries its own evidence with it. Plantinga quotes from *Institutes* I. 7. 5, a passage cited earlier in this chapter, in support of this. He understands Calvin to be saying not that we have knowledge or certainty with respect to propositions such as *The Bible comes to us from the very mouth of God*, or *The Book of Job is divinely inspired*, but rather with respect to the actual teaching, the internal cognitive content of the Bible, that it is the word of God. Nor, Plantinga thinks, is the certainty that the believer has with respect to such content the certainty that comes from the propositions of the Bible being self-evidently true, which they aren't. Nor does the idea of self-authentication mean that the believer sees that the Bible proves itself to be accurate or reliable.

However, although the relevant propositions are not self-evidently true there are respects in which the truths of the gospel resemble self-evident truths, namely that they have their evidence immediately, and not by inference from propositional evidence. Such evidence that the believer has of the divinity of the gospel he does not get from propositions external to the gospel, and the direct evidence he has is of a degree and kind so as to confer warrant. This, according to Plantinga, is what Calvin means.[64]

This account of Calvin is broadly along the right lines, and it is clear and perceptive. Where Plantinga seems to me to go astray (in respect of his interpretation of Calvin, or perhaps it would be better to say his estimation of Calvin, for we are not here concerned with his account as a free-standing contribution to religious epistemology) is in three respects. First (as we saw in Chapter 8), he imputes to Calvin an interest in rational justification, warrant (Plantinga's term in his later writings for what makes belief into knowledge), for which there is little or no evidence in Calvin's own words. Secondly, Plantinga's account of the warrant that self-authentication confers on the believer is rather different from Calvin's. Finally, he interprets

---

[63] *Warranted Christian Belief*, 259. [64] *Warranted Christian Belief*, 262.

Calvin's account of HSC as a case of externalist epistemology.[65] Let us take these points in turn.

Warrant

Plantinga's work is concerned with the rational justification of belief in God and in the Christian message (what he refers to as 'warrant'), and he argues that that message may have warrant for A, and that both belief in God and belief in the whole panoply of propositions which constitute the Christian faith may also have warrant and (if those propositions are true) the warrant is such as to confer knowledge if Christianity is true. This warrant does not require appeal to a body of propositions which are evidently true to any rational man, but rather to the proper working of cognitive faculties in a propitious environment. A central part of this programme is his claim that what the Scriptures teach, the 'great things of the gospel', have warrant in this sense for the believer. They do not require a successful, convincing natural theology, nor conviction that the Bible is the word of God that arises from 'external' sources such as evidence for its historical trustworthiness. It is here that he appeals to Calvin and to the idea of self-authentication.

It is not at all clear that in his account of self-authentication Calvin has rationality in mind. To be sure, as we have seen, he shows some interest in external proofs, even in what he calls 'rational proofs',[66] but only as secondary and inferior to the self-authenticating work of the Spirit, a judgement with which Plantinga concurs. And even if these references to reason are sufficient to show Calvin's interest in rationality, they also show that he has a very different idea of the rational justification of belief in Scripture from Alvin Plantinga. As we have seen, Calvin also contrasts two sorts of proofs, two-step proofs, via external testimony, and one-step proofs, an immediate perception of the divinity of Scripture for oneself. But it is not clear that he assesses these proofs in terms of some overarching criterion of warrant or rationality, or that he thinks that self-authentication is as reasonable or more (or less) reasonable than less direct ways of trying to establish the divine authenticity of Scripture. He thinks that these less direct ways are inferior because they cannot produce certainty but he shows little interest in their reasonableness or otherwise.

---

[65] Perhaps, in order to avoid possible confusion, it is worth noting that in this broad context of discussion 'externalism' is being used in two distinct senses. First, to characterize a sort of strategy for proving the Bible to be the Word of God, one that appeals to factors extraneous to the distinctive cognitive content of Scripture. Secondly, to characterize a certain kind of epistemological theory, one that claims that the epistemic justification (or warrant) of some proposition is the operation of a causal condition which produces the appropriate belief, working independently of any evidence that a person may in fact have for the truth of that proposition.   [66] *Inst.* 1.7.4.

No doubt Calvin would, if pressed, tell us that to accept the cognitive content of the Scriptures as the word of God on the testimony of the Holy Spirit is the most reasonable thing to do, since God is the source of all rationality. (This shows, incidentally, how flexible is the meaning of words such as 'reason' and 'rationality' in such a context.) Yet Calvin, paradoxically, claims that the knowledge which the self-authenticating Scripture gives is a conviction which requires no reasons, 'a knowledge with which the best reason agrees—in which the mind truly reposes more securely and constantly than in any reasons'.[67] However, such positive thoughts about reason that Calvin entertains would seem to be a *consequence* rather than a *ground* for taking the Bible to be divine. Rather than have a characteristically modern interest in reason and rationality, Calvin has a pre-modern concern with religious authority, and with different and competing sources of such authority. In particular, because of his polemical stance against the Church of Rome he is concerned to ground the authority of the Bible in itself rather than in some independently identifiable institution like a Church Council or the Roman Pontiff. Perhaps it is more rational to have the Bible grounded in itself rather than in something external to it, but that (for Calvin) is not the main point, and may not be the point at all.

The other thing which Calvin stresses at first sight comes nearer to Plantinga's own concerns. He is vitally interested in the religious aspect of this epistemological question of how we know that the Bible is the word of God. As we have noted, one theme throughout the early sections of book I of the *Institutes* is the contrast he draws between two sorts of knowledge of God. The sort which, as he puts it, 'merely flits in the brain',[68] and the knowledge and certainty 'which piety requires'.[69] And part of his argument for self-authentication is that it alone conveys true knowledge of God, knowledge which satisfies the conscience, which compels obedience, which penetrates the heart, which 'seriously affects us'.[70] 'By this power (of the divine majesty) we are drawn and inflamed, knowingly and willingly, to obey him, yet also more vitally and more effectively than by mere human willing or knowing!'[71] However, Calvin's conception of such knowledge is rather different from Plantinga's, as we shall now see.

Knowledge

We must not assume that when Calvin uses 'knowledge' he has in mind what Plantinga calls 'warrant'. Throughout *Warranted Christian Belief* Plantinga stresses that the warrant which the Christian faith has is sufficient for knowledge *if that faith is true*. As he argues, epistemology can only take us

---

[67] *Inst.* I. 7. 5.   [68] *Inst.* I. 5. 9.   [69] *Inst.* I. 7. 4.

[70] *Inst.* I. 7. 4–5.   [71] *Inst.* I. 7. 5.

so far; what constitutes knowledge is determined by what is true, and epistemology cannot show us what is true, that what we are warranted in believing is true.

There is, indeed, such a thing as truth; the stakes are, indeed, very high (it matters greatly whether you believe the truth); but there is no way to be sure that you have the truth; there is no sure and certain method of attaining truth by starting from beliefs about which you can't be mistaken and moving infallibly to the rest of your beliefs. Furthermore, many others reject what seems to you to be most important. This is life under uncertainty, life under epistemic risk and fallibility.[72]

That is, the Christian message may be true, (as Plantinga believes that it is), but warrant never ensures, nor can it ensure, the truth of the belief warranted. One may know, if what one warrantably believes is true, happens to be true. So one can never know that one knows.[73]

By contrast, when Calvin holds that HSC gives certainty or assured knowledge, he seems to have something stronger in mind, not just assurance that I am in such and such a cognitive state, or assurance that I have warrant, but assurance that I know. Unlike Plantinga, who thinks that warranted beliefs constitute conditional and fallible 'knowledge', because whether or not they constitute knowledge depends on the separate question of whether what is warranted is true, Calvin's view looks infallibilist. And it is precisely because the Holy Spirit conveys assured knowledge in this sense that for Calvin it is adequate from the point of view of religion or piety. Calvin thinks that the immediate self-evidencing character of the cognitive content of Scripture is truth-guaranteeing since it is immediate evidence from God who is himself infallible. Such a one-step approach is superior to multi-step approaches precisely because it does not depend upon fallible intermediaries nor the accumulation of probabilities.

In saying this, Calvin enters two caveats. The first is that this knowledge, though true knowledge, and partaking of the divine infallibility, is not comprehensive.

When we call faith 'knowledge' we do not mean comprehension of the sort that is commonly concerned with those things which fall under human sense perception. For faith is so far above sense that man's mind has to go beyond and rise above itself in order to attain it. Even where the mind has attained, it does not comprehend what it feels. But while it is persuaded of what it does not grasp, by the very certainty of its

---

[72] *Warranted Christian Belief*, 436–7 (see also 499).

[73] Cf. William Alston, 'On Knowing That We Know: The Application to Religious Knowledge', in C. Stephen Evans and Merold Westphal (eds.), *Christian Perspectives on Religious Knowledge* (Grand Rapids, Mich.: Eerdmans, 1993). 'What more reliable mode of belief formation could there be than one the accuracy of which is ensured by God? Hence, on a reliability theory, if the belief is indeed true it will count as knowledge' (21).

persuasion it understands more than if it perceived anything human by its own capacity.[74]

And as we saw when discussing the assurance of faith, Calvin recognizes (somewhat reluctantly, one feels) the need, on occasion, for the exercise of implicit faith.

We certainly admit that so long as we dwell as strangers in the world there is such a thing as implicit faith; not only because many things are as yet hidden from us, but because surrounded by many clouds of errors we do not comprehend everything . . . And in our daily reading of Scripture we come upon many obscure passages that convict us of ignorance.[75]

But despite these important qualifications Calvin believes that self-authentication gives the believer one-step certainty/knowledge that the Scriptures are the word of God and he would say that in the central, paradigm cases of self-authentication the believer enjoys the assurance of faith, despite his caveat about the possibility of presumption.[76]

Modern epistemology is centrally concerned with exploring methods of analysing rational justification or warrant, both internalist or externalist modes, which are of general application, and to which claims to a knowledge of God are obviously subject. It is argued[77] and at present widely accepted, that there is about all methods of gaining knowledge (internalist or externalist) an epistemic circularity. Any such method assumes its own reliability, and religious epistemology is not exempt from this assumption. One can only check the reliability of one sense perception against other perceptions, of one memory claim by consulting others, and so on. And religious epistemology is in the same boat. In making any positive epistemological claims about how God reveals himself (for example) one is assuming that God reliably communicates knowledge of himself. And hence it follows that although by pursuing one such method in religion one might gain knowledge of God, and believe that one has gained knowledge, one cannot know that one has, since one is overtly or covertly assuming the reliability of a particular mode of religious knowledge. This applies both to discursive proofs of God's existence, and to one-step appeals to self-authentication— each procedure assumes but cannot prove without circularity, the reliability

---

[74] *Inst.* III. 2. 14.

[75] *Inst.* III. 2. 4. Perhaps not so reluctantly, for he also says that he does not deny that 'most things are now implicit for us . . . In these matters we can do nothing better than suspend judgment and hearten ourselves to hold unity with the church' (*Inst.* III. 2. 3).   [76] e.g. *Inst.* III. 2. 11.

[77] e.g. by William Alston, 'On Knowing That We Know: The Application to Religious Knowledge'. Alston discusses these issues more generally in *The Reliability of Sense Perception* (Ithaca: Cornell University Press, 1993).

of our cognitive sources and procedures. This applies not only to knowledge, but to reasonable belief in all its varieties and strengths. One cannot step outside the circle. There is no vantage point outside the circle which will, so to say, guarantee the knowledge claims that one makes from within it. And so in making (tacitly or explicitly) the assumption about God's reliability in communicating truths about himself religious knowledge is in no better or worse position than other modes of knowledge, sensory perception of the external world, or the use of inductive and deductive inference, or memory.

It is not at all clear that Calvin is an epistemologist in this sense, concerned with methods of analysing the nature of rational justification or warrant. Calvin does not think that he has found a correct *method* for providing us with reliable religious knowledge. To be convinced with HSC that the Scriptures are the word of God is not the result of successfully employing the right epistemic strategy. It is, so to speak, a basic, brute fact. The character of such conviction is more like that of a sense-datum, which immediately and incorrigibly bears testimony to itself. The question of whether or not one possesses a method of detecting and displaying the reliability of such a conviction does not arise in his mind.

But other features of Calvin's case for self-authentication may seem to make him more hospitable to epistemological caution. For as we have seen he stresses (even though interpreters of Calvin differ among themselves about its exact significance) that the internal testimony of the Holy Spirit is parasitic on the text of Scripture. The doctrine is, after all, the doctrine of the self-authenticating character *of Scripture*. And (as we noted earlier) Scripture is a material object, or a set of such objects (just like *Great Expectations*, or Plato's *Republic*), parchments or pages containing words and sentences written in certain natural languages. And so the internal testimony of the Holy Spirit, whatever its exact epistemic status, presupposes and depends upon the exercise of sense perception, and a knowledge, however rudimentary, of the original languages of Scripture or the other natural languages into which they have been translated, and so on.

Calvin may reply that it is not necessary to know the exact meaning of a text to be convinced of its authenticity. Suppose that I have a rudimentary knowledge of German. I may come to be convinced that I hear someone speaking fluent, technical German while only having the haziest idea of what she is saying. In the same way, Calvin may retort, the believer may recognize something as the voice of God even when he is not at all clear what that voice is saying.

But it may be possible to press the objection further. Since the internal testimony of the Holy Spirit to Scripture depends upon perception, memory, and the like, the certainty which it conveys cannot be greater than the highest degree of certainty which perception, memory, and various ratiocinative processes are capable. Yet perhaps Calvin could afford to be rather relaxed in the face of the epistemic circularity claim. For it is not a consequence of that claim that we are never warranted in being certain about the claims we make, indeed of being very certain. I am very certain that I am now wearing trousers, very certain. The reliability of the means I have of establishing this and of checking it cannot be independently established, but is subject to other checks which themselves cannot be independently established, and so on. But this does not diminish the strength or the reasonableness of my belief, nor does it alter the comparative strength between it and other, less certain beliefs that I have about myself (for example, that I am a handsome chap, and a jolly good fellow). Calvin draws comparisons between the certainty of self-authenticating beliefs and other kinds of beliefs, beliefs of immediate perception for example. And all Calvin needs to establish his case is the claim that self-authenticated beliefs are, as regards their certainty, more like 'I am now feeling tired' than they are like knowing that Jim is unwell because Joe tells me that John knows that he is.

To this fact another must be added. Most of the examples of very certain or incorrigible beliefs cited by philosophers are of very obviously true or trivial or inconsequential matters; 'I have a head', 'I see a blue patch', $2 + 2 = 4$, and the like. But Calvin (and the tradition) is concerned with matters of abiding personal significance, and which otherwise are highly disputable. When Calvin says that the degree of certainty afforded by HSC is 'higher and stronger than any judgment'[78] it is not appropriate to take him to be holding that HSC is greater than the certainty which attaches to the claim, made under appropriate conditions, that I see a red patch, but that the degree of certainty is much greater than the certainty which attaches to other ways of establishing the truth of that which the Holy Spirit bears testimony to. Take the claim that a person will survive death. This is a matter of continuous philosophical and scientific debate resulting in a set of 'opinions' tending either to accept the truth or the falsity of that claim. What Calvin may be taken as saying, by contrast, is that if the Spirit bears testimony with HSC to the truth of the claim that we will survive death, then the person who is testified to is or is entitled to be more certain that he will survive death than he is when he is convinced by philosophical arguments, or impressed by reports of 'near-death' experiences, that he will survive the death of his body.

What Calvin is concerned about is the perception-like immediacy of such convictions, and with the source of the conviction that the Scriptures are

---

[78] *Inst.* I. 8. 1.

from God. He is chiefly interested in a contrast, familiar in all of the ways we acquire knowledge of anything, between believing or remembering or knowing something for oneself, and believing or remembering or knowing something because someone else has told one. Of course there are counter-examples to this contrast, cases where a person's first perceivings are corrected by more reliable or experienced sources of knowledge. But as a matter of logic not everything we (the human race) know or believe can be derived from someone else. And what Calvin needs is the plausibility of this contrast in its central, typical cases. For him the self-authenticating character of Scripture has this kind of certainty: it is the certainty that is conveyed like that when, looking directly in front of me, I see the window. It is as certain as anything that depends on my direct sense perception that there is a window in front of me. For Calvin, it is as certain as anything can be that depends on the reading of a text that this text is the Word of God. And this, he says, is because of the internal testimony of the Holy Spirit.

Externalism

As we have noted, in the latest phase of his work Plantinga interprets the SD and the internal testimony of the Holy Spirit in externalist fashion. Warrant does not depend on evidence that is consciously available to a person—this is the approach of internalism—but rather on the working of mechanisms which, in a favourable environment, produce warranted belief. In the later phases of his work Plantinga applies this externalist approach both to the operation of the SD and to the internal testimony of the Holy Spirit. However, there is this crucial difference between the externalism of the SD and the alleged externalism of the Scriptures; in the case of the SD certain phenomena (according to Plantinga) are the immediate occasion for the forming of the belief that there is a God, whereas in the case of the self-authenticating of the Scriptures being acquainted with the content of the Bible provides not only the occasion for the forming of an appropriate belief but also the cognitive content of what is believed. So (say) the text 'God was in Christ reconciling the world unto himself . . .' triggers (through the Holy Spirit) an immediate firm belief the cognitive content of which is 'God was in Christ . . .'.

Plantinga says that on this view the Bible is self-evidently true in the sense he characterizes. The evidence for the truth of the Bible is not other evidence, but the evidence of the Bible itself. In the technical sense used in modern epistemology, this is certainly not a species of evidentialism, for no reasoning from evidence is involved. Nevertheless the belief that the Scriptures are self-authenticating is evidence-relevant or evidence-pertinent, since one necessary condition of its being formed is the operation of perceptual and cognitive processes on a material object, the text of the Bible or some presentation of the meaning of that text. So what we have in Calvin (put in Plantinga's terms) is a two aspect epistemology: the operation of the Spirit in testifying to the truth of the Bible is externalist, but what the Spirit testifies to is evidence that is intrinsic to Scripture. It is hard to see how a person could, in these general circumstances, be convinced that God was in Christ reconciling the world without these words or their cognitive equivalents being evidence for that conviction.

When assessed in terms of the externalism–internalism contrast Calvin can at best be only a half-way house externalist; externalist with respect to the mechanism of the internal instigation of the Holy Spirit, but internalist with respect to the immediacy of the evidence on which the belief is grounded. When he refers to the divine side of self-authentication, to the faith-producing activity of the Holy Spirit, to his illumination of the mind, this has a distinctly externalist ring to it. The Spirit must 'penetrate into our hearts to persuade us', he seals the truth in our hearts, we must be 'illumined by his power'. But where he refers to the human side of things, this penetrating and sealing activity of the Spirit is manifested in discerning the majesty of God upon reading or hearing Scripture.[79] It is on account of the perception he has of this majesty and other connected matters that the believer forms the immediate conviction that this is the Word of God, but this conviction is formed and imbued in the mind by the illuminating work of the Spirit. So this looks not to be purely externalist in Plantinga's sense, but an externalist–internalist hybrid.

It is not plausible to suppose that for Calvin self-authentication is externalist such that it is sufficient for accepting the supreme authority of Scripture that God has implanted in that person a tendency to do so, and that the circumstances in which the tendency is made manifest occur. Such a version of externalism might account for the basicness of a belief, but not that belief's seeming to be self-authenticating. One reason is this: that it is upon reading the words 'God was in Christ reconciling the world to himself' that the believer forms the conviction that God was in Christ reconciling the world unto himself. The proposition does not act merely as an external belief-producing mechanism, or as part of such a mechanism, as attending to the intricacy of a tiny flower might immediately trigger the belief that God made this flower. Rather, there is an internal connection, a connection of meaning, between what the Holy Spirit witnesses to and what one believes.[80]

[79] *Inst.* 1. 7. 4, 5.

[80] This is not to say that internalism is totally absent in Plantinga's religious epistemology. When it comes to the idea of the experience of God, Plantinga writes of the internal testimony of the Holy Spirit enabling the believer to 'see the glory and beauty of the things of the gospel' (*Warranted Christian Belief,*

There is the danger of anachronism in making such comparisons. It may be that Plantinga and Calvin are talking past each other on this issue, for Plantinga is talking about warrant or rational justification of the sort that gives knowledge if what is warranted is true, while Calvin is talking not about knowledge in this modern sense, nor about knowledge in the classical sense of *scientia*, but about the certainty or assuredness of *notitia*. The danger of anachronism may be underlined by reminding ourselves that Calvin approaches an understanding of the internal testimony of the Holy Spirit as an epistemological infallibilist. His basic position is that HSC is as infallible as God himself. By contrast, for Plantinga our best epistemological endeavours are fallible. We only have knowledge if what has warrant for us is true, and we cannot presently know that it is. Nevertheless, despite his infallibilist tendencies Calvin has to walk a fine line here. On the one hand, he needs to maintain, against Rome, that 'Councils have erred', and thus to allow the possibility that he himself may err. On the other hand, he wishes to uphold a view of religious authority that is strong enough to be a live option to the infallibilist claims both of the Church of Rome and of the Anabaptists.

A FIDEIST CALVIN?

So far in our discussion of what Calvin means by the self-authenticating character of Scripture we have been treating him as an evidentialist, and debating how his evidentialism is to be best understood. However, John Beversluis has argued that Calvin is not an evidentialist but a fideist in respect of the authority of Scripture, someone who accepts the authority of Scripture without evidence, by an act of faith. He says: '[John Calvin] is a fideist through and through—a theologian who believes that, so far as fallen human beings are concerned, knowledge of God is the result of the internal illumination of the Holy Spirit and hence a gift of God to the elect.'[81] There are a number of points of Beversluis's treatment which prompt ready agreement. As we have seen, Calvin is not much interested in questions of rationality which have preoccupied discussions of religious epistemology since the Enlightenment. Further, Beversluis is correct to stress that Calvin's view is that the *sensus divinitatis* is corrupted, and does not deliver to anyone the basic belief that God exists in an untainted form, in a way that does not provoke resistance and repugnance, and therefore God's special revelation through the Bible is needed. We have also seen that Calvin places a great

---

304). These are the perception-like *consequences* of the work of the Spirit, what the Spirit testifies to, they are not themselves the grounds of belief.

[81] John Beversluis, 'Reforming the "Reformed" Objection to Natural Theology', 200.

deal of emphasis on the place of faith in accepting the Bible as a revelation from God. The internal testimony of the Holy Spirit is an aspect of his overall account of faith. Despite all this, there are at least two important reasons for shying away from classifying Calvin as a fideist.[82]

The first has to do with Calvin's account of faith. Suppose we say that for Calvin acceptance of the divine authority of Scripture as God's own revelation is an 'act of faith'; it is necessary to reflect a little on what Calvin means by this term. For Calvin faith is not a non-rational or irrational leap, in the spirit of Pascal or Kierkegaard, but faith for him is grounded on evidence in virtue of which the trust or reliance which is intrinsic to faith is called forth. In other words faith involves evidence, and the reliance is on account of what is believed. Here is a typical Calvinian statement about faith: 'We hold faith to be a knowledge of God's will toward us, perceived from his Word. But the foundation of this is a preconceived conviction of God's truth.'[83]

But perhaps Beversluis thinks that a 'fideist' is not someone who exercises a groundless leap of faith but one whose basic religious commitments are not open to independent rational scrutiny. The heart may have reasons which reason—understood as some form of evidentialism—knows not of. Understood in this way there is no denying that at first glance there are elements of fideism in Calvin. However, as we have seen, Calvin believes that Scripture evidences itself to the believer. And as we have also seen, keeping in step with the tradition, Calvin does have a place for arguments for the authority of Scripture, though he views the offering of such arguments for the acceptance of the Bible as God's revelation rather asymmetrically. These reasons or arguments can be operated *in defence* against attacks on the divine authority of Holy Scripture while not being necessary in establishing that authority *ab initio*.

Calvin is a particularist in the sense that the internally testifying activity of the Holy Spirit is not in fact enjoyed by everyone, and he steadfastly refuses to base his acceptance of divine revelation on external reasons generally available. But this does not mean that he scorns evidence, since he holds that the divinity of the Scriptures is *self-evident*; not a matter of inference from other evidence. Such *indicia* are intrinsic to the Bible, they bear their own evidence and so convey, by the internal testimony of the Holy Spirit, immediate, non-inferential conviction that the Bible is indeed the word of God.

---

[82] 'Fideism' has a variety of meanings in the literature. Here I am using it (as I believe Beversluis is using it) as a way of justifying belief and faith for which evidence is not necessary, but an act of the will is sufficient. For a discussion on other meanings of the term in the context of Calvin's thought see Arvin Vos, *Aquinas, Calvin and Contemporary Protestant Thought*, ch. 3.　　　[83] *Inst.* III. 2. 6.

Secondly, there is confusion over the use of the term 'evidence' in these discussions. In contemporary discussion of natural theology, the rationality of religious belief, and the like, 'evidentialism' is used in a fairly technical sense to refer to one's 'total evidence', the set of propositions which a person knows to be true or is justified in believing to be true.[84] And in this sense Calvin is certainly not an evidentialist with respect to the acceptance of the Bible as God's revelation. But this does not mean, as we have seen, that he does not think that there is evidence for the divine authority of Scripture since he holds that the Scriptures are self-evidently divine for those who have the Spirit-given eyes to see.

Having looked at both externalist and fideist interpretations of Calvin we are now, finally, in a position to say more about the exact nature of Calvin's evidentialism.[85]

CALVIN'S EVIDENTIALISM

In the light of our earlier discussion it seems clear that Calvin is making certain claims about the strength of the evidence in Scripture for its being God's word. He refers to the work of the Spirit as a powerful illumination which frees us from the need for and the weakness of mere human judgement, whether of our own or of someone else's. Just as we may judge, using our own unaided cognitive powers, that (it is likely that), on such and such grounds, the Scriptures are God's Word, so in a parallel but epistemically superior fashion the Spirit acts like a bright light illuminating the cognitive and other content of the Scriptures, and brings to our minds a degree of certainty higher than what results from any human procedure alone. This certainty is very high indeed, even though it does not amount to the incorrigibility beloved of many in modern epistemology.

As we saw, Calvin follows his treatment of the internal testimony of the Holy Spirit with a chapter[86] briefly surveying arguments for the authority of Scripture; for example, from its style, antiquity, miracles and prophecy, the preservation of the Bible, its simplicity and heavenly character, the testimony of the church and the witness of martyrs to it. In his praiseworthy endeavour to establish the evidential character of the internal testimony of the Holy Spirit, B. B. Warfield claims that these *indicia* provide the cognitive content of the internal testimony. According to him, they co-work with the internal

---

[84] *The Cambridge Dictionary of Philosophy*, ed. Robert Audi (Cambridge: Cambridge University Press, 1995), 'Evidentialism' (W. Hasker).

[85] For further discussion of Beversluis's reading of Calvin see Michael Czapkay Sudduth, 'Calvin, Plantinga, and the Natural Knowledge of God', *Faith and Philosophy* (1998).   [86] *Inst.* I. 8.

testimony to place the authority of Scripture above all controversy.[87] What the Spirit immediately conveys is the cognitive content of these *indicia*.

It is a matter of course that he should teach that the *indicia* are ineffective for the production of 'sound faith' apart from the internal operation of the Spirit correcting the sin-bred disabilities of man, that is to say, apart from the testimony of the Spirit. But what about the *indicia* in conjunction with the testimony of the Spirit? It would seem to be evident that, on Calvin's ground, they would have their full part to play here, and that we must say that, when the soul is renewed by the Holy Spirit to a sense for the divinity of Scripture, it is through the *indicia* of that divinity that it is brought into its proper confidence in the divinity of Scripture.[88]

Warfield immediately qualifies this by suggesting that Calvin appears to speak of the *indicia* as if they lay side by side with the testimony of the Spirit than acted along with it. Indeed he does. And he does so because the *indicia* on which he lays emphasis, and which form the evidential content regarding which the Spirit enlightens the mind, are side by side. The *indicia* which Calvin says the Spirit enlightens the mind about are not those elaborated in chapter 8, the external *indicia*, but those in the previous chapter, to which he attaches central importance, the internal *indicia*. The clue to this is the fact that, as noted earlier, Calvin sees the internal testimony of the Holy Spirit as being of a piece with saving faith. Calvin cuts short his discussion of the internal testimony at this place because essentially the same matter is taken up in his lengthy discussion of faith in book III, as we have seen. Warfield sees the importance that Calvin attaches to faith but for some reason does not follow it up.

There are in fact three reasons, two of which arise directly from what Calvin himself says, that suggest that in his eagerness to affirm that the internal testimony of the Holy Spirit is grounded in certain data, Warfield has somewhat overstated the case, or rather has managed to get Calvin's discussion back to front.

First, it seems clear that for Calvin the internal testimony of the Holy Spirit is not borne to the *proofs* of the divinity of Scripture which he discusses in *Institutes* I. 8. For as we have seen these proofs have a lesser importance, and a less direct function, despite the fact that Calvin treats them at some length in that chapter. The internal testimony of the Holy Spirit is not borne, say, to the fact that the martyrs sealed their confidence in Scripture with their own blood, or to the arguments for the antiquity of the Bible, but rather to the content of the Word itself, to its sublime, divine message. 'The same Spirit, therefore, who has spoken through the mouths of the prophets must

---

[87] 'Calvin's Doctrine of the Knowledge of God', in *Calvin and Calvinism*, 89.
[88] 'Calvin's Doctrine of the Knowledge of God', 87.

penetrate into our hearts to persuade us that they faithfully proclaimed what had been divinely commanded.'[89] And as we have also seen Calvin repeatedly stresses, in these same sections of the *Institutes*, that those illuminated by the Spirit do not need proofs. The testimony is 'more excellent than all reason'; 'it is not right to subject it [Scripture] to proof and reasoning'; 'we seek no proofs, no marks of genuineness on which our judgment may lean'. There is also the subsidiary point that if the *indicia* to which the Spirit bears testimony are the very same as those involved in external proofs, one would have expected Calvin to consider the external proofs before the internal.

Secondly, as we have already seen, in *Institutes* I. 8, which Calvin devotes to the external *indicia*, he prefaces his treatment with a strong separation between 'human judgment', 'arguments', 'helps', on the one hand, and the testimony of the Spirit, on the other. Nowhere, as far as one can judge, does Calvin say what B. B. Warfield takes him to be saying, that the external *indicia* are what the Spirit testifies to; rather the reverse. It is not the external *indicia* of the divinity of Scripture that the Spirit bears testimony to, but to that divinity itself, those internal and intrinsic marks, marks of style but particularly of content, that together make up its divine character. 'But our hearts are more firmly grounded when we reflect that we are captivated with admiration for Scripture more by grandeur of subjects than by grace of language.'[90]

Moreover,

Unless this certainty, higher and stronger than any human judgment, be present, it will be vain to fortify the authority of Scripture by arguments, to establish it by common agreement of the church, or to confirm it with other helps. For unless this foundation is laid, its authority will always remain in doubt. Conversely, once we have embraced it devoutly as its dignity deserves, and have recognized it to be above the common sort of things, those arguments,—not strong enough before to engraft and fix the certainty of Scripture in our minds—become very useful aids.[91]

This reflects the asymmetry in Calvin's treatment of external proofs of the divinity of the Bible that we have noted throughout this chapter. And Calvin underlines this separation between external and internal *indicia* in the concluding remarks of his treatment of the 'external proofs' of *Institutes* I. 8.

Therefore Scripture will ultimately suffice for a saving knowledge of God only when its certainty is founded upon the inward persuasion of the Holy Spirit. Indeed, these human testimonies which exist to confirm it will not be vain if, as secondary aids to our feebleness, they follow that chief and highest testimony.[92]

This could hardly be clearer; the cognitive content of the testimony of the Spirit is not the various human testimonies to the divinity of Scripture, the

---

[89] *Inst.* I. 7. 4.   [90] *Inst.* I. 8. 1.   [91] *Inst.* I. 8. 1.   [92] *Inst.* I. 8. 13.

external *indicia*, but the internal *indicia* which mark the true divinity of Scripture encapsulated in its salvific message.

But there is a final, more general reason, which we may infer from Calvin's more general position. As we have seen, for him the internal testimony of the Holy Spirit is an aspect of the gift of faith to God's elect.[93] Calvin adverts to this but tells us that he is postponing the full treatment of faith until later on in the *Institutes*. It is reasonable to think that among such people of faith there are those who would find it difficult to follow the arguments which Calvin sets out in *Institutes* I. 8, the external *indicia*, arguments to do with the antiquity of the Bible, about miracles and prophecy, about the consent of the church and the faithfulness of martyrs. But (presumably) Calvin would claim that nevertheless such an inability does not inhibit the Spirit in their case from testifying immediately to the divine character of the Scriptures. If appreciation of the external *indicia* are unnecessary in the case of some, it is hard to see why Calvin would consider them necessary in the case of some others.

[93] *Inst.* I. 8. 5.

10

The Angels

W E have now examined some central metaphysical and epistemological themes in Calvin. This chapter on angels involves a return to metaphysics (for what could be more purely metaphysical than discussion of the existence and status of angels?) but it will also act as a bridge between the metaphysical and the moral aspects of Calvin's thought which will occupy us in the next two chapters.

As we noted in the Introduction, close attention to Calvin's own words both in his writings and (more surprisingly, perhaps) in his sermons, reveals him to have an intimate knowledge of scholastic distinctions and their associated doctrines, and to have the mastery of them in the sense that he was prepared to endorse them, or to reject them, just as it suited him to do so. As Aquinas ran with Aristotle when he judged that it was appropriate, but parted company when he thought that revealed truth was at stake (on the eternity of matter say, or the nature of angelic intelligence), so Calvin, while often eschewing scholastic method, inhabited the thought-world of scholasticism.[1]

To illustrate and enforce these last two contentions we shall consult what may at first seem to be a surprising source, Calvin's *Sermons on Job*.

CALVIN ON JOB

In 1554–5 Calvin delivered a daily series of sermons on the Book of Job. These were taken down in shorthand by Denis Raguenier, a secretary employed by the French refugees in Geneva, and published in 1563, being translated into English by Arthur Golding and published in London in 1574. Passages citing Calvin's characteristic view of Job were first introduced into the *Institutes* in the 1539 edition. The sermons, delivered fifteen years later, can be regarded as an enormous expansion of these passages. As we shall see, what Calvin says at

---

[1] Although I find myself disagreeing with Susan E. Schreiner in the later part of this chapter, nevertheless the entire discussion here builds on and therefore presupposes ch. II 'The Angels Who Do His Bidding', of her *The Theater of His Glory*. On Calvin and angels, see also B. B. Warfield, 'Calvin's Doctrine of the Creation', in *Calvin and Calvinism*.

great length in the sermons is not at odds with what he had earlier taught in the *Institutes*.[2]

Like all commentators on Job, and anyone who has thought about the book, Calvin has to answer two basic questions; he has to explain in what way Job is righteous (even though he confesses his sin), and how, though Job is said to be 'perfect', the Lord may nevertheless righteously afflict him.

Briefly, Calvin's answer is that he believed that Job was a godly man, one who was upright or sound, though not perfect in the sense that he was sinlessly perfect. He was sound in that, as a believer, he kept all the commandments of God sincerely and conscientiously, even scrupulously, but not unerringly. Job may have had spasms of weakness, but he was never a hypocrite. Commenting on Job 1: 1 Calvin says:

It is sayd, that *He was a sound man.* This word *Sound* in the scripture is taken for a *playnnesse*, when there is no poynte to fayning, counterfayting, or hypocrisie in a man, but that he sheweth himself the same outwardly that he is inwardly, and specially when he hath no starting holes to shift himself from God, but layeth open his heart, and all his thoughts and affections, so as hee desireth nothing but to consecrate and dedicate himself wholly unto God. The sayd word hath also been translated *perfect*, as well by the Greeks as the Latins. But for as muche as the woorde *perfect* hath afterwarde bene misconstrued: it is much better for us to use the word *Sound.* For manie ignorant persones, not knowing how the sayde *perfection* is too bee taken, have thoughte thus: Beholde heere a man that is called perfect, and therefore it foloweth, that it is possible for us to have perfection in oure selves, even during the tyme that wee walke in this presente life. But they deface the grace of God, whereof wee have neede continually. For even they that have lived moste uprightly, muste have recourse to Gods mercie: and except their sinnes be forgiven them, and that God uphold them, they must needs all perishe.[3]

So it was right for Job to confess his sin, for he was a sinful person. He was, nevertheless, a 'sound man', without hypocrisy. Calvin also believed that while Job's comforters made the best of a bad case, using good material badly, in what he said in response to God and to his comforters Job himself made the worst of a good case.

But herewithall we have further to marke, that in al this disputation, Job maynteineth a good case, and contrarywyse his adversaries maynteyne an evill case. And yet it is more, that Job maynteyning a good quarell, did handle it ill, and that the other setting foorth an uniust matter, did convey it well. The understanding of this, will be as a key to open untoo us this whole booke.[4]

---

[2] For an at-length treatment of Calvin's view of Job see Derek Thomas, *Calvin's Teaching on Job* (Fearn, Ross-shire; Mentor, 2004).

[3] *Sermons on Job*, trans. Arthur Golding (London, 1574), 3. The original spelling of Golding's translation has been retained throughout this chapter.   [4] *Sermons on Job*, 1.

Calvin regards this remark as of some importance for his overall interpretation of the book, particularly of his understanding of the speeches of the comforters, but this aspect of the interpretation of the book of Job will not concern us in this chapter.

Calvin's response to the conundrum of the righteous Lord afflicting godly Job is to employ a theological distinction which *will* form the centre of our attention in what follows. References to this distinction recur throughout Calvin's sermons on Job, but we shall focus on his words in what seems to be the longest and most representative treatment of it, in his exposition of Job's response to Eliphaz in chapter 23, a response in which Job avers that, if he could, he would go to law with God, with the implication that if he did so he would win the case!

Calvin says this:

This matter would be hard to understand, if we called not too remembrance what hath been sayd heretofore: that is to wit, that although God be always righteouse, yet is it after two sortes. The one is that which he hath declared to us by his lawe, and that is the rightuousnesse whereby he dealeth with men and wherby he judgeth them ... Thus ye see one kind of God's Justice which will be granted to be rightfull without any gaynsaying. True it is that the wicked wil not ceasse to be always grunting against it: neverthelesse for all their grudging yet are their mouthes stopped forsomuchas their owne consciences do so condemne them. ...

There is also another kind of righteousnesse which we are lesse acquainted with: which is, when God handleth us, not according to his lawe, but according as he may do by right. And why so? Forasmuchas our Lord giveth us our lesson in his lawe, and commaundeth us to do whatsoever is conteined there: although the same do farre pass all our power, and no man be able to performe the things that he hath commaunded us: yet notwithstanding we owe him yet more, and are further bound unto him: and the lawe is not so perfect and peerlesse a thing, as is the sayd infinite rightfulness of God, according as we have seene heretofore, that by that he could find unrighteousnesse in the Angels, and the verie daysunne should not be cleere before him. Thus ye see how there is a perfecter righteousnesse than the righteousnesse of the lawe. And so God listed to use that: although a man had performed all that is conteyned in the lawe: yet shuld he not fayle to be condemned.[5]

Calvin draws this contrast between the righteousness of the law and the immaculate righteousness of God himself elsewhere; the *Institutes* from 1539 onwards recognized it, and we also find him in other places referring to the 'remarkable distinction made [in the book of Job] between that wisdom of God which is unsearchable and the brightness of which holds all human nature at an immeasurable distance, and that wisdom which is made manifest to us in His revealed and written law'.[6]

---

[5] *Sermons on Job*, 412–13.   [6] *The Secret Providence of God*, 327. Cf. Inst. III. 12.1

Having Job's own plight in mind, the distinction might be initially expressed as follows; God's own perfect righteousness is *a se*, underived and maximal, while Job's own righteous observance of the law is an instance of the creaturely righteousness of one who, though 'sound', is sinful and imperfect and who in any case has whatever goodness he has from God. It is both a creaturely and an imperfect goodness.[7] As Calvin expresses the point more generally a little later in the same passage:

Wee neuer do any good, wherin there is not some blemish insomuch that we shuld be faultie in al respects before God, if he listed to handle us rigorously. Howbeit, when God is so graciouse to us as to governe us by his holie spirit, he accepteth the goodnesse that he hath put into us, notwithstanding that it bee unperfect . . . Job knew well ynough that he was a wretched sinner, and he was not so blinded with pryde, as too beare himself in hand that he was throughly righteouse, and that God did but byte at him without cause. But his meening was if God would handle him after the ordinarie maner which he setteth foorth in his law, which is to blisse such as serve him, and too deale gently with them . . . he could well answer before him.[8]

This corresponds to remarks in the *Institutes* that 'the best work that can be brought forward from them [namely believers] is still always spotted and corrupted with some impurity of the flesh, and has, so to speak, some dregs mixed with it'.[9] 'There never existed any work of a godly man which, if examined by God's stern judgment, would not deserve condemnation.'[10]

These statements undergird and support Calvin's view of Job: he was, as Calvin repeatedly puts it, a 'believer', sincere and righteous and yet not sinlessly perfect. As such he was in broadly the same position as all 'believers'. Nor, even if he had been sinlessly perfect, would he have approached the righteousness of God himself. (Given Calvin's anti-perfectionism, and his conviction that appropriate actions are a necessary evidence of the reality of faith, it must follow that God accepts a less than perfect standard of righteousness from the believer.)

This view of Calvin's is sometimes referred to as one half of 'double justification'. Not only are Christian believers (and Calvin, disregarding the difference in dispensation, regards Job as such) justified by faith in Christ, but what that person does as a Christian, with all its attendant blemishes and imperfections, also stands in need of separate justification, and by God's grace receives it.[11]

Therefore, as we ourselves, when we have been engrafted in Christ, are righteous in God's sight because our iniquities are covered by Christ's sinlessness, so our works

[7] See *Inst.* 1. 14. 3, on God's self-existence. [8] *Sermons on Job*, 413. [9] *Inst.* III. 14. 9.

[10] *Inst.* III. 14. 11.

[11] For a helpful brief discussion of double justification in Calvin see Anthony N. S. Lane, *Justification by Faith in Catholic–Protestant Dialogue. An Evangelical Assessment* (Edinburgh: T. & T. Clark, 2002), 33–6.

are righteous and are thus regarded because whatever fault is otherwise in them is buried in Christ's purity, and is not charged to our account. Accordingly, we can deservedly say that by faith alone not only we ourselves but our works as well are justified.[12]

Thus finely balanced is Calvin's view of the spiritual life as this is instanced in the life of Job. He avoids evangelical perfectionism on the one hand and a theology of human merit on the other. Each of these extremes is unacceptable to him because each expresses the dangerous principle that it is possible for a person to perform unqualifiedly good actions, and even acts of supererogation.

So there are two ways in which we may think of the righteousnesses of God; the public righteousness expressed in his law for mankind, imperfectly achieved by even the best of saints; and the underived immaculate righteousness of God himself. Calvin refers to this as God's 'double righteousness'.[13] As Calvin puts it in his *Sermons on the Ten Commandments*, 'there is a righteousness of God's . . . that transcends that of the law'.[14] And it is by the standard of this immaculate righteousness that God justly afflicts righteous Job, afflicting him for his greater good.

This is double righteousness not in the sense that there are two standards of righteousness but two different intensities of the application of the same righteousness. By one application of his righteousness God accepts those who love and fear him, even though their obedience is imperfect: they do not fully keep the law. By another application of it the Lord is entitled to afflict even those who fear him.

But herewithall wee see also that good men are afflicted, that God impoverisheth such as have indevered too walk soundly, and that the man which is not given to any wickednesse, doeth neverthelesse linger in peyne all his life long, so as he hath much a do to go upon his leggs. And how comes that to passe? What is the cause of it? We cannot tell, nother are we able to determine. And why? For God reserveth the reason to himself. This therefore is no point of his ordinarie justice, nother must it be measured all after one rate.[15]

So it is not that the law sets forth a different standard of righteousness than that of God's righteous nature, but the law is an expression of the divine moral nature in its demand upon human beings, and so is not exhaustive of that nature itself.

---

[12] *Inst.* III. 17. 10.

[13] 'So wee see there is a double ryghtuousnesse in God: the one which is manifest unto us bycause it is conteyned in the lawe, and also hath some agreement with the reason that God hath given us: and the other which passeth all our understanding' (*Sermons on Job*, 455).

[14] *Sermons on the Ten Commandments*, trans. B. W. Farley (Grand Rapids, Mich.: Baker, 1980), 231.

[15] *Sermons on Job*, 456.

For we must alwayes bear in minde, that God's Maiestie is hidden from us, and that in the same Maiestie there is a certaine rightfulnesse whiche wee comprehende not. True it is that God hath well given us a patterne and image of rightfulnesse in his lawe, howbeit, that is but according to our capacitie.[16]

This distinction between incomprehensible and revealed wisdom is founded on the ontological difference between Creator and creature. It is because of our creatureliness that we cannot comprehend God's immaculate righteousness. Calvin is not saying that justice in God means something different from justice in man, but rather that we lack the evidence and the mental capacity and the moral insight fully to comprehend God's justice. Sometimes Calvin regards this incomprehensibility as a contingent matter, sometimes he sees it as arising from the nature of things.

But yet for all this, there is another higher righteousnesse in God: that is too say a perfect rightousnesse, whereuntoo wee bee not able too attayne, neyther can wee bee able too come any whitte neere it, untill we bee made like untoo him, and have the function of the glorie that is hid from us as yet, and which we see not but as it were in a glasse and darkely.[17]

This wil be a very straunge thing to our owne imagination. But what then? Seing that the Scripture telleth us so, it behoveth us to humble ourselves, and to wayte till the day come that we may better conceyvue Gods secretes which are incomprehensible to us at this day, and therfore we must learne to magnifie them, and to honour Gods judgements, having them in reverence and admiration, untill they may be better knowne unto us.[18]

One day we shall conceive of God's secrets better than we do today. But then he offers a qualification: 'Neverthelesse let us put the case that mans mynde were able too stye above the heavens, and that nothing coulde bee hidden from it: yet should we come short of Gods wisedome, bicause it is infinite: It cannot bee compared eyther with the deepes or wyth the heavens: for it farre outpasseth them all.'[19] But maybe the difference expressed in these quotations is one of degree, not one of kind. However, Calvin goes one step further, another *extra Calvinisticum*, as it were. One consequence of the imperfection of any level of Christian obedience is that:

Oure woorkes deserve too bee alwayes refuzed at hys hande . . . even when a man is governed by Gods spirite, and by hys grace doth walke in good woorkes; yet are all hys good works unperfecte, and God myght cast them off: yea and they are so farre off from any woorthynesse or deserving (as the Papistes imagin:) as there is nothing but fylthynesse in them . . . And therefore it foloweth that God maye damne us all. And so, wee must be fayne to hold downe oure heads, yea even without going any

---

[16] *Sermons on Job*, 171.

[17] *Sermons on Job*, 171.

[18] *Sermons on Job*, 22. See also 188, 212.

[19] *Sermons on Job*, 200.

further than to the lawe: and yet is that nothing if we come to Gods righteousnesse whiche is incomprehensible to us . . . Let us put the cace that a man had fulfilled the lawe, yet behoveth it him to reverence God with all humilitie, saying, Alas Lorde, I will still submit my selfe under thy hande, for I knowe well that all that I have done is of thee, and that there cannot so much as one droppe of goodnesse proveede out of me.[20]

When we say that it may rain we mean that there is some likelihood of it raining; and when we say that we may walk on the grass, we may mean that we have legal or moral permission to do so; walking on the grass is in accordance with the rules. When Calvin says that God may damn a Christian he does not mean that there is any likelihood of such damnation, for the Christian has imputed to him the immaculate righteousness of the God-man; nor does he mean that, morally speaking, God may punish the Christian. But he means that, having regard only to the imperfection of a Christian's subjective state, it is consistent with God's absolute righteousness to damn him since there are grounds for such judgement in his own remaining imperfection.

Calvin occasionally makes this point explicit:

But if we consider what Gods lawe is, wee shall finde that there is nothing but filthinesse and iniquitie in us. Yee see then wherefore God toucheth us after such a maner. But beholde there is yet a higher meening in this sentence, (according also as Job speaketh it for the perfecter sort:) that is to wit, that never any righteousnesse of the law shall be able to stand afore God, if hee list too deale rigorously with us. And heere a man might cast a doubt, and say: will God condemne men when they shall have performed that he commandeth and appointeth them? No, the matter is not what God will doo, but what he may doo. For surely he will not doo it.[21]

Can one not detect here a speculative tendency in Calvin, a fragment of scholastic abstraction which he was all too ready to condemn in others when he believed that they were straying from what the Scriptures actually teach? For is not Calvin here at least willing to consider the person of a Christian in abstraction from his actual standing in Christ? If there is no possibility of a person who is covered in Christ's righteousness being damned, what scriptural ground justifies Calvin in saying that God may in theory damn a person in Christ? However, even if this is speculative, it is not based upon the *potentia absoluta–potentia ordinata* distinction as Calvin understood this (and which we shall consider in the next chapter) and as he frequently condemned it. For Calvin is concerned with what God might do as the righteous God, not as a God whose will may be considered separately from his moral character. Nevertheless such speculation, for this is what (by Calvin's own standards) it seems to be, makes it easier to be convinced that the air that Calvin breathed contained the vapours of medieval scholasticism, and to see

---

[20] *Sermons on Job*, 187.   [21] *Sermons on Job*, 172.

how the later Reformed theology came to develop Calvin's theology in an atmosphere that was not altogether unreceptive to scholasticism. More on this later.

Whether or not they are tinged with a speculative spirit the basic positions that we have sketched seem quite consistent and they more or less anticipate what the final position will be on the question of how Calvin understood this idea of two righteousnesses. The views of Calvin as they have been considered so far are more or less those of the medieval tradition of the interpretation of Job, for example the position adopted by Thomas Aquinas, except for the implications his position has for human merit, or rather, for its absence. As Eleonore Stump puts it, 'When the biblical text says that Job is righteous, Aquinas takes the text to mean that Job was pure by human standards. By the objective, uncurved standards of God, even Job was infected with the radical human tendencies toward evil.'[22]

But before we can leave it at that there are a number of other issues that loom.

THE ANGELS

In chapters 2 and 3 of her book *Where Shall Wisdom Be Found?*[23] Susan E. Schreiner argues that matters are not as straightforward as I have made out. And reference to her book is the cue for the angels to make their entrance.

Schreiner's chief interest in these chapters is in Calvin's exegetical method. She points out that Calvin takes the same position as Thomas Aquinas in treating the Book of Job literally, that is, non-allegorically. Like Thomas, Calvin understands the trials of Job as tests, not as punishments; and like Thomas he sees the trials as having their ultimate rationale in the character of Job's life after death. But according to Schreiner he disagrees with Thomas over the view of divine providence to be found in the book. Thomas thinks of the Book of Job as an expression of the visibility of divine providence, Calvin of its invisibility.

It is not clear what she means by this contrast. Both Calvin and Aquinas have a clear doctrine of providence (as this is exemplified in the case of Job) and in that sense for each of them God's providence is visible in Job's afflictions. But each has a slightly different way of resolving Job's distress at the way that he is being handled. For Aquinas, the knot is untied by reference

[22] Eleonore Stump, 'Aquinas on the Sufferings of Job', F. Michael McLain and W. Mark Richardson (eds.) in *Human and Divine Agency* (Lanham, M.: University Press of America, 1999), 197.

[23] (Chicago: University of Chicago Press, 1994). These chapters are revised versions of two articles, ' "Through a Mirror Dimly": Calvin's Sermons on Job', *Calvin Theological Journal* (1986), and especially 'Exegesis and Double Justice in Calvin's Sermons on Job', *Church History* (1989).

to the fact of life after death and of the rewards and punishments then. For Calvin the stress lies on the contrast between human and divine standards of righteousness, Job forgetting (or not realizing) that his best efforts are imperfect and liable to Fatherly correction. But neither denies what the other stresses. And for both Calvin and Aquinas the moral framework in which Job is placed is strongly and clearly teleological.

What is of interest is that Schreiner thinks that Calvin's 'invisibilist' approach to the text of Job must in fact push him farther than the consistent position so far outlined, to the very limits of consistency, if not beyond them. How this view is in line with her proper stress[24] on Calvin's emphasis (again coinciding with the views of Aquinas) on the limits of human understanding of the ways of God is not made clear, but this need not detain us here. Schreiner says this:

Although Job is not punished for past sins, he was not blameless even according to God's lower or revealed justice. But we can see that the text pushes Calvin further by stating that even if one *were* just, God would still condemn him. Here Calvin must confront those verses which state that God could condemn both the just and the angels.[25]

Schreiner examines Calvin's procedure in connection with the interpretation of Job in an often illuminating comparison with the approaches of Gregory the Great and Thomas Aquinas. She shows that there are important points of connection (as well as of difference) both with Gregory (who treats the text of Job allegorically) and especially with Aquinas, who like Calvin approaches the text literally. What is significant for us is that both Gregory and Thomas work with the idea of a twofold justice in God; that is, a justice which is expressed in the law, and an immaculate or deeper justice which lies behind the law.

Gregory believed that these texts [parts of chapters 9 and 10 of Job] proved that God's justice so transcends human justice that 'all human righteousness would be proved unrighteous if it be judged by strict rules' . . . To describe the gulf that separates divine and human justice, Gregory argued that if judged by the 'secret judgments', 'strict inquiry' or 'standard of interior perfection', all the saints would be condemned.[26]

And similarly with Thomas Aquinas:

Aquinas also thinks the human justice found in a person such as Job could not withstand the scrutiny of divine judgment. According to Aquinas, when Job cried

[24] *Where Shall Wisdom be Found?* 94.

[25] *Where Shall Wisdom be Found?* 110. As we have seen, what Schreiner says here is not strictly speaking accurate. Calvin says that even if one were just God *may* still condemn him.

[26] *Where Shall Wisdom be Found?* 110–11.

that 'God would stain him with filthiness even if he were clean', he was confessing that human beings cannot claim purity before God because 'man's purity, however great it may be, is found deficient when referred to divine examination'. So too, Aquinas argued, 'divine justice exceeds human justice since the latter is finite and the former is infinite'.[27]

So Job said 'Although I were just, I could not answer him . . . he destroys the just and the wicked together . . . If I am just, still I cannot lift up my head.' Schreiner points out that according to the tradition beginning at least with Gregory the Great, such verses express the vast difference between divine and human righteousness.

And what of Calvin? Calvin 'agrees that these texts [Job 9 and 10] expose the deficiency of all human justice before God including the justice of the Law. 'Although God revealed a perfect rule for living in the Law, the Law is still only a "median" or "half justice" compared to the secret justice of God.'[28] Schreiner also points out that Calvin and Aquinas both account for at least some of Job's expostulations by his being overcome with passion or sorrow.[29] Aquinas claims that Job's reflections were 'impeded from the quiet contemplation of wisdom because of the sharpness of bodily pain',[30] and in a parallel way Calvin writes 'whensoever our affections overmyster us, it is unpossible that we shuld think of God and speake of him so reverently as we ought to do. Why so? For our affections are blind: and if we wil speake of God with such reverence as he deserveth: it behoveth us to gather our wits to us, and to keep them quiet and peasable.'[31] Other parallels can also be drawn. For example, both Aquinas and Calvin see Job's sufferings as being purposive for him.

So far, then, so similar; there is little to choose between Calvin and his medieval predecessors; all distinguish between divine and human righteousness; all think of Job's sufferings as purposive; and all hold that the righteous God could consistently afflict righteous Job whose righteousness was, in their collective view, though not perfect, yet a sincere obedience to the law of God. Each regards Job's language as evidence of the way in which his emotions led him to a distorted understanding. And Calvin adds, somewhat speculatively, as we have also seen, that despite his righteousness God may (but won't) justly damn Job for his remaining sin.

But according to Schreiner significant differences between Calvin and his medieval predecessors arise in connection with angels. Calvin departs from the medieval tradition in asserting that the angels referred to in Job 4: 18 are

---

[27] *Where Shall Wisdom be Found?* 111. [28] *Where Shall Wisdom be Found?* 112.
[29] *Where Shall Wisdom be Found?* 108. [30] Quoted in *Where Shall Wisdom be Found?* 78.
[31] *Sermons on Job*, 517. This is a recurring theme in the Sermons: see, for example, 189, 191, 257, 303, 417, 560, 579, 632.

unfallen. Aquinas, for example, commented on that verse (which, using the Vulgate, he understood to read 'Look! Those who serve Him are not stable, and in His angels He has found wickedness' (as Anthony Damico translates it)) as follows:

This statement is indeed plain according to the teaching of the Catholic faith, for the Catholic faith holds that all the angels were created good, of whom certain ones, through their own guilt, fell from the state of straightforwardness, whereas certain others achieved greater glory.

However,

Therefore since among all other creatures angels seem to cleave more and closer to God, inasmuch as they contemplate Him more subtly, they seem more stable than other creatures. Yet they were not stable. Hence, much less can inferior creatures, namely, men, be judged stable, however much they may seem to cleave to God by worshipping Him, which is to serve Him.[32]

So for Aquinas the text refers to the fallen angels, hardly surprisingly given the Vulgate *pravum quid*, and he holds that it expresses an a fortiori argument of the form: if the angels were unstable, how much more are people unstable.[33]

Calvin's view, according to which the angels referred to are *unfallen* angels, raises for Schreiner the terrifying question of whether according to Calvin God can override his lower justice and judge the angels according to the rigour of his secret justice.[34] Calvin

refuses to interpret these statements by Eliphaz [in Job 4. 18 and 15. 15] as references to the devils or fallen angels; Job 4. 18 charges the angels with 'vanity', not apostasy or rebellion. Therefore, Calvin contends, even the good angels are full of 'folly' or 'vanity' and are incapable of withstanding the severity of God's higher justice. If God willed, God could judge even the unfallen angels 'with rigor' and find them guilty, for 'what comparison is there between the finite and the infinite?'[35]

But does he raise that question? Well, let us enter the angelic realms and attempt to find out.

At first glance it would appear that Calvin is resolutely against speculation as far as the angels are concerned.

---

[32] Thomas Aquinas, *The Literal Exposition on Job*, trans. Anthony Damico, ed. Martin D. Yaffe (Atlanta: Scholars Press, 1989), 121–2. *Summa Theologiae*, 1a, 63. 1 contains a Reply to the assertion 'On the other hand we read in Job, He found wickedness in his angels'.

[33] A wide variety of terms is used to translate the Hebrew, among them 'blemish', 'defection', 'frailty', 'imperfection', and 'folly'. H. H. Rowley comments on the text 'even the purest angels are still impure in the presence of God'. H. H. Rowley, *Job* (rev. edn.; Greenwood, S. C: Attic Press, 1976), 55.

[34] *Where Shall Wisdom be Found?* 113.   [35] *Where Shall Wisdom be Found?* 112.

If we would be duly wise, we must leave those empty speculations which idle men have taught apart from God's Word concerning the nature, orders, and number of angels. I know that many persons more greedily seize upon and take more delight in them than in such things as have been put to daily use. But, if we are not ashamed of being Christ's disciples, let us not be ashamed to follow that method which he has prescribed. Thus it will come to pass that, content with his teaching, we shall not only abandon but also abhor those utterly empty speculations from which he calls us back.[36]

No doubt in adopting this attitude Calvin was taking his cue from Augustine at this point. In the *Enchiridion*, for example, Augustine has two chapters, 58, 'We Have No Certain Knowledge of the Organization of the Angelic Society', and 59, 'The Bodies Assumed by Angels Raise a Very Difficult, and Not Very Useful, Subject of Discussion'. Nonetheless, as we shall see, at least in his frequent and lengthy discussions of angels in the *Sermons on Job* Calvin lays claim, at least implicitly, to a good deal of knowledge about the status and nature of angels, knowledge which it is reasonable to think takes him some distance beyond what the Bible teaches about angels.[37]

We begin with some of Calvin's remarks on the focal verse already referred to, Job 4: 18: 'Behold, he findeth no steadfastness in his servants. And he hath put vanity in his angels.' Calvin says:

Beholde here the reason whiche hee addeth to confirme his doctrine, which is, that if God shoulde examine his Aungels, hee should finde fault in them, and he should not finde them stedfast: but they should perceive themselves to be vaine and weake creatures. Now if the Aungels be such: what shall become of men, which dwell in houses of Clay? . . . But we have too consider what is ment by the mention that is made here of Aungels. Some imagining it to be against reason that God should not finde his Aungels thoroughly righteous: have concluded, that it is not ment here concerning those Angelles that continued in their obedience to God, but of those that are falne and become renegades. For the Devils were once God's Aungels, But they kept not the state wherein God had created them, but fell an horrible fall, insomuch that they are faine to bee the mirrours of damnation . . . But we must not seke out forced expositions to magnifie the Angels. For this place speaketh of Gods servaunts, & the tytle is honorable . . . So then when all is well considered, no doubt

[36] *Inst.* I. 14. 4.

[37] There are places where Calvin touches on such metaphysical issues about angels. In his *Commentaries on Ezekiel*, for example, he claims that angels have a definite end. 'They go forward until they finish their allotted space, and then they return like lightning' (*Commentaries on the Prophet Ezekiel*, 1. 12.). I owe this reference to Richard A. Muller, 'Reformation, Orthodoxy, "Christian Aristotelianism", and the Eclecticism of Early Modern Philosophy', *Nederlands Archief voor Keerkgeschiedenis* (2001). Calvin also believed that there is an infinite number of angels. (*The Sermons of: Iohn Calvin Upon the Fifth Booke of Moses Called Deuteronomie*, trans. Arthur Golding (London, 1583; facsimile repr., Edinburgh: Banner of Truth Trust, 1987), 1187.)

but Eliphas speaketh heere, of the Aungelles that serve God, and give themselves wholly thereunto. And what meaneth he then by saying that there was no stedfast-nesse, but rather vanitie and unstedfastnesse in them?

When Sainct Paule sayth that there is none Immortall but onely God: it is certaine that hee excludeth all creatures. And yet we know that the Aungels are immortall spirites. But God hath created them of purpose, that they should not any more returne to nothing, no more than the soule of man may at any time die. Howe then shall we make these sentences agree, that the Aungelles are created to live ever-lastingly: and that there is none immortall but onely God? The solution is verie easie. For the Aungels are immortall, bicause they bee sustayned by power from above, and by cause God mainteyneth them, who beeing the immortall nature it selfe and the verie fountaine of life, is in them, as it is sayde in the Psalm (Ps. 36: 10) ... Then seeing there is no life but in God onely, and yet notwithstanding the same is no hinderance to the spredding of life into all creatures, bicause it proceedeth of his grace: wee perceyve howe the Aungelles are immortall, and yet have no stedfastnesse in themselves, but have need of God to strengthen them by his meere goodnesse.[38]

One can here observe a treatment of the angels which is parallel to his earlier treatment of Job, but with the significant difference that the remarks here apply to unfallen angels.

Calvin is here maintaining two theses: first, that the 'faultiness' of the angels lies in their nature as angels. It is not merely the fallen angels who are faulty. And secondly, that their 'faultiness' is due to their status as creatures. And so 'faultiness' (whatever exactly this is) is an essential or intrinsic feature of creatureliness.

Compare also Calvin's remarks in his sermon on 1 Timothy 6: 16:

So then it is true that the Angels are immortall Spirites, and that this qualitie also agreeth to our soules, but it is not naturall: For whatsoever had a beginning may have an ende, and maye come to decay, yea and to perish utterly. And as the Angels were made, so wee say that they have not an abiding state of nature as though they could not change, but this stedines whiche they have to continue and abide still in obedience to GOD, is a gifte given them from another, and so is also immortallitie.[39]

Is Calvin here asserting that such is God's sovereign righteousness that he may justly afflict the unfallen angels? A crucial question here is what Calvin means by God finding fault with the unfallen angels. Does he mean that God may blame them despite their unfallenness?

Schreiner says that on the basis of the Vulgate translation of Job 4: 18 'Gregory and Aquinas argued that the references to "instability" in these verses show that because the angelic nature is mutable, some angels fell and

---

[38] *Sermons on Job*, 73. See also 272–3.

[39] *Sermons of M. John Calvin, on the Epistles of S. Paul to Timothie and Titus*, trans. L.T. (London, 1579; facsimile repr., Edinburgh: Banner of Truth Trust, 1983), 621.

became wicked while others adhered to God through grace'.[40] And then contrasts this with Calvin.

> It is crucial to remember that Calvin does not place the insufficiency of creaturely justice in the context of the Fall, in terms of venial sins, or in the 'instability' of all creatures; even the unfallen angels could be condemned if God exercised the extreme rigor of his secret justice. For Calvin, the book of Job teaches that all creaturely perfection, even that of the angels, is 'accepted' by God only insofar as God 'contents' himself with the lower, median or created justice revealed in the law.[41]

Here Schreiner is bringing together in one category matters which should be kept separate: the question of the sinfulness of the creature, and the question of its instability. According to Calvin, God recognizes that the unfallen angels though not sinful are not self-sufficiently righteous but, being liable to fall are, compared with God himself, 'faulty' and in that sense unstable. 'Faulty' in this sense means liable to fail, or capable of failure, not actually failing or failed. An automatic washing machine that fails is faulty; but then so, on Calvin's view of faultiness, is a machine which though it does not break down, might do. It is potentially or inherently faulty. Only a machine that could not break down would be faultless. Developing the analogy, suppose there is a machine which is faulty in the sense that it will fail if not regularly serviced, but not otherwise. This is rather like Calvin's view of the relation of the inherent faultiness of angels to the divine upholding. As long as they are upheld, are regularly 'serviced' by the divine goodness, then their inherent faultiness will not result in actual failure. And in Calvin's view only God himself, in virtue of his *a se* righteousness, could not break down, and so is faultless. Being faultless is thus for Calvin a modal notion; someone is faultless not when they are as a matter of fact without fault, but when they are incapable of fault. And only God is incapable of fault in this sense.

The point might be expressed in terms of time; the medievals frequently explicated necessity and contingency in terms of time. Thus the reason why the unfallen angels are inherently faulty, unstable, is that their present unfallenness does not guarantee their future unfallenness. There could be a time when they fall. Will there be such a time? The only thing that guarantees future unfallenness is the divine upholding. So no unfallen angel can boast of its unfallenness; each is inherently indebted to God for continuing to remain unfallen. And what is true of the righteousness of the unfallen angels, the strongest case of creaturely righteousness as Calvin sees it, is true both of fallen humanity, and of restored Job. Job 'the believer' cannot rightfully boast or 'go to law' against God. For just like the angels, he depends upon the divine upholding for his continued righteousness.

---

[40] *Where Shall Wisdom be Found?* 112.   [41] *Where Shall Wisdom be Found?* 112.

We noted earlier that Calvin distinguishes between the righteousness of God and the righteousness of the law; the law is a derived righteousness, a transcript of divine righteousness as it is intended for men and women. The righteousness of God is underived, independent, and infallible. He underlines this distinction by emphasizing that the law is not meant for the angels.

> Let us marke then that the righteousnesse which is conteyned in the lawe, may well bee termed a perfect righteousnesse: yea, in respect of men, that is to say, according to their capacitie and measure. But this righteousnesse is not answerable to the righteousnesse of God, nor equall with it, it commeth farre short of it. As how? This will bee better knowen by the Angells. Ye see the Angells have no lawe written, and yet they frame themselves to the obeying of God. And heere ye see also why we say in our prayer, Thy will be done in earth as it is in heaven. For there is no gaynsaying, God is obeyed fully, and he reigneth in Heaven. Then do wee desire to be conformable to the Angels, and that ought to be ynough for us: for then shall we have such a perfection as ought to be in creatures. Yea but is that as much to say, as the Angels have a righteousnesse that may fully match and be compared with the righteousnesse of God? There is as great oddes betwixt them, as there is distance betweene heaven and earth. Although the righteousnesse of the Angels be perfect in respect of creatures: yet is it nothing but smoke when it commeth beefore the infinite majestie of God.[42]

Nothing but smoke because, like smoke, it is inherently likely to dissipate and vanish. Similar remarks are to be found in Calvin's sermon on Deuteronomy 5: 21, on the tenth commandment, in which he is arguing that the very conceiving of evil in the mind is sin. He says:

> For let us see if this bee to be founde in the Angels of heaven. No undoubtedly. And yet the righteousnesse of the Angels is hardly and feantly answerable to the Lawe of God. In deede there is a righteousnesse of God (as wee have seene in the Booke of Job) which surmounteth the righteousnesse of the Lawe. But though the Angels of heaven give themselves never so much to the keeping of Gods lawe: surely the uttermost that they can doe, is but to frame themselves to the rule that is given us here.[43]

It is clear why the 'law written' does not apply to the angels. Having no property, nor bodies, nor gender, nor parents, how could they steal, or commit adultery, or dishonour father and mother? Yet they are capable of coveting and so of breaking the tenth commandment. Aquinas makes the same point when he insists that the sins of the angels can only be spiritual sins. They have no passions, for without a body, a sensitive nature, passion is

---

[42] *Sermons on Job*, 186.

[43] *Sermons Upon Deuteronomie*, trans. Arthur Golding, 245. Calvin preached the sermon in July 1555.

impossible.[44] The primal sins of fallen angels are the sins of envy and pride. Though the letter of the law does not apply to them angels can do no better than observe its spirit.

So even granted the difference between Calvin and the medieval tradition of interpretation of the reference to angels which are not pure in the sight of God there is no material theological difference between the two positions. For whether the angels in question in Job 4: 18 are fallen or unfallen, the point that Calvin is making is that such righteousness as righteous angels have is, at best, a derived righteousness; they are creatures of God. If unfallen angels do not have an underived righteousness, a fortiori fallen angels do not. Both Calvin and the medieval tradition are (once again) at one here. Thus Aquinas can say, in the course of discussing the question 'Can there be moral evil in angels?'

Any creature endowed with intelligence, whether angel or not, if considered simply in its nature, can act wrongly; and if any be found impeccable, this is a gift of grace, it cannot be due to the creature's nature alone. And the reason is that a wrong act is simply one which deviates from the rightness that a given action ought to have, whether in the sphere of natural production or art or morals. There can only be one action that can never so deviate; namely that done by an agent whose power to act is one thing with the rule itself that should direct the action.[45]

The righteousness of any creature is a derived and dependent righteousness; it is not absolute and unconditioned. As Calvin puts it, in impeccably Calvinist fashion,

Monstrous indeed is the madness of men, who desire thus to subject the immeasurable to the puny measure of their own reason! Paul calls the angels who stood in their uprightness 'elect' [I Tim. 5: 21]; if their steadfastness was grounded in God's good pleasure, the rebellion of the others proves the latter were forsaken. No other cause of this fact can be adduced but reprobation, which is hidden in God's secret plan.[46]

No clearer proof could be given of Calvin's view that the elect angels' righteousness was derived, due to the good pleasure of God in confirming it. For the fallen angels fell on account of God's withholding his goodness in accordance with his decree of reprobation. Further, according to Calvin the righteousness of the unfallen angels is a righteousness for the continuance of which they are dependent moment by moment on the goodness of God for giving them that righteousness, or at least for not withholding it. While such dependence makes the angels 'subject to vanity', there is no suggestion here, in Calvin, any more than in Aquinas, that there is any chance of God

---

[44] *Summa Theologiae*, 1a, 63. 2 trans. Kenelm Foster.   [45] *Summa Theologiae*, 1a. 63. 1.

[46] *Inst.* III. 23. 4.

punishing the just angels, those very angels which he continued to uphold in righteousness by his goodness. In fact, according to Calvin the story is a little more complicated than this. It is not simply that the unfallen angels are upheld in righteousness. Calvin understands Christ's reconciliation of 'all things' (Col. 1: 20) to include the unfallen angels. The unfallen angels need a mediator, for they need pardoning.

It was however, necessary that angels, also, should be made to be at peace with God, for, being creatures, they were not beyond the risk of falling, had they not been confirmed by the grace of Christ. This, however, is of no small importance for the perpetuity of peace with God, to have a fixed standing in righteousness, so as to have no longer any fear of fall or revolt. Farther, in that very obedience which they render to God, there is not such absolute perfection as to give satisfaction to God in every respect and without the need of pardon. And this beyond all doubt is what is meant by that statement in Job iv. 18, *He will find iniquity in his angels* ... We must, therefore, conclude, that there is not on the part of angels so much of rightousness as would suffice for their being fully joined with God. They have, therefore, need of a peace-maker, through whose grace they may wholly cleave to God. [47]

There is a difference between the derived righteousness of the unfallen angels, then, and the righteousness of Job; each, being creaturely, is a dependent righteousness, but the righteousness of Job is not without blemish. Job's is the righteousness of a sincere though failed keeper of the law. Nevertheless, all, both Job and the unfallen angels, need to benefit from Christ's work of reconcilation.

Thus the 'fault' that God finds with the unfallen angels is not moral, nor aesthetic; it has a grounding in their creatureliness. For it is a fault which, given their natures, they could not avoid, not so much a moral fault as an ontological incapacity. It is not the defect of finitude per se; but it is the defect inherent in whoever has a derivative moral status. It is co-extensive with finitude and with creatureliness; it is a consequence or aspect of creatureliness. Nevertheless it does not render the angels liable to punishment.

If the angels' righteousness is derived, then a fortiori so is any creature's, and so is Job's. Being sincere and upright, a 'believer', as Calvin describes him, and a keeper of the law, Job cannot be retributively punished by the righteous God for his deficiencies. Nevertheless, because he is not without moral fault, he may be tested by divine righteousness in order to bring about in him a change for the better. Calvin makes an interesting direct application of the case of the angels to Job:

---

[47] *Commentary on the Epistle to the Colossians*, 156. I owe this reference to Jon Balserak. This commentary was published in 1548, 6 years before Calvin began preaching on the book of Job. Calvin notes in *Inst.* I. 12. 7 that the angels enjoy the headship of Christ.

Let us take the Angels for a mirrour. Behold, the angels indever to serve God: they are not tempted to euill affections as we bee: there is no rebelliousnesse nor sin in them: and yet notwithstanding, although the obedience which they yeeld unto God be pure in respect of us: it ceasseth not to bee imperfect if it be compared with the infinite maiestie of God . . . But now let us passe further. God hath promised to blisse such as walk in purenesse of hart and hand: yea, howbeit with condition to reserve always to himselfe the preheminence to iudge what is meete and expedient for oure welfare. For if God perceive that we have neede to be chastized, hee will do it: And although we have had the mind to serve him and have put our indeavoure thereto: yet will hee not therefore misse to handle us roughly sometimes, so as it shal seeme that we have offended him more greevously than the wickeddest of the world, by his punishing of us after this sort. But it is not as Job thought. And why? For it semed to him that God ought to have hild himselfe contented with the obedience that he had yelded him, and that Gods punishing of him proceedeth simply of an absolute power.[48]

But let us put the cace, that Job were as an Angell, and that he were able too go through to Godwarde according too the righteousnesse of the lawe: yet shoulde he alwayes finde himselfe behinde hande in respect of the secrete rightfulnesse that is in God. For it is sayde that the verie Angels are not able too stande afore him, if he listed to enter into reckening with them.[49]

So Calvin appears to be committed to the following argument:

(1) Only *a se* righteousness is perfect
(2) By definition, no creature can possess *a se* righteousness
(3) Only *a se* righteousness is perfectly faultless
(4) Therefore no creature is perfectly faultless
(5) Therefore no sinful creature is perfectly faultless
(6) Therefore, Anyone who is sinful but who is 'sound', as Job was, is nevertheless morally faulty
(7) Therefore, Anyone who is sound though morally faulty may be divinely chastised for their own good.

Calvin adds that the only moral justification for God's chastisement of a sound though morally faulty person is his *a se* righteousness. Further, to anyone other than God there may be no evidence at present to distinguish an act of chastisement from an act of punishment.

Somewhat strangely, given Calvin's stress on the righteousness of God being grounded in his uniqueness as God and Creator, there are places where he says that the redeemed in heaven will approach God's own righteousness. For example he says this:

For all this, there is another higher righteousnesse in God: that is to say a perfect righteousnesse, whereuntoo wee bee not able too attayne, neyther can wee bee able too come any whitte neere it, untill wee bee made like untoo him, and have the

---

[48] *Sermons on Job*, 414 (see also 273).　　　　　　　　[49] *Sermons on Job*, 172.

function of the glorie that is hid from us as yet, and which we see not but as it were in a glasse and darkely. For then shall wee bee a farre other thing, than wee bee nowe. Thus yee see why Job telleth us heere, that though hee wash himselfe, yet shall hee bee founde uncleane neverthelesse.[50]

From this it appears that the condition of *non posse peccare*, which the redeemed will enjoy in heaven in common with the unfallen angels now, is a 'coming near to' the divine righteousness. But if he is to be consistent Calvin cannot mean that this righteousness can ever be an attaining of the divine *a se* righteousness. The great ontological gulf between the Creator and any creature is forever fixed, and the righteousness of the creature is necessarily inferior to the righteousness of the Creator.

What is also rather strange is why Calvin needs to use the distinction of the twofold righteousness at all. For given his view that Job, though a sound law-keeper, is not sinlessly perfect, God could presumably afflict him for his good, justifying this by the fact that Job was not sinlessly perfect even by the standard of the law. And Calvin frequently makes this point. But in this case the very idea of a double justice in God becomes less applicable, perhaps not applicable at all. For double justice only creates even a prima-facie problem in the context of justice as retribution. If justice has to do with reform, with disciplining (and Calvin emphasizes that Job was not punished as a wicked offender[51]), then the moral connection between means and ends is much looser. Perhaps the ends would justify the means. So why does he need to emphasize the creatureliness of Job's righteousness as he does? Why does he not merely emphasize the imperfection of Job's righteousness?

Here are some suggestions. First, Calvin took seriously the question: What legitimizes God's affliction of a 'sound believer' such as Job? It is not Job's relation to the public moral law, for Job was a sincere though fallible keeper of that. It is clear that Calvin placed a great deal of value on the sincere though imperfect keeping of the law, valuing it to such a degree that he needed to invoke God's *a se* righteousness as a justification for the chastisement of anyone who, like Job, is a sincere law-keeper with a fallen nature. What legitimizes God's action is his possession of a higher righteousness, one possessed not even by the unfallen angels, but only by God himself.

Second, a clue to the answer to our question may be given by Calvin's reference to this righteousness as a 'secret' righteousness. For Calvin this is not a different kind of righteousness, but a righteousness that is administered according to God's secret will. As we shall see in the next chapter, the distinction between the secret and the revealed will of God is of prime importance for Calvin. Besides the purposes avowed or announced in the

---

[50] *Sermons on Job*, 171.   [51] *Sermons on Job*, 188.

standard of righteousness expressed in the law, or in the preaching of the gospel, God has a secret will or purpose.

Since God assumes to himself the right (unknown to us) to rule the universe, let our law of soberness and moderation be to assent to his supreme authority, that his will may be for us the sole rule of righteousness, and the truly just cause of all things. Not indeed that absolute will of which the Sophists babble, by an impious and profane distinction separating his justice from his power—but providence, that determinative principle of all things, from which flows nothing but right, although the reasons have been hidden from us.[52]

So it is always wrong for a believer to complain that he is afflicted by God's infinite power; if he does so 'hee playeth the horse that is broken looce' as Calvin put it;[53] but the believer may be right to conclude that, in order to test the genuineness or strength of his patience, or of some other virtue, he is being afflicted by God's secret righteousness.

Both here and in his remarks on the 'faultiness' of the unfallen angels Calvin incidentally throws some light on how in his view God in justice could permit the Fall. Because Adam's was a created and not an *a se* righteousness God had no obligation to maintain Adam in his original righteousness. Then Adam, having only a creaturely righteousness, could fall, and did fall.

So according to Calvin one cannot read off or deduce from the revealed will of God his secret will for individuals, not even what his disciplinary, restorative will is for sound believers. One has to rise up to God's secret righteousness to justify his ways with men and no creature can do this, for no creature has access to God's secrets.

The reason Calvin introduces and emphasizes the angels (apart from the fact that the relevant texts in Job do so!) may be that he believes that the obedience of the unfallen angels provides us with a test case of righteousness that does not consist in obedience to the revealed law of God. So righteous obedience cannot be *exclusively identified with* obedience to the Decalogue or anything similar. It is certainly not that, as Schreiner claims, there is a real possibility that God will override the lower justice and condemn the unfallen angels according to the rigour of his secret justice. It was *just because* the order of unfallen angels was righteous in another way than fallen mankind could ever be righteous in their pre-mortem state that the Lord's handling of Job could be righteous.

The unfallen angels provide Calvin with a model, a 'mirror' or paradigm case of the utmost of creaturely righteousness, and so they provide a standard against which the standard of God's *a se* righteousness, aspects of which Calvin refers to as his 'secret' righteousness, can be measured. In

---

[52] *Inst.* 1. 17. 2.   [53] *Sermons on Job*, 414.

Calvin's eyes this righteousness justifies God in taking two kinds of action: in charging his unfallen angels with 'folly' (Job 4: 18) because of their dependence upon him, though it does not justify him, in either a retributive or a reformative sense, in afflicting them. Secondly, it justifies God in afflicting Job for his own good because though (or even if) Job is 'perfect' or 'upright' or 'sound', these expressions refer to his sincerity or integrity, not to his perfect sinlessness, because he is not perfectly sinless. Not perfectly sinless, but still with the prospect of being less sinful than once he was.

> And so we see it was not his mind to handle Job according to his deserts, howbeit that we must alwaies conclude, that God even according to his law, could have sent Job an hundred times more adversitie, so as he shuld not have bin able to beare it. And why? The least offence that wee committe, trespasseth againste the maiestie of God. And I pray you what punishment is great ynough for so huge an offence, as the impeaching of God's maiestie and the casting downe of his iustice? . . . So then, Job reasoneth awry in saying that God handleth him not after the rule of his law.[54]

Schreiner goes on to claim that in the course of the sermons Calvin gradually becomes uneasy with his own theory of twofold justice because it looks suspiciously like the distinction between God's absolute and ordained power. It is hard to see what the evidence is for this. As we have already seen in earlier chapters, and will see in more detail in the next chapter, Calvin abhors the speculations that this distinction can give rise to and, if it implies in the hands of some theologians a distinction between the will of God and his nature, he refuses even to allow that the distinction could have any application. Not only that, it is somewhat ironic that on Calvin's view one of Job's failings was to imagine God's power to be lawless![55] Schreiner says that, uncomfortable with the distinction between the two justices, Calvin shifts from the idea of God punishing righteous Job in accordance with his secret, higher justice to God reforming Job by afflictions that are in accordance with it. But as we have seen on Calvin's view God does not retributively punish Job (though it is true that Calvin does refer to Job's afflictions as punishments) but afflicts him for reformative and refining purposes. But Aquinas said precisely the same, as Schreiner herself shows.[56]

It is not that Calvin draws back from taking a hard 'Calvinist' line to the effect that God could have punished righteous Job by the terms of his higher justice because he 'does not want his hearers to fear an unreliable God who would suddenly apply to them a secret justice, before which even the angels would perish'.[57] Nor is there any suggestion of incoherence or inconsistency

---

[54] *Sermons on Job*, 414   [55] *Sermons on Job*, 413–14, 422, 423.

[56] *Where Shall Wisdom be Found?* 77. Aquinas's teleological view of suffering is brought out clearly by Eleonore Stump, 'Aquinas on the Sufferings of Job'.   [57] *Where Shall Wisdom be Found?* 116.

in Calvin here. Rather, as Schreiner goes on to say (not altogether consistently on her part), Calvin is sure that God could do no such thing, not only because of God's inherent justice, but because he has covenanted not to do so. ('No, the matter is not what God will do, but what he may do. For surely he will not do it.'[58]) This is a standard application of the distinction between *potentia absoluta* and *potentia ordinata* showing, en passant, that Calvin thoroughly approved of such uses of that distinction as did not invite speculation, as we shall see in more detail in the next chapter.

So there is no evidence adduced by Schreiner which shows or even suggests that Calvin could or did say that the unfallen angels could have been found guilty and judged by God, or punished by him, or were liable to such punishment or judgement. Rather, Calvin is making an ontological point, and one fully in accord with the medieval tradition, that the unfallen angels did not have their justice *a se*. He is making an observation about the creaturely status of angels and a fortiori of unfallen angels.

Merit

Calvin disdains the idea of human merit, even deploring the use of the term.

Of course I would like to avoid verbal battles, but I wish that Christian writers had always exercised such restraint as not to take it into their heads needlessly to use terms foreign to Scripture that would produce great offense and very little fruit. Why, I ask, was there need to drag in the term 'merit' when the value of good works could without offense have been meaningfully explained by another term? How much offense this term contains is clear from the great damage it has done to the world. Surely, as it is a most prideful term, it can do nothing but obscure God's favor and imbue men with perverse haughtiness.[59]

He completely ignores the medieval idea that in order to be meritorious faith must be a free act. And here he pours scorn on the idea of merit because it is at the heart of the religious abuses that he wishes to rid the church of. Whatever the similarities in outlook between Calvin and the scholastic tradition in their interpretation of the story of Job, Calvin's views about merit take him in another direction. It appears that the phrase 'creaturely merit' is for Calvin a contradiction in terms. It is not that:

(1) Whoever has sinned cannot possess merit nor
(2) Whoever by grace avoids sin cannot possess merit; but rather
(3) Whoever could fall cannot merit; for
(4) Necessarily, all creatures could fall; and
(5) Whoever could fall and does not do so fails to sin only as a result of divine goodness.

---

[58] *Sermons on Job*, 172.   [59] *Inst.* III. 15. 2.

For these reasons to say that Calvin's disdain of merit is due solely to soteriological reasons misses the point. Similarly, to argue that his negative attitude to it is based on theological voluntarism, God by his will deciding that no human actions shall be meritorious, is also wide of the mark.[60] His objection to human or angelic merit is rooted not in the nature of salvation, nor in the operations of an arbitrary divine will (which in any case he rejects, as we have seen), but in the metaphysics of creatureliness. It is not accurate to say that Calvin's objection to merit is merely nominal, and that agreement between him and his Roman Catholic foes could be achieved by avoiding the word 'merit' and finding some other word or phrase, such as 'good works', even though Calvin would prefer that phrase.[61]

Calvin's position also has significance for the Reformed theology that followed. In the light of the way in which the doctrine of the covenant of works was developed by some in later Reformed theology as an account of how Adam would have merited eternal life if he had not fallen, it is significant that there is no mention of merit in Calvin's standard accounts of the Fall in *Institutes* and in the Genesis *Commentary*. The nearest that he comes to it is in the following rather incidental expressions. 'This exercising of the will would have been followed by perseverance'[62] and 'I speak only of the primal and simple knowledge to which the very order of nature would have led us if Adam had remained upright.'[63] There is no suggestion that Adam was put on probation to be rewarded by the divine blessing should he merit it by his obedience. Speculations about the sort of merit the obedience of Adam would have had, condign or congruous merit, for example, cannot therefore arise for Calvin and in any case would have been contemptuously rejected by him.[64] Rather Calvin seems to envisage the possibility, had there been no Fall, of an orderly progression in the knowledge of God and a progression in

---

[60] For such an interpretation see Anthony N. S. Lane, *Justification by Faith in Catholic–Proestant Dialogue*, ch. 1 'Traditional Protestant Doctrine: John Calvin'. 'If he [Calvin] is unable to see the inherent value of the death of Christ it is perhaps not surprising that he has a problem seeing any inherent value in human good works. This extends to the point where Calvin affirms that not even the holiness of unfallen angels would be acceptable to God if weighed in his heavenly scales' (39). To say that Calvin denies the meritoriousness of any creaturely works does not mean that he denied any inherent value to them.

[61] These claims are made for Calvin by Marijn de Kroon, *De eer can Goden heit heild van de mens* (2nd edn., 1996, trans. John Vriend and Lyle D. Bierma as *The Honour of God and Human Salvation: Calvin's Theology According to his Institutes*, 112, 116).

[62] *Inst.* I. 15. 8.   [63] *Inst.* I. 2. 1.

[64] Francis Turretin's remarks are consistent with Calvin's general outlook. Turretin says, 'Therefore there was no debt (properly so called) from which man could derive a right, but only a debt of fidelity, arising out of the promise by which God demonstrated his infallible and immutable constancy and truth . . . If therefore upright man in that state had obtained this merit, it must not be understood properly and rigorously. Since man has all things from and owes all to God, he can seek from him nothing as his own by right, nor can God be a debtor to him . . . ' (*Institutes of Elenctic Theology*, VIII. III. xvi–xvii).

virtue which for him is an aspect of or a consequence of the knowledge of God. Nor is he open to the argument 'Christ the last Adam merited salvation for us therefore by parity of reasoning the first Adam would have merited eternal life had he not fallen' since though Christ merited eternal life for us he was able to do so because he is God made flesh. There is no exact parity between the first and last Adams. This is why though in the *Institutes* he objects to the very term merit he is not shy about using it (earlier on) to characterize the work of Christ. Indeed he emphasizes its importance in that connection.[65] Why Calvin's willingness to consider the question of what would have happened had there been no Fall is not also speculative is that Calvin believes that he knows that God could have prevented the Fall by upholding Adam had he so chosen.

Earlier I referred to the terrifying question raised by Schreiner, the question of whether, given a twofold justice, God can override divine ordinary justice and judge according to the rigour of a divine secret justice that is purely arbitrary. In order to make headway at this point we need to make some distinctions. In particular to distinguish between what Calvin thought was Job's attitude to absolute power, and what Calvin's own attitude was.

On the first question there is no doubt that one way in which Calvin thought that Job made a bad job of a good case is in seeking to go to law with God (Job 23: 7). But Job's fault here, what Calvin repeatedly refers to as Job's 'old byasse',[66] is to accuse God of straight injustice, not to accuse God of absolute power. Job wished to contend with God because he thought that God was unjust in his dealings, and that he could prove this, something that he would have thought it useless to attempt had he thought only in terms of God's absolute power. No one can go to law with a tyrant, because a tyrant does not recognize law. The source of Job's 'bias' lies in thinking that he possessed a standard or resource of righteousness which justified him in complaining against God; Job fails to recognize that the unfallen angels have a greater righteousness than his and yet are still 'faulty'.

The verses just referred to are all occasions when Job seeks to vindicate himself. But he does not seek to vindicate himself because he thought he was faced with absolute power, but because he thought that he had a good case in law. He wrongly took this initiative because he failed, in Calvin's view, to make the crucial distinction between the two kinds of righteousness in God, and he failed to recognize that, when measured against God's secret righteousness, he was faulty.

This tells us something about Calvin's view of what it is to be self-righteous, to have righteousness from oneself. No creature can be truly

---

[65] Inst. II. 17. The whole of this chapter is an exposition of how Christ merited salvation for us.

[66] *Sermons on Job*, 412. See also Calvin's comments on Job 9: 35, 13: 22, 16: 21, 19: 7.

self-righteous, for Calvin, because such a state would presuppose a creaturely source of righteousness that is independent of God. The angels show this to be impossible in that though the unfallen angels are impeccable, they do not have such impeccability *a se*, as is shown by their 'folly'. The point may be expressed in terms of the language of rights. Like Duns Scotus before him, Calvin thought that God had no obligations to his creatures except, of course, those he bound himself to.[67] For Calvin, no creature however righteous has any inherent right before God. But the absence of such rights does not mean that God will deal with any creature arbitrarily, by acts of whimsy or tyranny. God has no duties to others, nevertheless all that he does is done in accordance with his righteous nature.

At other times, however, what seems to be a lapse on Job's part is explained differently by Calvin. For example, commenting on Job 9: 17 ('For he breaketh me with a tempest, and multiplieth my wounds without cause') Calvin says:

As concerning that he addeth *that God hath given him many wounds without cause*: it seemeth very rude geere. For that God should torment men after a sort without cause, is not only simple uniustice, but such a crueltie as he were not to be taken any more for iudge of the worlde, but rather for a tyrant. It seemeth that Job blasphemeth God here in saying that he was smitten and wounded without cause ... I have told you heretofore, that Gods Justice is knowne two wayes. For sometimes God punisheth the sinnes that are notorious to the worldward. Ye see that God chastizeth such a one. And why? For men have knowne him a shameful whoremaster full of filthinesse & dishonestie: men have knowne him to be a blasphemer and swearer: men have knowne him for a drunkard and ryotter: men have known him to be given to raking, to extortion, and to al unfaithfulnesse. Wel, when God executeth his Iustice upon such a one: there is no man but he seeth it, behold, God is a judge when he suffereth not crimes to scape unpunished. Also Gods iustice is knowne in his secret judgements, when wee see God smite and torment such folke as had no notable faults in them, but rather they had some vertues in them. Ye shal see sometimes that a whole Citie or a whole Countrie is put to havocke: yee see all is put to the fire and swoord, yea even the little babes in whom was nothing to bee seene but innocencie. Well, yee see things that to our seeming are straunge. In this cace we must glorifie God ... Yee see then what Job ment by these words *without cause*: his meening was not that God as in respect of himselfe doth punish men without cause. For (as I have sayd afore) that were an uniuste Tyrannie. But he taketh these woords [without cause] in respect of that which we perceyve.[68]

So the argument is, in a situation in which evils are public, God's punishment of these evils, when it occurs, will be correspondingly public. But God may publicly smite and torment people who have no notable or public faults

[67] For discussion on this point see Richard Cross, *Duns Scotus*, 93–4.   [68] *Sermons on Job*, 163.

(though they are sinful) according to his secret judgements. Here is another passage, from Calvin's sermon on Job 23: 4 ('I would order my cause before him, and fill my mouth with arguments'):

But looke mee heere upon Job who is a faithfull man and served God with a pure and rightmeening minde: and yet notwithstanding he is tormented with extremitie: it seemeth that God hath set him upon a scaffold to shewe there a dreadfull vengeance in him: to be short, for aught that man can conjecture, he was handled rougher than Cain or Judas. And what meeneth such a straunge maner of dealing? Hereupon Job sayeth that our Lord useth his secret Justice: that is to say, he useth not the ordinarie rule that is conteyned in his lawe, but intendeth to trie Jobs pacience, and to make him an example to the whole world. To be short, he intendeth to shewe what authoritie he hath over his creatures. Notwithstanding, in so dooing, he ceasseth not to bee rightuouse: I meene even although he deale altogither after that manner. For I have declared already, that God useth not the sayd extraordinarie Justice towards men: howbeit, Job thought so. Ye see then that God shal be righteouse still, although he proceede not according to the rule of his lawe. But now let us trie whither Job spake rightly in saying so: no surely, he overshot himself. And for proof thereof, let us take the sentence that is set downe heere: *He wil not debate with mee by force* (sayth he) *but there I shal have reason.* How, meeneth he that God wil not deale with him by force? It were to go too lawe with him if he would give him the hearing. Job then presupposeth that God useth an absolute or lawlesse power (as they terme it) towards him: as if he should say, I am God, I will doo what I list, although there be no order of Iustice in it but plaine lordly overruling. Herein Job blasphemeth God: for although Gods power bee infinite, yet notwithstanding, to imagin it to bee so absolute and lawlesse is as much as to make him a Tirant, which were utterly contrarie to his majestie. For our Lord will not use might without right, nother is he lesse rightfull than mightfull: his rightfulnesse and mightfulnesse are things inseparable. Therefore Jobs saying is evill.[69]

It seems that Calvin saw Job as wavering inconsistently from occasion to occasion. On some occasions Calvin appears to vindicate Job on the grounds that Job noted the distinction between the two kinds of justice; at other times he finds fault with Job for addressing God as if he were a tyrant. But there is no doubt about the consistency of Calvin's own position on the question of the distinction between the two righteousnesses, and the crucial role they play in his account of God's dealings with Job. In Calvin's view God dealt with Job according to this double standard, his public law and his secret justice; but it is also equally clear that God's secret justice is justice and not tyrannical power.

To say that Calvin saw Job wavering inconsistently is not to say that Calvin is himself inconsistent. Schreiner is inaccurate when she claims that Calvin was not wholly consistent, giving as the reason that:

[69] *Sermons on Job*, 413–14.

Calvin does not want his hearers to fear an unreliable God who would suddenly apply to them the divine secret justice, before which even the angels would perish. Therefore, he does not want to admit that God ever did this in any historical instance, including that of Job.[70]

We have already dealt with the angels. And far from Calvin wishing his congregation not to fear such an unreliable God we can see that for Calvin such a God was not unreliable, and that he was well prepared to warn his congregation, which no doubt included pious refugees from France, that on occasion God acts according to his secret justice to chastise even the righteous, to stiffen and strengthen their godly resolve.

There is a further reason in support of the view that Calvin did not believe that by his distinction between the double justice of God he was unleashing a capricious deity upon his congregation, namely Calvin's abhorrence of 'tyrannous power'.

True it is that men think they have a good cause too make complaints: yea, and they are so senselesse in that behalf, that when they have spewed up their blasphemies, they think they have gotten the victorie of God. But in the end they must be condemned whensoever God listeth too reply against them, and to make them feele his power and myght: not a tyrannouse power, as they have imagined, but yet an infinite power which sheweth not itself to our understanding, to say whither God be ryghtuouse or no, according too that which we perceyve of him. No, no. But God is ryghtuouse even then when we would condemne him.[71]

Wee see then that Gods using of this maner of speech, as thoughe hee were a mortall man, or were clad with our person: is to shew us that he plagueth us not like a Tyrant, ne dealeth with us by absolute authoritie, as the Popishe divines have surmized, which is a divelish doctrine. God useth no such absolute power, that is to say, no law-lesse power (as they terme it) which shoulde bee separated from hys rightfulnesse. But he useth all uprightnesse, insomuch that all mouthes muste bee stopped before him.[72]

We see here that Calvin carefully distinguishes between the *infinite* and the *absolute* power of God, and speaks approvingly of the first, while rejecting the second.[73] What is the distinction? Roughly, the infinite power of God is power that is modified by the other characteristics of God but the full understanding of which is beyond finite resources. Absolute power is the power of God considered in abstraction from the rest of his character. Why does Calvin reject the absolute power of God? Because he is not prepared to countenance, not even for dialectical purposes, the distinction between

---

[70] *Where Shall Wisdom be Found?* 116.

[71] *Sermons on Job*, 159. (See also 163; 455; 613, almightiness and tyranny; and 737, almightiness and will.)

[72] *Sermons on Job*, 302–3.　　　　　　　　　　　　　　　　[73] *Sermons on Job*, 13f.

potentia absoluta, the power of God understood as pure will, separated from the other elements of his character, and *potentia ordinata*, the power of God understood in the light of his character and purposes. The distinction understood in this way is a prime instance of the very type of those speculative distinctions that he was wont to reject both in his expositions of Scripture and in his theological reasonings. Whether this makes him an opponent of Scotus or not is, for the purposes of our argument, neither here nor there.[74]

Numerous instances can be cited of Calvin's abhorrence of the uses to which the scholastic distinction between *potentia absoluta* and *potentia ordinata* is put, though not his abhorrence of the distinction itself.[75] As we saw earlier he has to recognize the distinction. What abhorred him is the speculative thought that God might *now* act lawlessly, that he might in virtue of his absolute power, go against what he has covenanted to do. It is the divine *potentia absoluta*, understood as divine will separated from divine goodness, that Calvin repeatedly refers to as tyrannical,[76] because it is an instance of uncontrolled or unconditioned will, and so arbitrary, capricious, and lawless. The thought that such power might be attributed to God was for Calvin an utter blasphemy. But he was more hospitable to the distinction understood as that which God might have done and hasn't, and what he has in fact covenanted to do but might not have. We shall look in more detail at Calvin's attitude to the dialectic between the two powers in God in the next chapter.

As regards the infinite power of God, Calvin in effect endorses the medieval point that mankind and God are infinitely distant. For Calvin there is no question of anyone meriting anything in the eyes of God in his own right. To say that someone merited something from God would mean that God was indebted to that person, that he had an obligation to reward her, which was for Calvin an unacceptable thought. As it also seems to have been for Aquinas.

Now it is clear that there is the greatest inequality between God and man; they are infinitely far from each other, and man's whole good is from God. Thus there can be no justice between man and God in the sense of an absolute equality, but only in the sense of a proportionate relationship, so far, that is to say, as each works in his own

---

[74] A short overall assessment of the relation between Calvin and Scotus is offered at the end of Ch. 12.

[75] See, for example, *Concerning the Eternal Predestination of God*, trans. J. K. S. Reid (London: James Clarke, 1961), 117; *Institutes* III. 23. 2. *The Secret Providence of God* 'Therefore, with reference to the sentiments of the schoolmen concerning the absolute, or tyrannical, will of God, I not only repudiate, but abhor them all, because they separate the justice of God from His ruling power' (266).

[76] Calvin's abhorrence of the very idea of tyranny in God is echoed in his equal abhorrence of political tyranny, as expressed in *Inst.* IV. 20, for example.

mode. Now the mode and measure of human capacity is set for man by God. And so man can only merit before God on the presupposition of the divine ordination, of such a kind that by his work and action man is to obtain from God as a sort of reward that for which God has allotted him a power of action.[77]

In other circumstances than those that provoked the Reformation conflict perhaps Calvin could have endorsed such carefully qualified language. But he, in common with all the Reformers, was adamant that to countenance the language of human merit, however carefully circumscribed, was both unscriptural and spiritually disastrous. Mankind in a state of fallen nature was unable to merit anything, and in a state of grace is *simul iustus et peccator*. Good acts are the result of the work of God's grace within us. Even though Aquinas says that man can only merit something from God by his gift, and that man's whole power to do good he has from God,[78] nevertheless for Calvin the connotations of 'merit' were such that whatever might result from such a gift could not be said to have been merited.

CONCLUSION

Calvin's views on angels have importance for estimating his views on creaturely righteousness; they provide a kind of conceptual laboratory in which the powers of creatures can be examined under thought-experimental conditions, and tested to the limit. And an incidental feature of this is that we gain a renewed insight into Calvin's view of divine *a se* righteousness. But the chief conclusion to be drawn from our discussion is less direct than this; it is that here we find Calvin at home in a characteristic area of medieval debate. Although Calvin faults the scholastics for their profitless speculations, nonetheless here he clearly occupies the medieval thought-world without demur. He joins what he evidently regards as profitable conversations about angels. He takes over from the medievals a range of theses about the onto-logical and moral status of angels, theses which can hardly be said to have been drawn directly from the text of Scripture, however consistent they may be with Scripture.

While deliberately avoiding discussion of the orders of angels, or the relation of angelic beings to space and place (for example), Calvin nonethe-less subscribed to the view that angels were incorporeal beings, capable of intellectual and spiritual temptation, possessing, in the case of the unfallen angels, a necessary (because divinely guaranteed) righteousness which was therefore not possessed *a se*. Calvin's attitude to angels makes it easier to

---

[77] *Summa Theologiae*, 1a, 2ae, 114. 1, trans. Cornelius Ernst.
[78] *Summa Theologiae*, 1a, 2ae, 114. 2.

appreciate the strands of continuity between medieval and Reformed scholasticism, and the ease with which scholastic modes of thought reasserted themselves in the Reformed community.

But it would be wrong to convey the impression that this Reformed scholasticism represented a return to some of the extremes of the medieval period. Far from it. Francis Turretin, in his treatment of angels in his *Institutes of Elenctic Theology*, three tomes of 'Reformed Scholasticism', goes out of his way to warn against speculation; for example, on angelic knowledge he says, 'But it is more difficult to understand the mode of angelic knowledge, concerning which bold and anxious questions are raised by the Scholastics. Leaving these to them, we will only remark briefly.'[79]

There follows a reference to the question of how angels communicate with each other, on which he says, 'But what it is and how it is conducted, neither Scripture informs us, nor can any mortal affirm (whatever the Scholastics may here rashly prattle about the "speech of angels" as if they had heard them talking).'[80] And on the question of orders of angels, 'We do not deny that there is an order among the good angels, since there is no disorder in heaven . . . But what and of what kind that order is (Scripture being silent) no one ought curiously to inquire, much less rashly to define.'[81]

So while permitting ourselves to speak of 'Reformed Scholasticism' it is clearly a chastened and muted scholasticism by comparison with some of the extremes of medievalism; a scholasticism consciously conditioned by the limits of the scriptural revelation. This fact makes it all the more plausible to suppose that Calvin's thought, as exemplified in his treatment of angels, carrying with it a recognition of the central importance of *sola scriptura*, was a natural precursor of this later Reformed theology.

It should hardly be a surprise to us that Thomas Aquinas, the Angelic Doctor, could be said to have a doctorate in angelology. But what this chapter has demonstrated is the more startling thesis that the evidence of his *Sermons on Job* forces us to conclude that Master Calvin had at least a Master's Degree.

[79] Francis Turretin, *Institutes of Elenctic Theology*, VII. iii. vii.

[80] *Institutes of Elenctic Theology*, VII. iii. ix.   [81] *Institutes of Elenctic Theology*, VII. vii. ii.

11

The Power Dialectic

I T is commonly held that John Calvin took a voluntarist position over God's actions, holding that God's arbitrary will to command A or to bring about B is sufficient for the rightness of A or the goodness of B. Thus Keith Ward claims that 'One cannot satisfactorily ground the finite universe in a God whose values are wholly contingent, like Calvin's God, who could choose anything at all as a value, at the fiat of his arbitrary will.'[1]

We have already seen, in our treatment of Calvin's doctrine of God in Chapter 1, how wide of the mark such an assessment is, whether the charge is meant to refer either to God's command or to his decree. We have noted many expressions of Calvin's abhorrence of the idea that God's power might be arbitrary or tyrannical. In the next chapter we look at the question of the extent to which Calvin grounds ethical goodness in the will of God. Regarding the divine will we noted briefly in Chapter 1 that Calvin makes a distinction between the secret and the revealed will of God, one that roughly (but not entirely) corresponds to the medieval distinction between the will of God's sign and the will of his good pleasure.[2] But the secret will of God is not to be identified with what is arbitrary, but simply with what is not revealed, and perhaps not revealable.

One of Calvin's basic thoughts on the divine will in the sense of what God commands and also what he decrees is that the two sorts of divine willing form a unity. Calvin asserts the unity of the divine will in *Institutes* I. 18. 3 (no doubt thinking that this unity is itself a corollary of the divine simplicity) and discusses the objection that if nothing happens apart from what God wills to happen, and that in much of what happens God's will (in the sense of his command) is flouted, then it must follow that God has two wills which may

---

[1] Keith Ward, *Rational Theology and the Creativity of God* (Oxford: Blackwell, 1982), 172.

[2] e.g. Thomas Aquinas, *Summa Theologiae*, 1a, 19. 11, trans. Thomas Gilby. 'We draw a distinction between God's will in its proper and its metaphorical sense. The first is called his "will of good pleasure", the second is called a "will of sign", in that the sign is a pointer to his will.' So that God's will of sign is not a case of God's will properly speaking but is his will in that it consists of what is customarily taken to be evidence that a person wills. It is not accurate to suppose that 'secret' corresponds exactly with 'good pleasure' and 'revealed' with 'sign', since God may reveal some of what it is his good pleasure to do, and Calvin for one believed that he had.

conflict. Calvin says that 'it is easy to dispose of their first objection, that if nothing happens apart from God's will, there are in him two contrary wills, because by his secret plan he decrees what he has openly forbidden by his law'. Here as elsewhere we see Calvin taking the presence of an apparent contradiction very seriously, as constituting a powerful objection to his theology, and so he seeks to eliminate it.

The contradiction or apparent contradiction in this case is:

(1) God wills what he does not will.

Calvin's response to this apparent contradiction is in two phases. In the first phase he endeavours to show that there is no formal contradiction involved in God willing what he does not will, by, in the first place, distinguishing between God's perspective and the human perspective. 'Though his will is one and simple in him, it appears manifold to us because, on account of our mental incapacity, we do not grasp how in divers ways it wills and does not will something to take place.'[3] That is, our failure to discern the unity of the divine will is not because it does not have a unity, but because of our own incapacity to discern its unity.

In the second place Calvin argues that the appearance of contradiction is due to the fact that God's will (in the sense of what he decrees) is confused with his precept.[4] So that (1) is to be further glossed as (2):

(2) God willingly permits A to do what is against God's precepts.

That is, 'God's will' is ambiguous as between what God commands and what he decrees. The commands and decrees of God do not coincide. God wills (decrees) what is against his will to be done (what he commands) in that he incorporates creaturely actions that are against his law into the wider purpose of the fulfilment of his decree. (And he also wills, i.e. reveals features of his own intention which he does not actually intend, as in the biblical accounts of Hezekiah's death, or of Jonah, or of Abraham's binding of Isaac, as we noted in our earlier discussion of divine accommodation.) So those who perform acts which are against God's law, whoever they may be, are not God himself. So (1) is to be interpreted as (2).

So it is not the case that God unequivocally wills what he does not will. It can be objected that this does not by itself eliminate the apparent contradiction since (presumably) what God willingly permits he sincerely willingly permits, and what he commands he sincerely commands. So how can God sincerely willingly permit what is contrary to what he sincerely commands?

---

[3] *Inst.* 1. 18. 3.

[4] *Inst.* 1. 18. 4. Compare Aquinas: 'By metaphor God may be signified to will in us what he does not will properly speaking, and also to will what he does will, properly speaking' (*Summa Theologiae*, 1a, 19. 12).

It would be fallacious to suppose that the divine attitude must be the same overall and in every part. As Thomas Aquinas says, 'God, and nature, and any agent do what is better for the whole, and for each part as subserving the whole, yet not in isolation.'[5] Those events which are not best in every part God brings about in furtherance of some wider consideration which is best overall. Thomas reminds us that it is a fallacy to think that because some arrangement is wise, every detail of that arrangement, considered in isolation, must be wise. This is in fact an instance of Aquinas avoiding the fallacy of division, the fallacy of thinking that if the bag of sand is heavy then every grain of sand in the bag must be heavy. Although I have not been able to find a place where Calvin makes or endorses such a point, it is not difficult to imagine him doing so. What this would amount to, in Calvinian terms, is that both wills are subsumed under the one will of God's decree, for the response to what he commands, whether obedience or disobedience, is part of his decree.[6]

So one possible answer to the problem of God sincerely willing contrary things is that what God sincerely wills is the entire package. And it does not follow from the fact that he sincerely wills the entire package that he sincerely wills each item in the package separately. That is, Calvin may hold (or it might be argued on Calvin's behalf) that the question of whether God wills each separate item of the package sincerely is not a sensible question to ask. It would be like asking whether every thread in my tartan tie is tartan. Alternatively, Calvin might say that God sincerely decrees to command A and he sincerely decrees to permit X to disobey A. It is not clear that Calvin uses either of these tactics.

While Calvin attempts to overcome the prima-facie contradictoriness of the idea of two contrary wills in God, he draws the line at trying to *demonstrate* 'how God wills to take place what he forbids to be done'. In other words he indicates that we must distinguish between showing that the charge that there is a formal contradiction in some set of propositions can be rebutted, and demonstrating the consistency of the set. He believes, rightly or wrongly, that by his two arguments he has rebutted objections to the inconsistency in (1). However, demonstrating the consistency of a proposition is a much taller order than rebutting claims that it is inconsistent. For to demonstrate consistency one has to show that there is no possibility of inconsistency, whereas to rebut an apparent inconsistency involves showing that the grounds in fact offered for that apparent inconsistency are not in fact compelling. So while Calvin believes that it cannot be demonstrated

---

[5] *Summa Theologiae*, 1a, 48. 2, reply 3, trans. Thomas Gilby.

[6] Such issues are discussed further in Paul Helm, 'All Things Considered: Providence and Divine Purpose', in T. W. Bartel (ed.), *Comparative Theology: Essays for Keith Ward* (London: SPCK, 2003).

by us that there is no formal contradiction involved in God's willing what is against his will, he believes that he can rebut charges of inconsistency. Nevertheless we do not grasp how it is possible for God to will what is against his will, due to our mental incapacity.

Once we distinguish between God's command and God's decree, and having rebutted plausible objections to its consistency, Calvin believes that we can hold that the decree of God is a unity. What God decrees, as against what he commands, clearly has primacy for Calvin, as is clear in his doctrine of providence (as we saw in Chapter 4) and of course in what he says about predestination.

Calvin held the view (in common with the theological mainstream) that the unity of the divine will is consistent both with God decreeing that A occur at t1 and decreeing that not-A occur at t2. Thus God may decree that I type a particular letter this morning but that I do not type the letter tomorrow morning. And God may command at t1 what he forbids at t2. For Calvin believed (for example) that God commanded certain laws under the Old Testament dispensation which he abrogated under the New Testament dispensation. But he did not believe, indeed he strongly disbelieved, that God could decree what is formally self-contradictory. For he is at pains to address such apparent self-contradictions in the will of God. In Chapter 13 we shall discover another case of an apparent contradiction that troubles him, in his treatment of the atonement.

Two further questions now arise:

(1) Does Calvin hold that the arbitrary command of God is the highest good?

This question, whether God's will is arbitrary so that by his command God could make any action morally obligatory, are questions about the nature and scope of God's power. Let us call these the issues of *strong* arbitrariness. If Calvin's answer to this question is negative, it may still be the case that Calvin holds that:

(2) Could God have decreed other than he has in fact decreed?

Let us call this the issue of *weak* arbitrariness.

There is a third question about God's power and authority, namely, Is God's command sufficient to make what is commanded morally right? Calvin's attitude to the Divine Command Theory of ethics (as it is now called) will be discussed in the next chapter. However, before looking for answers to questions 1 and 2 in Calvin it will be helpful to have in mind features of the medieval debate about God's power, and in particular the distinction between his absolute and his ordained power. Having this distinction clearly in mind will help us to understand Calvin's position better.

THE DISTINCTION BETWEEN THE POWERS[7]

Basically, the distinction expressed in the contrast between God's absolute and his ordained power is between what God can do and what God in fact wills to do. The distinction was originally developed in the thirteenth century following a dispute about whether creation was a free act. Abelard had argued that God can only do what he had in fact done, being controverted by Lombard, who argued that God has the power to do what he has in fact not done. In an effort to uphold the divine freedom a distinction was drawn between God's ordained (or ordered) power and his absolute power. What God does and can do in the universe he has created is put down to his ordered power. But he can (or could have) done other things which do not form part of his creative plan. Thomas Aquinas expresses this in the following terms:

> Accordingly we should state that by his absolute power God can do things other than those he foresaw that he would do and pre-ordained to do. Nevertheless nothing can come to pass that he has not foreseen and pre-ordained; for his doing falls under his foreknowing and pre-ordaining, not the power of his doing, for that is his nature, not his choice. Why he does something is because he wills to do it; why he is able to do it is because such he is by nature, not because he wills it.[8]

Aquinas sees the divine ordered power ranging over all particularities of the actual world; as Marilyn Adams puts it 'a completely determinate plan of action describing everything that God ever did, does, or will do'.[9]

Perplexity about God's power may arise not only from a consideration of the scope of divine freedom, but also from a more human source. Impressed by the regularity of the natural order someone might ask, given that God has created this natural order (perhaps one that it is believed follows the contours of Aristotle's physics) can he now change it (say, by performing a miracle)? Aquinas would refer the questioner back to God's ordination. God can ordain a miracle, and if he has, then he can act and will act contrary to the natural order. But this miracle, should it occur, is clearly not an exercise of the divine *potentia absoluta*, but of the *potentia ordinata*.[10]

---

[7] I am grateful to my former colleague Martin Stone for help with this section and also to the excellent discussion of the distinction in Gijsbert van den Brink, *Almighty God: A Study of the Doctrine of Divine Omnipotence* (Kampen: Kok Pharos, 1993). See also William J. Courtenay, 'Nominalism and Late Medieval Religion', in C. Trinkaus and H. A. Oberman (eds.), *The Pursuit of Holiness in Late Medieval and Renaissance Religion* (Leiden: 1974), and H. A. Oberman, *The Harvest of Medieval Theology: Gabriel Biel and Late Medieval Nominalism* (3rd edn.; Grand Rapids, Mich.: Baker, 2000), ch. 1.

[8] *Summa Theologiae*, 1a, 25. 5, trans. Thomas Gilby.

[9] Marilyn M. Adams, *Ockham* (Notre Dame: University of Notre Dame Press, 1987), 1195.

[10] For discussion of this point, see Edward Grant, *God and Reason in the Middle Ages* (Cambridge: Cambridge University Press, 2001), ch. 5.

So one of the chief motivations for the introduction of this distinction is to safeguard the divine freedom; or put differently, to safeguard the contingency of what God has in fact willed. What God has in fact willed is the consequence of his own free decision, for it is inconceivable that he should have been externally constrained to will what in fact he has willed, not even 'constrained' by his own nature to the extent that what he has willed he could not have failed to have willed. No, what he has willed he might not have willed: this is the essence of the two powers distinction.

The reference to 'two powers' can, however, be misleading insofar as it suggests that God possesses two separate powers, operating alongside each other in harmony or at odds. Rather the distinction represents a conceptual distinction, two different ways of viewing divine power. One way to view it is in the abstract, and to ask what God viewed in this fashion could will. Another way of thinking about divine power is with reference to what God has willed, or promised, or otherwise decreed. So the question 'Can God do . . . ?' is ambiguous as between 'Can God in principle do . . . ?' and 'Given what he has done or promised or otherwise decreed, can God do . . . ?'

So it is important to understand that those who in the earlier medieval period employed the distinction as just outlined did not suggest that God may *now* act *de potentia absoluta*, overriding or conflicting with what his ordained power committed him to do.[11] For one thing, since God only acts willingly, he would not now act *de potentia absoluta* since what he has brought to pass through the exercise of his *potentia ordinata* he has willingly brought to pass. There is only one divine power and it is currently exercised in upholding and governing what God has created and promised or otherwise revealed his decree to be. The 'other' divine power is not actually 'other' in the sense that it is now exercisable, but reference to it enables us to ask hypothetical or counterfactual questions about the will of God, questions of the form, 'Granted that God has not done such and such, could he have?'

The invocation of *potentia absoluta* in the earlier medieval period (roughly, before the condemnations of 1277) was therefore used as a basis of thought experiments and consequent conceptual clarifications about the power and will of God. However, the distinction as later developed by Duns Scotus, following the condemnations of 1277, is more like that of two powers existing side by side.[12] The distinction is made by Scotus in legal terms.

[11] On the development of the idea of the two powers and the way in which it was sometimes used to suggest that God might now act by his absolute power, see the literature cited in fn. 7.

[12] In 1277 Stephen Tempier, Archbishop of Paris, issued 219 propositions threatening excommunication against anyone holding them. They were chiefly levelled against those believed to be under the influence of Averroism and Averroist interpretations of Aristotle. On the likely influences of the 1277 condemnations see Martin W. F. Stone, 'Moral Psychology After 1277: Did the Parisian Condemnation

Ordered power is the ability to act *de jure*, absolute power as the ability to act outside the same law. And evidently law for Scotus has a general scope. So God has the power, the absolute power, to supplant rule by one law with rule by another.

> Therefore, not only in God but in every free agent which can act according to the dictates of the right law and outside such a law or contrary to it—ordered and absolute power must be distinguished. Therefore, the jurists say that someone can do this *de facto*—i.e. with respect to absolute power—or *de jure*—i.e. with respect to power ordered according to the law.[13]

Because both divine ordered and absolute power are law-governed, whatever is the rule is not arbitrary, but the choice to supplant one rule by another is not itself an expression of a rule. And since the rule is general, there are alternative, equally legal possibilities. Driving within a speed limit of 30 m.p.h. I can equally legally drive at 25 m.p.h. or 20 m.p.h. I can also choose to flout the law and drive at 40 m.p.h. But I cannot choose an alternative law according to which it is legal to drive at 40 m.p.h. whereas previously it wasn't. However, the lawgiver can; that is, the lawgiver could enact an alternative law according to which whereas it was previously illegal to drive at 40 m.p.h. now it is legal to do so. Scotus would say that the lawgiver can do this by his absolute power.

> His [God's] absolute power for something does not extend to anything other than what He would do in an orderly fashion according to this order if He did it— certainly they would be done in an orderly fashion according to another order, which order the divine will could thus establish, just as it can act.[14]

Further, Scotus distinguishes between laws and judgements. Laws have a general character, governing acts of a certain type. Judgements apply the law to particular cases. So the focus of attention in Scotus's understanding of ordered power is on general laws on the basis of which God makes particular judgements.

Whereas for Aquinas, say, the ordered power of God is immutable, issuing from the immutable will of God, Scotus envisages the possibility of a change in God's ordered power, one order supplanting an earlier order.

Make a Difference to Philosophical Discussions of Human Agency?', in Jan A. Aertsen, Kent Emery, Jr., and Andreas Speer (eds.), *After the Condemnation of 1277. Philosophy and Theology at the University of Paris in the Last Quarter of the Thirteenth Century: Studies and Texts* (Berlin: Walter de Gruyter, 2001).

[13] Duns Scotus, *Ordinatio*, I d. 44 q.u.n. 3, cited by Marilyn Adams in *Ockham*, 1190. Adams gives an excellent discussion of the distinction between God's ordered and absolute power 1195f. to which I am greatly indebted. See also William J. Courtenay, 'The Dialectic of Omnipotence in the High and Late Middle Ages', in Tamar Rudavsky (ed.), *Divine Omniscience and Omnipotence in Medieval Philosophy* (Dordrecht: Reidel, 1985).

[14] Ibid. n. 8; cited by Adams, *Ockham*, 1193.

For example, He established that no one should be glorified unless he first receives grace. When His action is ordered according to this law, He acts according to His ordered power. And he cannot act otherwise except by ordaining and establishing another law—which He can do, since He contingently willed that every sinner should be damned. Thus, by doing the contrary, He establishes another law, according to which He acts in an orderly fashion.[15]

So it appears that God could act now to supplant an existing law by another law, and he can do this by an exercise of his absolute power, not in an illegal or disorderly fashion, but in virtue of freely laying down another law and acting in accordance with this new enactment. It is not clear whether Scotus thinks that this power to lay down another law is 'arbitrary' in a pejorative sense; if it is true that whatever God ordains by his power he does in some orderly sense or other, then any idea of arbitrariness must be carefully qualified. This power must of course be distinguished from the power God has to ordain that the ceremonial and judicial laws of the Old Testament are changed at the coming of Christ, a power which Aquinas explicitly recognizes. But for Aquinas that change is a temporally indexed variation within the divine, immutably willed creation.

There is a third way of making the distinction between the absolute and the ordained power of God: to think of God as a God of pure will, totally excluding other features of his character such as wisdom and justice. It is of the distinction understood in this third sense that Peter Geach has written:

A much more restrained version of the same sort of thing (the idea that God can do something wicked) is to be found in the Scholastic distinction between God's *potentia absoluta* and *potentia ordinata*. (There are various acceptations of this distinction; I am here considering only one.) The former is God's power considered in abstraction from his wisdom and goodness, the latter is God's power considered as controlled in its exercise by his wisdom and goodness. Well, as regards a man it makes good sense to say: 'He has the bodily and mental power to do so-and-so, but he certainly will not, it would be pointlessly silly and wicked.' But does anything remotely like this make sense to say about Almighty God? If not, the Scholastic distinction I have cited is wholly frivolous.[16]

Geach is surely correct to call it frivolous, though in the next section of this chapter we shall see it (perhaps unwittingly) being taken seriously by a contemporary theologian. But some of the reasons for it being frivolous will become apparent. It is something very similar to Geach's 'Scholastic' distinction that later on we shall find Calvin scornfully rejecting.

So our question 2: Could God have decreed other than he has in fact decreed? can be taken in various senses. The narrowest view involves making

[15] Scotus, *Ordinatio*, I d. 44 q.u.n. 4, cited by Adams, *Ockham*, 1195.

[16] *Providence and Evil* (Cambridge: Cambridge University Press, 1977), 19–20.

no attempt to separate the will of God from his essential nature. Employing the distinction in this narrowest way we may still ask, say, though God has made atonement for sin through the death of his incarnate Son, might he have made atonement in some other way? This question is certainly not wholly frivolous. Later on we shall see that Calvin has some time for this question, though not much. For somewhat ironically Calvin himself can occasionally be found using the distinction in the less narrow sense, for example in his earlier views regarding the necessity of Christ's death for atonement. Then there is the less narrow, Scotist way of understanding the distinction, according to which God could *now* ordain an alternative system of laws. There is not much evidence that Calvin would be sympathetic to this view, though not much evidence against, either, since he concentrates his attention almost wholly on what is in fact the case. But he never seems to countenance the idea that what is now the case might suddenly be countermanded by divine fiat, and supplanted by another law. Such a view would be repugnant to him and we shall not pay it much more attention in what follows.

The widest view, that God has the power (in abstraction from other features of his essential nature) to decree other than he has in fact decreed Calvin regards as not so much frivolous as pointless and even mischievous, since we do not have the materials to answer the counterfactual or counter-scriptural questions we might raise by means of using it. And as a consequence of our ignorance any attempts to provide answers to such questions will be fruitless distractions from what God has in fact done and said, expressions of the divine *potentia ordinata*.

The Distinction Misunderstood

Alister McGrath has claimed that the idea of the divine covenant between God and the human race emerges as a significant theological model or motif in late medievalism as the preferred way of resolving the dialectical tension that arises from the power distinction, the distinction between the *potentia absoluta* and *potentia ordinata*. As we have seen, in first elaborating the distinction the medievals argued that on its accepted understanding God by his absolute power could do anything that does not entail a contradiction. But if all we know of what God might will (in the sense of what he might decree) is that it will not take the form of a formal contradiction then clearly this might be thought to leave us in a situation of radical uncertainty, not knowing from moment to moment what God might will. On the other hand, the thought that God might act out of necessity seems intolerable because it appears to be a clear infringement of his sovereignty and aseity. How is this tension to be resolved?

According to McGrath, it is resolved by God, by his ordained power, promising certain things, and so binding himself in respect of the future, thus establishing himself a reliable and faithful God. The uncertainty of the naked will of God on the one hand and the certainty of a will bound by a necessity external to it on the other is resolved, in dialectical fashion, by the idea of God's covenant promise.

McGrath writes:

> The essential point made by those who appealed to the dialectic between the powers of God was that the present created order, including the order of salvation, did not result from God acting out of necessity. Out of an initial set of potentialities open to actualization by God, only a subset was thus actualized. The argument runs thus. Before his decision concerning which potentialities should be actualized, God was at liberty to select any, subject solely to the condition that this should not involve contradiction. The fact that it is impossible to construct a triangle with four sides is thus not understood to involve a restriction upon God's course of action. Once God has determined which potentialities shall be actualized, and executed this decision, however, he is under a self-imposed restriction in regard to his actions. In other words, once God has created a certain order, he is under an obligation to himself to respect this order.[17]

This diagnosis of how the appeal to divine absolute power is to be resolved, though widely held, seems to be somewhat implausible, at least as McGrath explains it. For if the fundamental dialectical tension is between God's absolute power, a tyrannical and arbitrary power, limited only by what is abstractly possible from a logical point of view and by no other consideration, and on the other hand what God has in fact ordained, a covenantal framework, how could the fact that God has made a covenant guarantee its reliability since, *ex hypothesi*, a tyrant has ordained it? The covenant is the product of God's strongly aribitrary will. This is even more the case if what God might conceivably will is temporally indexed. Might God will at one time what he forbids at some later time? For on this understanding of *potentia absoluta* the ordination at a time must itself be an act of arbitrary power, and therefore liable to be rescinded or countermanded by divine whim at any later time. Where does the 'self-imposed restriction to respect the established order' come from if not from God's self? But how could this be relied upon if God, *ex hypothesi*, is a tyrant? Does someone who rules by arbitrary fiat recognize obligations? Such power to countermand cannot be

---

[17] Alister McGrath, *The Intellectual Origins of the European Reformation* (Oxford: Blackwell, 1987), 20. See also Alister McGrath, *Justitia Dei: A History of the Christian Doctrine of Justification* (2nd edn.; Cambridge: Cambridge University Press, 1998), 120.

resolved by indexing God's will to what he wills at some particular time, the enacting of a covenant, say, but arises from God's arbitrary will.

The only explanation for McGrath's argument is that he is understanding the two powers distinction in its wide sense,[18] the sense regarded by Geach as frivolous and the one that (as we shall see in due course) Calvin has no time for. Only on this reading of the distinction can McGrath say, 'While the divine freedom was safeguarded through the absolute power of God, the divine reliability was safeguarded through the ordained power, as expressed in the *pactum*.'[19] But as we have seen this proposal fails.

McGrath's frequent linking of *potentia ordinata*, the covenant theme, and divine reliability[20] carries the obvious converse that in his exposition of the emergence of the covenant motif from the power dialectic he sees the *potentia absoluta* linked with divine *un*reliability. But why should this be? Only by reading the distinction in the wider, 'frivolous', sense. Read in the narrower way, though God is free (as the distinction between the two powers allows him to be), what he has freely chosen to will (and any alternative he might have freely chosen to will) will each be in accordance with his wise and good nature and so will be paradigmatically reliable. So on this narrower sense, the limits of divine power are narrower than the limits of logic; for according to this sense God cannot do evil, or act foolishly or unreliably, say.

So McGrath's discussion[21] on the logical relation between the dialectic between the two powers, the development of covenant theology, and the onset of what he calls theological pluralism in late medievalism seems inept. Perhaps God could freely have chosen to actualize other potentialities than this, the actual world. We shall shortly come to see the significance of this possibility. But any alternative world actualizable by God must be consistent with God's nature whatever character that nature has, tyrannical or otherwise. Put otherwise, the fact that a God possessed of absolute power alone ordains X will not prevent the possibility of his absolute power countermanding X at some arbitrary point in the future, then reinstating it, then countermanding the reinstatement, and so on.

We noted in the last chapter, in the discussion of angels, that Calvin rejects the idea of merit in the creature, whether human or angelic, because a creature necessarily depends upon God for uprightness. Nothing that could

---

[18] This is plausible from a historical perspective in that in the later medieval period, after Ockham, the distinction tends to be understood as widely as possible. So it was asserted (by Gabriel Biel, for example) that God could *de potentia absoluta* without injustice annihilate someone who loves him, make someone hate him, lie, assume human nature and then allow it to become the nature of another person. (These examples are taken from Gijsbert van den Brink, *Almighty God*, 84.)

[19] McGrath, *Justitia Dei*, 127.   [20] McGrath, *Justitia Dei*, 121, 124, 127.

[21] McGrath, *Intellectual Origins*, 20–1.

(apart from the divine upholding) fall into sin can act meritoriously, for such an individual fails to sin only by God's efficacious support. So any covenantal arrangement with the race cannot be on the basis that God will faithfully reward meritorious acts. But to say that Calvin could find no place for creaturely merit does not mean that any covenant God made was simply in order to domesticate his otherwise untameable, capricious nature, or that any such arrangement was purely an act of God's arbitrary will.

Perhaps there has been some confusion in the interpretation of Calvin's view of the divine will due to the fact that, as McGrath's discussion suggests, on one interpretation the divine *potentia ordinata* is made *equivalent* to God's revealed will, in McGrath's case to God's covenant promise. It would seem that if one side of the distinction is understood in this way then it is natural to understand the other side, *potentia absoluta*, as being what gives rise to the secret will of God. Whatever the plausibility of this as a way of understanding some uses of the distinction (and it has to be said that it does not seem very plausible), this way would not satisfy Calvin, since for him the secret will of God is so merely because some of what God has decreed he has also, for good reason, kept to himself. In other words, as we saw in earlier discussion, the distinction between the secret and the revealed will is an epistemological one, not a distinction in the divine nature itself. The fact that God possesses absolute power does not mean that God might choose now to will simply anything, even though what he wills may surprise us. So we may rest easy in our beds.

Elsewhere[22] McGrath makes a more convincing point. Deploying the distinction between the absolute and the ordained power of God (provided that the distinction is not being used in its widest sense) is one way of saying that while God does not act out of necessity he nevertheless acts reliably. This distinction can have a theological use even among those who, like Calvin, regard God's creative and redemptive activities as being free and so not necessitated. The covenant is what God has freely chosen to establish. And because whatever he freely chooses to do must be immutable, since God is immutable, his covenant promise is immutable; it has about it the necessity of the consequent, as Calvin shows in his adoption of the *necessitas consequentis–necessitas consequentiae* distinction elucidated once again by his favourite illustration about Christ's bones.

What God has determined must necessarily so take place, even though it is neither unconditionally, nor of its own peculiar nature, necessary. A familiar example presents itself in the bones of Christ. When he took himself a body like our own, no sane man will deny that his bones were fragile; yet it was impossible to break them

---

[22] McGrath, *Intellectual Origins*, 78.

[John 19: 33, 36]. Whence again we see that distinctions concerning relative necessity and absolute necessity, likewise of consequent and consequence, were not recklessly invented in schools, when God subjected to fragility the bones of his Son, which he had exempted from being broken, and thus restricted to the necessity of his own plan what could have happened naturally.[23]

There is another way of cutting this particular cake. All in the medieval period are agreed that not even God who is omnipotent can do what is logically impossible. But what is logically possible depends on two things. One is the formalities of logic. Not even God can bring it about that something can both exist and not exist, be both round and not round, and so forth. The other factor is what we might call the requirements of the nature of things, if any. If man is essentially rational, then not even an omnipotent God can create a man who is not rational. If man is essentially animal, then not even an omnipotent God can create a man who is not an animal. If time is essentially unidirectional, then not even God can bring it about that what happened did not happen, and so on.

While all may fairly readily agree on the formalities of logic, the impositions of the requirements of the nature of things are obviously much more debatable, since they raise fundamental metaphysical issues. Perhaps there are no essences; perhaps there are essences but we never know what they are; perhaps we confuse essences with *de facto* regularities. There is plenty of room for debate here, and therefore plenty of room for differing over what the exact scope of divine power might be, over what God could exercise *potentia absoluta*. But these debates will inevitably be subordinate to the wider and the narrower readings of such power. Suppose someone who takes divine *potentia absoluta* in the narrowest sense, and is a metaphysical anti-essentialist about creatures; even for such a person God will not and cannot ordain what is inconsistent with his nature.

This touches on another reason for Calvin's dislike of speculation: it is due to his refusal to get embroiled in detailed questions about the nature of things, other than the divine nature, either because he thought that they were inherently profitless, or (more likely) because he thought that they were the business of the philosopher, not of the theologian.

THE DISTINCTION AFFIRMED

After this rather lengthy *excursus* we now return to our two questions: (1) Does Calvin hold that the arbitrary will of God is the highest good? and

---

[23] *Inst.* I. 16. 9. Besides its use in *A Defence of the Secret Providence of God* (235), noted in Ch. 4, Calvin also employs it in *Concerning the Eternal Predestination of God*, 170.

(2) Could God have decreed other than he has in fact decreed? It may seem that an affirmative answer to (1) would entail that God could have willed anything not formally self-contradictory. For the whole force of asserting (1) is to make the point that God's arbitrary willing of something could have been other than it is, and that therefore some other value could have been the highest good than those values that are at present good. But it is possible to hold that God's willing of something could have been other than it is in a non-frivolous sense, a sense in which it entails (2). God could have decreed other than he has in fact decreed, without being committed to (1). For it is perfectly possible to hold that what is brought about by God or willingly permitted by him is not the result of God's arbitrary fiat, and good because of that, while at the same time holding that God could have willed other than he has in fact willed. For otherwise the denial of (2) would entail a necessitarianism such that the actual world is the only world that God could have created. And while Calvin holds that the will of God is the necessity of things, he repeatedly tells us that he does not hold that God's willing of X is itself necessary.

Even though Calvin nowhere discusses the freeness of God in creation in formal terms we may refer to Calvin's discussion of the creation in *Institutes* I. 14 for clues about its freeness. There Calvin touches on the question of why God did not create the universe earlier. Evidently he held the view that there were times before the first moment of creation for he talks about God 'delaying' the creation. He does not, as Augustine did, dismiss this idea either on the grounds that the very idea of a delay is incoherent or on the grounds that creation is *cum tempore*, even though he was clearly aware of Augustine's discussion.[24] Nor does he simply say that God was not free to create the universe sooner or later than he actually did, but he deploys the characteristically Calvinian argument that such an inquiry is unlawful and of no benefit.

And indeed, that impious scoff ought not to move us: that it is a wonder how it did not enter God's mind sooner to found heaven and earth, but that he idly permitted an immeasurable time to pass away, since he could have made it very many millenniums earlier, albeit the duration of the world, now declining to its ultimate end, has not yet attained six thousand years. For it is neither lawful nor expedient for us to inquire why God delayed so long, because if the human mind strives to penetrate thus far, it will fail a hundred times on the way. And it would not even be useful for us to know what God himself, to test our moderation of faith, on purpose willed to be hidden. When a certain shameless fellow mockingly asked a pious old man what God had done before the creation of the world, the latter aptly countered that he had been building hell for the curious.[25]

---

[24] Augustine, *Confessions*, XI. x. 12.   [25] *Inst.* I. 14. 1.

What Calvin implies is as significant as what he says. It is unlawful and useless to inquire why the universe was not created earlier not because the universe could not have been created earlier but because the question is profitless. So the universe could have been created earlier. So God was free to create the universe earlier had he so wished. So the creation of the universe was (to this extent at least) free. So the universe is not necessitated in every detail by the divine nature because the time of its creation, a not insignificant detail, was not necessitated. As we might expect, Calvin does not inquire further into how such contingency is consistent with divine eternity in the way that many medievals did;[26] nevertheless, the freedom of God in creation is implied if not asserted here. We ought not to exceed the bounds of God's operations in time and space to ask 'What if?' questions, even though the questions themselves may be perfectly intelligible.

Further, for Calvin to deny divine freedom would seem to be at odds with the freeness of God's grace which is so central to his evangelical theology. Divine freeness not only in the sense that there was nothing in creation that required God to be gracious, but freeness because nothing in God himself required it and because it is (according to God's unfathomable election) freely bestowed on some human beings and not on others. God could have justly withheld his mercy, and he could have been merciful to Smith rather than to Jones.

Who then, I pray, will say it is not meet that God should have in his own hand and will the free disposing of his graces, and should illuminate such nations as he wills? To evoke the preaching of his Word at such places as he wills? To give progress and success to his doctrine in such way and measure as he wills? To deprive the world, because of its ungratefulness, of the knowledge of his name for such ages as he wills, and according to his mercy to restore it when he again wills?[27]

This is indeed Calvin's position. He denied (1) and affirmed (2) in its first sense. So let us look further at his attitude to (1).

In the course of dealing with objections to the doctrine of predestination[28] Calvin discusses the righteousness of God's will. He claims that, in the matter of election and reprobation, God's will is the rule of all righteousness.

For his will is, and rightly ought to be, the cause of all things that are. For if it has any cause, something must precede it, to which it is, as it were, bound; this is unlawful to imagine. For God's will is so much the highest rule of righteousness that whatever he wills, by the very fact that he wills it, must be considered righteous. When, therefore, one asks why God has so done, we must reply: because he has willed it. But if you

---

[26] See, for example, Norman Kretzmann, 'Ockham and the Creation of the Beginningless World', *Franciscan Studies*, (1985) and the literature cited therein.

[27] *Inst.* II. 11. 14.					[28] *Inst.* III. 23. 2.

proceed further to ask why he so willed, you are asking for something greater and higher than God's will, which cannot be found.[29]

This may seem to be a version of theological voluntarism implied in (1). Some have thought that they detected the influence of Scotus or other kinds of voluntaristic influences at points such as these, and Calvin may be thought to be under the influence of Scotistic forms of thought, as has often been said.[30] However, Calvin is emphatic that he is not prepared to separate the will of God from the character of God. For he goes on to state:

And we do not advocate the fiction of 'absolute might'; because this is profane, it ought rightly to be hateful to us. We fancy no lawless god who is a law unto himself. For, as Plato says, men who are troubled with lusts are in need of law; but the will of God is not only free of all fault but is the highest rule of perfection, and even the law of all laws. But we deny that he is liable to render an account; we also deny that we are competent judges to pronounce judgment in this cause according to our own understanding.[31]

This could hardly be clearer. And it could hardly be clearer that in saying what he does Calvin shows himself to be familiar with the medieval power distinction, even if he was familiar with it in what he regarded as its nadir, its use in the Geachian frivolous sense (in late medieval discussion and especially by his contemporary theologians of the Sorbonne) rather than in its earlier and more acceptable use.

When Calvin says that if you proceed to ask why God has willed as he has you are asking for something higher than God, he is presumably also making a point about the regress of explanation. While it makes sense to answer the question 'Why did God ordain X?' with the answer 'Because God willed it so', it makes no sense to ask 'Why did God will it to be so?' Asking that question suggests that the questioner has not understood the previous answer. There is no higher cause. This point would hold independently of theological commitments: every explanation comes to a halt at some point. However, in addition to this Calvin held that the will of God which is the rule of righteousness is the will of a holy God. In virtue of his godhood he is not liable to give an account of his ways; and in any case in view of the poverty of our understanding we are not competent to plumb the depths of his will. Nevertheless we can be sure, in virtue of who God is, that what he wills is just.

---

[29] *Inst.* III. 23. 2.

[30] For example, François Wendel, *Calvin: The Origins and Development of his Religious Thought*, 127–9. A. N. S. Lane also favours such a voluntarist understanding (*Justification*, 39), though he himself has shown how scanty the documentary evidence is for any direct influence of Scotus's writings on Calvin (*John Calvin: Student of the Church Fathers*, 24). The lack of Scotus's influence here is reinforced by the very different positions Scotus and Calvin took on the question of free will as we shall note in the brief Excursus at the end of this chapter. [31] *Inst.* III. 23. 2.

This general conclusion about Calvin's theology (which we already advanced in Chapter 1) is further borne out by his remarks on the ill-advisedness of pitting God's might against his truth[32] and of not separating justice from power,[33] and his insistence that the divine ordinances are just, even though this justice may be presently hidden from us.[34]

So Calvin denies (1) but—as we shall now go on to see—he affirms (2) in its non-frivolous sense. It is in terms of his affirmation of (2) that we must understand his doctrine of the covenant (and of the atonement of Christ which is at the heart of his understanding of the covenant). We shall consider aspects of the atonement later. In maintaining this idea of the covenant it becomes clear that Calvin is firmly in one line of medieval discussion of the matter. God could have ordained some other arrangement than the covenant of grace. But given that he has ordained or decreed this covenant, then it has an immutability of necessity to it, the necessity of the consequent, and an immutability that is based not upon the arbitrary will of God but on his utter trustworthiness.

THE DISTINCTION DENIED

Contrary to this understanding of God's power, and rather surprisingly, David Steinmetz has argued in a couple of places[35] that Calvin rejects any distinction between the absolute and the ordained power of God. 'Like Scotus and Ockham, Calvin wishes to preserve the transcendent freedom of God and to stress the radical contingency of the world and of all created being. It therefore comes as a shock that Calvin refuses to accept the very distinction they used to safeguard God's transcendent freedom and to underscore the world's radical contingency.'[36] In line with the previous discussion my argument will be that Calvin does not reject all versions of the distinction but that he accepts the first version. Indeed, 'accepts' hardly does justice to the central role that this idea plays in his theology.

Steinmetz claims later that Calvin's rejection of the distinction between the absolute and ordained power of God is a rejection of the distinction as such and not a protest against its abuse.[37] But this is a misunderstanding. It is true that Calvin does not like the term 'absolute power' any more than he favours talk of creaturely merit or free will. 'Absolute power' or 'absolute will' (*absoluta voluntas*) has been used by the Sorbonnists in a bad,

---

[32] *Inst.* II. 7. 5.   [33] *Inst.* I. 17. 2.   [34] *Inst.* III. 23. 9.

[35] 'Calvin and the Absolute Power of God', in *Calvin in Context* (New York: Oxford University Press, 1995) and 'The Scholastic Calvin' in Carl R. Trueman and R. S. Clark (eds.), *Protestant Scholasticism: Essays in Reassessment* (Carlisle: Paternoster Press, 1999).

[36] *Calvin in Context*, 41.   [37] *Calvin in Context*, 49.

blasphemous sense, and so it is better not to use it at all. But this does not mean that Calvin rejects the thought that God's power is not conditioned by anything outside himself. We shall see in a moment that in this connection he prefers to speak of the 'infinite power' of God.

Furthermore, before being tempted to go along with Steinmetz's suggestion we need to reflect on what the wholesale rejection of every distinction between the absolute/infinite and the ordained power of God would amount to. Steinmetz presumably does not simply mean that Calvin recognizes that there is such a distinction but refuses to apply it. The distinction may be rejected because it is thought that every expression of God's power is an expression of his absolute power. It is not hard to see that Calvin, with his love of 'order' and his contempt for the Sorbonnists, finds this totally unacceptable. Or it may be thought that every expression of God's power is to be thought of as an expression of his ordained power, perhaps conveying the Abelardian point that God can only do what he has in fact done. Neither of these possibilities, viewed a priori, looks very appetizing. So let us look at the evidence from Calvin which Steinmetz cites in support of his view that Calvin rejects the distinction as such.

Steinmetz cites a number of passages where Calvin appears to reject the distinction. The first is from Calvin's commentary on Genesis 18: 18 ('Is anything too hard for the Lord?').

In this way the Papists plunge themselves into a profound labyrinth, when they dispute concerning the absolute power of God. Therefore, unless we are willing to be involved in absurd dotings, it is necessary that the word should precede us like a lamp; so that his power and will may be conjoined by an inseparable bond.[38]

It seems clear that here Calvin is simply reaffirming what we have seen that he maintains in the *Institutes* and elsewhere, that discussion of God's power in abstraction from what he has in fact willed is speculative and profitless. But his words ought not to be taken as a claim that there is no distinction between God's power and his will to be made. Otherwise his objection to the 'Papists' makes no sense. For Calvin is clearly endorsing a distinction between absolute power on the one hand and inseparable power and will, which is, he believes, how we are taught about God's will in his word. But if Steinmetz is correct, and Calvin rejects the distinction *tout court*, then this for Calvin amounts to a distinction without a difference. Whatever Calvin may be saying in this passage, what he is not doing is denying that God could have willed what he did not in fact will.

And the second is from Calvin's commentary on Isaiah 23: 9:

---

[38] Quoted in Steinmetz, *Calvin in Context*, 46.

The invention which the Schoolmen have introduced, about the absolute power of God, is shocking blasphemy. It is all one as if they said that God is a tyrant who resolves to do what he pleases, not by justice, but through caprice. Their schools are full of such blasphemies, and are not unlike the heathens, who said that God sports with human affairs.[39]

Again, what Calvin is objecting to is not the freedom of God to have done other than he has done, a freedom that is absolutely central to his own theology but rather, as Steinmetz notes,[40] to the consideration of the power of God in abstraction from the other features of his essence, notably (in this instance) his justice, and he further objects to the employment of that abstract possibility (perhaps in a Scotist form of it) as a warrant for claiming that it is now possible for God to do things which manifestly he has covenanted not to do, or not covenanted to do; or (less boldly) employing the distinction in a way that might provide grounds for speculating about what God might have decreed but has not.

The third context cited is predestination. Discussing the election of Jacob and the rejection of Esau in Romans 9 Calvin says:

And yet Paul does not, by thus reasoning, impute tyranny to God, as the sophists tri-flingly allege in speaking of his absolute power. But whereas he dwells in inaccessible light, and his judgments are deeper than the lowest abyss, Paul prudently enjoins acquiescence in God's sole purpose; lest, if men seek to be too inquisitive, this immense chaos should absorb all their senses.[41]

Clearly, in discussing election and predestination Calvin must be allowing that God could have done other than he in fact did. But, Calvin says, this is not tyranny and cannot be. God acts from reasons, he has 'judgment', a 'purpose'. So the implication is that God could have chosen Esau over Jacob had he had a good reason to do so even though we cannot possibly imagine what his reason for choosing the one rather than the other might be. The sophists triflingly allege that God could act as a tyrant when they consider God's absolute power, but (the implication surely is) one can and must use that distinction non-triflingly.[42] God cannot act tyrannically, but he could have acted differently. Why he did not choose to do so is hidden from us but (obviously) not from God himself.

So a careful reading of these passages, taking into account what we have seen that Calvin says elsewhere, shows that he is not committing himself to a wholesale rejection of the distinction between the absolute and the ordained

---

[39] Quoted by Steinmetz, *Calvin in Context*, 47.   [40] *Calvin in Context*, 49.

[41] Quoted by Steinmetz, *Calvin in Context*, 47.

[42] For a reference to Calvin's distinction between God having a reason and us discerning that reason, see R. J. Mouw, *The God Who Commands* (Notre Dame: University of Notre Dame Press, 1990), 64.

power of God. What he does (as might be expected from our previous discussion) is to recognize the fact of God's absolute power (as for example Aquinas did),[43] but to refuse to speculate or dispute about it in an abstract way, and most certainly never to countenance a theological method that understood God's power in purely voluntaristic, tyrannical terms. God's power and the other features of his character are necessarily joined, (because God is one, is simple) and this (Calvin would say) is sufficient for us for present purposes. The trouble is not with the absolute power of God as such, but with inventions about it, or speculations based on the idea of the pure will of God in abstraction from his wisdom and justice, or speculations about what God might have done but has not. The schoolmen, he says, have invented certain things *about* the absolute power of God and in the process have distorted the idea.

What bothers Calvin about such scholastic inventions is that they open the door to two unwelcome possibilities. By their isolation of the power of God from other features of his essence the scholastics allow tyranny to be imputed to God, and this is blasphemous. Further, such speculations have the potential to attract our attention. If we find ourselves attracted by such inventions and speculations we will be distracted from what God has in fact ordained, and especially what he has made known to us in his word. But refusing to be attracted by sophistical distortions of an idea does not warrant a principled rejection of God's absolute power where this is properly understood, and Calvin sees this.

Despite all of this, however, it may seem that occasionally Calvin himself adheres to a fairly tyrannical view of God, as in the previously (and frequently) cited sentence 'God's will is so much the highest rule of righteousness that whatever he wills, by the very fact that he wills it, must be considered righteous'.[44] But this sentence can be readily interpreted in a way which is consistent with what he elsewhere holds about the nature of God's power. It is mistaken, in my view, to take Calvin as saying that if in the expression 'A decrees X' (where X is any action we may care to substitute and 'God' is substituted for A) then X is thereby rendered a morally good action. This is the fiction of absolute power that he rejects. Rather what he is saying is something weaker and less startling than this, that if in fact God decrees X or has decreed X then by that very fact his decreeing of it is righteous even though we may not immediately see this, may not know the reasons that he has for decreeing it, and may in fact think what he has done cannot be just. This is compatible with the claim that, necessarily whatever God decrees he

[43] *Summa Theologiae*, 1a. 25. 5: 'We conceive of understanding and wisdom as directing, will as commanding, and power as executing; as for what lies within power as such, God is said to be able to do it by his absolute power.'   [44] *Inst.* III. 23. 2.

has reasons for decreeing, while the 'fiction' of divine absolute power is not compatible with this. For Calvin the inscrutable decree of God is therefore not a decree of pure power divorced from all other features of the divine nature, it is the decree of a necessarily holy and righteous God. We cannot presently scrutinize the reasons for the decree because they have not been made available to us. Clearly the significant point for Calvin is that there must be reasons for what God does, reasons consistent with and expressive of his entire nature, and therefore this cannot be the sort of absolute power which, according to Calvin, the scholastics profitlessly dispute about.

Here is Calvin making this very point (in Arthur Golding's stylish translation) in his 88th sermon on the Book of Job (and at the same time, incidentally, affirming the unity of the divine nature):

Undoutedly whereas the doctors of Sorbon say that God hath an absolute or lawlesse power, it is a divelish blasphemie forged in hell, for it ought not once to enter into a faithfull mannes head. Therfore we must say that God hath an infinite or endlesse power, whiche notwithstanding is the rule of all righteousnesse. For it were a rending of God in peeces, if we shuld make him almightie without being alrighteous. True it is, that his righteousnesse shall not always be apparant unto us, but yet ceaseth it not too continue evermore sound and unnappayred. Wee must not measure Gods ryghteousnesse by our own conceyte, (for that were too great a streytening of it:) but we muste alwayes bee fully resolved, that Gods myghtfulness can not be separated from his ryghtfulnesse, bycause God can not be dismembred.[45]

And again from his *Bondage of the Will*:

While creatures by nature have many attributes which are not within the scope of the will and are not subject to the choice of the will, yet to imagine anything comparable in God is a blasphemous fabrication. For he is what he is by nature in such a way that he wills to be so, and he also wills what he wills in such a way as to have it naturally. For since God's goodness, wisdom, power, righteousness, and will are united together by a kind of, so to speak, circular connection, it is the work of a wicked, devilish imagination to break this bond apart. Since, then, God wills to be whatever he is, and that of necessity, there is no doubt that just as he is good of necessity, he also wills to be so, a state which is so far from coercion that in it he is to the greatest degree willing.[46]

But it does not follow from this that whatever God ordains in creating and sustaining the universe, he necessarily ordains.

Steinmetz also claims that on this point one of Calvin's successors in Geneva, Francis Turretin, is obliged to explain away Calvin's rejection of the distinction.[47] But what Turretin says is entirely in accord with the inter-

---

[45] *Sermons on Job*, 415.   [46] *The Bondage and Liberation of the Will*, 148.

[47] Steinmetz, 'Calvin and the Absolute Power of God', *Calvin in Context*, 50.

pretation of Calvin we have offered. He says that Calvin objects to a certain way of making the distinction, not to the distinction itself. And what he objects to, according to Turretin, is the idea of God's absolute power as the power to:

do whatever can be imagined by us whether good or evil, contradictory or not; for instance, that he could lie and sin; that he could do what would be repugnant to the nature of things. Calvin rightly denies this absolute power because it would not belong to power and virtue, but to impotency and imperfection. But he was unwilling to deny that God (by absolute power) can do more things than he really does by his actual power.[48]

Turretin underlines the earlier claim that there is at least one version of the *potentia absoluta–potentia ordinata* distinction which Calvin accepts, and that (by implication) it is mistaken to think that Calvin has a root and branch objection to it.

CALVIN, DIVINE POWER AND ATONEMENT

In this final section of the chapter we shall apply what we have learned to aspects of Calvin's discussion of the atonement.

As we have seen earlier, according to Calvin it is not the theologian's job to speculate about what God might have done but has not done, but to be concerned only with what God has done, in particular with what God has revealed. We can draw out this remark about speculation by some comments on the opening words of *Institutes* II. 12.

Now it has been of the greatest importance for us that he who was to be our Mediator is both true God and true man. If someone asks why this is necessary, there has been no simple (to use the common expression) or absolute necessity. Rather, it has stemmed from a heavenly decree, on which men's salvation depended. Our most merciful Father decreed what was best for us . . . The situation would surely have been hopeless had the very majesty of God not descended to us, since it was not in our power to ascend to him. Hence it was necessary for the Son of God to become for us 'Immanuel, that is, God with us'(Isa. 7: 14; Matt. 1: 23).[49]

Anticipating some of the features of Calvin's discussion, there are three questions about divine power that arise in connection with the atonement (and its covenantal framework) and its necessity. The first is, was it necessary that God atoned for sin? Secondly, could God have atoned for sin without an incarnation of the Son? And thirdly, would the Son of God have become incarnate even if there were no need for redemption? (There are other questions that are pertinent to divine power and the atonement which

---

[48] *Institutes of Elenctic Theology*, III. xxi. v.   [49] *Inst.* II. 12. 1.

Calvin does not discuss. For example, why did God decide to atone at all? And why do the effects of Christ's atonement affect people differently?)

To the first question Calvin answers, in the passage just cited, that there was no absolute necessity for the incarnation, no 'simple necessity', but that it came from the decree of God. We might say that there was no overriding necessity. God might, consistently with his own nature, have chosen not to redeem. He freely decreed to redeem. So God could have done other than he in fact decreed to do. If God freely decreed to redeem he could equally freely have decreed not to redeem. Calvin does say that God decreed what was best for us, but it would be a serious mistake to suppose that Calvin thought that the decree was necessitated by that fact.

To the second question Calvin answers that it was necessary for the Son of God to become for us Immanuel, otherwise our situation would have been hopeless. That is, Calvin is asserting that 'If our situation were not to be hopeless God had to become incarnate'. The necessity in question here is what might be called conditional or hypothetical necessity; necessity that is required for the fulfilment of some antecedent condition or requirement. It is in this sense that the Incarnation 'was of the greatest importance for us', that the Father 'decreed what was best for us'. And it may be necessary in a further, Anselmian sense, that if there is to be an atonement for sin then nothing less than the sacrifice of the incarnate Son of God is sufficient. Calvin makes this further point in the following section:

For the same reason it was also imperative that he who was to become our Redeemer be true God and true man. It was his task to swallow up death. Who but the Life could do this? It was his task to conquer sin. Who but very Righteousness could do this? It was his task to rout the powers of world and air. Who but a power higher than world and air could do this? Now where does life or righteousness, or lordship and authority of heaven lie but with God alone? Therefore our most merciful God, when he willed that we be redeemed, made himself our Redeemer in the person of his only-begotten Son.[50]

So by the rhetorical intent of these words Calvin seems to imply that granted that an atonement was decreed, God can only atone through the God-man and in no other way. That is Calvin's answer to our second question.

On the second question it has been suggested that there is a similarity of view between Calvin's view of merit and that of Duns Scotus.[51] Scotus claimed that apart from God's good pleasure Christ could not merit anything. The *acceptio* of God is both necessary and sufficient for merit. If

---

[50] *Inst.* II. 12. 2.

[51] See McGrath, *The Intellectual Origins of the European Reformation*, 104–5. Also E. David Willis, 'The Influence of Laelius Socinus on Calvin's Doctrines of the Merits of Christ and the Assurance of Faith', in J. A. Tedeschi (ed.), *Italian Reformation Studies in Honor of Laelius Socinus* (Florence: Le Monnier, 1965).

God accepts X as meritorious, whatever X is, then X is meritorious. Scotus says 'If it had pleased God, a good angel could have made satisfaction by an offering which God could have accepted as sufficient for all sins. For every created offering is worth exactly what God accepts it for and no more.'[52]

Whether due to the influence of Scotus or not there is some evidence in the overall corpus of Calvin's work that, for a time at least, he favoured a voluntarist approach to the atonement, as in this comment on John 15: 13:

God might have redeemed us by a single word, or by a mere act of his will, if he had not thought it better to do otherwise for our own benefit, that, by not sparing his own well-beloved Son, he might testify in his person how much he cares for our salvation.[53]

Alister McGrath has maintained that:

It will therefore be clear that the theology of the *via moderna* demands that human merit in general, and the merit of Christ in particular, must be recognized as depending totally upon the divine good pleasure. It is therefore of considerable interest to note that Calvin himself appears to adopt precisely this position, where he might have been expected to adopt the earlier medieval position. This only becomes clear in the *Institutio* of 1559 (II. 17. 1–5), a section which is based upon an exchange of letters between Calvin and the Italian Laelius Socinus.[54]

The strongly voluntarist emphasis of Calvin's thought in general, and in his discussion of the *ratio meriti christi* in particular, unquestionably points to a continuity between his thought and that of the *via moderna* (and, on this specific point, it may be said, also with those of the *schola Augustiniana moderna*). No reason may be given for the meritorious nature of Christ's sacrifice, apart from the fact that God has ordained to accept it as meritorious. The exclusive location of the propriety of this matter in the will of God by Calvin, as by the *moderni*, raises the question of the theological significance of the *potentia Dei absoluta* in Calvin's thought, a question we cannot pursue here.[55]

But as we are in the course of seeing there is no evidence of Calvin favouring divine *potentia absoluta* in that sense. Further, as we saw in our discussion of angels, Calvin grounds merit not in the will but in the being of God and (in the case of the absence of merit) in the being of the creature. As we shall

---

[52] Quoted in E. David Willis, 'The Influence of Laelius Socinus on Calvin's Doctrines of the Merits of Christ and the Assurance of Faith', 235.

[53] Calvin, *Commentary on John's Gospel*, 15. 13. I am grateful to Carl Trueman for this reference. It is such an isolated passage as this, which appears to be almost unique in Calvin's writings, that warrants M. M. Adams's remark that for Calvin nothing binds God as to what soteriological scheme (if any) he establishes ('The Problem of Hell: A Problem of Evil for Christians', in Eleonore Stump (ed.), *Reasoned Faith* (Ithaca: Cornell University Press, 1993), 304).

[54] Alister McGrath, 'John Calvin and Late Medieval Thought', *Archiv für Reformationsgeschichte*, 1986 (75–6).   [55] 'John Calvin and Late Medieval Thought', 77.

shortly see, in Calvin's view there is not even a proportionate merit between Christ and the creature. Christ, being divine, has infinite merit, the creatures no merit at all. And in this connection McGrath's appeal to *Institutes* II. 17. 1–5 is questionable.

In any case it is much more likely that the source of Calvin's remarks on John 15: 13 lies not in Scotus or in late medieval voluntarism but in Augustine:

Those then who say, What, had God no other way by which He might free men from the misery of this mortality, that He should will the only-begotten Son, God co-eternal with Himself, to become man, by putting on a human soul and flesh, and being made mortal to endure death?—these, I say, it is not enough so to refute, as to assert that that mode by which God deigns to free us through the Mediator of God and men, the man Christ Jesus, is good and suitable to the dignity of God; but we must show also, not indeed that no other mode was possible to God, to whose power all things are equally subject, but that there neither was nor need have been any other mode more appropriate for curing our misery.[56]

The atonement by the God-man, Augustine says, is highly appropriate or fitting, but not strictly speaking necessary. Calvin seems to have agreed, at least in his *Commentary on John* published in 1553. But when this is compared with what he wrote later there is evidence of some change of emphasis due perhaps to his correspondence with Laelius Socinus which, though it began in 1549, only culminated in 1555 in Calvin's *Responsio ad aliquot Laelii Socini senensis quaestiones*. As McGrath points out, the 1559 *Institutes* contains fuller discussion regarding the merits of Christ, provoked by Calvin's exchange with Socinus and drawn from the *Responsio*, than appear in previous editions of the *Institutes*.[57]

Part of Socinus's argument was that if the justification of sinners is due to the sheer mercy of God then surely Christ's merit was unnecessary and references to it obscure God's grace. Calvin answered that Christ's atonement is an expression of God's mercy. Christ was appointed to merit salvation for us.

In discussing Christ's merit, we do not consider the beginning of merit to be in him, but we go back to God's ordinance, the first cause. For God solely of his own good pleasure appointed him Mediator to obtain salvation for us.

Hence it is absurd to set Christ's merit against God's mercy. For it is a common rule that a thing subordinate to another is not in conflict with it. For this reason nothing hinders us from asserting that men are freely justified by God's mercy alone, and at the same time that Christ's merit, subordinate to God's mercy, also intervenes on our behalf. Both God's free favor and Christ's obedience, each in its degree, are

---

[56] *On the Trinity*, XIII. x, trans. A. W. Haddan, 324.

[57] David Willis indicates that *Inst.* II. 17. 1–5 incorporates Calvin's response to Socinus on the merits of Christ more or less verbatim.

fitly opposed to our works. Apart from God's good pleasure Christ could not merit anything; but did so because he had been appointed to appease God's wrath with his sacrifice, and to blot out our transgressions with his obedience. To sum up: inasmuch as Christ's merit depends upon God's grace alone, which has ordained this manner of salvation for us, it is just as properly opposed to all human righteousness as God's grace is.[58]

These words do not imply that Christ had merit only because God willed so, though they have been taken in that sense, but that Christ's death only had merit *for us* because God willed it. So Christ was appointed by God the Father as a subordinate cause to merit salvation for us by appeasing divine wrath.

Support for this is found in the way Calvin writes of Christ's merit. It is striking that while denying that the creature can merit anything Calvin waxes eloquent on what Christ has merited.[59] To explain this difference on the grounds that by his mere will God chose to accept Christ's work as meritorious and human work as never meritorious does not seem very plausible. (Could it, one wonders, have been the other way round?) Rather, as we saw in Chapter 10, Calvin holds the view that no creature can be a source of merit. So the absence of merit is grounded in the nature of things. It is hardly likely that if this is what he thought he also held that Christ's work had merit simply because of the exercise of the divine *acceptio*. Rather it too was grounded in the nature of things: Christ's work had merit because of who Christ was, not a creature but the eternal Word. What Christ did and suffered is in virtue of his divine nature infinitely meritorious.

How does this misunderstanding, this voluntaristic interpretation of Calvin's mature views on the atonement arise? Perhaps because there is an inherent ambiguity in saying, as Calvin does, that apart from God's good pleasure, Christ could not merit anything (*quia mero beneplacito Mediatorem statuit qui nobis salutem acquireret*). On the one hand, it might mean that it is only in virtue of the divine will that Christ's death had merit. Had God willed otherwise, then it would not have had merit. This is the voluntaristic interpretation. But alternatively, and more plausibly, what Calvin is saying by these words is that it is only in virtue of God's good pleasure *to give his Son for us* that the atonement has value, thus linking the love of God and the offering of Christ closely together. ('I admit, if anyone would simply set Christ by himself over against God's judgment, there will be no place for

---

[58] *Inst.* II. 17. 1. For a clear statement of Calvin's view of Christ's merit see Paul van Buren, *Christ in Our Place* (Edinburgh: Oliver & Boyd, 1957), 61–2.

[59] 'Surely the only reason why Christ's flesh is called "our food" [John 6: 55] is that we find in him the substance of life. Now that power arises solely from the fact that the Son of God was crucified as the price of our righteousness' (*Inst.* II. 17. 5).

merit.')[60] It is not God the Father's *accepting* Christ's atonement, in Scotist fashion, which procures merit, but his *providing* of it.

So in the 1559 *Institutes*, after more reflection, and no doubt under some pressure from Socinus, Calvin roundly rejects as speculative what has been called the Scotist interpretation of the merit of Christ.[61] He holds that since the action of the Son on the cross was an act of obedience to the will of his Father, what he accomplished was in accordance with the Father's good pleasure and the Father's provision and was accepted precisely because it was an act of obedience to the Father. It would have had no atoning value other than as such an act of obedience. As Calvin repeatedly points out in *Institutes* II. 17, the love of the Father and the work of the Son are indissolubly linked, linked by the decree to redeem; it is in this sense and this sense only that what Christ merited was in accordance with the Father's good pleasure; his meriting of human redemption was not at all due to the Father's arbitrary whim, giving value to what otherwise would have no value. Therefore it is in this vein that we are to understand the following words:

Apart from God's good pleasure Christ could not merit anything; but did so because he had been appointed to appease God's wrath with his sacrifice, and to blot out our transgressions with his obedience. To sum up: inasmuch as Christ's merit depends upon God's grace alone, which has ordained this manner of salvation for us, it is just as properly opposed to all human righteousness as God's grace is.[62]

'Depends upon God's grace alone', not on God's mere will.

I take it to be a commonplace that if Christ made satisfaction for our sins, if he paid the penalty owed by us, if he appeased God by his obedience—in short, if as a righteous man he suffered for unrighteous men—then he acquired salvation for us by his righteousness, which is tantamount to deserving it.[63]

Quite apart from the internal evidence that we have been citing to the contrary, it would in any case be odd for Calvin to espouse theological voluntarism in connection with the atonement in the course of correspondence with Laelius Socinus (as he is alleged to have done) when in the very same correspondence he warned Socinus of the dangers of speculation. In any case to suppose that Calvin upheld such theological voluntarism is to reinterpret him in terms of a reading of the *potentia absoluta–potentia ordinata* distinction that as we have already seen he would have repudiated. Were it to have been put to him that 'If God were to accept the offering of an angel as satisfaction for the sins of the world, then that offering would have been

---

[60] *Inst.* II. 17. 1.

[61] With what justice? Willis quotes Scotus's commentary on the *Sentences*, III. 19, I, 7. (235)

[62] *Inst.* II. 17. 1.

[63] *Inst.* II. 17. 3.

sufficient', he would (at least in his later reflection, following his interchange with Laelius Socinus) have rejected the thought with horror.

However, when it comes to answering the third question, 'Would the Son of God have become incarnate even if there were no need for redemption?'[64] Calvin does not, it seems to me, keep clear of all speculation himself (that is, even on his own understanding of what speculation is). For he had earlier claimed that 'Even if man had remained free from all stain, his condition would have been too lowly for him to reach God without a Mediator'.[65] The counterfactual which Calvin permits himself ('had man remained free from all stain') here is precisely of the sort that he forbids to others, on the grounds that it invites speculation and is 'profitless'. How could Calvin know that the proposition 'Even if man had been sinless he would still have needed a Mediator' is true?

At first glance Calvin's thought does not seem to be very dissimilar from those entertained by Osiander in his treatise *An filius Dei fuerit incarnandus* (1550) which Calvin subjects to merciless critique in the *Institutes*. Calvin asserts that Osiander taught the 'speculation' 'that Christ would still have become man even if no means of redeeming mankind had been needed'.[66] Given what he himself appears to maintain about the necessity for mediatorship, Calvin's argument against Osiander seems weak unless he has in mind something which he does not seem to tell us about, that unfallen mankind, needing a mediator, would or could have had a mediator other than the Son of God. If he does have such a thought in mind, then his biblical citations in refutation of Osiander are beside the point, for they all refer to what has in fact happened for human salvation, not what might have happened had there been no Fall.

Calvin does have one interesting further argument, however, which significantly separates his own position from Osiander's. In answer to the objection that the Son of God may nevertheless have become incarnate even though he did not need to be incarnate for our reconciliation, he answers that the two—the Incarnation, and our reconciliation—are joined together by God's eternal decree. When Paul discusses the purpose of the Incarnation

---

[64] *Inst.* II. 12. 5.

[65] *Inst.* II. 12. 1. There are several other places where Calvin offers similar speculative remarks. As well as his treatment of the angels, already noted in Ch. 10, see also his brief suggestions in his sermons on Galatians, that God could have created us stronger and more perfect than he chose to, and that God could have ensured that only Adam fell (*Sermons on Galatians*, trans. Kathy Childress (Edinburgh: Banner of Truth Trust, 1997), 329–30). These sermons were preached in 1557 and first published in 1563. There are also instances of more well-founded speculations, as when Calvin says that although God created the universe in six days he could easily have completed the work in a moment (*Inst.* I. 14. 22). And he appears to condone some speculation when, writing about angels, he warns his readers against 'speculating more deeply than is expedient' (*Inst.* I. 14. 3). [66] *Inst.* II. 12. 4.

he does not envisage the decree to become incarnate as a response in time to Adam's actual Fall in time but as an eternal decree with the Fall in mind. 'It is what God determined before all ages that is shown, when he willed to heal the misery of mankind.'⁶⁷ In other words, as far back as one can think God's revelation always has connected the Incarnation with the accomplishing of redemption. 'It is as if he [Paul] were purposely setting bars about our minds so that whenever Christ is mentioned we should not in the least depart from the grace of reconciliation.'⁶⁸ And even more explicitly, 'For if Adam's uprightness had not failed, he along with the angels would have been like God; and it would not have been necessary for the Son of God to become either man or angel.'⁶⁹

But this, once again, seems to be a speculation by Calvin's own standards of what counts as one. And so it is rather strange that a little later Calvin should have condemned in Osiander a speculation of a rather similar type to that which he himself had briefly indulged in some few pages earlier. The one possible explanation is that in the brief earlier passage reference to a Mediator is a reference to the Son of God unincarnated nevertheless taking on the role of mediator. In support of this interpretation is Calvin's later remark in response to Osiander:

As if the Kingdom of God could not stand had the eternal Son of God—though not endued with human flesh—gathered together angels and men into the fellowship of his heavenly glory . . . As the angels enjoyed his Headship, why could Christ not rule over men also by his divine power, quicken and nourish them like his own body by the secret power of his Spirit until, gathered up into heaven, they might enjoy the same life as the angels!⁷⁰

Here Calvin seems to envisage a mediatorial role for the unincarnated Son of God in a thought that seems to be at least as speculative as Osiander's! If so, he is flouting his own rule never to match someone else's speculation with a counter speculation of one's own.

Apart from such asides, however, what these discussions bring into relief and underscore is Calvin's view that the Incarnation was conditionally necessary, its requirement being conditioned upon human sin and upon the will of God to redeem. However, might not this also be a piece of speculation? It is one thing to say, as Calvin does, that 'it was of the greatest

---

⁶⁷ *Inst.* II. 12. 5.

⁶⁸ *Inst.* II. 12. 5. Incidentally Calvin's point here has little to do with the infralapsarian–supralapsarian issue, despite the editorial claim in the Battles's translation that the passage briefly shows Calvin as favouring the supralapsarian as opposed to the infralapsarian view of the decrees of God (469 n. 5). What Calvin is in fact discussing are two forms of infralapsarianism, one in which the decree to redeem is an eternal decree, another in which it is a decree formed at a time after Adam's fall. He favours the former.

⁶⁹ *Inst.* II. 12. 7.   ⁷⁰ *Inst.* II. 12. 7.

importance for us that he who was to be our Mediator be both true God and true man'. This assertion might be said to be based upon reasonable inferences drawn from the New Testament. But it is another thing to say that 'it was necessary, [even conditionally necessary], for the Son of God to become for us "Immanuel, that is, God with us" '. How can Calvin be so confident that it was impossible for God not to redeem in some other way? Is this Anselmian claim not itself making a tacit reference to the *potentia absoluta* in a way that he elsewhere regards as inadmissible, in that he is implying that it was absolutely impossible for God to redeem in some other way? How does Calvin know this? Has he been drawn by his opposition to one particular speculation to rebut it with (what is by his own standards) a piece of unwarranted dogmatism? To be consistent with his own strictures on speculation he should on principle restrict himself to the data of Scripture to support his position. But where does Scripture assert this impossibility, or make the inference a reasonable one to make? Perhaps, if pressed, Calvin would say that the need for a divine mediator even had the race not fallen is a necessity, and not a matter of the divine willing. But how might he know that?

However this may be, we can say that the Incarnation, and the covenant of grace that it is at the centre of, are both for Calvin instances of God's ordained power, and the necessities that attach to them are so attached in view of his free and yet utterly reliable ordination. Calvin's overall position, which occasionally (as we have seen) he himself flouts, is that we are not to attempt to go behind this decree to speculate on what God in his absolute power, the power not of God's will in abstraction from his nature, but of the entire divine nature, might have decreed. It is for this reason also that Calvin condemns as 'madness' the speculation of some, such as Ockham, over whether the Son of God could have taken upon himself the nature of an ass.[71]

Excursus: Calvin's 'Scotism'

It is possible now to bring together the various brief discussions of Scotus and Scotism to try to assess the claim that Calvin's theological ideas owe a significant debt to those of Duns Scotus.[72] We have already noted the absence

[71] *Inst.* II. 12. 5.

[72] As we have seen, the view was given currency by François Wendel in his study of Calvin's theology. It has also been given support by T. F. Torrance, though this was in the belief that Calvin was a pupil of John Major's. At the other extreme, there are those who see a 'paradigm change' between the thought of Calvin, whom Scotus had little or no influence on, and the later Reformed Scholasticism which was allegedly heavily indebted to Scotus's views on radical contingency (see, for example, Antonie Vos,

of hard evidence that Calvin actually read Scotus, or that he was taught by a Scottish Scotist, John Major. Nonetheless, if Scotist emphases were 'in the air' and if in that period even Aquinas was interpreted in a Scotist fashion (as Allan Wolter claims[73]), the influences of Scotism on Calvin cannot be ruled out a priori.

In order to assess the extent of the influence of Scotus on Calvin in the areas of his thought covered by this book I shall offer a brief résumé of Calvin's thought in four areas: divine freedom in creation, *potentia absoluta* and the divine command theory of ethics, human action, and the relation between merit and the atonement.

Divine freedom in creation

As we have seen, Calvin's thought on creation (as on redemption) is governed by his idea of the divine decree. Is the decree free? There is no suggestion of necessitarianism or emanationism in Calvin, and we have seen that while he does not address the question of the divine freedom directly, what he says implicitly supports the view that for Calvin both creation and redemption are metaphysically contingent arrangements. He also stresses the divine incomprehensibility, this being at least one of the senses in which providence and predestination are for him 'secret'. If one were to ask what Calvin thinks things are like behind this veil of ignorance then we have seen that he frequently draws attention to the fact that God has reasons for decreeing this or that, even though these reasons are for us 'unfathomable'. Of course someone may have reasons for doing what they do, but not do what they do for those reasons. But it is hard to see how this is possible in the case of God. If God has unfathomable reasons for decreeing what he does then it is reasonable to suppose that Calvin thought that God did what he did for those reasons. So this strongly suggests an 'intellectualist' rather than a 'voluntarist' understanding of divine freedom.

Though Calvin is said by some to be supralapsarian in his account of the decrees, there is nothing in Calvin that resembles later reflection on the ordering of the decrees, and so it cannot be said that Calvin makes use of anything that corresponds to Scotus's idea of eternal moments, any more than there is evidence that he thinks that God in creating the universe actualizes one of a set of possible worlds. So while, like Scotus (and like Aquinas and indeed the mainstream tradition), Calvin thought of creation

'Scholasticism and Reformation' in Willem J. van Asselt and Eef Dekker (eds.), *Reformation and Scholasticism: An Ecumenical Enterprise* (Grand Rapids, Mich.: Baker, 2001).

[73] Allan B. Wolter, 'Scotism', in Hans Burkhardt and Barry Smith (eds.), *Handbook of Metaphysics and Ontology* (Munich/Philadelphia/Vienna: Philosophia Verlag, 1991), 816–18.

and redemption as metaphysically contingent, there is no reason to think that he approached the idea of contingency in a distinctively Scotist manner.

Potentia absoluta *and the Divine Command Theory*

It is perhaps in the areas of divine power that Scotist influences are most readily imputed to Calvin. Calvin's sentence in the *Institutes*, 'God's will is so much the highest rule of righteousness that whatever he will, by the very fact that he wills it, must be considered righteous,' has frequently been taken to imply Scotism.[74] But we have seen that the seeming voluntarism of these remarks must be tempered by Calvin's commitment to the idea of divine simplicity (as presumably it must be by Scotus), but especially by the inseparability of God's will and his justice. So we must understand his sentence not as a bald statement of theological voluntarism but as in effect saying, 'In the absence of the provision to us of divine reasons for decreeing this or commanding that, we must accept God's will as the highest rule, because his will and his righteousness are inseparably joined together.' François Wendel, in claiming Scotist influence on Calvin in this area, has also, it seems to me, provided an inaccurate account of what he takes to be the opposite of Scotism. He thinks that the opposite view is that God's command is subject to 'external causality',[75] presumably the external causality of necessary and immutable moral values which constrain the divine choice. But, being in the tradition of Augustine and Anselm, Calvin certainly does not hold such a position; rather, God's majesty uniquely instantiates the principles of perfection. So for Calvin there is no question of God being subject to the external constraints of immutable moral principles existing independently of his being any more than God's willing can be seen as an act of absolute power.

On the further question of whether God by his absolute power can *now* act against what he has ordained, it is surely clear that Calvin would regard the question as speculative, simply because for him whatever happens does so in virtue of God's decree, and in his theology Calvin resolutely intends to adhere to what God has in fact revealed, and he almost always succeeds in that intention. The unfolding of that decree in time contains some surprises for us, but the surprises are not due to God's going against what he has decreed, by supplanting it with another decree, but because of the unanticipatable complexity of the original decree.

[74] For example what Calvin says here is appealed to both by François Wendel, *Calvin: The Origins and Development of his Religious Thought*, 128, and by John Hare, *God's Call*, (Grand Rapids, Mich.: Eerdmans, 2001), 51.

[75] Wendel, *Calvin: The Origins and Development of his Religious Thought*, 129.

We have seen that several thinkers have claimed that Calvin endorses a version of the Divine Command Theory of ethics. But if he does so, Calvin's version bears little resemblance to that of Scotus. Calvin thinks, in common with the tradition, including the views of Scotus, that the Decalogue is an expression of the 'inward law', natural law. He makes no principled distinction between the necessity of the first table of the Decalogue and the contingency for us of the second table,[76] and even where (as with the ceremonial laws of the Old Testament), he recognizes that though having been commanded they are now countermanded, the purpose of these laws remains, though no doubt that purpose is itself a contingent matter. The most we can say, as will be shown in the next chapter, is that by and large Calvin defends an epistemic version of the Divine Command Theory of morality: the divine command makes clear to us and enforces what are the immutable principles of the divine nature.

Human action

It is a well-known fact about Scotus that he took the view that the human will (and the divine will) is self-determined in the libertarian sense; it has the power of contrary choice, the liberty of indifference, contra-casual freedom—however this power is described, it is the power in a given situation to choose either A or not-A.[77] No one to my knowledge has claimed that Calvin is a Scotist in this sense. As we have seen in the chapter on free will, the best way of understanding Calvin's position (when viewed in terms of the age-old polarity between determinists and libertarians) is as a compatibilist. He thinks that a person acts freely when he acts in a non-coerced fashion. Human action is compatible with some form of determinism, and with human responsibility, and such actions as occur do so in accordance with God's decree, God remaining untainted by evil.

Dewey Hoitenga has argued that though Calvin was not a Scotist, but in the intellectualist tradition of Thomas Aquinas, he would have been better advised to have been a Scotist! Hoitenga provides a 'Scotist gloss' on Calvin, offering 'the view I think he would have taken, had he thought about locating his concept of the will in the medieval tradition that produced him'.[78] Hoitenga's suggestion is motivated by what he thinks is an inconsistency

---

[76] Though we noted in the last chapter that he believed that much of the second table is not applicable to angels.

[77] Douglas Langston's claim that Scotus held a non-libertarian view of human action, in at least part of his writings, is very much a minority view: Douglas C. Langston, *God's Willing Knowledge* (University Park and London: Pennsylvania State University Press, 1986), ch. 3. But then if this is Scotus's view, it is hard to see how the alleged influence of Scotus on Calvin could be distinguished from the influence of other scholastic thinkers on him.   [78] Dewey Hoitenga, *John Calvin and the Will*, 65.

between Calvin's account of the unfallen and the fallen will, but as we have seen in the chapter on the soul there is in fact no inconsistency there in the first place.

Merit and the atonement

Evidently Scotus took the view that the passion of Christ had no intrinsic value, but that it had value only because of what was conferred upon it by the divine will. God chose to regard Christ's passion as meritorious even though it had no intrinsic merit. Wendel says that this is Calvin's view in his correspondence with Laelius Socinus and in the *Institutes*. He quotes from a section of the *Institutes* where Calvin says that:

> In discussing Christ's merit, we do not consider the beginning of merit to be in him, [*non statuitur in eo principium*], but we go back to God's ordinance, the first cause. For God solely of his own good pleasure appointed him Mediator to obtain salvation for us.[79]

Wendel says that this amounts to saying that the Christ was able to deserve our salvation only because God would have it so.[80] But there is another, more obvious way to take what Calvin says. He is discussing and rejecting the views of those who would 'have Christ as a mere instrument or minister, not as the Author of leader or prince of life, as Peter calls him [Acts 3: 15]'.[81] What is his argument? He cites Augustine to the effect that the man Christ Jesus is predestined by God to be the Saviour. The merit of Christ's human nature did not originate with him; the human nature was not united to the divine because it deserved to be, but solely because of God's predestining grace. Calvin is not saying that Christ had merit simply by divine fiat—the fiat of God is not under discussion—but that he has the office of mediator because he was predestined to it by God's grace. There is therefore no opposition between the grace of God and the office of Christ, for Christ has his office because God destined him to it. 'Hence', Calvin goes on to say, 'it is absurd to set Christ's merit against God's mercy.'

In any case, it is hardly likely that in a passage drawn from his correspondence with Laelius Socinus and inserted into the 1559 *Institutes* Calvin would be found agreeing with Socinus that the death of Christ had no intrinsic merit. Rather, as we noted earlier in this chapter, this controversy with Socinus seems to have marked a shift away from Calvin's earlier view of the atonement which may have been more Scotist, but may also have reflected Augustine's view that the atonement of Christ was a good and suitable means

---

[79] *Inst.* II. 17. 1.
[80] Wendel, *Calvin: The Origins and Development of his Religious Thought*, 228.
[81] *Inst.* II. 17. 1.

of our salvation, but not strictly necessary. Prior to that controversy Calvin seems to have some sympathy with this view, and even with the idea that God might have redeemed us by a mere word. But not afterwards.

In evaluating Calvin's alleged Scotism we have not touched on all the distinctive aspects of the thought of Duns Scotus.[82] Nothing has been said about synergistic views of grace, or on the radical priority of Christ over Adam, or, indeed, on the immaculate conception (one of Scotus's favourite doctrines). But perhaps enough has been said to show that hard evidence of the direct influence of Scotus's ideas on Calvin's is minimal, and that (if Calvin is to be pigeon-holed) it is wiser to think of him, if not as an eclectic, then as being in the tradition of the intellectualism of Thomas Aquinas, even though he rarely cites him.

[82] More comments on Calvin's relation to Scotus are to be found in the following chapter.

12

Equity, Natural Law, and Common Grace

CALVIN's treatment of natural law, and the central place that the idea of equity plays in this, may be understood as part of his account of the natural knowledge of God. As we saw earlier, his position on such knowledge was the subject of fierce debate in the twentieth century; some of the debate was prompted, it seems, less by a desire to establish Calvin's own position, than to have him as an ally in implementing some current theological agendum. For instance, there have been those who, in the interests of upholding the supremacy and sufficiency of special revelation, have denied that Calvin taught that it is possible to have a natural knowledge of what is right and wrong apart from that revelation. In this chapter we shall try to show that this position is, to say the least, somewhat exaggerated.[1]

A DIVINE COMMAND THEORIST?

One aspect of this debate is that denying natural knowledge of right and wrong appears to commit one to some form of the Divine Command Theory of ethics. For if the knowledge of what is right and wrong depends upon supernatural knowledge, what God tells us in his word, then this looks as if some ethical position is right simply because God commands it, wrong simply because God forbids it. And perhaps this commits us to a form of the Divine Command Theory according to which the command issues not from a God whose moral character we can count on, but one whose goodness is wholly inscrutable. Thus Alasdair Macintyre: 'Calvin too presents a God of whose goodness *we* cannot judge and whose commandments we cannot interpret as designed to bring us to the τέλος to which our own desires point; as with Luther, so with Calvin, we have to hope for grace that we may be

---

[1] It is striking that in part II, ch. 2 'The Failure of Nature', of his *Calvin's Doctrine of the Knowledge of God* (Grand Rapids, Mich.: Eerdmans, 1959), T. H. L. Parker does not even mention Calvin's attitude to natural law. The book is written in the shadow of the Karl Barth–Emil Brunner debate on natural theology, siding throughout with the Barthian interpretation of Calvin, and conflating throughout knowledge of God with the saving knowledge of God. The trajectory of the present chapter is more in sympathy with the earlier study of Josef Bohatec, *Calvin und das Recht* (Feudingen in Westfalen: Buchdruck- und Verlags-Anstalt, 1934).

justified and forgiven for our inability to obey the arbitrary fiats of a cosmic despot.'[2] We shall see that this blood-chilling picture of Calvin is far from the truth, and that it is doubtful that Calvin presents a strong form of the Divine Command Theory, if one at all. To start with, it would be hasty to draw the conclusion that a Divine Command Theory is entailed by the fact, if it is a fact, that our knowledge of what is right and wrong depends upon what God tells us in his word. Even if one held that the knowledge of right and wrong is due solely to special revelation, one may hold this consistently with a denial of any form of the Divine Command Theory of ethics. For one may hold that we depend upon divine revelation not to establish by divine command what is right and wrong, but to disclose to us something that unaided human reason or conscience cannot discern, namely, what is immutably right and wrong, that which God's command will (and must) conform to.

Let us say that a Divine Command Theory of ethics is one which holds that the divine command is necessary and sufficient for the rightness of some action. In her anthology on divine command ethics[3] J. M. Idziak quotes two passages from the *Institutes* which she regards as favouring the Divine Command Theory. Let us look at these to begin with.

First, part of Calvin's exposition of the moral law.

The Lord, in giving the rule of perfect righteousness, has referred all its parts to his will, thereby showing that nothing is more acceptable to him than obedience. The more inclined the playfulness of the human mind is to dream up various rites with which to deserve well of him, the more diligently ought we to mark this fact.[4]

Calvin is here claiming that the moral law is a 'rule of perfect righteousness' which God wills that we keep. The law certainly has the force of a command, but is this an instance of a Divine Command Theory of ethics? It may seem so. Calvin says that in delivering the law of righteousness the Lord has 'referred all its parts to his will'. But this surely does not necessarily mean that what is good depends solely on the divine will but, as the context makes clear, that his will is *sufficient* for obedience. It is not to be added to, or diminished. But Calvin says nothing here about the divine command being *necessary* for making a rule a good or righteous rule, though of course it is necessary for righteousness taking the form of obedience to God.

The second passage, from *Institutes* III. 23. 1, concerns Calvin's treatment of divine election, and particularly the idea of reprobation. Why are some elect, some reprobate? Calvin's answer is that Paul (in Romans 9) 'gives the ultimate sovereignty to God's wrath and might, for it is wicked to subject to

---

[2] *A Short History of Ethics* (London: Routledge, 1967), 123.

[3] *Divine Command Morality: Historical and Contemporary Readings* (New York: Edward Mellen Press, 1979).   [4] *Inst.* II. 8. 5.

our determination those deep judgments which swallow up all our powers of mind'. But it ought to be noted that the passage concerns God's decree, not God's command. It has nothing at all to do with human obligations nor in what their obligatoriness is grounded. Secondly, Calvin makes one of his favourite points, not that the mere fact of God's decreeing is necessary and sufficient for the rightness or justice of that decree, but that God's will is inseparable from his justice and the divine justice is profound, beyond human powers of discernment. So his argument has nothing to do with commands as such, but with God's decree. And he grounds the decree not in God's mere will, but in a justice too deep for the human mind. So the passages cited by Idziak are not persuasive.

Others have also claimed to discern a Divine Command Theory in Calvin. In *God's Call*[5] John Hare defends a version of the Divine Command Theory drawn mainly from Duns Scotus which he believes is consonant with Calvin's outlook. He takes Calvin to be in the Scotist rather than the Thomist tradition, seeing coincidence between Calvin and Scotus on the centrality of the will or heart in religion, the emphasis upon divine sovereignty, and in their distrust of attempts to limit by reason what God can and cannot do.[6] So he thinks that Calvin would endorse the theory that what makes something obligatory for us is that God commands it. God's command is a 'pull to the good', and our evaluative judgements, positive or negative, are our response to that pull. We respond positively when we want to make God's announced will, his call, our own. The final end of the divine command is not mere obedience, but loving union with God, and because of this a person may care what God wills or commands, even when it cuts across his own immediate happiness, or what he otherwise thinks is the right thing to do, because of this. Hence for Hare it is more appropriate to refer to God's 'call' rather than to his 'command'. Such a positive response is often and usually a constrained response in that it comes to us as a recognition of obligation, but that is because of the Fall.[7] He thinks that all this is consonant with Calvin's outlook.

Hare contrasts this with natural law theory, in that version according to which the second table of the Decalogue can be 'read off', that is deduced from the natural law. He argues that Scotus's version of the divine command theory consists in prescribing to us ends independent of our own prescribing, ends which will, if followed, culminate in our enjoyment of true fulfilment. This objective route for us is contingent, it is not grounded in the necessity of things. God might have chosen some other route, therefore, but

---

[5] (Grand Rapids, Mich.: Eerdmans, 2001).   [6] Hare, *God's Call*, 50–1.

[7] Hare, *God's Call*, 49

his choosing the route that he has in fact chosen is what makes it the right route for us.[8] Coupled with this is a view on the sources of moral motivation: for Scotus these are other than our own happiness (eudaemonism), being focused on the need to uphold divine justice.

As far as Scotus is concerned these remarks apply at best to the second table of the Decalogue and to the judicial and ceremonial laws of the Old Testament.[9] They cannot apply to the first table since Scotus holds that there are some things which God cannot command, those matters having to do with his own nature. He cannot command blasphemy or idolatry, for example. For Scotus the first table comprises the natural or eternal law.[10]

Does Scotus hold that the divine command is necessary and sufficient for the rightness of an action that is not required or forbidden by natural law, acts of the second table? Richard Cross says that for Scotus the divine command is sufficient for certain otherwise morally good acts, acts that express principles which are contingently true.[11] But if God could command the opposite of these, as Scotus holds, then his command in these instances would be both necessary and sufficient for the obligatoriness of the act. For although without the command we ought not perform an action of that type, because it is in conflict with something which normally we ought to do, we are by the command obliged to perform it.

In respect of the judicial and ceremonial laws Calvin is perhaps a divine command theorist of sorts. These Old Testament laws are indexed to the Mosaic era, and it is necessary and sufficient for their obligatoriness that God has commanded them. It is hard to suppose that the specific laws about clothing and diet (for example) are other than arbitrary, being in no sense an expression of God's righteousness (even supposing that his righteousness is mainly hidden from us). Yet this needs some qualification, because Calvin interprets many of these details, for example the dress of the High Priest, as typically foreshadowing Christ.[12] While an alternative form of dress

---

[8] Hare, *God's Call*, 84.

[9] One clue as to how 'Scotist' Calvin's ethics is may perhaps be found in his attitude to the Decalogue. He rejects the Subtle Doctor's division of the Ten Commandments into two tables consisting of the first three commands (the third being the command regarding the Sabbath) and the remaining seven (achieved by splitting the tenth command into two) respectively. Calvin rejects this division as absurd (*Inst.* II. 8. 12). However, this way of dividing was not distinctive of Scotus but was general, following Lombard. Calvin, following (he believes) Origen and Augustine, prefers a division consisting of a preface, then four commands of the first table, six of the second. For more on Calvin's alleged 'Scotism' see the Excursus at the end of ch. 11.

[10] On Scotus on divine command ethics, see Richard Cross, *Duns Scotus*, 89ff.

[11] Cross, *Duns Scotus*, 93.

[12] See, for example, Calvin's discussion of Exod. 28 in his *Commentaries on the Four Last Books of Moses Arranged in the Form of a Harmony* (vol. 1, 187f.). I owe this point to David Searle.

which served an equally effective typological function might be imagined, nevertheless there is an appropriateness to this particular set of commands, and so the commands are not simply 'arbitrary'. So it is not surprising that Calvin does not write of the abrogation of the ceremonial and judicial laws in an unqualified way. He sees, instead, a certain parallel between how the moral and ceremonial laws change as a result of the coming of Christ. He distinguishes between the *use* of a law, and its *effect*. The Mosaic ceremonial legislation was abrogated, but its evangelical or Christological focus remains.

In a parallel way, the moral law comprising the ten commandments given to Moses possessed (under the Old Testament dispensation) a condemnatory function as long as the law itself remains in force.

What Paul says of the curse unquestionably applies not to the ordinance itself but solely to its force to bind the conscience. The law not only teaches but forthrightly enforces what it commands. If it be not obeyed—indeed if one in any respect fail in his duty—the law unleashes the thunderbolt of its curse. For this reason the apostle says: 'All who are of the works of the law are under a curse; for it is written, "Cursed be every one who does not fufill all things"' [Gal. 3: 10; Deut. 27: 26]. He describes as 'under the works of the law' those who do not ground their righteousness in remission of sins, through which we are released from the rigor of the law. He there-fore teaches that we must be released from the bonds of the law, unless we wish to perish miserably under them.[13]

So the moral law now no longer condemns us, because of Christ. Though it retains the power to condemn, its use is not to condemn, but to point to Christ. So the moral law is not abolished in use, but in effect, or in one of its effects.

By contrast, according to Calvin the ceremonial law is abrogated in use, but not in effect. For it does not follow that the fact of arbitrary laws about diet and clothing is itself an arbitrary matter.

The ceremonies are a different matter: they have been abrogated not in effect but only in use. Christ by his coming has terminated them, but has not deprived them of anything of their sanctity; rather, he has approved and honored it. Just as the ceremonies would have provided the people of the Old Covenant with an empty show if the power of Christ's death and resurrection had not been displayed therein; so, if they had not ceased, we would be unable today to discern for what purpose they were established.[14]

What these nuances reveal is that Calvin's approach to ethics, or to the part played by the revealed law of God in ethics, is heavily influenced by his understanding of the progress of revelation and of the successive eras of God's unfolding redemptive purposes. This makes a straight comparison

[13] *Inst.* II.7.15.   [14] *Inst.* II.7.16.

between his views and those of the medievals, who understood divine law in a rather more formal and abstract way, somewhat difficult.

If we turn attention to the moral character of the Decalogue as such we may now ask, Is the second table a part of natural or eternal law, for Calvin? Or could God, consistently with the natural or eternal law, command an action which contradicted a command of the second table? Calvin does not seem to address the question discussed by Scotus about the contingency of the second table of the law, except in his discussions of angels which we examined in Chapter 10. However, he recognizes that there is a contingent, or at least a time-conditioned feature of the first table, namely the command regarding Sabbath observance. However, if anything the evidence goes the other way; Calvin uses language which, if anything, points to the non-contingent character of both tables (with the exception of the Sabbath). Thus in his prefatory remarks on the Decalogue he writes of the law that has been handed down to us to teach us perfect righteousness,[15] and that the two tables contain 'the whole of righteousness'.[16] Further, when his discussion of the division of the law into two tables gives him the opportunity to make the Scotist point, there is no suggestion of it, no suggestion that for us there is a difference in ethical or metaphysical character between the two tables. Finally, Calvin sees the Decalogue as a spelling out of that one 'inward law . . . written, even engraved upon the hearts of all' which 'in a sense asserts the very same things that are to be learned from the two Tables'.[17] Shortly we shall examine such claims in more detail.

There are some more general considerations which may at first sight point in the opposite direction. For Calvin believes that we are not in the best position, because of our ignorance and our sin, to discern what is right and wrong. And given what we have learned about what Calvin thought about God's power, he may seem to be hospitable to the idea of divine commands as a source of moral obligation provided that the unity of God's character is safeguarded. No absolute might!

According to Robert Merrihew Adams, William of Ockham held the view that those acts which we call 'theft', 'adultery', and 'hatred of God' would be meritorious if God had commanded them.[18] So God could command them even though Ockham himself was assured that God never would in fact do so. It is clear by now that Calvin would not countenance such possibilities: he would reject them as speculative in the worst sense, if not blasphemous. He would probably refer to Ockham as a 'madman'. As we saw in the last chapter Calvin eschews theological voluntarism, any attempt to separate the will of

---

[15] *Inst.* II. 8. 5.   [16] *Inst.* II. 8. 11.   [17] *Inst.* II. 8. 1.

[18] Robert Merrihew Adams, 'A Modified Divine Command Theory of Ethical Wrongness', in Paul Helm (ed.), *Divine Commands and Morality* (Oxford: Oxford University Press, 1981), 85.

God from his righteous character. And it would seem that any version of 'weak' voluntarism which we have identified as Calvin's view is insufficiently strong to ground a version of the Divine Command Theory of ethics. For since on this view God epitomizes or instantiates supreme goodness he could not command what is not in accordance with this goodness.

But perhaps he would have more sympathy with what Adams calls a Modified Divine Command Theory of ethics, a theory according to which if an action is contrary to the command of God then it is wrong to do that action only if it is assumed, what Ockham apparently did not assume, that the God who commands has the character of loving his creatures. Calvin emphasizes not only the love of God but his righteousness or justice, even though that righteousness is often inscrutable to us. Such an emphasis might lead us to suppose that he would favour such a modification; for Calvin, an action would be wrong if contrary to the command of a loving and righteous God. So long as we hold that God is loving and righteous, then whatever he commands is, by the fact that he commands it, something that we ought to do.

There is a certain initial plausibility to this suggestion given not only Calvin's emphasis on the righteousness of God but also his more general appeal to divine sovereignty. However, there is no suggestion in what Calvin says that he had in mind anything as sophisticated as the modified theory that Adams develops. According to this theory, if notwithstanding my belief that God is a loving and righteous God I came to believe that he commanded, say, cruelty for its own sake, my concepts of ethical wrongness and permittedness would break down. Calvin never seems to countenance such a possibility. The situations of moral perplexity that he envisages arising from the command of God never include the extreme possibility that God might command cruelty for its own sake, and his characteristic way of handling those perplexities he does envisage is to appeal to the inscrutable but inherent justice or righteousness of God. So it is implausible to reconstruct Calvin as holding a Modified Divine Command Theory of the sort suggested by Adams.

Perhaps the chief evidence for denying Calvin's commitment to the Divine Command Theory is the nature of his appeal to equity and to natural law and the fact that he attributes equity to God's own character. 'The ordinance of God . . . has its own equity—unknown, indeed, to us but very sure.'[19] We shall need to inquire more precisely what Calvin means by 'equity'.

This emphasis does not mean that Calvin utterly disconnects the command of God from moral obligation. For he holds that God's command

---

[19] *Inst.* III. 23. 9.

is sufficient for *knowing* what we ought to do. But it is not necessary because we already have a more general though more inchoate guide to the divine will, besides God's explicit command, an innate awareness of natural law and the possession of a sense of equity. So that God's command supplements our understanding of what we ought to do that is derived from natural law and equity, it does not overrule it. It would not be realistic to suppose that natural law and the sense of equity are divine commands innately instilled into us. Calvin's general approach to the relevance of God's command to obligatoriness is epistemic throughout; because of our ignorance, we need his word. So Calvin's commitment to the Divine Command Theory (except in the case of the ceremonial laws already discussed) is, at best, to one or other of its epistemic versions. He does not hold that an action is morally good or bad solely in virtue of God's command.[20] What God commands refines and informs the deliverances of the natural law and of our general sense of equity, it does not supplant these. This would appear to be Calvin's general position.

The argument here, then, is not that what Calvin says is flatly inconsistent with the Scotist view, for Calvin does not reject it in so many words. But the temper and inclination of these remarks, taken together, do not point in a Scotist direction and they make an interpretation of Calvin as a divine command theorist in other than an epistemic sense that much less plausible.

Excursus: The Binding of Isaac

In view of the seemingly widespread belief that Calvin was a divine command theorist in ethics it is worth looking at his treatment of what is sometimes regarded as a *locus classicus* of this view, the Lord's command to Abraham to sacrifice Isaac (Genesis 22). It is a striking fact that Calvin's exposition of this story contains hardly a single reference or allusion to the question of whether God's command is a logically necessary and sufficient condition for ethical rightness. Much less does Calvin think that God's command to Abraham to sacrifice Isaac is an instance of the Divine Command Theory at work. In what follows I shall draw out the main features of his exposition and then suggest that insofar as the story presents a logical problem Calvin sees it not as the problem posed by a dilemma, the Euthyphro Dilemma, but as one generated by an apparent self-contradiction. And this concern over self-contradictoriness is also another incidental piece of evidence for Calvin's concern for self-consistency in theological thinking. The presence of contradictions or apparent contradictions always causes him concern.

---

[20] For a clear discussion of the Divine Command Theory as an epistemic thesis see Michael J. Harris, *Divine Command Ethics: Jewish and Christian Perspectives* (London: Routledge Curzon, 2003), 10ff.

According to Jerome Gellman the history of discussion of the binding of Isaac can be divided into pre-Kierkegaardian and post-Kierkegaardian eras. Before Kierkegaard, reflection on the story was largely concerned with God, particularly with the implications of the story for his moral character and also for his omniscience.[21] After the publication in 1843 of Kierkegaard's *Fear and Trembling*, reflection on the story focuses on Abraham, on his experience both of an ethical demand not to sacrifice his son and on the command of God precisely to do so. Morality imposes an obligation on Abraham that conflicts with God's command to sacrifice his son. The problem is the problem of two conflicting requirements, though not of two ethical requirements. God's command is a religious not an ethical requirement. The focus of the story, then, is the decision of Abraham to 'suspend the ethical', to become a Knight of Faith when he decides to prefer the religious to the ethical, and to sacrifice his son. Such at least is the standard interpretation of Kierkegaard. And Gellman says that hand in hand with this shift in interest since Kierkegaard there has been a tendency to allegorize the story.

Calvin's interpretation of the story does not fall easily into either of these interpretative traditions. He is not at all concerned to vindicate God's moral character and he even brushes aside any problem that the story poses for God's omniscience. There is no 'problem for God' for Calvin, not at least in these abstract terms. By contrast he does focus a great deal on Abraham, on his developing and sometimes confused state of mind, but the crisis for Abraham is not read in terms of any kind of contrast between religion and ethics. And of course he interprets the story literally: there is no attempt to allegorize it.

As Calvin understands it, what mattered chiefly to Abraham was not the moral crisis posed by the command to lose his only son by violence inflicted by his own hand, but the recognition that the loss of his son in obedience to such a command would be the failure of the divine promise to him that through Isaac he would be the father of many nations.

'God . . . requires the death of the boy, to whose person He himself had annexed the hope of eternal salvation. So that this latter command was, in a certain sense, the destruction of faith.'[22] So as Calvin sees it, the conflict is produced by two conflicting *words* from God: the word of promise to Abraham, and the word of command to him to sacrifice Isaac. Certainly in Calvin's view that God has the right to command—or more precisely the right to put Abraham to the test—is not in doubt, any more than is the fact of Abraham's utter certainty that the word of command to him is God's word.

---

[21] Jerome Gellman, *The Fear, the Trembling and the Fire. Kierkegaard and the Hasidic Masters on the Binding of Isaac* (Lanham, Md: University Press of America, 1994).

[22] *Commentary on the Book of Genesis*, I. 560.

'For the expression before us ["Behold, here I am"] is as much as if he said, Whatever God may have been pleased to command, I am perfectly ready to carry into effect. And, truly, he does not wait till God should expressly enjoin this or the other thing; but promises that he will be simply, and without exception, obedient in all things.' 'This, certainly, is true subjection, when we are prepared to act, before the will of God is known to us.'[23] The will of God here is understood as what he in fact brings to pass. Mere recognition that God has the right to command is not of course equivalent to any plausible version of the Divine Command Theory of ethics.

The problem for Abraham was posed by God's assuming 'a double character, that, by the appearance of disagreement and repugnance in which He presents Himself in his word, he may distract and wound the breast of the holy man'.[24] So the conflict in Abraham's mind can be expressed as the conflict between the two following propositions:

(1) Abraham knows that God has promised that through the progeny of Isaac all nations will be blessed; and
(2) Abraham knows that God has commanded him to sacrifice Isaac.[25]

The promise is more basic than the command not simply because it is earlier but because it is the unconditional ground of all that follows it in the life of Abraham. But there comes a time when to Abraham this does not *seem* to be so, because of (2). So in other words the crisis for Abraham is not primarily a moral crisis, nor is it a purely logical crisis, but it is an epistemic crisis. Only more information will solve it. The climax of the story gives him what he needs to reconcile (1) and (2). Abraham knows that there must be a resolution, but he does not know what or when this will be.

So the crisis created by the command to sacrifice Isaac is not as Calvin sees it a conflict between religion and morality, not even between a command and a norm, but between the knowledge of an earlier divine promise and of a later divine command. It is striking that Calvin presents Abraham as having little or no concern with the morality of killing Isaac but only with its instrumental wrongness.[26] Rather, according to Calvin, as Abraham sees things the divine command to kill Isaac appears to get in the way of the fulfilment of the earlier, more basic promise. Had Abraham refrained from

---

[23] *Commentary on the Book of Genesis*, I. 562.   [24] *Commentary on the Book of Genesis*, I. 561.

[25] Olivier Millet points out that the idea that Abraham was faced by two conflicting or apparently contradictory words from God is to be found in Martin Luther, and claims that Calvin 'follows Luther', 'Exègèse Évangélique et Culture Littéraire Humaniste: Entre Luther et Bèze: *L'Abraham Sacrifiant* selon Calvin', *Études Théologiques et Religieuses* (1993–4), 371. I owe this reference to Jon Balserak. It is interesting that *Abraham Sacrifiant* is the title of a play written by Theodore Beza.

[26] As far as I can see there is only one reference to Abraham's recognition of God's command to him as involving 'shameful cruelty' (*Commentary on the Book of Genesis*, I. 564).

being prepared to sacrifice Isaac because it was wrong, or for any other reason, then he would have failed the test of his faith. Calvin focuses on Abraham's paternal love, but never on the immorality of murder, but this is not because murder if commanded by God is not immoral. God has the right to command, and more basically he has the right to put his people to the test, but the rightness of what he commands does not follow from the mere fact that he commands it but is grounded in his character as the God of the covenant. The question for Abraham was, can he entrust his son to God? As Calvin sees it this is the point of the Lord's saying, at the climax of the story, that he knew that Abraham would not withhold his son from him (v. 12). To withhold his son would have been to have failed to entrust Isaac to the God who had promised an innumerable progeny through him.

Calvin sees Abraham as obeying God's command to sacrifice not because Abraham believed that it cancelled the promise but because it was conditioned by the promise. The command to sacrifice Isaac has an interim status. Obedience to it does not represent the final form of God's will for Abraham, because of the precedence of God's other word to him, his word of promise. So there has to be a way out. The test of Abraham's faith is in obeying God in this interim situation. His faith is seen in obeying the command while believing that this could not be God's last word. So the faith of Abraham is displayed in acting in the belief that the impending contradiction between the two 'words' of God will be resolved while not knowing presently how this will happen.

His mind, however, must of necessity have been severely crushed, and violently agitated, when the *command* and the *promise* of God were conflicting within him. But when he had come to the conclusion, that the God with whom he knew he had to do, could not be his adversary; although he did not immediately discover how the contradiction might be removed, he nevertheless, by hope, reconciled the command with the promise; because being indubitably persuaded that God was faithful, he left the unknown issue to Divine Providence. Meanwhile, as with closed eyes, he goes whither he is directed.[27]

His eyes were closed because at this stage they had not been enlightened by any word from the Lord as to how this impending contradiction between word and promise might be resolved. Abraham 'was unwilling to measure, by his own understanding, the method of fulfilling the promise, which he knew depended on the incomprehensible power of God'.[28] So,

(3) Abraham knew that God could reconcile (1) and (2) by his incomprehensible power, incomprehensible, that is, prior to the climax of the story.

---

[27] *Commentary on the Book of Genesis*, I. 563. [28] *Commentary on the Book of Genesis*, I. 564.

For Abraham learnt how God would reconcile (1) and (2) only when the story reached its climax.

Another striking feature of Calvin's interpretation is the seriousness with which he takes the 'real time' aspect of the story. Because this is a story about Abraham's testing he can only be tested (as anyone can only be tested) by being held in epistemic suspense regarding the outcome. So when the text says that Abraham tells his men that he will return with his son (v. 5) Calvin prefers to think of this not as Abraham's dissimulation, nor as a supernaturally imparted insight into the outcome, but as a sort of double-mindedness or self-deception or plain confusion on Abraham's part.

When, however, he says, that he will return with the boy, he seems not to be free from dissimulation and falsehood. Some think that he uttered this declaration prophetically; but since it is certain that he never lost sight of what had been promised concerning the raising up of seed to Isaac, it may be, that he, trusting in the providence of God, figured to himself his son as surviving even in death itself. And seeing that he went, as with closed eyes, to the slaughter of his son, there is nothing improbable in the supposition, that he spoke confusedly, in a matter so obscure.[29]

The reason for Calvin favouring this interpretation is that were it to be taken as a prophetic insight into the resolution of the conflict then the contradiction would have been prematurely solved, and the test of Abraham would have been aborted. He allows that Abraham's state might be interpreted as believing that God would resolve the contradiction at a time subsequent to the death of Isaac by raising him from the dead, 'as surviving even in death itself'.[30] But this is an interpretation that Calvin does not seem to favour.

At this stage, were Abraham to have believed that he would return with his son there would have been no test. The interim character of the epistemic contradiction which constituted the heart of the testing would have been lost, as it would have been had Abraham believed that God would raise Isaac from the dead.[31] Similarly, if for whatever reason Abraham were to have believed that he would not return with his son then likewise there

[29] *Commentary on the Book of Genesis*, I. 567.   [30] *Commentary on the Book of Genesis*, I. 567.

[31] It is interesting that in his *Commentary on Hebrews* (published in 1549, five years before his *Commentary on Genesis*), Calvin comments on Hebrews 11: 17–19 ('accounting that God was able to raise him up, even from the dead; from whence also he received him in a figure'), taking a rather different line. 'How is it that Abraham's faith is praised when it departs from the promise? for as obedience proceeds from faith, so faith from the promise . . . This question, which would have been otherwise difficult to be solved, the Apostle explains by adding immediately, that Abraham ascribed this honour to God, that he was able to raise his son again from the dead. He then did not renounce the promise given to him, but extends its power and its truth beyond the life of his son; for he did not limit God's power to so narrow bounds as to tie it to Isaac when dead, or to extinguish it. Thus he retained the promise, because he bound not God's power to Isaac's life, but felt persuaded that it would be efficacious in his ashes when dead no less than in him while alive and breathing.'

would have been no test. For Calvin what is integral to the drama is that until the angel intervenes Abraham has no confident belief about how the contradiction would be resolved. Abraham's later word to Isaac, the word that resolves the apparent contradictoriness of (1) and (2), that God will provide himself a lamb (v. 7) is taken by Calvin to be Abraham taking refuge in divine providence. By the provision of a lamb, together with the accompanying 'word', God delivers Abraham from the obligation to fulfil the command, thus resolving the contradiction.

So Calvin sees the story neither as making a contribution to the logical problem of evil, nor as an instance of the Divine Command Theory of ethics. but it is a special case of what is now referred to as the 'evidential problem of evil'. The 'evil' for Abraham is due to ignorance, and it is removed by the imparting of information at the critical moment.

It may be argued in objection to this that epistemic problems to do with conflicting norms do not entail the denial of the Divine Command Theory of ethics. And this is true: there may be two arbitrary commands which appear to be inconsistent but which are as a matter of fact consistent and can be shown to be so. However, in view of what we know from elsewhere about Calvin's views this option is not one that would be at all attractive to him. For Calvin the resolution of the impending contradiction comes about because of compelling evidence that the components of the impending contradiction are consistent with the goodness of the divine nature, and so consistent with each other, not simply that two arbitrary commands are as a matter of contingent fact found to be consistent.

Calvin's view is rather similar to that of Rabbi Leiner as quoted by Gellman:

The trial of the *akedah* has do with the greatness of Abraham's faith in God: even though God had told him [that his seed would be great] and that the covenant would be established through Isaac, and now he is being told to offer him up as a burnt offering, nonetheless, he believed in the first promises as before, and did not lose faith in them. And this faith is beyond human grasp.[32]

As Gellman comments, Abraham expects the sacrifice not to transpire, because God had made a promise inconsistent with its taking place. However, it is pressing things a bit too far to say, as Gellman does in commenting

---

[32] *The Fear, the Trembling and the Fire*, 77–8. For an interpretation of the *akedah* that intersects with Calvin's see Michael J. Harris, *Divine Command Ethics: Jewish and Christian Perspectives*, 'On the reading of Genesis 22 I am suggesting, then, God's purpose in testing Abraham has to do with Abraham's willingness to perform an act which God also deems immoral, and which He never intends that Abraham actually carry out. Once Abraham has passed the test, therefore, and it is clear that he is willing to give up Isaac at God's bidding, God naturally instructs Abraham not to perform the immoral act. On this heading of the episode, God at no point desires or intends that Abraham kill Isaac . . .' (127).

on Leiner's remarks, that Abraham believes in two contradictory outcomes, and that it is as a consequence of that his faith is 'beyond human grasp', being in human terms absurd. It is precisely because according to Calvin he does not believe in two contradictory outcomes that his faith is not paradoxical, a faith which defies coherent characterization. Abraham's faith is very great. As Calvin says in his *Commentary on Hebrews*, Abraham's faith is 'a singular instance of firmness, so that there is hardly another like it to be found'.[33] Abraham's faith is extraordinary, but it is not incoherent.

THE NATURE OF EQUITY

We now turn to look in more detail at Calvin's appeal to equity and to natural (or 'inward') law, and at the connection of these to the moral law. Here are two representative passages.

It is a fact that the law of God which we call the moral law is nothing else than a testimony of natural law and of that conscience which God has engraved upon the minds of men. Consequently, the entire scheme of this equity of which we are now speaking has been prescribed in it. Hence, this equity alone must be the goal and rule and limit of all laws.

Whatever laws shall be framed to that rule, directed to that goal, bound by that limit, there is no reason why we should disapprove of them, however they may differ from the Jewish law, or among themselves.[34]

So equity (whatever exactly this is) provides a rule, a goal, and a limit which actual laws ought to reflect. And Calvin suggests that different systems of law may reflect equity in different ways. How widely Calvin's approval of diverse systems of law is to be expressed is not clear. Let us suppose that it is equitable that husbands and wives should show mutual respect and devotion. Does this mean that Calvin might say we ought not to disapprove of the Hindu practice of Suttee, of wives being immolated on the funeral pyres of their dead spouses? We can be pretty sure that this is not, as he would see it, a permissible form of wifely devotion. Perhaps he gives evidence of what his reply would be to such a question in the following passage. Arguing that not only the ceremonial laws but also the judicial laws of Israel contained elements peculiar to their era, he says:

But if this is true, surely every nation is left free to make such laws as it foresees to be profitable for itself. Yet these must be in conformity to that perpetual rule of

---

[33] *Commentary on Hebrews*, 11: 17.

[34] *Inst.* IV. 20. 16. Cf. The relation of the moral law 'the true and eternal rule of righteousness' to natural law. All laws are founded on equity which 'is natural, cannot but be the same for all' (*Inst.* IV. 20. 15–16).

love, so that they indeed vary in form but have the same purpose. For I do not think that those barbarous and savage laws such as gave honour to thieves, permitted promiscuous intercourse, and others both more filthy and more absurd, are to be regarded as laws. For they are abhorrent not only to all justice, but also to all humanity and gentleness.[35]

So laws which flout the second table of the moral law are *ipso facto* inequitable, and so we should not exaggerate the pluralism that may seem to be implicit in what Calvin sometimes says. The point is, then, that different systems of laws may express the same values, even the same basic laws, in different ways, perhaps through varying kinds of rewards and punishments. So long as they express the moral law fairly they are to be approved. Calvin's conviction that it is the duty of the magistrate to uphold the moral law is clearly in evidence here. Aquinas makes a very similar point. 'Owing to the great variety of human affairs the common principles of natural law do not apply stiffly in every case. One outcome is the diversity of positive laws among different peoples.'[36]

'Equity' and 'equitable', when used as moral terms, can be applied either to persons or to law or laws. An equitable person is, roughly, a person who does not insist upon his own rights. But it is equity in the administration of law that we shall be concerned with here.

In the *Nicomachean Ethics* Aristotle discusses the relation between equity and justice. Equity is a kind of justice, and yet is better than one kind of justice. How so?

The reason is that all law is universal but about some things it is not possible to make a universal statement which shall be correct. In those cases, then, in which it is necessary to speak universally, but not possible to do so correctly, the law takes the usual case, though it is not ignorant of the possibility of error . . . When the law speaks universally, then, and a case arises on it which is not covered by the universal statement, then it is right, where the legislator fails us and has erred by over-simplicity, to correct the omission—to say what the legislator himself would have said had he been present, and would have put into his law if he had known. Hence the equitable is just, and better than one kind of justice—not better than absolute justice, but better than the error that arises out of the absoluteness of the statement. And this is the nature of the equitable, a correction of law where it is defective owing to its universality.[37]

[35] *Inst.* IV. 20. 15.

[36] *Summa Theologiae*, 1a, 2ae, 95. 2, trans. Thomas Gilby. Such views have their source in Augustine, for instance in his *Confessions*, 'I also did not know that true inward justice which judges not by custom but by the most righteous law of almighty God. By this law the moral customs of different regions and periods were adapted to their places and times, while that law itself remains unaltered everywhere and always. It is not one thing at one place or time, another thing at another', III. vii (13) trans. Henry Chadwick, 44.

[37] Aristotle, *The Nicomachean Ethics*, trans. David Ross, 5. 10 (133).

So Aristotle envisages two types of case where equity is to be employed as a higher kind of justice. The appeal to equity may perform a logical role, having to do with the qualifying or temporizing of the law, which is necessarily general in form, to particular 'hard' cases. The appeal to equity may, in addition, perform an epistemological role, where a given law is judged unfair because of the legislator's lack of foresight of possible circumstances. Had he possessed that foresight the law though remaining general in form would have been couched in different terms.

In his discussion of the concept of equity in Calvin's ethics Guenther Haas glosses Aristotle's use of equity here as the 'rectification of the law',[38] but this does not seem quite right because it suggests that the application of equity to the law in question must invariably result in the law being changed; this may cover the epistemological cases, but not the logical, and perhaps neither. Appeal to equity to override the provision of law in particular circumstances does not overturn the law, though no doubt many such overridings would weaken it.

In the *Summa Theologiae* Aquinas discusses the issue of equity mainly in two places; 2a, 2ae, 120, 'Epieikeia, or equity', and 2a, 2ae, 60. 5, 'Should judgment always be passed according to written laws?' In the first of these sections he asks whether equity is a virtue and a part of justice. In answering these questions he closely follows Aristotle in arguing that laws are necessarily general in form and equity seeks the interpretation of law in hard cases according to what it is believed the intention of the lawmaker would have been. According to equity, therefore, though it is part of the law that one should give back to the owner what one has borrowed from him it would be wrong to give back a borrowed sword to the owner who demanded it while in a fit of madness. Equity is therefore a form of justice; indeed, as with Aristotle, it is a higher form of justice than that which is to be found in those laws which equity is required to interpret or qualify.

As for epieikeia being, as Aristotle says *one form of justice*, it is a part of justice taken in the widest sense. In this way it is clearly a subjective part. And it is called justice in a fuller sense than legal justice, because epieikeia is a norm over and above legal justice. Epieikeia thus stands as a kind of higher rule for human actions.[39]

In the second of the sections Aquinas deals more explicitly with written law. He notes that some written laws are unjust, and once more makes the Aristotelian point that no written law can cover every individual happening.

Even as unjust laws of themselves conflict with natural right always or for the most part, so, too, laws that are rightly enacted fall short in cases when to observe

---

[38] Guenther H. Haas, *The Concept of Equity in Calvin's Ethics*, 88.
[39] *Summa Theologiae*, 2a, 2ae, 120. 2, trans. T. C. O'Brien.

them would be to offend against natural right. In such cases judgment should be delivered, not according to the letter of the law, but by recourse to equity, this being the intention of the lawgiver.[40]

So Aquinas contrasts written and unwritten law here, and claims that equity is part of natural law, the law that is in us by nature. He also makes the distinction between just and unjust laws more clearly than Aristotle, though as we have seen such a distinction may be said to be implicit in Aristotle.

CALVIN ON EQUITY

Haas claims and to my mind conclusively shows that Calvin clearly recognized and approved of the use of equity in such non-Christian sources as Aristotle, and that he also recognized the positive normative worth of equity. Calvin follows Aristotle in general terms (not necessarily directly, though he was familiar with the *Nicomachean Ethics*, but perhaps as mediated by the tradition[41]) in seeing a role for equity in the interpretation of law, and also in providing a place for equity among the virtues.[42] Haas shows effectively that for Calvin the recognition of equity, the sense of equity that we all possess, is a basic principle of natural law. The recognition of such a sense of equity on the part of Calvin is surely strong evidence, if evidence were needed, of his recognition of natural law, which as we have noted forms part of a person's natural knowledge of God. We shall return to the significance of this later on.[43]

So, like Haas, I am making what is surely a reasonable assumption, that this coincidence of view on the relation of equity to natural law in Calvin is evidence that the discussions of equity in Aristotle and Aquinas (and also Seneca) which we have been noting (and countless other scholastic

[40] *Summa Theologiae*, 2a, 2ae, 60. 5, trans. T. Gilby.

[41] As Irena Backus points out, in *Calvin's Commentary on Seneca's De Clementia* (published in 1532) he uses *aequitas* as a synonym for *epieikeia* though she claims that it does not seem to have altogether the same sense here as in some of Calvin's later works: 'Calvin's Concept of Natural and Roman Law', *Calvin Theological Journal*, (2003), 16.

[42] *The Concept of Equity in Calvin's Ethics*, 19, 88, 105. Because this chapter focuses on the relation between equity and law we shall pay almost no attention to the virtue of equity, to passages such as 'But suppose it be clear to all that Christ, in order to urge his followers more cogently to equity and concord, meant to show the many dangers and evils to which men expose themselves who obstinately prefer to demand the letter of the law rather than to act out of equity and goodness' (*Inst.* III. 5. 7).

[43] For recent account of Calvin's appeal to natural law in relation to providence see Susan E. Schreiner, *The Theater of His Glory*. Chapter 5 is especially valuable for showing the importance of natural law in Calvin's moral and social thought. A briefer, more general treatment by Schreiner, 'Calvin's Use of Natural Law', is to be found in Michael Cromartie (ed.), *Preserving Grace* (Grand Rapids, Mich.: Eerdmans, 1997).

discussions of the same themes), filtered through late medieval ethics and jurisprudence and were part of the cultural air that Calvin breathed. It must also be borne in mind that Calvin was a student of law at Orléans in 1528–9.[44] There seems to be no evidence which goes the other way, which suggests that Calvin repudiated this general outlook.

Haas claims that the two uses of the concept of equity in law in Aristotle influenced Calvin, but one more than the other. As we have noted Aristotle sees equity as an interpreter of human law where the application of the law in its generality or universality would lead to injustice in individual cases. And equity corrects or ought to correct any law which fails to attain to the standard of justice. According to Haas, Calvin uses equity as a benign interpreter of law, tempering its rigours with considerations of mercy and clemency, rather than (for example) in the rectification of positive law. It is not so obvious that one can separate these two uses as clearly as Haas thinks, though he is certainly correct in saying that Calvin sees no role for equity as a corrector of divine law, which is for Calvin the 'perfect rule of righteousness'.[45]

Law is essentially general in its scope; it does not make reference to individuals as such, nor to sets of circumstances peculiar to an individual, but to classes of individuals and to types of circumstances. Law is therefore too rough and clumsy a template to be imposed on all actions without qualification, and it is the role of equity to provide that qualification, to temper the rigours of the generality of law to the individual circumstances of a case. The appeal to equity in such cases would appear to be necessarily benign, since it is only called into play when the generality of law makes for harshness and arouses our disquiet. So while Haas contrasts the use of equity in softening the generality of law with the use of equity as a corrector of positive law, perhaps the two uses are connected in that the application of the formal aspect of equity (as Haas calls it) leads not to the abandoning of the law but to a modification in the *application* of law. So with a minor modification to Haas's account it is plausible to think that Calvin employs equity in each of these two senses and that in fact the two senses are not easily separable.

All this is certainly true when Calvin deals with some of the Mosaic judicial legislation. When Calvin comes to interpreting the Decalogue itself there is

---

[44] On this period of Calvin's career see Alexandre Ganoczy, *The Young Calvin*, trans. David Foxgrover and Wade Provo (Philadelphia: Westminster Press, 1987), ch. 3.

[45] Haas, *The Concept of Equity*, 88. Backus says that one use of *aequitas* for Calvin is 'consensus', as when the ethical systems of different cultures coincide. But there is more to the idea than a mere *de facto* correlation. For Calvin such coincidence is literally *de jure*, a reflection of the underlying influence of natural law ('Calvin's Concept of Natural and Roman Law', 16).

an interesting shift. Whereas it would be reasonable, a priori, to suppose that according to Calvin the Aristotelian point about the generality of law holds for all laws, including the Decalogue, in the case of the Decalogue, Calvin appeals to the intent of the lawgiver. By such an appeal Calvin does not limit the application of the law but enlarges its scope. This shift echoes earlier treatments of the Decalogue, for example Bonaventure's interpretation of the precept 'Do not kill'.

Accordingly, the Legislator, in this mandate 'do not kill', prohibits firstly anger breaking out in destructive injuries to natural life; secondly, to unmolested life, namely an injury done through words or through wounds; and thirdly, to honourable life, such as the injury which is done through open or hidden destruction indicated by some sign.[46]

Calvin follows this approach. He says nothing about any hard cases that the application of the Decalogue might give rise to, though it is not difficult to think of some, for example, where one commandment cuts across another, where the command to be truthful is in conflict with the command not to kill. But his chief concern is to argue that the particularities of the Decalogue ought to be generalized and intensified.

We must, I say, inquire how far interpretation ought to overstep the limits of the words themselves so that it may be seen to be, not an appendix added to the divine law from men's glosses, but the Lawgiver's pure and authentic meaning faithfully rendered. Obviously, in almost all the commandments there are such manifest synecdoches that he who would confine his understanding of the law within the narrowness of the words deserves to be laughed at. Therefore, plainly a sober interpretation of the law goes beyond the words; but just how far remains obscure unless some measure be set.[47]

As Allen Verhey succinctly puts it in his remarks on Calvin on natural law,

The basic ethical principle, I suggest, is equity. Equity validates certain fixed points, the commandments of the second table. From those fixed points it is possible to move rationally according to the principle of synecdoche, contraries and intention, to what is required of full neighbor love.[48]

So in the case of the Decalogue reference to the intention of the lawgiver intensifies and widens the scope of the law, it does not (as it may in the case of

---

[46] *Collationes de decem praeceptis*, vi. 4, quoted in Jean Porter, *Natural and Divine Law* (Grand Rapids, Mich.: Eerdmans/Novalis, 1999), 139.

[47] *Inst.* ii. 8. 8. In the passage from which this extract is taken Calvin refers explicitly to the Lesbian rule also referred to by Aristotle in his treatment of equity in book v of the *Nicomachean Ethics*. For a discussion of the generality versus particularity issue see J. R. Lucas, 'The Lesbian Rule', *Philosophy* (1955). See also Haas, *The Concept of Equity*, 88.

[48] 'Natural Law in Aquinas and Calvin', in Clifton J. Orlebeke and Lewis B. Smedes (eds.), *God and the Good* (Grand Rapids, Mich.: Eerdmans, 1975), 86.

other laws) limit or diminish it. Further, we can reasonably assume that in Calvin's eyes it would be wrong to attribute to the Divine lawgiver what Aristotle understandably attributes to some human legislators, namely a lack of foresight. However, there is no appeal to equity or to any other overriding value to ground the discussion.

In his treatment of some Old Testament legislation Calvin does use equity as a corrector of such legislation not (as with Aristotle) merely on account of its generality but because as it stands it is an inadequate measure of the true meaning of the law of God as revealed in the Decalogue and supremely in Christ. He applies the Thomistic point, something which he himself endorses, that written laws may be criticized on moral grounds, on the grounds of equity, and applies this to laws (other than the Decalogue) enunciated by God himself, as we noted in our earlier discussion of divine accommodation.

Commenting on the legislation about slavery set out in Exodus 21 Calvin writes:

Their enfranchisement is, therefore, enjoined, but with an exception, which Moses expresses in the first passage but omits in the latter, *i.e.* that if the slave had married a bond-woman, and had begotten children, they should remain with the master, and that he should alone be free. Whence it appears how hard was the condition of slaves, since it could not be mitigated without an unnatural exception (*sine prodigio*); for nothing could be more opposed to nature than that a husband, forsaking his wife and children, should remove himself elsewhere. But the tie of slavery could only be loosed by divorce, that is to say, by this impious violation of marriage. There was then gross barbarity in this severance, whereby a man was disunited from half of himself and his own bowels. Yet there was no remedy for it . . . The sanctity of marriage therefore gave way in this case to private right.[49]

And further:

From this passage, as well as other similar ones, it plainly appears how many vices were of necessity tolerated in this people. It was altogether an act of barbarism that fathers should sell their children for the relief of their poverty, still it could not be corrected as might have been hoped.[50]

It seems that Calvin believes that what God could command (with the expectation that the command would be obeyed) is constrained by cultural circumstances. God cannot in all cases command what he would prefer to command. Nevertheless, his command is obligatory, even though 'inequitable'. In other words there are situations in which the social conditions are such that not even the Lord can legislate in accordance with his nature but rather has to go with the grain of institutions such as slavery.

---

[49] *Harmony on the Four Last Books of Moses*, III. 159–60.
[50] *Harmony on the Four Last Books of Moses*, III. 80–1.

Such passages seem to identify a third use of equity for Calvin, not only to temper the generality of law, and to criticize positive law as unjust, but even to offer a critique of divinely sanctioned positive law. Medieval philosophers and theologians such as Aquinas do not seem to use the appeal to equity in this third function; but Calvin certainly does.

However, one ought not to get too excited about Calvin's sense of equity. It has an important function in his ethics, as we have seen, but for him its meaning falls rather short of what equity has come to mean in the modern world. This is vividly illustrated by an examination of the Registers of the Consistory of Geneva. During the early years of the Reformation in Geneva the Consistory met every Thursday in Geneva as a civil court and Calvin was usually present as a member. There is no evidence in the Records that the Consistory was sensitive to the rules of evidence, to the need for the accused to have legal representation, or to the need for the presumption of innocence. Not surprisingly in this as in much else Calvin was a child of his time.[51]

CALVIN, THE MEDIEVAL OUTLOOK, AND NATURAL LAW

We now turn to Calvin's attitude to natural law. In doing so we do not turn away from the idea of equity, not at least in Calvin's eyes, but attend to its development. For him natural law seems to have three essential main components. It is normative, setting forth values, standards, rights, etc. rooted in human nature and in its *telos*. Secondly, the law thus set forth is to some degree accessible to humankind in general, the naturalness of the norms being recognized by all without recourse to revelation. And thirdly, the norms apply to everyone irrespective of the epoch or culture in which they live. It will be helpful to have these three features in mind as we reflect further on Calvin's attitude to natural law.

Any attempt to discuss Calvin's relation to the natural law has certain initial obstacles to overcome. For there are those who have argued that Calvin makes 'an entire break from the Scholastic conception of creation and existence'.[52] Two arguments are offered by T. F. Torrance for this sweeping view. The first is that Calvin has a view of God's relation to the world as being dynamic rather than static. What this means, according to Torrance, is that in Calvin's theology the idea of secondary causation has no real place. But this would mean that Calvin's own express commitment to secondary causation has to be explained away, and that his theological position then becomes indistinguishable from occasionalism or even perhaps from

---

[51] *Registers of the Consistory of Geneva in the Time of Calvin*, Vol. i, *1542–4*, ed. R. M. Kingdon, T. A. Lambert, I. M. Wart, trans. M. W. McDonald (Grand Rapids, Mich.: Eerdmans/The Meeter Center, 2000).

[52] T. F. Torrance, *Calvin's Doctrine of Man* (London: Lutterworth Press, 1949), 29.

pantheism. For a theology in which there is no secondary causation is one in which God is the only cause of everything that happens. It would follow that rather than it being the case that I am the cause of this chapter being typed God is the cause of it. While such claims are characteristic of occasionalism Calvin does not entertain them. To appeal, in support of such an interpretation of Calvin's theology, to his remarks about God's constant upholding of the creation is not in point here, since similar remarks can be found in the allegedly 'static' medieval tradition.[53]

Calvin makes frequent appeals to the distinction between God the primary cause, and secondary causes, sometimes rather elaborately. As we noted in Chapter 4, in his introduction to *A Defence of the Secret Providence of God* he refers to the various kinds of relation of the power of God to the creation as 'with their means', 'without their means', or 'contrary to their means'.[54]

As all inferior and secondary causes, viewed in themselves, veil like so many curtains the glorious God from our sight (which they too frequently do), the eye of faith must be cast up far higher, that it may behold the hand of God working by all these His instruments.[55]

We must here also carefully bear in mind that principle which I have before laid down, that when God displays His power through *means (media)* and *secondary causes*, that power of His is never to be *separated* from those means or inferior causes.[56]

A clear endorsement of the distinction between primary and secondary causes.

The second argument which Torrance offers for the alleged break between Calvin and his medieval past is that Calvin understands the doctrine of God in terms of verbs rather than abstract qualities or properties. This is not universally true of Calvin's treatment of God,[57] but even if it were, the alleged distinction between the static and the dynamic ignores the fact that for the medievals, with their supposedly static view of God, God is *pure act*, and it skates over the question of *what* verbs are used to explain the character of God.

Putting such arguments to one side, then, we shall orientate the discussion of Calvin's views by first considering the medieval position on natural law as typically expressed by Aquinas. Aquinas discussed the theme of natural law

---

[53] T. F. Torrance, *Calvin's Doctrine of Man*, 29. 'The second [way in which a thing may be kept in being by another] is a per se and direct way of preserving a thing in existence, insofar, namely, as the thing preserved is so dependent that without the preserver it could not exist. This is the way that all creatures need God to keep them in existence. For the *esse* of all creaturely beings so depends upon God that they could not continue to exist even for a moment, but would fall away into nothingness unless they were sustained in existence by his power, as Gregory puts it' (*Summa Theologiae*, 1a, 104. 1, trans. T. C. O'Brien).

[54] *The Secret Providence of God*, 230.   [55] *The Secret Providence of God*, 231.

[56] *The Secret Providence of God*, 235.   [57] e.g. *Inst.* I. 10. 2.

at great length in *Summa Theologiae*, 1a, 2ae, 98–105. In considering what he calls 'the Old Law', that is, the legal system of the Old Testament, he maintains the following four positions:

(i) 'The Old Law clearly set forth the obligations of the natural law, and over and above these added certain precepts of its own.'[58]

The setting forth of the natural law in the Old Law was entirely appropriate since though with regard to those precepts of the natural law which are absolutely, universally accepted, 'man's reason could not be misled in principle . . . it could be confused by the effect of habitual sin as to what ought to be done in particular cases'.[59] Here, as with Calvin, there is recognition of a partial overlap between Old Law (the Decalogue) and the content of the natural law. And more surprisingly, perhaps, Aquinas believed that the identification and application of natural law is spoiled by sin.

(ii) There is a threefold distinction to be drawn between moral, ceremonial, and judicial precepts of the Old Law.

This distinction provides that basic framework within which Aquinas then discusses the nature of law.

(iii) 'The moral precepts, as distinct from the ceremonial and judicial, are concerned with matters which, of their very nature, belong to right conduct.'[60]

(iv) Because the precepts of the Decalogue are, in all essentials, the natural law, they can be understood by natural reason.

Thus two kinds of precepts are not comprised in the Decalogue: the primary and general which, being inscribed in natural reason as self-evident, need no further promulgation, such as that one should do evil to no one, and others such; and those which are found, on careful examination on the part of wise men, to be in accord with reason—these are received by the people from God by instruction from the wise. Nevertheless, both these kinds of precept are contained in the precepts of the Decalogue, though in different ways. Those which are primary and general are contained in them as principles in their proximate conclusions: while, conversely, those which are mediated by the wise are contained in them as conclusions in their principles. Hence: 1. These two precepts are primary and general precepts of the law of nature, self-evident to human nature, whether by nature or by faith. Consequently all the precepts of the Decalogue are related to them as conclusions to general principles.[61]

The precepts, therefore, contained in the Decalogue are those the knowledge of which man has in himself from God. They can be known straight away from first general principles with but little reflection.[62] The precepts of the

---

[58] Thomas Aquinas, *Summa Theologiae*, 1a, 2ae, 98. 5, trans. David Bourke and Arthur Littledale.

[59] Aquinas, *Summa Theologiae*, 1a, 2ae, 99. 2.   [60] Aquinas, *Summa Theologiae*, 1a, 2ae, 100. 1.

[61] *Summa Theologiae*, 1a, 2ae, 100. 3.

Decalogue are concerned with matters which the mind of man can grasp instantly.[63]

Finally,

The moral precepts derive their force from the dictate of natural reason, even if they had not been expressed in the Law. Now they fall into three groups. Some are absolutely certain, and so evident as not to need promulgation, such as the commandments about love of God and one's neighbour, and others of the sort, as we have said, which constitute, as it were, the end of the precepts; and so no one could be mistaken about them. Others are more determinate in character, yet the reason for them can easily be seen even by the most ordinary intelligence. Yet since, in a few cases, human judgment may be misled about them, they need to be promulgated. These are the precepts of the Decalogue.[64]

Reading these words of Aquinas one cannot fail to be struck by a number of evident similarities and equally evident dissimilarities between his position and Calvin's. What are these similarities and differences? We must make a broad and rough distinction between the ontological status of natural law, what the natural law is, its epistemological status, how it is known, and thirdly, how it is to be applied. The relation between Aquinas and Calvin might roughly be expressed as one of considerable agreement about the first, of some disagreement about the second, and agreement about the third.

In English 'natural' can be contrasted with 'supernatural', used as equivalent to universal, to innate, to sinful, and as opposed to contrived or designed, and these are but a few of its most prominent meanings. This should make us cautious in saying what Calvin's view of natural law was. When Calvin uses the term it means, at least 'a law that is not in fact specially i.e. verbally revealed by God, though one that is revealable in this way'. In addition he seems to mean that this law is 'universally distributed', known to all mankind. We have seen that he thinks that the content of the natural law has a rough correspondence with the second table of the Decalogue in the sense that societies can arrive at such laws unaided by divine revelation. Most strikingly of all, perhaps, there are places where he equates natural law with the Golden Rule. Here are two references to that equation from his *Sermons on the Ten Commandments*, the first one from the point where he is discussing theft.

---

[62] Aquinas, 1a, 2ae, 100. 3. Compare Bishop Joseph Butler, 'Yet let any plain honest man, before he engages in any course of action, ask himself, Is this I am going about right, or is it wrong? Is it good, or is it evil? I do not in the least doubt but that this question would be answered agreeably to truth and virtue, by almost any fair man in almost any circumstance' (*Fifteen Sermons Preached at the Rolls Chapel*, III. 4 (London: G. Bell & Sons Ltd., 1967), 63).   [63] Aquinas, *Summa Theologiae*, 1a, 2ae, 100. 6.

[64] Aquinas *Summa Theologiae*, 1a, 2ae, 100. 11.

Furthermore, seeing that we should not operate in such a way by either finesse or subtlety, it is crucial for us to return to that natural law, (*equité naturelle*) which is, that we ought to do unto others as we want them to do unto us. When we follow that rule, it is unnecessary to have thick tomes in order to learn not to steal, for, in brief, everyone knows how he ought to walk with his fellowman, that is, that he should not harbor malice, or attempt to enrich himself at his neighbor's expense, or gain for himself substance which is not his own.[65]

Without being aware of Jesus' teaching everyone knows what the Golden Rule teaches. Later there is a reference to the natural law of not doing anything to anyone unless we would want them to do the same to us.[66] So Calvin appears to hold that the law of nature is that law of God concerning man's relationship to God, and the relationship of people with each other which is known to some degree by all human beings, for even 'barbarians' are not as barbaric as could be.

We have already seen that it is difficult to keep apart questions about what the natural law is and how that law is to be apprehended or understood. How do those who are aware of the natural law learn it? When Calvin says that 'to begin with, God's image was visible in the light of the mind, in the uprightness of the heart, and in the soundness of all the parts'[67] what he says clearly has implications for human knowledge. Was the knowledge that such an enlightened and fully integrated individual possessed innate? It would seem so, in that Calvin goes on to say that knowledge of the heavenly life 'was engraved upon his soul'. 'Man in his first condition excelled in these pre-eminent endowments, so that his reason, understanding, prudence, and judgement not only sufficed for the direction of his earthly life, but by them men mounted up to God and eternal bliss.'[68]

But whatever the exact position was originally, whether the knowledge of the natural law was innate or acquired, Calvin is clear that at present, in his sinful and fallen condition, man is unable by the exercise of his own powers alone (action that is 'natural' in yet another sense) to reacquire and retain the knowledge of God's natural law in its entirety. Calvin is emphatic on this point, as being the plight of fallen humankind, all 'in Adam'. Yet he characteristically adds that through the continued activity of conscience each man knows enough of God's original, natural law, as a result of which he is rendered inexcusable before God for his sin.

As to the natural law itself, there are important similarities between the two theologians. Each bases his view on Romans 2: 14–15. Each maintains that the Decalogue contains the natural law clearly set forth. Each subscribes

---

[65] *John Calvin's Sermons on the Ten Commandments*, trans. B. W. Farley (Grand Rapids, Mich.: Baker, 1980), 189.   [66] *John Calvin's Sermons on the Ten Commandments*, 247.

[67] *Inst.* I. 15. 4. See also II. 8. 1.   [68] *Inst.* I. 15. 8.

to the threefold distinction between moral, ceremonial, and judicial precepts of the Mosaic Law.[69] Both ground the goodness of natural law both in the character of God and in human nature, whose flourishing the natural law promotes. However, there is one crucial difference. When we turn to the extent to which the natural law is naturally known Aquinas is much more sanguine than is Calvin about whether human reason unaided by special grace can identify it, and the degree to which it recognizes its obligatoriness. The natural law allows men and women to have the knowledge of good and evil. For Aquinas the natural law is natural both in the sense that it is a divine law for human nature given at the creation, and in the sense that it may now be successfully apprehended as a set of precepts, by unaided fallen reason alone. This is one reason why Aquinas does not stress as much as Calvin does the importance of the enlightening and focusing character of the Decalogue upon the natural law. The other reason is that for Calvin the natural knowledge of the natural law is expressed in terms of tendencies and dispositions.[70]

So for Aquinas the Decalogue has an epistemologically subordinate role to the clearly apprehensible (but not always clearly apprehended) precepts of the natural law. Natural law is knowable and known by the natural reason of man as he now is. The knowledge of the content of the Decalogue in precise terms is not, it would seem, innate, but it follows at once from the knowledge of first principles. Thus from the self-evident moral principle that one should do evil to no one it follows that one should not kill. Aquinas says that 'all the precepts of the Decalogue are related to them [the primary and general precepts of the law of nature] as conclusions to general principles'.[71] This is true even of the fourth commandment, which follows from (to Aquinas) the self-evident principle that some time ought to be set aside for the worship of God. What is *not* part of the natural law is that this span of time should be one day in seven, or that it should comprise the seventh day of each week, but then both these features, according to Aquinas (and certainly the fact of the obligatoriness for Jews in the Old Testament of worship on the seventh day), are ceremonial precepts due to the historically conditioned circumstances in which the Decalogue was promulgated.

So for Aquinas the Decalogue supplements natural law. It provides a primary set of applications from the natural law (*precepts of the short range*) which each person could have worked out for himself by the use of his reason drawing upon his innate moral principles, his personal endowment of the moral law, at least insofar as they do not (as with the fourth commandment)

---

[69] At *Inst.* IV. 20. 15 Calvin recognizes the 'common division' of laws between moral, ceremonial, and legal.   [70] On this point see Backus, 'Calvin's Concept of Natural and Roman Law', 11–12.

[71] *Summa Theologiae*, 1a, 2ae, 100. 3.

involve a ceremonial element. Let us call the laws which contain a divinely commanded ceremonial element *precepts of the middle range*. In addition there are *precepts of the far range* which 'wise men' find by careful examination to be implied by both the basic moral principles and the precepts of the middle range. Such a principle might perhaps be that it is permissible to kill an enemy in the prosecution of a just war.

The contrast with Calvin at this point is fairly sharp. For Aquinas the revelation of the Decalogue complements the natural law which is recognizable by all. For Calvin, though those without benefit of special revelation know that there is a natural law and have some sense of its content, nevertheless what that moral law is can as a result of the Fall only be known clearly through a reasoned understanding of special revelation. It is only with the hindsight that special revelation provides that the content of natural law can now be recognized for what it is. So Calvin moves in the opposite direction from Thomas. For Thomas, the Decalogue expresses particular instances of the natural law, which we know as well as or even better than the Decalogue. Calvin recognizes the fact of natural law, and the limited though essential role that it plays, but the Decalogue has a more fundamental epistemological position. From its particularities more general principles, covering a wide range of conduct, may be derived. Nonetheless, even for Calvin the natural law functioning in those bereft of special revelation has a positive effect.

Yet this is perhaps too pessimistic an estimate of Calvin's view of our natural knowledge of natural law. In his *Commentary* on Romans 2: 14, 15 he says (v. 15) that there is not in men a full knowledge of the law, only some seeds of what is right implanted in their nature, some notions of justice and rectitude. Yet these seeds grew and blossomed. All nations 'of themselves and without a monitor, are disposed to make laws for themselves', 'laws to punish adultery, and theft and murder, they commended good faith in bargains and contracts'.[72] So while the seed of religion that remains in fallen human nature has a moral dimension this seed does not remain dormant but expresses itself in laws which fairly closely shadow the laws of the Decalogue.[73]

[72] *Commentaries on the Epistle to the Romans*, 96, 98.

[73] According to Harro Höpfl, 'Calvin thought that "nature" or "natural sense" or "reason" teaches the authority of fathers over wives and children, the sanctity of monogamous marriage, the duty to care for families, breast-feeding, primogeniture (albeit with qualifications) the sacrosanctity of envoys and ambassadors, the obligation of promises, degrees of marriage, the need for witnesses in murder trials, the need for a distinction of ranks in society; and natural law prohibits incest, murder, adultery, slavery, and even the rule of one man. And again, nature itself teaches the duty to award honours only to those qualified, respect for the old, equity in commercial dealings and that religion must be the first concern of governors' (*The Christian Polity of John Calvin* (Cambridge: Cambridge University Press, 1982), 180). He provides textual support for each of these claims.

So maybe it is exaggerated to think that for Calvin the Decalogue has an epistemological primacy. We have already noted that he thinks that it exercises a condemnatory function. But the recognition of natural obligations apart from revelation exercises a restraining influence. Allen Verhey sums up the contrast between Aquinas and Calvin on this point in the following suggestive way:

Thomas's natural law claims to lead to the fulness of the good life minus only the theological virtues. Calvin's natural law claims only to protect the boundaries of human nature, beyond which the image of God is lost entirely. Thomas provides ends to be sought by man. Calvin provides limits to the actions of men seeking their own ends. In both, however, the law is instrumental to grace.[74]

Irena Backus thinks that despite similarities of terminology Aquinas's and Calvin's concepts of natural law do not have a great deal in common[75] but in fact there is simply a difference of degree between them, one which no doubt is due to different degrees of confidence in unaided human powers. Each grants some unaided understanding of at least the second table of the Decalogue, and each allows that this unaided understanding may be skewed by differences in culture and civilization. Calvin's emphasis on conscience, which Backus thinks is significant, echoes Paul's, and is explained by the fact that he gives greater weight to the power of our natural knowledge of the natural law to render a person inexcusable than does Aquinas. For Calvin this is the main theme of Romans 2: 14, 15. Yet however we weigh the differences in emphasis between the two on the knowledge of natural law they agree on the vital point that a person's recognition of the obligation to keep the commandments is 'confused by the effect of habitual sin'. So a person needs grace fully to identify his obligations and to be motivated to discharge them.

What Calvin says about the 'civic' use of the law, its function as a socially enforced deterrent against evil, is consistent with what he says about the relation between natural law and the Decalogue. He does not argue that the law is obeyed because it is in fact seen to be reasonable, and disobeyed because it is judged to be unreasonable, but it deters (where it does) because of the sanctions of the law.

But they are restrained, not because their inner mind is stirred or affected, but because, being bridled, so to speak, they keep their hands from outward activity, and hold inside the depravity that otherwise they would wantonly have indulged.

---

[74] 'Natural Law in Aquinas and Calvin', 82.

[75] 'Calvin's Concept of Natural and Roman Law', 12. She says at one point that Calvin removes natural law in all its expressions from the purview of the church (11). But if for Calvin the moral law is an expression of the natural law it is hard to see what plausibility this claim has.

Consequently, they are neither better nor more righteous before God. Hindered by fright or shame, they dare neither execute what they have conceived in their minds, nor openly breathe forth the rage of their lust. Still, they do not have hearts disposed to fear and obedience toward God.[76]

So it is only with the motivation and the moral power that regenerating grace gives that there is even the *prospect* of a properly motivated obedience to moral law. Aquinas would broadly agree with this.[77] (There is only the prospect of this, never of complete fulfilment in this life, because, as Calvin's interpretation of Romans 7 indicates, he takes the broadly Augustinian position that the life of the regenerate is characterized by conflict between the awareness of moral weakness and aspirations to keep the law of God.) So that intellectually the natural, unregenerate man fails to recognize the moral law for what it is, and particularly the first table of the moral law, and morally fails to keep it. 'If we want to measure our reason by God's law, the pattern of perfect righteousness, we shall find in how many respects it is blind!'[78] For even such general understanding and keeping of the second table as there is is superficial and one-sided, wrongly motivated and without true self-knowledge. Such understanding has, as Calvin repeatedly stresses, a civic use, but it cannot bring a person to God.

For the natural man refuses to be led to recognize the diseases of his lusts. The light of nature is extinguished before he even enters upon this abyss. While the philosophers label the immoderate incitements of the mind as 'vices', they have reference to those which are outward and manifest by grosser signs. They take no account of the evil desires that gently tickle the mind.[79]

The difference between Aquinas and Calvin regarding the apprehension of the law of nature encapsulates important aspects of the Reformation conflict. It was a conflict about the primacy and sufficiency, or otherwise, of the Bible considered as God's special revelation, about the extent of human sinfulness, and about the need for the power of God's regenerating grace. Calvin holds that there is an under-estimation of the noetic effects of sin possibly in the likes of Aquinas and certainly in the case of the classical philosophers more generally. He thinks that the idea that sin is solely a matter of sensuality prevails with them whereas for Calvin sin affects the understanding, not by destroying it but by depraving it. In particular the moral understanding is not completely wiped out, but it is choked with ignorance and prejudice, as a result of which without divine grace the will cannot strive after what is right.

---

[76] *Inst.* II. 7. 10.

[77] See, for example, *Summa Contra Gentiles*, III. 147. 5, quoted in Arvin Vos, *Aquinas, Calvin, and Contemporary Protestant Thought*, 137–8.   [78] *Inst.* II. 2. 24.   [79] *Inst.* II. 2. 24.

The relative positions of Calvin and Aquinas on natural law have a parallel in their respective views on natural theology. We might legitimately discuss what importance Aquinas's natural theology has for his religious epistemology as a whole[80] but there is no denying the fact of his natural theology. By reason alone, starting from self-evident principles, any sufficiently intelligent rational man with sufficient time may demonstrate that God exists. This is what Aquinas thought Paul was teaching in Romans 1. Natural theology is possible but not necessary for faith, and some must accept as *opinio*, even though with a considerable degree of certitude, what for others is *scientia*.

Calvin is much more cautious. As we saw in Chapter 8 it would be wrong to suppose that he thinks that there is no natural knowledge of God. But it would be exaggerated to suppose that there is firm evidence that Calvin is committed to a full-orbed natural theology, even though he occasionally endorses it.[81] Rather what we find in Calvin here is precisely what we find in his treatment of the natural law, that man has from the creation around him clues about the existence of God and of his law, clues which he—predictably but culpably—fails to follow up.

But why, if natural law plays the subordinate and residual role that we have been arguing for in Calvin, does he find it important to insist on it? Was it indeed important? Or are the references in Calvin to natural law stray references which are alien to his real view? What is the force of saying that some particular injunction is a part of the natural law, if the apprehension of that natural law is at present hedged about with such difficulties, and in fact can only be apprehended with the help of the special revelation? Why not rest satisfied with an appeal to the commands of special revelation?

There are two answers to these questions. One answer is in terms of the distinction between nature and convention. To suppose that the Sabbath and all divine laws were only explicit specially revealed commands, with no grounding in the created nature of things, would allow that they were merely conventional, a law made merely as a result of divine fiat, and perhaps of an arbitrary, temporary, and adventitious character. But as we saw earlier, in our discussion of the Divine Command Theory, it appears that though for Calvin the judicial and ceremonial laws are indexed, the moral law arises out of the very nature of God and of the creation. This is why he is not a Divine Command Theorist in any than an epistemological way. The second reason is that only by assigning some priority to natural law which everyone has some knowledge of can a satisfactory account be given of the inexcusability of everyone, both those who have special revelation and those without

---

[80] For discussion of such points see Paul Helm, *Faith and Understanding*.

[81] Cf. B. B. Warfield, *Calvin and Calvinism* (New York: Oxford University Press, 1931), 41–2.

benefit of it, and only thus can the need for divine grace be secured. This is what Calvin believes Paul teaches in Romans 1 and 2.

We saw in Chapter 8 that according to Calvin the human race has a corrupted *sensus divinitatis* in both its metaphysical and its moral aspects. How does this bear on the idea of the sense of equity to which Calvin frequently appeals? Whether or not Calvin has a much more positive account of the natural awareness of equity—the employment of the moral aspects of the *sensus divinitatis*—than of the metaphysical in the early chapters of the *Institutes*, there is no doubt about his positive estimate of equity and the force of his appeal to it in passages such as those from his commentary on the last four books of Moses. Yet the commentary passages show that in Calvin's view though equity is a natural endowment it is not equally distributed. According to his appeal to equity in these passages the awareness of natural law serves not simply to make a person responsible before God for his actions, but results (where social conditions permit it) in laws of permanent moral value even though these laws may differ markedly from one society to another, and from one time to another.

But there is nothing as positive as this in the case of the perverted *sensus divinitatis* in its metaphysical apprehensions. We have seen that Calvin recognizes that the *sensus* in its metaphysical apprehensions is perverted to such an extent that it may manifest itself in polytheistic beliefs, or even in avowed atheism. So whereas for Calvin the sense of equity functions as a hermeneutical control of his understanding and acceptance of the ethical force of certain passages of Scripture (a sense of equity that is natural, and therefore also possessed by those who are not beneficiaries of special revelation, or who do not wish to avail themselves of its benefits), it is difficult if not utterly impossible to imagine Calvin endorsing a similar line of argument with respect to the metaphysical-cognitive aspects of the *sensus divinitatis*. As far as I am aware Calvin never argues that the ancient Israelites' conception of God (or anyone else's conception of God, for that matter) is corrigible in the light of what men generally know of the nature of God, and it is hard to imagine him arguing thus.

But in the absence of such arguments the interpreter of Calvin is faced with a dilemma, or perhaps a straight choice. Either he must say that for Calvin the degeneration of the moral aspects of the natural knowledge of God was much less serious than the degeneration of the metaphysical aspects, or he must say that the account given by Calvin of the moral effects of the Fall in the early chapters of the *Institutes*, an account which seems to echo that which he gives of the effects of the Fall on our knowledge of the nature and reality of God, is at odds with what he writes elsewhere. Let us now consider this point in a little more detail.

Without stretching things unduly the two aspects of the *sensus divinitatis* may be said for Calvin to correspond to an intuitive awareness of the commands of the first and second table of the Decalogue respectively. The moral component of the *sensus*, that which chiefly concerns us here, concerns the awareness of certain obligations arising out of the knowledge of the fact that God is the source of all goodness. Such an awareness conveys a sense of obligation to those who are made in the image of God. Among the remaining traces of the moral knowledge of God is the sense of equity which as we have seen is universally if not equally distributed.

So perhaps the view that Calvin's accounts of the metaphysical and the moral aspects of the corrupted *sensus divinitatis* are parallel is misplaced. Evidence for this might be found in the fact that whereas the corrupted *sensus*, as far as it concerns metaphysical issues, is marked by a lack of consensus, the corrupted *sensus* as far as it concerns moral matters is fairly uniform in the verdicts that it delivers. The metaphysical aspect of the *sensus*, when corrupted, expresses itself in polytheism, in animism, even in atheism, whereas the moral aspect, even when corrupted, expresses itself (with certain notable exceptions, namely in those whom Calvin refers to as 'the barbarians') in a certain minimal understanding and respect for the law of God though not necessarily *as* the law of God, and a widely dispersed sense of equity. 'The human mind sometimes seems more acute in this [the "knowledge of the works of righteousness"] than in higher things... There is nothing more common than for a man to be sufficiently instructed in a right standard of conduct by natural law.'[82] So we may conclude from this that although the *sensus* remains in the members of fallen humanity the moral aspect of the *sensus* is more deeply embedded than is the metaphysical aspect, though even this does not function equally in all. For whereas it is possible to be an atheist, it is usually not possible to avoid the activity of the conscience and conscience is the voice of equity, even though it is a voice that is often distorted and out of tune.

---

[82] *Inst.* II. 2. 22. Here I find myself dissenting from what can only be regarded as an eccentric interpretation of Calvin, that of Dewey Hoitenga. In his *John Calvin and the Will*, Hoitenga claims that there is a strong asymmetry between Calvin's claim (in such places as *Inst.* II. 2. 13) that since the Spirit is the sole fountain of truth we dishonour the Spirit if we do not give due recognition to the truth wherever it appears, and an unwillingness to invite us similarly to accept moral goodness wherever it appears (120). But in my view the asymmetry is, if anything, the other way. Calvin recognizes the widespread influence of the natural law even in places where there is no recognition of the truth of God's existence, or a very distorted recognition. As if in confirmation of the eccentricity of his interpretation of Calvin, Hoitenga proceeds on the very next page to acknowledge that in fact Calvin does recognize that 'fallen human beings are still social and political animals and that they can frame their earthly lives in accord with the second table of the law' (121).

Natural Law and the Laws

So far we have looked at the conceptual context in which Calvin developed his ideas of natural law. In this section we shall consider further what he says about natural law, having in mind its relation to other kinds of law.

Writing about the Fourth Commandment Calvin distinguishes between those features of it which are ceremonial from those that are moral (and hence in some sense natural). By Christ's coming the ceremonial part of this commandment was abolished (implying that the non-ceremonial part of it was not). And Calvin proceeds to identify the non-ceremonial elements. Later in the *Institutes* he further elaborates his treatment of the law, making a distinction between moral, ceremonial, and legal commands.

In certain important respects the detailed content of God's revealed law goes beyond the natural law. While natural law finds embodiment in the Decalogue, the Decalogue is not simply a verbalizing of the natural law, but contains non-natural, conventional, ceremonial elements, particularly relating to the Sabbath. 'By the Lord Christ's coming the ceremonial part of this commandment was abolished',[83] indicating that the Mosaic re-publication of the law of nature contained figurative and proleptic features suited to that era of redemptive special revelation.

Of course a thinker such as Aquinas would agree with this. The fact that he had a more sanguine view than Calvin about our ability to apprehend and fulfil the elements of the natural law does not mean that he believed that the revealed moral law is useless. And with Calvin he holds that although men and women can, in their fallen state, obey the law, they cannot do so out of charity, love for God and man, without grace.

In a second way the commandments can be fulfilled not only as regards the substance of the action but also as regards the mode of action, such that these actions are done out of charity. And in this sense man cannot fulfil the commandments without grace, either in the state of intact nature or in the state of spoiled nature . . . in both states men need in addition the assistance of God moving them to fulfil the commandments, as was said.[84]

Does this mean that the New Testament amendment of the Sabbath teaching of the Decalogue amounts to a return to the pre-Mosaic law of nature? Not for Calvin, since for him the Lord's Day of the New Testament is inextricably bound up with the fact of Christ's resurrection. So it might be said that while the law of nature, in Calvin's view, obliges all men to keep one day in seven, and perhaps obliged them to keep the seventh day (in Calvin's commentary on Genesis the seventh-day Sabbath is regarded as a 'creation ordinance'[85]),

---

[83] *Inst.* II. 8. 31.　　　[84] *Summa Theologiae*, 1a, 2ae, 109. 4 (trans. Cornelius Ernst).

[85] *Commentary on Genesis*, 2: 3.

it does not oblige all men everywhere and at all times to keep the seventh day as the Sabbath as the Jews under Moses ought to have and did, nor to keep the first day as in Calvin's view the Christians ought to.

In fact in his discussion of the Sabbath Calvin's emphasis does not fall on the one-day-in-seven principle being a 'creation ordinance'. For the Christian Sunday does not replace the Jewish Sabbath. Sunday is not a Christian Sabbath. Rather Sunday serves the practical function as the agreed day for Christian worship and as a day or rest. But the Jewish Sabbath was one of those 'days' which, according to Paul (Col. 2: 17, Gal. 4: 10–11), Christians have no obligation to keep.[86] Even had the emphasis fallen on the Sabbath as a creation ordinance Calvin could not consistently have held that this is an aspect of natural law, since the fact of the Lord's resting on the seventh day is not knowable by unaided reason, but it is revealed. As the Old Testament Sabbath arrangement as expressed in the Decalogue contained ceremonial elements, so there are other commands of God which are not at all moral, namely the ceremonial laws. 'The ceremonial law was the tutelage of the Jews, with which it seemed good to the Lord to train this people, as it were, in their childhood, until the fullness of time should come.'[87]

We can see from these statements, incidentally, the far-reaching hermeneutical consequences of Calvin's reliance upon natural law. The knowledge of the natural law, with which mankind was endowed at the creation, is of permanent validity. It is re-expressed in the Decalogue. It cannot, therefore, be that law which was the schoolmaster of the Jews to bring them to Christ, and which according to Galatians 3: 24, 25 is done away with in Christ. But what are done away with are the ceremonial laws or elements of laws which are non-natural or purely conventional in character. The natural law, shorn of its ceremonial and judicial elements, is re-expressed, endorsed, and highlighted by Christ (for example, in the Sermon on the Mount, and especially in the Golden Rule), and by the Apostles in their correspondence.

Finally, what of the relation of the natural law to the judicial law? For Calvin the judicial law is connected with the idea of civil government, which in turn is connected to his idea of the two kingdoms, the 'spiritual and inward Kingdom of Christ' and 'civil government'.[88] He is concerned to uphold civil government against Anabaptistic moves to establish the kingdom of Christ on earth which are, for Calvin, the product of an unwarranted perfectionism. The idea of two governments or kingdoms is also connected with Calvin's idea of Christian freedom.[89] Also Calvin's body–soul dualism, which we discussed in Chapter 5, has a rather surprising application here.

---

[86] *Inst.* II. 8. 33. For further discussion of Calvin's view of the Sabbath see Richard B. Gaffin, *Calvin on the Sabbath* (Fearn, Ross-shire: Mentor, 1998).

[87] *Inst.* IV. 20. 15.   [88] *Inst.* IV. 20. 2.   [89] *Inst.* III. 19. 15.

Christ's kingdom is concerned with the soul while civil government has to do with the concerns of the present life. Christ's kingdom has to do with the inner life, civil government with outer behaviour.[90]

Whoever knows how to distinguish between body and soul, between this present fleeting life and that future eternal life, will without difficulty know that Christ's spiritual Kingdom and the civil jurisdiction are things completely distinct. Since, then, it is a Jewish vanity to seek and enclose Christ's Kingdom within the elements of this world, let us rather ponder that what Scripture clearly teaches is a spiritual fruit, which we gather from Christ's grace; and let us remember to keep within its own limits all that freedom which is promised and offered to us in him.[91]

Given what we have already learnt it is no surprise that Calvin refers to the legitimacy of diverse types of government.[92] However, these various types of polity have a common scope. They are concerned not simply with the second table of the law but with both tables. What is interesting and rather surprising is that Calvin grounds the magistrates' concern for religion not only in Scripture but in an appeal to common consent.

And thus all have confessed that no government can be happily established unless piety is the first concern; and that those laws are preposterous which neglect God's right and provide only for men. Since, therefore, among all philosophers religion takes first place, and since this fact has always been observed by universal consent of all nations, let Christian princes and magistrates be ashamed of their negligence if they do not apply themselves to this concern.[93]

His attitude to the judicial law is rather different from that to the moral law but parallels what he thinks about the ceremonial law. Calvin agrees with the 'ancient writers' that the ceremonial and judicial laws could be changed without affecting morals.[94] In keeping with this as we have seen Calvin holds that the Mosaic ceremonial law is abolished, while the moral law is upheld and intensified (though Calvin thinks that for the Christian the emphasis should fall not on the obligatoriness of the moral law but on a person's freedom to keep it.)[95] In the case of the judicial law Calvin argues, invoking his two Kingdoms idea, that upholding it is a legitimate, indeed an essential concern of the civil magistrate (and therefore the Christians should respect the magistrate),[96] but that it may be legitimately refracted through the variety of polities that there happen to be. The judicial law is no longer an expression of theocracy, for Calvin expressly repudiates the idea that no commonwealth can be formed which neglects the political system of Moses.[97] But what is it that is refracted in the varied circumstances of differing societies? 'Equity, because it is natural, cannot but be the same for all, and therefore, this same

---

[90] *Inst.* III. 19. 15.   [91] *Inst.* IV. 20. 1.   [92] *Inst.* IV. 20. 8.   [93] *Inst.* IV. 20. 9.

[94] *Inst.* IV. 20. 14.   [95] *Inst.* III. 19. 3, 7.   [96] *Inst.* IV. 20. 14.   [97] *Inst.* IV. 20. 14.

purpose ought to apply to all laws, whatever their object. Constitutions have certain circumstances upon which they in part depend. It therefore does not matter that they are different, provided all equally press toward the same goal of equity.'[98] He sees equity as something to be striven after. By the differences Calvin chiefly has in mind different kinds and degrees of punishments.[99] However, as we saw, laws which 'gave honor to thieves, permitted promiscuous intercourse, and others both more filthy and more absurd, are not to be regarded as laws. For they are abhorrent not only to all justice, but also to all humanity and gentleness'.[100] Nevertheless, Calvin is notably cagey about the rights of people who are oppressed by such barbarities to overthrow the governments who uphold them.

> But we must, in the meantime, be very careful not to despise or violate that authority of magistrates, full of venerable majesty, which God has established by the weightiest decrees, even though it may reside with the most unworthy men, who defile it as much as they can with their own wickedness. For, if the correction of unbridled despotism is the Lord's to avenge, let us not at once think that it is entrusted to us, to whom no command has been given except to obey and suffer.[101]

NATURAL LAW AND COMMON GRACE

There has been a strong tendency among some interpreters of Calvin and of the Reformed tradition to see Calvin's views about ethics, and particularly about the ethical capacities of those who are outside the church, in terms of the operation of what has been called 'common grace'. Common grace has been defined by one theologian in this tradition as follows:

> Those general operations of the Holy Spirit whereby He, without renewing the heart, exercises such a moral influence on man through his general or special revelation, that sin is restrained, order is maintained in social life, and civil righteousness is promoted.[102]

Such interpreters have often drawn an opposition between natural law, which they believed that Calvin eschewed, and common grace, which they believe that he embraced, though such an opposition is by no means implied by Berkhof's definition. Working with a caricature of Thomas Aquinas's

---

[98] *Inst.* IV. 20. 16.

[99] Backus argues that Aquinas and Calvin significantly differ in that Aquinas 'makes a distinction between principles of natural law which naturally lead to human laws, and those that need to be applied in various ways depending on context, civilization, and so forth, such as the type of punishment to be administered for a certain type of crime. Calvin's main concern, on the other hand, is to establish a direct link between pagan consciences,—the seat of natural moral law,—and the civil laws they produced' ('Calvin's Concept of Natural and Roman Law', 12–13). But as we can see, Calvin's concern in fact corresponds closely to Aquinas's.   [100] *Inst.* IV. 20. 15.   [101] *Inst.* IV. 20. 31.

[102] Louis Berkhof, *Systematic Theology* (Grand Rapids, Mich.: Eerdmans, 1941), 436.

view an opposition is made between nature and grace.[103] Thomas is thought to teach that 'nature' comprises those areas of human life mostly untouched by the effects of sin . 'Nature' thus understood is regarded by the Calvinistic proponents of common grace as an area of human life which is autonomous, self-propelled, where God and his grace are not needed. So divine grace is said to presuppose and build on nature, it does not supplant it. Rejecting this picture of nature and grace they argue that the whole of life is so infected and skewed by sin that the restraining and gifting of God are not to be explained in terms of the workings of nature, but they are the result of God's 'common', that is, non-saving grace.

But Calvin, the Calvin of the *Institutes* rather than the Calvin of later tradition, would have been quite bemused by such a picture of his ideas. Quite apart from whether he would have recognized the view of Aquinas adopted by later Calvinists as authentic, he himself shows no signs of making a sharp antithesis between 'nature' and 'common grace'. Thus natural law and the sense of equity on which it is based are the gifts of God. They are not untouched by the Fall, nevertheless their continued efficacy is the result of God's goodness undeserved by its recipients. When God engraved the moral law on the minds of men,[104] this was a gift to them. Insofar as this continues, though affected by sin, the gift remains. In giving or not withdrawing these gifts God restrains sin, and these mechanisms of law are in turn ways for the further restraining of sin and of providing the basis on which tolerable lives can be lived and human culture can flourish.

The inability to see Calvin's references to nature and natural law for what they are is vividly seen in what is probably the fullest discussion in English of the theme of common grace in Calvin, H. Kuiper's *Calvin on Common Grace*.[105] Calvin's references to nature are simply counted in with all the other expressions in Calvin of God's common goodness which Kuiper records[106] and so the elements in Calvin's thought which are clearly continuous with features of the medieval tradition are obliterated and a novelty is imputed to his views which is not there. Kuiper invokes the view of Herman Bavinck as claiming that 'Calvin was the first one to overcome the unwarranted dualism between nature and grace which is inherent in the Romish system of thought . . . Calvin's logical mind could not put up with this dualism'.[107] Kuiper's own bias is revealed in the comparison he draws between Luther and Calvin.

---

[103] This caricature is well portrayed by Arvin Vos, *Aquinas, Calvin, and Contemporary Protestant Thought*, ch. 6. The later emphasis of some Reformed theologians on common grace stems from the pioneering work of Abraham Kuyper (1837–1920) and Herman Bavinck (1854–1921).

[104] *Inst.* IV. 20. 16.   [105] (Grand Rapids, Mich:, Smitter Book Company, 1928).

[106] *Calvin on Common Grace*, 26, 183.   [107] *Calvin on Common Grace*, 2.

Luther did not entirely do away with this dualism although he emphasised the truth that the opposite of grace is sin rather than nature. The great German Reformer sought to leave room for the good found with natural man by drawing a sharp line of demarcation between things heavenly and things earthly.[108]

But the very similar line of demarcation to be found in Calvin between earthly things (*res terrenas*) and heavenly things (*res caelestes*)[109] is simply treated by Kuiper as one instance among many others of 'common grace'. If Luther exhibits remnants of dualism then so does Calvin. But in fact there is no dualism there, not if by dualism is meant an opposition between nature and grace. For Calvin nature is God's gift.

For we have noted that Calvin's attitude to natural law is by no means negative or dismissive. He does not draw attention to natural law and equity simply to eliminate these notions; rather he has a positive view of them. Nor is he using 'natural law' in a way that equivocates on the scholastic use. Rather we have seen several significant points of similarity (as well as points of difference) with, for example, Thomas Aquinas's usage. We have seen that the main point of difference is that Calvin has a dimmer view of the powers of fallen mankind to discern what is morally right from the natural law, and to be motivated to do it. So the difference between them is one of degree rather than one of principle.

Nevertheless, alongside the references to natural law, its relation to the revealed moral law of God, the importance of equity, and so on, there are numerous references in Calvin to the moral and other effects of 'common' or 'general' or 'heavenly' grace.[110] Clearly, if Calvin is consistent, there is a way of interpreting such references which does not negate what he says about natural law. We must not think of the grace in 'common grace' as a repudiation of what he says about natural law. But nor must we quickly conclude that the best 'model' for their relationship is a foundationalistic one in which what is natural provides, ontologically and epistemically, the foundations, and on which common grace is built. But before considering in more detail what this relationship is or might be, we should consider some representative statements of Calvin's on common grace.

To sum up: We see among all mankind that reason is proper to our nature; it distinguishes us from brute beasts, just as they by possessing feeling differ from inanimate things. Now, because some are born fools or stupid, that defect does not

---

[108] *Calvin on Common Grace*, 2.   [109] *Inst.* II. 2. 13.

[110] On 'heavenly' grace, see *Inst.* I. 5. 3. Calvin does not use the phrase 'common grace' very often, if at all. *Inst.* II. 2. 17 has a reference to the 'general grace of God'. A further reason for hesitation over Calvin's views on 'common grace' is provided by the fact that we find that not only do references to natural law and God's restraining and enriching goodness sit side by side, but Calvin sometimes refers to such goodness as instances of both the general grace of God and of his 'special graces'. (See *Inst.* II. 3. 4.)

obscure that general grace of God. Rather, we are warned by that spectacle that we ought to ascribe what is left in us to God's kindness. For if he had not spared us, our fall would have entailed the destruction of our whole nature. Some men excel in keenness; others are superior in judgment; still others have a readier wit to learn this or that art. In this variety God commends his grace to us, lest anyone should claim as his own what flowed from the sheer bounty of God. For why is one person more excellent than another? Is it not to display in common nature God's special grace, which, in passing many by, declares itself bound to none? Besides this, God inspires many special activities, in accordance with each man's calling. Many examples of this occur in The Book of Judges, where it says that 'the Spirit of the Lord took possession' of those men whom he had called to rule the people [ch. 6: 34]. In short, in every extraordinary event there is some particular impulsion.[111]

Calvin seems to be saying two different things in passages such as this. First, that following the Fall things are not as bad as they could be, for they could, consistently with divine justice, have resulted in total death and destruction. That they did not do so is due entirely to the goodness of God, and so it is an expression of his grace. It is this aspect of Calvin's thought which those who emphasize the restraining aspect of common grace appeal to.

In every age there have been persons who, guided by nature, have striven toward virtue throughout life. I have nothing to say against them even if many lapses can be noted in their moral conduct. For they have by the very zeal of their honesty given proof that there was some purity in their nature . . . These examples, accordingly, seem to warn us against adjudging man's nature wholly corrupted, because some men have by its promptings not only excelled in remarkable deeds, but conducted themselves most honorably throughout life. But here it ought to occur to us that amid this corruption of nature there is some place for God's grace; not such grace as to cleanse it, but to restrain it inwardly.[112]

This restraining influence need not be expressed only in negative terms.

There are at hand energy and ability not only to learn but also to devise something new in each art or to perfect and polish what one has learned from a predecessor. This prompted Plato to teach wrongly that such apprehension is nothing but recollection. Hence, with good reason we are compelled to confess that its beginning is inborn in human nature. Therefore this evidence clearly testifies to a universal apprehension of reason and understanding by nature implanted in men. Yet so universal is this good that every man ought to recognize for himself in it the peculiar grace of God.[113]

So restraint works in the provision of the gifts of reason and understanding, a universal or almost universal provision. (Calvin thinks that the creation of 'fools' is an exception). God's restraining of evil can also be expressed as his

[111] *Inst.* II. 2. 17.   [112] *Inst.* II. 3. 3.   [113] *Inst.* II. 2. 14.

promoting the good in *leaving* gifts to human nature even after the Fall.[114] The fact of restraint by itself tells us nothing at all about the mechanisms of restraint, and it is perfectly consistent with such 'common grace' that the vehicle of such restraint should be such things as the recognition by the conscience of various features of the 'inward law' or natural law instigated at the creation, the recognition of the general sense of equity among men and women, and so on. Calvin draws attention to such mechanisms when he refers to what God has 'implanted' in human nature.[115]

In this he is in line with the sort of thing Aquinas says. Considering the question of whether man can will and do good without grace Aquinas says:

But in the state of spoiled nature man falls short even of what he is capable of according to his nature, such that he cannot fulfil the whole of this kind of good by his natural endowments. Yet since human nature is not wholly spoiled by sin so as to be deprived of the whole good proper to nature, man can indeed, even in the state of spoiled nature, perform some particular good actions by his natural powers, such as building houses, planting vines and the like. He cannot however perform the whole good which is connatural to him, so as to fall short of nothing. So a sick man is capable of some movement by himself, yet he cannot move perfectly with the movement of a healthy man unless he is healed by the aid of medicine.[116]

The second thing that Calvin is saying is that there are besides the general effects of divine restraint and goodness, special effects, so to speak. Particular individuals are gifted with wit, or special artistic or other creative skills, or with gifts of leadership and sagacity.[117] These are not generally dispersed, but given selectively and sovereignly by the operation of God's grace. Although they are consistent with the general restraint exercised on all mankind, the presence of these gifts cannot be accounted for in terms of such restraint but rather in terms of a particular gifting by God of certain individuals at certain times.

That Calvin may have these two things in mind by expressions such as 'general grace' or 'common grace' is borne out, for example, by his remarks on Genesis 4: 20, which states that Jabal is the father of such as dwell in tents.

I, however, understand Moses to have spoken expressly concerning these arts, as having been invented by the family of Cain, for the purpose of showing that he was not so accursed by the Lord but that he would still scatter some excellent gifts among his posterity . . . Moses, however, expressly celebrates the remaining benediction of God on that race, which otherwise would have been deemed void and barren of all good. Let us then know, that the sons of Cain, though deprived of the Spirit of

---

[114] *Inst.* II. 2. 15.　　　　[115] e.g. *Inst.* II. 2. 12.　　　　[116] *Summa Theologiae*, 1a, 2ae, 109. 2.

[117] 'Because sculpture and painting are gifts of God, I seek a pure and legitimate use of each, lest those things which the Lord has conferred upon us for his glory and our good be not only polluted by perverse misuse but also turned to our destruction' (*Inst.* I. 11. 12.)

regeneration, were yet endued with gifts of no despicable kind; just as the experience of all ages teaches us how widely the rays of divine light have shone on unbelieving nations, for the benefit of the present life; and we see, at the present time, that the excellent gifts of the Spirit are diffused through the whole human race. Moreover liberal arts and sciences have descended to us from the heathen. We are, indeed, compelled to acknowledge that we have received astronomy, and the other parts of philosophy, medicine, and the order of civil government, from them.[118]

So Calvin has a variety of ways of expressing the fact of 'common grace'; the restraint of evil, the giving or leaving of the gifts of intelligence and moral sense in the human race, and the gifting in unusual or exceptional ways of individual men and women in the sciences and fine arts, in government and in philosophy. As one might expect from Calvin the common factor in all this is a theological point. It is that all these gifts, which in themselves fall short of or are certainly different from the gift of regeneration and are no guarantee of it, are gifts which are properly to be attributed to the Spirit of God, as in this fine passage:

Whenever we come upon these matters in secular writers, let that admirable light of truth shining in them teach us that the mind of man, though fallen and perverted from its wholeness, is nevertheless clothed and ornamented with God's excellent gifts. If we regard the Spirit of God as the sole fountain of truth, we shall neither reject the truth itself, nor despise it wherever it shall appear, unless we wish to dishonor the Spirit of God. For by holding the gifts of the Spirit in slight esteem, we condemn and reproach the Spirit himself. What then? Shall we deny that the truth shone upon the ancient jurists who established civic order and discipline with such great equity? Shall we say that the philosophers were blind in their fine observation and artful description of nature? Shall we say that those men were devoid of understanding who conceived the art of disputation and taught us to speak reasonably? Shall we say that they are insane who developed medicine, devoting their labor to our benefit? What shall we say of all the mathematical sciences? Shall we consider them the ravings of madmen? No, we cannot read the writings of the ancients on these subjects without great admiration. We marvel at them because we are compelled to recognize how pre-eminent they are. But shall we count anything praiseworthy or noble without recognizing at the same time that it comes from God?[119]

[118] *Commentary on Genesis*, 4: 20, 21.

[119] *Inst.* II. 2. 15. The entire section from Inst. II. 2. 12–16 is devoted to this theme. There are numerous incidental references to the same point throughout his writings. For example, this comment on Exod. 28: 3, 'We shall speak more fully hereafter, what I will touch upon now, as to the wisdom of the artificers, viz, that all who from the foundation of the world have invented arts useful to the human race, have been imbued with the Spirit of God; so that even heathen authors have been compelled to call them the inventions of the gods. But inasmuch as in this Divine work there was need of rare and unwonted skill, it is expressly spoken of as a peculiar gift of the Spirit' (*Commentaries on the Four Last Books of Moses Arranged in the form of a Harmony*, II. 195).

So how are to relate what we earlier saw Calvin saying about equity and natural law, and what he also says about common grace? My suggestion is that for the most part when Calvin is referring to equity and natural law he is talking about structures, usually ethical and political structures. By contrast, his references to 'common grace' and equivalent expressions are references to gifts, usually to gifts to individuals or to classes of individuals, though not exclusively so; sometimes gifts given to almost the entire race. The distinction is thus one of direction and emphasis, and it would be unwise for any interpreter of Calvin to attempt to polarize Calvin's ideas around one as opposed to the other idea; to affirm natural law *and not* common grace, or common grace *and so not* natural law.

13

Faith, Atonement, and Time

A CENTRAL theme of the previous chapters is that Calvin freely drew on medieval philosophical and theological ideas where it suited him to do so while remaining critical of what he regarded as the over-subtlety and sophistry of some scholastic discussions. The effect of these chapters, if the argument is convincing, is to draw a tighter link between Calvin and medieval philosophy and theology than is usually done.

But John Calvin was also, and foremost, a Protestant Reformer who with Luther and the other Reformers broke decisively with the Roman Church over justification by faith alone and the unwillingness or inability of that Church to reform itself by Scripture, which the Reformers regarded as a sufficient rule of faith and practice. And so it is fitting that in this last chapter some attention is paid to Calvin's distinctively Protestant ideas on faith and the atonement of Christ. We shall find that even here Calvin makes use of inherited ideas in formulating his position.

In exploring some of the aspects of Calvin's views on the relation between faith and the work of Christ we shall particularly have in mind what he says about the nature of the change in status of the believer that coming to have faith in Christ's atonement brings with it. In Calvin's account of this, time, change and causation each play a role, and we shall see him once more using the idea of divine accommodation to address some of the intellectual problems that employing these ideas brings. He employs notions of causation familiar to the medievals to elaborate the distinctive ideas of the Reformation, and we find him once more taking the problem of apparent contradiction with as much seriousness as any scholastic might. Later in the chapter we shall contrast Calvin's ideas at this point with Karl Barth's.

CALVIN AND CONTRADICTION

A contradiction is a proposition which cannot be true, under any circumstances. 'This man is a woman'; 'All dogs are tables'; 'At least one bachelor is married'—these are all contradictory propositions. There is no possible world in which they can be true. How a theologian handles contradictions, and apparent contradictions, is a good test of his commitment to the fundamental principles of logic and therefore of his theological method as well as of his view of one important aspect of the relation between faith and reason.

Apart from the blank refusal to consider an apparent contradiction that arises in the course of theological reflection, we may distinguish between two rather negative theological approaches to apparent contradictions about God, and one positive approach. One negative response is to say that God, in virtue of his power, is above contradiction. With God all things are possible, impossibilities included. So that by virtue of his power God can make it the case that there is a possible world in which, say, at least one bachelor is married. The defence of such an unbounded conception of divine power goes back at least to Descartes[1] while in its modern form reserving such powers to God highlights the centrality of paradox in theology. But this is not Calvin's approach to contradiction or apparent contradiction, despite what is often asserted to the contrary.

A second negative response to the appearance of logical difficulties is to say that there is an apparent contradiction in some state of affairs only because of our epistemic position, as human beings whose knowledge and intelligence range is limited. Such limits may be features of our present epistemic position or of our all-time epistemic position. Because of who and where we are, we may not see the consistency of some set of claims even though they must be consistent because God has asserted each of these claims as true. God can see their consistency, even if we cannot, in the way in which a mathematical or formal logician might see the consistency of a proof to which the rest of us are blind. It is not clear that Calvin typically makes such an argument in connection with logical difficulties even though he makes frequent appeal to the idea of God's incomprehensibility in connection with, say, our ability to understand how his judgements are just, or what God knows when he knows himself.

It is sometimes claimed by commentators that Calvin willingly embraced self-contradictions, and that he subordinated logic to Scripture, and rejected logic as a device to understand what is beyond the limits of the revealed

---

[1] Compare Descartes, 'The mathematical truths which you call eternal have been laid down by God and depend on Him entirely no less than the rest of his creatures. Indeed, to say that these truths are independent of God is to talk of Him as if He were Jupiter or Saturn and to subject Him to the Styx and the Fates . . . In general we can assert that God can do everything that we can comprehend but not that he cannot do what we cannot comprehend. It would be rash to think that our imagination reaches as far as His power.' (Letter to Mersenne, 15 Apr., 1630), Descartes, *Philosophical Letters*, trans. and ed. Anthony Kenny (Oxford: Clarendon Press, 1970), 11–12. Calvin would, I believe, have agreed with the last point but not that it carried the inference which Descartes drew.

mysteries. There are, in fact, three separate claims here.[2] Let us look at them in reverse order.

Did Calvin reject logic as a device for understanding what is beyond the limits of the revealed mysteries? There is considerable evidence of this attitude in Calvin; it is part and parcel of his rejection of speculation as being profitless, at least for the Christian theologian. As we have seen more than once, for Calvin such speculation is useless and may be positively harmful because according to him we do not have the materials necessary to make progress in our speculations. But this is not by itself a rejection of logic; for Calvin rejected any device, such as the deploying of acute conceptual discriminations characteristic of some scholastics, that were then used in an attempt to take us beyond what he regarded as the limits of what is revealed, or to distract and so waste the time of the Christian theologian. But he did use logic to draw out inferences from revealed mysteries, as we have discovered in his discussion of the Trinity and the Incarnation.

Secondly, did Calvin subordinate logic to Scripture? This claim, understood in one way, is the corollary of the first point. But whether this subordination of logic to Scripture represents the demotion of logic depends partly on what one takes Scripture to teach or imply about logic in the first place. For if Scripture itself teaches what is clearly self-contradictory, then to subordinate logic to Scripture is to be willing for such self-contradictions to remain. But it is hard to see that this is Calvin's attitude. He recognized forms of argumentation used by the canonical writers. And he held, that since God is truth, his word is true and therefore consistent.

Thirdly, did Calvin willingly embrace self-contradictions which occurred in the course of his theological inquiries? A good test of Calvin's reaction to self-contradiction is to observe his response when he finds what he takes to be a self-contradiction, or as he sometimes puts it, 'a certain appearance of contradiction'[3] in the teaching of Scripture. In general, we can say that Calvin at places specifically rejects the idea that God by his omnipotence can bring about a contradictory state of affairs and so the appearance of contradiction is for him always a cause for concern. In his discussions regarding the correct understanding of the body of Christ in connection with the Lord's Supper Calvin says:

What is the nature of our flesh? Is it not something that has its own fixed dimension, is contained in a place, is touched, is seen? And why (they say) cannot God make the same flesh occupy many and divers places, be contained in no place, so as to lack measure and form? Madman, why do you demand that God's power make flesh to

---

[2] Each of them is made rather indiscriminately in editorial footnote 6, p. 234 of the Battles' translation of the *Institutes*.   [3] *Inst.* 1. 18. 4.

be and not to be flesh at the same time! It is as if you insisted that he make light to be both light and darkness at the same time![4]

In the course of our study of Calvin so far we have identified a number of instances where he is troubled by the appearance of contradiction. For Calvin, then, not even God by his power can bring about a contradiction, making something both to be flesh and not to be flesh, and the demand that he do so is a form of madness.

THE ATONEMENT

Another case of what Calvin regards as an apparent contradiction will occupy us for the remainder of this chapter. When considering the atonement Calvin says, there is a 'sort of contradiction' about it. How does Calvin respond? Consistently with his general approach he seeks to eliminate the appearance of contradiction here, and he has a rather more optimistic attitude to the prospect of doing this than he has in the case of the unity of the divine will considered in Chapter 11.

Calvin sets out the problem as follows:

But, before we go any farther, we must see in passing how fitting it was that God, who anticipates us by his mercy, should have been our enemy until he was reconciled to us through Christ. For how could he have given in his only-begotten Son a singular pledge of his love to us if he had not already embraced us with his free favor? Since, therefore, some sort of contradiction arises here, I shall dispose of this difficulty.[5]

He says something very similar in his *Commentary on Romans* 5: 10:

We were enemies, he says, when Christ interposed for the purpose of propitiating the Father: through this reconciliation we are now friends . . . But the Apostle seems here to be inconsistent with himself; for if the death of Christ was a pledge of the divine love towards us, it follows that we were already acceptable to him; but he says now, that we were enemies.[6]

What is the 'sort of contradiction' which arises here? Presumably that between:

    (A) We were enemies of God until we were reconciled to Christ; and
    (B) God had already embraced us with his free favour.

That is, there is an apparent change in God when he ceases to be our enemy that seems to be at variance with the eternality of his love. How could God at

---

[4] *Inst.* IV. 17. 24.   [5] *Inst.* II. 16. 2.

[6] *Comm. on Romans*, 197–8. See also Calvin's commentaries on John 17: 23 and 2 Cor. 5: 19. I am indebted to Robert A. Peterson, *Calvin and the Atonement*, for these references.

any time be our enemy if he eternally loves us? How, Calvin asks, can these statements both be true? To be sure, there is evidence for each of them. For the first, the evidence is the need for the atonement of Christ. For what need could there be of atonement if those atoned for were not enemies of God? What need of reconciliation if there was no reconciliation needed? The evidence for the second statement is the coming of Christ as the pledge of the Father's love. How could God give the pledge of his love in Christ if he did not already love us? So it seems that we are both the enemies of God and in need of reconciliation, and also loved by God, not needing reconciliation, and this is, as Calvin rightly says, 'some sort of contradiction'. For it is plausible to assume that no one can both be an enemy of God and be loved by God, both need reconciliation and not need reconciliation.

How are we to interpret Calvin here? In particular, how are we to interpret his attempt to dispose of the difficulty? First is an example of how not to interpret him, that provided by G. C. Berkouwer.

It is remarkable that Calvin does not attempt here to arrive at a rational and speculative synthesis, but remains throughout fully conscious of the *ineffabili modo*, the mode in which the Spirit usually speaks in Scripture. He offers a solution which is in accordance with the teaching of Scripture and which does justice to both God's justice and his love. Calvin's object in these seemingly paradoxical statements is to respect the limits which Scripture imposes . . . Within these limits Calvin is conscious of the fact that he can only stammer when speaking of both God's love and his wrath.[7]

A careful reading of the *Institutes* (as well as of Calvin's comment on Romans 5: 10 and his comments elsewhere) shows that Calvin takes the idea of apparent contradiction or paradox with greater seriousness than Berkouwer here allows. He does not merely 'stammer' but as we shall see he offers a way in which the paradox or apparent contradiction can be eliminated.

Calvin addresses this 'sort of contradiction' by an appeal to his principle of accommodation, a principle which (as we have seen) is variously invoked throughout his writings to cover issues of language about God, apparent ethical relativism in the Scriptures, and much else. Calvin explicitly says that this is how he proposes to solve the appearance of contradiction. But exactly how does the appeal to accommodation help?

Expressions of this sort have been accommodated to our capacity that we may better understand how miserable and ruinous our condition is apart from Christ. For if it had not been clearly stated that the wrath and vengeance of God and eternal

---

[7] G. C. Berkouwer, *The Work of Christ*, trans. Cornelius Lambregste (Grand Rapids: Eerdmans, 1965), 269.

death rested upon us, we would scarcely have recognized how miserable we would have been without God's mercy, and we would have underestimated the benefit of liberation.[8]

That the wrath and vengeance of God rested on us is a statement that is accommodated to our capacity. It is an accommodation because Calvin believes that such a statement is not strictly true.

Robert Peterson thinks that accommodation is only a partial answer to the problem of the 'sort of contradiction'. 'Accommodation is not the final answer. It cannot be, because Calvin takes the holiness of God and the sinfulness of men and women with utter seriousness.'[9] But Calvin does not say it is a partial answer. He says (or rather strongly implies) that it is the whole answer. So how is the device of accommodation working here? What is it about these expressions that is accommodated to us? The answer, it seems, is that each of these passages describes a transition, in time, from wrath to grace. At one time, Christians were enemies and are now, at a later time, reconciled. To avoid misunderstanding it is important to note that Calvin does not for one moment deny that liberation is a change in us. But such liberation does not describe a change in God's relation to us. It is the idea of a change in God's relation to us that Calvin says is an 'accommodation'. It does not represent the strict truth of the matter; for strictly speaking there is no change in that relation.[10] What is true is that we ought to believe there is a change in God's relation to us in order not to underestimate the benefit of our liberation. I shall now try to develop this point.

There are in principle four positions that one might take on the issue of whether reconciliation involves a change in us and a change in God: (1) that when a person is reconciled there is a change in both God and that person; (2) that there is a change in that person but not in God; (3) there is a change in God but not in the person; finally, (4) that there is no change in either. I think we can rule out (3) and (1), in present circumstances, straight away because Calvin holds that God's redemptive plan is unchanging. 'God once established by his eternal and unchangeable plan those whom he long before determined once for all to receive into salvation.'[11] In due course it will be argued that (2) represents Calvin's position, and I shall then substantiate

---

[8] *Inst.* II. 16. 2.   [9] Peterson, *Calvin and the Atonement*, 22.

[10] It is undeniably difficult to characterize exactly the distinction between what is a 'real' change in something and what is not. But there is an obvious, intuitive difference between someone who changes as a result of losing a leg and someone who changes as a result of becoming a grandfather. Losing a leg may be said to be a real change in that person in a way in which becoming a grandfather is not. (For this distinction, see 'What Actually Exists' and 'Praying for Things to Happen', in Peter Geach, *God and the Soul.*) Calvin thinks that the language of Scripture is accommodated because it refers to a real change in God.   [11] *Inst.* III. 21. 7.

this by a comparison with what Karl Barth says on the matter, for he takes position (4).

Perhaps we may think of the accommodated expressions that Calvin refers to telling us the truth but not the whole truth about the atonement and its relation to the Christian. According to Calvin it is true that each of us deserves the wrath of God. But it is not the whole truth, for the whole truth is that God has loved us from eternity, and as a consequence has sent Christ as the expiation for our sins. That is the full truth. But if we were told the full truth at once then in Calvin's judgement certain undesirable consequences would follow: we would presume on God's mercy and not seek reconciliation for ourselves. So God accommodates himself to us in order to produce desirable changes in us. Calvin explains this at some length in his commentary on 2 Corinthians 5: 19:

> For so long as God imputes to us our sins, He must of necessity regard us with abhorrence; for he cannot be friendly or propitious to sinners. But this statement may seem to be at variance with what is said elsewhere—that we were loved by Him before the creation of the world, (Eph. i. 4,) and still more with what he says, (John iii. 16,) that the love, which he exercised towards us was the reason, why He expiated our sins by Christ, for the cause always goes before its effect. I answer, that we were loved before the creation of the world, but it was only *in Christ*. In the mean time, however, I confess, that the love of God was first in point of time, and of order, too, as to God, but with respect to us, the commencement of his love has its fountain in the sacrifice of Christ. For when we contemplate God without a Mediator, we cannot conceive of Him otherwise than as angry with us: a Mediator interposed between us, makes us feel, that He is pacified towards us. As, however, this also is necessary to be known by us—that Christ came forth to us from the foundation of God's free mercy, the Scripture explicitly teaches both—that the anger of the Father has been appeased by the sacrifice of the Son, and that the Son has been offered up for the expiation of the sins of men on this ground—because God, exercising compassion towards them, receives them, on the ground of such a pledge, into favour.[12]

So the truth about atonement, about reconciliation to God, has to be represented to us as if it implied a change in God, and so an inconsistency, an apparent contradiction, in his actions towards us.[13] But in fact there is no change in God; he loves us from eternity. There is, however, a change in us, a change that occurs as by faith Christ's work is appropriated. The change is not from wrath to grace, but from our belief that we are under wrath to our belief that we are under grace. 'As God hates sin, we are also hated by him as far as we are sinners; but as in his secret counsel he chooses us into the body

---

[12] *Comm.* on 2 Cor. 5: 19. See also the second half of *Inst.* II. 16. 2.

[13] Calvin's approach here is similar to that he applied to God's attitude to Hezekiah's prayer which we discussed in Ch. 7.

of Christ, he ceases to hate us: but restoration to favour is unknown to us, until we attain it by faith.'[14]

God does not cease to hate us at some time. God does not change. But we change when, by the exercise of faith, we experience restoration to the favour of God. As Wendel correctly observes:

The sacrifice offered in time by the Christ modifies, at least considered from the human point of view, the attitude of God himself towards men. In reality, that attitude is unchanged and immutable; it cannot therefore be influenced *a posteriori* by the work of Christ. That work is limited to the removal of the obstacle that prevents the divine love from making its way to men. The initiative remains moreover with God, and it is his love for men which has removed the barrier constituted by sin, and the divine wrath that was the consequence of it, by deciding to accept the satisfaction to be offered by Jesus Christ.[15]

Why does Calvin not think that there is such a transition in God? He has two reasons for this, one (to me) more surprising than the other. The first, more familiar reason, is that both in terms of the eternal counsels of God, and in terms of what has happened in time, in the past, God loves us. He has eternally loved us in Christ, and Christ has died to expiate our sin. It is in both of these senses that 'God anticipates us by his mercy'.[16] 'By his love God the Father goes before and anticipates our reconciliation in Christ.'[17] There is no change in God because the love of God is eternal. Nothing that God does or says in time can actually contradict what is eternal even though it may appear to do so.

There is another possible way of meeting the apparent contradiction which Calvin does not take. He could have said that God eternally decreed to hate us at one time (for our sin) and eternally decreed to love us at a later time, when we came to faith in Christ. There is no contradiction in this formulation. But the reason why he does not go down this route is that, as we have seen, he does not believe that God eternally decreed to begin to love us at such and such a time, rather he eternally loved us. There wasn't a time when God began to love us, and so there wasn't a time in a person's life when God began to love her.

The second, more surprising reason, for denying a transition in God is that Calvin insists[18] that texts such as Rom. 5: 10 and Gal. 3: 10 are deliberate exaggerations because they are too black and white. Despite our sin and unrighteousness, which make us guilty before God and hateful in his sight, there is still something lovable about us: 'But because the Lord wills not to

---

[14] *Comm.* on Romans 5: 10.

[15] Wendel, *Calvin: the Origins and Development of his Religious Thought*, 231.

[16] *Inst.* II. 16. 2.   [17] *Inst.* II. 16. 3.   [18] *Inst.* II. 16. 3.

lose what is his in us, out of his own kindness he still finds something to love. However much we may be sinners by our own fault, we nevertheless remain his creatures. However much we have brought death upon ourselves, yet he has created us unto life.'[19] That is, though we do not merit God's love (there is no suggestion of this in Calvin here or elsewhere) nevertheless, in virtue of our creatureliness as those made in the image of God (Calvin does not say this, but he must mean something like this) we remain, so to speak, appropriate (in the ontological sense) recipients of God's love, despite our sin, in a way in which plants and non-human animals could never be appropriate objects of such love. God eternally loves us but manifests that love to us at some time in our lives, the time when we are reconciled in faith.

This second reason is rather surprising because Calvin usually paints a blacker picture of mankind under divine wrath than this. Also, the thought expressed in the quotation just given rather diminishes the force of what Calvin frequently says, that believers are eternally loved in Christ, though it is not inconsistent with it. It becomes clear[20] that Calvin is closely following Augustine at this point.

As we have noted, Robert Peterson thinks that accommodation is only a partial answer for the Reformer. It is only partial because it does not, for Calvin, negate God's wrath. He says that for Calvin the expressions about the wrath of God are expressions about present realities, and so the divine accommodation can only be partial.

There is no doubt that accommodation is an important concept in Calvin's theology. Calvin emphasizes it in the discussions of the love/wrath dilemma not only in the *Institutes*, but also in the commentaries. And yet accommodation can be overemphasized to the place where God's wrath loses its reality. Calvin is careful not to do this. Accommodation is only a partial answer for the Reformer—it did not negate God's wrath.[21]

But now we can see that this is not quite correct. In fact, it is back to front. For accommodation is invoked by Calvin precisely *not* to negate God's wrath, but to stress its reality, and hence to enable it to play what for Calvin is its necessary pedagogic, preparatory role. God accommodates himself by appearing as wrathful until, by faith, the believer apprehends the merit of Christ and as a consequence comes to realize that God has eternally loved him. Before that, though it is true that God eternally loved him the believer has no good reason to think that he does, and plenty of reasons to think that he doesn't, because the wrath of God rests on the sinner.

As we noted in the earlier chapter on accommodation it does not follow from Calvin's idea of accommodation that if something is an accommodated

---

[19] *Inst.* II. 16. 3.   [20] *Inst.* II. 16. 4.   [21] *Calvin and the Atonement*, 22.

expression it is not to be taken seriously or literally. Rather, for an expression to be accommodated is for it not to be appropriately qualified by other expressions. So there is a roughness to an accommodated expression, it does not have the nuance or finesse or finality that the unaccommodated expression has. So Peterson has got hold of the wrong end of the stick when he says 'Accommodation is not the final answer. It cannot be, because Calvin takes the holiness of God and the sinfulness of men and women with utter seriousness.'[22] This should be 'Accommodation is the final answer because by invoking it Calvin is able to take the holiness of God and the sinfulness of men and women with full seriousness.'

Peterson also says that we must not neglect the element of mystery. According to his understanding, accommodation is part of the answer, the invoking of mystery is the other. In this he appears to want to understand Calvin as hospitable to paradox or contradiction. 'Mystery' here looks to indicate a metaphysical category, not a word indicating human ignorance. But the data which he cites from Calvin do not bear this out. For example he refers to what he calls Calvin's quotation of Augustine's expression 'In some ineffable way, God loved us and yet was angry toward us at the same time',[23] as if this was Calvin's final word on the matter. But Calvin goes on to say that:

The explanation of this mystery is to be sought in the first chapter of the letter to the Ephesians. There, after Paul has taught us that we were chosen in Christ, he adds at the same time that we acquired favor in the same Christ (Eph. 1: 4–5). How did God begin to embrace with his favor those whom he had loved before the creation of the world? Only in that he revealed his love when he was reconciled to us by Christ's blood. God is the fountainhead of all righteousness. Hence man, so long as he remains a sinner, must consider him an enemy and a judge.[24]

There is therefore an important change in the beliefs of people when they exercise faith in Christ. They change from regarding God as a judge to regarding him as a Saviour, even though (unbeknown to them) God eternally loves them in Christ. This takes divine wrath seriously; at least, it warrants people taking divine wrath seriously. They need to 'embrace his benevolence and fatherly love in Christ alone' and so to escape 'the imputation of our sins to us—an imputation bringing with it the wrath of God'.[25]

---

[22] *Calvin and the Atonement*, 22.

[23] *Inst.* II. 17. 2. In fact there is no direct reference to Augustine here, but *Inst.* II. 16. 4 quotes very similar words from Augustine: 'Thus in a marvelous and divine way he loved us even when he hated us. For he hated us for what we were that he had not made; yet because our wickedness had not entirely consumed his handiwork, he knew how, at the same time, to hate in each one of us what we had made, and to love what he had made.' Though this is a 'marvel' for Augustine it nonetheless has an explanation.

[24] *Inst.* II. 17. 2.   [25] *Inst.* II. 16. 2, 3.

So I am arguing that in view of the Father's eternal love for the elect, the belief that any of them has that they are under the divine wrath before they come to faith in Christ is a divine accommodation to them. Theirs is a justified belief in the sense that they have good reason to believe that they are under divine wrath and no good reason (yet) not to believe it. It preserves all that needs preserving of the recognition of the divine wrath, according to Calvin, for this belief is necessary, in the case of the elect, to enable them to 'embrace' Christ, or at least to embrace him more fervently,[26] and so to experience God's love and to recognize that God has eternally loved them. Calvin thus implies that without the belief in God's wrath no one would bother to embrace Christ. Such a change, from believing that we are objects of God's wrath to believing that he loves us in Christ, is a real change in us, but not a change in God.

The embrace of faith is thus, for Calvin, in some sense a condition of salvation. Without faith, we have no good reason to believe that God is our Father and that we are reconciled to him. To understand this more fully we need to look more closely at what Calvin says about causes and conditions in faith and justification, and then, to bring what he says more sharply into relief, we shall compare his position with that of Karl Barth.

CALVIN ON CAUSES AND CONDITIONS

In the *Institutes* Calvin deals with justification in book III, chapters 11 and following. There he tells us that justification is a reckoning righteous;[27] that that person is justified who 'excluded from the righteousness of works, grasps the righteousness of Christ through faith'.[28] There follows a brief refutation of Osiander's view, and, as part of this, in section 7 there is a discussion of the place of faith in justification. According to Calvin faith only justifies insofar as it receives Christ. It is not itself a work, and has no intrinsic power. 'We compare faith to a kind of vessel; for unless we come empty and with the mouth of our soul open to seek Christ's grace, we are not capable of receiving Christ . . . faith, which is only the instrument for receiving righteousness.'[29] To Calvin's mind, Osiander, with his doctrine of the essential indwelling of Christ in the believer, confuses two kinds of cause, the instrumental and the material cause of our justification. 'Therefore, I say that faith, which is only the instrument for receiving righteousness, is ignorantly confused with Christ, who is the material cause and at the same time the Author and Minister of this great benefit.'[30] In making this remark, in distinguishing

---

[26] *Inst.* II. 16. 2. [27] *Inst.* III. 11. 2. [28] *Inst.* III. 11. 2. [29] *Inst.* III. 11. 7.

[30] *Inst.* III. 11. 7. Calvin has a variety of ways of using this causal terminology. So in discussing Christ's merit he says that God's love is the highest cause of our salvation, faith in Christ is the second and

between two kinds of cause in justification, Calvin signals that he is prepared to elucidate and defend his account of justification using features of the Aristotelian fourfold causal schema (familiar to him from medieval theologians, no doubt).

However, it is interesting that Thomas (for example) in his brief treatment of justification in the *Summa Theologiae* does not apply the Aristotelian fourfold causal scheme to justification, though he does use some Aristotelian expressions. Aquinas refers to God as the cause of justification, and of course his language of infusion, the infusion of grace which Thomas believes is necessary for justification, is causal language. So Christ causes our salvation by grace and grace is instrumentally caused by the sacraments and principally by the power of the Holy Ghost working in the sacraments, according to John 3: 5.[31] Calvin by contrast transposes such causal language into the forensic understanding of justification characteristic of the Reformation.

The fourfold causal distinction, used in connection with the believer's appropriation of the work of Christ, occurs in *Institutes* III. 14. 17.

The philosophers postulate four kinds of causes to be observed in the outworking of things. If we look at these, however, we will find that, as far as the establishment of our salvation is concerned, none of them has anything to do with works. For Scripture everywhere proclaims that the efficient cause of our obtaining eternal life is the mercy of the Heavenly Father and his freely given love toward us. Surely the material cause is Christ, with his obedience, through which he acquired righteousness for us. What shall we say is the formal or instrumental cause but faith? And John includes these three in one sentence when he says: 'God so loved the world that he gave his only-begotten Son that everyone who believes in him may not perish but have eternal life' [John 3: 16]. As for the final cause, the apostle testifies that it consists both in the proof of divine justice and in the praise of God's goodness . . . Since we see that every particle of our salvation stands thus outside of us, why is it that we still trust or glory in works? The most avowed enemies of divine grace cannot stir up any controversy with us concerning either the efficient or the final cause, unless they would deny the whole of Scripture. They falsely represent the material and the formal cause, as if our works held half the place along with faith and Christ's righteousness. But Scripture cries out against this also, simply affirming that Christ

proximate cause. Does this mean that Christ is only the formal cause? Certainly not. 'For if we attain righteousness by a faith that reposes in him we ought to seek the matter [*materia*] of our salvation in him', clearly an allusion to Christ being the material cause of salvation (*Inst.* II. 17. 2). Calvin seems ready to use this Aristotelian causal scheme in a variety of contexts. His exposition of Eph. 1: 4–8 is structured in terms of fourfold causation. God's eternal election is the first cause of 'our calling and of all the benefits which we receive from God'. The material cause of election and of God's love revealed to us is Christ. The efficient cause is 'the largeness of the divine kindness, which has given Christ to us as our mediator'. Finally, the formal cause is 'the preaching of the gospel, by which the goodness of God overflows upon us' (*Commentary on Ephesians*, 197–203).   [31] *Summa Theologiae*, 1. 2ae, 112–113.

is for us both righteousness and life, and that this benefit of righteousness is possessed by faith alone. [32]

Here Calvin seems to take a rather relaxed approach to these distinctions when he says that faith is the formal or instrumental cause. In the original Aristotelian scheme the formal cause of a sculpture is the plan in the sculptor's mind, the material cause is the stone, the efficient cause is the sculptor's skill, and the final cause is, say, the honouring of Caesar. However, the instrumental cause, the sculptor's hammers and chisels, are for Aristotle one kind of means (the 'tools') of carrying out the plan. The use of 'formal cause' here may simply be a slip, for in Calvin's theological scheme the formal cause must be the divine plan of redemption. For Aristotle tools such as surgical instruments are for the end of keeping fit but are to be distinguished from 'works'.[33] As we shall see, Calvin's distinction between the other causes and the instrumental cause is crucial for his account of the place of faith in justification.

These words of Calvin are not so much a statement of justification by faith as of the place that Christ plays in salvation, a place, says Calvin, sufficient to exclude all works, and the benefits of which are appropriated by faith. Nevertheless, despite the absence of the word 'justification', the thing itself is in the forefront of Calvin's concern. There can be no doubt what Calvin is discussing; justification, and the place of faith in justification.

So despite the undoubted fact that Calvin was not a scholastic theologian he does not hesitate to use here the Aristotelian account of fourfold causation—efficient, material, formal, and final—and even to attribute

---

[32] Note also Calvin's distinction between primary, secondary, and formal causes in relation to Christ's work (*Inst.* II. 17. 2). A later writer in this Calvinian tradition distinguishes two sorts of efficient cause. The principal efficient cause of justification is God himself. The instrumental efficient cause is (on God's part) the ministry of the word and sacraments, and on our part faith, 'the hand of the receiver'. George Downame, *A Treatise on Justification* (London, 1633), bk. I, ch. 2, 'The Efficient Causes of Justification'.

[33] 'According to one way of speaking, that out of which as a constituent a thing comes to be is called a cause; for example, the bronze and the silver and their genera would be the causes respectively of a statue and a loving-cup. According to another, the form or model is a cause; this is the account of what the being would be, and its genera—thus the cause of an octave is the ratio of two to one, and more generally number—and the parts which come into the account. Again, there is the primary source of the change or the staying unchanged: for example, the man who has deliberated is a cause, the father is a cause of the child, and in general that which makes something of that which is made, and that which changes something of that which is changed. And again, a thing may be a cause as the end. That is what something is for, as health might be what a walk is for. On account of what does he walk? We answer, "To keep fit", and think that, in saying that, we have given the cause. And anything which, the change being effected by something else, comes to be on the way to the end, as slimness, purging, drugs, and surgical instruments come to be as means to health: all these are for the end, but differ in that the former are works and the latter tools' (Aristotle, *Physics* II. 3, 194ᵇ23–195ᵃ21, trans. W. Charlton (Oxford: Clarendon Press, 1970).

to the Apostle John the use of the idea of the final cause of justification! Sometimes he adds a fifth cause, faith is sometimes said to be the instrumental cause, sometimes (rather oddly) said to be the formal cause. No doubt Calvin's tactic here is *ad hominem*; to draw out the Reformed doctrine of grace against the Catholic ideas he was combating on a template familiar to and accepted by his opponents. The mercy of God is the efficient cause of our salvation; Christ is the material cause; faith is the formal or instrumental[34] cause; and the final cause is the praise of God's goodness. That is to say, salvation is brought about by the mercy of God (that mercy is the necessary and sufficient causal condition of salvation); it is procured by the obedience and death of Christ (the work of Christ is itself the effect of God's mercy); it is appropriated by faith (no one (adult?) personally benefits from the saving mercy of God without faith); and it issues in the vindication of the divine righteousness (since Christ's work is itself an expression of divine righteousness).

If you buy me a meal which you don't owe me, your generosity is the efficient cause, the result of the activity of the chef is the material cause, the knives and forks are the instrumental cause, and the final cause is (let us say) the solidifying of our friendship. The knives and forks are part of the meal, but not in the same sense in which the sprouts and sausages are.[35]

Each of these senses of cause has an element in common with the others as well as differences. The similarities and differences can be brought out as follows. If X is any kind of cause of Y, then it follows that if X does not occur

---

[34] Compare the wording of the *Westminster Confession of Faith*, 'Faith, thus receiving and resting on Christ and his righteousness, is the alone instrument of justification . . . ' (ch. XI. ii) (*Documents of the English Reformation*, ed. Bray, 496).

[35] Calvin's attitude to this causal language is rather different when he discusses the Council of Trent on justification. In his *Antidote* to the first seven sessions of the Council of Trent, published in 1547, Calvin comments that the enumeration of causes of justification by the Council is 'frivolous and nugatory' (116), and objects particularly to baptism being the instrumental cause of justification, and to the confusion (as he judges it) between justification and sanctification. Despite this comment he is content to discuss justification in terms propounded by the Council. In the seventh section of the Sixth Session the Council states, 'The causes of Justification are these:- The final cause is the glory of God and Christ, and eternal life: the efficient cause is a merciful God, who freely washes and sanctifies, sealing and anointing with the Holy Spirit of promise, which is a pledge of our inheritance: The meritorious cause is his beloved, only-begotten Son, our Lord Jesus Christ, who, when we were enemies, because of the great love wherewith he loved us, by his own most holy passion on the wood of the cross, merited justification, and gave satisfaction to the Father for us: The instrumental cause is the sacrament of baptism, which is the sacrament of faith, without which justification is never obtained.' (*Selected Works of John Calvin, Tracts and Letters*, ed. Henry Beveridge and Jules Bonnet (Edinburgh, 1844, Philadelphia, 1858; repr. Grand Rapids, Mich.: Baker, 1983, iii. 95–6) While Calvin denies that baptism is the instrumental cause of justification he does not of course deny that there is an instrumental cause (116).

then Y does not occur.[36] So if the efficient cause of justification were absent (but all other causes were present), there would be no personal justification; if the material cause were absent (but all other causes were present), there would be no personal justification; if the instrumental cause were absent (but all other causes were present), there would be no personal justification; and if the final cause were absent, (but all other causes were present) there would be personal justification. Each of the four senses of 'cause' highlighted by Calvin sets up a corresponding condition, and the character of the condition varies according to the character of the cause. So Calvin needs a distinction between justification in some objective sense and the personal appropriation of that justification. We shall discuss this distinction later on.

However, as well as this similarity between the causes there are differences, differences in the way these causes operate, differences in their powers or values. If the efficient cause of personal justification were absent, then there would be no personal justification because there would be no effective source of justification; if the material cause were absent, though there was an effective source of personal justification, such justification would not actually be secured or procured; if there were efficient and material causes of personal justification but no instrumental cause, then though justification had an effective source and was secured it would not be personally appropriated; and if there were efficient, material, and instrumental causes of personal justification, but no final cause, then though personal justification had an effective source, was secured and appropriated, it would be without purpose or end.

Another way of understanding Calvin's (and Aristotle's) use of this causal language is in terms of levels or kinds of explanation. How is justification to be explained? It is on account of the mercy of God, that's one way of explaining it. It is on account of Christ. That's another way. It is on account of faith. That's another way. It is to praise God's goodness, another way. These 'ways' are not interchangable: they don't all have the same value. Rather they are explanations of different levels, bringing out the roles that the different aspects of one complex whole play in the achieving of that whole.

In Calvin's thought each of these causes builds upon the former in the sense that any cause is a necessary condition of the operation of the next one. (So Calvin would not welcome the thought that we entertained earlier, that one cause of justification might not occur while all the others did.) For Calvin there can be no material cause of personal justification without an

---

[36] The converse is not true. Suppose that in the past whenever X has occurred, then Y has. Suppose now that X does not occur, and also Y does not occur; the explanation may be that X and Y are non-causal concomitants or correlates.

efficient cause, no instrumental cause without a material cause, no final cause without an instrumental cause. Given the divine decree to save sinners through Christ, we may even say that each cause is a necessary and sufficient condition of the next. The mercy of God ensures the mediation of Christ which ensures saving faith in the elect, which ensures the vindication of the divine righteousness. Furthermore, for Calvin the logical ordering of the causes is due to the fact that the existence and operation of each cause is equally due to divine grace. One way of characterizing the later Calvinist–Arminian controversy is as a disagreement over the causal necessity and sufficiency of divine grace for the operation of the instrumental cause of justification.

In Chapter 4 we argued that Calvin does not favour a view of theology in which predestination is the axiom from which we can deduce all else. For one thing, because predestination is 'secret' it cannot function that way. But were we to know the content of the divine decree in detail, as God himself knows it (something which is necessarily hidden from us), then we would understand what outworking in history is implied in it.

Besides a logical ordering of these causes, is there also an obvious temporal ordering of them? Is each logically prior cause also temporally prior? Not obviously. The efficient cause is an eternal decree, a timelessly divine decree. It may look safe to say that any material cause is always temporally before any instrumental cause, though not if Calvin takes the view, as he does, that men and women who lived before Christ were justified by faith then. The final cause looks to be logically first but temporally last.

In order to make full sense of what Calvin is saying here it is necessary to keep in mind the achieving of justification by Christ, and the personal appropriation of justification, the distinction between justification and personal justification introduced earlier. Justification is what the efficient and material causes of salvation procure; personal justification is what faith, the instrumental cause, is additionally necessary for. Faith appropriates the benefits of Christ 'existentially', thus ensuring the personal justification of the believer. The three causes are together sufficient for personal justification and for the vindication of the divine righteousness. Without faith the justification procured by Christ is not personally appropriated. There is no personal justification. 'We compare faith to a kind of vessel; for unless we come empty and with the mouth of our soul open to seek Christ's grace, we are not capable of receiving Christ.'[37]

It is possible to see from this how in Calvin's eyes faith can be a cause, even a condition of personal justification, and yet not be a contributing cause or

---

[37] *Inst.* III. 11. 7.

condition. To suppose that it was a contributing cause or condition would be to confuse two and possibly three kinds of cause. It would be to confuse the instrumental and the material cause, and possibly the instrumental cause and the efficient cause; it would be like confusing the cutlery with the sausages. Calvin accuses his opponents of just this confusion. 'Therefore, I say that faith, which is only the instrument for receiving righteousness, is ignorantly confused with Christ, who is the material cause and at the same time the Author and Minister of this great benefit.'[38] To suppose that faith was a contributing cause would be to suppose that without faith something would be lacking in the material cause of justification, that the obedience and righteousness of Christ required supplementation. But Calvin vehemently rejects any such idea.

Later on Calvin repeats his reference to the fourfold cause of justification in connection with his treatment of the place of good works in justification, neatly attributing each of the first three causes to a different person of the Trinity, the fourth cause to the Trinity itself.

The fact that Scripture shows that the good works of believers are reasons why the Lord benefits them is to be so understood as to allow what we have set forth before to stand unshaken: that the efficient cause of our salvation consists in God the Father's love; the material cause in God the Son's obedience; the instrumental cause in the Spirit's illumination, that is, faith; the final cause, in the glory of God's great generosity. These do not prevent the Lord from embracing works as inferior causes.[39]

Calvin here goes so far as to call works a 'cause' of salvation, but an 'inferior cause'. What does he mean? Ordinarily, those destined for mercy (as Calvin puts it) reach their inheritance by means of good works; that is, their good works precede their glory. So, in the order of time, works precede the enjoying of the final inheritance and 'what goes before in the order of dispensation he ("the Lord") calls the cause of what comes after'.

In this way he sometimes derives eternal life from works, not intending it to be ascribed to them; but because he justifies those whom he has chosen in order at last to glorify them [Rom. 8: 30], he makes the prior grace, which is a step to that which follows, as it were the cause. But whenever the true cause is to be assigned, he does not enjoin us to take refuge in works but keeps us solely to the contemplation of his mercy.[40]

[38] *Inst.* III. 11. 7.

[39] *Inst.* III. 14. 21. With such a passage in mind it is not difficult to see how those Reformed theologians who later on developed covenant theology might reasonably conclude that their theology had precedent in the thought of Calvin himself. For Calvin's attribution of a different cause of justification to each member of the Trinity corresponds closely to and may even be said to imply the eternal *pactum salutis* between the persons of the Trinity which is at the heart of covenant theology.   [40] *Inst.* III. 14. 21.

What comes before in time is called the cause of final salvation but it is not the 'true cause' and so 'by these expressions sequence more than cause is denoted'.[41] Works are the sign of grace; and so 'if no works then no glory' is to be understood in the way we usually understand 'if no spots then no measles'. The spots do not cause the measles, any more than the works merit the glory; spots are a sign of measles, a consequence of having measles, as good works are a consequence of grace, and so not meritorious.

Here, a different sense of 'condition' is to be understood from those considered earlier, the rather paradoxical sense in which a consequence may be said to be a condition. Note that Calvin distinguishes carefully between faith and works. Faith is a cause, the instrumental cause, of personal justification, while works are evidence of personal justification, an 'inferior cause', and so are a consequence, a causal consequence of it which occurs later in time. We can say 'if no faith then no justification' just as we can say 'if no works then no justification' but if we do so we are using the if-thens very differently. Consistently with this Calvin says, in commenting on the well-known passage in the Epistle of James about Abraham being justified by works (James 2: 21), 'We must understand the state of the question, for the dispute here is not respecting the cause of justification, but only what avails a profession of faith without works, and what opinion we are to form of it.'[42] We can connect this with our earlier discussion of change as follows. Because of its causal efficacy as an instrument, in exercising faith there is a change in the one who exercises that faith, but not a change in God.

KARL BARTH ON CAUSES AND CONDITIONS

When we turn from John Calvin to Karl Barth, though there are striking similarities, certainly striking similarities of terminology, there are also strong differences in their treatment of justification,[43] and by implication a different understanding of the apparent contradiction which Calvin finds in Paul's treatment of the atonement of Christ.

Here, to begin with, is a striking similarity:

There is always something wrong and misleading when the faith of a man is referred to as his way of salvation in contrast to his way in the supposed good works of false faith and superstition. Faith is not an alternative to these other ways. It is not the way which—another Hercules at the cross-roads—man can equally well choose and enter, which he can choose and enter by the same capacity by which he might go

---

[41] *Inst.* III. 14. 21.   [42] *Comm.* James 2: 20.

[43] 'Justification by Faith Alone' is the title of a shortish (34 pages) chapter, which forms s. 61 of ch. XIV, 'Jesus Christ, The Lord as Servant', of *The Doctrine of Reconciliation*, vol. iv, part 1 of the *Church Dogmatics*, ed. G. W. Bromiley and T. F. Torrance, trans. G. W. Bromiley (Edinburgh; T. & T. Clark, 1956).

any other way. Even in the action of faith he is the sinful man who as such is not in a position to justify himself, who with every attempt to justify himself can only become the more deeply entangled in his sin.[44]

That is, faith is not a work, not (to use Calvin's terms) part of the material cause of justification; or (to use Barth's words again) 'He [the man of faith] is as little justified in faith as in his other good or evil works.' And Barth goes on to applaud Calvin's insistence that faith cannot contribute anything to our justification.

Of the Reformers Calvin made this distinction with particular sharpness. Faith as such cannot contribute anything to our justification: *nihil afferens nostrum ad conciliandum Dei gratiam* (*Inst.* III. 13. 5). It is not a *habitus*. It is not a quality of grace which is infused into man (on Gal. 3. 6; *C.R.* 50, 205). *La foi ne justifie pas entant que c'est une œuvre que nous faisons.* If we believe, we come to God quite empty (*vuides*), *non pas en apportant aucune dignité ni mérite à Dieu.*[45]

We have already seen that as far as Calvin is concerned we may distinguish between justification and personal justification. For justification it is neces- sary and sufficient to have the operation of what Calvin calls the formal and the material causes of justification, the mercy of God and the death of Jesus Christ respectively. But for personal justification more is needed, another cause, the instrumental cause of justification. By the operation of this cause, faith, the justification effected by the formal and the material causes, is 'conveyed' (Calvin's word) to the person who has the faith. So there can be justification without personal justification, and until a person exercises faith there *is* justification without personal justification.

It would seem that Barth would refuse to countenance such a distinction. For him there is no justification that is not also personal justification. For Barth faith is the recognition of personal justification, it is not what conveys or transacts personal justification.

But the self-demonstration of the justified man to which faith clings is the crucified and risen Jesus Christ who lives as the author and recipient and revealer of the justification of all men. It is in Him that the judgment of God is fulfilled and the pardon of God pronounced on all men. In the second and third sections of this part, and therefore in our whole description of the term justification, we have been speaking of Him and therefore of justified man, of His history and therefore of our own, of His transition from the past to the future, from sin to right, from death to life, and therefore of ours, of His present and therefore of ours.[46]

And so while for Barth faith is important for justification, it does not have the central importance that it does for Calvin and the other Reformers.

[44] Barth, *Church Dogmatics*, iv/1. 616.
[45] Barth, *Church Dogmatics*, iv/1. 617.
[46] Barth, *Church Dogmatics*, iv/1. 629.

One reason for this is that for Barth faith is not the *sine qua non* of being personally justified, it is merely the recognition or acknowledgement of a personal justification already acquired.[47]

> It happened that in the humble obedience of the Son He took our place, He took to Himself our sins and death in order to make an end of them in His death, and that in so doing He did the right, He became the new and righteous man. It also happened that in His resurrection from the dead He was confirmed and recognised and revealed by God the Father as the One who has done and been that for us and all men. As the One who has done that, in whom God Himself has done that, who lives as the doer of that deed, He is our man, we are in Him, our present is His, the history of man is His history, He is the concrete event of the existence and reality of justified man in whom every man can recognise himself and every other man—recognise himself as truly justified.[48]

Here the emphasis is clearly on recognition rather than on appropriation. The reason for this insistence on Barth's part is that he wishes to take further, to give (as he sees it) a greater measure of consistency to the Reformation principle of *sola gratia* than did the Reformers themselves. For the Reformers, as Barth correctly perceived, and as we have seen for ourselves in the case of Calvin, faith conditionalizes justification. But for Barth such conditionalizing, however hedged about and qualified it may be, however confined to mere instrumentality, is a compromise of the principle of *sola gratia* in that it interposes between a gracious God and a sinful soul a condition that must be fulfilled by the sinful person, even though that condition is instrumental, and even though (for Calvin at least)

[47] There is an interesting similarity in language between Barth and some of the more antinomian of the Puritan theologians during the time of the Commonwealth. Thus John Eaton in *The Honey-Combe of Free Justification by Christ Alone* (London, 1642) wrote of justifying faith not as the instrumental means by which one is personally justified, but as the recognition that one has been justified: 'The first [of "four principall things" of faith] is the right object, ground and matter of faith, whereupon faith must rest, which is a promise of God giving a real being of the thing, to be already so indeed as he hath spoken it before himself, although to outward sense, sight and feeling it seems not' (176). John Saltmarsh, *Free-Grace: Or, The Flowings of Christ's Blood Freely to Sinners* (6th edn.; London, 1649): 'Christ is not ours by any act of our own, but God's; God imputing and accounting: to make Christ ours, is an *Almighty work*, and not the work of anything created. So as Christ is ours *without faith*, by a *power* more glorious and infinite but we cannot have known him to be ours, but by *believing*; nor partake of him as ours, but by *believing*' (188–9), John Saltmarsh, *Sparkles of Glory* (London, 1648): 'Christ hath taken away all *sin* by his *offering* once for all; and that *faith* in the *believer* doth nothing, no not instrumentally, as to *justification*, but as by way of *revelation* and *manifestation* of that *justification*' (141–2). The similarity in language arises from a similarity of conception of Christ as the one who has provided full justification. Many of these writers accepted a version of the teaching of eternal justification, that the elect were justified in Christ from eternity, and also that holiness was purchased by Christ and imputed to the elect. The similarities with Barth are obvious; the differences equally so.

[48] Barth, *Church Dogmatics*, iv/1. 629–30.

it is God the Holy Spirit who in grace gives the faith that is instrumentally necessary.

Another reason,[49] perhaps a more fundamental reason, is Barth's desire to safeguard and preserve God's freedom. For Barth *sola gratia* is an expression of God's utter freedom, which has logical priority over everything else. Only God in his freedom can make available unconditional salvation in Jesus Christ.

We have to think something after the following fashion. As God was in Jesus Christ, far from being against Himself, or at disunity with Himself, He has put into effect the freedom of His divine love, the love in which He is divinely free. He has therefore done and revealed that which corresponds to His divine nature . . . It corresponds to and is grounded in His divine nature that in free grace He should be faithful to the unfaithful creature who has not deserved it and who would inevitably perish without it, that in relation to it He should establish that communion between His own form and cause and that of the creature, that He should make His own its being in contradiction and under the consequences of that contradiction, that He should maintain His covenant in relation to sinful man (not surrendering His deity, for how could that help? but giving up and sacrificing Himself), and in that way supremely asserting Himself and His deity.[50]

So if Barth denies the conditional, causal character of faith, and yet gives central importance to faith, what role does faith perform? The answer—as is clear in the earlier quotation—is that faith is the way (or perhaps a way) of recognizing or acknowledging personal justification, it is not its instrumental cause. For Barth the propositional object of faith is 'that Christ is God's justification for everyone' not (as with Calvin) 'that Christ is necessary and sufficient for my justification'.

This is not a mere verbal difference between Calvin and Barth. For there is an important logical distinction between recognition and appropriation. Recognition, as Barth uses it, is an epistemic term. To recognize that something is the case is to learn something that one did not know before. (There is of course an interesting ambiguity in 'recognize' in English; it can be used purely epistemically, as when someone recognizes that the bird hovering above is a kestrel. Or it can be used in the sense of 'give recognition to' as when the UK government recognizes the state of Ruritania.) Barth is

---

[49] As Myron Penner pointed out to me.

[50] Barth, *Church Dogmatics*, iv/1. 186–7. See also *Church Dogmatics*, iv/1. 39: 'In the atonement in which the presupposition is revealed, "I will be your God" this [i.e. God's freedom] is clear beyond any possible doubt . . . Man cannot bring forward a Jesus Christ in which his atonement with God can take place. If it is to take place, it must be from God, in the freedom of God and not of man, in the freedom of the grace of God, to which we have no claim, which would necessarily judge and condemn us because we have sinned against it and always will sin against it, because we have shown ourselves unworthy of it. Atonement is free grace.'

using it in the first sense. By contrast, appropriation, though it no doubt contains an epistemic element, is chiefly causal, as we have seen in our analysis of Calvin.

For Calvin personal justification is secured by an action, the exercise of faith in Christ (though for him that action is itself the effect of the efficacious grace of God). Upon believing, a person is personally justified who was not justified before. So for Calvin faith is *transactional*, resulting in the personal appropriation of the grace of God (but not, for Calvin, resulting in a change in God). Hence Calvin's concern with the reality of this change in the believer, and with the apparent contradiction that this generates when it is misunderstood. But for Barth justification is a state; indeed, on a plausible reading of Barth, justification is an eternal state of the Son of God, an eternal state made manifest in the *Geschichte* of the God-man. Christ is the justified man, eternally so and manifest as such in time. He is the representative man, and may even be said to embody humanity in himself, and so, as the justified one, to secure the justification of humanity. So faith in no sense begins or brings about personal justification; faith is trust in God, but it is not trust in God for anything. Rather, in humility and obedience it acknowledges and recognizes the fact of justification.

It will become clear that Barth must be using 'recognition' in the purely epistemic sense; for Barth to use it in the diplomatic sense would, it seems to me, compromise the principle of *sola gratia* equally as much as considering faith as an instrumental cause would. To recognize (in the epistemic sense) something implies that it was so before it was recognized to be such; the kestrel was a kestrel before I recognized that it was. But to give recognition to Christ in the diplomatic sense would put things back to front for Barth, in a God-dishonouring way. For Barth it is not so much that sinners ever give recognition to Christ as that Christ gives recognition to them.

In confirmation of this interpretation, in the section 'Faith and Its Object' Barth stresses that faith is purely epistemic, it accepts everything as it is:

Faith is at once the most wonderful and the simplest of things. In it a man opens his eyes and sees and accepts everything as it —objectively, really and ontologically—is. Faith is the simple discovery of the child which finds itself in the father's house and on the mother's lap. But this simple thing is also the mystery of faith because only in Jesus Christ is it true and actual that things are as man discovers them, and because man's own discovery can itself be an event only in the fact that man is again awakened by Him to see and accept everything as it is: that the night has passed and the day dawned; that there is peace between God and sinful man, revealed truth, full and present salvation. This simple thing, and this mystery, constitutes the being of the Christian, his being by the One in whom he believes.[51]

[51] Barth, *Church Dogmatics*, iv/1. 748.

Faith opens the eyes, it grants the discovery that the night has passed, and that there is peace with God. It shows that we have all the time been in our father's house and on our mother's lap. And yet Barth goes on to insist that in the action of faith there begins and takes place a new and particular being of man. But this change is a change brought about by the realization that faith discerns, a realization of what is already true; the change that involves incorporation into the Christian community.

> As a human act it [faith] consists in a definite acknowledgement, recognition and confession. As this human act it has no creative but only a cognitive character. It does not alter anything. As a human act it is simply the confirmation of a change which has already taken place, the change in the whole human situation which took place in the death of Jesus Christ and was revealed in His resurrection and attested by the Christian community. But it obviously belongs to the alteration of the human situation which Christian faith can only confirm, that it does find this confirmation, that there are men who do recognise and acknowledge and confess it, who can be the witnesses of it—in other words, that there are individual Christian subjects.[52]

So for Barth there cannot be even the appearance of a contradiction between God's wrath and God's mercy as we have seen that there is for Calvin. Unfortunately the appearance of contradiction is replaced by a real contradiction, for incompatible properties are ascribed to Christ; he is both elect and reprobate. Because Christ as the reprobate one has been condemned, and as the elect one has been justified, his work (indeed, his eternal character as the justified one), is sufficient for justification and actually secures the personal justification of men and women, whether or not they have faith in Christ. If they do have faith, that faith is a recognition in the epistemic sense, an acknowledgement of what is already true.[53]

> There is not one for whose sin and death He did not die, whose sin and death He did not remove and obliterate on the cross, for whom He did not positively do the right, whose right He has not established. There is not one to whom this was not addressed as his justification in His resurrection from the dead. There is not one whose man He is not, who is not justified in Him. There is not one who is justified in any other way than in Him—because it is in Him and only in Him that an end, a bonfire, is made of man's sin and death, because it is in Him and only in Him that man's sin and death are the old thing which has passed away, because it is in Him and only in Him that the right has been done which is demanded of man, that the right has been

---

[52] Barth, *Church Dogmatics*, iv/1. 751–2.

[53] 'Christ is the *locus* in which the true knowledge of the human situation is disclosed, the *speculum* or mirror in which man sees himself reflected. For Barth, Christ's incarnation, passion, death and resurrection cannot in any way be said to change the relationship between God and man—they merely disclose the Christologically determined situation to man' (Alister E. McGrath, *The Making of Modern German Christology 1750–1990* (Oxford: Blackwell, 1986), 110).

established to which man can move forward . . . There is not one for whom He has not done everything in His death and received everything in His resurrection from the dead.

Not one. That is what faith believes. And in believing that it is justifying faith, i.e., a faith which knows and grasps and realises the justification of man as the decision and act and word of God. It is faith in Jesus Christ, who was crucified and raised again for us—faith in Him as the One in whom our judgment has taken place, our pardon has been pronounced. Faith comes about where Jesus Christ prevails on man, and in Jesus Christ the self-demonstration of the justified man. Faith knows him and apprehends Him. It lets itself be told and accepts the fact and trusts in it that Jesus Christ is man's justification.[54]

These moving words make it clear why for Barth faith does not accomplish anything; faith is essentially epistemic recognition of what another has accomplished, or the recognition that nothing needs to be accomplished. Barth's view of the place of faith in justification might be expressed in the immortal words of Paul Tillich: 'Do not seek for anything; do not perform anything; do not intend anything. Simply accept the fact that you are accepted!'[55]

For Barth the temporal order of justification is very straightforward. The reconciliation of mankind in Christ is eternal, and is made known in time. Justification is therefore one eternal act, with no temporal components.[56] However, the epistemic recognition of justification (on the part of those who do recognize it) is an event in time. For Barth faith is faith in Christ as the justified man; for Calvin, faith is faith in Christ described as the one who has in history procured our justification. And faith appropriates that justification personally, and by such appropriation the believer becomes what he was not before, a personally justified person.

FAITH AND CONDITIONALITY

Calvin's account of faith in *Institutes* III. 2 is prefaced by the following paragraph:

But it will be easy to understand all these matters after a clearer definition of faith has been presented, to enable our readers to grasp its force and nature. We may well recall here what was explained before: First, God lays down for us through the law what we should do; if we then fail in any part of it, that dreadful sentence of eternal

---

[54] *Church Dogmatics*, iv/1. 630–1.

[55] Quoted in William Lad Sessions, *The Concept of Faith* (Ithaca: Cornell University Press, 1994), 249.

[56] 'The diverse aspects and elements of the question of the person and work of Christ are inextricably interwoven, in that God is merely declaring to man what he had consummated in eternity, by a decree which anticipates everything temporal' (McGrath, *Modern German Christology*, 109).

death which it pronounces will rest upon us. Secondly, it is not only hard, but above our strength and beyond all our abilities, to fulfill the law to the letter; thus, if we look to ourselves only, and ponder what condition we deserve, no trace of good hope will remain; but cast away by God, we shall lie under eternal death. Thirdly, it has been explained that there is but one means of liberation that can rescue us from such miserable calamity: the appearance of Christ the Redeemer, through whose hand the Heavenly Father, pitying us out of his infinite goodness and mercy, willed to help us; if, indeed, with firm faith we embrace this mercy and rest in it with steadfast hope.[57]

Christ the Redeemer will help us, says Calvin, if we embrace this mercy with firm faith. Otherwise, we shall lie under eternal death. We return to what is for Calvin the reality and the seriousness of the change that takes place when faith is exercised in Christ. For Calvin it is therefore of the utmost importance that we have faith, and that if at all possible we know that we have it. But what is faith? Any account of Calvin's views on faith and assurance must start with his celebrated definition.

Now we shall possess a right definition of faith if we call it a firm and certain knowledge of God's benevolence toward us, founded upon the truth of the freely given promise in Christ, both revealed to our minds and sealed upon our hearts through the Holy Spirit.[58]

Calvin here seems to bracket together faith and assurance, to make nothing of the distinction that later Calvinists made so much of. For faith is the knowledge 'of God's benevolence toward us'. Faith is knowledge, not a conjecture or a mere hope, and it is (or includes) knowledge that God is benevolent toward us. But it is not knowledge in the merely epistemic sense that we found in Barth. It is knowledge that God is benevolent towards us because, in the very exercise of faith, we come to enjoy that benevolence towards us. It carries with it not merely the conviction that God is benevolent, but that he is benevolent toward the very one who has such faith.

But surprisingly perhaps, in view of his definition of faith, this is not all that Calvin says on the nature of faith, as we noted in our earlier discussion in Chapter 9. A little after the passage just quoted he writes:

Surely, while we teach that faith ought to be certain and assured, we cannot imagine any certainty that is not tinged with doubt, or any assurance that is not assailed by some anxiety. On the other hand, we say that believers are in perpetual conflict with their own unbelief.[59]

Therefore the godly heart feels in itself a division because it is partly imbued with sweetness from its recognition of the divine goodness, partly grieves in bitterness from an awareness of its calamity; partly rests upon the promise of the gospel, partly

---

[57] *Inst.* III. 2. 1.   [58] *Inst.* III. 2. 7 and III. 2. 15.   [59] *Inst.* III. 2. 17.

trembles at the evidence of its own iniquity; partly rejoices at the expectation of life, partly shudders at death. This variation arises from imperfection of faith, since in the course of the present life it never goes so well with us that we are wholly cured of the disease of unbelief and entirely filled and possessed by faith.[60]

Calvin here makes clear that his earlier definition of faith has a normative character. In the later quotations he recognizes that even where the objective grounds of faith are not in doubt the 'godly heart' may nevertheless be assailed by anxiety when it reflects upon the evidence of its own iniquity. Though convinced of the divine benevolence, a person may, through reflecting on his remaining sinfulness, doubt that divine benevolence is toward him. But he ought not to doubt, for in the case of the true believer the objective grounds of the promise ought to overwhelm the evidence that he may have of his own continuing sinful state. Nevertheless Calvin recognizes that though faith ought not to be mixed with such doubt, it nonetheless often will be.

When we turn to Barth, and remind ourselves that for Barth faith is the acknowledgement of what is already true, it is little wonder that he pays scant attention to the relation between faith and the assurance of faith. Though he is bound to acknowledge the conceptual distinction between the two, despite what he says to the contrary, the importance of that distinction for him is vanishingly small. For a person's justification could not be put in jeopardy if for some reason he fails, by a failure of faith, to recognize it. Faith is not for Barth, as it is for Calvin, a life or death matter. A person might lack faith in Christ but nevertheless conclude, by an inference, that since in Christ humanity is justified, he is. But for Calvin a person who reasons like this puts his soul in jeopardy.

Barth goes beyond Calvin in claiming that justification is jeopardized only by human belief in self-justification by works, and not also, as Calvin claimed, by the absence of faith. It appears that it is possible according to Barth to lack justifying faith, not to have faith in one's own works, and nevertheless to be justified.[61]

Could he [Paul] have forbidden it to a Christian as a *vana et omni pietati remota fiducia*, the very words of the Tridentium (*c.* 9), to cling in faith and to find comfort in the fact that his sins are forgiven? Could he have regarded it as a 'heretical and schismatic' opinion that Christian faith has an unconditional and not a conditional assurance of this, and that so far as it does not have this unconditional assurance it is not the true Christian faith which justifies a man? Where did he ever say, and how could he possibly have said, that (*c.* 9) although the Christian ought not to doubt the mercy of God, the merits of Christ and the power of the sacraments, yet in view of his

---

[60] *Inst.* III. 2. 18.   [61] Barth, *Church Dogmatics*, iv/1. 632.

own *infirmitas* and *indispositio* even in faith there can be no absolute assurance *de sua gratia*, in the question of whether there is grace for him?[62]

And:

Faith ceases to be faith, it becomes its opposite, unbelief, hating and despising God, rejection, the crucifying afresh of the One in whom He gave Himself for us, if it looks anywhere but to Him, if the believer tries to look at himself and to rely and trust on his own activity and accomplishment.[63]

How might Calvin himself respond to these charges, the charges that the assurance of faith is unconditional and that conditional faith invariably involves the believer looking to himself and relying and trusting on his own activity and accomplishment? In order to consider this, let us think about the following sentences in the light of our earlier conclusion that for Calvin faith is the instrumental cause of justification.

(1) If X does not believe, he is not personally justified.
(2) Whether or not X believes, provided that he does not seek justification by his own efforts, he will be justified.

(1) is a statement of Calvin's position on justification by faith, at least for any X that is adult, while (2) is my reconstruction of Barth.[64] Why for Barth are expressions of type (1) conditionalizings of grace subverting its unconditional character? According to Calvin, for justification to be gracious it most certainly cannot be conditioned on any prior state of the recipient; this much is surely not in doubt. But as it stands that expression is ambiguous. It may mean: *justification* cannot be conditioned upon any prior state of the recipient of it; or, the *application* or *personal enjoyment* of justification cannot be conditioned. Why are expressions of type (1) regarded by Barth as being necessarily equivalent to: If X does not trust Christ then X believes that the grace of God in Christ is insufficient for his justification? In supposing that they are equivalent to such a sentence there seems to be an insufficient appreciation of the diverse ways in which conditions may be invoked.

[62] *Church Dogmatics*, iv/1. 625. Barth is here echoing in detail the wording of the Decrees of the Council of Trent.   [63] *Church Dogmatics*, iv/1. 632.

[64] My warrant for this reconstruction are these remarks of Barth: 'If he believes in Him, he knows and grasps his own righteousness as one which is alien to him, as the righteousness of this other, who is justified man in his place, for him. He will miss his own righteousness, he will fall from it, if he thinks he can and should know and grasp and realise it in his own acts and achievements, or in his faith and the result of it. He will be jeopardising, indeed he will already have lost, the forgiveness of his sins, his life as a child of God, his hope of eternal life, if he ever thinks he can and should seek and find these things anywhere but at the place where as the act and work of God they are real as the forgiveness of his sins, as his divine sonship, as his hope, anywhere but in the one Jesus Christ' (*Church Dogmatics*, iv/1. 631).

Of course if faith were the material cause of justification according to Calvin, that which actually procures justification, then there would be substance to the charge that he was putting faith in the place of Christ, and also to the charge that such a person was depending upon faith for salvation, rather than upon Christ. But as we have seen Calvin is at pains to make the distinction between the material and the instrumental cause of salvation as clear as he can, and so he cannot be fairly accused of making this mistake.

So Calvin could with perfect consistency say that to suppose that looking for signs of assurance is relying upon and trusting on one's own activity and accomplishment, involves a simple confusion between being in a state of trust and having evidence that one is in that state. To take note of the evidence that one is trusting God is not to substitute that evidence for God, to trust it instead of him. It is to have good reason to think that one is in fact trusting God.

Inasmuch, therefore, as this reliance upon works has no place unless you first cast the whole confidence of your mind upon God's mercy, it ought not to seem contrary to that upon which it depends. Therefore, when we rule out reliance upon works, we mean only this: that the Christian mind may not be turned back to the merit of works as to a help toward salvation but should rely wholly on the free promise of righteousness. But we do not forbid him from undergirding and strengthening this faith by signs of the divine benevolence toward him.[65]

[65] *Inst.* III. 14. 18.

Bibliography

Sources in Calvin

The Bondage and Liberation of the Will, ed. A. N. S. Lane, trans. G. I. Davies (Grand Rapids, Mich.: Baker, 1996).

Calvin: Theological Treatises, trans. J. K. S. Reid (London: S. C. M. Press, 1954).

Calvin's Calvinism, trans. Henry Cole (London: Sovereign Grace Union, 1927).

Calvin's Commentary on Acts, trans. John W. Fraser (Edinburgh: Oliver & Boyd, 1966).

Calvin's Commentary on Romans, trans. Ross Mackenzie (Edinburgh: Oliver & Boyd, 1961).

Calvin's Commentary on Seneca's De Clementia with Introduction, Translation, and Notes, ed. F. L. Battles and A. M. Hugo (Leiden: E. J. Brill, 1969).

'Christ the Mediator: Calvin versus Stancaro', trans. Joseph N. Tylenda, *Calvin Theological Journal* (1973).

Commentaries (Edinburgh: Calvin Translation Society, 1843–55; repr. Grand Rapids, Mich.: Baker, 1981).

Concerning the Eternal Predestination of God (1552), trans. with an Introduction by J. K. S. Reid (London: James Clarke, 1961).

'The Controversy on Christ the Mediator: Calvin's Second Reply to Stancaro' trans. Joseph N. Tylenda, *Calvin Theological Journal* (1973).

Institutes of the Christian Religion (1559), ed. J. T. MacNeill, trans. F. L. Battles (London: S. C. M. Press, 1961).

Institutes of the Christian Religion (1559), trans. Henry Beveridge (Edinburgh, 1845; repr. Grand Rapids, Mich.: Eerdmans, 1966).

Institution of the Christian Religion (1536), trans. F. L. Battles (Atlanta: John Knox Press, 1975).

Ioannis Calvinis Opera Quae Supersunt Omnia, ed. G. Baum, E. Cunitz, and E. Reuss (Brunschwig and Halle: Schwetschke, 1834–60).

John Calvin's Sermons on the Ten Commandments, trans. B. W. Farley (Grand Rapids, Mich.: Baker, 1980).

John Calvin, Treatises Against the Anabaptists and Against the Libertines, trans. and ed. B. W. Farley (Grand Rapids, Mich.: Baker, 1982).

Selected Works of John Calvin, Tracts and Letters, ed. Henry Beveridge and Jules Bonnet (Edinburgh, 1844, Philadelphia, 1858; repr. Grand Rapids, Mich.: Baker, 1983).

Sermons on Galatians, trans. Kathy Childress (Edinburgh: Banner of Truth Trust, 1997).

Sermons of Maister Iohn Caluin, upon the Booke of Job, trans. Arthur Golding (London, 1574; repr. in facsimile, Edinburgh: Banner of Truth Trust, 1993).

Sermons of M. John Calvin, on the Epistles of S. Paul to Timothie and Titus, trans. L. T. (London, 1579; facsimile repr. Edinburgh: Banner of Truth Trust, 1983).

The Sermons of M. Iohn Calvin Upon the Fifth Booke of Moses Called Deuteronomie, trans. Arthur Golding (London, 1583; facsimile repr. Edinburgh: Banner of Truth Trust, 1987).

A Warning Against Judiciary Astrology and Other Prevalent Curiosities, trans. Mary Potter, *Calvin Theological Journal* (1983).

'The Warning That Went Unheeded. John Calvin on Giorgio Blandrata', trans. Joseph N. Tylenda, *Calvin Theological Journal* (1977).

Secondary Sources

ADAMS, EDWARD, 'Calvin's View of Natural Knowledge of God', *International Journal of Systematic Theology*, 3 (2001).

ADAMS, MARILYN MCCORD, *Ockham* (Notre Dame: University of Notre Dame Press, 1987).

—— 'The Problem of Hell: A Problem of Evil for Christians', in Eleonore Stump (ed.), *Reasoned Faith* (Ithaca and London: Cornell University Press, 1993).

—— 'The Resurrection of the Body according to Three Medieval Aristotelians: Thomas Aquinas, John Duns Scotus, William Ockham', *Philosophical Topics*, 20 (1992).

—— and ADAMS, ROBERT MERRIHEW (eds.), *The Problem of Evil* (Oxford: Oxford University Press, 1990).

ADAMS, ROBERT MERRIHEW, 'A Modified Divine Command Theory of Ethical Wrongness', in Paul Helm (ed.), *Divine Commands and Morality* (Oxford: Oxford University Press, 1981).

ALSTON, WILLIAM, 'Can We Speak Literally of God?', in *Divine Nature and Human Language: Essays in Philosophical Theology* (Ithaca and London: Cornell University Press, 1989).

—— 'How to Think About Divine Action', in Brian Hebblethwaite and Edward Henderson (eds.), *Divine Action: Studies Inspired by the Philosophical Theology of Austin Farrer* (Edinburgh: T. & T. Clark, 1990).

—— 'On Knowing That We Know: The Application to Religious Knowledge', in C. Stephen Evans and Merold Westphal (eds.), *Christian Perspectives on Religious Knowledge* (Grand Rapids, Mich.: Eerdmans, 1993).

—— *The Reliability of Sense Perception* (Ithaca and London: Cornell University Press, 1993).

ANTOGNAZZA, MARIA ROSA, 'The Defence of the Mysteries of the Trinity and the Incarnation: An Example of Leibniz's "Other" Reason', *British Journal of the History of Philosophy*, (2001).

AQUINAS, THOMAS, *Commentary on the Gospel of St. John*, trans. James A. Weisheipl and Fabian Larcher (Albany, NY: Magi, 1980).

—— *The Literal Exposition on Job*, trans. Anthony Domico, ed. Martin D. Yaffe (Atlanta: Scholars Press, 1989).

—— 'On the Eternity of the World', in *Thomas Aquinas: Selected Writings*, trans. Ralph McInerny (London: Penguin Books, 1998).

—— *Summa Contra Gentiles, Book One, The Doctrine of God*, trans. Anton C. Pegis (Garden City, NY: Image Books, 1955).

—— *Summa Theologiae*, Latin text and English translation, various translators (Blackfriars, in conjunction with London: Eyre & Spottiswoode, New York: McGraw-Hill Book Company, 1963–80).

ARISTOTLE, *Nicomachean Ethics*, trans. David Ross, revised by J. L. Ackrill and J. O. Urmson (Oxford: Oxford University Press, 1980).

—— *Physics Book II*, trans. W. Charlton (Oxford: Clarendon Press, 1970).

ARMSTRONG, BRIAN G., *Calvin and the Amyraut Heresy: Protestant Scholasticism and Humanism in Seventeenth Century France* (Madison: University of Wisconsin Press, 1969).

ATHANASIUS, *On the Incarnation of the Word*, trans. A. Robertson, in Edwards R. Hardy (ed.), *Christology of the Later Fathers* (Philadelphia: Westminster Press, 1954).

AUGUSTINE, *The City of God*, trans. John Healey, ed. R. V. G. Tasker (London: Dent & Sons, 1945).

—— *Confessions*, trans. Henry Chadwick (Oxford: Oxford University Press, 1992).

—— *Letters*, vol. iii, trans. Sister Wilfrid Parsons (Washington, DC: Catholic University of America Press, 1953).

—— *On the Trinity*, trans. A. W. Haddan (Edinburgh: T. & T. Clark, 1873).

BACKUS, IRENA, 'Calvin's Concept of Natural and Roman Law', *Calvin Theological Journal* (2003).

BARR, JAMES, *Biblical Faith and Natural Theology* (Oxford: Clarendon Press, 1993).

BARTH, KARL, *Church Dogmatics, i/2: The Doctrine of the Word of God*, trans. G. T. Thomson and Harold Knight, ed. G. W. Bromiley and T. F. Torrance (Edinburgh: T. & T. Clark, 1956).

—— *Church Dogmatics, iv/1: The Doctrine of Reconciliation*, trans. G. W. Bromiley, ed. G. W. Bromiley and T. F. Torrance (Edinburgh: T. & T. Clark, 1956).

—— and BRUNNER, EMIL, *Natural Theology*, trans. Peter Fraenkel (London: Geoffrey Bles, 1946).

BATTLES, FORD LEWIS, 'God was Accommodating Himself to Human Capacity', in Donald K. McKim (ed.), *Readings in Calvin's Theology* (Grand Rapids, Mich.: Baker, 1984).

BEARDSLEE III, J. W. (trans. and ed.), *Reformed Dogmatics* (New York: Oxford University Press, 1965).

BENIN, D. STEPHEN, *The Footprints of God* (Albany, NY: SUNY Press, 1993).

BERKELEY, GEORGE, *Alciphron* (1734), ed. David Berman (London: Routledge, 1993).

BERKHOF, LOUIS, *Systematic Theology* (Grand Rapids, Mich.: Eerdmans, 1941).

BERKOUWER, G. C., *The Work of Christ*, trans. Cornelius Lambregste (Grand Rapids, Mich.: Eerdmans, 1965).

BERMAN, DAVID, 'Cognitive Theology and Emotive Mysteries in Berkeley's *Alciphron*', in David Berman (ed.), *George Berkeley, Alciphron in Focus* (London: Routledge, 1993).

BETHUNE-BAKER, J. F., *An Introduction to the Early History of Christian Doctrine* (3rd edn.; London: Methuen, 1923).

BEVERSLUIS, JOHN, 'Reforming the "Reformed" Objection to Natural Theology', *Faith and Philosophy*, (1995).

BLOCHER, HENRI, 'Yesterday, Today, Forever; Time, Times, Eternity in Biblical Perspective', *Tyndale Bulletin* (2001).

BOHATEC, JOSEF, *Calvin und das Recht* (Feudingen in Westfalen: Buchdruck- und Verlags-Anstalt, 1934).

BRAY, GERALD, *The Doctrine of God* (Leicester: Inter-Varsity Press, 1993).

—— 'The Patristic Dogma', in Peter Toon and James D. Spiceland (eds.), *One God in Trinity* (Westchester, Ill.: Cornerstone Books, 1980).

BROADIE, ALEXANDER, *The Shadow of Scotus* (Edinburgh: T. & T. Clark, 1995).

BROADIE, SARAH, *Ethics With Aristotle* (New York: Oxford University Press, 1991).

BROWN, DAVID, *The Divine Trinity* (London: Duckworth, 1985).

—— 'Trinitarian Personhood and Individuality', in Cornelius Plantinga and Ronald Feenstra (eds.), *Trinity, Incarnation and Atonement* (Notre Dame: University of Notre Dame Press, 1989).

BRÜMMER, VINCENT, 'Calvin, Bernard and the Freedom of the Will', *Religious Studies*, 30 (1994).

—— 'On Not Confusing Necessity with Compulsion: A Reply to Paul Helm', *Religious Studies*, 31 (1995).

BURKETT, DELBERT, *The Son of Man Debate: A History and Evaluation* (Cambridge: Cambridge University Press, 1999).

BURRELL, DAVID, *Knowing the Unknowable God: Ibn-Sina, Maimonides, Aquinas* (Notre Dame: University of Notre Dame Press, 1986).

BUTIN, PHILIP W., *Revelation, Redemption and Response: Calvin's Trinitarian Understanding of the Divine–Human Relationship* (New York: Oxford University Press, 1995).

BUTLER, JOSEPH, *Fifteen Sermons Preached at the Rolls Chapel* (London: G. Bell & Sons Ltd., 1967).

The Cambridge Dictionary of Philosophy, ed. Robert Audi (Cambridge: Cambridge University Press, 1995).

CICERO, *The Nature of the Gods*, trans. Horace C. P. McGregor (London: Penguin Books, 1972).

COURTENAY, WILLIAM J., 'The Dialectic of Omnipotence in the High and Late Middle Ages', in Tamar Rudavsky (ed.), *Divine Omniscience and Omnipotence in Medieval Philosophy* (Dordrecht: Reidel, 1985).

—— 'Nominalism and Late Medieval Religion', in C. Trinkaus and H. A. Oberman (eds.), *The Pursuit of Holiness in Late Medieval and Renaissance Religion* (Leiden: E. J. Brill, 1974).

CRAIG, WILLIAM LANE, *The Problem of Divine Foreknowledge and Future Contingents from Aristotle to Suarez* (Leiden: E. J. Brill, 1988).

CROSS, RICHARD, '*Alloiosis* in the Christology of Zwingli', *Journal of Theological Studies*, NS 47 (1996).

—— *Duns Scotus* (New York: Oxford University Press, 1999).

—— *The Metaphysics of the Incarnation* (Oxford: Oxford University Press, 2002).

DE KROON, MARIJN, *The Honour of God and Human Salvation: Calvin's Theology According to his Institutes*, trans. J. Vriend and Lyle D. Bierma (Edinburgh: T. & T. Clark, 2001).

DESCARTES, RENÉ, *Philosophical Letters*, trans. and ed. Anthony Kenny (Oxford: Clarendon Press, 1970).

Documents of the English Reformation, ed. Gerald Bray (Cambridge: James Clarke, 1994).

DOWEY, E. A., *The Knowledge of God in Calvin's Theology* (expanded edn., Grand Rapids, Mich.: Eerdmans, 1993).

DOWNAME, GEORGE, *A Treatise on Justification* (London, 1633).

DUNS SCOTUS, *Duns Scotus on the Will and Morality*, ed. Allan B. Wolter (Washington: Catholic University Press of America, 1986).

EATON, JOHN, *The Honey-Combe of Free Justification by Christ Alone* (London, 1642).

EDWARDS, JONATHAN, 'Essay on the Trinity', in *Treatise on Grace and Other Posthumous Writings of Jonathan Edwards*, ed. Paul Helm (Cambridge: James Clarke, 1971).

EDWARDS, PAUL, 'Common Consent Arguments for the Existence of God', in Paul Edwards (ed.), *The Encyclopaedia of Philosophy* (London: Macmillan, 1967).

FISCHER, J. M. (ed.), *God, Foreknowledge and Freedom* (Stanford, Calif.: Stanford University Press, 1989).

—— and RAVIZZA, MARK (eds.), *Perspectives on Moral Responsibility* (Ithaca and London: Cornell University Press, 1993).

———— *Responsibility and Control* (Cambridge: Cambridge University Press, 1998).

FRANKFURT, HARRY, *The Importance of What We Care About* (Cambridge: Cambridge University Press, 1988).

—— *Necessity, Vision and Love* (Cambridge: Cambridge University Press, 1999).

GAFFIN, RICHARD B., *Calvin on the Sabbath* (Fearn, Ross-shire: Mentor, 1998).

GANOCZY, ALEXANDRE, *The Young Calvin*, trans. David Foxgrover and Wade Provo (Philadelphia: Westminster Press, 1987).

GEACH, PETER, *God and the Soul* (London: Routledge, 1969).

—— *Providence and Evil* (Cambridge: Cambridge University Press, 1977).

GELLMAN, JEROME, *The Fear, the Trembling and the Fire. Kierkegaard and the Hasidic Masters on the Binding of Isaac* (Lanham, Md.: University Press of America, 1994).

—— 'Identifying God in Experience: On Strawson, Sounds and God's Space', in Paul Helm (ed.), *Referring to God* (Richmond, Surrey: Curzon Press, 1999).

GRANT, EDWARD, *God and Reason in the Middle Ages* (Cambridge: Cambridge University Press, 2001).

GRISLIS, EGIL, 'Calvin's Use of Cicero in the *Institutes* I: 1–5 — A Case Study in Theological Method', *Archiv für Reformationsgeschichte*, 62 (1971).

HAAS, GUENTHER, *The Concept of Equity in Calvin's Ethics* (Carlisle: Paternoster Press, 1997).

HARE, JOHN E., *God's Call* (Grand Rapids, Mich.: Eerdmans, 2001).

HARRIS, MICHAEL J., *Divine Command Ethics: Jewish and Christian Perspectives* (London: Routledge Curzon, 2003).

HASKER, W., 'Evidentialism', in R. Audi (ed.), *The Cambridge Dictionary of Philosophy* (Cambridge: Cambridge University Press, 1995).

—— Basinger, D., and Dekker, Eef (eds.), *Middle Knowledge, Theory and Applications* (Frankfurt: Peter Lang, 2000).

HELM, PAUL, 'All Things Considered: Providence and Divine Purpose', in T. W. Bartel (ed.), *Comparative Theology: Essays for Keith Ward* (London: SPCK, 2003).

—— 'Calvin (and Zwingli) on the Providence of God', *Calvin Theological Journal* (1994).

—— *Eternal God: A Study of God without Time* (Oxford: Clarendon Press, 1988).

—— *Faith and Understanding* (Edinburgh: Edinburgh University Press, 1997).

—— 'Omnipotence and Change', *Philosophy*, (1976).

—— 'On Grace and Causation', *Scottish Journal of Theology*, (1979).

—— 'The Problem of Dialogue', in G. E. Ganssle and D. M. Woodruff (eds.), *God and Time: Essays on the Divine Nature* (New York: Oxford University Press, 2002).

HICK, JOHN, *Evil and the God of Love* (London: Macmillan, 1966).

—— *Faith and Knowledge* (London: Macmillan, 1966).

—— *An Interpretation of Religion* (London: Macmillan, 1989).

—— 'Religious Faith as Experiencing-As', in G. N. A. Vesey (ed.), *Talk of God* (London: Macmillan, 1969).

HILARY OF POITIERS, *The Trinity*, trans. Stephen McKenna (Washington, DC: Catholic University Press, 1954).

HOITENGA, JR., DEWEY J., *Faith and Reason from Plato to Plantinga* (Albany, NY: SUNY Press, 1991).

—— *John Calvin and the Will: A Critique and Corrective* (Grand Rapids, Mich.: Baker, 1997).

HÖPFL, HARRO, *The Christian Polity of John Calvin* (Cambridge: Cambridge University Press, 1982).

HUGHES, CHRISTOPHER, *On a Complex Theory of a Simple God* (Ithaca: Cornell University Press, 1989).

IDZIAK, J. M., *Divine Command Morality: Historical and Contemporary Readings* (New York: Edward Mellen Press, 1979).

JAMES III, FRANK, *Peter Martyr Vermigli and Predestination* (Oxford: Clarendon Press, 1998).

JANZ, DENIS R., *Luther and Late Medieval Thomism: A Study in Theological Anthropology* (Waterloo: Wilfrid Laurier University Press, 1983).

JEFFREYS, DEREK S., 'How Reformed is Reformed Epistemology? Alvin Plantinga and Calvin's "Sensus Divinitatis"', *Religious Studies*, (1997).

KANT, IMMANUEL, *Religion Within the Limits of Reason Alone*, trans. T. M. Green and H. H. Hudson (New York: Harper & Row, 1960).

KELLY, J. N. D., *Early Christian Doctrines* (5th edn.; London: A. & C. Black, 1977).

KLAUBER, MARTIN I., and SUNSHINE, GLENN S., 'Jean-Alphonse Turretini on Biblical Accommodation: Calvinist or Socinian?', *Calvin Theological Journal*, (1990).

KRETZMANN, NORMAN, *The Metaphysics of Creation* (Oxford: Clarendon Press, 1999).

—— *The Metaphysics of Theism* (Oxford: Clarendon Press, 1997).

—— 'Ockham and the Creation of the Beginningless World', *Franciscan Studies*, (1985).

—— 'Warring Against the Law of My Mind: Aquinas on Romans 7', in T. V. Morris (ed.), *Philosophy and the Christian Faith* (Notre Dame: University of Notre Dame Press, 1988).

KUIPER, H., *Calvin on Common Grace* (Grand Rapids, Mich.: Smitter Book Company, 1928).

LANE, ANTHONY N. S., *Calvin and Bernard of Clairvaux* (Princeton: Princeton Theological Seminary, 1996).

—— *John Calvin: Student of the Church Fathers* (Edinburgh: T. & T. Clark, 1999).

—— *Justification by Faith in Catholic–Protestant Dialogue: An Evangelical Assessment* (Edinburgh: T. & T. Clark, 2002).

LANGSTON, DOUGLAS C., *God's Willing Knowledge* (University Park and London: Pennsylvania State University Press, 1986).

LECERF, AUGUSTE, *An Introduction to Reformed Dogmatics* (London: Lutterworth Press, 1949).

LEFTOW, BRIAN, 'Anti Social Trinitarianism', in S. T. Davis, Daniel Kendall and Gerald O'Collins (eds.), *The Trinity* (Oxford: Oxford University Press, 1999).

—— *Time and Eternity* (Ithaca and London: Cornell University Press, 1991).

LOCKE, JOHN, *An Essay Concerning Human Understanding*, ed. J. Yolton (London: Dent, 1961).

LUCAS, J. R., *Freedom and Grace* (London: SPCK, 1976).

—— 'The Lesbian Rule', *Philosophy* (1955).

LUTHER, MARTIN, *The Bondage of the Will*, trans. J. I. Packer and O. R. Johnston (London: James Clarke, 1957).

McCORMACK, BRUCE, 'Grace and Being: The Role of God's Gracious Election in Karl Barth's Theological Ontology', in John Webster (ed.), *The Cambridge Companion to Karl Barth* (Cambridge: Cambridge University Press, 2000).

McFague, Sallie, *Metaphorical Theology: Models of God in Religious Language* (Philadelphia: Fortress Press, 1982).

McGrath, Alister E., *The Intellectual Origins of the European Reformation* (Oxford: Blackwell, 1987).

—— 'John Calvin and Late Medieval Thought: A Study in Late Medieval Influences upon Calvin's Theological Development', *Archiv für Reformationsgeschichte*, (1986).

—— *Justitia Dei: A History of the Christian Doctrine of Justification* (2nd edn.; Cambridge: Cambridge University Press, 1998).

—— *A Life of John Calvin* (Oxford: Blackwell, 1990).

—— *The Making of Modern German Christology 1750–1990* (Oxford: Blackwell, 1986).

Macintyre, Alasdair, *A Short History of Ethics* (London: Routledge, 1967).

Maimonides, Moses, *Guide of the Perplexed*, trans. with an introd. and notes by Shlomo Pines, with an introductory essay by Leo Strauss (Chicago: University of Chicago Press, 1963).

Mallinson, Jeffrey, *Faith, Reason, and Revelation in Theodore Beza (1519–1605)* (Oxford: Oxford University Press, 2003).

Millet, Olivier, 'Exégèse Évangélique et Culture Littéraire Humaniste: Entre Luther et Bèze: *L'Abraham Sacrifiant* selon Calvin', *Études Théologiques et Religieuses* (1993–4).

Molina, Luis de, *On Divine Foreknowledge, Part IV of the Concordia*, trans. with an Introduction and Notes by Alfred J. Freddoso (Ithaca and London: Cornell University Press, 1998).

Moonan, Lawrence, *Divine Power* (Oxford: Clarendon Press, 1994).

Morris, Thomas V., 'Duty and Divine Goodness', in Thomas V. Morris (ed.), *The Concept of God* (Oxford: Oxford University Press, 1987).

—— *The Logic of God Incarnate* (Ithaca and London: Cornell University Press, 1986).

Mouw, R. J., *The God Who Commands* (Notre Dame: University of Notre Dame Press, 1990).

Muller, Richard A., 'Calvin and the Calvinists: Assessing Continuities and Discontinuities Between the Reformation and Orthodoxy, Part I', *Calvin Theological Journal* (1995).

—— 'Calvin and the Calvinists: Assessing Continuities and Discontinuities Between the Reformation and Orthodoxy, Part II', *Calvin Theological Journal* (1996).

—— *Christ and the Decree: Christology and Predestination in Reformed Theology from Calvin to Perkins* (Durham, NC: Labyrinth Press, 1986).

—— *God, Creation and Providence in the Thought of Jacobus Arminius* (Grand Rapids, Mich.: Baker, 1991).

—— 'The Myth of "Decretal" Theology"', *Calvin Theological Journal* (1995).

—— *Post-Reformation Reformed Dogmatics*, 4 vols. (Grand Rapids, Mich.: Baker, 2003).

—— 'Reformation, Orthodoxy, "Christian Aristotelianism", and the Eclecticism of Early Modern Philosophy', *Nederlands Archief voor Keerkgeschiedenis*, (2001).

—— *The Unaccommodated Calvin*, (New York: Oxford University Press, 2000).

MURRAY, JOHN, *Calvin on Scripture and Divine Sovereignty* (Grand Rapids, Mich.: Baker, 1960).

OBERMAN, H. A., *The Dawn of the Reformation: Essays in Late Medieval and Early Reformation Thought* (Edinburgh: T. & T. Clark, 1986).

—— *The Harvest of Medieval Theology: Gabriel Biel and Late Medieval Nominalism* (3rd edn.; Grand Rapids, Mich.: Baker, 2000).

OWEN, PAUL, 'Calvin and Catholic Trinitarianism', *Calvin Theological Journal* (2000).

PARKER, T. H. L., *Calvin's Doctrine of the Knowledge of God* (Grand Rapids, Mich.: Eerdmans, 1959; 2nd edn.; Edinburgh: Oliver & Boyd, 1969).

PARTEE, CHARLES, *Calvin and Classical Philosophy* (Leiden: E. J. Brill, 1977).

—— 'Calvin on Universal and Particular Providence', in Donald K. McKim (ed.), *Readings in Calvin's Theology* (Grand Rapids, Mich.: Baker, 1984).

PETERSON, ROBERT A., *Calvin and the Atonement* (2nd edn.; Fearn, Ross-shire: Mentor, 1999).

PINK, THOMAS, 'Reason and Agency', *Proceedings of the Aristotelian Society*, NS 97 (1996–7).

PLANTINGA, ALVIN, 'Advice to Christian Philosophers', *Faith and Philosophy*, (1984).

—— 'Divine Knowledge', in C. Stephen Evans and Merold Westphal (eds.), *Christian Perspectives on Religious Knowledge* (Grand Rapids, Mich.: Eerdmans, 1993).

—— *Does God Have A Nature?* (Milwaukee: Marquette University Press, 1980).

—— 'Reason and Belief in God', in Alvin Plantinga and Nicholas Wolterstorff (eds.), *Faith and Rationality* (Notre Dame: University of Notre Dame Press, 1983).

—— 'The Reformed Objection to Natural Theology', *Proceedings of the American Catholic Philosophical Association*, (1980).

—— *Warranted Christian Belief* (New York: Oxford University Press, 2000).

PLANTINGA, CORNELIUS, 'Social Trinity and Tritheism', in Cornelius Plantinga and Ronald Feenstra (eds.), *Trinity, Incarnation and Atonement* (Notre Dame: University of Notre Dame Press, 1989).

PORTER, JEAN, *Natural and Divine Law* (Grand Rapids, Mich.: Eerdmans/ Novalis, 1999).

RAHNER, KARL, *The Trinity*, trans J. Donceel (New York: Herder & Herder, 1970).

REARDON, P. H., 'Calvin on Providence: The Development of an Insight', *Scottish Journal of Theology*, (1975).

Registers of the Consistory of Geneva in the Time of Calvin, vol. i 1542–4, ed. R. M. Kingdon, T. A. Lambert, I. M. Wart, trans M. W. McDonald (Grand Rapids, Mich.: Eerdmans/The Meeter Center, 2000).

REID, J. K. S., *The Authority of the Bible* (London: Methuen, 1957).

RICHARD OF ST VICTOR, *La Trinité*, Latin text, introd., and notes by Gaston Salet (Paris: Éditions du Cerf, 1959).

ROWLEY, H. H., *Job* (Greenwood, SC: Attic Press, 1976).

SALTMARSH, JOHN, *Free-Grace: Or, The Flowings of Christ's Blood Freely to Sinners* (6th edn.; London, 1649).

SALTMARSH, JOHN, *Sparkles of Glory* (London, 1648).

SANDERS, JOHN, *The God Who Risks* (Downer's Grove, Ill.: Inter Varsity Press, 1998).

SCHAFF, PHILIP, *Creeds of Christendom* (6th edn.; New York: Harper, 1919; Grand Rapids, Mich.: Baker, 1977).

SCHOFIELD, M., 'Preconception, Argument and God', in M. Schofield, M. Burnyeat, and J. Barnes (eds.), *Doubt and Dogmatism: Studies in Hellenistic Epistemology* (Oxford: Clarendon Press, 1978).

SCHREINER, SUSAN E., 'Calvin's Use of Natural Law', in Michael Cromartie (ed.), *Preserving Grace* (Grand Rapids, Mich.: Eerdmans, 1997).

—— *The Theater of His Glory* (Durham, NC: Labyrinth Press, 1991).

—— *Where Shall Wisdom be Found?* (Chicago: University of Chicago Press, 1994).

SEEBERG, R., and HAY, CHARLES E., *Textbook of the History of Doctrines* (Philadelphia: Lutheran Publications Society, 1905).

SESSIONS, WILLIAM LAD, *The Concept of Faith* (Ithaca and London: Cornell University Press, 1994).

STEINMETZ, DAVID C., *Calvin in Context* (New York: Oxford University Press, 1997).

—— *Luther in Context* (Grand Rapids, Mich.: Baker, 1995).

—— 'The Scholastic Calvin', in Carl R. Trueman and R. S. Clark (eds.), *Protestant Scholasticism: Essays in Reassessment* (Carlisle: Paternoster Press, 1999).

STEPHENS, W. P., *The Theology of Huldrych Zwingli* (Oxford: Clarendon Press, 1986).

STONE, MARTIN W. F., 'Moral Psychology After 1277: Did the Parisian Condemnation Make a Difference to Philosophical Discussions of Human Agency?', in Jan A. Aertsen, Kent Emery, Jr., and Andreas Speer (eds.), *After the Condemnation of 1277: Philosophy and Theology at the University of Paris in the Last Quarter of the Thirteenth Century. Studies and Texts* (Berlin: Walter de Gruyter, 2001).

STUMP, ELEONORE, *Aquinas* (London: Routledge, 2003).

—— 'Aquinas on the Sufferings of Job', in F. Michael McLain and W. Mark Richardson (eds.), *Human and Divine Agency* (Lanham, Md.: University Press of America, 1999).

—— 'Augustine on Free Will', in Eleonore Stump and Norman Kretzmann (eds.), *The Cambridge Companion to Augustine* (Cambridge: Cambridge University Press, 2001).

—— 'Sanctification, Hardening of the Heart and Frankfurt's Concept of Free Will', *Journal of Philosophy*, (1988).

SUDDUTH, MICHAEL L. CZAPKAY, 'Calvin, Plantinga, and the Natural Knowledge of God', *Faith and Philosophy* (1998).

—— 'The Prospects for "Mediate" Natural Theology in John Calvin', *Religious Studies*, (1995).

SWINBURNE, RICHARD, *Atonement and Responsibility* (Oxford: Clarendon Press, 1988).

—— *The Christian God* (Oxford: Clarendon Press, 1994).

—— *The Coherence of Theism* (Oxford: Clarendon Press, 1977).

THOMAS, DEREK, *Calvin's Teaching on Job* (Fearn, Ross-shire: Mentor, 2004).

TORRANCE, T. F., *Calvin's Doctrine of Man* (London: Lutterworth Press, 1949).

—— 'Calvin's Doctrine of the Trinity', *Calvin Theological Journal* (1990).

—— *The Christian Doctrine of God* (Edinburgh: T. & T. Clark, 1996).

—— *Space, Time and Incarnation* (New York: Oxford University Press, 1969).

TRUEMAN, CARL R., and CLARK, R. S. (eds.), *Protestant Scholasticism: Essays in Reassessment* (Carlisle: Paternoster Press, 1999).

TURRETIN, FRANCIS, *The Institutes of Elenctic Theology*, trans. G. M. Giger, ed. J. T. Denison (Phillipsburg, NJ: P. and R. Publishing, 1992–7).

TYLENDA, JOSEPH N., 'Calvin's Understanding of the Communication of Properties', *Westminster Theological Journal*, 38 (1975).

TYÖRINOJA, REIJO, 'God, Causality and Nature: Some Problems of Causality in Medieval Theology', in Eeva Martikainen (ed.), *Infinity, Causality, and Determinism* (Frankfurt am Main: Peter Lang, 2002).

VAN ASSELT, WILLEM J., 'The Fundamental Meaning of Theology: Archetypal and Ectypal Theology in Seventeenth-Century Reformed Thought', *Westminster Theological Journal*, (2002).

VAN BUREN, PAUL, *Christ in Our Place* (Edinburgh: Oliver & Boyd, 1957).

VAN DEN BRINK, Gijsbert, *Almighty God: A Study of the Doctrine of Divine Omnipotence* (Kampen: Kok Pharos, 1993).

VAN INWAGEN, PETER, *God, Knowledge and Mystery: Essays in Philosophical Theology* (Ithaca and London: Cornell University Press, 1995).

—— *Material Beings* (Ithaca: Cornell University Press, 1990).

VERHEY, ALLEN, 'Natural Law in Aquinas and Calvin', in Clifton J. Orlebeke and Lewis B. Smedes (eds.), *God and the Good* (Grand Rapids, Mich.: Eerdmans, 1975).

VERMIGLI, PETER MARTYR, *The Philosophical Works*, trans. Joseph C. McClelland (Kirkville, Mo.: Sixteenth Century Essays and Studies, 1996).

VOS, ANTONIE, 'Scholasticism and Reformation', in Willem J. van Asselt and Eef Dekker (eds.), *Reformation and Scholasticism: An Ecumenical Enterprise* (Grand Rapids, Mich.: Baker, 2001).

VOS, ARVIN, *Aquinas, Calvin, and Contemporary Protestant Thought* (Grand Rapids, Mich.: Eerdmans, 1985).

WAINWRIGHT, WILLIAM J., 'The Nature of Reason: Locke, Swinburne and Edwards', in Alan G. Padgett (ed.), *Reason and the Christian Religion* (Oxford: Clarendon Press, 1994).

—— *Reason and the Heart* (Ithaca: Cornell University Press, 1995).

WARD, KEITH, *Rational Theology and the Creativity of God* (Oxford: Blackwell, 1982).

WARFIELD, B. B., *Calvin and Calvinism* (New York: Oxford University Press, 1931).

WEINANDY, THOMAS, *Does God Suffer?* (Edinburgh: T. and T. Clark, 1999).

WENDEL, FRANÇOIS, *Calvin: The Origins and Development of his Religious Thought* (London: Fontana Library, 1965).

WESTPHAL, MEROLD, 'On Taking St. Paul Seriously: Sin as an Epistemological Category', in T. Flint (ed.), *Christian Philosophy* (Notre Dame: University of Notre Dame Press, 1990).

WHITE, ROGER, 'Notes on Analogical Predication and Speaking about God', in Brian Hebblethwaite and Stewart R. Sutherland (eds.), *The Philosophical Frontiers of Christian Theology. Essays presented to D. M. Mackinnon* (Cambridge: Cambridge University Press, 1982).

WILLIS, E. DAVID, *Calvin's Catholic Christology* (Leiden: Brill, 1966).

—— 'The Influence of Laelius Socinus on Calvin's Doctrines of the Merits of Christ and the Assurance of Faith', in J. A. Tedeschi (ed.), *Italian Reformation Studies in Honor of Laelius Socinus* (Florence: Le Monnier, 1965).

WOLTER, ALLAN B., 'Scotism', in Hans Burkhardt and Barry Smith (eds.), *Handbook of Metaphysics and Ontology* (Munich/Philadelphia/Vienna: Philosophia Verlag, 1991).

WOLTERSTORFF, NICHOLAS, 'Can Belief in God be Rational If It Has No Foundations?', in Alvin Plantinga and Nicholas Wolterstorff, *Faith and Rationality* (Notre Dame: University of Notre Dame Press, 1983).

WRIGHT, D. F., 'Accommodation and Barbarity in Calvin's Old Testament Commentaries', in A. G. Auld (ed.), *Understanding Poets and Prophets: Essays in Honour of George Wishart Anderson* (JSOT Supplement Series 152, Sheffield: JSOT, 1993).

—— 'Calvin's Accommodating God', in W. Neuser (ed.), *Calvinus Sincerioris Religionis Vindex* (Kirksville: Sixteenth Century Journal Publisher, 1996/7).

—— 'Calvin's "Accommodation" Revisited', in P. de Klerk (ed.), *Calvin as Exegete* (Grand Rapids, Mich.: Calvin Studies Society, 1995).

—— 'Calvin's Pentateuchal Criticism: Equity, Hardness of Heart and Divine Accommodation in the Mosaic Harmony Commentary', *Calvin Theological Journal* (1986).

WYKSTRA, STEPHEN J., 'Rowe's Noseeum Arguments from Evil', in D. Howard-Snyder (ed.), *The Evidential Argument from Evil* (New York: Oxford University Press, 1996).

ZACHMAN, RANDALL, 'Calvin as Analogical Theologian', *Scottish Journal of Theology* (1998).

ZWINGLI, ULRICH, *On Providence and Other Essays*, ed. William John Hinke for Samuel Macauley Jackson (1922; repr. Durham, NC: Labyrinth Press, 1983).

Index